Adapting Superman

Adapting Superman

Essays on the Transmedia Man of Steel

Edited by JOHN DAROWSKI

McFarland & Company, Inc., Publishers
Jefferson, North Carolina

LIBRARY OF CONGRESS CATALOGUING-IN-PUBLICATION DATA

Names: Darowski, John, editor.
Title: Adapting Superman : essays on the transmedia man of steel / edited by John Darowski.
Description: Jefferson, North Carolina : McFarland & Company, Inc., Publishers, 2021 | Includes bibliographical references and index.
Identifiers: LCCN 2021011626 | ISBN 9781476677255 (paperback : acid free paper) ∞
ISBN 9781476642390 (ebook)
Subjects: LCSH: Superman (Fictitious character)—In mass media. | BISAC: LITERARY CRITICISM / Comics & Graphic Novels | PERFORMING ARTS / Film / History & Criticism
Classification: LCC P96.S94 A35 2021 | DDC 700/.451—dc23
LC record available at https://lccn.loc.gov/2021011626

BRITISH LIBRARY CATALOGUING DATA ARE AVAILABLE

ISBN (print) 978-1-4766-7725-5
ISBN (ebook) 978-1-4766-4239-0

© 2021 John Darowski. All rights reserved

No part of this book may be reproduced or transmitted in any form or by any means, electronic or mechanical, including photocopying or recording, or by any information storage and retrieval system, without permission in writing from the publisher.

Front cover image: Poster art for *Superman IV: The Quest for Peace* (1987) (Warner Bros./Photofest)

Printed in the United States of America

McFarland & Company, Inc., Publishers
Box 611, Jefferson, North Carolina 28640
www.mcfarlandpub.com

To Mom,
who bought me my first comic book

Table of Contents

Introduction
    John Darowski — 1

The Dawn of the Man of Tomorrow: How Adapting Superman into Different Media Created America's Superhero
    William J. Lorenzo — 7

Secret Origins: The Birth of Superman and Tintin as National Icons
    Alexandre Desbiens-Brassard — 27

Forging an *S* into a Myth: Adaptations of Superman Across Media
    Liam Webb — 41

Superman Takes to the Air: The Radio Adaptations of the Man of Steel
    John Darowski *and* Joseph J. Darowski — 57

Adapting the Clan to the Klan: Modern Confrontations of White Nationalism in Young Adult Superman Comics
    J. Richard Stevens — 76

Adapting American Values: Contextualizing *Superman and the Mole Men* and *Superman IV: The Quest for Peace*
    Fernando Gabriel Pagnoni Berns — 90

A European Superman
    Lars Konzack — 101

Superman vs. The Soap Opera: The Success of *Lois & Clark: The New Adventures of Superman*
    Nicole Freim — 110

Adaptation, Fandom and Gender: What Counts, Who Counts and Why
    Anna F. Peppard — 127

The Man of Steel: A Modern Hero in Crisis
    Simon Harold Walker — 144

No Tights, No Flights: How *Smallville* Put the "Human" in "Superhuman"
    Christopher Maverick — 158

Through the Lens of Dr. Frankenstein: Luthor as Prometheus
  DANIEL PERETTI   173

Lois Lane in Three Acts: Zack Snyder's Key to a Modern Portrait of *The Daily Planet*'s Reporter
  SANDRA ECKARD   185

Branded a Tyrant: Rescuing Superman Video Games with the *Injustice* Series
  CARL WILSON   194

Superman, a Super Freak: Returning the Man of Steel to the Circus in *DC Bombshells*
  CHRISTINA M. KNOPF   207

Forging Kryptonite: Lex Luthor's Xenophobia as Societal Fracturing, from *Batman v Superman* to *Supergirl*
  IAN BOUCHER   216

Anxiety Burning Bright: Exploring the Genealogy of the Evil Superman in *Brightburn*
  DEBADITYA MUKHOPADHYAY   235

Appendix I: Adaptations Starring Superman or the Superman Family   245
Appendix II: Adaptations Featuring Superman or the Superman Family   259
Appendix III: Unproduced Adaptations Starring or Featuring Superman or the Superman Family   270
About the Contributors   273
Index   277

Introduction

John Darowski

The May 5, 1938, edition of the Gary Larson's *The Far Side* comic features a silent panel of a man in a phone booth, his shirt undone to reveal a distinctive S-shield, checking the coin slot for loose change (299). The incongruity of Superman captured in a mundane moment as well as this paragon of virtue displaying such a human foible creates a humorous irony. However, the context for this comedy, Superman changing in a phone booth, is not from the comic books, the medium where he originated and is most associated with, but from his adaptations. The image of Superman changing into his costume in a phone booth was created for the Fleischer cartoon shorts in the 1940s and reintroduced to popular culture by the Christopher Reeve *Superman* films in the late 1970s and '80s.

Created by writer Jerry Siegel and artist Joe Shuster, Superman first appeared on the cover of *Action Comics* #1 (June 1938). But the world's first superhero quickly broke free of the confines of a single medium at an almost unprecedented rate for any character in popular culture. Within five years of his publication, Superman had been adapted into a newspaper comic strip, a radio show, a series of animated short films, and a novel, as well as appearing in many advertisements and on numerous toys. His adventures were already exported internationally to Canada, England, France, Belgium and the Philippines.[1] Superman, Inc., established by National Allied Publications (later DC Comics) to oversee Superman merchandising and adaptations, reportedly employed 250 people in various enterprises by 1941 (Kobler 74). The number has grown exponentially since. In the eighty-plus years since his inception, every decade has had multiple Superman adaptations, often keeping up with the latest innovations in technology and entertainment.

The rapid adaptation of the Man of Steel occurred before the character and storyworld were fully developed on the comic book page. Rather than a definitive ur-text, adapters had more a set of guidelines to be adjusted not only according to the dictates of each distinct medium but by the whims of the creators. To paraphrase film theorist André Bazin:

> [Superman comic books] simply serve to supply the filmmakers [and creators] with characters and adventures largely independent of their literary framework. [Superman] has become part of a mythology existing outside of the [comic books. He] enjoys in some measure an autonomous existence of which the original works are no longer anything more than an accidental and almost superfluous manifestation [53].[2]

Without a definitive source, fidelity is no longer an issue. Instead of a hierarchy of adaptation, prioritizing the original over subsequent interpretations, each story can exist independently and equally alongside each other.

This makes Superman extremely versatile when it comes to adaptation. Creators may draw on the characters and concepts of the storyworld and, as long as they stay true to certain immutable aspects, are free to tell any variety of story. And this is key to Superman's longevity. Not only can he be transformed to suit any medium, but can adjust geographically and temporally to reflect the culture of the audience.

The following essays are focused on the adapted adventures of the Man of Steel, though this does not exclude comic books. The scholars expand the approaches to adaptation studies by not just studying how a text moves from one medium to another but applying cultural historicism, economic practices, and fan studies, among other disciplines, to contextualize and illuminate a wide variety of works. While many of the Superman texts analyzed may be popular, several essays focus on adaptations that have not received critical attention. Others put adaptations in dialogue with each other to examine their unique refractions.

The essays in this collection are presented largely in chronological order. Where an essay analyzes more than one adaptation, it is positioned according to the earliest text. A historiography of Superman adaptations can be broadly categorized into three periods: Early (1939–1970), Middle (1970–2000), and Late, or at least latest (2000–present).[3] The Early period covers the experimental phase beginning in 1939, when the cast, characterizations, and even Superman's powers were not yet defined, through their codification in the late forties to the fifties and on to a somewhat fallow time in the sixties. Though Superman achieved his classical form during this period, I include those works with the early experimental texts because many of the same creators and actors participated in the adaptations throughout these decades. The Middle period are adaptations at their most classical, highlighted by the Christopher Reeve film cycle (1978–1987). By this point, Superman had achieved an iconic status as a paragon of truth, justice, and the American way, so there was little need to explain who he was or why he acted for the benefit of mankind. The Late period is marked by deconstruction of the Superman archetype and more focus on the human side of the character. Although the deconstruction of the superhero had begun in comic books in a previous era, precipitated by Alan Moore and Dave Gibbons' *Watchmen* (1986–1987), it did not transfer to other media until the new millennium. This Late era features not only an interrogation of why Superman acts but whether his action actually benefits mankind.

William J. Lorenzo provides an historical survey of Superman adaptations in the 1940s and '50s in "The Dawn of the Man of Tomorrow: How Adapting Superman into Different Media Created America's Superhero." This overview shows the progression of adaptations from comic book to comic strip, radio show, novel, film and film serials, and finally television. Each of the several adaptations contributed to the Superman mythos and eventual codification of the character while mirroring the transformation of the media landscape.

In "Secret Origins: The Birth of Superman and Tintin as National Icons," Alexandre Desbiens-Brassard examines how the differing cultural contexts of Belgium and the United States in the 1930s and '40s allowed two very different characters to become popularized and identified with each nation. The superhero and the reporter-adventurer were both initially published in the years leading up to World War II. Comparing how each character adopted their respective cultural values provides insight into how they became and continue to be national symbols through an iconization process.

Liam Webb's "Forging an *S* into a Myth: Adaptations of Superman Across Media" examines the evolution of both Clark Kent's character and Superman's powers from their earliest incarnation in a 1933 short story through to a close reading of the Fleischer/Famous Studios animated film shorts (1941–1943) and the 1943 novel *The Adventures of Superman* by George Lowther. While these early adaptations contributed several important elements to the Superman mythos, just as many ideas were never canonized. Webb's extensive analysis reveals that the 1930s and '40s truly were an experimental era for the Man of Steel, particularly when other creators beside Siegel and Shuster began to contribute.

"Superman Takes to the Air: The Radio Adaptations of the Man of Steel" by John Darowski and Joseph J. Darowski looks at the transition from image to sound through multiple Superman radio series. *The Adventures of Superman* radio program (12 Feb. 1940–1 Mar. 1951) not only significantly contributed to the Superman mythos and his popularity, it also demonstrated the superhero's versatility to be modified to suit different contexts. This essay discusses the process of adapting the Man of Steel to radio and the history of the programs in the United States, Australia, and Great Britain.

One of the most famous stories from *The Adventures of Superman* radio show is "The Clan of the Fiery Cross" (10 June–1 July 1946), in which Superman battles racism and intolerance through a confrontation with a thinly veiled stand-in for the Ku Klux Klan. J. Richard Stevens analyzes this story as well as its modern comic book adaptation, *Superman Smashes the Klan* (Oct. 2019–Feb. 2020) by Gene Luen Yang and Gurihiru, in "Adapting the Clan to the Klan: Modern Confrontations of White Nationalism in Young Adult Superman Comics." Though created more than seventy years apart, Superman's message of inclusion resonates as much today as it did after World War II.

Fernando Gabriel Pagnoni Berns transitions from the Early to Middle period by tackling two of the most overlooked and maligned Superman adaptations in "Adapting American Values: Contextualizing *Superman and the Mole Men* and *Superman IV: The Quest for Peace*." Placing these films in their respective cultural contexts of 1951 and 1987 reveals how each film addressed the contemporaneous concerns about racism and paranoia on the one hand and, on the other, nuclear proliferation at the end of the Cold War. By putting these two texts in dialogue, Pagnoni Berns examines how the core American values which Superman represents are fluid and allow for a more complex reading as they adjust over time.

To celebrate Superman's 50th anniversary in 1988, DC Comics launched several initiatives, one of which was to invite foreign publishers to create their own Superman comic book. Only one such comic was published, the 48-page Danish *Superman og Fredsbomben* (directly translated: *Superman and the Peace Bomb*), which has never been translated into English. In "A European Superman," Lars Konzack examines how this story reflects a European mindset toward Superman and American culture toward the end of the Cold War.

One of the ways Superman has stayed relevant over the decades is to have the superhero genre reinvigorated by borrowing from other genres. "Superman vs. The Soap Opera: The Success of *Lois and Clark: The New Adventures of Superman*" by Nicole Freim explores how the 1993–1997 television show borrowed soap opera conventions to create a modern interpretation of the classic romance that focuses more on the human side of the characters in a precursor to the Late period. By doing so, the show made Clark Kent and Lois Lane reflect the contemporary gender ideologies of second-wave feminism and the new man.

4 Introduction

Anna F. Peppard takes the idea of adaptation studies a step further by considering the role of fan fiction in "Adaptation, Fandom and Gender: What Counts, Who Counts and Why." This exploration considers how fans are able to celebrate and critique *Lois & Clark* through the online continuation of the series in writings of Seasons 5 and 6. In including fan fiction as adaptation, Peppard tackles the gender ideology of *Lois & Clark* as well as the role of gender in fandom.

Moving into the Late period, Simon Harold Walker discusses the gradual darkening of the Superman character and storyworld in the 21st century in "The Man of Steel: A Modern Hero in Crisis." Walker investigates the changes to costume, morality, and, in an element exclusive to adaptations, musical scores. Though the bleaker interpretations mirror several comic book storylines, the question remains as to whether these "more realistic" characterizations humanize the superhero or make him less heroic. Walker considers whether a virtuous character like Superman can continue to resonate in an increasingly post-modern world.

In "No Tights, No Flights: How *Smallville* Put the 'Human' in 'Superhuman,'" Christopher Maverick writes about how the 2001–2011 show revitalized 21st-century superhero media by focusing on the fallible, human side of the characters rather than the exceptional, wish-fulfillment aspect. The series not only chronicles Clark Kent developing his powers but also the moral code which would lead him to become a superhero. Maverick applies moral philosophy to the changing media landscape to help understand why more ethical complexity in leading characters has proved increasingly popular as an allegory for the human condition

Daniel Peretti expands the scope of this collection by focusing on Superman's arch-nemesis, Lex Luthor. In "Through the Lens of Dr. Frankenstein: Luthor as Prometheus," Peretti contrasts Luthor's personal analogies to the ancient myth of Prometheus in *Superman Returns* (2006) and *Batman v Superman: Dawn of Justice* (2016). Through a comparative reading, Peretti reveals that, though Luthor views himself as similar to the mythic figure, the villain is more akin to Mary Shelley's modern Prometheus, Dr. Frankenstein.

Almost as iconic as the Man of Steel himself has been his consistent love interest, Lois Lane. In "Lois Lane in Three Acts: Zack Snyder's Key to a Modern Portrait of *The Daily Planet*'s Reporter," Sandra Eckard argues that, though director Zack Snyder's DC films have had a mixed reception, the portrayal of Lois Lane is one of the bright spots and forms a lynchpin for the shared storyline. Eckard's analysis reveals that this interpretation of Lois Lane, as portrayed by Amy Adams, to be a 21st-century feminist: a protagonist in character and story who is not defined by her relationship with either Clark Kent or Superman.

One area of media in which Superman has been the least successful in adaptation has been video games. He has found recent success in the art form, coinciding with the apex of the darkening of the character, as the Tyrant Superman in the *Injustice* video games (2013, 2017). Carl Wilson traces the technological, economic, and business factors which hindered the Man of Steel's appearances in video games before achieving critical acclaim in "Branded a Tyrant: Rescuing Superman Video Games with the *Injustice* Series."

Christina M. Knopf tackles one of the more interesting acts of adaptation, a line of statues turned into a comic book series, in "Superman, a Super Freak: Returning the Man of Steel to the Circus in *DC Bombshells*." DC Collectibles' *Bombshells* statues reimagined various superheroines by combining them with 1940s and '50s iconography. In doing so, they returned Superman to his inspirational roots as a circus strongman. Knopf examines the *DC Bombshells* comic book series (Aug. 2015–June 2018), set during World War II, in terms of its intersectionality with circus culture and queer lifestyles.

Ian Boucher returns us to Lex Luthor to examine how the villain has weaponized xenophobia in the 21st century for his own political and personal ends. "Forging Kryptonite: Lex Luthor's Xenophobia as Social Fracturing, from *Batman v Superman* to *Supergirl*" contextualizes these stories of the 2010s to reveal how they mediate the damage done to society and especially families through fear of otherness. Though the resolution of these problems requires much more than punching a villain, the fictional perspective provided by characters like Lex Luthor, Superman, and Supergirl provide much-needed catharsis and can contribute to the development of empathy and understanding.

Superman is one of the most frequently imitated characters in popular culture; every superhero universe seems to have some iteration of the Man of Steel.[4] The 2019 film *Brightburn* takes the premise of Superman and places it, to borrow parlance from the television show *Community*, in the darkest timeline. When a teenage boy discovers his alien heritage and superpowers, he becomes a murderous psychopath. In "Anxiety Burning Bright: Examining the Genealogy of the Evil Superman in *Brightburn*," Debaditya Mukhopadhyay analyzes how the film's focus on the protagonist's otherness highlights contemporary anxieties concerning immigration and alienness as a refraction of Superman's own history.

The volume concludes with a set of appendices providing bibliographical information on adaptations in which Superman has appeared. Divided into three parts, "Appendix I: Adaptations Starring Superman or the Superman Family" lists adaptations starring Superman or members of the Superman family, "Appendix II: Adaptations Featuring Superman or the Superman Family" lists adaptations featuring Superman or members of his family as part of a team, and "Appendix III: Unproduced Adaptations Starring or Featuring Superman or the Superman Family" lists projects that were proposed or announced but never either entered or completed production. The lists are presented by medium in chronological order. The presented lists are thorough but not necessarily complete. Priority is given to narrative adaptations, and the appendices do not include: action figures, toys, advertisements, theme park rides, picture books, role-playing games, trading cards, etc.

Superman is one of the most adapted characters in popular culture. The essays presented in this collection represent a small portion of potential topics on the Man of Steel and adaptation but are a significant contribution to the intersectionality of comic book and media studies. Superman will continue to have new stories told in a plethora of media for years to come. An understanding of how the world's first superhero has and will continue to endure, by adapting not only across media but to new cultural contexts, will only become more important.

Notes

1. Reprints of the Superman comic books appeared in Great Britain beginning on 5 Aug. 1939 in Amalgamated Press's *Triumph* #772 and appearing in issues #772–792 (1939) and #807–814 (1940). The stories were recut to fit the British style, with text appearing beneath the images, which would have required some redrawing (Murray 59–60, 65). The *Superman* comic strip was reprinted in the Belgium *Spirou* beginning on 2 Mar. 1939 through an undetermined point in 1941. In France, reprints began on 7 Mar. 1939 in *Aventures*. However, the title was changed from *Superman*, with its overtones of the German *übermensch*, to the science-fiction sounding *Yordi*. These strips were also recut to fit the national format. The Belgium and French reprints ceased at an undetermined point in 1940 due to the German occupation (Gavaler). Canada also likely

received reprints of the comic books and comic strips. Canada and the Philippines received transcription broadcasts of the *Superman* radio show beginning in 1940 ("'Superman' for Canada").

2. Bazin's original quote utilized Alexandre Dumas's D'Artagnen and Victor Hugo's Javert as examples.

3. I see ambiguity as a feature of bracketing historical periods, not a detriment. If a work was released in 1970, it should be discussed which period it may better belong to rather than reading the dates as though on 1 Jan. 1970, the world changed its approach to adapting Superman. The overlap of dates recognizes the ambiguity of the transition period that should be embraced and debated.

4. Examples of other superheroes following the Superman archetype, to name a few, include: Hyperion in Marvel Comics; Prime in the Ultraverse of Malibu Comics; Supreme from Image Comics; Apollo in Wildstorm Comics; Samaritan from the *Astro City* comic book series; and the Will Smith film *Hancock* (2008).

Works Cited

Bazin, André. *What Is Cinema?* trans. Hugh Gray. University of California Press, 1967.

Gavaler, Chris. "How Do You Say 'Superman' in French?" *The Hooded Utilitarian*, 20 Sept. 2014. https://www.hoodedutilitarian.com/2014/09/how-do-you-say-superman-in-french/. Accessed 12 May 2020.

Kolber, John. "Up, Up and Awa-a-y! The Rise of Superman, Inc." *The Saturday Evening Post*, 21 June 1941, pp. 14–15, 70–78. http://www.saturdayeveningpost.com/wp-content/uploads/satevepost/rise-of-superman.pdf. Accessed 2 Feb. 2020.

Larson, Gary. *The Complete Far Side: 1980–1994*. Vol. 1, Andrews McMeel Publishing, 2003.

Murray, Chris. *The British Superhero*. University of Mississippi Press, 2017.

"'Superman' for Canada." *Variety*, 8 May 1940. https://archive.org/details/variety138-1940-05/page/n89/mode/2up/search/superman. Accessed 11 Apr. 2020.

The Dawn of the Man of Tomorrow

How Adapting Superman into Different Media Created America's Superhero

WILLIAM J. LORENZO

Building the Superman Mythos

The world knows Superman as the star superhero who fights "a never-ending battle for truth, justice, and the American way." But it took decades for the comic book character to become the superhero that is known throughout the world. In fact, it was only with the help of various converging media throughout the first two decades of his existence that Superman became the superhero that he is today. Not only was the Superman that first appeared in *Action Comics* #1 (June 1938) a very different character, but his success story is contingent upon the various early adaptations of the character and specific alterations that were made along the way. The earliest conception of the character, in writer Jerry Siegel and artist Joe Shuster's self-published science fiction short story "Reign of the Superman" (Jan. 1933), was more of a villain than a hero. Once Superman debuted as an archetypal superhero, the character was ripe for a myriad of adaptations. It was the various early adaptations of that character in radio, cartoon shorts, comic strips, a novel, film serials, a movie, and a television series that expanded and enhanced the Superman mythos in order to create a mold of this character that would thereafter remain largely unchanged.

Superman will forever be considered the all-American superhero. He was quickly lauded as such ever since he rather abruptly came into the collective consciousness in 1938 with the publication of *Action Comics* #1. The socio-political connection to the character would change through the subsequent tumultuous times in American history. He became a champion of the people at the tail end of the Great Depression, fought against the Nazis during World War II, and kept citizens safe and secure by defending American ideologies during the Cold War era. With such integral ties to the common man in America, Superman instantly became an innate part of American popular culture (Steranko 34–41). This can easily be seen in the simple fact that Superman was able to cross into multiple media within the first 15 years of the character's debut. From his first comic book appearance in 1938 to his first television appearance in 1952, Superman became available in every available form of American media, which still remains an impressive feat.

From one medium to the next, Superman was adapted by new authors, artists, animators, dramatists, producers, and filmmakers, with each and every adaptation adding layers to Jerry Siegel and Joe Shuster's original creation. These adaptations at times permanently altered the character for each subsequent iteration. This initial 15-year period of various adaptations across media platforms, coinciding with the Golden Age of superheroes, saw each individual medium distinctly impact the character in a profound and unique way. Rather than solely drawing inspiration from the comics, each new adaptation specifically sought to draw inspiration from the preceding adaptation. This, in essence, took every singularly unique element of the character adapted for one specific medium and made it part of the overall Superman mythos.

We can study the unique aspects of the characterization of Superman by examining early entries into each medium—from his artistic appearances in Siegel and Shuster's comic books and comic strips (*Superman*, 1939–1966) to Max Fleischer's animated adaptation (17 shorts, 1941–43), George Lowther's literary adaptation (*The Adventures of Superman*, 1942), Bud Collyer's radio (*The Adventures of Superman*, 1940–1951) and animation voice-over work, the two film serializations (*Superman*, 1948; *Atom Man vs. Superman*, 1950), all the way to Superman's first feature film (*Superman and the Mole Men*, 1951) and television appearance (*Adventures of Superman*, 1952–58). More specifically, we can observe how the initially unique aspects from each medium from 1938 to 1952 contributed to and is maintained forever as part of the Superman mythos, culminating with George Reeves' portrayal of Superman in the film and the television series as the quintessential superhero.

The Superman mythos drastically evolved due to the various unique alterations made across adaptations. This can only happen when there are so many adaptations, all becoming so integral to the character mythology, that all preceding adaptations eventually become altered as well. The adaptation of any story or character from one medium to another presents multiple challenges to the creators and the audience; making the move from comic book to any other medium is particularly challenging. The comic book is, in itself, a visual medium, and an unusual one at that. In the comic book medium, time and space play an important role in how the reader interprets the story, but they do not move in a standardized manner. A comic book page is composed of panels; from one panel to another, the characters can move through any amount of time or space (McCloud 62, 65–66, 100). Superman can jump out the window of the Daily Planet in one panel and, just an inch to the right, land on the moon. A few pages later, Superman could jump over a car in one panel and land across the street in the next. The trips can be made quite simply from an artist's perspective; they need only to draw two panels. Yet it's quite intricate from the reader's perspective because they interpret the entire journey made by Superman as he moves across blank space between one panel and the next, called the gutter. The gutter is filled with invisible action that the reader fills in through closure (McCloud 66–67). Superman can travel nearly a quarter of a million miles or only a few feet. And the amount of time between journeys would also be drastically different. The comic book reader is actively filling in bits and pieces of the narrative and the characters' movements. What makes comics so different from any other medium is that each reader will interpret the action that takes place in the gutters in significantly different ways. Taking that control away from the reader makes it difficult to adapt comics into any other medium, where the audience will be passively shown or told.

The issues of time, space, and reader interaction are not the only hurdles to adapting a comic book. One also must consider that the adaptation is being made from a visual medium with characters that have a certain appearance. This appearance needs to be relatively standardized between all adaptations, both visual and otherwise, in order to establish a certain level of intertextual continuity. Any subtle differences that shape Superman between his first appearance in 1938 and his television appearance in 1952 are primarily in story and characterization, generally making sure his particular appearance remains intact.

It is also difficult to establish a character mythos and continuity of story across multiple media platforms. But the interesting dichotomy with Superman is that any adaptations of the character become uncomplicated due to these very same peculiarities. Specific circumstances regarding the character can be slightly altered from one form of media to the next, effectively allowing a certain amount of deviation without changing the overall character. Depending on the medium, Superman will not move in the same manner, his behavior might be altered, etc. His powers will change dramatically by the 1950s due to the various interactions with each form of media. But before we see the character of Superman become fully realized by the early 1950s, we must begin in the early 1930s, with Siegel and Shuster working on their original idea for the character that would become Superman.

Superman Before Action Comics #1

Two childhood friends, writer Jerry Siegel and artist Joe Shuster, had sought to sell their stories to publishers as teenagers, only to have their work rejected. In 1932, Siegel wrote "The Reign of the Superman" which, along with Shuster's art, they self-published in a mimeographed fanzine of their own creation: *Science Fiction: The Advance Guard of Future Civilization* #3 (Jan. 1933). In the story, the vagrant Bill Dunn takes a potion given to him by a mad scientist, gaining telepathic superpowers that make him determined to take over the world. Needless to say, this "superman" bore virtually no resemblance (in both artistic likeness and character traits) to their superhero creation that they would fully realize years later (Daniels 11–15).

In part inspired by the burgeoning comic book market and in part inspired by the popular pulp strongman Doc Savage (who himself was called "Superman" in advertising blurbs and even retired to a "Fortress of Solitude"), Siegel and Shuster realized that if their "superman" was a force of good, as opposed to a villain, their stories would be more commercially successful. They began seeking a publisher for an original comic the likes of which had never been seen. Later in 1933, Siegel and Shuster pitched their idea to Humor Publishing Company, the only company offering original comic book stories in their tabloid-sized title *Detective Dan* (Feiffer 11–21). They titled their comic *The Superman* and touted the character as a physical marvel. This early version of the character resembled a carnival strongman, wearing pants and a shirt as opposed to a costume, and he sought to save the day using incredible feats of strength. But *Detective Dan* wasn't selling well and, with no previous commercial success in superheroes, Siegel and Shuster's comic was scrapped. Siegel saved the cover art of that issue from Shuster's irate destruction of the rest of the book, leaving us the only image of this initial characterization (Steranko 19, 34–37).

Siegel and Shuster continued to try to sell *Superman*, this time as a comic strip, but the character was rejected by every major newspaper syndicate in the country. The Bell

Syndicate claimed that Superman did not have extraordinary appeal and Esquire Features, Inc. went so far as to insult Joe Shuster's art, claiming it was crude (Steranko 39). Eventually, Siegel and Shuster were only able to sell different pulp-like characters and stories to one comic book publishing company, National Allied Publications. There they were able to gain some commercial success first with *Doctor Occult, Ghost Detective* (*New Fun Comics* #6 [Oct. 1935]) and then with FBI agent Steve Carson in *Federal Men* (*Adventure Comics* #2 [Jan. 1936]). Their next success also happened to be a significant commercial success for DC Comics in private detective Slam Bradley, debuting in *Detective Comics* #1 (Mar. 1937) (12–13, 39).

By 1937, the comic book industry was beginning to become more commercially viable than it had been. Major Malcolm Wheeler-Nicholson (founder of National Allied Publications) sold a majority share of the company to Harry Donenfeld (pulp publisher and magazine distributor) in order to keep such titles as *Adventure Comics* and the newly created *Detective Comics* alive. This new company was renamed Detective Comics, Inc. Wheeler-Nicholson and Donenfeld were both looking to make money, so they quickly put together an ashcan comic titled *Action Comics* #1 in late 1937. Ashcan comics were solely created and submitted to the US Patent and Trademark Office in order to trademark the name and were not meant for sale. The cover of the *Action Comics* ashcan featured a ghoulish, vampire-like creature wielding a bloody knife, which resembled the cover of a pulp as opposed to what would become a superhero comic book. Harry Donenfeld was familiar with Siegel and Shuster's often-rejected character from his dealings with the McClure Newspaper Syndicate, particularly their agent M.C. Gaines. At the same time, Wheeler-Nicholson was in the process of being ousted with a forced bankruptcy lawsuit in which Donenfeld (and his accountant Jack Liebowitz) bought National Allied Publications and Detective Comics, Inc., in their entirety, a conglomeration which would soon colloquially become known as DC Comics (Wheeler-Nicholson 244–47).

In the early months of 1938, Siegel and Shuster began editing and re-working their improved Superman submissions to the McClure Syndicate into a 13-page story to be featured in *Action Comics* #1 (Wheeler-Nicholson 244–47). The extensive origin of the character was cut down to just the first page of the comic book: In the first panel, a spaceship is launched from a then-unnamed doomed planet. The rocket ship is quickly recovered and the infant inhabitant taken to an orphanage. By the fourth panel, Superman has already reached adulthood and his powers were being explained to the reader—the abilities to leap one-eighth of a mile, raise tremendous weights, run faster than a train, and nigh-invulnerability, with only a bursting shell able to penetrate his skin (Siegel and Shuster's initial origin story would not be printed for almost another year in the *Superman* syndicated comic strip.) With the first printing of *Action Comics* #1, published in April 1938 with a June cover date, Superman was finally unveiled.[1] It took only a few short months for the popularity of the character to launch him into a whirlwind of adaptations for generations to come.

Superman in the Panels and the Papers

There were a few aspects of the character that were solidified in *Action Comics* #1. On the origin page, the reader was told that Clark Kent decided he must use his strength to benefit mankind in his costumed identity of Superman, a champion of the oppressed who devoted his existence to helping those in need. This mission is a character trait of Superman's that would remain largely unchanged. At this time in American history, Superman was often helping the American everyman fight everything from small town crooks to corrupt corporations. These stories were representative of America's uncertainties during the era of the Great Depression. Within a few years, Superman would get into the war effort and would be helping American servicemen fight the Nazis during World War II, though not fighting in the war itself. As American sentiments and the cultural landscape of the country changed, Superman would adapt along the same lines, but still always helping those in need as a champion of the oppressed (Steranko 39–41).

In addition, another element of the Superman mythos that would remain largely unchanged is his appearance: black hair, often with a distinctive curl, in a blue costume with red cape, trunks, and boots, and an S-shield emblazoned on his chest. Though there are occasionally minor alterations to Superman's and Clark Kent's costume and physical appearance, the S-shield undergoing the most transformation, they do stay relatively consistent across all media adaptations for the period of time that shaped the Superman mythos.

With the unprecedented success of Superman in *Action Comics* titles, Harry Donenfeld began working on the expansion of the character property through merchandising, adaptations, etc., under the auspices of Superman, Incorporated. The first of these adaptations was simply turning the property back over to the McClure Syndicate, from which Donenfeld first discovered the character, for a daily newspaper comic strip (Steranko 39–41). The *Superman* daily comic strip began running in McClure's newspapers on January 16, 1939, with color Sunday strips to follow later in the year on November 5, 1939, though a teaser origin Sunday page appeared a week earlier on October 29, 1939. These daily strips were the first adaptation of the character of Superman into a medium other than comic books. Siegel and Shuster decided to run their original expanded origin story of Superman as the first twelve strips, ten of which feature the destruction of the planet Krypton for the first time. It is here that we are introduced to a named Krypton, scientist Jor-L, wife Lora, and baby Kal-L. By the tenth strip, the spaceship leaves Krypton in a panel similar to the first origin panel in *Action Comics* #1.

The *Superman* daily comic strip offered Siegel and Shuster an opportunity to further develop Superman stories that could run serialized over the course of days or weeks. No longer confined to the constraints of an individual story within a comic book, these comic strips can be seen as the first example of story serialization with regards to Superman, which would become key in just about all of the character's later adaptations. These daily *Superman* strips became so popular that they aided in the sales of *Action Comics*. Due to the increase in circulation and the popularity of the character, Donenfeld decided that Superman should be the first superhero to receive his own self-titled comic book series in addition to his appearance in *Action Comics* (Steranko 34–41). *Superman* #1 (Summer 1939) mostly reprinted stories from the first 2 issues of *Action Comics*, but there were some new pages added, including a new 2-page origin story. In this origin, Krypton (now named in the comic books) explodes as an infant is sent to Earth to be found by two farmers. This is the first time that Ma and Pa Kent are depicted, though their names and stories are different than what they would become. These farmers deliver the infant to an orphanage and then later adopt him. They are only shown in three panels on the first page, followed by their gravestones on the second page. The second page also features the same listing of powers as *Action Comics* #1, and the same claim about Superman using his power to help those in need. With these four major print titles (*Action Comics*, the *Superman* comic book, the *Superman* daily strip, and the *Superman* Sunday strip), DC Comics employee Whitney Ellsworth was tasked with editorial duties on all Superman titles. Superman was about to branch out into multiple new non-print media, and Whitney Ellsworth was about to play an even bigger role in the enhancement of the Superman mythos.

Superman Over the Airwaves

After the quick success of Superman comics, Harry Donenfeld felt that it was about time for Superman to make the move into another form of media. He hired Robert Maxwell, a former pulp writer, to oversee Superman, Inc. and its various marketing campaigns and licensing efforts associated with the character to maximize on his popularity: toys, figures, puzzles, clothing, and a wide array of other products. Donenfeld decided that Maxwell was the perfect employee to work on getting Superman on the airwaves and into yet another medium (Tye 88–93).

The first recording of Superman is a series of unaired audition discs, which were enough to get the radio series sponsored. The first episode premiered as a syndicated show on February 12, 1940, on New York's WOR radio station.[2] The radio show went on to both Mutual and ABC during its more than ten-year run and eventually picked up its most prolific sponsor, Kellogg's Pep cereal. In an act of synergy, Kellogg's went on to sponsor other Superman products, broadcasts, and tie-ins as well. As early as the first episode's audition tape, listeners were told that the stories of Superman would carry a similar socio-political ideology as the comic books and strips. Superman was still fighting for the American everyman as the era of the Great Depression came to a close, and within the first two minutes of the audition tape (and eventually the first aired episode, as well), listeners were told that Superman, "champion of the oppressed, has sworn to devote his existence on Earth to helping those in need" ("The Baby from Krypton"). This is a principle that any listener could get behind, just as readers did in the comic books, and was instrumental in the initial production and ultimate success of the radio series.

The first audition tape begins with a version of an opening narration which would become virtually synonymous with the character of Superman. The first line of the audition tape featured the narrator's call: "faster than an airplane, more powerful than a locomotive, impervious to bullets—up in the sky, look, it's a giant bird, it's an airplane, it's Superman." By the time the first episode, titled "The Baby from Krypton," premiered, the "giant" was removed and "airplane" simply became "plane." By the second episode, "Clark Kent, Reporter," the series opened with a tagline that would resonate with the character forever: "Up in the sky, look, it's a bird, it's a plane, it's Superman!" From the very start, before any character even speaks, the Superman mythos is permanently altered with this simple catchphrase that will be uttered by onlookers for generations in virtually every adaptation.

The Superman mythos was impacted in a drastic manner from these radio shows. The most obvious is that of Bud Collyer, the voice artist portraying Superman/Clark Kent. As this is the first adaptation to feature actors of any kind, the principal hurdle was figuring out a way to portray Superman and Clark Kent as the same person, one an alter ego of the other. Initially, Maxwell was bringing in voice actors for Superman only, intending to hire another person to provide the voice for Clark Kent. But then Bud Collyer comes along and all the pieces fell into place. Bud Collyer was a fairly well-known radio voice artist and soap opera announcer, though his role as Superman would ultimately become his most prolific voice role, later reprising it in the DC Comics/Filmation animated television series of the late 1960s.[3] What made Collyer perfect for the role of Superman, however, was his ability to lower his voice from that of a tenor to more of a baritone (Tye 86–87). He would change his voice from relatively high-pitched speech as Clark Kent to a much deeper, commanding voice as Superman. This change in vocal range would sometimes occur mid-sentence, further accentuating the differences between the alter ego and the superhero. Listeners would easily be able to tell the difference between Superman and Clark Kent, but since they were voiced by the same person, listeners would also clearly be able to tell that the two personas belonged to the same individual.

The *Superman* radio series also made multiple alterations to the Superman origin story and overall mythos, some of which would later be ignored, but most were incorporated into later adaptations. In the very first episode, Jor-L warns a Kryptonian governing council about the planet's impending doom, and he and Lara send the baby Kal-L to Earth. Though the permanent spelling of Jor-El and Kal-El would have been indecipherable to listeners and would not change in print for a few more years, the radio series does change Lora's name to Lara, which would become the ultimate name of Superman's birth mother. This adaptation is also noteworthy due to the depiction of Jor-L's interaction with the Kryptonian council and his final moments on Krypton. Prior to this airing, such an origin only appeared briefly in the *Superman* daily strips.

After the rocket ship leaves Krypton for Earth, the radio series does alter the origin story in a way that helped accelerate the story for the purpose of moving the radio show along, but an alteration that would nonetheless almost always be disregarded by later adaptations. In the first and seconds episodes, listeners are told that Krypton is a planet in our own solar system, hidden behind the Sun; furthermore, by the time baby Kal-L reaches Earth, listeners are told that he has grown to adulthood inside the rocket ship, making him ready to become Clark Kent and Superman by the second episode's end. This is a sped-up and rather strange way to present the origin story, but by the third episode, *Superman* was beginning to introduce so many elements to the Superman mythos that the imperfect arrival on Earth pales in comparison to what the series will accomplish. When the radio series was relaunched on the Mutual Broadcasting System as *The Adventures of Superman* on August 31, 1942, the origin was retold, complete with Superman arriving on Earth as a baby.

The Adventures of Superman radio series was responsible for creating many of the most well-known supporting characters in the Superman mythology. Shortly after the series began, Whitney Ellsworth came on board, as he was slowly becoming DC Comics' point man on all Superman media adaptations. By the end of the second episode of the series, Clark Kent was hired by Perry White to work as a reporter for the *Daily Planet* (originally Paris White of the *Daily Flash* in the second audition tape). Thus, Perry White was created for the radio series and the newspaper, originally called the *Daily Star* in the comics, was permanently renamed the *Daily Planet*. White's curmudgeonly character traits were present from his very first spoken line. Due to Ellsworth's involvement with the production of the radio series and his editorial involvement with all of the Superman print titles, both the character of Perry White and the newly-renamed *Daily Planet* began instantly appearing in the comic book and the comic strips. A few weeks into the radio series, in an April 15, 1940, episode entitled "Donelli's Protection Racket," copy boy and soon-to-be cub reporter Jimmy Olsen makes his debut; it took him about a year to be introduced into the comic books in *Superman* #13 (Nov.–Dec. 1941).[4] Primarily added as a way to include more regularly appearing supporting characters in a radio series that ran multiple times per week, the characters of Perry White and Jimmy Olsen would become integral characters in every later adaptation (Hayde 19–25).

The Adventures of Superman radio series also introduces its listeners to Kryptonite in the story "The Meteor from Krypton" story, beginning June 3, 1943. Kryptonite would be later used as a plot device to incapacitate Superman long enough to either give Bud Collyer some vacation time or to focus mainly on other characters. Furthermore, Inspector Bill Henderson was created for the radio series, depicting Superman working with local law enforcement, in this case the Metropolis Police Department. Though the character would just barely make it into the comics decades later, he played an integral role in the quintessential Superman adaptation, the TV series *Adventures of Superman*, as portrayed by actor Robert Shayne.

The Adventures of Superman program was so successful that the subsequent adaptations were actually adaptations of the radio series itself and not the comic books or strips. This radio series soon led to Superman appearing in two separate prose literary adaptations of the character, "Superman in Radio" in the *Radio and Television Mirror* magazine (Jan. 1941–Apr. 1942) and *The Adventures of Superman* novel by George Lowther in 1942, before it ultimately became the springboard for a multiple film and television adaptations which set the standard for the Superman mythos.

Superman in Text

The quick success of *The Adventures of Superman* radio series initially led to a monthly text feature written for a popular radio magazine, *Radio and Television Mirror*. These issues presented prose stories, some adapted directly from the stories presented on the radio series and some written specifically for the magazine (including the occasional romantic bend), in an ongoing column entitled "Superman in Radio." The short stories ran for 16 months, beginning in the January 1941 issue and ending in April 1942. These monthly stories, each featuring Superman illustrations, were able to demonstrate that Superman could be successful in prose form, as well as in the comics.

Readers and listeners were eager to hear Superman's origins, as all of the origin stories up until that point were relatively lackluster for such an exhilarating character. These origin story deviations, particularly those of the radio series, wound up being "corrected" by one of the radio series' writers and eventual directors, George Lowther. His 1942 novel, *The Adventures of Superman*, would present the most in-depth origin story of Superman, one that would soon become the basis of his origin across all media, including the comics. With this first prose novel adaptation, Superman's origin tale occupies one-third of the book with the other portion featuring Superman battling a Nazi spy, reflecting the shift from Depression-era to wartime themed stories in other Superman media. Joe Shuster provided four full-page color and six full-page black-and-white illustrations, as well as numerous sketches, for the novel.

Lowther begins by assigning Superman and his birth parents the names that would continue to be used perpetually: Kal-el, Jor-el, and Lara.[5] When the newly standardized

Kryptonian spelling made its way into comic books in 1945, the "e" in "el" would become capitalized. The first chapter features an in-depth look at Jor-el attempting to convince the "Council of One Hundred" of Krypton's impending doom, only to be ignored. This novel also presents Jor-el as Krypton's preeminent scientist who builds the prototype spaceship for the salvation of the planet's population but only has the time to launch his infant son to Earth. When the spaceship reaches Earth, it is discovered by Sarah and Eben Kent. This becomes the first time the story of Superman's youth on the Kent farm is told. In *Superman* #1, the Kents are only barely mentioned in three panels and given no real story. In the novel, readers are given the story of Clark Kent being raised by Ma and Pa Kent on the Kent farm. It is also the first time that Smallville makes an appearance, though it is not named and only referenced as a rural suburb of Metropolis. It is important to note that even though the Kents are named Sarah and Eben, these are the same characters as Jonathan and Martha Kent. They would go through a plethora of name changes in the comics before finally being named Jonathan and Martha in 1952, yet their characterizations remain the same.

In the comic books and strips, Superman was depicted as being raised in an orphanage due to the space constraints of the mediums. Similarly, Superman grows to adulthood aboard his spaceship in the radio series due to time constraints. But a novel has no such constraints and Lowther was able to tell an extremely elaborate story about Superman's birth on Krypton and his childhood and adolescence on the Kent farm. Lowther details Clark's gradually learning to use and control his powers as a teenager, beginning with his use of x-ray vision when he accidentally looks through the desk of his schoolteacher Miss Lang.[6] Lowther depicts Clark learning to fly in his home at the Kent farm, beginning with his jumping across the house in excitement and ending with him flying around the room. This story also gives readers the chance to see the beginning of the origin of Superman's costume, when Ma Kent sews together a costume, which is described to look exactly like Superman's costume, so a teenage Clark could attend a masquerade party.

Lowther's novel also depicts the first Pa Kent's death in a detailed chapter. This origin story takes place on a Depression-plagued, middle-American farm. When Clark is seventeen, he finds out that the Kent farm is failing financially and that the family is broke. Pa Kent decides to vie for the $500 prize in a strength contest at a state fair, which he was ill-equipped to win. In a turn of events, Clark winds up winning the prize for the farm after he easily lifts an anvil above his head, in the process meeting the *Daily Planet*'s Perry White. But Eben Kent suffers a heart attack trying to lift the anvil over his head and died later at the Kent farm. Pa Kent tells Clark to hide his identity from the world but to use his strength to keep helping those in need, and just before Eben dies, he tells Clark to call himself Superman.

Lowther's version of the Superman origin story was adapted, in part, in *Superman* #53 (Aug. 1948). Due to the length afforded Lowther in writing a prose novel, he was able to elaborate on Krypton's and young Clark Kent's origin story in a way that would not be possible in any other medium. With many of the pieces falling into place, Superman was ready to be adapted as a moving image on the silver screen. Just prior to the publication of this novel, Superman animated cartoons came to American theaters and proved that the property could be a massive success on screen. With the animated shorts, the novel, the radio series, and the comics, there was enough source material to eventually progress into live-action motion pictures a few years later with two Superman serials, quickly followed by a feature-length film.

Superman's Giant Leap for DC Comics

Back in the DC Comics offices in 1940, Whitney Ellsworth was becoming more and more involved with all of the various media adaptations of Superman, as well as his position editing Superman properties.[7] Ellsworth was beginning to make the character less morally ambiguous in the comic books, imposing a rule that Superman cannot kill or otherwise thrash a villain, as he and other superheroes had performed some pretty questionable acts of justice prior (Grossman 114–115, 160–163). It was also around this time that Ellsworth became the point man for anyone adapting Superman, seeing as how he was involved with the creation of all of the adaptations up to that time. He was in contact with Republic Pictures, who were interested in making a proposed live-action Superman serial in 1940 and 1941. But that serial never came to fruition due to the fact that Paramount, a more recognized studio with a much wider distribution, offered to produce a series of animated Superman shorts in color when cartoon studios were still producing many of their shorts in black and white due to the cost of the expensive Technicolor process. Paramount was the distributor of Fleischer Studios' productions, who would be responsible for making the animated shorts.

Fleischer Studios was a renowned East Coast animation studio operating in the United States from 1921 to 1942. As the studio responsible for such animated series as Popeye, Betty Boop, Koko the Clown, Screen Songs, Color Classics, and more, Fleischer Studios would rival Disney as the greatest animation studio in America during the 1930s. To further challenge Disney, in 1939, Fleischer Studios released their full-length animated feature *Gulliver's Travels* and in 1942, *Mr. Bug Goes to Town*.[8] With all of the aforementioned series and a feature film in production, studio head Max Fleischer was reluctant to take on the Superman shorts due to the responsibility associated with such a mammoth property and to the level of sophistication that would need to go into making these cartoons featuring realistic human characters. Fleischer intentionally inflated the production budget he requested from Paramount in an effort to try and avoid making the shorts. The approximate budget for a Popeye cartoon was $20,000, so Fleischer told Paramount that he would need $100,000 to make each Superman cartoon (Maltin 79–120). Surprisingly, Paramount agreed to enter into negotiations with Fleischer and DC, eventually approving a vast budgetary increase giving Fleischer $50,000 to make the first Superman cartoon (Barrier 304).

Fleischer and his animators immediately began production on the series of Superman shorts. Superman model sheets are dated as early as January 1941 and after an extensive production period, the first Superman cartoon, simply titled "Superman," was released on October 26, 1941. Both in an effort to establish continuity between adaptations and because of the unparalleled success of the radio series, due in no small part to its voice actors, Bud Collyer and Joan Alexander were hired by Fleischer Studios to reprise their voice roles as Superman and Lois Lane in the animated shorts. But now the Fleischers needed to devise methods of distinguishing between Clark Kent and Superman beyond those of previous adaptations. The comics need only show one in a suit and the other in a costume, and the radio series needs only to offer a subtle, yet distinguishable voice change. Bud Collyer will continue slightly altering his voice, often mid-sentence, when changing from Clark Kent to Superman, giving him his oft-used catchphrase "This looks like a job—*for Superman*." The shorts, of course, depict Clark Kent in a suit and Superman in his costume, but animation has the added burden of visually showing the character change. No other medium yet needed to specifically detail Clark Kent's changing out of his suit and into his costume to become Superman. Therefore, we are introduced to many familiar sequences of Clark Kent changing into Superman, often in silhouette behind closed doors, in alleyways, and, most notably, in a phone booth. In the very first short, Clark Kent steps into the stock room of the Daily Planet in order to change into his Superman costume, and in the second short, "The Mechanical Monsters" (Nov. 1941), Superman used a phone booth. These two methods of transition from one identity to another become a fundamental part of the Superman mythos, so much so that it would become a moment of comic relief in a well-known scene from Richard Donner's *Superman: The Movie* (1978).

In addition to what appears on the screen, Fleischer Studios needed an element that was not necessary in any other component—music. Though the radio series needed sound effects, it did not have any music yet.[9] The Fleischers used their in-house music director, Sammy Timberg, to compose the score used throughout all seventeen animated shorts, including the famed theme melody "Superman March." This music would eventually be used on the radio series, as well, and it will also be used as the basis for many a Superman score. Another component of Superman's characterization that was first introduced in these animated shorts is scenes depicting Clark Kent breaking the fourth wall and interacting with the viewer. In almost every short, Clark Kent cracks a joke, smirks, or winks directly at the viewer, a character trait that would carry over to the TV series *Adventures of Superman*.

The Fleischer cartoons are also responsible for one of the prototypical superpowers associated with Superman—the power of flight. Superman was never able to fly prior to these animated shorts, but not for the lack of trying. From the earliest explanation of Superman's powers in *Action Comics* #1, readers are told that Superman could only jump great distances. This was sufficient in the comic books and comic strips, but eventually his leaps began to evolve. Instead of jumping from point A to point B, Superman began to change direction mid-jump, sometimes more than once. In *Superman* #10 (June 1941), Superman is jumping all over the place and moving in so many different directions, it is indistinguishable from his later flying sequences in the comics. But the issue goes out of its way to tell the readers that Superman cannot fly despite these movements. The cover of the UK magazine *Triumph* #772 (Aug. 1939), a reprint of early Superman comics, features an image of him leaping high above the Earth as drawn by British artist Jock McCail, the first published art of Superman by someone other than Joe Shuster. Again, it created the appearance of flying, but he is still clearly jumping, albeit much higher than one-eighth of a mile. The radio series featured the now famous catchphrase "up, up, and away," and even featured Superman "hovering" in his origin story, but this series continually mentions Superman's ability as leaping or jumping great distances, even though the radio series would often flirt with the power of flight.

As early as the second and third episodes of the series, Superman is described as an "eagle of the sky," the verb "wings" is used to describe his movements by the narrator, and he is described as "flying" by onlookers ("Clark Kent, Reporter," "Keno's Landslide"). Yet after all of these mentions of flight, in the third episode Superman narrates in detail his attempt to board a moving train, describing how he must "drop down" to "leap on board," and to do so he runs alongside the train, jumps up and grasps hold of a guard rail to hoist himself onto the train—hardly the actions of someone who is allegedly flying moments prior. The series will continue to utilize the ambiguity associated with this aural medium throughout. Without being able to visually depict Superman either flying or leaping, the series constantly utilizes a whirling/whooshing sound effect, which often creates the illusion of the character's flight. Yet that sound effect, too, is misleading, as the series uses the same sound effect constantly, even when Superman himself states that he is running, fighting, etc., and cannot be relied upon to indicate flight. Since Collyer was often delivering dialogue in describing his own actions, it would have been verbally clumsy to distinguish between flying and leaping, so the whooshing sound effect is constantly used for any action. As early as episode 9 of the series, "Threat to the Planet Building," Lois describes Superman as "flying in the air," yet nearly a year later in episode 147, "The Black Pearl of Osiris, Pt. 1," we hear onlookers scream "look at him jump, did you see the leap that guy made," complete with his "flying" sound effect. In episode 165, "The Dragon's Teeth, Pt. 9," at the same time Fleischer Studios was producing shorts that were visually depicting Superman flying, the radio narrator continues to ambiguously describe his movements with the statement "high above the countryside, a figure leaps forward in curious flight." Also, the series frequently uses the verb fly in a less literal or more colloquial manner by observers used to simply mean that Superman is in the air and/or moving fast. Since Superman's mobility on the radio series is variously described in many ways, it makes the act of "flying" ambiguous throughout the series. It is this same ambiguity that would be present in the first few animated shorts, before they explicitly described and depicted Superman in definitive flight, changing his arsenal of powers forever. But by the time of Lowther's 1942 novel and *Action Comics* #65 (Oct. 1943), Superman is undoubtedly and explicitly able to fly. And it was Fleischer Studios that brought about this change.

Fleischer Studios used an animation technique called rotoscoping, invented by Max Fleischer, to animate some of the characters' movements. This technique called for the filming of live-action actors and then tracing their bodily movements frame-by-frame from the film in order to give their animated characters more life-like movement. But Superman's superpowers could obviously not be performed by live-action actors to be rotoscoped, so those scenes relied solely on the animators. Fleischer animators realized early on in the production process that Superman did not look like a superhero with superhuman powers when he was hopping and jumping around (Maltin 79–120). They felt so strongly they asked their DC contact Whitney Ellsworth if it would be acceptable to give Superman the power of flight. Ellsworth recognized their concern and agreed (Steranko 40–41). In the first five Superman shorts, the viewer can see Superman both jumping great distances and exhibiting the power of flight. By the sixth short, "The Magnetic Telescope," released April 1942 though Fleischer productions were in gestation for approximately nine months prior to release, Superman had abandoned jumping and was routinely flying. By the eighth short, "Volcano" (July 1942), Fleischer changed the phrase "able to leap tall buildings in a single bound" in the cartoon's opening narration to "able to soar higher than any plane." Akin to many of the other alterations made, Ellsworth soon saw to it that in each and every adaptation, Superman was given the power of flight.

These animated shorts attained unparalleled levels of success. They were so successful, in fact, that the fourth story in *Superman* #19 (Nov. 1942), "Superman, Matinee Idol," featured a "sequel" to the first Fleischer Studios short. The story, drawn inside film strips as panels, saw Clark Kent and Lois Lane going to the movies to see this Fleischer cartoon about the escape of the mad scientist, during which Clark had a faux coughing fit and kicks Lois' purse under a chair in a dark theater in order to distract her from seeing him change into Superman on the silver screen. The story ends with a panel depicting an on-screen Superman winking at the theater audience, just as an on-looking Clark Kent winks at the reader.

Still admired today by fans and scholars alike, the Fleischer Superman shorts brought to the medium a new genre, the animated adventure film, and never pander to a moment of comic relief. Unlike the one-reel funny cartoons, these shorts were serious in nature, which led famed animator Shamus Culhane to say "that's some of the best work that was done at Fleischer's, on those pictures" (Culhane and Waldman). The first of these Fleischer Studios shorts was so well received that it was nominated for an Academy Award and they were all poised for future adaptations. But shortly after the shorts began being released, a corporate takeover was about to inhibit the series, leading to its premature conclusion.

In a move similar to that of Harry Donenfeld at DC Comics, Paramount called their loans that Max Fleischer accrued from the studio's move to Miami along with production advances, demanding reimbursement from Fleischer Studios and forcing Max Fleischer to sign a new contract handing ownership of his studio over to Paramount. Paramount also forced Max and Dave Fleischer to write letters of resignation, which Paramount held to be used at their discretion. Halfway through the production of the Superman shorts Fleischer Studios was renamed Famous Studios, and at the same time, Paramount decided to accept the forced resignation letters of the Fleischers. Though the animation staff was primarily kept intact, Max and Dave Fleischer's names were removed from all subsequent productions, making the ninth short, "Terror on the Midway" (Aug. 1942), the final Max Fleischer and Fleischer Studios cartoon. Within a few years, the sophistication and ingenuity of Fleischer Studios was all but obliterated by Paramount, who essentially forced Famous Studios to churn out lackluster cartoons in order to turn a profit. Unlike Donenfeld, who was carefully creating an empire at DC Comics with his new property, Superman, Paramount chose to abandon the expensive Superman series in favor of another licensed property, a series of cartoons based on the Little Lulu comic panels. Had the Fleischers remained a part of the studio, the series of Superman shorts may have continued longer, but Paramount only completed the remaining shorts in their contract with DC, making the seventeenth Superman short, "Secret Agent" (July 1943), the final one (Fleischer 111–123). Rather fittingly for the character, it ends with Superman flying past a large American flag and saluting it. By the time the series of animated shorts came to a close, Whitney Ellsworth and DC Comics were already looking to conquer the next medium adapting Superman.

Superman Lights Up the Silver Screen

After the Fleischer Studios animated shorts ended, Whitney Ellsworth sought to have Superman adapted as a serial. Republic Pictures had previously attempted to obtain the rights to make a live-action Superman serial prior to the series of Fleischer animated shorts. It took a few years, but Sam Katzman eventually obtained the rights in 1947. Ellsworth again served as DC Comics' representative on the project and it quickly went into production. This serial wanted to adapt the radio series as the source instead of the comic books. They did just that, with the exception of the origin story, which was adapted from Lowther's novel. Kirk Alyn was eventually cast in the titular role based mainly on his headshots and an audition at Columbia, and Noel Neill was cast as Lois Lane, in a serial that would launch her career (Grossman 19–29).

The serial, titled *Superman*, was successful despite its relatively small production budget. Since there was not enough money for a great deal of special effects, Superman's flying sequences and the spaceship featured hand-drawn animation combined with the live action footage (Grossman 36–42). As Columbia Pictures released the serial, Columbia's in-house animation department animated the sequences, led by staff animator Howard Swift (Beck). When Superman (now voiced and portrayed by Kirk Alyn) used the line made famous by Bud Collyer, "up, up, and away," he turned into a cartoon and Superman was animated until he landed, usually behind some object so that a live-action Alyn could emerge. This catchphrase did not play well on screen, as Collyer only used that catchphrase on the radio when listeners could not see that he was jumping or flying away.

The serial was broken up into fifteen chapters, the first two of which were adapted from Lowther's origin and the rest from the radio series. The main villainess was the Spider Lady, a version of the radio series' Scarlet Widow ("The Scarlet Widow," 6 Sept.–10 Oct. 1945). On the radio series, the Scarlet Widow is responsible for the creation of the Atom Man. In response to the success of the 1948 *Superman* serial Columbia produced a sequel, *Atom Man vs. Superman*, in 1950. The second serial capitalized on the success of the first, with the actors and production team all returning save for director Tommy Carr, who wanted to transition from serials to the new medium of television. Though they were able to slightly improve upon the special effects with Kirk Alyn live-action flying sequences, they still combined hand-drawn animation with the live action for the majority of the special effects, which again left a lot to be desired. This second serial is noteworthy due to the inclusion of Superman's arch-nemesis Lex Luthor, portrayed for the first time on screen by Lyle Talbot. Curiously, the serial makes Luthor the Atom Man, which is not the case in the radio episodes on which the serial is based, "The Atom Man"/"The Atom Man in Metropolis" (11 Oct.–3 Dec. 1945), which were sequels to "The Scarlet Widow" (Grossman 47–56).

Both serials utilize the mandatory concept of a cliffhanger ending for each chapter, which led the stories to become serialized in nature. The fifteen chapters basically form one massive story when put together, as opposed to fifteen individual complete stories. Serialization was an imperfect model for the Golden Age Superman, who thrived from a more episodic approach. Ellsworth began development on a Superman television program, which he knew would be a successful format for an adaptation of the character, due to the episodic nature of television alone. In 1951, Robert Lippert, Barney Sarecky, and Robert Maxwell were responsible for the production of a feature film that served as a backdoor pilot for a Superman television series adaptation (Grossman 110–111).

Superman and the Mole Men was released on November 23, 1951 with a script written by "Richard Fielding." The screenplay was actually penned by both Whitney Ellsworth and Robert Maxwell, who used the name Fielding (Mrs. Maxwell's maiden name) as an alias (Grossman 157). It was the first feature film to feature DC Comics characters: Superman/Clark Kent (George Reeves) and Lois Lane (Phyllis Coates). The original story proved that a Superman production can be made without necessarily utilizing the stories from any other medium but specifically adapting the characters and their unique personalities.

George "Superman" Reeves

The television industry, which all but obliterated serials, shorts, and scripted radio series, was ripe for a Superman adaptation. After the filming of the *Superman and the Mole Men* feature film, Harry Donenfeld, Whitney Ellsworth and Robert Maxwell began production on 24 television episodes that would be used two years later as the first season of *Adventures of Superman*. Robert Maxwell served as creative producer for the first season and Bernard Luber came on to the project as Paramount's money man. The entire season was shot in August and September of 1951 at the rate of four episodes every ten days. Tommy Carr, who had made the move to television after the first *Superman* serial, was now in a position to direct episodes of the new *Adventures of Superman* TV series. He would serve as director for over a third of the episodes made during the entire series' run. Lee Sholem, director of *Superman and the Mole Men*, would direct the rest of the first season episodes, splitting the directorial duties with Carr (though the split was uneven, with Carr directing many more) (Grossman 14–117). Reeves and Coates would reprise their roles as Superman and Lois, and the rest of the main cast was rounded out with Jack Larson as Jimmy Olsen, John Hamilton as Perry White, and Robert Shayne as Inspector Bill Henderson. Donenfeld, Ellsworth, and Maxwell again secured a lucrative sponsorship with Kellogg's and the stage was set for the first season of *Adventures of Superman* on television in 1952.

The first season of *Adventures of Superman* sets the stage for the later seasons, which are the gold standard for the depiction of Superman in any medium. But the first season is certainly different than the remaining seasons due in no small part to producer Robert Maxwell. Maxwell only produced the first season of the show, with DC's Whitney Ellsworth taking over the remaining five seasons. Maxwell sought an adult audience and a primetime timeslot for the series and the atmosphere of the first season is reflective of such. Bodies were dropping left and right, much to the chagrin of both DC, who wanted the series marketable towards children, and Whitney Ellsworth, who himself was responsible for imposing Superman's moral code in the comics (Grossman 160–163). By the time the second season of the series aired, many changes were made. However, the first season provides many of the elements that would solidify the series as the foremost adaptation of Superman.

Adventures of Superman would be able to boast a cast of actors who would all become closely associated with their roles from this series. George Reeves and Phyllis Coates were cast as Superman and Lois Lane, roles that would become the principal role of both their careers. George Reeves would become so closely identified with the role that periodicals and tabloids would often caption his picture "George 'Superman' Reeves." After the first season, Coates was replaced by Noel Neill as Lois Lane, who would also always be associated with the role. John Hamilton, a veteran character actor with well over 300 credits to his name, will forever be associated with his portrayal of Perry White. Much like the radio and Fleischer portrayals of the character, Hamilton portrays Perry White as the ultimate curmudgeon, leading to his often-repeated catchphrases "don't call me chief" and "great Caesar's ghost." But Hamilton introduces a certain likability to the character that led to a definite camaraderie between Perry White and his *Daily Planet* staff. Jack Larson's Jimmy Olsen would define the innocence and enthusiasm of the cub reporter. Robert Shayne portrays police Inspector Bill Henderson in a role adapted from the radio series. Each of the actors associated with the series portrayed the Superman characters in a manner that was representative of all the best aspects of previous character iterations and would become the standard that all future Superman adaptations' actors would strive to emulate.

The opening title sequence of the TV series borrows phrasing and text from all the preceding adaptations in order to craft the archetypal introduction. Taking pieces from the Fleischer Studios shorts and the radio series, the opening narration (voiced by Bill Kennedy) would become the frequently quoted standard for a description of any Superman media:

> Faster than a speeding bullet, more powerful than a locomotive, able to leap tall buildings at a single bound! "Look, up in the sky!" "It's a bird!" "It's a plane!" "It's Superman!" Yes, it's Superman—strange visitor from another planet, who came to Earth with powers and abilities far beyond those of mortal men. Superman, who can change the course of mighty rivers, bend steel in his bare hands, and who, disguised as Clark Kent, mild-mannered reporter for a great metropolitan newspaper, fights a never-ending battle for truth, justice, and the American way!

This opening narration would remain unchanged throughout the entire six-season run.

The first episode, "Superman on Earth," adapts George Lowther's origin story in a screenplay that was written by "Richard Fielding" (Maxwell and Ellsworth) (Grossman 157). Both Maxwell and Ellsworth would pen later episodes of the series as well, though they were both primarily involved as series producers; Ellsworth took over Maxwell's duties from the second season on (Grossman 160–167). Ellsworth allowed Superman to be the most powerful he has been to date, ushering in even more superpowers than all the previous adaptations, such as: splitting in two, walking through walls, becoming invisible, and travelling through phone lines. These powers were not part of Superman's staple set of abilities: super strength, flight, super speed, x-ray vision, super hearing, super vision, super breath, and near invulnerability; his only weakness being Kryptonite (Grossman 116–117).

By the time the show reached its second season there were two major changes, and they came in the form of Noel Neill and Whitney Ellsworth. Ellsworth, due to his mantra of morality, made the rest of the series much more child-friendly. Phyllis Coates left the series due to other commitments, and was replaced by an actress familiar with the role of Lois Lane, Noel Neill, who portrayed Lois in both the Columbia serials. The change in actresses similarly mirrors Ellsworth's changes, for as much as Noel Neill was a child-friendly Lois Lane, Phyllis Coates played a Lois that was much more adult-oriented. While Noel Neill's Lois would scream and do nothing before being rescued by Superman, Phyllis Coates' Lois would scream and take a swing at the henchmen. In fact, Coates' feisty Lois was in so many a fight sequence that the actress herself actually took a knockout punch from a henchman in a scene from the episode "Night of Terror" (Grossman 144–145).

The TV series continues to depict Clark Kent changing into Superman in a manner more closely related to the Fleischer Studios shorts than to even the live-action serials—Clark Kent most often ducks into the store room or into an alleyway to change into Superman. Though not shown in silhouette, the viewer is shown Clark Kent removing his glasses, loosening his tie, and beginning to remove his jacket before a jump cut shows Superman coming out of the alleyway or leaping out the window of the Daily Planet building. As Superman flies, the theme music is used as a leitmotif. The flying sequences in the series use special effects (courtesy of effects designer Si Simonson) that were far superior to anything that was being done on television at the time, and they were inarguably the best Superman special effects used in any adaptation to that date, as the serials' effects left much to be desired (Grossman 287–291). Starting with the third season of the series in 1955, *Adventures of Superman* was given the color treatment. Color television was a relatively new phenomenon but the success of the first two seasons warranted the change. By the time the series made the transition to color, Ellsworth began shooting even more child-friendly episodes, mirroring the humor that was being introduced into the comics during this time period, before eventually reverting back to a more serious tone (Grossman 250–251).

Though the series was initially cancelled, a two-season revival was in the works, even with the death of actor John Hamilton occurring in the interim. When the series was tragically brought to a close by George Reeves's death, it was a staple series in the U.S., especially in homes with children. All of the actors that participated in this series would best be remembered for their roles in Superman as opposed to their other work. In fact, since George Reeves was so closely associated with the character of Superman, he was only referred to as "Superman" when he guest starred on a 1957 episode of *I Love Lucy* (Grossman 274–275). The ultimate success of *Adventures of Superman* was due in no small part to the performance of actor George Reeves. George Reeves was perfectly cast as Superman and his mild-mannered counterpart, Clark Kent. He played Superman as a tough, but personable superhero helping those in need, while he played Clark Kent as a very capable newspaper reporter. Reeves' Kent may have been mild-mannered, but he was no bumbling, stumbling klutz, and he was as serious a reporter as Lois Lane, in addition to being a superhero. He played both characters with a level of wit that was unparalleled, which was always evident in the moments when he would break the fourth wall. In an element first used extensively in the Fleischer Studios shorts, George Reeves' Clark Kent would often joke with and wink at the viewer as the series' episodes came to a close.

George Reeves was able to give the character of Superman a personality unlike any he had in prior adaptations. Reeves (nicknamed "Honest George" by his cast and crewmates) had such profound congeniality that it was certain to carry over into his portrayal of Superman and Clark Kent. Prior to his portrayal, Superman was fairly rigid and detached, only bringing truly amiable moments when he would break the fourth wall and address the viewer. But Reeves' own personality helped to make the character himself more friendly and likeable than he had ever been before. Recurring series director Tommy Carr said of George Reeves nearly three decades after the series ended: "I couldn't then, and still can't, think of anyone in the world who would have been a better Superman" (*Fifty*... 25). Of all that can be said regarding the *Adventures of Superman* television series, Reeves' portrayal of Superman is certainly at the center of the series' success.

By utilizing all of the specific alterations made to each and every medium's adaptation of Superman up until that point, the television series *Adventures of Superman* takes every singular change made to the character and incorporates each into the series in a unique way. All of these minor alterations were incorporated into the Superman mythos along the way. Each medium utilized its own inherent strengths, while at the same time revealing their own particular limitations, as well. When Siegel and Shuster's Superman appeared in *Action Comics* #1, it was in a rather unique medium—the comic book. The comic is a medium which combines the storytelling power of a prose medium and a moving image medium into an atypical combination of the two, shortening the extent of the text and using still images as a stand-in for moving action. Through a succession of sequential panels, comics can imply motion and through the use of word balloons and onomatopoeic image blasts, comics can indicate dialogue and sound. But a comic book is limited by its specific size and story constraints, which is why it took until Lowther's novel for a much more complete Superman origin story to appear.

The *Superman* radio series presents a very distinct set of problems with no visuals to depict and an approximately 10-minute runtime, initially airing thrice weekly. The radio's one inherent strength—sound—did introduce many important elements into the Superman mythos. It was because of the nature of radio that Bud Collyer was hired to differentiate Clark Kent and Superman by only his voice, a differentiation that would expand and develop over the course of many other adaptations, most notably the Fleischer Studios animated shorts. These shorts made Superman a movie star and proved that the character could triumph on the big screen. The two subsequent *Superman* serials were able to deliver a live-action Superman to audiences, while their imperfect special effects left audiences eager for something more. Soon thereafter, audiences were given *Superman and the Mole Men*, which would ultimately be the springboard for the *Adventures of Superman* TV series, which was the final frontier in a long line of different media that Superman needed to conquer. By the time *Adventures of Superman* lit up the television screens in America, every other medium had already tackled the character and each made its mark.

Observing how each initially unique aspect from each medium is maintained forever as part of the Superman mythos, we can see how the character of Superman has evolved into the superhero presented in *Adventures of Superman*. The strengths and weaknesses of each medium itself all helped to shape and develop the character along the way into what he would become. With the final media hurdle of television, the final piece of the puzzle is introduced. Taking the strengths of each medium in stride, and mending each one's weaknesses, the refined character of Superman was adapted into a television series that would everlastingly set the standard for the character mythos. With an astonishing ensemble of actors creating archetypical interpretations of every character, coupled with a production team that was capable of bringing Superman stories to a preeminent level, the character of Superman that was vitalized by George Reeves was cemented in history as the model for all future adaptations. The Superman mythos is from this time forth standardized forever in such a way that George Reeves' portrayal of Superman in the television series *Adventures of Superman* has eternally become the prototypical portrayal of the character which will forever be at the heart of the Superman mythos.

Notes

1. Comic books are postdated to indicate when vendors should remove unsold copies. For *Action Comics* #1, it was printed in Apr. 1938, went on sale in May, and was meant to be removed by the cover date of June.

2. All episode dates for the radio show come from *Radio Drama: A Comprehensive Chronicle of American Network Programs, 1931–1962* (2000) by Marty Grams.

3. Collyer later went on to become a well-known on-screen personality in his hosting of 1950s and 1960s game shows *Beat the Clock* and *To Tell the Truth*. He reprised his Superman voice role on the DC Comics/Filmation animated television series *The New Adventures of Superman* (1966–1970) and Justice League of America segments of *The Superman/Aquaman Hour of Adventure* (1967–1968), with guest appearances on *Aquaman* segments.

4. An unnamed, blond-haired "office boy" wearing a bow tie appeared in *Action Comics* #6 (Nov. 1938). Some have retroactively credited this as the first appearance of Jimmy Olsen.

5. The origin story in *Radio and Television Mirror* features the names "Jorel" and "Kal-el," after leaving out

Lara altogether. That origin is somewhat of a transcription of the first radio series episode written by a magazine staff writer; therefore, Lowther is actually the person who standardized the names of Superman's family.

    6. Coincidentally, Clark Kent would later have a teenage romantic interest named Lana Lang.

    7. With Ellsworth taking on more roles outside of the DC Comics offices coupled with the growing success of DC Comics, additional editorial staffing was about to take place. Soon, DC Comics would hire the future famed editor Julie Schwartz, who himself co-published the first exclusively sci-fi fanzine *The Time Traveller* in the early 1930s with future Superman editor Mort Weisinger and Forry Ackerman, though Schwartz wouldn't work on Superman properties until the Justice League came into existence.

    8. These two Fleischer Studios features were the only two non-Disney animated feature films produced in America until the 1950s, with RKO's stop motion animated film *Hansel and Gretel* (1954) and UPA's traditionally hand animated film *1001 Arabian Nights* (1959).

    9. The radio show would add organ accompaniment beginning on 16 Apr. 1946 with first episode of "The Hate Mongers' Organization" (episode 1254).

WORKS CITED

"The Arctic Giant." Directed by Dave Fleischer, voice performances by Joan Alexander and Bud Collyer, Fleischer Studios, 1942.
Atom Man vs. Superman. Directed by Spencer Gordon Bennet, performances by Kirk Alyn, Tommy Bond, Noel Neill, Lyle Talbot, and Pierre Watkin, Columbia Pictures, 1950.
"The Baby from Krypton." *The Adventures of Superman*, episode 1. WOR, New York City, 12 Feb. 1940.
Barrier, Michael. *Hollywood Cartoons: American Animation in Its Golden Age*. Oxford University Press, 2003.
Beck, Jerry. "Sam Katzman's Animated Superman." CartoonResearch.com. Accessed 17 Sep. 2013.
Bifulco, Michael J. *The Original Superman on Television*. Independent Publishing Platform, 2011.
"The Black Pearl of Osiris, Pt. 2." *The Adventures of Superman*, episode 147. WOR, New York City, 17 Jan. 1941.
Cabarga, Leslie. *The Fleischer Story*. Da Capo, 1988.
Cameron, Don (w), Ed Dobrotka (p), and George Roussos (i). "The Million-Dollar Marathon," *Action Comics* #65 (Oct. 1943). DC Comics, 1943.
"Clark Kent, Reporter." *The Adventures of Superman*, episode 2.WOR, New York City, 14 Feb. 1940.
Couperie, Pierre, and Maurice C. Horn. *A History of the Comic Strip*. Crown Publishers Inc., 1967.
Culhane, Shamus, and Myron Waldman. "Fleischer Production in the 1930s." Society for Animation Studies Conference Panel Discussion. Sheridan College, Ottawa, Canada, 1990.
Daniels, Les. *Superman: The Complete History: The Life and Times of the Man of Steel*. Chronicle Books, 1998.
"Donelli's Protection Racket, Pt. 1." *The Adventures of Superman*, episode 28. WOR, New York City, Apr. 1940.
"The Dragon's Teeth, Pt. 9." *The Adventures of Superman*, episode 165. WOR, New York City, 28 Feb. 1941.
Feiffer, Jules. *The Great Comic Book Heroes the Origins and Early Adventures of the Classic Superheroes of the Comic Books*. The Penguin Press, 1967.
Fifty Who Made DC Great. DC Comics, 1985.
Finger, Bill (w), Wayne Boring (p), and Stan Kaye (i). "The Origin of Superman," *Superman* #53 (Aug. 1948). DC Comics, 1948.
Fleischer, Richard. *Out of the Inkwell: Max Fleischer and the Animation Revolution*. University Press of Kentucky, 2011.
Grossman, Gary H. *Superman: Serial to Cereal*. Popular Library, 1977.
Hayde, Michael J. *Flights of Fantasy: The Unauthorized but True Story of Radio & TV's Adventures of Superman*. BearManor Media, 2009.
Jenkins, Henry. *Convergence Culture: Where Old and New Media Collide*. New York University Press, 2016.
"Keno's Landslide." *The Adventures of Superman*, episode 3. WOR, New York City, 16 Feb. 1940.
Lowther, George Francis. *The Adventures of Superman*. Random House, 1942; Reprint, Applewood Books, 1995.
"The Magnetic Telescope." Directed by Dave Fleischer, voice performances by Joan Alexander and Bud Collyer, Fleischer Studios, 1942.
Maltin, Leonard. *Of Mice and Magic: A History of American Animated Cartoons*. Penguin Books, 1987.
McCloud, Scott. *Understanding Comics: The Invisible Art*. Kitchen Sink Press, 1993.
"The Mechanical Monsters." Directed by Dave Fleischer, voice performances by Joan Alexander and Bud Collyer, Fleischer Studios, 1941.
"The Meteor from Krypton." *The Adventures of Superman*, episode 249. WOR, New York City, 03 Jun. 1943.
"Secret Agent." Directed by Seymour Kneitel, voice performances by Joan Alexander and Bud Collyer, Famous Studios, 1943.
Siegel, Jerry (w), Leo Nowak (p), and the Shuster Shop (i). *Superman* #10 (June 1941). DC Comics, 1941.
Siegel, Jerry (w), and Joe Shuster (a). "Superman, Champion of the Oppressed," *Action Comics* #1 (June 1938). DC Comics, 1938.

26   Adapting Superman

_____. *Superman* #1 (June 1939). DC Comics, 1939.
_____. *Superman: The Dailies: Strips 1–966, 1939–1942*. New York: Sterling Publishing Co., Inc., 2006.
Siegel, Jerry (w), John Sikela (p), and Ed Dobrotka (i). *Superman* #19 (Nov. 1942). DC Comics, 1942.
Steranko, Jim. *The Steranko History of Comics*. Supergraphics, 1970.
Superman. Directed by Spencer Gordon Bennet and Thomas Carr, performances by Kirk Alyn, Tommy Bond, Carol Forman, Noel Neill, and Pierre Watkin, Columbia Pictures, 1948.
"Superman." Directed by Dave Fleischer, voice performances by Joan Alexander and Bud Collyer, Fleischer Studios, 1941.
Superman and the Mole Men. Directed by Lee Sholem, performances by Phyllis Coates and George Reeves, Lippert Pictures, 1951.
"Superman in Radio." *Radio and Television Mirror*, Jan. 1941–Apr. 1942.
"Superman on Earth." *Adventures of Superman*, season 1, episode 1, syndication, 19 Sept. 1952.
Superman: The Movie. Directed by Richard Donner, performances by Gene Hackman, Margot Kidder and Christopher Reeve, Warner Bros., 1978.
"Terror on the Midway." Directed by Dave Fleischer, voice performances by Joan Alexander and Bud Collyer, Fleischer Studios, 1942.
"Threat to the Planet Building." *The Adventures of Superman*, episode 9. WOR, New York City, 1 Mar. 1940.
Triumph #772 (Aug. 1939). UK: Amalgamated Press, 1939.
Tye, Larry. *Superman: The High-Flying History of America's Most Enduring Hero*. Random House, 2013.
"Volcano." Directed by Dave Fleischer, voice performances by Joan Alexander and Bud Collyer, Fleischer Studios, 1942.
Waugh, Coulton. *The Comics*. University Press of Mississippi, 1994.
Wheeler-Nicholson, Nicky. *DC Comics Before Superman: Major Malcolm Wheeler-Nicholson's Pulp Comics*. Hermes Press, 2018.

Secret Origins: The Birth of Superman and Tintin as National Icons

ALEXANDRE DESBIENS-BRASSARD

The secret origin—also known as the origin story or, simply, the origin—is one of the most common tropes found in American superhero comics. The secret origin reveals how a character acquired superpowers and decided to put on a costume and fight crime. The origin story is not necessarily the first story ever published about a character, but it is almost always the most retold story about that character—and therefore the most adapted. The explosion of Krypton and the crashing of its sole survivor in Kansas, for example, has been retold more than a dozen times across various movies, tv series, and video games, to the point where an entire television series, *Krypton* (2018–2019), was made to tell the origin of that origin. Interestingly, with each retelling, the origin gets revised and rewritten slightly—only the main outline remains constant. Why Krypton was destroyed and how many Kryptonians survived that destruction are malleable details, but there are very few Superman adaptations out there where Jor-El and his wife are still on an intact Krypton.

This chapter, however, is not concerned with Superman's fictional origin as the last son of Krypton. Rather, I am interested in Superman's meta-origin as a national icon. In other words, I am interested in how a fictional character like Superman can break the confine of his original stories and, through an intermingled chain of adaptations and evolutions, become a national icon imbued with ideological meanings and connotations that transcend the comic book medium. The meta-origin story is a lot less spectacular, but a great deal more interesting, than a rocket ship escaping an exploding planet. It takes place over years and over hundreds of stories in different media, making it hard for the average reader to perceive the evolutionary through line undergirding it all. In order to better outline the thematic trends behind Superman's evolution, I thus decided to add a comparative element to the analysis. As Superman is the forefather of the American comic book tradition, it made sense to compare him to another such forefather from a different comic book tradition. Since the Franco-Belgian and American comic book traditions developed conterminously and share many traits, Tintin, from Belgian writer and artist Hergé (George Rémi), appeared to me as the obvious choice to act as a comparative mirror to Superman. In both the United States and francophone Europe, comic books emerged during roughly the same period, targeted mostly the same young audiences and were published in similarly serialised fashion in magazines or newspapers. These qualities make the American and Franco-Belgian comic book tradition a fertile ground for a comparative analysis of the development of new national icons through popular culture.

Consequently, the goal of this chapter is to chart the meta-origin story of Superman and the Franco-Belgian character Tintin: how the characters came to be, what they originally represented, and how or why the characters evolved beyond that origin as popular comic book characters and into national icons with worldwide recognition in a variety of medium. What themes, connotations, and symbolic significances were originally attached to a character that have since been forgotten or intentionally taken out? And which ones have endured until today? These are the kind of questions I aim to answer.

What is a national icon? Semiotically, cultural studies scholars Keyan G. Tomaselli and David Scott defines icons as "signs that resemble their objects whether their object is a thing in the real world, an idea, or another sign" and as signs that "include indexical and symbolic functions in that they point to their objects and often become conventional signs" (18). National icons, therefore, are repeated representations of a thing, a person, an idea, or a symbol that both point to and connote a specific nation or particular characteristics of that nation, depending on the context. There are various types of visual signs that can be represented as national icons, including monuments, works of art, historical artifacts, animals, living or dead individuals, and cultural symbols. The latter category includes objects or images such as flags, seals, coat of arms or, most importantly for my purpose, allegorical figures. An allegorical figure is a personified embodiment of a particular nation; examples include Uncle Sam for the United States, the stereotypical square-jawed Mountie figure for Canada, or Britannia for Great Britain. Since these fictional characters do not have to mimic a real-world individual, they allow for greater artistic freedom in how they are represented. However, since icons are supposed to be "signs that resemble their object," this freedom can prove problematic. While it might be easy to see how, for example, a representation of the Statue of Liberty in a painting denouncing American capitalism represents its object—the real monument on Liberty Island—it is harder to understand how a fictional character can resemble anything but itself. David Scott attempts to solve this problem by insisting on the indexical function of icons:

> If an icon is a sign that resembles its object, one might ask what is the "object" that Britannia resembles? An armor-clad woman, clutching a shield emblazoned with the Union Jack flag and brandishing a trident—does she resemble anything more than herself? The Britannia icon manages to escape this congenital tautology, however, by using two *indexical* strategies: she includes within her regalia other signs—for example, that of the national flag, the Union Jack—that point to the country with which she is associated; and she herself as a figure is usually placed in a minimal context—waves or stretch of shoreline with naval warships in the offing—signs that are also indexes of the country she represents (Britain the island maritime power) [136].

In addition to the two strategies Scott mentions, there is a third indexical strategy that can be employed to make fictional characters resemble their object (i.e., their nation): the insertion of those characters into a *narrative* that points to the nation they represent. This is where media that fuses visual and narrative elements—like cinema and comic-books—come into play and enable national icons to exploit their full indexical and symbolic tendency in ways a single lone picture or object cannot.

It is not a coincidence that Superman and Tintin, two of the comic-book medium's most recognizable national icons, are also two of the oldest comic-book characters, since "[t]he longer the history of the icon, the richer the layering of indexical and symbolic significances organically attached to it" (Tomaselli and Scott 19). However, before these layers could pile on, the characters as originally created and the stories told about them had to have embodied a certain vision of their nation that the mainstream public could identify with. In other words, it had to resemble its object. However, since the process of "[i]conization eliminates contradiction, celebrates the unity of surface appearance, and denies history," many of these elements have since been altered or excised (Tomaselli and Scott 20). The Superman and Tintin of the 1930s and 1940s can thus be considered different characters than the icons modern readers are familiar with. As such, from this point on, the early versions of the characters will be referred to as the "original" Superman and Tintin and the current versions as the "iconic" Superman and Tintin.

Before progressing further, a brief note on the corpus under study is needed. As is undoubtedly clear by now, this chapter is interested only with the earliest adventures of each character, as befit an origin story. While Superman's early stories have been well-preserved, warts and all, the colored versions of Tintin stories that can be purchased today were redrawn during the fifties by Hergé and his collaborators and rewritten slightly in order to tighten the pacing and remove some of the more objectionable elements of the original stories. Therefore, this essay will analyze the original black and white versions of all the Tintin stories published before and during World War II, as reproduced in the multiple volumes of the relatively rare *Archives Hergé* collection, rather than the colored versions available today.

The Political Beginnings of Superman and Tintin

To say that Superman is as much an American icon as the Statue of Liberty or Abraham Lincoln is not very controversial. Being an American, and a patriotic one at that, is so intrinsic to Superman's character that a short story in *Action Comics* #900 (June 2011) in which Superman renounced his American citizenship was aggressively denounced by right-wing pundits as treason (McKay). However, though Superman's American-ness is an intrinsic part of the character today, it was not always the case. When Joe Shuster and Jerry Siegel created the character, they did not intend to use him to glorify America as a model for and savior of the rest of the world. On the contrary, Siegel used the character to critique many aspects of his country, from large scale problems like white collar crime and arms smuggling to smaller personal problems such as domestic violence. As the opening narration of his early stories put it, he was the "saviour [or champion, depending on the story] of the helpless and oppressed" who battled "the forces of evil and injustice!" (Siegel and Shuster, "Challenge" 65). The Fleischer cartoons were more succinct, with each episode beginning with the following pronouncement: "Possessing remarkable physical strength, Superman fights a never-ending battle for truth and justice disguised as a mild-mannered reporter, Clark Kent!" In addition to not being as much of a patriot, the original Superman was also much less of a big blue boy scout than his iconic counterpart. Indeed, if the iconic Superman is coded as morally righteous to the point that showing him killing a villain in *Man of Steel* caused serious controversy and "divided the fan community between those who claim that Superman never kills, and those who defend David Goyer and Zack Snyder's creative choices as necessary to the storyline" (Salkowitz 1; see also Hughes), the original had a lot fewer scruples when pursuing what he saw as justice. While he used more aggressive negotiation tactics, however, the original Superman rarely, if ever, killed criminals directly. Rather, they always died by their own hands. In other words, namely those of comic book writer and Superman expert Mark Waid, rather than the superhero archetype the character is credited with inventing, the Superman of the late thirties bore a greater resemblance to a "super-anarchist" who "reveled in his strength, who clearly enjoyed a little hell and who didn't care who got in his way as he bounded through Metropolis meting out his own brand of justice" (Waid 5). The original Superman did not uphold of the system; he was there when the system failed. An excellent example of this is found in *Superman #3* (Winter 1939). In the issue's first story,[1] Clark and Lois investigate a state orphanage where they know abuses are being perpetrated. When they fail to find the solid evidence they need to take down the crooked superintendent, Superman takes charge and brings down the entire orphanage—literally (he had it evacuated first, of course). This is an anarchic, even revolutionary move. On the ruins of the old orphanage—which, being state-run, is representative of the system—a new, better, fairer orphanage—and thus system—is built (Siegel and Shuster, "Superman and the Runaway" 381). The original Superman was not the All-American wonder-boy that he is today, but simply an American, who, like millions of others, wanted to be a good person and help others. The iconization process, however, forced Superman to transform from *an* American to *the* American.

Contrary to the original Superman—and to his own iconic self—the original Tintin was nothing more nor less than the littlest Belgian patriot. Indeed, when he first appeared—in the January 10, 1929, issue of *Le Petit Vingtième (The Little Twentieth)*, the youth supplement of Belgian French-language Catholic newspaper *Le Vingtième Siècle (The Twentieth Century)*—Tintin was a pretty transparent mouthpiece for the most popular worldviews present in Hergé's francophone, Catholic, monarchist, colonialist, anti-communist, and altogether right-wing milieu. Hergé himself willingly admitted that he was very receptive to external ideas: "I'm very permeable, very impressionable, which makes me an excellent medium. All my books carry traces of the time when they were drawn" (qtd. in Peeters 46). In the first few years of Tintin's life, the biggest influence on Hergé was Abbot Norbert Wallez, who ran *Le Vingtième Siècle*. Hergé borrowed a lot of his political ideas from Wallez who, unlike the writer, was politically active. In fact, according to Hergé's biographer Benoît Peeters, Wallez was "[m]uch more passionately interested in political problems than in questions of religion" and was a "fervent admirer of Mussolini" (27). More than simply influencing Hergé's political views, Wallez also played a pivotal role in the creation of Tintin. It was Wallez who asked Hergé to create Tintin after seeing two drawings of a young boy and a white dog that Hergé had done as freelance work for another publication. Likewise, it was the abbot who decided that Tintin's first adventure should be set in Soviet Russia. If that adventure reads like anti-communist propaganda, that is because this was exactly what Wallez wanted it to be. The abbot even gave Hergé a copy of the virulently anti-communist book *Moscou sans voiles (Starless Moscow)*, from which Hergé "borrowed" most of the anti-communist scenes in *Tintin in the Land of the Soviets* (1930),[2] sometimes word for word (Peeter 35–36, 55).

Tintin in the Land of the Soviets was a huge success for the newspaper, and so Wallez ordered a second Tintin story. Once again, Wallez himself decided where to send the boy reporter and he chose the Belgian Congo. The abbot wanted to use the story to inspire more Belgians to take on the colonial mantle and to influence a public opinion that was mostly indifferent to the remote African colony (98). Hergé thus dutifully sent his hero on what Marc McKinney, in his book on colonial themes in French comics, calls a "colonial voyage." McKinney, borrowing from Edward Said, defines the colonial voyage as "an imperialist 'ceremony of reappropriation' of the colony by the colonizer" that "expresses a geographic relationship between an imperialist metropolis and its colonies" (McKinney 8). *Tintin in the Congo* (1931), in other words, was a way of reifying the link between Belgium and the Congo by bringing the colony to Belgian children's doorstep so that those children could experience and, Abbot Wallez hoped, develop a strong interest for that colony. As a result, Tintin acts in this second adventure according to "paternalistic notions of superiority [that] were widely taken for granted in colonialist Europe, not least in the right-wing Roman Catholic circles around Abbé Wallez; after all Belgium did not lose the Congo until 1960" (Screech 20). That the strong, noble, and intelligent Tintin represents all Belgians in his nobility is made explicit in the final panel of the adventure, when a distraught Congolese villager says that "in Belgium, all the young whiteys are like Tintin" (293; my translation).[3]

In short, in these early adventures Tintin was a strictly Belgian hero upholding the values of his country abroad. The best example of this, however, is not found in Tintin's comic-book adventures but in the marketing stunts organized by *Le Vingtième Siècle* to celebrate the end of the character's first two stories. The last page of *Tintin in the Land of the Soviets* featured Tintin arriving back from Russia and exiting the train at the Gare du Nord in Brussels (Hergé 1: 180). In what could be termed the first live-action adaptation of Tintin,[4] the newspaper hired an actor to play Tintin and had him actually exit a train at that very station. The event was so successful that another was organized when *Tintin in the Congo* ended, with a different actor, even though this time the arrival in Brussels was not in the comic story itself. However, after *Tintin in the Congo*, no other event of this nature was ever organized again, probably because Tintin had started becoming popular in France and thus such local events were no longer considered the best way to promote the character anymore. This was the first time that Tintin's Belgian colonialism and nationalism was toned down as a way to universalize the character. As such, this shift in marketing represented the first step on the road that lead to the iconic version of Tintin, who shies away from explicit reference to Belgium while still representing Belgian values and who educates children about the lives and problems of others rather than promote a specific nationalist and colonialist ideology to the next generation of Belgians. Further universalizing steps were taken in the subsequent few adventures—all of which had their destination and theme chosen by Hergé himself—but the iconization process would not start in earnest until the eve of World War II, which, not coincidentally, is also when Superman started turning into his iconic self in a decisive way.

The War and the Start of the Iconization Process

The topic of war had been present in Superman stories since *Action Comics* #2 (July 1938). However, in that story and in a handful of others from the same era, Superman was always against war as a concept and took no sides.[5] In *Action Comics* #2, Superman encounters munitions magnate Emil Norvell, who is paying off congressmen to get the United States embroiled with a war in the (fictional) South American country of San Monte. Superman kidnaps Norvell and forces him to enlist in the San Monte army. After a few weeks in the army, Norvell grows to detest war and vows that "from now on, the most dangerous thing [he]'ll manufacture will be a firecracker!" (Siegel and Shuster, "Revolution" 33). Superman then kidnaps the commanders of both armies and orders them to fight each other, causing the two commanders to realize they have no reason to fight and had been manipulated into doing so in order, as Superman puts it, "to promote the sale of munitions" (34). In light of this epiphany, the commanders agree to stop fighting and the war ends.

Speaking out against wars and war profiteers was so important for Siegel and Shuster that, less than a year after *Action Comics* #2 was published, they wrote an almost identical story for another medium, namely the syndicated newspaper strip featuring their hero. That story, entitled "Superman Champions Universal Peace," was first published as a newspaper strip from May 1 to June 10, 1939, and then reprinted in *Superman* #2 (Fall 1939). The fact that this story has a title is quite unusual—most stories of this period did not have an individual title when originally published (though anthologies sometimes give them one for ease of reference). The story begins as a scientist invents "the most deadly weapon modern warfare has ever seen!" but refuses to sell it to anyone (272). Rather, the scientist intends to give his weapon (a deadly gas) to the United States government freely "but only in the case of a defensive war!" (273). Unfortunately, the scientist is murdered and the weapon gets stolen by another munitions magnate named Lubane who wants to cash in on another war raging in another fictional South American country, Boravia. When Superman confronts Lubane, he is definitely not in a merciful mood: "I'm going to give you the fate you deserve, Lubane, for promoting this war and profiteering upon the death and misery of others!" (289). Terrified by the sight of the superhero advancing on him, Lubane accidentally drops the vial of deadly gas he was holding, killing himself. Superman does not waste any time shedding a tear for a "vulture" like Lubane (290). Instead, he flies away and, just like in *Action Comics* #2, forces the commanders of both armies to come together and end the war.

The message of these two stories is pretty clear: war is only a way for unscrupulous men to make money by causing others needless suffering. For the original Superman, strength and physical force was to be exerted only in the pursuit of social justice, not to advance the interests of the American elite, be they senators or businessmen. All this, however, would change quickly as the Second World War gained in intensity. In 1940, "Superman was still concentrating on smaller-scale problems for the most part, as Siegel continued to explore the idea of how a good man with supernatural powers could change the social conditions of the contemporary United States" (Goulart 4). Come 1941, most of Superman's stories now featured the caped hero fighting against Fifth Columnists and other perceived enemies of the United States. Superman was to stay as violent as he had been—that aspect of the iconization process would not happen until the mid-fifties and the appearance of the Comics Code—but that violence would be diverted from social issues and refocused into patriotic efforts, even before Pearl Harbor. The most blatant example of this in the comics themselves was in *Superman* #9 (Mar.–Apr. 1941) in which Superman fought against a "Committee Against Militarism," whose public plea for "no rearmament in the U.S., and no aid to warring democracies" is quickly revealed to be a sham. The Committee was in reality "in the employ of a warring totalitarian nation" aiming to "tak[e] over America" (Siegel and Cassidy, "Phony" 114). The conscientious objection to war lionized in *Action Comics* #2 was now an act of treason that Superman had to stop. The change in attitude was striking, to say the least. And so, from 1941 onward, Superman was no longer described as a champion of the oppressed, but as the "foe of all interests and activities subversive to this country's best interests" or a variant thereof (Siegel, Boring and Shuster, "Dukalia" 240).

This shift in attitude impacted the adaptations of Superman even more strongly than it did the comics. The most long-lasting change made to the original Superman to make him more patriotic happened in September 1942 when *The Adventures of Superman*—the second radio show about the character—started airing. The writer of the show, Robert Maxwell, had very much liked the aforementioned introductory sentence used by all of Fleischer Studio's Superman cartoon shorts and decided to borrow it from his show, with only one small change: "The Superman cartoons had begun with a narrator intoning the phrase 'Superman fights a never ending battle for truth and justice!' Maxwell's emendation was 'a never-ending battle for truth, justice, *and the American way*'" (Weldon 57, emphasis mine). As for the Fleischer cartoon themselves, they were not immune to this attitude shift either. Two of the original shorts had Superman fighting the Axis: "Japoteurs" (Sept. 1942) and "The Eleventh Hour" (Nov. 1942). "Japoteurs" is a fairly standard war-time yarn, with Superman fighting Axis agents trying to sabotage the American war effort on American soil, this time by stealing a new bomber plane. Superman stops the saboteurs, of course, and rescues Lois Lane, as usual. What distinguish "Japoteurs" from contemporary comic-book stories is that the saboteurs are explicitly "Japs," as Lois Lane says in the cartoon. The Japanese characters are therefore depicted according to the racist caricatural conventions of the era, all buckteeth, slanted eyes and clumsy "Engrish" accent. The cartoon was released about 6 months before the most blatant and well-known of such depictions in the comics: the cover to *Action Comics* #58 (Mar. 1943), which proudly proclaimed that "Superman says you can slap a Jap with war bond and stamps!" Between this short and the radio show, it is clear that, during the iconization process, it was adaptations of Superman that led the charge and the comics simply followed suit.

Meanwhile, "The Eleventh Hour" is particularly significant because it takes place in Japan itself. The short opens in a military shipyard in Yokohama. For some unspecified reason, Clark and Lois are prisoners in a local hotel and Superman decides to take this opportunity to do some sabotage of his own. He wrecks warships every night until the Japanese threaten to kill Lois, at which point he sabotages some more ships before flying in to save Lois, sending her back home, and heading back to Yokohama to destroy some more of Japan's military assets. Seeing Superman wage war behind the front lines in this short is extremely unusual considering that, as a very consequence of his newfound patriotic obligations, the character was not allowed to leave the home front in his own comics. At first glance, having Superman wage war alongside brave American soldiers seems a logical choice. Even if he did not do so by his own choice—unlikely, since by this time he had become "patriot number one" (Siegel, Nowak and Sikela, "Grotak" 49)—Clark Kent would certainly get drafted. On the other hand, Superman, with all of his powers, was clearly no match for the Axis. Therefore, if Superman went to war, he would have to either restrain himself, which was no way for a patriot to act in defense of his nation, or end the war in a single story, which "could be easily construed as trivializing the grim work that soldiers faced" (Weldon 54). This problem was made even worse when the United States government decided to send copies of *Superman* and *Action Comics* to deployed soldiers, as a contemporary issue of *Times* magazine explained:

> Superman is now in a really tough spot that even he can't get out of. His patriotism is above reproach. As the mightiest, fightingest American, he ought to join up. But he just can't. In the combat services he would lick the Japs and Nazis in a wink, and the war isn't going to end that soon. On the other hand, he

can't afford to lose the respect of millions by failing to do his bit or by letting the war drag on ["Superman's Dilemma"].

As a solution, Siegel and Shuster devised a way for Clark Kent get exempted from drafting. In what might seem like a weird choice in retrospect, that solution was not published in an issue of *Action Comics* or *Superman*, where deployed soldiers might have read it, but in the syndicated newspaper strip (i.e., in an adaptation). In a series of strips starting on February 16, 1942, Clark Kent reports to the army recruitment center to enlist. So excited is Superman to be doing his duty as an American that he inadvertently uses his X-Ray vision to read the eye chart in the next examination room, rather than the one he is in. This causes the doctor to declare Clark as unfit for service for being "blind as a bat" (Weldon 53–4). Thus, Superman was kept out of the war with his honor and patriotic credentials still intact.

Having Superman and the war in a single story, however, was too good a fantasy for the wartime propaganda machine to pass up. Consequently, stories from outside the comics came in to fill a niche the comics could not. A year and a half before "The Eleventh Hour," *Look* magazine commissioned Siegel and Shuster to create a story about what would happen if Superman intervened in World War II. The 2-page story, aptly titled "How Superman Would End the War," was published in the February 17, 1940, issue of *Look*. In it, the Man of Steel charges into Germany with no care for its defenses and picks up Adolf Hitler before heading to Russia and picking up Joseph Stalin.[6] He then brings them both in front of the League of Nations, who promptly declares them "guilty of modern history's greatest crime—unprovoked aggression against defenseless countries" (13). The story was billed as nothing more than a thought exercise, yet its cultural impact was big enough that it has been continuously reprinted in collections, even one bearing the title *Superman: The Greatest Stories Ever Told* (2004).

In summary, Superman's might was catalyzed as a propaganda tool both in his comics stories and in his adaptations, allowing him to bolster his countrymen and fight his nation's enemies on two fronts: at home in the comics and abroad outside of them. During and after World War II, Superman became a super-patriot and the super-patriot became a national icon. However, in order to become this icon, Superman had to give up something—his political consciousness. In the words of Umberto Eco, he had to become "a perfect example of civic consciousness, completely split from political consciousness" (123). After all, "[t]here was a war on, so the time for social crusades was over. Where he once agitated and chafed against the status quo, Superman was now determined to reinforce it" (Weldon 55). Superman could not be both a super-patriot and a "super-anarchist." As a whole, this shift in attitude regarding the status quo and the established authorities happened over a span of about ten to twelve years. It started during the war, as I have shown, and ended when psychiatrist Fredric Wertham accused Superman of "undermin[ing] the authority and the dignity of the ordinary man and woman in the minds of children" in his now infamous 1953 book *Seduction of the Innocent* (97–98). That book immediately intensified a moral panic about comic books that led the American comic book industry to establish its own censor—the Comics Code Authority—which, among other things, stated that "policemen, judges, government officials, and respected institutions shall never be presented in such a way as to create disrespect for established authority" (United States 36). In various pre-war stories, Superman fought corrupt politicians regularly.[7] After the war, and especially after the passage of the Comics Code, the Man of Steel was now busy by preference, not against blackmarket drugs, nor, obviously against corrupt administrators or politicians, but against bank and mail-truck robbers. In other words, *the only visible form that evil assumes is an attempt on private property* [Eco 123, emphasis in the original].

In the end, Superman could not beat the system he originally denounced; he had to join it. In a way, this was the first and only fight Superman ever lost.

Once again, the evolution of Tintin from his beginnings to his current iconic form was in many ways the mirror opposite of Superman's. If the American super-hero was transformed from a social crusader to a super-patriot by the iconization process, then Tintin transformed from "*Le Petit Vingtième*'s star journalist" and resident colonialist Belgian patriot into "a righter of international wrongs" (Screech 20).

Peeters identifies the first signs of Tintin's new attitude, which he calls "the protection of the weak," in *Tintin in America* (1932) but notes that it is only from *The Blue Lotus* (1936) onward that this attitude become an important part of the plots (56). *The Blue Lotus* is the fifth story starring Tintin and revolves around Tintin defending the weak, in this case the Chinese, from British, American, and Japanese oppressors. Hergé's Japanese villains are drawn almost identically to those that would later appear in the aforementioned "Japoteurs,"[8] but the Americans and the British are also depicted as unflatteringly as possible. For example, the first person Tintin encounters in Shangai is a fat and foul-mannered British man whom Tintin has to stop from beating a Chinese citizen who had accidentally bumped into him. When the man complains about the incident to his European colleagues, he is the very picture of the "paternalistic notions of superiority [that] were widely taken for granted in colonialist Europe" (Screech 20) and that Hergé himself had glorified only a few years beforehand in *Tintin in Congo*:

> Keeping me from beating a Chink! Intolerable, isn't it! What is the world coming to if we can't teach these dirty Yellows a thing or two about politeness?… To keep us from trying to civilize these barbarians a little…. It would mean that we wouldn't have any more control over them!… We, who give them the benefits of our wonderful Western civilization! [Hergé 3: 154–5; translation from Peeters 77]

The Blue Lotus was also the first Tintin story to contain fictionalization of and commentary on real events, another of the iconic Tintin's defining traits that was absent from the characters' earliest stories, which preferred to borrow from propaganda or to indulge in over-the-top slapstick. In this case, the event in question is the Mukden incident, a staged railway attack used by the Japanese army as a pretext to invade Manchuria (Hergé 3: 182–3). While, with the benefit of hindsight, we can determine that Hergé's version was close to the historical events, it is paramount to note that when Hergé wrote the book, the fact that the incident was "a complete fabrication of the Japanese army" was hotly debated (Ferrell 69). Hergé's version was not a neutral depiction of the events; the author was deliberately siding with the Chinese version of the events, in opposition to the Japanese version, which made the story quite controversial when first published.[9]

Likewise, *The Broken Ear* (1937), the adventure that followed *The Blue Lotus*, features another barely disguised fictionalization of a real event, this time "the war of Gran Chaco, which pitted Bolivia and Paraguay against each other from 1932 to 1935. This bloody conflict had been stirred up by two oil companies, and as in the book, the expected oil deposits had finally proven unusable" (Peeters 90). *The Broken Ear* is especially interesting because it parallels the original Superman's attitude towards war and warmongering while using a lot of the same plot elements Siegel and Shuster would later use in their own anti-war stories. Like "Superman Champions Universal Peace," *The Broken Ear* features a conflict between two fictional South American countries, "San-Theodoros" and

"Nuevo-Rico," and contains a highly critical depiction of a weapon merchant who sells ammunition to both sides. However, unlike the entirely fictional arms dealer that Superman fought, the warmonger seen in *The Broken Ear* is a thinly-veiled caricature of the real and infamous Bazil Zaharoff, a ruthless businessman often described as a "merchant of death" and nicknamed "The Mystery Man of Europe" (Dash). Hergé changed his name from Zaharoff to Mazaroff and the name of the company he worked for from Vickers to Vicking but made sure to keep the man's likeness intact (Hergé 4: 213–5).

However, as with Superman, while Tintin had already taken steps towards becoming his iconic Franco-Belgian self before World War II, it is the war which sounded the —not entirely voluntary—death of the character's original self. Superman had been obligated to become a super-patriot by the U.S. War Department, which had to approve the script for every issue of the comic-book, every newspaper strip, and every episode of the radio show before their release. Consequently, even if his creators had been against their creation participating in the war, they would not have had much choice; fortunately, they were all for it (Weldon 54). Hergé and Tintin, however, found themselves in a much more delicate situation than Siegel, Shuster, and their creation. In May 1940, Germany invaded and took over Belgium, placing it under the direct supervision of the *Wehrmacht. Le Vingtième Siècle* was closed down, leading Hergé to accept to write Tintin stories for *Le Soir (The Evening)*, Belgium's biggest newspaper, which was now entirely controlled by the Germans. Hergé has always denied that his decision to work for *Le Soir* was an act of collaboration and considered himself as having been neutral and passive during the war, rather than actively acting for one side or another. He consequently applied this self-imposed neutrality to the stories he wrote for *Le Soir*, eschewing criticism of real-world events in favor, not of a return to Belgian patriotism, but of fantastic, larger-than-life adventures replete with elements taken from fantasy or science-fiction, with a small degree of "defense of the weak" sprinkled in. The real world was never farther than during this period—both the slapstick of *Tintin in the Land of the Soviets* and the (then impossible) trip to the moon of the later *Destination Moon* (1953)/*Explorers on the Moon* (1954) two-part story were more grounded than many of the elements featured in the war-time stories (*The Crab with the Golden Claws* (1941), *The Shooting Star* (1941), *The Secret of the Unicorn* (1943), *Red Rackham's Treasure* (1944), and *The Seven Crystal Balls* (1948). Despite the shift in direction, the sales and popularity of Tintin books were higher during the war than they ever were before. In the eyes of many, Hergé had succeeded in boosting the morale of his fellow Belgians during the occupation:

> It is a surprising paradox that sales of Tintin books saw a remarkable rise during the Second World War. One common explanation given by people who actually experienced this tragic historical event is that the stories transported them to a different universe, allowing them to dream of a better world and escape for a while from the desperate reality they faced [Maricq 41].

Bolstered by this success, the defense of the weak against more powerful enemies indeed came back after the war, starting in the reworked and completed *Land of the Black Gold* (1950), as well as in stories like *The Red Sea Sharks* (1958)[10] and the last completed story, *Tintin and the Picaros* (1976), which came back to themes first touched upon in *The Broken Ear* and fictionalized the revolutionary wars then happening in South and Central America. Screech even characterized the later Tintin as "a valiant force of goodness, crusading against villains whom we still know only too well: warlike dictators, drug smugglers, gun runners, people traffickers, corrupt politicians, criminal businessman" (48).

It is as if the iconic Tintin had picked up the slack after the iconic Superman had been forced to dedicate himself to the American Way.

Conclusion

Throughout this chapter, for the sake of clarity, I have presented the evolution of both characters as a straight, continuous chronological line. In truth, the process of transition from the original Superman and Tintin to the iconic Superman and Tintin was a little messier, with later stories sometimes going back to prior characterization or theme, counter to the general narrative trend of the period. For example, the Fleischer cartoon short that directly followed "The Eleventh Hour," "Destruction, Inc.," featured another story of saboteurs trying to frustrate the United States' war effort, but this time the saboteurs are never explicitly or implicitly characterized as agents from Germany, Japan, or any other Axis countries. There are no highly symbolic shots of the Statue of Liberty transforming into a flag of Imperial Japan, as in "Japoteurs." In fact, apart from a single shot of white-suited navy officers watching a torpedo test, the army is not a presence in this short, despite having an ammunition factory as a setting. The final scene, with the saboteurs being taken away in handcuff in a regular police truck, looks ripped from a 1939 comic-book Superman stories rather than the contemporary war-themed stories.

As for Tintin, no stories better exemplify this sort of step backwards than *King Ottokar's Sceptre*, the last complete story published before the war. At first, the story seems to fit into the era's trend of Tintin stories fictionalizing and commenting on a real event, in this case the *Anschluss*, the annexation of Austria by Nazi Germany. However, a more thorough analysis of the stories shows that *King Ottokar's Sceptre* (1939) is the most nationalist Tintin story since *Tintin in Congo*. Indeed, the story's setting, Syldavia, was not only a metaphor for Austria, but also "a metaphor for Belgium, threatened in its neutrality. King Muskar XII, whose throne Tintin saves, bears a resemblance to young Léopold III. More than an antifascist book, *King Ottokar's Sceptre* is an exaltation of the constitutional monarchy in Belgium" (Peeters 100). Maricq, similarly, calls *King Ottokar's Sceptre* "a story that expressed [Hergé's] appreciation of monarchies" (Maricq 34), and especially the Belgian monarchy, in opposition to the fascist populism that was growing everywhere in Europe, Belgium included.

As one can see, my retelling of Superman and Tintin's iconization process, like the iconization process itself, glossed over some details to present a more homogeneous picture than what actually happened. This was intentional, as my goal was not to detail each character's history. A number of scholarly treatises have already done that work superbly, many of which you can find in this chapter's Works Cited. Rather, my goal in outlining the process of iconization of each character was to (a) show how much adaptations have always been a privileged vector of change for the character of Superman, even in his earliest days, and (b) show how much Superman and Tintin were, most likely entirely coincidentally, mirrors of the other. Both characters went through the same evolution at roughly the same time, but in the opposite direction. If I smoothed over the rough edges of the real iconization process in my retelling, thus, it was only to highlight these two facts.

Another criticism one could lobby at this chapter is that I never attempt to prove that Superman and Tintin are national icons, that I just took this fact for granted. I did so because I do not feel that this is a fact that still needs proving: once again, the amount of scholarly work done on both characters has already proved it so much better than I could in a single chapter. However, if there is one proof I can add to the debate, it is that, in another interesting parallel, both Superman and Tintin were first acknowledged as powerful icons not by favorable critics but by decidedly hostile ones. Indeed, even those who, after the war, accused Hergé of having collaborated with the Nazis recognized the importance of Tintin as an icon to young Belgians and made sure to recuperate him in a parody strip published in the anti–Nazi magazine *La Patrie* (*The Homeland*) shortly after Hergé was temporarily forbidden to work for any newspaper because of his wartime work in *Le Soir*. Entitled "The Adventures of Tintin and Snowy in the Land of the Nazis," the strip sees Tintin, Snowy, and Captain Haddock celebrating the departure of Hergé. "Captain, we are finally free, Hergé's gone," says a dancing Tintin. In the following two panels, each character declares that Hergé was not able to change their nature—Haddock is still an "anglophile," Tintin still likes cowboys, and Snowy is still not a German Shepherd.[11] This denunciation of an alleged "meddling" of Hergé with the characters is strange, since it implies that Tintin, Snowy and Haddock have an essence that pre-existed their creation by Hergé and exists independently from him. As Peeters points out "[t]he publication is strange and highly symptomatic; it is as if the cartoonist had to be attacked in order to redeem his characters. Already, it seemed, Belgium needed them" (160).

As for Superman, so great was his power as a patriotic icon that, in another moment of near perfect mirroring of Tintin, his opponent—the Nazis themselves—felt compelled to respond to it. Their critique, published on April 25, 1940, in *Das schwarze Korps*—the official newspaper of the *Schutzstaffel* (SS)—is, unsurprisingly, little more than a vicious anti–Semitic attack on Superman's creators. The concluding paragraph of the article is nevertheless extremely interesting, since it acknowledges that Superman's impact on American minds is not to be ignored:

> Well, we really ought to ignore these fantasies of Jerry Israel Siegel, but there is a catch. The daring deeds of Superman are those of a Colorado beetle. He works in the dark, in incomprehensible ways. He cries "Strength! Courage! Justice!" to the noble yearnings of American children. Instead of using the chance to encourage really useful virtues, he sows hate, suspicion, evil, laziness, and criminality in their young hearts. [...] Woe to the American youth, who must live in such a poisoned atmosphere and don't even notice the poison they swallow daily ["Jerry Siegel Attacks!" 8].

What is most interesting about this critique is that it was not written in response to the comic-books themselves, but to one of their adaptations—namely the story in *Look* magazine. Clearly, even the anonymous Nazi who authored this piece knew how potent Superman could be if he was ever unshackled from the bounds of the comic-book medium and transformed—or rather, *adapted*—into a national icon. As the rest of this book proves, this Nazi was right—the only thing a Nazi was ever right about.

Notes

1. The self-titled *Superman* series was originally published as over-sized issues with multiple stories and initially released on a quarterly basis before shifting to bi-monthly issues starting with issue 6. As was common practice at the time, most of the stories are untitled. Modern collected editions, however, sometimes give them one for ease of reference. In this case, the title given is "Superman and the Runaway."

2. The publication dates provided for Tintin are for the original black and white collections, not their serializations.

3. Like many, though far from all, of *Tintin in Congo*'s most problematic moments, this final panel is greatly edited in the color version available today.

4. In another extremely interesting parallel, Superman's first live-action appearance was also at a public event: Superman Day, organized on July 3, 1940, as part of the New York's World Fair. The identity of the actor inside the suit is still subject to debate, though most credit actor Ray Middleton (Bureau international des expositions). Interestingly, the BIE, who organizes the World Fairs and World Expos since 1931, mentions in their official description of Superman Day that "at a time of international conflict and tragedy, Superman was more than just a comic book character, he also gave hope to adults and children alike," a statement that goes very well with the rest of this chapter (and this book).

5. Technically, the topic of war has been present in Superman stories since "The Reign of the Superman," an illustrated short story written by Siegel and Shuster and eventually released as a fanzine by the two men after multiple rejections from publishers. In that story, "Superman" is a homeless man who is given superpowers by a mad scientist and uses them for evil. His final, and most evil, act in the story is to use mind-control in order to sabotage a peace summit between all nations of the world and instead "send the armies of the world to total annihilation against each other" (Siegel and Shuster, "Reign" 14).

6. This story was written before Hitler tore up the non-aggression treaty he had with Stalin and invaded Russia, hence why Stalin is here depicted as an Axis rather than an Allied power.

7. For examples, see the stories listed in the Works Cited as "The Construction Scam," "The Exploding Citizens," and, most pertinently, "Superman's Cleanup Campaign."

8. It should be noted that, while undoubtedly racist caricatures, the visual depiction of the Japanese villains in both *The Blue Lotus* and *Japoteurs* is quite tame compared to some of the extremes to which American comic-books went during the war. Many early issues of *Captain America*, for example, had the future Avenger go against Japanese villains with simian visages, vampiric fangs, and names like "Captain Okada, Oriental Master of Evil" (Simon 297) or "The Fang, Archfiend of the Orient," (367).

9. See Peeters 79 for a sampling of contemporary reactions to the story.

10. A story denouncing the contemporary slave trade, *The Red Sea Sharks* was criticized for its problematic depictions of African characters. However, while I acknowledge that the execution may have been lacking, the intent behind the story is much closer to the iconic Tintin's nature as a righter of international wrongs than to the racist Belgian colonialism of *Tintin in Congo*. It should be noted that, as he did with earlier stories, Hergé did alter some of the more problematic elements for the collected edition still sold today.

11. The anonymous strip is reproduced in Thompson. It is the ninth illustration found between pages 96 and 97. The translation is mine.

Works Cited

Bureau International des Expositions. "Superman Day: When a Comic Superhero Came to Life" *Blog of the Bureau International des Expositions*, 3 July 2016, https://www.bie-paris.org/site/en/blog/entry/superman-day-when-a-comic-superhero-came-to-life-1. Accessed 16 Feb. 2020.
Dash, Mike. "The Mysterious Mr. Zedzed: The Wickedest Man in the World." *Smithsonian.com*, Smithsonian Institution, 16 Feb. 2012, https://www.smithsonianmag.com/history/the-mysterious-mr-zedzed-the-wickedest-man-in-the-world-97435790/. Accessed 9 Nov. 2019.
"Destruction, Inc." Directed by Isidore Sparber, Famous Studios and Paramount Pictures, 1942.
Eco, Umberto. "The Myth of Superman." *The Role of the Reader: Explorations in the Semiotics of Texts*, Hutchinson, 1979, pp. 107–124.
"Eleventh Hour." Directed by Dan Gordon, Famous Studios and Paramount Pictures, 1942.
Ferrell, Robert H. "The Mukden Incident: September 18–19, 1931." *The Journal of Modern History*, vol. 27, no. 1, 1955, pp. 66–72, www.jstor.org/stable/1877701. Accessed 9 Nov. 2019.
Goulart, Ron. Foreword. *Superman Archives* Vol. 3, by Jerry Siegel and Joe Shuster, Archives Editions-DC, 1991, pp. 3–5.
Hergé. *Archives Hergé*. 4 vols, Casterman, 1973.
Hughes, Mark. "Why Superman Can Kill: In Defense Of 'Man of Steel.'" *Forbes*, 17 Mar. 2016, https://www.forbes.com/sites/markhughes/2016/03/17/why-superman-can-kill-in-defense-of-man-of-steel/#7e8250831c7d. Accessed 1 Nov. 2019.
"Japoteurs." Directed by Seymour Kneitel, Famous Studios and Paramount Pictures, 1942.
"Jerry Siegel Attacks." Translated by Randall Bytwerk. *Das schwarze Korps*, 25 Apr. 1940, p. 8. *German Propaganda Archive*, Calvin University, 1998, https://research.calvin.edu/german-propaganda-archive/superman.htm. Accessed 16 Nov. 2019
Maricq, Dominique. *Hergé and the Treasures of Tintin*. Edited and translated by Stuart Tett, Goodman, 2013.
McKay, Hollie. "Superman Renounces His U.S. Citizenship in 900th Issue of Action Comics." *FoxNews.com*, Fox News Network, 28 Apr. 2011, https://www.foxnews.com/entertainment/superman-renounces-his-u-s-citizenship-in-900th-issue-of-action-comics. Accessed 1 Nov. 2019.
McKinney, Mark. *The Colonial Heritage of French Comics*. Liverpool UP, 2011.
Peeters, Benoît. *Hergé, Son of Tintin*. Translated by Tina A. Kover, John Hopkins University Press, 2012.

Salkowitz, Rob. "Warner Brothers Destroyed Superman's Brand For Their New Franchise. Will It Pay Off?" *Forbes*, 18 Mar. 2016, https://www.forbes.com/sites/robsalkowitz/2016/03/18/warner-brothers-destroyed-supermans-brand-for-their-new-franchise-will-it-pay-off/#6f5d57653365. Accessed 1 Nov. 2019.

Scott, David. "The Semiotics of Cultural Icons: The Example of Britannia." *Cultural Icons*, edited by Keyan G. Tomaselli and David Scott, Left Coast Press, 2009, pp. 135–153.

Screech, Matthew. *Masters of the Ninth Art: Bandes Dessinées and Franco-Belgian Identity*. Liverpool UP, 2005.

Siegel, Jerry (w), and Joe Shuster (a). "The Challenge of Luthor." *Superman* Vol. 1 #4 (Spring 1940). *Superman: The Golden Age* Volume 2, edited by Robin Wildman, DC Comics, 2016, pp. 65–77.

_____. "The Construction Scam." *Superman* Vol. 1 #6 (Sep.–Oct. 1940). *Superman: The Golden Age* Volume 2, edited by Robin Wildman, DC Comics, 2016, pp. 296–308.

_____. "How Superman Would End the War." *Superman: The Greatest Stories Ever Told*, DC Comics, 2004, pp. 12–13.

_____. "The Reign of the Superman." *Science Fiction: The Advance Guard of Future Civilization* Vol. 1 #3 (Jan. 1933), pp. 4–14. *University of Florida Digital Collections*, https://ufdc.ufl.edu/UF00077088/00001. Accessed 16 Feb. 2020.

_____. "Revolution in San Monte, Part 2." *Action Comics* Vol. 1 #2 (July 1938). *Superman: The Golden Age* Volume 1, edited by Paul Santos, DC Comics, 2016, pp. 22–34.

_____. "Superman and the Runaway." *Superman* Vol. 1 #3 (Winter 1939). *Superman: The Golden Age* Volume 1, edited by Paul Santos, DC Comics, 2016, pp. 358–381.

_____. "Superman Champions Universal Peace." *Superman* Vol. 1 #2 (Fall 1939). *Superman: The Golden Age* Volume 1, edited by Paul Santos, DC Comics, 2016, pp. 271–294.

Siegel, Jerry (w), Joe Shuster (p), and Wayne Boring (i). "The Exploding Citizens." *Superman* Vol. 1 #7 (Nov.–Dec. 1940). *Superman: The Golden Age* Volume 2, edited by Robin Wildman, DC Comics, 2017, pp. 353–365.

Siegel, Jerry (w), Leo Nowak (p), and John Sikela (i). "The Grotak Bund." *Superman* Vol. 1 #12 (Sep.–Oct. 1941). *Superman: The Golden Age* Volume 4, edited by Tyler-Marie Evans, DC Comics, 2018, pp. 49–61.

Siegel, Jerry (w), and Paul Cassidy (a). "The Phony Pacifists." *Superman* Vol. 1 #9 (Mar.–Apr. 1939). *Superman: The Golden Age* Volume 3, edited by Robin Wildman, DC Comics, 2017, pp. 105–117.

Siegel, Jerry (w), and Wayne Boring (a). "Superman's Cleanup Campaign." *Superman* Vol. 1 #7 (Nov.–Dec. 1940). *Superman: The Golden Age* Volume 2, edited by Robin Wildman, DC Comics, 2017, pp. 366–378.

Siegel, Jerry (w), Wayne Boring (p), and Joe Shuster (i). "The Dukalia Spy Ring." *Superman* Vol. 1 #10 (May–June 1941). *Superman: The Golden Age* Volume 3, edited by Robin Wildman, DC Comics, 2017, pp. 240–252.

Simon, Joe (w), Jack Kirby (w, p), Al Avison (p), Syd Shores (i), and George Klein (i). "The Gruesome Secret of the Dragon of Death!" *Captain America Comics* Vol. 1 #5 (Aug. 1941). *Golden Age Captain America Omnibus* Volume 1, edited by Cory Sedlmeier, Marvel Comics, 2014, pp. 297–311.

Simon, Joe (w), Jack Kirby (w), Al Avison (p), Syd Shores (i), and George Klein (i). "Meet the Fang, Arch Fiend of the Orient." *Captain America Comics* Vol. 1 #6 (Sept. 1941). *Golden Age Captain America Omnibus* Volume 1, edited by Cory Sedlmeier, Marvel Comics, 2014, pp. 367–375.

"Superman's Dilemma." *Times*, vol. 39, no. 15, 1942, p. 80. *EbscoHost*, 24 Nov 2016, http://search.ebscohost.com.proxy1.lib.uwo.ca/login.aspx?direct=true&db=a9h&AN=54831238&site=ehost-live. Accessed 16 Nov. 2019.

Thompson, Harry. *Tintin: Hergé and His Creation*. Hodder, 1991.

Tomaselli, Keyan G., and David Scott, editors. *Cultural Icons*. Left Coast Press, 2009.

United States, Congress, Senate, Committee on the Judiciary. *Comic Books and Juvenile Delinquency: Interim Report*. Government Printing Office, 1955. *HeinOnline*, https://heinonline.org/HOL/P?h=hein.congrec/cmcbks0001&i=1. Accessed 9 Feb. 2020.

Waid, Mark. Foreword. *Superman: The Action Comics Archives* Vol. 1, by Jerry Siegel and Joe Shuster, Archives Editions-DC, 1997, pp. 5–8.

Weldon, Glen. *Superman: The Unauthorized Biography*. Wiley, 2013.

Wertham, Fredric. *Seduction of the Innocent*. 1953. Main Road Books, 2004.

Forging an S into a Myth
Adaptations of Superman Across Media

LIAM WEBB

Superman was an instant success when first published in *Action Comics* #1 (cover date June 1938). Two more "versions" were quickly added, creating three "groups" of Superman media in the late 1930s to early 1940s: the comic book and comic strip, both written by Jerry Siegel; the radio show and novel, written and/or directed by George Lowther; and the cartoon by Fleischer Studios. The character was adapted for *The Adventures of Superman* radio show which premiered on February 12, 1940, just a year and eight months after the character's *Action Comics* debut. On September 26, 1941, three years and three months from debut, the first Superman cartoon hit theaters. In 1942, the first novel about Superman was published; it was written by a writer and director of the radio show, George Lowther, and it was also titled *The Adventures of Superman*. The Superman character was quickly adapted into four different kinds of media outside of its initial media form.

Please note that I say "four" here, and this does not include the *Superman* newspaper comic strip which debuted on January 16, 1939. The count is four because the comic book version itself (including the original, unpublished 1933 comic) was actually the second cross-media adaptation of Superman; Jerry Siegel and Joe Shuster originally created Superman as a comic *strip* hero for the newspapers and not for the comic *book* market. The comic book market was just beginning in 1933 when they first came up with Superman (or at least his name and original concept) as a short story character, and a villain at that. Three of these adaptations—the comic book, the radio show, and the novel—had distinct effects on the character, most notably in the characterization of Clark Kent. Looking at the development of the character from initial concept to first publicly printed Detective Comics, Inc./DC comic,[1] and then at the early issues of the comic books *Action* and *Superman*, the published comic strip, the Fleischer serials, and the Lowther novel, I will note and compare the differences and chart the developments of the varying interpretations of the character between and within media, to show which media "early version" contributed what to Superman's final, solidified character. Make no mistake, the Superman that was first published in *Action Comics* #1 was not completely done developing as a character. The vast majority of the character of course came from his co-creators Siegel and Shuster, but as we will see, others informed on the "final draft version" of the Man of Steel that the public has come to accept as the "definitive" version. I will focus on the Fleischer serials and the Lowther novel and see how they compare, contrast, and provide additions to the comic version as acts of adaptation and convergence in media.

Mankind has told itself stories for millennia, yet there are only a finite number of themes, characters, and plots in storytelling, and these are retold with ever-new variations to please ever-changing tastes and times. Naturally, as time progresses and people's reference points change, stories are not retold just in different formats but also with different characters or items.[2] Retelling a story's theme or moral with new characters, plot, and/or storyline, or even retelling the same story in a different format, is known as adaptation. In *A Theory of Adaptation* (2006), Linda Hutcheon defines adaptation as "...a text [that is] ... created and then received in relation to a prior text. This is why adaptation studies are so often comparative studies" (6). Adaptation is "...not slavish copying; it is the process of making the adapted material one's own. In both, the novelty is in what one *does with* the other text" (20). When people do this, they "...tak[e] possession of another's story, and [filter] it ... through [their] own sensibilit[ies], interests, and talents. Therefore, adapters are first interpreters and then creators" (18). In adaptation, elements of a story remain the same; the overall story is the core and common element, and different adaptions highlight different aspects (10); many incidentals will change, either through the later storyteller's choices or as a requirement of the new format. "Because adaptation is a form of repetition without replication, change is inevitable, even without any conscious updating or alteration of setting" (xvi).

As mentioned above, the history of adapting Superman was unexpectedly long in the first nine years of his existence. Each time the Superman story was told, it was adapted to a different medium or format while simultaneously being worked on/revised by his co-creator, Jerry Siegel, to be more popular. Once Superman became popular, other creators began telling stories about him. However, these later creators had different concerns regarding their stories and how to make them profitable, not only due to the medium they worked in but the later input (meddling?) by the DC corporate structure. But this is necessary, since "[g]eneral economic issues, such as the financing and distribution of different media and art forms, must be considered in any general theorizing of adaptation," and "...stories adapt just as they are adapted" (Hutcheon 30). This is because adapters want "safe bets" that are "reliable—that is, already financially successful—" (5) for risk avoidance and to make a profit. These new storytellers added to the Superman mythos in their interpretations/adaptations, and the additions that proved the most popular were kept and converged into the overall mythos, while others were dropped quickly.[3]

When something is added to the Superman mythos (or to any mythos) it is known as convergence, a subset of adaption, because it was kept and included in future stories permanently; the idea was "converged" into the total idea of the character. In his early years, the Superman concept was new and so still had plasticity: as the public learned more about the character, they were willing to believe more about the character, and so things were added/converged. The things that converged were not only held to a popularity standard but also to a "truthfulness" about the character. This truth of correspondence is "...not to any 'real world' but to the universe of a particular adapted text" (Hutcheon 14). In other words, adaptions must be true to the concept and/or original intent. Each adaption is a palimpsest on a character and sometimes "[p]alimpsests make for permanent change" (29); if an adaption proves popular enough with the audience then, in their opinion, it becomes part of the "real" character.

During Superman's early years, the different media were cooperating through DC corporate to greater and lesser extents under the auspices of Superman, Inc, which had been created in October 1939 to protect the Superman trademark (Tye 38). While the Superman property was changed to fit different media, one thing that Superman, Inc./DC Comics didn't keep strict control on between media adaptations was the personality/characterization of Clark Kent; other notable items are the emotional stability of Superman, the varying verbosity of Superman, and Superman's attitude towards himself and towards criminals.

As stated in his "Welcome to Convergence Culture" blog, Henry Jenkins' theory of convergence culture addresses "the flow of content across multiple media platforms, the cooperation between multiple media industries, and the migratory behavior of media audiences."[4] In this theory, the audience is a participant in convergence because "…convergence represents a shift in cultural logic, whereby consumers are encouraged to seek out new information and make connections between dispersed media content" (Jenkins). It is this cooperation of the platforms and the audiences' behavior/contribution which make convergence distinct from and, for my purposes a subset of, Hutcheon's audience reception component of adaptation, in which audiences become collaborators/creators through interaction.

This study, however, will limit the "audience" to those who worked in a branch of the entertainment industry. This distinction means that while a person may be a creator in one media, he is the "audience" for another: for instance, Siegel worked in comics, not in film, so is the film's "audience"; the Fleischers who worked in film were the comics' "audience." Especially important among this "audience" were press agent Allen Ducovny and writer Robert Maxwell, the latter who DC Comics' publisher Harry Donenfeld personally drafted "into Superman, Inc., first to oversee the licensing of toys and other products, then to bring the superhero into the world of broadcast" (Tye 88) and who together created the audition radio show.

Though Jenkins' crafted his theory for new media and not the media of the 1940s, convergence theory is applicable since anyone who didn't participate in the creation of a work (such as the Superman comic book or comic strip in relation to Lowther or the Fleischer staff) is technically in the audience, even if they were later hired to create content for a property. In a complementary fashion, Siegel and Shuster, who had little direct contact with Lowther or the film studio,[5] later became consumers of their own creation.[6] During Superman's first few "formative years," the audience gave feedback to the creators directly and indirectly. While fan letters were not printed in comics until 1940 ("Letter Columns"), "[a]nother staple of 1930s serial fiction was the junior fan club" (Ricca 110). Siegel created a junior fan club for his *Federal Men* feature in *New Adventure Comics* in 1937, and Siegel and Shuster themselves received fan mail about Superman (Ricca 149), so DC may have also received unpublished letters during this time.

DC Comics did ask for direct feedback from readers when they asked the readers' preferences of character in a survey printed in *Action Comics* Vol. 1 #4 (Sept. 1938) to determine which character was the greatest draw in the book and, therefore, the most bankable. DC also received indirect feedback by tracking sales through penny postcards to retailers to see how many comics they sold (Tye 36). This feedback may explain why some powers (like the newspaper strip Superman's ability to change his face like Plastic Man) would only be featured once while others continued and expanded in scope. This informal process is what allowed the different adaptations, or "versions," of Superman to ultimately converge into the "full" story of who and what Superman was as a character.

This fan feedback was not the first influence on the character's evolution; in reality, it was close to the last influence. The original conception of Superman, in general idea if not spirit, presented itself to Jerry Siegel in late 1932 and was published in Siegel and Shuster's self-published fanzine *Science Fiction: The Advanced Guard of Future Civilization* as the illustrated short story "The Reign of the Super-Man" (Jan. 1933). "[A] mastermind with enhanced mental powers who manipulated ordinary mortals" (Stern xi), this original, villainous Super Man was Bill Dunn, an unemployed man who was experimented on by a scientist named Professor Ernest Smalley who "…feeds Dunn … a serum derived from 'what he [Smalley] suspected to be a new element; that he [Smalley] distills from a 'fragment of a meteor.' This element 'exerted a strange influence' that sounds radioactive" (Ricca 70). Elements from this story can be seen in the later Superman comics: Shuster's original illustration "was a clear template for future foe Lex Luthor" (Ricca 68); a "meteor fragment"; and the scientist is named Smalley, which, I conjecture, might have been repurposed in the name of Smallville when Siegel later wrote his Superboy stories. As noted by Brad Ricca in *Super Boys* (2013), "…all of it was there in 'Reign': the one man as two, the powers, the importance of goodness over greed, and the realization, of Dunn and now Jerry [Siegel], that a hero would be a much better choice than a villain" (97). One thing that wasn't present in the "Reign" story but may have been immediately after was alliteration in the main character's name. Siegel and Shuster's use of the name "Bill Dunn" is an echo of the similarly named "Dan Dunn," which was running in his own newspaper strip from September 25, 1933, to October 2, 1943, and was published as a proto-comic book, *Dan Dunn: Secret Operative No. 48* (May 1933), by Humor Publishing, the same company Superman's creators unsuccessfully pitched their character to in 1933. When Superman was later submitted to DC his civilian name was the now-alliterative "Clark Kent"; the creators may have made this alliterative adaptation to capitalize on the alliteration/popularity of the character Humor accepted (Dan Dunn) while their Superman was rejected. This alliteration of name was later continued with many LL characters in the mythos.

This first 1932 story of Siegel's has an antecedent and so is itself adapted from a "borrowed" idea, which is why I chose to say "the concept presented itself to him" above. Siegel had read the November 11, 1931, issue of *Wonder Stories* which contained a story by George Henry Weiss (as "Frank Flagg") titled "The Superman of Dr. Jukes (75)." This pulp story concerns a destitute former mob hit man who accepts the job of "test subject," is given injections and thereby imbued with intelligence, mental powers, strength, superspeed, and keen sight (Ricca 75).

Still taken with the idea of an all-powerful figure after publishing "Reign," Siegel rethought the premise and, modeling him on comic-strip star Flash Gordon, "turned him into a hero" (Greenberger, "Remembering the Millennium: Action Comics #1—The Birth of the Superhero" [Feb. 2000]). And where did Siegel and Shuster take their literary inspiration to change Superman into a force for good? Well, Siegel and Shuster were both "…saps for the endless newspaper comics, dime novels, science fiction tales, and cliff hanger movies they took in as kids…" (Tye 32). They "adapted" many elements from the *Doc Savage* pulps and from the science fiction novel *Gladiator* (1930) by Phillip Wylie. From Doc Savage came a first name of Clark, superhuman strength, a no-killing rule (unless there was no other way), and the nickname "Man of Steel," derived from Savage's "Man of Bronze." In *Gladiator*, the main character Hugo Danner could hurdle across rivers, make great leaps in the air, and lift a car by the bumper; most tellingly, the exact same comparison to insects is used to explain the main characters' great strength (Tye 32–33).

Siegel and Shuster then created a comic book titled "The Superman" and presented it to Humor Publishing Company (Vance, "A Job for Superman" 8). This version of Superman "...performed his amazing feats clad in slacks and a t-shirt..." (8) and was "'a genius in intellect, a Hercules in strength, a nemesis to wrong-doers'" (Steranko 4), but that was all. The co-creators' next attempt was to make their own comic, the unpublished *Popular Comics* (1933), "was really *Science Fiction* 2.0: an independently produced magazine, but this time with comics instead of stories" (Ricca 84). *Popular* also featured a revival of Siegel's junior high paper character, *Jerry the Journalist*, which was "...a much more romanticized role of the press" (Ricca 86); this romanticism would be carried over into the final Superman product. It was from Popular Comics that they began to take inspiration for the nature of Superman's heroics from their own work. Another feature in their *Popular Comics* book was *Interplanetary Police* which had "an emphasis on X-ray vision, which was rapidly becoming a favorite science fiction trope among teenage boys" (Ricca 85). Superman is a holdover from that book as the published DC version could be seen as a literal "interplanetary policeman," though belonging to no formal force.[7] On that note, in Siegel and Shuster's *Federal Men* strip for DC's *New Adventure Comics* #12 (Jan. 1937), "Federal Men of Tomorrow," the main character is a "space lawman named Jor-L" (Ricca 110).

After the cancelled Humor Publishing "plain clothes hero" Superman drawn by Shuster in 1933, Siegel rewrote the script and attempted a partnership first with Leo O'Mealia and then with Russell Keaton (Tye 18). In this revised script, Superman was initially the last man on Earth sent back in time, and then the baby of the last man on Earth sent back in time and found by motorists Sam and Molly Kent, sent to an orphanage, and then adopted by the Kents and named Clark (Tye 18). Here we see Siegel adapting and evolving the origin story of the character from its original (from Dunn the unemployed man to a time travelling adult Earthman to time travelling baby). When these proposed partnerships fell through, Siegel went back to Shuster and decided to try again with a more extreme character. "Jerry decided his only hope lay in crafting a hero so super that no publisher could resist, one whose story was just unbelievable enough to be credible" (19). It was at this point, Siegel came up with a dying alien planet, Clark as a reporter, and Lois Lane (19).

Much to his credit, Siegel kept developing the idea, and he improved on his original story while borrowing from other stories and from real life. "In the 1920s and 1930s, strongmen such as [Siegmund] Breitbart toured the country as celebrities" (Ricca 122). Like professional wrestlers (and some pop stars) of our day "[t]hey wore colorful costumes to show off their muscles and had one-word names," (ibid). These men would perform feats of strength such as manually "pound[ing] in railroad spikes" and "bend[ing] iron bars into shapes and letters," (ibid). Most significantly for this study of the sources of Superman's convergence, one strongman named Sandow "...would wrap his chest in chains—and then break them apart by exhaling" (ibid).[8]

Prior comic heroes wore space suits with chest emblems and "[t]he tights are a mixture of the strongman's outfit and the attire of wrestlers and boxers, who frequently wore tights with shorts, often differently colored, on the outside. [...] The cape was born of many sources: weightlifters, swashbucklers, and perhaps the cover of [Siegel and Shuster's] high school yearbook, where it was combined with a single initial" (Ricca 128). The cape and emblem were first imported into their *Doctor Occult* work for DC Comics, namely a short cape and a triangular power symbol on his chest (Ricca 107). The Occult strip also featured a police contact and a beautiful assistant, who are in similar positions to Occult as Perry White and Lois Lane are to Clark Kent, though Lois Lane is an "inverted" adaptation, as she is more competitor than assistant in news gathering.

All of these literary and real life pieces and "spare parts" were infused into their idea so that their next adaption/revision of Superman was as a heroic, red-and-blue costumed comic strip character, partly because a newspaper strip was more lucrative and stable work at the time compared to the "tiny" and "shaky" comic book market (Vance, "A Job for Superman" 8). The creators "doggedly sent numerous versions to newspaper syndicates, all of which rejected the strips as crude or immature" (Steranko 3). Even though Siegel and Shuster submitted other work to Detective Comics, Inc., for comic books which was accepted,[9] they still only "occasionally flirted with the notion of submitting their creation to the fledgling comic book industry—but both were firmly convinced that the proper home for Superman was in the pages of the nation's newspapers" (Vance, "A Job for Superman" 7). When Superman was finally taken notice of and advocated for by Sheldon Mayer, "Siegel and Shuster chopped up their syndicate submission [read: comic strip], cropping some panels, expanding others, and pasting the whole thing up into a thirteen-page story" (9). The first appearance of Superman in *Action Comics* #1 was itself an adaptation of what the creators thought was his truest or best form, the newspaper comic strip.

By the time this built-up, cancelled, formerly plain-clothes Superman appeared in his 1938 comic book (almost) in the form we know today, he was also able to "hurdle skyscrapers ... leap an eighth of a mile ... raise tremendous weights ... run faster than a streamline train ... and nothing less than a bursting shell could penetrate his skin!" (Siegel and Shuster, *Superman* #1 10). And his powers grew from there. *Superman* #1 (June 1939) was the first mention of "keen telescopic vision" in the text story (71).[10] In *Action Comics* #8 (Jan. 1939), super-hearing is first conceptualized as "sensitive ears" ("Superman in the Slums" 109) which would later turn into "super-acute hearing" by *Superman* #2 (Sept. 1939) ("The Redemption of Larry Trent," *The Superman Archives Vol 1* 88).[11] *Superman* #2 also features the first use of x-ray vision, called "telescopic, X-ray eyesight," in a text story ("Superman" 136).

Siegel would later adapt his original villainous Super-Man in the DC comic book Superman's first supervillain, the Ultra-Humanite: "*Action Comics* #13 [June 1939] ... leads Superman to a dark cabin where he finds a bald man in a white scientist frock, confined to a wheelchair. The fiery eyes of the paralyzed cripple burn with terrible hatred and sinister intelligence..." (Ricca 177). And like Superman before (after?) him, Ultra-Humanite's power would grow; grow so much, in fact, that "the character [Ultra] lapsed into a level of incredulity that began to separate Superman from his urban roots" (Ricca 177–178).

Once Superman was a smash hit in comic books, he was finally given what Siegel and Shuster originally wanted, his own comic strip in the newspapers. This comic strip, the "second/revised original" adaptation of Superman, immediately began building on the mythos and these items were immediately converged into the overall Superman mythos/canon. "That April 1938 backstory [in *Action Comics* #1] got more interesting the following January, with the launch of the Superman newspaper comic strip. Word one on day one gave his home planet a name, Krypton, followed by an elaborated context" (Tye 40). It was the newspaper strip, not the comic books, that first gave Kryptonians their names which were immediately converged into the lore (Tye 40–41). Superman's father was given the name, Jor-L, and in this first naming was called "Krypton's foremost scientist" (notably like the senior Mr. Danner in *Gladiator*), his mother was named "Lora," and baby Superman was finally given his native Kryptonian name of "Kal-L" (Siegel and Shuster, *Superman: The Dailies, 1939–1940* 13).

However, this convergence was not one-sided. Baby Kal-El was not adopted by the Kents until *Superman* #1, his second comic book series. In both *Action Comics* #1 and the newspaper strip, the Kryptonian baby was found by "a passing motorist" (Siegel and Shuster, *Action Comics* #1 1; *The Dailies: 1939–1940* 18) who was a "walk-on character" and left the baby at an orphanage. In both of these versions, Superman was never adopted by the Kents, nor was it made clear why he had the name "Clark Kent." The Kents finally appeared in *Superman* #1, but the father wasn't given a name and the mother was named Mary. Nor did they immediately adopt him in this first appearance; rather, they left him at an orphanage but later came back to adopt him (Siegel and Shuster, *Superman* #1 1).

In the first issues of *Action Comics*, Superman was a "butt-kicking New Dealer.... Superman was neither kind nor gentle [with criminals]" whose "nearer and more apt role model ... was Eliot Ness." Siegel took the position that criminals "didn't deserve a Bill of Rights, and they wouldn't get one with Superman" (Tye 45); this is more akin to his pulp incarnation (now with a heroic moral code). As Superman's powers grew over the years, so did his intellect: he had a photographic memory; he could hypnotize entire groups simultaneously; and he could communicate with mermaids (Tye 43–44). This was likely another adaptation held over from the original 1933 concept instead of just a logical step of everything else growing about the character because the expanded mental capacities are in line with that concept.

The progressive building of Superman's powers was not new to the super-powered adventure genre. On radio, the adventure character The Shadow "...had nebulous superpowers, but the character was very radio-ambiguous and could change depending on the peril..." (Ricca 94). Fittingly, when Superman appeared on the radio, his powers would continue to grow with plasticity like his radio-predecessor, the Shadow. The syndicated *Superman* is the first adaptation of Superman by someone other than his co-creator Jerry Siegel. Ben Peter Freeman is credited as the head writer of the radio series but George Lowther also wrote and directed the radio show in 1942 (Tollin 12, 27–60).[12] Lowther would soon write the novel which "solidified and clarified the *Superman* mythology and served as a 'bible' for later radio, comic and television writers" (12). Here we see the first likely convergence between the radio and comic versions of Superman, with Lowther as "creator" close on the heels of his being "audience."

As creators, Lowther and Freeman radically adapted Superman's Earthly origins in interest of more (and immediate) action. Lowther had Superman step *fully grown* from the rocket which brought him to Earth in the second episode! Like *Action Comics* #1 and the comic strip but unlike *Superman* #1, the radio adaptation featured no adoption and no Kents, but they took it even further by saying that Superman had no youth on Earth at all. In the radio show, he saves a man and boy (the boy was coincidentally named Jimmy) as one of his first acts on Earth, and Jimmy pulls the name "Clark Kent" from out of the blue with no reason or backstory. Furthermore, there was no explanation as to why Superman understood and spoke English before setting foot on Earth that morning. These changes are adaptation in that they were better suited to the radio environment to which it was transposed. This origin had implicit if not explicit convergence since the radio industry had to have the cooperation of the comic industry through Superman, Inc.'s agent Robert Maxwell (Tollin 5). However, even this isn't the final word in the radio adaptation, as the radio show would later re-tell and change his arrival on Earth to being an infant (an early retcon) in 1942. The series would also name Clark's adoptive father "Eben Kent" from the Lowther novel, showing that the second radio version converged the information from the novel and also adapted it to Eben dying in a fire, not in his bed as in the novel ("Eben Kent Dies in Fire, Clark Goes to Metropolis").

This first, radically different arrival on Earth and the introduction of new characters were part of radio's contributions as a medium. A radio adaption of a work "...brings the importance of the aural to the fore.... The issues common to all dramatizations come into play, with distillation uppermost; because each character/voice must be aurally distinguishable, there cannot be too many of them. For this reason, most radio plays concentrate on primary characters alone and therefore simplify the story and time-line" (Hutcheon 41). The first show certainly simplified the timeline. And the needs of the medium helped dictate Perry White, Jimmy Olsen, and Inspector Henderson becoming main/recurring characters, so as not to confuse listeners with ten editors giving reporters jobs and twenty policemen helping investigate using knowledge the listener may not remember each new policeman had.

Siegel himself became "audience" after the radio show premiered, and while he didn't change Superman's origins to fit the (much more compact) radio narrative, he and others did ultimately incorporate some radio firsts into the comics. The radio show introduced Jimmy Olsen, Perry White, Inspector Henderson, and kryptonite itself (Tollin 9). However, concluding that kryptonite was created for the radio show is debatable. Siegel wrote an unpublished story in 1940 which utilized "K-metal," a meteor chunk from Krypton which can cause Superman to lose his powers. It was unpublished because the story would have made Clark reveal his identity to Lois. It is unknown whether Freeman or Lowther spoke with Siegel or another knowledgeable DC employee or read DC's files. However, "Whitney Ellsworth, who edited the K-metal story, was National [DC]'s adviser on the radio show. This would not be the first time that elements of a rejected Siegel manuscript would seemingly later be used without permission" (Ricca 191–193). Suffice it to say that the adaptations and convergences were by this time a two-way street. Like other elements of the Superman mythos, K-metal as kryptonite was expanded later from simply taking away his power to fully incapacitating him to outright killing him.

Another "lane" on this "street" was the Fleischer Superman cartoons, first exhibited in September 1941. Though the studio was given a high budget to make the films, they still needed to economize. In part, they accomplished this by not animating the extra frames needed to show Superman "jumping" and instead animated him as simply flying up off the ground (Cronin, *Was Superman a Spy?* 22). Even though the cartoons' introduction still stated that he "could leap tall buildings in a single bound" and not actually fly, this was the first "purposeful" time Superman flew in a *visual* medium; later, the introduction would be changed to "soar higher than any plane" ("Terror on the Midway"). He had, however, been implied as flying in the radio show—"hovering in the air"—since 45 seconds into the second episode on February 14, 1940 ("Clark Kent, Reporter"). He was still only leaping in the comics at that time since Siegel was writing him. The one comic book exception was in *Superman* #10 (June 1941) when he was drawn as flying, but only accidentally, since an artist made a mistake (Cronin, *Comic Book Legends Revealed* #373). The Fleischer cartoons were a huge hit, but it wasn't until after they had finished in July 1943 that full flight converged into the comic (Cronin, *Was Superman a Spy?* 22). Superman wouldn't actually fly in the comic books until *Action Comics* #65 (Oct. 1943) (Tye 92).

The Fleischer cartoons adapted the characterization of Superman in a significantly different way than in the comics. To begin with, Superman hardly ever spoke. Having watched and counted in every film, I found that in 12 of the 17 films Superman doesn't say a single word; in "Jungle Drums" (Mar. 1943) he says just four words; in "Japoteurs" (Sept, 1942) five words (all in one sentence); in "The Magnetic Telescope" (Apr. 1942) and "Destruction, Inc." (Dec. 1942) just eight words each; and in "The Arctic Giant" (Feb. 1942) he says a whopping 24 words.[13] Superman speaks all but five of these words to Lois; that one exception is when he speaks to trick a saboteur, in "Japoteurs": "Okay, little man, you win." The Supermen of the comic book, comic strip, and certainly radio were all vastly more talkative.

Moreover, the Fleischer character of Clark Kent was not timid but rather manly. In "The Mechanical Monsters" (Nov. 1941), Kent says "Lois, what are you doing here?" (3:33–3:35) in either an angry or shocked tone, but clearly not a fearful or passive one. He does not display timidity or cowardice as Kent in the entire film series. This characterization may have been due to the studio's belief that timidity in the hero, even as a disguise, wouldn't be well received with movie audiences or it may have confused them, but this is merely my conjecture. His timidity is clearly extinct by the last film, "Secret Agent" (July 1943), when Clark runs after his just-stolen car and jumps on the trunk, riding on the outside of the car, and then Clark (not Superman) wrestles a gun away from a criminal inside the car when said criminal stuck the gun out of the rear window. The Clark Kent of the comics was a timid person who would never dream of doing those things in his Kent persona: in *Action Comics* #1, the very first thing he says to Lois is "W-what do you say to a—er—date tonight, Lois?," then does not defend Lois from someone who wants to cut in on their dance and is afraid to fight the thug when challenged (Siegel and Shuster, "Superman, Champion of the Oppressed" 19–20).

In the Fleischer films, the Lois and Clark romantic plot is barely hinted at and never directly stated or even used as it had been in the comics since *Action Comics* #1.[14] This may have been due to the fact that they are only ten minute action cartoons, some which, by my observation, had as little of ninety seconds of Superman in action ("Underground World"; "Secret Agent"). Any extra time spent on a romantic plot may have eliminated the super-action completely. Besides this, due to the sales of the comic being over one million copies (Tollin 5), the studio could safely assume the target audience was familiar with the romantic plot and knew it wasn't the focus of the character.

The Fleischer films also adapted the original origin of Superman. The first film, "The Mad Scientist" (Sept. 1941), shows the baby sent to Earth and states: "A passing motorist found the uninjured child and took it to an orphanage. As the years went by, and the child grew to maturity, he found himself possessed of amazing physical powers," (1:42–1:51). As in *Action Comics* #1, but not *Superman* #1, in the cartoons Kal-El was never adopted by the Kents nor does the series ever give an explanation why his name is Clark Kent; here, we are led to believe that he grew up in an orphanage. This completely mirrors, and is possibly directly lifted from, the Superman newspaper comic strip (Siegel and Shuster, "Episode 1. Superman Comes to Earth" 18) which the studio may have reasoned more people saw and knew about and so decided not to change it, though this itself *was* a change from the previously-printed comic book. But the Fleischer films didn't just appropriate from previous sources, they also made a few additions which converged into the Superman mythos. These additions include the phrases "faster than a speeding bullet" and "more powerful than a locomotive"; also Clark's changing to Superman in a phone booth, which was first done in the second cartoon, "The Mechanical Monsters."

Finally, I note that Superman's power level varied from film to film. In "The Mad Scientist," he flies against and punches back a full-power energy ray after being knocked back once, yet the beam in "The Magnetic Telescope" gives him more trouble. In "Electric Earthquake" (May 1942), electricity doesn't seem to bother him at all (even underwater), yet the electricity of the dynamite charge wires in "Volcano" (July 1942) cause him great strain. There are times when he is flying outright and other times, such as at the end of "The Mad Scientist," when he is in much more of a "jumping" attitude and arc of motion. This may be due to the varying concepts of the character that the studio had from different conversations and reading different comics (if read at all); maybe one staffer read *Superman* #10 where an artist mistakenly drew flying panels and/or listened to the radio serial, while another read only the Shuster-drawn comics for research. Maybe at the end of producing "The Mad Scientist" they simply had enough money left to spend on the extra frames to show the "jumping" positions, so they did. Of course, in explaining these inconsistencies it behooves us to remember that, despite the money they received, they simply didn't care enough to iron out these power level discrepancies since it could have been "just a job" to many of them. As a man who has written creatively on deadlines, I can vouch for the fact that absolute, painstaking, perfect detail can quickly take second place to on-time completion. Beyond these possibilities, we must consider the restrictions and requirements of their media form. "Usually adaptations, especially from long novels [or in this case, a plethora of comics], mean that the adapter's job is one of subtraction or contraction…" (Hutcheon 19). In their films, the Fleischers drastically contracted the talkativeness of Superman and subtracted many extra frames of animation (as a cost saving measure) to make the character appear to fly instead of make multiple large leaps.

Now, let's turn our attention to the 1942 novel titled, like the radio show, *The Adventures of Superman*. The title page of the book says "based on the cartoon character," which is misleading to our modern understanding of that term. Since Lowther worked on the radio show, presumably read some comics to prepare for that, and that an *absolute maximum* of five short films were released by the time Lowther could have started the book,[15] the term "cartoon character" most likely referred to the Superman property as a whole and not strictly the Fleischer adaptation.

Lowther was very creative in this novel and did much to build upon the Superman mythos, and that from whole cloth. What is first striking about this adaptation is that it spends 58 of 215 pages, a full 26.9 percent of the book, on Clark Kent's origin and youth. This was a drastic departure from any of the prior adaptations, especially since the radio show (which the book's author was a part of) re-wrote it so that Superman had no youth on Earth.

In Chapter One, Lowther writes that Krypton will explode like a volcano, and not from earthquakes as in the films and comics (Lowther 7).[16] This contrasts with Siegel's statement that Krypton will "crumble and die" and that the volcanic eruptions "were a warning" and not the main cause of Krypton's destruction (Siegel and Shuster, "Episode 1. Superman Comes to Earth" 15). Lowther had Kryptonians wear togas color-coded to signify a person's profession (7) as opposed to the regular clothes seen in the Superman newspaper strip (Siegel and Shuster, "Episode 1. Superman Comes to Earth" 13).[17] Beyond being "the peak of human perfection" per the Fleischer films ("The Mad Scientist" 1:14–1:15), Lowther gives to every Kryptonian flight, strength, intellect, and the ability to breathe underwater (10–11). This last power may have been converged from "The Electric Earthquake" Fleischer film: in it, Superman had no problem acting underwater nor were his cheeks visibly puffed out as if he was holding his breath, so it's possible Lowther took/misinterpreted this ability of Kryptonians to breathe underwater.

Lowther changes the spelling of Superman's Kryptonian parents from "Jor-L" and "Lora" to "Jor-el" and "Lara" (Lowther, 4, 13), which the comic books would later converge with and adapt once more by capitalizing the "e" in "El." He is also the first to give names to *both* of Superman's Earth parents: Eben and Sarah, who speak in drawls (20, 23)[18]; this would, years later, be changed to Jonathan and Martha.

Lowther establishes that it was Eben who rescues the baby from the burning rocket, and adds that Eben was severely burned in doing so (23–25). Clark has no powers until he is 13, when his x-ray vision manifests (27–30). Another major change in Lowther's novel adaptation is that Clark first meets Perry White when the latter is a reporter and Clark a teenager (48). They meet because Clark was *publicly* exhibiting his strength by lifting an anvil over his head on a stage at a county fair (48), but Clark did this only after his *first* exhibition of strength, which was private, interpersonal violence. In the novel, Clark and his father were at the fair so that the elder Kent could attempt lifting the anvil to win money to help save their farm (34). Due to his age Mr. Kent is ridiculed, most sharply by the town strongman. The novel's first exhibition of Clark's super-strength is to have Clark punch and knock out this strong man, named only "The Bull," who mercilessly taunted Mr. Kent. Furthermore, when Clark did this, he had "tears of rage" in his eyes (44–45). This is a far cry from the emotionally stable and secure character in the Fleischer films and the stable-but-pretending-cowardice version of Clark in the comics. In the rest of the novel, the adult Clark is flat personality-wise and yet still far more emotionally labile than in any other adaption. He is described as "surprised" (62, 71), "worried" (63), "pretending fear" (65), "walking on air" (72) and giving "a grim smile" (75). Later, he feels "white hot anger" *and* "the joy of being Superman" on the same page (103)! However, even his emotions seem inconsistent as he is described as not having any emotional reaction to seeing a supposed ghost ship and skeleton captain (80).

Unlike in the radio show or either of the comics formats, the first-person Clark helps with his superpowers is his adoptive father, who collapses from the effort of raising the anvil (Lowther 51); this is also when he realizes that his powers are a serious responsibility. As in the comic book, death inspires Clark's move to the city to be a reporter in order to better help as Superman; here, it is the death of only his father rather than both parents. Furthermore, his adoptive father talks to Clark at length as he dies in bed and, while talking, gives him the Superman name (57).[19] This novel is also the first adaptation to give an origin to Superman's costume: his adoptive mother sewed it for him from ordinary materials (60). Later comic books would converge this into their stories, but they would again adapt it by saying that she wove it from indestructible cloth from the Kryptonian rocket.

The novel does keep something from the radio program, which is Perry White's "gruff, perpetually angry voice" (Lowther 61). This seems to be modeled on the original editor from the comic books, George Taylor, who was still the editor of the paper in the comic books when the radio show aired. Unlike the radio version, the novel's adult Clark Kent is more like the comic book counterpart in that in his first heroic act in Metropolis, Clark "faints" his way into stopping a gunman and Lois thinks he is a coward (65–68). The entire novel is an origin of Clark's adult life, as the story that Clark is assigned to cover by Mr. White is a try-out to see if he is good enough to work for the paper (71). This deviates from the comic strip in that his try-out there was to get an interview with

Superman (Siegel and Shuster, "Episode 2. War on Crime" 21). In the comic book he wasn't given a try-out at all; he simply got the scoop on a lynching he heard about by eavesdropping on the outside of the Daily Star building (*Superman* #1 13). This different try-out was created to help move the novel plot along and also likely to keep from repeating the story from the comic book/strip the audience already read so that the company could sell more copies.

Another addition in the novel adaptation is Superman's ability to "sense danger" (Lowther 62–63, 74, 81, 90, 92, 138, 140, 150, 160). This is written not as a reporter's "hunch" but as a separate super-power. This is the only story I could find where Superman displays this power.[20] The Superman mythos was growing at that time and this novel did increase Superman's powers, but inconsistently. The novel lists him having a super-brain and "supersensory powers" (108), thus expanding/adapting prior instances of "sensitive" hearing and "x-ray telescopic" vision into all five of his senses. Lowther may have advanced these sensory powers to all of Superman's senses since Lowther definitely knew about the x-ray vision of the films and likely knew of the "sensitive" hearing. However, later (likely just to increase the plot's tension) Lowther has Superman unable to realize what it was he saw that was important and had him wrack his "super-brain" for 27 pages (190–207). Though logically the comic book origin would include genius as part of "the peak of human perfection," the comic books wouldn't truly converge this super-brain concept until the later 1950s and with gusto in the 1960s.[21] As with the "super-brain" omission, Lowther didn't have Kent/Superman use his x-ray vision later on in the novel to look through two different doors (130, 162) but did use it on the very next page from the second door so Superman could find a submarine (163). These may have been editorial gaffes left in due to an approaching deadline or just to build dramatic tension, but let's remember that this was, after all, "just a kids' novel" to those adults producing it.

Regarding Superman's dual identity, Lowther's Kent is more aligned with the early radio and comic book version since "he had forgotten himself, almost to the point of revealing he had been the ghostly apparition [who saved a ship foreman]" (136) and he is "tougher" in his Superman personality. Clark's personality is initially more like the comics; when first meeting Mr. White and Lois at the Daily Planet he pretends meekness and even cowardice but after that one scene, he is much more like his Fleischer version. This looks to be a convergence of the "two Clarks" into one in this novel. But Lowther may have, like the super-senses, taken the "tough guy" persona further than necessary or is well-advised since at the end of the story it reads as if Superman killed the villain with a punch. The sentences are written ambiguously but probably just for "plausible deniability" should any parents get upset: "His fist snapped up against the shipyard owner's jaw, and this time he did not pull his punch. Lowell slumped to the floor without a word, without a sound. Lowell disposed of; Superman regained the deck…." (200). Considering the strength of Superman, who destroys submarines barehanded in this book, and the use of the phrases "did not pull his punch" and "disposed of," it is fairly obvious to a modern reader that this Superman will kill villains (here, Nazi spies) if needed.

The similarities and differences in the Supermen, and especially the Clarks, in different media shows that the character was adapted to both story and media needs, and possibly Lowther's personal taste. When before he was only jumping, he clearly flew in the Fleischer films due to economic needs of that medium; he became significantly more emotional in the novel so the author could provide more "colorful" language as this was the first time the character was in a black and white, mostly non-visual, text medium[22];

and even co-creator Siegel himself dispensed with Superman's adoptive parents to accommodate the needs of the more tightly-written newspaper comic strip. Some items grew over time (from "sensitive" to "super" hearing) as a natural progression and for story's sake; others were created or randomly included or omitted, just to help the story.[23] Over time, popular or useful ideas were kept and converged into other media, like Jimmy Olsen being added to the comics; others, like the ability to sense danger, were ignored. This is where convergence interacts with the adaptations—the new powers, characters, or concepts were added to the character and his world over time.[24]

The only exception to this was Superboy, who was added/converged to the comic books partly so DC Comics could keep the legal rights to the younger iteration of the character. In 1945, "the editors began considering ways in which the Superman franchise could be expanded. The answer was adventures of Superman when he was a boy, an idea that had been under consideration since 1941," and was treated as "an integral part of the Superman mythos," (Greenberger, "Remembering the Millennium: More Fun Comics #101—Superboy Earns His Own Future" [Nov. 2000]). The idea was inherent in the super-baby panel in *Action Comics* #1; Siegel later claimed origination of this idea such that once DC printed the Superboy feature in a comic he complained to Liebowitz that he should have gotten credit for this "old idea" of his (Tye 63).[25]

On a whole, the characters in the Lowther novel read more closely to the radio and film versions than the comics versions. On page 68, after Clark pretends to faint to stop a gunman, Lois believes he is a coward, but this isn't brought up again in the book. Nor is Clark enamored of Lois. Only on the penultimate page does it say: "As their eyes met for a second, Kent decided that he liked Lois Lane more than he had thought" (214). Clark is more confident and assured, similar to how he is in the Fleischer films and the early radio shows, and still tries to keep his Superman identity a secret, as he did in the first comics. The novel's story was set at the start of Clark's adulthood—Clark was also hired by *The Daily Planet* on the penultimate page—so that may explain his secretiveness regarding his alter ego, but not the more assured personality. The novel mentions "the higher-pitched voice" of Clark Kent (76), a clear inheritance from the radio show that kept consistent in the cartoons as both were voiced by Bud Collyer. The book ends with Clark, while discussing the inconsistencies in his story that are explained by superpowers to the rewrite man, telling him "Well, figure them out for yourself, old man, figure them out for yourself" (215). This is something that the comics versions, book or strip, would never and could never have done so as to have Clark remain "meek and mild."

One thing to keep in mind about this convergence and adaptation between sources in Superman's early years is that it was organic and not intentional:

> There was no master plan for the related but distinct storylines of the *Action* and *Superman* books and the *Superman* strip. No one had known that *Action* would catch on enough for the McClure Newspaper Syndicate, which had turned the strip down twice before, to come begging to bring Superman to the funny pages. Neither Harry [Donovan] nor Jack [Liebowitz] had planned for a separate *Superman* comic book, or for that to be ongoing [Tye 41].

As a result, writing the character consistently became more difficult for Siegel and later writers: "each installment needed to seem original yet part of a whole, stylistically and narratively," (Tye 41). The adaptation(s) and convergence were all happening at once. In a real way, Siegel and Superman, Inc., were just trying to control the character who was getting a bit out of hand due to popularity and frequent, diverse production, and didn't seem to give much thought to any goal other than doing what sold best.

The early development of the Superman and Clark Kent characters and the mythos surrounding him was a very plastic thing early in his history. The five adaptations of the story—in comic books, comic strips, film, novel, and radio—changed some things to better fit their media, their audience, and in some cases it seems just to fit the tastes of the creators. Popular ideas were kept and ideas that didn't strike a chord with people were forgotten about. Over time, these four media came together to organically develop the character of Superman as America knew him for decades to come. The novel seems equally indebted to the radio and early comic book versions, but it also adds to the mythos and is itself absorbed into the comic books in later years. It is an interesting process to examine, and in its own way, typifies the collaborative spirit of the "melting pot" that is America which perfectly suits the character, who, in the final analysis, should embody the good in all of us and be someone we could all strive to emulate.

Notes

1. The company that published Superman was known as Detective Comics, Inc. at that time, only informally referring to themselves as "DC Comics."
2. For instance, historians have found that Cinderella's glass slipper was likely originally made of fur, and was changed/mispronounced over time from the French for fur, *fourrure*, to glass, *verre*.
3. Such as Superman's "super-muscular control" to change his appearance in *Superman* #44 (Mitchell).
4. Thanks to John Darowski for initially recommending I look at Jenkins' theory.
5. At least, I could not find any hard evidence stating they had direct contact.
6. Add to this the fact that, having been so incredibly popular a character, Superman was most assuredly talked about among his audience of children and teenagers, and was presumably talked about in adult circles as well, even if those adults were at first limited to only those in the creative industries or the parents of the child audience (which was incredibly large); later of course, the audience expanded to GIs during World War II, which is a bit "late" for my purposes here, as July 1943 was the debut of the last Fleischer film.
7. For formality, we would have to wait until the 1960s and Green Lantern (Hal Jordan) and the Green Lantern Corps.
8. Note that Superman is shown doing the exact same chest expansion trick on the back cover of *Superman* #1. The image was subsequently used in the 1941 printed ad for his radio show (Vance, "The Superman Bandwagon" 10).
9. These were Dr. Occult, Henri Duval, Radio Squad, Federal Men, and Slam Bradley (Vance, "A Job for Superman" 8–9).
10. Early comic books included a short text story in order to meet postal code requirements.
11. The stories in *Superman* #2 were repackaged from the *Superman* comic strip. "The Comeback of Larry Trent" was originally published as strips 31–54 (20 Feb.–18 Mar. 1939).
12. Lowther had previously worked as a radio play writer for two other comic strip properties: *Dick Tracy* and *Terry and the Pirates* (Tollin 3).
13. In "The Arctic Giant" Superman says "Lois?" (1 word), "You'd better get back to your office where you'll be safe. I've got some work to do." (17) "Lois!" (1) "Now this time, stay put," (5). Oddly, in his last line as Clark Kent, he still uses his deeper "Superman" voice, but I discount that since it was Clark in his office at that time. In "The Magnetic Telescope" Superman says "Are you all right?" (4) and "Miss Lane, the controls!" (4). In "Japoteurs" Superman says "Okay, little man. You win," (5). In "Destruction, Inc." Superman says "Miss Lane! Miss Lane! Are you all right?" (8). In "Jungle Drums" Superman says "Lois!" (1) and "Stay down, Lois," (3).
14. The original Humor Publishing submission was destroyed by Shuster (Vance 8) so we will never know if Lois, or even a proto-Lois, was in that story.
15. I could not find an exact month of release of the novel, so this maximum comes from my supposing the book was released on 1 Dec. 1942, giving six months to edit, print, and distribute country-wide and two months to write, which brings us to the beginning of Apr. 1942 as a starting date, and even that is likely far too fast.
16. Also note that this volcano hearkens back to the protagonist's demise in *Gladiator* (the Phillip Wylie novel that may likely have helped inspire Superman's creation). Siegel denies reading the book, but he made this denial after Superman became a financial success, and an admission on Siegel's part could have opened up a lawsuit from Wylie (Ricca 130). Wylie actually consulted his lawyer about suing over Superman, but declined due to the chance of small renumeration from DC Comics (Tye 44).
17. Notably, Kryptonians wearing togas is something that John Byrne would use again in his 1980s reboot of Superman; though in his version, the togas were not multicolored.

18. In *Superman* #1, the wife was named Mary and the husband was never named.

19. This scene in the novel would be converged and adapted years later in *Action Comics* #500 (Oct. 1979), though this time Clark would already have become Superboy (Bridwell, *The Great Superman Comic Book Collection*).

20. I, for one, am grateful this is its only instance because the phrase "My super-sense ... tingling!" just isn't as catchy, true believer.

21. Such as in the much-reprinted *Superman* #162 (July 1963) when, split in two, his two selves of Superman Red and Superman Blue use "super-calculation."

22. The novel included nine color illustrations, five full-page black & white illustrations, and quick sketches at the start and/or ends of the chapters.

23. Superman uses his x-ray vision only once in the Fleischer films, in "The Mechanical Monsters," to expressly find Lois inside the robot. This is never used or mentioned again in the other 16 films, even when Lois was under rubble in "The Arctic Giant."

24. Or, arguably, recycled/adapted concepts like kryptonite from K-metal.

25. At the "Superman Day" arranged by National Periodicals' publicist Allen Ducovny for the 1940 World's Fair, there was a physical fitness event that crowned a "Super-Boy" and a "Super-Girl" (Ricca 187).

Works Cited

"The Baby from Krypton." *Superman*, WOR, New York City, 12 Feb. 1940.
Bridwell, E. Nelson (w), Carmine Infantino (a), Curt Swan (a), and Murphy Anderson (a). "The Origin of Superman." *Action Comics* Vol. 1 #500 (Oct. 1979). *The Great Superman Comic Book Collection*, edited by Laurie Sutton, DC Comics, Inc., 1981, pp. 1–15.
"Clark Kent, Reporter." *Superman*, WOR, New York City, 14 Feb. 1940.
Cronin, Brian. "Comic Book Legends Revealed #373." *CBR.com*, 29 June 2012, https://www.cbr.com/comic-book-legends-revealed-373/. Accessed 10 Jan. 2020.
_____. "Comic Legends: When Did Superman First Fly?" *CBR.com*. 3 Dec 2016. https://www.cbr.com/comic-legends-when-did-superman-first-fly/. Accessed 10 Jan. 2020.
_____. *Was Superman a Spy? And Other Comic Book Legends Revealed*. Plume, 2009.
"Eben Kent Dies in a Fire, Clark Goes to Metropolis." *The Adventures of Superman*, Mutual Broadcasting Network, New York City, 1 Sept. 1942.
Greenberger, Robert. "Remembering the Millennium: Action Comics #1—Birth of the Superhero," *Millennium Edition: Action Comics* #1 (Feb. 2000). DC Comics, 2000.
_____. "Remembering the Millennium: More Fun Comics #101—Superboy Earns His Own Future," *Millennium Edition: More Fun Comics* #101 (Nov. 2000). DC Comics, 2000.
Hutcheon, Linda. *A Theory of Adaptation*. Taylor & Francis, 2006.
Jenkins, Henry. "Welcome to Convergence Culture." *Confessions of an Aca-Fan*, 19 June 2006, https://henryjenkins.org/blog/2006/06/welcome_to_convergence_culture.html. Accessed 20 Dec. 2019.
"Letter Columns." *Comic Vine*. https://comicvine.gamespot.com/letter-columns/4015-56165/. Accessed 27 Feb 2020.
Lowther, George. *The Adventures of Superman*. Illustrated by Joe Shuster, 1942. Applewood Books, 1995.
Max Fleischer's Superman, 1941–1942. Directed by Dave Fleischer, Warner Bros., 2009.
Mitchell, Nigel. "Superman: 15 Powers You Didn't Know He Had." CBR.com, 20 Feb 2017, https://www.cbr.com/superman-powers-you-didnt-know/. Accessed 29 Feb 2020.
Ricca, Brad. *Superboys: The Amazing Adventures of Jerry Siegel and Joe Shuster—The Creators of Superman*. St. Martin's Press, 2013.
Siegel, Jerry (w), and Joe Shuster (a). "Episode 1. Superman Comes to Earth," Strips 1–12 (16–28 Jan. 1939). *Superman: The Dailies, Strips 1–996, 1939–1942* Vol. 1, Sterling Publishing Co., Inc., 2006, pp. 12–18.
_____. "Episode 2. War on Crime," Strips 13–30 (30 Jan.–18 Feb. 1939). *Superman: The Dailies, Strips 1–996, 1939–1942* Vol. 1, Sterling Publishing Co., Inc., 2006, pp. 19–28.
_____. "Superman, Champion of the Oppressed!" *Action Comics* #1 (June 1938). *The Golden Age Superman Omnibus* Vol. 1, edited by Rowena Yow, DC Comics, 2013, pp. 14–27.
_____. "Superman in the Slums," *Action Comics* Vol. 1 #8 (Jan. 1939). *The Golden Age Superman Omnibus* Vol. 1, edited by Rowena Yow, DC Comics, 2013, pp. 108–121.
_____. *Superman* Vol. 1 #1 (July 1939). *The Superman Archives* Vol. 1, DC Comics, 1989, pp. 7–72.
_____. *Superman* Vol. 1 #2 (Fall 1939). *The Superman Archives* Vol. 1, DC Comics, 1989, pp. 73–138.
_____. *Superman* Vol. 1 #10 (June 1941). *The Superman Archives* Vol. 3. DC Comics, 1991, pp. 73–138.
Steranko, Jim. Forward. *The Superman Archives* Vol. 1, by Jerry Siegel (w) and Joe Shuster (a), DC Comics, 1991, pp 3–6.
Stern, Roger. Introduction. *Superman: The Sunday Classics—Strips 1–183, 1939–1943*, by Jerry Siegel (w) and Joe Shuster (a), Kitchen Sink Press, 1998, pp ix–xv.

Tollin, Anthony. *Superman with Batman & Robin on Radio*. Radio Spirits, 1999.
Tye. Larry. *Superman: The High-Flying History of America's Most Enduring Hero*. Random House, 2013.
Vance, James. "A Job for Superman." *Superman: The Dailies—Strips 1–966, 1939–1942* Vol. 1, by Jerry Siegel (w) and Joe Shuster (a), Sterling Publishing Co., 2006, p. 6–11.
_____. "The Superman Bandwagon." *Superman: The Dailies—Strips 1–966, 1939–1942* Vol. 2, by Jerry Siegel (w) and Joe Shuster (a), Sterling Publishing Co., 2006, p. 7–13.

Superman Takes to the Air
The Radio Adaptations of the Man of Steel
JOHN DAROWSKI *and* JOSEPH J. DAROWSKI

Faster than a speeding bullet! More powerful than a locomotive! Able to leap tall buildings in a single bound! Look, up in the sky! It's a bird! It's a plane! It's Superman! Yes, it's Superman—strange visitor from the planet Krypton who came to earth with amazing physical powers far beyond those of mortal men. And who, disguised as Clark Kent, mild-mannered reporter for a great metropolitan newspaper, wages a never-ending battle for truth, justice, and the American way!

Audiences listened to variations of this introduction for decades through Superman radio and television shows.[1] It provides a neat summation of the essential elements of the Superman mythos: powers, origin, secret identity, and mission statement. Many phrases from the sequence, as well as the catchphrase "Up, up, and away!," have entered the popular lexicon, conjuring fantasies of athletic prowess or the romance of flight. But the power of the introduction lies not solely in its narrative but in its aurality. The emphatic narration and the accompanying sound effects of a gunshot, train whistle, and whistling wind, all combine to quicken the imagination in ways that words printed on a page never could. The soaring popularity of Superman in the United States throughout the 1940s, as well as his dissemination internationally, must be attributed—at least in part—to such aural elements, provided primarily by his radio show.

Airing in the United States from February 12, 1940, through March 1, 1951, the five iterations of the *Superman/The Adventures of Superman* radio programs became the primary text for the Man of Steel at a time when multiple transmedia sources were creating and refining the Superman mythos.[2] Radio was the largest disseminator of popular culture at the time that Superman first appeared in comic books and began transforming American entertainment. As noted in *The Superman Radio Scripts Vol. 1*: "In a world without Internet access, video games, or network television, children and their parents would gather around the family radio to listen to the exploits of their favorite characters. [...] Though Superman's widely circulated comic books had made him famous, it was his radio show that made him a household name" (iii). The show ran for long enough that many young fans grew up with Superman as a constant presence on the radio. Many radio programs of the 1930s and '40s serve as a cultural record reflecting the United States' transition from the Great Depression to World War II to post-war prosperity. Superman, in his fight for the American way, chronicled the changing values of what it meant to be

American. Though Superman is synonymous with the American way, his radio adventures facilitated his international influence and universal appeal through simultaneous broadcasts in Canada and the Philippines ("'Superman' for Canada"), an Australian version (1949–1954), and later BBC adaptations (1988–1993). An examination of the Superman radio programs reveals the dynamics of transmedia adaptations, especially from a print to aural medium, and the challenges of reflecting American values in changing times.

Superman was the creation Jerry Siegel and Joe Shuster, two Cleveland teenagers who struggled to find work during the Great Depression. The duo utilized their respective writing and drawing skills to enter the nascent comic book industry, though they really wanted to break into the lucrative newspaper comic strip field. Popular comic strips were read by millions of readers and made creators such as Chester Gould, Alex Raymond, and Al Capp into wealthy celebrities (*Superheroes*). Cultural cachet was not achieved solely through the comic strips, but through multimedia enterprises which adapted characters such as Dick Tracy, Flash Gordon, and Lil' Abner into radio shows, movie serials, and comic books, with the radio reaching the largest audience by far.[3] Radio was the mass entertainment medium of the era, but as cultural historian Russel Nye recounts, "radio took few chances. Whatever was popular in other media it took for its own use, absorbing or imitating it" (400). The reason Superman was considered for adaptation into radio was his already existing popularity. The convergence between radio, comic strips, pulp magazines, and film, especially in science fiction and fantasy stories, would achieve an apex in the invention of the world's first superhero.

The image of a man in blue and red tights lifting a car over his head which graced the cover of *Action Comics* #1 (June 1938) was an evocative illustration, capturing the imagination of children all over the country. This initiated a superhero boom that brought the comic book medium into its own; as one DC Comics staffer observed: "Superman literally created the industry" (Ashby 261). Superman's explosion in popularity, with his comic books grossing almost a million dollars in 1940, quickly brought appearances far beyond the comic book page. In 1939, the McClure Syndicate bought the rights to a Superman comic strip, with Siegel, Shuster, and their studio providing the stories. The radio show premiered in February 1940 and within a year had over twenty million listeners (*Look! Up in the Sky!*). In that same year, a record-breaking 36,000 children attended the New York World's Fair's "Superman Day" on July 3rd (Kobler 15), which featured the specialty comic book *New York World's Fair Comics* #2 (June 1940),[4] a live radio broadcast, and the first live appearance of Superman, credited to actor Ray Middleton. That holiday season brought a rather bloated, eighty-feet tall balloon figure to the Macy's Thanksgiving Day Parade (Maslon 57–8)[5] and a Superman-themed Christmas exhibit at the Macy's department store in New York City (Kobler 15). The subsequent years brought short story companions to the radio serials, "Superman in Radio," to *Radio and Television Mirror* magazine (Jan. 1941–Apr. 1942), cartoon shorts from Fleischer/Famous Studio (Sept. 1941–July 1943), and the novel *The Adventures of Superman* (1942) by George Lowther—a writer and director for the radio show—as well as a host of merchandising.

The popular perception of Superman quickly began to be shaped in a constellation of texts rather than from the original stories in *Action Comics*. The Superman brand became a type of transmedia storytelling, which media scholar Henry Jenkins describes as: "Stories that unfold across multiple platforms, with each medium making a distinctive contribution to our understanding of the storyworld; a more integrated approach to franchise development" (334). Because of this exponential transmedia expansion, Siegel and Shuster were joined by many other creators in crafting the Superman mythos. National Allied Publications (later DC Comics) established Superman, Incorporated, overseen by press agent Allen Ducovny and former pulp writer Robert Maxwell, to manage all merchandising and media licensing (Hayde 15; Scivally 16).[6] Author Tom De Haven has argued that Maxwell, who guided the production of the radio series as well as the first season of television's *Adventures of Superman* (1952–1958), "may well have been the most responsible for establishing the character as an American icon whose persona fuses decency, civility, and the democratic ideal" (104–5). Maxwell was also responsible for the more violent content in the radio and television show, contributing to him being let go after the television show's first season (Tye 141–142).[7] In a very short period of time there were multiple adaptations from dozens of creators while the comic book source text continued printing new adventures, which resulted in Superman going through a refining process on a compressed time scale. Every iteration brought new elements to the canon until a self-consistent mythology was established across all media by the mid–1940s.

Historian Daniel Boorstin relates the process of refining and codifying American folklore:

> At least two crucial distinctions, then, mark the American making of a popular legendary hero. First, there was a fantastic chronological abridgement: from elusive oral legend to printed form required here a few years rather than centuries. Legends hastened into print before they could be purified of vulgarities and localisms. Second, the earliest printed forms were in a distinctly American form; they were not in literature but in "subliterature" [328].

While Boorstin was discussing Davy Crockett in the nineteenth century, his analysis could equally apply to Superman—"a progenitor in the pop folklore of the twentieth century," as *The Washington Post* once described him (Arnold)—albeit with an inversion of the oral to print sequence. However, that inversion was a key aspect of the golden age of radio. Cultural critic Susan Douglas explains: "Radio introduced a new orality to American culture, in which ancient ways of conveying myths, heroic stories, or morality tales intermixed with more modern ways of conveying information, through text and images" (12). The result is that American popular culture during the 1930s and '40s developed both a strong literate and oral/aural tradition.

The blending of literate and oral traditions may have been especially appealing to children, the key demographic for the Superman comic book and radio show. Each source provides partial information—images by the comic book and sound by the radio. Only by actively engaging the imagination can a complete formulation of Superman be constructed. A 1989 *New York Times* opinion piece later explained:

> We recognized the familiar swoosh of Superman landing, red cape streaming behind him. We identified the voices of our heroes as easily as our own families. Though comic books and publicity pictures give us a visual image to start with, radio completes the process by providing the imagination's animation [...] Sparked by the words, the sounds, the intonations, and the silences, the radio creates the landscape for us and the action and special effects of the heroic world [Scinto].

The radio and the comic book then reinforce each other, with the audience applying the sounds of the radio to reading a comic book and imagine the images of the comic book while listening to the radio, bringing the character to life in the theater of the mind.

In adapting Superman to radio, it was never the case that a storyline from the comic book was translated into the new medium. Rather, *The Adventures of Superman* were re-imaginings that were both related to and independent from the source material. In

Film Adaptation and its Discontents (2007), Thomas Leitch posits at least two criteria for how characters like Superman can achieve an autonomous existence. First, it can happen with strong iconic representation that celebrates the power of the visual or audible to display what printed words can only present indirectly; second, the character may come from a less-than-respectable source (97). As to Leitch's first point, the power of the imagination can create an iconic representation based on both visual and audible information. Radio is a purely aural medium. The act of listening, not just hearing, creates a livelier experience because voice can relay emotion, emphasis, and personality much more effectively than a static image. "It is incomparably more interesting to hear the message delivered than to read it in the next morning's paper" or comic strip (qtd. in Douglas 102). Imagination is also required in order to activate dimensional listening. Through the use of sounds, dialogue, and narration, the listener's mind is able to create complete images of what is being portrayed. Audio producer Dirk Maggs describes the process: "If skillfully written and produced, audio bypasses the optic nerve, sneaks through the side door via the ear drum and paints pictures using the human brain, the greatest imaging computer ever invented" (Mulrain). This makes the listener personally involved in the creation of the story alongside the actors and sound engineers. Radio programs then become a unique experience for each individual, as the imagery will be of their own invention.

As to Leitch's latter argument, comic books, by their very nature, were cheap, disposable, mass-consumer literature.[8] The medium has long possessed a cultural stigma as being crude and juvenile. Radio, being both more popular and ostensibly serving a role of public service, possessed more cultural value than the comic book, though it had its own issues with respectability. Even though every episode of the radio show acknowledged that Superman was published by DC Comics at the end of the program, Superman as a character could exist autonomously from that source material.

The image of a man in blue tights and red trunks, inspired by circus strongmen, with a red cape, to imply effortless motion, is powerful iconography. The image is so memorable that the radio program need only occasionally reference the costume elements to conjure the entire image of Superman in the imagination. Likewise, the distinctive whistling sound of the wind on the radio show creates the image of Superman in motion. This sound was one of the more difficult to create effectively, the soundmen experimenting with different techniques before finding the right one. Originally a simple hand-cranked wind machine, it was ultimately produced through mixing a recording of a wind tunnel played backwards, the roar of a dive-bombing plane, and newsreel footage of an artillery shell whistling through the air from the Spanish Civil War (Tye 90). The time and effort put into creating the aural soundscape of the radio show resulted in a distinct interpretation of Superman. This version of the character shaped the public perception of the icon and has become part of the cultural formulation of who Superman is.

Transmedia storytelling is "the integration of multiple texts to create a narrative so large that it cannot be contained within a single medium" (Jenkins 95). In the early years, each new source added to the Superman mythos, sometimes in contradictory ways, until it could be codified. *Action Comics* #1 introduced the most basic elements in the characters of Superman: his origin and powers; his alter ego Clark Kent; and his love interest Lois Lane. The *Superman* comic strip introduced his doomed homeworld of Krypton and his birth parents, Jor-L and Lara. George Lowther's novel *The Adventures of Superman* included an account of Clark Kent's early years of being raised on a farm by Eben and Sarah Kent (instead of at an orphanage) and discovering his powers.[9] And the Fleischer cartoons began the tradition of Superman using a phone booth to change costumes.

But it was the radio show that had the most extensive and lasting impact on the mythos. The program introduced key supporting characters in newspaper editor Perry White ("Clark Kent, Reporter" [14 Feb. 1940]) and cub reporter Jimmy Olsen ("Donelli's Protection Racket, Pt. 1" [15 Apr. 1940]), as well as changing Clark Kent's place of employment from the comic book's *The Daily Star* to *The Daily Planet* (deForest 169, Scivally 19).[10] Whereas Superman could only leap long distances in the comic book, radio implies the power of flight as early as the second episode ("Clark Kent, Reporter"), which was much easier to convey with just sound.[11] The show also created kryptonite, the one element that could weaken Superman ("The Meteor from Krypton" [3–11 June 1943]).[12] The series featured the first team-up between Superman, Batman, and Robin in "The Mystery of the Waxmen" (28 Feb.–15 Mar. 1945), over seven years before they would meet in the comic books in *Superman* #76 (May 1952). Both kryptonite and Batman and Robin would later be utilized to give the regular cast, especially Superman actor Bud Collyer, some much needed vacations.[13] When kryptonite was used, "listeners sat in rapt attention as Superman did little more than moan in the background" and Collyer enjoyed a break from the series as the moans could be provided by another actor (Rosen 3).

While these examples demonstrate the radio origins for now well-known aspects of the Superman mythology, some ideas never made it far beyond the radio. For example, in the initial syndicated broadcasts, Superman arrived on earth as an adult and in full costume in order to plunge him into the action as quickly as possible ("Clark Kent, Reporter"). The radio show also introduced Inspector Henderson (named both Charles and William), voiced at different times by Matt Crowley, Earl George, and Ned Wever, as a law enforcement contact to reassure parents that Superman was not a vigilante.[14] Though the character continued on to the *Adventures of Superman* television show (1952–1958) played by Robert Shayne,[15] he only made sporadic appearances in the comic book and never achieved the supporting character status of Perry White and Jimmy Olsen. One supporting character that never made it further than radio was Poco ("Planet Utopia" [16 Nov.–4 Dec. 1944]), a peace-loving alien who speaks in rhyme and becomes Perry White's butler but is now largely forgotten.

The Superman mythos was spreading nationwide by 1943, when the radio show moved from syndication to a live national broadcast, changing its original title, *Superman*, to the more famous *The Adventures of Superman*. Drawing on multiple sources, the series synthesized a new origin story, complete with Kal-El arriving on Earth as an infant, when the show began to air on the Mutual Broadcasting System. George Lowther, now a director for the show, even drew on his novel and named Clark Kent's parents Eben and Sarah ("Eben Kent Dies in Fire, Clark Goes to Metropolis" [1 Sept. 1942]). With this codification of Superman's origin, the radio series became privileged as the primary source for the Superman mythos, even over the comic books. One reason for this is that the radio reached a larger audience than the comic books ever achieved. In 1941, issues of *Action Comics* were selling 900,000 copies and *Superman* over 1,300,000 (Daniels 35); at the same time, *Superman* was being listened to by over 20,000,000 (*Look! Up in the Sky!*). The series had a broader audience than comics, too. Common household logistics often meant only one radio in a home, so shows drew an entire family to listen. "[O]ne phone poll showed that 35 percent of [*Superman*'s] audience was composed of adults" (Rossen 4). Also, the radio show was produced more frequently, creating a daily ritual. While *Action Comics* was published once a month, the self-titled *Superman* series initially published on a quarterly schedule for its first five issues (June 1939–June 1940) before switching to a bi-monthly with #6 (Sept.–Oct. 1940). Even appearing in more than one title (*Action Comics, Superman, World's Finest* [#1 (Mar. 1941)],[16] as well as guest appearances), Superman would appear, at best, once a week on the newsstand. Though supported by a daily newspaper strip, there was no guarantee that every newspaper would carry the three-to-four panel short strips nor that children would read it every day.[17] Airing five times a week between when children came home from school and before dinner on the most popular medium of the time, *The Adventures of Superman* was in the perfect position for maximum exposure. Cliffhangers were used to draw the listener back every day. Even if an episode was missed, the radio show's omniscient announcer would concisely summarize the previous episodes' events so the listener would never be lost in the storyline. As comic book historian Jon Morris notes: "The genuine value of the radio show is that it made Superman (and his cast of characters) personable. By becoming part of the aural landscape of thousands—and even millions—of American homes, the familiar sounds and peculiar phrasings of the cast were engraved onto the public consciousness. [...] If the original audience has ever felt an emotional intimacy with the Man of Steel, much of it had to do with his radio incarnation."

The process of bringing Superman to the radio began in 1939, soon after publisher Harry Donenfeld realized the character was a hit. One of the biggest initial challenges was finding an actor who could play both Superman and Clark Kent. The producers, Allen Ducovny and Robert Maxwell, even considered hiring two actors, one for each part. But they found unexpected success in Clayton "Bud" Collyer (born Clayton Heermance). Collyer had extensive radio experience, appearing on several shows each week (Scivally 17). He also had the ability to play Clark Kent as a tenor before dropping down to a baritone mid-sentence to become Superman, allowing him to proclaim: "This looks like a job— FOR SUPERMAN!" Being able to hear Superman and Clark Kent performed by the same actor was crucial, as the dual identity is an essential part of the superhero appeal; there is something primal at play through a wish-fulfillment by proxy. Superman's double life as Clark Kent was a secret readers and listeners could both share and project onto themselves (deForest 168). Collyer was initially reluctant to take the part as he already had a full schedule, but also didn't want to be associated with a kiddie program. Maxwell convinced him to take the part for the audition tapes and then simply told the actor, "You're Superman" (Scivally 18). Though the cast was not credited on the broadcast, Collyer was regularly reported as voicing Superman.[18] However, his name did not become synonymous with the superhero until 1946 when he began speaking publicly, such as to Youthbuilders, Inc., in support of the show's new social messages (Hayde 72). This coincided with national interest in the show following a post-war story in which a group called The Guardians of America attempted to make different races and religions fear and hate each other ("The Hate Mongers Organization" [16 Apr.–20 May 1946]). Though he largely stayed out of the public spotlight, Collyer played Clark Kent and Superman in over two thousand episodes of the radio show.

After casting Collyer, Ducovny and Maxwell brought *Superman* to the radio networks, but no one was initially interested. *Variety* reported on January 24, 1940:

> There will be no radio serial based on the comic strip, Superman as far as the networks are concerned. Erwin, Wasey & Co. picked on this new type of Dick Merriwell character as a medium to sell kid listeners on Hecker cereals but the webs have thumbed it down as a protagonist of too much horror stuff. The webs also didn't like the proposed script's war and spy theme.
>
> The "Superman" character is clothed with unlisted physical and mental powers and performs the

most amazing feats of daring. He can cope with planes attacking him with death rays and hold up bombed skyscrapers until the occupants of top stories make their way to safety. All this and much more was deemed by the networks as too much to unload on adolescent listeners, or unworthy of inciting further kickbacks from parents and teacher associations.

This brief article is intriguing for what it reveals about the general cultural awareness of Superman before the radio show. Despite a meteoric rise in popular culture, the concept of Superman, especially his superpowers, were only vaguely understood as a generic science fiction idea. A review of the initial broadcasts in *Variety* from 24 Feb. 1940 lists Superman's powers as: "He's a man with seven-league boots. He can make himself invisible and visible at will. He can read men's minds and nothing daunts, because, after all, this visitor from another planet is a superman" (Odec). A review of *Superman* from TIME magazine on February 26, 1940, also raises concerns: "Mother's clubs have their eyes on him, the Child Study Association of America feels that his occasional rocket and space ship jaunts are a bit too improbable. By radio's own war rules, he must remain neutral, may mix in no international intrigues, rub out no Hitlers" ("H-O Superman"). The only spaceship jaunt by that point had been Superman's arrival on Earth in the second episode, though that would hardly be the only improbable action in the series. Though the war and spy themes would be central after the U.S. entered World War II, even in 1940 they were deemed inappropriate as the country was still neutral in the conflict.

Most pertinent in the above articles is the appeasement towards parents, teachers and other cultural guardians. By the 1930s, there was rising concern about the morally corruptive effect of thriller, horror, and other genre radio programs on youth. Authorities on the issue fell into two camps. On the one hand were experts who viewed such listening as a cathartic experience and vicariously meeting important emotional needs in children. On the other were critics that saw the radio shows as stimulating negative emotions and promoting juvenile delinquency (Dennis 38–40).[19] However, little relevant psychological research was produced during the period for either side of the argument. As listening to such programs or reading comic books was so prevalent during the forties, little difference could be discovered between those who participated in such practices and those that did not (33, 39). Comic book companies and radio show producers, including those responsible for *The Adventures of Superman*, attempted to shield themselves by consulting with psychologists and having civic groups, such as the Child Study Association of America, review each script (Hayde 72). Alternatively, executives and sponsors could defend themselves by stating that the popularity of such books and shows were proof that they were giving young people what they wanted or that parents weren't supervising their children's reading and listening for comics and programs never intended for children (Dennis 42). However, accusations of being too violent or containing "too much horror stuff" would haunt Superman throughout its radio run and beyond.

Even without a network, the program was able to begin broadcast in syndication on February 12, 1940, on WOR in New York, with transcription disks sent out to other stations. The recorded fifteen-minute episodes aired three times a week and quickly became one of the most popular children's radio shows, gaining a main sponsor in Hecker's HO Oats on the East Coast with other sponsors in various regional markets (Scivally 17). Over the following episodes, the cast was rounded out with Joan Alexander as Lois Lane, Jackie Kelk as Jimmy Olsen, and Julian Noa as Perry White.[20] The other essential cast member was the narrator. First voiced by head writer George Lowther, the narrator initially only opened the episode and gave the closing tease, leaving Superman to awkwardly stop the action to monologue about what he was doing and why. Having Lois Lane or Jimmy Olsen around to talk to and save helped alleviate this some, but it wasn't until Jackson Beck became the narrator in the fall of 1943, providing a much fuller account of the action throughout the episode, that the awkwardness was relieved (Tye 87–8). Bud Collyer and Joan Alexander would reprise their respective roles for the Fleischer/Famous Studios animated film shorts (1941–1943) and three novelty records during the radio show's run.[21]

As a daily show being produced with a limited lead time, current events naturally influenced what stories were being told. The listener can sense the themes of the series shift as World War II becomes a reality for America. *The Adventures of Superman* can be demarcated with the pre–World War II episodes, the War episodes, and the post–War episodes. The pre–War episodes feature the hero battling against petty criminals or gang bosses with elaborate schemes. The villains were selfish—prizing personal profit and wealth above all else—and hurt the common man through their plotting. This echoed the early Superman comic book's New Deal themes by championing public welfare over injustice and greed, which filled a powerful need in the alienated and dispossessed during the Great Depression. This, in part, led to the show becoming a hit (Ashby 261). *Variety*'s February 24, 1940, review noted: "The only thing that all concerned have to worry about is whether the serial's plot and hard-hitting level of excitement won't incur the kickback from parent-teachers associations or kindred groups. The chances are pretty much in the affirmative" (Odec).

The rising popularity of *Superman*, as well as the Mutual Broadcasting System's loss of their number one youth program "Jack Armstrong, the All-American Boy" to the NBC Blue Network (later ABC), led to a move from syndication to a national broadcast on August 31, 1942 ("Hi-Yo, Silver, Plated"). This transition brought several changes. The program had already switched to a five-day-a-week schedule on August 25, 1941, but being on a network meant that the show was performed live rather than recorded for transcription. The show gained a new sponsor in Kellogg's Pep, which would remain with the program for the majority of its run (Scivally 20). These factors contributed to softening of the violence and more emphasis on comedy relief, which may have led to things like the introduction of the alien Poco (Hayde 49, 56). And, of course, the show began addressing the Second World War. Many programs integrated propaganda messages into their plots under the direction of the Office of War Information (Russo 269). Famously, the phrase "…and the American way" was added to the introduction to help strike the right chords of patriotism (Tye 89).

The war was an added challenge to Superman, who could have easily ended it with his powers, as illustrated in a two-page comic strip for *Look* magazine by Siegel and Shuster in 1940. "How Superman Would End the War" saw the Man of Steel leap into Europe, grab Hitler and Stalin, and take them to the world court (Siegel and Shuster 12–13). The war would have been over in a day before the United States had entered it. It would be a notable omission for Superman stories to ignore the war, but also tone deaf if Superman ended the war in fiction while real battles raged on the frontlines. As the April 13, 1942, *TIME* article "Superman's Dilemma" explains: "As the mightiest, fightingest American, he [Superman] ought to join up. But he just can't. In the combat services he would lick the Japs and Nazis in a wink, and the war isn't going to end that soon. On the other hand, he can't afford to lose the respect of millions by failing to do his bit or by letting the war drag on." This was an issue that had to be navigated in the comic books, the radio show, and the animated film shorts.

In the comic book, Clark Kent is declared 4-H for bad eyesight because he accidently used his x-ray vision to read the eye chart in the next room over. While Clark Kent may not be able to join the fight, in the comics and on the radio Superman was commissioned as an undercover Secret Service operative ("Superman's Dilemma"). *The Adventures of Superman* took on more international storylines as Superman fought to prevent Nazi's from sabotaging the Allied war effort around the world. This would sometimes lead to Superman having to choose between saving his friends or saving the troops: "Jim[my Olsen] and Poco are important, but not as important as that convoy of troops" ("The Space Shell, Pt. 8" [21 Feb. 1945]). A few previous storylines were recycled, merely replacing the criminals with Nazis or "Japs" (Hayde 51, 55).[22] Of course, the propaganda of this era is not only pro–Ally but also explicitly anti–Axis powers. Not all recordings of the radio show survive to this day, but there are a few episodes from the War-era that feature Japanese enemies. The voice work for the Japanese characters—which Asian culture scholar Todd S. Munson describes as "heavy 'Yellowface' accents" that "leave no doubt as to their nationality and mission" (11)—is cringe-inducing for modern audiences far separated from the propaganda of World War II. One Japanese soldier, amazed at seeing bullets bounce off of Superman cries out "He will not take me! I go to my ancestors! I die honorable death!" and shoots himself. Superman simply says, "Well, that's *one*" ("The Mystery of the Sleeping Beauty, Pt. 2" [16 Jan. 1945]).

In 1942, Bud Collyar was also exploring how Superman would engage in the war effort in his voice work for Fleisher studios. Earlier animated shorts had seen Superman battling mad scientists and natural disasters, but after the United States entered the war the hero faced off against "Japanese stereotypes" in narratives that were fueled by "the raucous patriotism of a nation mired in war" (Rossen 12). The first Superman animated short to explicitly address the war was "Japoteurs" (Sept. 1942), which saw Superman stopping Japanese spies from stealing a U.S. war plane. Thus, Superman aided the war cause in a specific instance, but the U.S. military was prepared to continue the battle. A subsequent short, "The Eleventh Hour" (Nov. 1942), begins with Lois and Clark being held prisoner in Japan. Each night, Clark sneaks out and, as Superman, commits an act of sabotage against the Japanese military. Eventually, notices are put up that Lois will be executed if Superman does not cease his attacks. Superman saves Lois and returns her to America. The short ends with Lois revealing that Clark Kent is still being held in Japan. The implicit message is that Superman's never-ending battle for truth and justice has shifted to a never-ending battle against America's war-time enemies. In this telling, Superman can harm the Japanese forces but not defeat them entirely.

As the war ended, Superman would face his greatest challenge as a Nazi scientist uses Kryptonite to create the Atom Man, the first true supervillain to appear on the radio show (though many villains had used codenames). The saga of Superman versus the Atom Man ran for 77 episodes from September 24, 1945, to January 8, 1946.[23] As an antagonist, Atom Man differs from the gangsters, mad scientists, and hate-mongers that populated the radio show in that he possesses superpowers that make him a physical threat to Superman. A Nazi scientist named Der Teufel obtains kryptonite from a villain called the Scarlet Widow ("The Scarlet Widow" [26 Sept.–10 Oct. 1945]). Teufel liquifies the kryptonite and injects the kryptonite into Hienrich Milch, a Nazi soldier who received the Iron Cross from Hitler for his service to Germany during World War II. Milch develops the power to shoot destructive energy from his hands and infiltrates the United States as Henry Miller ("The Atom Man" [11 Oct.–6 Nov. 1945]). In the finale, Superman flies Atom Man into the sky, but Atom Man's kryptonite-infused body weakens Superman and they both fall to the earth. Atom Man is killed in the impact, but Superman survives and quickly revives to his usual power levels ("The Atom Man in Metropolis, Pt. 19" [3 Dec. 1945]). Coming less than two months after the atomic bombs were dropped on Japan, the serial can be interpreted as showing that Superman, and by extension America, was stronger than that weapon (*Look, Up in the Sky!*). Denouncing Atom Man's message about one group being superior to others would also serve to inform the next several years of serials.

After the war, *The Adventures of Superman* shifted from an international to a domestic focus. On April 14, 1946, *The New York Times* reported:

> Superman has been enlisted in the fight against juvenile delinquency. Beginning this Tuesday, the format of the Superman episodes will be changed from straight "adventure" into stories dealing with racial intolerance, school absenteeism and other problems of child behaviorism.
> The new series represents an experiment in embodying an educational message in an entertaining, exciting presentation, and as such, is said to be of great interest to educators, religious leaders and organizations concerned with juvenile problems [Lohman].

The new direction for the series was part of what producer Robert Maxwell termed "Operation Intolerance." The opening narration was changed beginning in February 1945 to reflect this new social justice message. Following the traditional preamble, the narrator now stated: "Yes, it's Superman! Strange visitor from another planet, who came to Earth with powers and abilities far beyond those of mortal men. Superman, defender of law and order, champion of equal rights, valiant courageous fighter against the forces of hate and prejudice!" ("The Radar Rocket, Pt. 1" [15 Feb. 1946]). Superman preached against prejudice and anti–American behavior through storylines such as "The Hate Mongers' Organization" (25 episodes, 16 Apr.–20 May 1946), "Knights of the White Carnation" (14 episodes, 26 Feb.–17 Mar. 1947), and, most famously, "The Clan of the Fiery Cross" (16 episodes, 10 June–1 July 1946), a not-so-subtle allusion to the Ku Klux Klan.[24] Some have attributed this Superman serial as leading to a decrease in the KKK's power and influence in the following years. One Klansman reportedly said:

> When I came home one night, there was my kid and a bunch of others, some with towels tied around their necks like capes and some with pillowcases over their heads. The ones with capes were chasing the ones with pillowcases all over the lot. When I asked them what they were doing, they said they were playing a new kind of cops and robbers called Superman against the Klan. Gangbusting, they called it! Knew all our secret passwords and everything. I never felt so ridiculous in all my life! Suppose my own kid finds my Klan robe some day? [Levitt and Dunbar 65].

Superman's message of tolerance reflected a re-evaluation of the American way after the war as the beginnings of the civil rights movement fought against discrimination. But this wasn't the only motivation for the programs. They were also to appease parent and civic groups' increasing concerns about the radio thriller. Superman's approach to such controversy through social responsibility proved effective. A spokesman for Kellogg's explained: "We had been getting a lot of complaints about the blood and thunder stuff until we decided to put in these social episodes. Now all the parents' organizations are congratulating us on the show. The psychologists tell us we're planting a 'thought egg' in the kids' minds" (Tye 85). These civic episodes were intermixed with regular adventure stories, now often featuring team-ups with Batman and Robin.[25] After World War II, sales of superhero comic books plummeted as other genres gained in popularity. It is in a large part thanks to the radio show that both Superman and Batman remained in print.[26]

Another transmedia adaptation was developed in the late 1940s in the movie serials *Superman* (1948) and *Atom Man vs. Superman* (1950). The title cards for the serials open with the cover of a Superman comic book and state that the stories are "Based on the Superman Adventure Feature Appearing in the magazines 'SUPERMAN' and 'ACTION COMICS'" but that they are "Adapted from the Superman Radio Program" ("Superman Comes to Earth"; "Superman Flies Again"). Specifically, they borrowed from the Atom Man saga, with the first serial changing a radio-show's villain name from Scarlet Widow to the Spider Lady and the second utilizing the villainous Atom Man. However, the movie serial's Atom Man is quite a divergence from the radio show's, as this Atom Man is not a Nazi science experiment but rather Lex Luthor in a glittery mask. Actor Alyn Kirk, who portrayed Superman, was strongly influenced by Bud Collyer's vocal performance: "I visualized the guy I heard on the radio. That was a guy nothing could stop. That's why I stood like this, with my chest out, and a look on my face saying 'Shoot me'" (Tye 98). While the two serials were popular, they were not successful enough to warrant another sequel. This was a sign of the waning popularity of both movie and radio serials with the advent of the new technology of television.

By 1949, *The Adventures of Superman* began to go through an experimental phase trying to find continued success after nearly a decade on the air. It first changed from a fifteen-minute live serialized broadcast five days a week to thirty-minute transcribed, self-contained episodes airing three times a week, from February 7 to June 24, 1949. After a short gap, the series returned, albeit in a new format on a new network. ABC reimagined the series as a short-lived crime drama. This iteration aired on Saturdays for thirteen weeks from October 27, 1949, to January 21, 1950 (Tye 93). However, as ABC was focusing most of its money on the burgeoning television market, the network would only pay the radio actors scale. This led to the loss of most of the cast (Hayde 113), though Bud Collyer, Joan Alexander, and Jackson Beck would later reprise their roles as Superman/Clark Kent, Lois Lane, and narrator, respectively, on *The New Adventures of Superman* cartoon television series (1966–1970).[27] But ABC still saw potential revenue in the radio series, perhaps in conjunction with the proposed *Adventures of Superman* television series. To survive the budget cuts, this final iteration, airing twice a week, reused the scripts from the 30-minute format and replaced most of the cast: Superman/Clark Kent was played by Michael Fitzmaurice, Jimmy Olsen by Jack Grimes, and the show was narrated by Ross Martin. This last version of *The Adventures of Superman* managed to use all of the half-hour scripts for a seventy-eight-episode run from June 5, 1950, to March 1, 1951. The Man of Steel soon returned to American living rooms in the syndicated *Adventures of Superman* television show.

As the radio show was leaving the airwaves in the United States, it was being picked up elsewhere. *Superman* premiered on the Australian radio network 2GB on May 30, 1949. According to media studies scholar Kevin Patrick: "While Americans had grown weary of superheroes, they had become an exciting new phenomenon to young Australian readers." Superman was likely introduced to the Australian audiences during World War II, when the comic book was included as part of the care packages for servicemen, almost one million of whom were stationed there (Patrick). Due to wartime import restrictions, the character was not the immediate success he was in the United States but rather experienced a slow roll-out. Reprints of the Sunday comic strip began appearing in Australian newspapers in 1943.[28] After the import restrictions were lifted, K.G. Murray licensed the comic book stories for his Colour Comics Pty. Ltd. in 1947. Initially published in color, the title soon changed to black and white, a format which continued for twenty-five years ("Superman").[29] Though selling 150,000 copies paled in comparison to sales figures in the United States, these were record numbers in Australia at a time when superhero comic books were on the wane in America. The dissemination of Superman content continued with the introduction of the radio show.

The exportation of *The Adventures of Superman* was organized by Paul Talbot. In 1946, Talbot, who also wrote for DC Comics,[30] established Fremantle Overseas Radio (later Fremantle Media) to export American radio and television content internationally. Talbot's company did not sell recordings, but rather the scripts to the shows which could be transposed into a local context. For *Superman*, this meant performing the series' scripts with Australian actors in the roles. Leonard Teale played Superman/Clark Kent with Margaret Christensen as Lois Lane. Jimmy Olsen was played at different points by Ron Faulkner, John Mellion, and Morris Unicombe with Perry White voiced by Alfred Bristow and Reginald Collins. Recordings reveal that the performances had neither a distinct Australian accent nor a performative American accent but rather a neutral radio voice.

The radio show was announced in *The Standard* on March 10, 1949, as follows:

> *Superman*, the recently-acquired AW 6 o'clocker, not only makes a better radio serial than a newspaper strip, but it is also more healthy for children than most of the serials currently broadcast. Of course, our magnetic friend, Clark Kent still performs miracles, but then you expect that sort of thing in *Superman*, and it merely seems part of the fun. It is also so fantastic as to present no worry to mothers with sensitive youngsters [qtd. in Gonzalez].

This is a far cry from *Variety*'s 1940 report when the radio show was first trying to get on the air. Due to the gradual circulation of Superman content, it is assumed that the superhero is a known quantity to the audience, needing no explanation. And though Australia had the same concerns as to whether radio content could be harmful to children (Arneil), it is here a non-issue.

The Australian *Superman* broadcast approximately half of the stories of *The Adventures of Superman* program, utilizing 1040 scripts starting at the beginning of the radio show, complete with Superman arriving on Earth as an adult. Sticking to the fifteen-minute episodes, the Australian cast did not record the series in chronological order but skipped around the catalog as they included Batman (voiced by Bruce Beeby) and Robin (Trader Faulkner), most of whose adventures occur in the second half of the original run. As the episodes are also listed under different names, it is unclear if the cast performed the war or the social justice stories or kept to the adventure scripts.[31] If they did record the war stories, the series would have come across more as historical rather than contemporary adventures. The scripts also possess a distinctly American flavor, especially during the "Operation Intolerance" stories, and it is unknown how the Australian audience responded to this. The interest was obviously there as the show aired for exactly five years, May 30, 1949, to May 30, 1954.

It would be thirty-four years before Superman would be heard on the radio again. Unlike in the United States, the tradition of audio drama never disappeared from British radio. In honor of Superman's fiftieth anniversary in 1988, the British Broadcasting Corporation (BBC) aired the special *Superman on Trial* (5 June 1988).[32] This tale of Superman on trial before one of the cosmic Guardians of Oa for "crimes against humanity," with Lex Luthor as prosecutor and Lois Lane as the defense attorney, was one of the first productions by now legendary audio writer-director Dirk Maggs and helped him begin work with the BBC Light Entertainment Department. Maggs, who had grown up reading comics (Hunt), drew on Superman's comic book adventures for evidence as well as testimonies from then-DC President Jeanette Kahn, comic book artist Dave Gibbons, and Batman actor Adam West as themselves,[33] to write this single-episode docu-drama. Directed by Neil Cargill, the story featured Stuart Milligan as Superman, William Hootkins as Lex Luthor, Vincent Marzello as Jimmy Olsen, Shelley Thompson as Lois Lane, and Lorelei King as Lana Lang. Through a somewhat confusing look at Superman's history, including the fabrication for trial reasons that Superman was raised in Kansas as Clark Kent's brother, the Man of Steel is acquitted of all charges and allowed to continue as a superhero.

The success of *Superman on Trial* led the BBC to produce more "audio movies," Dirk Maggs's term for giving radio a three-dimensional sound more like film (Hunt), based on superheroes.[34] Maggs describes his process of adaptation as: "Write the movie you want to see, then worry about how you're going to make it work in sound alone," relying on the audience to draw on pre-existing visual references (Gottlieb). In addition to radio series based on Batman and Spider-Man, Maggs wrote and directed two series of *The Adventures of Superman* (1990–1991) and one series of *Superman: Doomsday and Beyond* (1993).[35] Maggs reunited the cast of *Superman on Trial* for these new productions, albeit switching the roles of Shelley Thompson and Lorelei King as Lois Lane and Lana Lang. The twelve episodes of *The Adventures of Superman* were loosely based on John Byrne's 1986 *Man of Steel* comic book mini-series, which revamped the Superman mythology for a contemporary audience.[36] *Superman: Doomsday and Beyond* was an active, though abbreviated, adaptation of *The Death and Return of Superman* storyline (1992–1993). Adapting the storyline as it played out in the comics meant that Maggs worked more closely than usual with DC Comics, even receiving the scripts and layouts of the comic books before they were published (Mulrain). Though the death of Superman was and remains one of the character's most popular storylines, it was not enough to save him on the radio as superhero stories were soon phased out by the BBC.

No audio adaption of the Man of Steel has been produced since 1993, but the potential is still there. The relatively new podcast format, created in 2000 and popularized by 2007, has created a veritable explosion of new audio fiction. Marvel Comics has found success in recent years in adapting its characters to this format and is expanding its productions with various entertainment partners.[37] In February 2021, DC Comics announced a partnership with Spotify to produce an audio drama starring Superman and Lois Lane, as well as several other podcast projects.

The Adventures of Superman radio program was the centerpiece of early transmedia adaptations that created the Superman mythos and established the superhero as a prominent figure in American and international popular culture. Without the show capturing a mass audience, it is likely the comic book and perhaps the entire superhero genre would not have survived to this day. The waning popularity of the superhero genre in comic books after the conclusion of World War II saw almost all the costumed do-gooders disappear from the medium. The broader appeal of Superman in other media helped to ensure the character's long-term viability in the entertainment industry. At the same time, popular contemporary masked men such as the Shadow, the Green Hornet, and the Lone Ranger were soon leaving the airwaves. While there have been periodic revivals of each of those characters, none have had the consistent presence in popular culture that Superman has enjoyed.

The importance of *The Adventures of Superman* in entertainment history is not just its popularity; there were, after all, more popular radio shows from that era that featured characters and stories which have largely been forgotten in the intervening decades. It's importance also does not lie in the introduction of new aspects of the Superman mythos, though it certainly did that. With a character that has endured for almost a century, there have been many subsequent additions to the mythos as well, and the core modern Superman mythology does not exactly match what can be heard in the old radio adventures. The success of the radio shows definitively establish the versatility of Superman as the anchor of a multimedia franchise. The radio shows helped to ensure that familiarity with Superman was a necessary aspect of cultural awareness in the 1940s and beyond, but the ability for Superman to resonate in subsequent media has made the character a cultural touchstone for generations.

NOTES

1. Variations of the this introduction, which became standardized in 1943, appeared in *Superman/The Adventures of Superman* radio show, the Fleischer/Famous Studios cartoons (1941–1943), *Adventures of Superman* television show (1952–1958), *The New Adventures of Superman* animated television series (1966–1970), *Superman* animated television series (1988), and the BBC radio productions (1988–1993). It is also referenced in the title of the Broadway musical *It's a Bird!...It's a Plane!...It's Superman!* (1966).

2. For more on how transmedia adaptations developed the Superman mythos, see William J. Lorenzo's "The Dawn of the Man of Tomorrow: How Adapting Superman into Different Media Created America's Superhero" and Liam Webb's "Forging an S into a Myth: Adaptations of Superman Across Media" in this volume.

3. *Dick Tracy* was created by Chester Gould, who wrote and drew the comic strip from 4 Oct. 1931–25 Dec. 1977. During that time, *Dick Tracy* was adapted into a radio show (4 Feb. 1935–16 July 1948), four film serials (1937–1941), five films (1937–1947), and numerous comic books. *Flash Gordon* was created by Alex Raymond to compete with the popular *Buck Rogers* comic strip. Raymond drew parts of the comic strip from 7 Jan. 1934–30 Apr. 1944. During that time, *Flash Gordon* was adapted into three film serials (1936–1940), which were condensed into three films, a radio show (22 Apr. 1935–6 Feb. 1936), and reprinted as a comic book. Al Capp created and drew *Li'l Abner* from 13 Aug. 1934–13 Nov. 1977. *L'il Abner* was adapted into a radio show (20 Nov. 1939–6 Nov. 1940), a film (1940), five cartoon shorts (1944), a Broadway musical (1956), and numerous comic book reprints.

4. Two issues of *New York World's Fair Comics* were published by DC Comics, both featuring a Superman story. Issue #1 (Apr. 1939) misprints Superman with blond hair in the cover inset. The cover for issue #2 is the first illustration to feature Superman, Batman, and Robin together. Batman and Robin were not featured in issue #1 because they had not yet been created at that point.

5. This Superman balloon, the tallest to appear in the Macy Thanksgiving Day Parade, only appeared in 1940 before it was redesigned as a football player. Superman made two subsequent appearances as a balloon in the parade: 1966–1970 and 1980–1987.

6. As was standard practice at the time, Siegel and Shuster sold the rights to Superman to National Periodicals. They expected to receive a cut of the profits, which was very quickly in the millions of dollars, but were never given as much as they should have earned (Kobler 76). The pair spent subsequent decades trying to unsuccessfully reclaim the rights to the character. The legal battle is carried on to this day by their families.

7. The first season of *Adventures of Superman* cost twice as much as the proposed budget, which also contributed to Robert Maxwell being let go as a producer (Tye 142).

Maxwell also penned the novelty polka song "Superman" (1941), performed and recorded by Freddie Fisher and his Orchestra.

8. It was only decades later that some comic books became valuable consumer commodities.

9. Superman's adoptive parents went through several names over the years. In an unused pitch to comic strip artist Russell Keaton in 1934, Shuster named the parents Sam and Molly (Tye 18). In *Action Comics #1*, an unidentified "passing motorist" took the recently-arrived infant to an orphanage, where he was apparently raised (the motorist seems to not have questioned why the baby was in a rocket ship). In *Superman #1* (July 1939), the passing motorists take the infant to an orphanage and then adopt him; the husband is unnamed while the wife is named Mary. In the 1942 novel *The Adventures of Superman*, George Lowther names the couple Eben and Sarah; these names were also used on the radio show ("Eben Kent Dies in a Fire, Clark Goes to Metropolis" [1 Sept. 1942]) and on the *Adventures of Superman* television show ("Superman on Earth" [19 Sept. 1952]). The 1948 *Superman* movie serial named the couple Eben and Martha. The first extensive comic

book retelling of Superman's origin in the tenth anniversary *Superman* #53 (July–Aug. 1948) identify the couple as John and Mary. It wasn't until the adventures of Superboy, wherein Ma and Pa Kent would be regular supporting characters, that they became Jonathan and Martha. Jonathan Kent is first named so in *Adventure Comics* #148 (Feb. 1950) and Martha in *Superboy* #12 (Jan.–Feb. 1951).

10. In the pilot transcripts, which were created to find sponsors and not for broadcast, Perry White was Paris White of *The Daily Flash* (Hayde 16). An unnamed, bow-tie wearing office boy appeared in *Action Comics* #6 (Nov. 1938) and some have credited this as the first appearance of Jimmy Olsen. However, the character did not receive a name nor personality until the radio show.

The broadcast dates and episode numbers for the radio show are from the "Superman Radio Episode List" on the *Superman Homepage*.

11. In the comic books, Superman's power was constrained to leaping until *Action Comics* #65 (Oct. 1943). In "Clark Kent, Reporter," Superman is described as "hovering" in the opening scene. At the end of the episode, he leaps from a twentieth-story window to travel 2000 miles and is described as "an eagle in the sky." Though the episode does not explicitly state that Superman is flying, these phrases, as well as the comparisons to a bird and plane, accompanied by the sound effect of whistling wind imply flight. For more on this ambiguity, see William J. Lorenzo's "The Dawn of the Man of Tomorrow: How Adapting Superman into Different Media Created America's Superhero" in this collection.

12. In 1940, Jerry Siegel submitted a comic book story titled "The K-Metal from Krypton," involving a meteor that robbed Superman of his powers. It was rejected due to the fact that the climax involved Clark Kent being forced to reveal his secret identity to Lois. George Lowther, head writer for the radio show, had access to the Superman files at National and may have seen this story and been inspired to create Kryptonite (Hayde 56–57).

13. It has been often repeated the kryptonite was created to allow Bud Collyer to have a vacation. However, Collyer was present for the entirety of "The Meteor from Krypton" (7 episodes, 3–11 June 1943), the story that introduced kryptonite.

14. It is unknown which episode Inspector Henderson first appeared on. Many of the 2088 episodes are missing recordings, though the number varies by source. Henderson was likely introduced in one of these missing episodes.

15. Inspector Henderson did not appear in the comic books until *Action Comics* #422 (Dec. 1974), where he briefly served as Superman's main police contact. He also was a supporting character in the first *Black Lightning* comic book series (Apr. 1977–Oct. 1978). Henderson has also appeared on television as a recurring character on the first season of *Lois and Clark: The New Adventures of Superman* (1993–1997), played by Mel Winkler (who also voiced the character on an episode of *Superman: The Animated Series* [1996–2000]), Brent Jennings, and Richard Belzer, though the latter bizarrely changed the character from African-American to white. Henderson also appeared on *Black Lightning* (2018–2021), played by Damon Gupton.

16. Following the success of *New York World's Fair Comics* #2, DC Comics began publishing *World's Finest Comics* (titled *World's Best Comics* on first issue) as an anthology with various superhero stories. Initially a quarterly, each issue featured their most popular characters, Superman, Batman, and Robin, on the cover and inside. During the Golden Age of superhero comic books (1938–1954), these characters had separate strips. In the Silver Age (1954–1970), the page length was shortened to feature only one story wherein Superman and Batman would team up beginning in *World's Finest Comics* #71 (July 1954).

17. In 1942, *TIME* Magazine estimated that the comic books would be passed around approximately 10 times, giving them a projected readership of 12,000,000. The daily and Sunday strips (the Sunday strip was longer at half a page but were their own separate continuity), were assessed as being read by 25,000,000 ("Superman's Dilemma"). How *TIME* arrived at these statistics is not revealed in the article.

18. One legend about the radio show is that Bud Collyer's identity as voicing Superman was kept a secret for years (Barron). However, *Variety*'s review of the radio program from 24 Feb. 1940 lists Bud Collyer as the lead actor, clearly implying he is voicing Superman/Clark Kent (Odec). *TIME*'s 25 Feb. 1940 review explicitly states Collyer as radio's Superman ("H-O Superman") while their 14 Sept 1942 piece "Superman in the Flesh" is an entire write-up about the actor as Superman.

19. Similar debates existed around comic books throughout the period.

20. Lois Lane was initially performed by Rollie Bester (wife of *Superman* and *Green Lantern* comic book writer Alfred Bester) for six episodes (26 Feb.–8 Mar. 1940) and then Helen Choate for approximately eighteen episodes (18 Mar.–26 Apr. 1940) before Joan Alexander took over on 9 June 1940 for the majority of the radio shows run. At one point, producers became unhappy with Alexander's performance and fired her, but after a blind audition process resulted in Alexander being selected, she was retained for the remainder of the series (Rosen 3).

21. The unnamed newspaper editor in the Fleischer/Famous shorts was voiced by Jackson Beck, who would soon become the narrator for the radio series. The record *Superman's Christmas Adventure* (1941) labels the voice actors as "the Superman Radio Players." *Superman: The Flying Train* (1947) and *Superman: The Magic Ring* (1947) were both record and book sets "in song and adventure with the radio voice cast."

22. Mutual, after broadcasting a new two-part origin, retold Superman's first radio adventure thwarting the Wolfe from sabotaging trains, only now the Wolfe is a Nazi and the trains are full of soldiers ("The Wolfe" [2–16 Sept. 1942]). "Lighthouse Point" (22 Feb.–1 Mar. 1944) was also a recycled story that replaced the criminals with Nazis (Hayde 51, 55).

23. The Atom Man saga ran through "The Meteor of Kryptonite" (2 episodes, 24–25 Sept. 1945), "The Scarlet Widow" (11 episodes, 26 Sept.–10 Oct. 1945), "The Atom Man" (19 episodes, 11 Oct.–6 Nov. 1945), "The Atom Man in Metropolis" (19 episodes, 7 Nov.–3 Dec. 1945), and "Looking for Kryptonite" (26 episodes, 4 Dec. 1945–8 Jan. 1946). The dangling plot thread concerning the last piece of kryptonite is picked up a year-and-a-half later in "Superman vs. Kryptonite" (33 episodes, 14 May–27 June 1947).

24. Much has been documented about Stetson Kennedy's infiltration of the KKK and passing on secret codes and signs for use in the Superman radio show, notably in Rick Bowers' *Superman Versus the Ku Klux Klan* (2012), which is the subject of forthcoming film and podcast adaptations. In *Flights of Fantasy* (2009), Michael J. Hayde argues that, while Kennedy may have been in contact with the producers, little of the actual content reflected any specialized knowledge of the Klan (Hayde 77–8).

For an in-depth analysis of "The Clan of the Fiery Cross," see J. Richard Stevens's "Adapting the Clan to the Klan: Modern Confrontations of White Nationalism in Young Adult Superman Comics" in this volume.

25. Batman and Robin also appeared in the subsequent stories "Is There Another Superman?" (13 episodes, 29 Jan.–14 Feb. 1946), "The Story of the Century" (12 episodes, 29 Mar.–15 Apr. 1946), "Horatio F. Horn, Detective" (14 episodes, 2–19 July 1946), "The Dead Voice" (15 episodes, 26 Sept.–16 Oct. 1946), "The Secret Letter" (7 episodes, 25 Nov.–3 Dec. 1946), "Monkey Burglar" (10 episodes, 12–25 Feb. 1947), "Superman vs. Kryptonite" (33 episodes, 14 May–27 June 1947), "Pennies for Plunder" (19 episodes, 27 Nov.–28 Dec. 1947), "Batman's Great Mystery" (11 episodes, 3–17 Feb. 1948), "The Mystery of the Stolen Costume" (17 episodes, 10 Mar.–1 Apr. 1948), "Secret of Meteor Island" (17 episodes, 14 June–6 July 1948) and "The Voice of Doom" (18 episodes, 7–30 July 1948).

There was an attempt to create a Batman radio show, *Batman Mystery Club*, in 1950. This would have been closer in format to the chiller anthology series like *Lights Out* (1934–1947) and *Suspense* (1940–1962), with Batman telling a scary mystery story only to reveal the logical explanation for the supernatural elements. A pilot episode was recorded but never aired.

26. The only other superhero to remain in continuous publication throughout this period was Wonder Woman.

27. Jackson Beck would also voice Lex Luthor and Perry White on *The New Adventures of Superman* animated television series. Joan Alexander voiced Lois Lane for the first and last season, with Julie Bennett playing the role for the middle two seasons. Jack Grimes, who took over the radio role of Jimmy Olsen from Jackie Kelk in 1950, would return to voice the *Daily Planet* copyboy again.

Joan Alexander, Jackson Beck, and Jack Grimes also reprised their roles for the specialty record *The Official Adventures of Superman* (1966), though Superman was voiced by Bob Holiday, who played Superman in the original Broadway production of the musical *It's a Bird!...It's a Plane!...It's Superman*!

28. The *Superman* Sunday comic strip first appeared in the *Sunday Telegraph* in Melbourne on 7 Mar. 1943 (Cliffe). *The Mail* in Adelaide began republishing strips on 7 Oct. 1944 (Best), though these were rearranged to fit the more vertical format of their comic page. The first strip actually used panels from the first comic strip with block text to introduce the character readers in a style akin to the British comic strips of the time.

29. These reprints initially went by several titles: *Superman All Color Comic* (#1, 5, 6, 9, and 14); *Superman Color Comics* (#2–4 and 20–33; ironically, issue #33 is when they switched to the black and white format); *Superman All Color Comics* (#7–8, 10–13, and 15–19); *Superman Comics* (#34–36 and 38–39); before settling on the eponymous *Superman* (#37 and 40–147) ("Superman"). The title then became *Superman's Supacomic* (#1–5) and *Superman Supacomic* (#6–202) ("Superman Supacomic"). Colour Comics Pty. Ltd. also published several other DC Comics titles under the banner *Superman Presents*....

30. During the Golden Age of comic books (1938–1954), most creators did not receive printed credit for their work. The authors have been able to verify that Paul Talbot wrote the Green Arrow back-up strips for *Adventure Comics* #156–160 (Sept. 1950–Jan. 1951). He has also been attributed to working on Superman, Batman, and Aquaman stories. In some places, this has been conflated with his radio enterprise into him writing for the Superman, Batman, and Aquaman radio shows (Moran and Avenyard). As the latter two never existed, that he wrote for the Superman radio show is unlikely.

31. This is based on the list of Australian radio titles found on "Superman on Radio in Australia" on the *Superman Homepage*.

32. Other parts of the BBC's celebration of Superman's anniversary included an airing of the CBS's television special *Superman's 50th Anniversary* (1988), an airing of an episode of the original *Superman* radio series, and special edition of the *Radio Times*, the weekly magazine which published radio and television listings. The 4–10 June 1988 edition of the *Radio Times* included a cover and two-page comic strip drawn by Dave Gibbons, which set up *Superman on Trial*, and a poem by Roger Woddis, "The Zarathustra Factor."

33. According to Maggs: "Jeanette Khan was stunningly easy to get—I phoned, asked, she said yes. All we had to do was find a New York studio where she could be recorded giving her testimony. Dave Gibbons [...] was hugely enthusiastic about the project and able to get to the studio to record and interact with the cast. [...] West was an unexpected bonus. He was in the UK promoting repeats of the *Batman* TV show and happened to turn up at Broadcasting House. I literally ran down three flights of stairs, buttonholed him as he was about to go in for his interview, asked if he could spare five minutes after he had finished, ran back to my office, wrote some questions for him and grabbed him into a little self-op studio when he emerged" (Mulrain).

Though Adam West appeared as himself, Batman was performed by Bob Sessions, who would reprise the role in the BBC radio productions *Batman: The Lazarus Experiment* (1989) and *Batman: Knightfall* (1994), both of which were written and directed by Dirk Maggs.

34. The success of the *Superman* radio programs also led author Douglas Adams to hand-pick Dirk Maggs to adapt his final three *A Hitchhiker's Guide to the Galaxy* novels for radio (the first two novels were based on Adams's original radio series). Additionally, Maggs adapted Eoin Colfer's addition to H2G2, *And Another Thing...* (2009).

35. *Superman: Doomsday and Beyond* was released in the U.S. as *Superman Lives!* (1993).

36. This was actually the second audio adaptation of *The Man of Steel*. In 1989, DC Comics released a special edition of the mini-series. Each of the six issues came packaged with an audio cassette containing a full-cast dramatic performance of the issue complete with soundtrack.

37. Marvel has produced the scripted podcasts *Wolverine: The Long Night* (2018), *Wolverine: The Lost Trail* (2019), and *Marvels* (2019) with Stitcher Premium. They have partnered with Serial Box/Realm for the scripted series *Thor: Metal Gods* (2019), *Black Widow: Bad Blood* (2020), *Jessica Jones: Playing with Fire* (2020), and *Black Panther: Sins of the Ki*n (2021). They have also announced a partnership with Sirius XM and Pandora to create scripted podcast series based on Wolverine, Hawkeye, Black Widow, and Star-Lord, and *Wastelanders*, set in the world of Old Man Logan.

Works Cited

The Adventures of Superman, episodes 1–12. BBC Radio 4, London, 1990–1991.
Ashby, LeRoy. *With Amusement for All: A History of American Popular Culture Since 1830*. The University Press of Kentucky, 2006.
Arneil, Chris. "Horror Radio Featuring The Shadow and The Witch of Salem." *National Film and Sound Archive of Australia*, https://www.nfsa.gov.au/latest/radio-horror-and-thriller-serials-1940s-and-50s. Accessed 27 Mar. 2020.
Arnold, Gary. "Hollywood's Super Holiday." *The Washington Post*, 10 Dec. 1978, https://www.washingtonpost.com/archive/lifestyle/1978/12/10/hollywoods-super-holiday/720c75c8-c10b-40bb-ac2e-97df82dfa9e1/. Accessed 6 Feb. 2020.
"The Atom Man." *The Adventures of Superman*, episodes 1122–1140. Mutual Broadcasting Network, New York City, 11 Oct.-6 Nov. 1945.
"The Atom Man in Metropolis." *The Adventures of Superman*, episode 1184. Mutual Broadcasting Network, New York City, 8 Jan. 1946.
Barron, James. "Turn That Dial Back in Time: Superman & Co. Return!" *The New York Times*, 24 Oct. 1988, https://www.nytimes.com/1988/10/24/nyregion/turn-that-dial-back-in-time-superman-co-return.html. Accessed 27 Mar. 2020.
Best, Daniel. "Superman's First Appearance in Australia (Kind of)." *20th Century Danny Boy*, 2 Aug. 2011, https://ohdannyboy.blogspot.com/2011/08/supermans-first-appearance-in-australia.html. Accessed 27 Mar. 2020.
Boorstin, Daniel J. *The Americans: The National Experience*. Vintage Books, 1965.
"The Clan of the Fiery Cross." *The Adventures of Superman*, episodes 1293–1308. Mutual Broadcasting System, New York City, 10 June–1 July 1946.
"Clark Kent, Reporter." *Superman*, episode 2. WOR, New York City, 14 Feb. 1940.
Cronin, Bryan. "Comic Book Legends Revealed #414," *CBR.com*. 12 Apr. 2013, https://www.cbr.com/comic-book-legends-revealed-414/. Accessed 27 Mar. 2020.
deForest, Tim. *Storytelling in the Pulps, Comics, and Radio*. McFarland, 2004.
DeHaven, Tom. *Our Hero: Superman on Earth*. Yale University Press, 2011.
Dennis, Paul M. "Chills and Thrills: Does Radio Harm Our Children? The Controversy Over Program Violence During the Age of Radio." *Journal of the History of Behavioral Sciences*, Vol. 38, no. 1, 1998, pp. 33–50.
"Donelli's Protection Racket, Pt. 1." *Superman*, episode 28. WOR, New York City, 15 Apr. 1940.
Douglas, Susan J. *Listening In: Radio and the American Imagination*. Minneapolis: University of Minnesota Press, 2004.
"Eben Kent Dies in Fire, Clark Goes to Metropolis." *The Adventures of Superman*, episode 327. Mutual Broadcasting System, New York City, 1 Sept. 1942.
"The Eleventh Hour." Directed by Dan Gordon, Famous Studios and Paramount Pictures, 1942.
Freeman, Matthew. "Up, Up and Across: Superman, the Second World War, and the Historical Development of Transmedia Storytelling." *Historical Journal of Film, Radio, and Television*, Vol. 35, no. 2, 2015, pp. 215–239, http://libs.illiad.library.louisville.edu/illiad/ILL/illiad.dll?Action=10&Form=75&Value=900509. Accessed 2 Feb. 2020.
Gottlieb, Akiva. "Who Is This Dirk Maggs, and Why Does He Rule so Hard?" *Audible Range*, 3 Aug. 2017, https://www.audible.com/blog/arts-culture/who-is-this-dirk-maggs-and-how-does-he-rule-so-hard. Accessed 1 Apr. 2020.

Gonzalez, Miguel. "Aussie Superman: The True Blue Aussie Fighting the Forces of Evil on Radio." *National Film and Sound Archive of Australia*, https://www.nfsa.gov.au/latest/meet-aussie-superman. Accessed 27 Mar. 2020.

"The Hate Mongers Organization." *The Adventures of Superman*, episodes 1254–1278. Mutual Broadcasting Network, New York City, 16 Apr.-20 May 1946.

Hayde, Michael J. *Flights of Fantasy: The Unauthorized but True Story of Radio and TV's Adventures of Superman*. BearManor Media, 2009.

Hunt, James. "Dirk Maggs Interview: Hitchhiker's Douglas Adams, Superman, Batman, & more…" *Den of Geek*, 18 June 2013, https://www.denofgeek.com/books/dirk-maggs-interview-hitchhikers-douglas-adams-superman-batman-more/. Accessed 1 Apr. 2020.

"Japoteurs." Directed by Seymour Kneitel, Famous Studios and Paramount Pictures, 1942.

Jenkins, Henry. *Convergence Culture: Where Old and New Media Collide*. New York University Press, 2006.

Kolber, John. "Up, Up and Awa-a-y! The Rise of Superman, Inc." *The Saturday Evening Post*, 21 June 1941, pp. 14–15, 70–78. http://www.saturdayeveningpost.com/wp-content/uploads/satevepost/rise-of-superman.pdf. Accessed 2 Feb. 2020.

Leitch, Thomas. *Film Adaptations and Its Discontents: From* Gone with the Wind *to* Passion of the Christ. The Johns Hopkins University Press, 2007.

Levitt, Steven D., and Stephen J. Dubner. *Freakonomics: A Rogue Economists Explores the Hidden Side of Everything*. William Morrow, 2005.

Loham, Sidney. "One Thing and Another." *The New York Times*, 14 Apr. 1946, https://www.timesmachine.nytimes.com/1946/04/14/910944389.html?pageNumber=55. Accessed 16 Apr. 2020.

Look, Up in the Sky! The Amazing Story of Superman. Dir. Kevin Burns. Warner Bros., 2006. DVD.

"Looking for Kryptonite." *The Adventures of Superman*, episodes 1160–1184. Mutual Broadcasting System, New York City, 4 Dec. 1945–8 Jan. 1946.

Maslon, Laurence. *Superheroes: Capes, Cowls and the Creation of Comic Book Culture*. Crown Archetype, 2013.

"The Meteor from Krypton." *The Adventures of Superman*, episodes 522–528. Mutual Broadcasting System, New York City, 3–11 June 1943.

Moran, Albert, and Karina Aveyard. "From Marginal Trader to Corporate Giant: The Emergence of FreMantleMedia." *New Patterns in Global Television Formats*, edited by Karina Aveyard, Albert Moran, and Pia Majbritt Jensen. Intellect Ltd., 2016.

Morris, Jon. "The Adventures of Superman Radio Serials—December 1949." *The Chronological Superman*, https://thechronologicalsuperman.tumblr.com/post/139052811938/the-adventures-of-superman-radio-serials. Accessed 17 May 2020.

Mulrain, Stuart. "A Movie Without Pictures…" *True Believers Comic Festival*, 19 Mar. 2015, http://oktruebelievers.com/articles/2015/2/28/superman-at-the-bbc?rq=dirk%20maggs. Accessed 1 Apr. 2020.

Munson, Todd S. "'Superman Says You Can Slap a Jap': The Man of Steel and Race Hatred in World War II." *The Ages of Superman: Essays on the Man of Steel in Changing Times*, edited by Joseph J. Darowski, McFarland, 2012, pp. 5–15.

"The Mystery of the Sleeping Beauty, Pt. 2." *The Adventures of Superman*, Mutual Broadcasting Network, New York City, 16 Jan. 1945.

"The Mystery of the Waxmen." *The Adventures of Superman*, episodes 967–978. Mutual Broadcasting System, New York City, 28 Feb.–15 Mar. 1945.

Nye, Russel. *The Unembarrassed Muse: The Popular Arts in America*. NY: The Dial Press, 1970.

Odec. "Superman." *Variety*, 24 Feb. 1940, https://archive.org/details/variety137-1940-02/page/n133/mode/2up/search/superman. Accessed 4 Apr. 2020.

Patrick, Kevin. "Age of Atoman: Australian Superhero Comics and Cold War Modernity." *The Superhero Symbol: Media, Culture, and Politics*, edited by Liam Burke, Ian Gordon, and Angela Ndalianis, Rutgers University Press, 2019.

"Planet Utopia." *The Adventures of Superman*, episodes 895–906. Mutual Broadcasting Network, New York City, 16 Nov.–4 Dec. 1944.

"The Radar Rocket, Pt. 1." *The Adventures of Superman*, episode 1212. Mutual Broadcasting Network, New York City, 15 Feb. 1946.

Russo, Alexander. "A Dark(ened) Figure on the Airwaves: Race, Nation, and *The Green Hornet*." *Radio Reader: Essays in the Cultural History of Radio*, edited by Michael Hilmes and Jason Loviglio, Routledge, 2002, pp. 257–276.

"The Scarlet Widow." *The Adventures of Superman*, episodes 1112–1121. Mutual Broadcasting Network, New York City, 26 Sept.–10 Oct. 1945.

Scinto, Helen. "The Good Old Days of Radio Serials." *The New York Times*, 15 Oct. 1989, https://www.nytimes.com/1989/10/15/nyregion/connecticut-opinion-the-good-old-days-of-radio-serials.html. Accessed 6 Feb. 2020.

Scivally, Bruce. *Superman on Film, Television, Radio and Broadway*. McFarland, 2008.

Siegel, Jerry (w), and Joe Shuster (a). "What If Superman Had Ended the War?" *Superman: The Greatest Stories Ever Told*, edited by Anton Kawaski, DC Comics, 2004, pp. 12–13

"The Space Shell, Pt. 8." *The Adventures of Superman*, episodes 962. Mutual Broadcasting System, New York City, 21 Feb. 1945.
Superheroes: A Never-Ending Battle. Dir. Michael Kantor. PBS, 2013. DVD.
Superman. 2GB, Sydney, 30 May 1949–30 May 1954.
"Superman." *AusReprints*, https://ausreprints.net/series/110. Accessed 27 Mar. 2020.
"Superman Comes to Earth." *Superman*, chapter 1. Directed by Spencer Gordon Bennett and Thomas Carr, performance by Kirk Alyn, Columbia Pictures, 1948.
Superman: Doomsday and Beyond, episodes 1–5. BBC Radio 5, London, 1993.
"Superman Flies Again." *Atom Man vs. Superman*, chapter 1. Directed by Spencer Gordon Bennett, performance by Kirk Alyn, Columbia Pictures, 1950.
"'Superman' for Canada." *Variety*, 8 May 1940. https://archive.org/details/variety138-1940-05/page/n89/mode/2up/search/superman. Accessed 11 Apr. 2020.
"Superman on Radio in Australia." *Superman Homepage*, https://www.supermanhomepage.com/radio/radio.php?topic=radio-aus. Accessed 13 Apr. 2020.
Superman on Trial. BBC Radio 4, London, 5 June 1988.
"Superman Radio Episode List." *Superman Homepage*, https://www.supermanhomepage.com/radio/radio.php?topic=radio-episode-list. Accessed 18 May 2020.
Superman Radio Scripts, The. Vol. 1: Superman vs. the Atom Man. Watson-Guptill Publications, 2001.
"Superman Supacomic." *AusReprints*, https://ausreprints.net/series/0/9407. Accessed 27 Mar. 2020.
"'Superman' Too Heroic for Radio." *Variety*, 24 Jan. 1940, https://archive.org/details/variety137-1940-01/page/n275/mode/2up. Accessed 7 Feb. 2020.
Superman Radio Scripts, The. Vol. 1: Superman vs. the Atom Man. NY: Watson-Guptill Publications, 2001.
Tye, Larry. *Superman: The High-Flying History of America's Most Enduring Hero*. Random House, 2013.

Adapting the Clan to the Klan

Modern Confrontations of White Nationalism in Young Adult Superman Comics

J. Richard Stevens

In 1946, *The Adventures of Superman* radio show took on the Ku Klux Klan in a series titled "Clan of the Fiery Cross" that broadcast cross America's airwaves. Informed by activist Stetson Kennedy, the show portrayed Klan techniques, arguments, rituals, and strategies for a popular audience, and was credited with helping cause a decline in Klan membership and influence. Seventy-three years later, that radio series was adapted by DC's children's imprint DC Zoom into *Superman Smashes the Klan*, a three-part serial graphic novel by writer Gene Luen Yang and artistic team Gurihiru. Chronicling the struggles of a Chinese American family against the Klan, the story presents its 8-to-12-year-old target audience with messages about racial tolerance and social justice. This chapter explores the adaptation of the 1946 radio drama into a contemporary young adult comic format, considering adjustments to modern representations of immigrant families and the super-immigrant's struggle against the clandestine forces of white nationalism.

Transmedia Narratives and Adaptation

Thomas Andrae observed that while iconic heroes like Superman—whom Gary Engle describes as deeply representative of American character (90)—tend to reinforce dominant ideology, they also offer social criticism (Andrae 124–138). But that balance appears to emerge over time, as the constant need for reinterpretation of characters and stories becomes "part of [their] survival code" (Glock 13). Superman is an exemplar of such evolutionary adjustments, particularly as the character has been adapted across different media formats. In part, Superman's pro-social values were embedded in his narratives from the very beginning. Superman's first appearance in *Action Comics* #1 (June 1938) showed the hero confronting contemporary social issues like unjust imprisonment, spousal abuse, and corrupt government officials. Co-creator Jerry Siegel explained these issues appeared in the early Superman comics because the character was "very serious about helping people in trouble and distress," because of a "tremendous feeling of compassion [co-creator] Joe [Schuster] and I had for the downtrodden" (Daniels 35).

Over time, Superman would evolve to be a symbolic bellwether icon for America, or as Peter Lloyd described:

> Superman is a mirror to American society. He reflects the moral and technological expectations of Americans. And the American public re-absorbs the ideal that Superman represents. It's a two-way-exchange. As American society has changed, Superman has changed. In the Golden Age, Superman had a robust view of justice that reflected the opinions of the average American citizen. If there were to be superheroes, this is how they would behave [181].

However, Superman did not achieve this iconic state in the pages of comic books, which Art Spiegelman describes as "the bastard offspring of art and commerce" (106). Superman's rise to iconography was largely a function of his transmedia endurance, as many different forms of the character appeared in many different media for many different audiences over many years.

Marsha Kinder introduced the term "transmedia entertainment" in her study of children's franchises *Playing with Power in Movies, Television and Video Games* (1993), though Henry Jenkins popularized the term and defined it as "stories that unfold across multiple platforms, with each medium making distinctive contributions to our understanding of the storyworld; a more integrated approach to franchise development" (334). Transmedia narratives recognize the centrality of narrative or characters, but adapt the expression of both to new media spaces, a process that usually results in new dimensions and characteristics. Adaptations between print and other media are usually expected to remain faithful (Welsh xxiii–xxiv), and good adaptations reinforce the canonical status of the texts they adapt (Sanders 120). However, transmedia installments differ from mere adaptation in that each expression offers its own unique contribution (Cardwell 9), contributions that often flow back and forth between media versions.

Superman became one of the earliest American transmedia properties when comic strips began to appear in newspapers in January 1939, featured in 300 newspapers by 1941 (Freeman 218). The comic strip expanded on the Superman mythos by introducing his homeworld of Krypton (which circled a "tiny blue star," in contrast to the radio version's "burns like a green star in the endless heavens," and this in contrast to the consistently shown planet circling a large red star that would later become the firm mythos) and established explanations for Superman's powers. The comic strips also gave Superman's parents' names (Jor-El and Lara), as well as his own native name (Kal-El), additions that would then be introduced in the pages of Superman comic books.

But the comic strips were merely the first of many media extensions for the Superman narrative. Harry Donenfeld founded Superman, Inc., a subsidiary of DC Comics to handle the licensing of Superman. It wouldn't be long before Superman appeared across merchandise, novels, and would eventually make his way to the radio and television airwaves. As Superman spread out across American culture, he achieved a cultural saturation that transcended the direct exposure his stories (Bazin 46), until he eventually became recognized all over the world.

The Superman radio program, however, was the most instrumental leap in making the Man of Steel a household name. In comics, Superman's mythology and continuity can be tied to his creators, the editorial management of DC editors like Mort Weisenberg (Proctor 52–61), or perhaps the publisher. But in radio, the successes of Superman narratives came at the hands of many more hands and market forces. For example, a radio series like "Clan of the Fiery Cross" was shaped by Kenyon and Eckhardt, the advertising agency that represented Kellogg's sponsorship of the program; William B. Lewis, vice president and radio director for Kenyon & Eckhardt; Robert "Bob" Maxwell, the "former pulp writer who had been put in charge of Superman, Inc." (Daniels 47); Ben Peter Freeman, the writer and journalist who wrote scripts; and Josette Frank, the education consultant with DC who approved content for educational value. And of course, central to the construction of the radio narratives were the actors, performers and production staff of the broadcast performances themselves.

The Adventures of Superman premiered on February 12, 1940, initially airing as a pre-recorded program on individual stations to which DC licensing could sell it. Beginning on August 31, 1942, the series ran as a live broadcast performance on the Mutual Broadcast System, before moving to ABC in 1949 (Gordon 7). Radio made Superman All-American, and the media of the day noticed the difference: "...parents who haven't been keeping up with Superman may not be aware of the high moral tone pervading his exploits, or aware that a serious minded committee, including educators and psychologists, advise on editorial policy" (MacKenzie 22).

The focus on educational value and social messaging would not be the only change to Superman's formula. Some longstanding conventions and narrative elements were introduced in the radio drama because of the different forms of storytelling needed. For example, the radio broadcasts introduced new characters like Perry White and the idea of Kryptonite (Tollin 1–2). *Daily Planet* Editor-in-Chief Perry White was introduced in the second episode ("Clark Kent, Reporter" [14 Feb. 1940]), where he replaced the comic book continuity editor George Taylor. White was a new character created by Bob Maxwell and Allen Ducovny and voiced by Julian Noa, whose performance framed the essential characteristics of the character for decades and eventually across all media (Maralli). Though he was an invention for radio and his personality formed around the actor who voiced him, Perry White would be introduced to the comic book continuity in *Superman* #7 (Nov. 1940), when Taylor was fired in the comic narrative and White took over the *Daily Planet*. While an unnamed copy boy who would retroactively be called Jimmy Olsen was introduced in *Action Comics* #6 (Nov. 1938), it was in the radio dramas where Olsen's name, personality and relationship with Clark Kent was established in ways that soon trickled back into the comic book narratives.

Kryptonite was introduced in the radio drama, and would later serve to give Superman actor Bud Collyer a two-week vacation (Rossen 3). During those episodes, Superman was incapacitated and could only be heard moaning during broadcasts. Six years later, Kryptonite appeared in *Superman* #61 (Nov.–Dec. 1949) and became a mainstay of Superman lore. But perhaps the biggest change to the radio version of Superman was one of the most essential: flight. When Superman was introduced in *Action Comics* #1, he could not fly, he merely leapt great distances. In fact, the recorded introduction for the first radio drama reflects the leaping convention:

> Faster than an airplane! More powerful than a locomotive! Impervious to bullets!
> "Up in the sky—look!" "It's a bird." "It's a plane." "It's SUPERMAN!"
> And now, Superman—A being no larger than an ordinary man but possessed of powers and abilities never before realized on Earth: able to leap into the air an eighth of a mile at a single bound, hurtle a 20-story building with ease, race a high-powered bullet to its target, lift tremendous weights and rend solid steel in his bare hands as though it were paper. Superman—a strange visitor from a distant planet: champion of the oppressed, physical marvel extraordinary who has sworn to devote his existence on Earth to helping those in need ["The Baby from Krypton"].

Future episodes would open with the truncated recorded introduction, which most long-standing fans of Superman would recognize:

> Faster than a speeding bullet! More powerful than a locomotive! Able to leap tall buildings in a single bound!
> Look! Up in the sky!
> It's a bird!
> It's a plane!
> It's Superman!
> Yes, it's Superman—strange visitor from another planet who came to Earth with powers and abilities far beyond those of mortal men. Superman—defender of law and order. champion of equal rights, valiant, courageous fighter against the forces of hate and prejudice, who disguised as Clark Kent, mild-mannered reporter for a great metropolitan newspaper, fights a never-ending battle for truth, justice and the American way ["Clan of the Fiery Cross, Pt. 1"].

Superman's flight was easier to produce with the sound effects available to the radio performers, and the visualization of flight would become so associated with the radio version of Superman (many more people listened to the radio program than read the DC comics narratives), and then the Fleischer cartoons (1941–1943), that eventually Superman would remain aloft in every medium he inhabited.

Though the radio era would eventually give way to television and film versions of the character, *The Adventures of Superman* represents a liminal moment in the character's history, when the Man of Steel was still hardening into a more permanent form. Other versions would evolve and even retcon various aspects of the character's mythos, but from the radio narratives on, the Superman formula would be more consistent than not.

Part of the evolutionary change occurred because of the vastly different media experience between printed comics (and comic strips) and radio drama. Radio competes for the listener's attention, as listeners multitask and divide their attention. For this reason, scholars noted that dramatic structures in radio narratives were more effective than other formats in holding listener attention (Lynch and Lo 167–172). As one researcher noted, "[r]adio has popularly been referred to as the theater of the mind because of its perceived ability to paint pictures in the imagination of listeners" (Bolls 537).

Though we think of radio as an auditory medium, the primary function of narrative structure is the descriptive function (Rodero 242–252), the use of audio to produce a reconstruction of reality. This mode of engagement can be more compelling than a comic book, as the "act of visualizing an event can make the event seem even more likely" (Macinnis and Price 480). Radio dramas have scripts but also utilize layers of sound to "situate listeners in space" (Dunn 201) and create a sense of location (Gaver 5). Additionally, sound effects can form iconic meaning in narratives (Crisell 150), such as the particular wind tunnel noises used to create Superman's flying sounds effects. Overall, the various elements of a radio drama produce "a complex sound picture painted by the use of dialogue, music, sound effects, and silence—each artistically integrated with the others to produce the most vivid picture possible in the mind of the listener" (Mackey 41).

Most of these auditory elements had to be created new for the radio broadcast. The radio version of Superman thus brought many innovations that would become standing conventions of the Superman mythos, some to solve production problems, some to solve narrative problems, and some to solve character problems.

The Second Rise of the Ku Klux Klan

In many ways, it's appropriate that Superman would combat the Ku Klux Klan in popular culture, for the second version of the Klan had risen to prominence itself with the help of popular culture. Though the original Klan had died out in the 1870s, a new generation was called together by William J. Simmons, the son of a Confederate veteran. Simmons timed the announcement of reemergence of the Klan with the Atlanta premiere of *Birth of a Nation*. On December 16, 1915—after the opening screening, audience left the theater to be confronted by more than 100 Klansmen with rifles standing on Peach Street (Bowers 66).

The modern Klan was as much as marketing campaign as a social movement, as Bessie Clark Tyler and Edward Young Clarke of the Southern Publicity Association played a pivotal role in marketing the Klan, starting in 1920. To the original ideological goals of suppressing African-Americans and Jewish people, Tyler and Clarke targeted Catholics, Asians, Mexicans, labor union organizers, socialites and Wall Street tycoons (Bowers 71). Their firm produced films for local theaters, launched advertising campaigns to place in newspaper ads and billboards, and organized large rallies. One year after the campaign began, 100,000 men had paid $10 membership dues; within a few years, four million Americans had joined the Klan, and revenues exceeded $75 million (72).

However, many Americans opposed the new Klan, among them Stetson Kennedy. Over a period of years, Kennedy infiltrated the Klan, rising through the ranks and taking detailed notes of Klan rituals that he would later publish in books. Kennedy's expressed goal was demystifying Klan cultural practices and rituals for the public. As one biographer noted, "[t]he main idea was to make bigotry obnoxious" (Bulger 189). But, as mentioned above, print circulation pales in comparison to broadcast audience. Kennedy began looking for more high-profile ways to ridicule the Klan. What resulted was an alliance between Kennedy, the Anti-Defamation League and the New York producers of *The Adventures of Superman*, as Kennedy began to pass along Klan materials for inclusion in the 1946 radio narratives (Kennedy 92).[1]

Because of the need for attention (and because each episode aired only once), repetition in dialogue and storytelling is very important to aiding the listening process for radio drama (Miller 327). For that reason, it is relatively easy to discern what themes and messages are built into the narratives, as characters repeat certain phrases over and over to each other. Additionally, the narrator summarizes key plot points at the beginning of each episode.

By the time Superman's adventures could be heard on the radio, DC Comics and Superman, Inc. had already been using the character to promote childhood literacy (Tilley 251–263). But by the mid–1940s, Superman was increasingly including pro-social themes. This focus took an explicit turn on the radio in the April–May 1946 series, "The Hate Mongers Organization." In that series, Superman battled the "Guardians of America," a group opposed to racial integration. As Clark Kent explains to Jimmy Olsen,

> It isn't just the Catholics, or the Jews, or the Protestants they're after. Their game is to stir up hatred among all of us—to get the Catholic to hate the Jew and the Jew to hate the Protestant, and the Protestant to hate the Catholic. It's a dirty, vicious circle, and like Hitler and his Nazi killers, they plan to step in and pick up the marbles while we're busy hating one another and cutting each other's throats. It's an old trick, but for some reason a lot of us still fall for it [Wall 163].

"The Hate Mongers Organization" was the top-rated children's program, and national media began to praise the socially aware programming. "Superman is the first children's program to develop a social conscience. Officials for both sponsor and network are relieved when the show's plea for tolerance began attracting the highest ratings in the history of the series." The *Newsweek* article that published that statement also featured quotes by Bud Collyer, who played Superman on the show, with the actor pledged the tolerance crusade would continue ("It's Superfight").

"Clan of the Fiery Cross"

The "Clan of the Fiery Cross" began on June 10, 1946, and stretched across 16 episodes each lasting about 15 minutes (though 4–5 minutes of each episode was Kellogg's Pep advertising). The story followed the struggle of a Chinese-American family who were repeatedly harassed by the Clan.[2] Tommy Lee is a star pitcher and quickly is invited to join the Unity House baseball team, displacing a boy named Chuck Riggs. Chuck, jealous at being displaced from his starting pitcher role, goads Tommy during batting practice and crowds home plate, resulting in Tommy accidentally hitting him. An altercation breaks out and Jimmy Olsen, who manages the team, sends Chuck home to cool off. At home, Chuck encounters his uncle Matt, who after hearing Tommy's last name begins to spin Chuck's story into an act of malice.

This relationship would serve as one of the fulcrums for the series, as Chuck is constantly pressured by Matt to accept racist interpretations of various events. The narrator consistently frames Chuck as struggling between what he knows to be right (the equal treatment of all Americans) and his loyalty to his uncle, who consistently tries to indoctrinate him into the Clan's views.

The second episode begins with Matt and Chuck driving to a secluded location. Matt spends the trip "carefully grilling his nephew to make him to believe the false version of the baseball incident." As they arrive, Chuck gasps as he sees his first Clan rally: "In a glade—casting weird shadows over the nearby hills and lighting the sky above—burns a huge wooden cross. Before it kneels half a hundred men clothed in long robes. Pointed hoods slit only at the eyes cover their heads and faces, and a low guttural chant issues harshly from their hidden lips, sending an uneasy chill through Chuck's blood." Matt, it turns out, is the Grand Scorpion, the local Clan leader. He explains the mission of the Clan to Chuck as "a great secret society pledged to purify America. America for 100% Americans only—one race, one religion, one color" ("Clan of the Fiery Cross, Pt. 2"). He had Chuck repeat for the assembled Clansmen the rehearsed story, which motivates the Clan into action.

That action would result in a cross being burned in the Lee's front yard (the narrator described this as an "Unamerican attack on Tommy Lee's family"), which the listener hears recounted from Tommy the next morning. Jimmy Olsen is shocked by Tommy's account (in the radio series, Jimmy serves as the naïve avatar for the children in the audience, the character to whom everyone explains the significance of events).

When Jimmy asks Clark Kent why the Clan would terrorize the Lees, Kent responds, "Because the Clan of the Fiery Cross is made up of intolerant bigots, Jim. They don't judge a man in the decent American way, by his own qualities, they judge him by what church he goes to, and by the color of his skin" ("Clan of the Fiery Cross, Pt. 3"). The phrase "what church he goes to, and by the color of his skin" would be repeated many times throughout the series, by several different characters.

Tommy's bicycle is rigged with a bomb, but Superman saves him. On the baseball diamond, a player connected to the Clan "accidentally" throws a bat at Tommy, and Kent saves Tommy with his superspeed. Next, Tommy is kidnapped by the Clan, who intends to tar and feather him. Tommy escapes, but breaks his arm and leaps into a fast-moving river. Superman saves him from drowning.

Daily Planet editor Perry White publishes a scathing editorial, gets a cross burned on his lawn, and is kidnapped by the Clan along with Jimmy Olsen. When the duo discover that the Grand Scorpion is Matt Riggs, they are sentenced to death. Defiant, White launches into a speech over the objections of the assembled Clansmen:

> Now you listen to me, I happen to love my country and what it stands for. Equal rights and privileges for all Americans, regardless of what church they choose to worship God in, or what color skin God give them. The United States was founded on that principle. And we've just fought a Second World War to preserve it. You and others like you with your diseased minds want to tear down what we built and fought to keep. But you can't do it! I'll fight you to the last breath! And so will every other American worth his salt! We'll flush you and your hate-peddling goons out from behind your dirty sheets and clap you in jail where you belong! ["Clan of the Fiery Cross, Pt. 9"].

Meanwhile, Chuck Riggs tells Kent what he knows. Superman rescues White and Olsen and rounds up the Clan Action Committee, but Matt Riggs escapes and make his way to the home of Segret Wilson, the Grand Imperial Mogul of the Clan. It is this encounter which exposes Kennedy's critique of the KKK as Wilson complains about the money the organization will lose because of Riggs' failures and Riggs reacts negatively to the proposition that the financial impact of the night's events would be the focus. It is in this moment that Wilson lays bare Kennedy's judgement of the KKK as a marketing campaign aimed at profit in narrative form:

> SEGRET WILSON: "Wait a minute. Is it possible that you really believe all that stuff about getting rid of the foreigners? That 'one race, one religion, one color' hokum?"
> MATT RIGGS: "Hokum? Why, it's the absolute truth. We've got to save America from foreign elements!"
> SEGRET WILSON: "Well, I'll be—I thought you had brains, Riggs. But you've become drunk on the slop we put up for the suckers."
> MATT RIGGS: "Suckers? Who are you calling—"
> SEGRET WILSON: "Our members, Riggs. The poor fish who want to hate and blame somebody else for their failures in life. The saps who believe drivel such as, a man is a dangerous enemy because he goes to a different church. The little nobodies who want to believe some other race is inferior so they can feel superior. The jerks who go for that '100% American' rot."
> MATT RIGGS: "Rot? You mean you don't believe?"
> SEGRET WILSON: "Of course not. You must know there is no such thing as what we call 100% American. Everyone here except the Indians is descended from foreigners."
> MATT RIGGS: "Why, blast you, Wilson. You sound like a dirty foreigner yourself!"
> SEGRET WILSON: "I'm running a business, Riggs. And so are you. We deal in one of the oldest and most profitable commodities on Earth. Hate" ["Clan of the Fiery Cross, Pt. 14"].

Riggs kills Wilson, collects a rifle, and attempts to assassinate Perry White, Jimmy Olsen, and Chuck at the final baseball game. But Superman intercepts the fired bullets and delivers Riggs to the police. The youths celebrate their victory on the baseball field, and deliver to Tommy Lee a golden baseball as a memento.

The "Clan of the Fiery Cross" achieved high ratings. The Ku Klux Klan was reportedly angry at the show and attempted to boycott Kellogg's Pep cereal in protest, but ultimately the radio program hurt Klan recruiting and led to a decline in Klan membership (Kennedy 3).

Superman Smashes the Klan

Though Superman began his existence in print, the idea to adapt a radio narrative into a print format represents no small undertaking. Just as the radio version of Superman needed innovation and reconfiguration of Superman's conventions to meet the needs of the medium, much of what made the radio drama compelling would not translate directly to graphic storytelling. And yet, Yang and Gurihiru could not wholly leave the radio narrative behind. Historical adaptations must preserve the right amount of intertextual reference to the original while also allowing for the intratextual connections for transmedia storytelling. As the radio narratives had not been accompanied by visuals in the first place, a visual approach to the story needed to signify both nostalgic styling while appealing to the target audience: middle schoolers.

Superman Smashes the Klan draws heavily on the costume designs from the Fleischer serial cartoons of the mid–1940s yet the art style appears drawn in a manga style, which is an interesting choice given the prominence of the Chinese-American family characters. These choices were intentional, according to Yang: "Early on, the editor and I talked about going for an art style that's just like the old Fleischer Superman cartoons but mixed with a manga influence, and I feel like they totally delivered on that. That's exactly what they did" (McMillan). As a transmedia project, the graphic novel style brings into orbit classic Superman animation styling and imagery consistent at time with the 1950s television series, but filtered through a styling never before used in prominent Superman narratives.

The comic opens with Superman battling Atom Man at the Metropolis reservoir, a scene taken from the end of the 1945 "Superman vs. the Atom Man" radio saga. In the radio drama, Atom Man was a Nazi supervillain, created by a Nazi mad scientist who put liquid kryptonite into his veins. Superman had been defeated by Atom Man in their first encounter and rendered helpless for days. In his absence, the Atom Man had begun to terrorize Metropolis and was preparing to destroy the dam holding up the Metropolis reservoir, drowning thousands. Superman arrived and waged a desperate battle with Atom Man which concluded when the Man of Steel flew Atom Man high into the air, but was weakened by the kryptonite in Atom Man's weaponry. The two fell to earth. Superman survived the fall, the Atom Man did not (Korté 200–203).

But in the opening of the first issue of *Superman Smashes the Klan* (Oct. 2019), the Atom Man is shown damaging the dam that borders the reservoir. Lois Lane and Jimmy Olsen distract him long enough for Superman to arrive and quickly overpower the Atom Man. But several key narrative elements differ from the radio broadcast: this is the first encounter between Superman and the Atom Man, Superman is unaware of the existence of kryptonite, and most strikingly, Superman cannot fly. Or rather, we quickly learn that Superman CAN fly, but that he has obscured that ability from humans:

> LOIS LANE: "Superman's faster than a speeding bullet—"
> JIMMY OLSEN: "'—more powerful than a locomotive, able to leap tall buildings in a single bound!' I've read your article many times."
> LOIS: "Then you know that even Superman has his limits. The highest he's ever leapt is 20 stories. It's not like he can fly" [Yang and Gurihiru, *Superman Smashes the Klan* #1 5].

This Superman may look like the 1940s Fleischer cartoon version, but he's at a different point in his career than any of the 1940s media had portrayed him. This Superman has not told anyone his origins and the reader soon learns he doesn't actually know much about his Kryptonian heritage. He vaguely responds to questions about where he comes from or what his abilities are, all in an effort to conform to human norms. In fact, Superman discovering details about his origin and how his immigrant story informs his own performance of identity is a central theme of *Superman Smashes the Klan*. Yang and Gurihiru may be referencing popular texts from the radio drama series, but they are updated into a new narrative and style.

In many ways, *Superman Smashes the Klan* re-examines and plays with 1940s conventions. Though green kryptonite has long been used as a "weakening" agent for Superman, in the original radio series dramas, it also sometimes rendered Superman incoherent or delusional (such as in the "Superman vs. the Atom Man" saga, when Lois Lane had Clark Kent committed to an institution because his reactions to kryptonite were perceived as a mental breakdown). When Superman is exposed to the Atom Man's kryptonite (Superman's first exposure to kryptonite), he weakens but immediately begins to have hallucinations that would appear unexpectedly over the following days. Parts of Superman's body occasionally turning green, he sometimes sees an alien face in the mirror, and out of the corner of his eye he keeps thinking he's seeing green aliens. Additionally, he complains of a peculiar smell, one that threatens to make him throw up. Encountering a piece of his homeworld unsettles Superman and he struggles through unpredictable visions and painful memories related to the emergence of his powers and his alien otherness throughout the series.

Another change to the radio series concerns the focus on Roberta Lee as a primary character. Though the "Clan of the Fiery Cross" radio drama mentioned that Tommy Lee had a younger sister, that character is never named nor ever is voiced in the original series. *Superman Smashes the Klan* focuses more on this character than perhaps any other. Roberta is introduced to the reader as the youngest and most inexperienced family member, but also the one most resistant to leaving Chinatown behind and moving to Metropolis. She's car sick (and her weak stomach is at time paralleled to Superman's kryptonite-induced queasiness), but more observant than her family or peers. As she struggles to fit into a social world unlike any she's ever known, her outsider status provides a critical distance, one that features into the plot in key ways.

Much of the *Superman Smashes the Klan* narrative does adapt the radio drama elements. The core conflict is still over amateur baseball; Tommy Lee displaces Chuck and hits him during batting practice. Matt Riggs still repeatedly pressures Chuck into framing these events in terms of ethnic warfare, but in this version, the pressure is more overt. Whereas the radio recounted the cross burning at the Lee home in retrospect, the scene is portrayed in the graphic text. Chuck is present in a Klan hood and asked to throw a Molotov cocktail at the Lee home to burn it down. His throw is off the mark but is witnessed by Roberta, who recognizes Chuck's red boots (Yang and Gurihiru, *Superman Smashes the Klan* #1 39–40). The aftermath of the cross burning is also shown, as African-American police inspector William Henderson investigates. Inspector Henderson is another character introduced by the radio program than became part of Superman lore. The comic's version of the character first appeared in *Action Comics* #442 (Dec. 1974), and was a supporting character for both Superman and Black Lightning comic book stories. In the radio and comic book narratives, Henderson is a white character, but in *Superman*

Smashes the Klan, Henderson is a black police inspector whose presence informs both interracial tensions and solidarity throughout the narrative.

Chuck is also given more interaction with his peers, and those encounters provide his with opportunities for exchanges that illustrate the social pressure he's under while questioning his own emerging ideology:

> CHUCK: "Hey Tommy …? I've been thinking … what happened at the Unity House was absolutely wrong, of course. But … is it really all that bad to want to live around only people who look like you?"
> TOMMY: "Wait. What are you saying, Chuck?"
> CHUCK: "I … I don't know. I'm just trying to make sense of it all!"
> TOMMY: "A broken arm's not enough? You want me to quit the team?!"
> CHUCK: "No, No! That's not—!"
> TOMMY: "You want my family to move back to Chinatown, is that it?!"
> CHUCK: "I … I …!"
> TOMMY: "Spit it out!"
> CHUCK: "I want to know that my family's not evil!" [Yang and Gurihiru, Superman Smashes the Klan #3 (Feb. 2020) 14–15].

Chuck's dilemma, performed in radio broadcasts with quivers in his voice when he spoke to his mother and uncle, are rendered more explicitly with perspiration and expressions in the pages in exchanges with Tommy Lee. Chuck wants to be a good friend, but he is also sensitive to his own identity politics tied to his family. Each of the young protagonists (Tommy Lee, Roberta Lee, and Chuck Riggs) struggle with challenges to their sense of belonging, torn between cultures and families, on display for young readers to witness.

Tommy Lee is still abducted by the Klan, but this version has Roberta convincing Chuck to talk to Superman, and she accompanies them on Superman's mission (Yang and Gurihiru, *Superman Smashes the Klan* #2 [Dec. 2019] 1–7). When Perry White is abducted, Inspector Henderson is taken with him, and he leaves a clue that Roberta figures out. Every character contributes in key situations to help bring down the Klan.

Roberta also confronts Superman about how he's using his powers. Roberta has noticed that Superman can fly but chooses not to and tells him she thinks he's holding back to fit in (Yang and Gurihiru, *Superman Smashes the Klan* #3 30–31). She explains his underuse of his powers threatens lives. Superman then embarks on a journey to discover his birth parents and learn about his heritage. The experience gives him newfound confidence in his identity, which eventually allows him to use the full extent of his powers in public. Matt Riggs also challenges Superman's identity, telling Superman that his powers must be tied to his superior Aryan blood. This comment helps Superman realize that his vagueness regarding his identity and limitation of his powers has allowed the Klan members to assume his symbolic whiteness as supportive of their positions. In his desire to suppress his otherness, his conformity enable exclusionary impulses in the society to which he is trying to conform.

Riggs also experiences his own conflict of identity. The third issue re-enacts his confrontation with the Grand Imperial Mogul, almost verbatim from the radio broadcast. Riggs also kills the Mogul and collects an advanced kryptonite weapon to use at the final baseball game to eliminate the threats he sees to his mission of a pure white America.

Initially the kids turn the tables on Riggs, with Chuck, Roberta and Tommy all striking him in unison. Riggs regains the upper hand with his weaponry, but then Superman arrives, floating above the baseball diamond and using the heat vision he has hidden since he was a child, finally revealing himself as an alien to the citizens of Metropolis

(Yang and Gurihiru, *Superman Smashes the Klan* #3 61–62). Superman battles Riggs, who uses the kryptonite ray, a bomb, and a kryptonite knife to weaken Superman. The final confrontation actually mirrors the final battle between Superman and the Atom Man from the radio series, as Superman weakens and drops Riggs. But in the graphic version, Superman uses his powers to save Riggs from death at the last moment (the radio Superman was unable to save the Atom Man from a similar fall). The *Daily Planet* publishes a story revealing Superman's immigrant origins, and Superman ends the series closer to the familiar form of the modern Superman formula.

The changes to the graphic version of the narrative allow each character to visually struggle with their dual identities, a tension writer Gene Luen Yang explained as

> ... vacillating between two different identities, having two different names, having two different sets of cultural expectations.... I saw it with my own parents; they came here and people perceived them as "foreign," [and] they were always cognizant of this. The way they dealt with that was by trying to be perfect citizens. I think Superman does the same thing; the reason he tries to be a perfect citizen is because he knows he's an alien [McMillan].

Embracing the duality of immigrant citizens allows Superman to serve as an even more effective symbol opposed to the Ku Klux Klan than the radio version did in 1946. Of all the characters struggling with dual identities (Roberta, Tommy, Chuck, even Matt Riggs to some extent), Superman is the only technical non–American, a fact that initially brings insecurity he must overcome. And yet, once that insecurity is banished by the acceptance of his own dual heritages, Superman's outsider status also makes him a compelling figure as a representation of America. Gary Engle previously argued that Superman's immigrant status was central to his appeal: "Superman's powers make the hero capable of saving humanity; Kent's total immersion in the American heartland makes him want to do it," which Engle says results in "an optimistic myth of assimilation but with an urban, technocratic setting" (85).

And this duality goes both ways. When comparing the characterizations of Clark Kent and Bruce Wayne (alter ego of Batman), Lou Anders observed that Clark Kent's dual identity made him more of an icon for America, and that his Kansas upbringing informs his alien identity:

> Kent was the product of a vanishing America., the Jeffersonian ideal of small farms owned by individual farmers. Early to bed and early to rise makes a man healthy, wealthy and wise. Bacon and eggs, and football games, and town socials church on Sunday and be sure to say your prayers at night. And while the legend will inevitably have to be modified as the world marches on, you can bet Smallville will be the last place on earth to have drug problems, street gangs, or teen pregnancies [71].

It is from the Kents that Superman originally gets his heroic mission (Siegel and Shuster, *Superman* #1 [June 1939]), but Yang focuses on his immigrant identity, one he has suppressed, and one that makes Superman a more compelling figure. Lawrence Watt-Evans states: "It's long been recognized that this is part of what makes him boring sometimes, or at least hard to write stories about; he's *too* powerful, too perfect. No menace can really endanger him—he's invulnerable. His moral choices are never really difficult; the Kents gave him so strong a sense of right and wrong that there's not much room for self-doubt" (1). Yang repositions Superman, in both identity and power. Superman may be ultimately powerful, but feeling he can't use those powers makes his struggles more realized than some of Superman's more contemporary adventures.

From 1938 to the present, Superman's adventures in various media formats demonstrate the ongoing process of mythological creation and revisionism. But more importantly, such stories put on display underlying ideologies of the age in which they achieved popularity because they present "in mythic style the ideals that are widely felt but that are no longer articulated in more sophisticated circle" (Jewett 10). Yang's transmedia creation in *Superman Smashes the Klan* pays homage to the radio drama version of Superman even as it alters its formula. The medium that gave Superman the power of flight for technical storytelling reasons is adapted to serve as a story of why Superman chooses to fly freely. By announcing his otherness, Superman becomes connected to the community that he defends. As he battles Matt Riggs above the baseball diamond, he observes directly into the literal representation of divisive hate: "...we *are* bound together. The Lees and I ... our friends at the *Daily Planet* and the Unity House and the police department ... *everyone* down there, really. We are bound together by the *future*. We all share the *same tomorrow*" (Yang and Gurihiru, *Superman Smashes the Klan* #3 61–67). The narratives of Superman have always contained pro-social concerns at their root, and the hero's dual identity has always allowed him to improbably represent a country and people that he is both similar to and quite different from. Transmedia moves across media formats have generally resulted in opportunities for the most foundational changes to the character, and adapting the radio version to print proved no different. By drawing upon the history, conventions, prior articulations and mythos of Superman, Yang and the Gurihiru team both recreate and reestablish Superman for a new generation in a story that adapts multiple media conventions from Superman's past in a manner that presents history as a teacher into the lives of its middle school audience.

Notes

1. This is according to Kennedy, but accounts of who initiated the flow of information, and the precise pattern vary according to different accounts.
2. Fearing a lawsuit, the produced decide that the "Clan of the Fiery Cross" was a safer title for the hate organization than the actual Ku Klux Klan.
3. A brief note on radio program episode numbers is warranted. The numbers provided here conform to the *Old Time Radio Downloads* site which houses most of the audio files for the show. But there are actually several competing systems for radio episodes, all of which are flawed. Some scholars use the 2000 Martin Grams, Jr., edited volume, though it miscounts the number of episodes of "The Radar Rocket" series, throwing off all subsequent episode numbers by 2. Some scholars use Jerry Haendiges' radio log at *The Vintage Radio Place*, though it miscounts several episodes. The *Superman Homepage* maintained by Steve Younis adapts the Grams list, but it makes corrections to observed miscounts and missing episodes. None of these indexes and lists use studio production codes, all are compiled by the archivists in question. There is not yet a single standard for listing episode numbers for "The Adventures of Superman" radio programs.

Works Cited

"Adventures of Superman, The." *Old Time Radio Downloads*. 2007. https://www.oldtimeradiodownloads.com/adventure/superman-the-adventures-of.
Anders, Lou. "A Tale of Two Orphans: The Man of Steel vs. The Caped Crusader." *The Man from Krypton: A Closer Look at Superman*, edited by Glenn Yeffeth, Benbella, 2005, pp. 69–76.
Andrae, Thomas. "From Menace to Messiah: The History and Historicity of Superman." *American Media and Mass Culture*, edited by Donald Lazere, University of California Press, 1987, pp. 124–138.
"The Baby from Krypton." *Superman*, episode 1. WOR, New York City, 12 Feb. 1940.
Bates, Cary (w), and Curt Swan (a). "The Midnight Murder Show!" *Action Comics* Vol. 1 #442 (Dec. 1976). DC Comics, 1976.
Bazin, André. "Adaptation, or the Cinema as Digest." *Bazin at Work: Major Essays and Reviews from the Forties and Fifties*, edited by André Bazin and Bert Cardullo, Routledge, 1997, pp. 41–52.
Bolls, Paul D. "I Can Hear You, but Can I See You?" *Communication Research*, vol. 29, no. 5, 2002, pp. 537–563.

Bowers, Rick. *Superman Versus the Ku Klux Klan*. National Geographic, 2012.
Bulger, Peggy. *Stetson Kennedy: Applied Folklore and Cultural Advocacy*. University of Pennsylvania, 1992.
Cardwell, Sarah. *Adaptation Revisited: Television and the Classic Novel*. Manchester UP, 2002.
"Clan of the Fiery Cross, Pt. 1." *The Adventures of Superman*, episode 1308. Mutual Broadcasting System, New York City, 10 June 1946.[3]
"Clan of the Fiery Cross, Pt. 2." *The Adventures of Superman*, episode 1309. Mutual Broadcasting System, New York City, 11 June 1946.
"Clan of the Fiery Cross, Pt. 3." *The Adventures of Superman*, episode 1310. Mutual Broadcasting System, 12 June 1946.
"Clan of the Fiery Cross, Pt. 9." *The Adventures of Superman*, episode 1316, Mutual Broadcasting System, New York City, 20 June 1946.
"Clan of the Fiery Cross, Pt. 14." *The Adventures of Superman*, episode 1321, Mutual Broadcasting System, New York City, 27 June 1946.
Crisell, Andrew. *Understanding Radio*. Routledge, 1994.
Daniels, Les. *Superman: The Complete History*. Chronicle Books, 2004.
Dunn, Anne. "Structures of Radio Drama." *Narrative and Media*, edited by Helen Fulton, Cambridge University Press, 2005, pp. 191–202.
Engle, Gary. "What Makes Superman So Darn American?" *Superman at Fifty: The Persistence of a Legend*, edited by Dennis Dooley and Gary Engle, Octavia, 1987, pp. 88–95.
Finger, Bill (w), and Al Plastino (a). "Superman Returns to Krypton!" *Superman* Vol. 1 #61, (Nov.–Dec. 1949) DC Comics, 1949.
Freeman, Matthew. "Up, Up and Across: Superman, the Second World War and the Historical Development of Transmedia Storytelling." *Historical Journal of Film, Radio and Television*, vol. 35, no. 2, 2015, pp. 215–239.
Gaver, William W. "What in the World Do We Hear? An Ecological Approach to Auditory Event Perception." *Ecological Psychology*, vol. 5, no. 1, 1993, pp. 1–29.
Glock, Geoff. *How to Read Superhero Comics and Why*. Continuum, 2002.
Gordon, Ian. *Superman: The Persistence of an American Icon*. Rutgers University Press, 2017.
Grams, Martin, Jr. *Radio Drama: A Comprehensive Chronicle of American Network Programs, 1932–1962*. McFarland, 2000.
Haendiges, Jerry. "Jerry Haendiges Vintage Radio Logs." *The Vintage Radio Place: Jerry Haendiges' Vintage Radio Site*. 1 Mar. 1997. http://otrsite.com/logs/logs1023.htm.
"It's Superfight." *Newsweek*, 29 Apr. 1946, p. 61.
Jenkins, Henry. *Convergence Culture: Where Old and New Media Collide*. New York University Press, 2016.
Jewett, Robert. *The Captain America Complex*. 2nd ed., Bear & Co., 1984.
Kennedy, Stetson. *The Klan Unmasked*. Florida Atlantic University Press, 1954.
Kinder, Marsha. *Playing with Power in Movies, Television, and Video Games: From Muppet Babies to Teenage Mutant Ninja Turtles*. University of California Press, 1993.
Lloyd, Peter B. "Superman's Moral Evolution." *The Man from Krypton: A Closer Look at Superman*, edited by Glenn Yeffeth, Benbella, 2005, pp. 181–198.
Lynch, Mervin D., and Dahren Lo. "Effect of Combining Styles of Composition on Recall and Image of Radio Scripts." *Journal of Broadcasting*, vol. 7, no. 2, 1963, pp. 167–172.
Macinnis, Deborah J., and Linda L. Price. "The Role of Imagery in Information Processing: Review and Extensions." *Journal of Consumer Research*, vol. 13, no. 4, 1987, pp. 473–491.
MacKenzie, Catherine. "Movies—and Superman." *The New York Times*, 12 Oct. 1941, p. 22.
Mackey, David R. *Drama on the Air*. Prentice-Hall, 1951.
Mallari, Junelle. "Smallville: The Mythology of Perry White." *IJPC Student Research Papers*, 2011, www.ijpc.org/uploads/files/IJPC%20Student%20Journal%20Junelle%20Mallari.pdf.
McMillan, Graeme. "How 'Superman Smashes the Klan' Updates a Piece of DC History." *The Hollywood Reporter*, 10 July 2019. https://www.hollywoodreporter.com/heat-vision/gene-luen-yang-talks-superman-smashes-klan-1223354.
Miller, Bonnie M. "'The Pictures are Better on Radio': A Visual Analysis of American Radio Drama from the 1920s to the 1950s." *Historical Journal of Film, Radio and Television*, vol. 38, no. 2, pp. 322–342.
Proctor, William. "Transmedia Comics: Seriality, Sequentiality and the Shifting Economies of Franchise Licensing." *The Routledge Companion to Transmedia Studies*, edited by Matthew Freeman and Renira Rampazzo Gambarato, Routledge, 2018, pp. 52–61.
Rodero, Emma. "Point of Listening in a Radio Fiction: The Eternal Problem." *Revista Observatorio (OBS*) Journal 10*, vol. 3, no. 3, pp. 242–252.
Rossen, Jake. *Superman vs. Hollywood: How Fiendish Producers, Devious Directors and Warring Writers Grounded an American Icon*. Chicago Review Press, 2008.
Sanders, Julie. *Adaptation and Appropriation*. Routledge, 2006.
Siegel, Jerry (w), and Joe Schuster (a). "The Coming of Superman." *Action Comics* Vol. 1 #1 (June 1938). DC Comics, 1938.
⸺. "Superman's Phony Manager." *Action Comics* Vol. 1 #6 (Nov. 1938). DC Comics, 1938.

_____. "Two Page Origin of Superman." *Superman* Vol. 1 #1 (Summer 1939). DC Comics, 1939.
_____. "The Three Kingpins of Crime." *Superman* Vol. 1 #7 (Nov. 1940). DC Comics, 1940.
Spiegelman, Art. "The Birth of Comics." *The New Yorker*, Dec. 24–Jan. 2, 1994, pp. 106–107.
The Superman Radio Scripts, Vol. I: Superman Vs. the Atom Man. Edited by Korté Steven, Watson-Guptill Publications, 2001.
Tilley, Carole L. "'Superman Says, 'Read!'" National Comics and Reading Promotion." *Children's Literature in Education*, Vol. 44, 251–263.
Tollin, Anthony. *Superman on the Radio.* Smithsonian Institution Press, 1997.
Wall, Wendy, L. *Inventing the "American Way": The Politics of Consensus from the New Deal to the Civil Rights Movement.* Oxford University Press, 2008.
Watt-Evans, Lawrence. "Previous Issues." *The Man from Krypton: A Closer Look at Superman*, edited by Glenn Teffeth, Benbella, 2005, pp. 1–8.
Welsh, James M. "Introduction: Issues of Screen Adaptation: What is Truth?" *The Literature/Film Reader: Issues of Adaptation*, edited by James Michael Welsh and Peter Lev, Scarecrow Press, 2007, pp. i–xxiv.
Yang, Gene Luen (w), and Gurihiru (a). "Superman Smashes the Klan, Part One." *Superman Smashes the Klan* #1 (Oct. 2019). DC Comics, 2019
_____. "Superman Smashes the Klan, Part Two." *Superman Smashes the Klan* #2 (Dec. 2019). DC Comics, 2019.
_____. "Superman Smashes the Klan, Part Three." *Superman Smashes the Klan* #3 (Feb. 2020). DC Comics, 2019.
Younis, Steve. "Superman Radio Episode List." *Superman Homepage*. 1994. https://www.supermanhomepage.com/radio/radio.php?topic=radio-episode-list.

Adapting American Values
Contextualizing Superman and the Mole Men *and* Superman IV: The Quest for Peace

FERNANDO GABRIEL PAGNONI BERNS

Since his birth in the late 1930s, Superman has been considered the perfect, law-abiding, American Boy Scout. He was, and still is, the embodiment of American values. Some argue that the Man of Steel's personality "might eventually be exploited to further the agendas of United States government" (Romagnoli and Pagnucci 30) since the hero "protects the status quo" (Toth 176) when he praises law and elected officials of order. As argued by Paul Kohl, Superman's vision of the world was rather simplistic and slightly "blind" (170) regarding problems which do not involve supervillains.

This linkage of Superman with American values is kept, through varying degrees, in all the passages from the comic book to other mediums. Ranging from cartoon to film to television, Superman stands next to the president to help him defeat all those who attack America. However, the processes of adaptation taking place through the social and cultural contexts of different decades allow for more complex readings of how "conservative" Superman is. American values, rather than a fixed, univocal set of assumptions, are presented as a fluid corpus of principles which vary through time, from adaptation to adaptation. Each transposition of the Superman mythos is centered around a different core of American values; these principles, in turn, vary according the social and cultural context in which the adaptation took place.

In this chapter, I will analyze two film adaptations of Superman's mythos to note how American values are re-interpreted in each case. *Superman and the Mole Men* (Lee Sholem, 1951) revolves around Clark Kent (Georges Reeves) and Lois Lane (Phyllis Coates) arriving to the small town of Silsby to witness the drilling of the world's deepest oil well. The drill, however, has penetrated the underground home of a race of mole men, who come to the surface at night. The mole men might be radioactive, so scared townsfolk form a mob to kill them. Only Superman has a chance to prevent tragedy while fighting for the right of being different amidst conservative strictures of normalcy. Opening amidst the Cold War and the beginning of the paranoia about any form of difference, the real villains of the story are the conservative American townspeople. In the much-maligned *Superman IV: The Quest for Peace* (Sidney Furie, 1987), the fourth and final Christopher Reeve Superman film, the Man of Steel tries to rid the world of nuclear weapons. One of the countries unilaterally "attacked" by the man from Krypton includes the United States. Rather than avoiding interventionism as he was doing right up to that point, Superman takes more extreme (and leftist) ideas to ensure global peace once and for all.

As Glenn Jellinek argues, the process of adaptation is a complex act that involves not only the source but also "the sociocultural moments that produce and consume them" (40). Adaptation is both a strategy of hermeneutic intervention and a form of political reading where there is no "original" and "illustration" but two completely different works. The different films, I will argue, do not adapt just the adventures of Superman but also American values for new social and cultural contexts, each depiction claiming to represent the best of American ethical principles.

Adapting Values

The term "American values" is ambiguous in its content and, as such, it may vary from interpretation to interpretation. There is not a univocal definition of what American values are and how to read them. Larry Trapp defines American values as "the most important standards and principles by which Americans live"; he admits, however, they change through time. Further, "we cannot generalize the values that may be unique to our individual spheres of interests" (16). This last statement emphasizes one particular problem: American values are highly subjective. Since they are not written in stone, every American can assume as important some values that other American feel as secondary or of a "lesser" degree. The *Academic Listening Encounters: American Studies Teacher's Manual* for intermediate courses breaks down the American values as follows: "hard work, self-reliance, equality, freedom, individualism, and democracy" (46). Some may argue, however, that these values represent neoliberalism rather than America as a whole. American values offer models to identify with—equality, tolerance, etc.,—but the exact interpretation remains individual. Further, some values, such as chastity, are deemed passé; new climates of opinion encouraging new values elevated from the ashes of burned ones.

In this scenario, I may ask: which American values are best represented by Superman? Like Captain America does for Marvel Comics, he seems to be the personal "bodyguard" of America and all its presidents. Unlike Batman (a vigilante), Wonder Woman (a truly complex avatar for global peace), Spider-Man (a teenager framed by teen angst) or the X-Men (a group of pariahs escaping heteronormativity), Superman is depicted with the American flag moving behind him, a bald eagle resting in his arm, the sun shining bright over his head. He is the embodiment of the America soul.

Still, Superman is not indifferent to this "fluidity" of American values. Each apparition of the Man of Steel in film highlights a determinate set of ethical principles, but not necessarily the same ones. Audiences and readers alike can find some core values in all transpositions, such as considering human life as sacred; other ethical principles, however, are more mobile. *Superman and the Mole Men* and *Superman IV*, for instance, share worries about nuclear energy and the dangers of spilled radioactivity. Thorough broad strokes, it is possible to point that the main menaces of the two films are radioactive glowing monsters. Fear about nuclear holocaust is present in the two films, separated by more than 35 years.

Yet, the Man of Steel of *Superman and the Mole Men* is not the same hero leading

Superman IV. His interests seem to have changed. He is still the embodiment of American values, but while he emphasizes the standards of equality within United States in one film (*Superman and the Mole Men*), he highlights the principles of peace in the other (*Superman IV*), coming to the extreme of global interventionism. In the film of 1951, Superman's main goal is stopping xenophobia in a little, sleepy town. By 1987, Superman is adamant in stopping global warfare, even if the president of US (both the fictional and the real) is interested in keeping the arms race going on.

These differences in attitude and goal are direct responses to the social and cultural climates in which the films were produced and made: one amidst the beginning of the Cold War, one at the end of this ideological battle. The first film was geographically localized deep within America, while the second film is global in scope. What makes this difference of values fascinating is that both claim to speak for America, its core principles, and for a majority of Americans that remain unheard. Both films claim correctly to be representing the Constitution and the American values of democracy, equality, and the freedom of speech. Regardless of the rhetoric and the social contexts, the two films are equally American.

Superman and the Mole Men: *Seeds of Paranoia, Values of Equality*

Superman and the Mole Men was filmed in the first years of the 1950s, with the Cold War dominating the ethos of Americans and foreign relationships. The beginning of the Cold War had a profound impact on the daily life in America. Communist nations, such as the Soviet Union, were depicted as bearers of extreme difference right up to the point of being considered dangerous for American health. Americans must protect their rights and properties from an extreme alterity, highly evocative of forms of sick monstrosity. Beginning with the presidency of Harry Truman, it was determined that communism should be contained to avoid an infectious "spree" through the world. As part of this philosophy, communists became the Others, bearers of an economic and political philosophy that ran counter to everything Americans held dear. Capitalist America represented democracy and the freedom to think and speak, while the Soviet region represented homogeneity of thinking and oppression. The Marshall Plan helped stimulate economies through Europe but also win friends to America in its war against the many evils of communism.

Ironically, one of the ideological strategies America used in its war against communism was shaping its own sense of homogeneity. Much of American life during the 1950s reflected an increasing sense of uniformity and conformity of middle-class values. The fifties were a decade still known for a striking image: little white houses, all them alike, localized in a seemingly never-ending row with white fences at the front and a happy housewife cooking apple pie within each house. This imagery enhanced the divide between Us and Them but, curiously, was basically homogenization versus homogenization. The intolerance toward difference surpassed just the fear towards communism. It was bigger than that: fear against religious difference, sexuality, ideas and race shaped the decade, as difference itself was considered ideologically wrong, something evil. The pressures for conformity made any form of difference something suspicious.

As argued by Athan Theoharis, the Truman era was where the seeds of McCarthyism were sown. "The Truman administration committed itself to victory over communism and to safeguarding the nation from external and internal threats; the rhetoric of

McCarthyism was in this sense well within the framework of Cold War politics" (vii). Soon, blacklists were produced and circulated to highlight the new ethos: being different is being evil.

Within this scenario, *Superman and the Mole Men* opens. It navigates between the complete distrust about difference and the acceptance of foreign forms of life. The film opens with a montage of images of outer space. Planets and comets cross the galaxy, thus insinuating that the main menace of the story, the Mole Men, were extraterrestrial in nature. The film's poster emphasizes this supposition, as the Mole Men of the title are tinted green. The creatures, however, will be revealed as terrestrial, part of an underground human race who has survived at the Earth's core through millennia. Another layer of ambiguity is added after the end of the opening credits: the "outer space" montage refers, in fact, to Superman, as a voice-over tells viewers about the extraterrestrial nature of the superhero. Superman is the real embodiment of difference, as is he the only non-human being in the whole film. The recounting of his story (how he come to America, his fight against evil, and his camouflage as Clark Kent) ends with an American flag fluttering behind Superman, a symbol of the hero's "Americanness." He may be alien, but American by adoption (of ideological principles). "Superman represents the assimilationist rhetoric of America towards its immigrants: to be in America is to adopt American values" (Nayar 104). In fact, the voice over ends telling viewers that Superman defends "the American way." The phrase was not an original idea of the film's writers; it was, in fact, a phrase added to the openings of the Superman radio serials through its third season in 1942, becoming quickly associated with the hero from Krypton (Gordon 43). Thus, Superman was de-territorialized from his native planet and Americanized.

It remains to be defined what the American way is by the standards of the 1950s. American values were inextricably anchored through the decade to ideals of sameness and fears about forms of difference. Being American was being foreign to any philosophy of ideological alterity to the capitalist ethics. On March 22, 1947, a permanent employee loyalty program was established which "legitimized the idea of judging an employee's loyalty on the basis of his previous associations, activities, and beliefs" (Theoharis 102). Federal employees, regardless of the importance of their jobs, were to be investigated on grounds of suspicion of disloyalty against America. In 1951, the program was adjusted to make it even stricter: "when the program came under attack for not achieving absolute loyalty, the limited safeguards to individual liberties originally written into it were further circumscribed" (103). In April 1951, the administration amended the dismissal provision to read "reasonable doubts" rather than certainties. Thus, "the amendment subordinated individual rights to internal security, and internal security itself to internal suspicion" (103). Being suspect of carrying some form of difference was, by 1951, a crime. Soon, America was framed by paranoia, as anyone could be the enemy within trying to infiltrate "red" ideas in the veins of the country. As John Jackson argues, race, ideological and sexual paranoia is "constituted by extremist thinking, general social distrust, the non-falsifiable embrace of intuition, and an unflinching commitment to contradictory thinking" (15). Denouncing or warning against any form of difference was, then, an American value. The U.S defended equality and freedom; it was important to shut down any voice against this freedom.

Paranoia runs rampant in the little village of Silsby (population 1430), "home of the world's deepest oil hole." To the town comes Lois Lane and Clark Kent to write an article on the oil pit, only to learn from Bill Corrigan (Walter Reed), the man in charge, that the camp is closing abruptly and without much explanation. While Lane express her resentment after traveling many miles only to see an oil pit closing down, Clark is quick to retort that the shutdown must, probably, obey some good reasons. Always the good American, Clark/Superman believes the government is choosing the best for the country, even if closing the pit is killing Silsby's economic life. In later scenes, Lane cruelly mocks Silsby's boring life (she ironically calls the place "big thing" and emphasizes the fact that she can live without seeing the place, preferring rather resting in her room at a humble hotel) while Clark (raised in Smallville, part of "small" America) is respectful of the tranquil atmosphere. While Lane is a modern girl from the city who seemingly despises little towns, Clark is depicted as the perfect offspring of the country. Superman is a mythic character who intertwines together cultural traditions of small-town American with wider national values.

Pop Shannon (Farrell MacDonald), one of the men guarding the pit, is found dead later that night by Lois and Clark. The town suspects foul play, especially after Lois observes mysterious creatures walking around the shed. Lois is the first one to come to the wrong conclusion: these weird-looking creatures surely killed Pop. There is little evidence to support this idea, except for the strange aspect of the beings. Thus, their physical difference (small, bald, thick eyebrows, greenish skin,[1] paw-like hands covered by hair) goes vis-a-vis with evilness. It will be later revealed that Pop actually died from a heart attack, the Mole Men innocent of any crime.

Investigating further, Kent finds the truth: Corrigan has decided close down the oil pit after some clues lead him to think that there is life in the Earth's core. Further, the life forms habiting the center of the planet are radioactive and, as such, potentially dangerous for human life. This explanation taps into two anxieties framing the 1950s: the fear about difference in one hand and the anxieties born from scientific development involving radiation and atomic science in the other. Both were intertwined through the decade: "while the general public may have supported the build-up of atomic weapons in response to the apparent Soviet threat, fears of radiation were obvious and widespread" (Carlisle 54). Both fears are embodied by the mole men, whose touch can spread radioactivity (sickness) to humans. The idea of "spreading sickness" was a useful image to contain communism through the 1950s and 1960s, as the "red scare" was imagined as a disease that could touch and pervert anyone.

Like the communists, the Mole Men came from another place where everyone think-alike and behave-alike. All the creatures wear black attire, their faces a mirror of each other. They move in a group and are highly suspicious of the Americans populating the town. Soon, all the creatures are hunted down by the different villagers, who start a witch hunt to end the "menace" of the Mole Men. Paranoia abounds, as many residents accuse the Mole Men of scaring and even attacking them. At this point in the story, it is left clear that their fears are unfounded, as the little Mole Men have not yet arrived to town; thus, the fear is the offspring of paranoia rather than a reality.

Only Clark Kent tries to stop the mob which wants to hunt and kill the Mole Men. There is little indication that the creatures are evil, but neither is there a reason to believe them inoffensive. Kent, however, is adamant in protecting the creatures from the vicious townspeople, who are uninterested in hearing any word in favor of the "monsters." Even Lois Lane tells Kent that the townspeople "know what they do," thus placing herself firmly within the dialectic Us versus Them. Clark, however, wants to hear from the creatures rather than hunting them down like criminals.

As the narrative progresses, it is clear that the real antagonists of the story are not the Mole Men but the xenophobic townspeople. Their attitude towards difference evokes images of lynching. Although violence against African Americans decreased through the postwar period, racial prejudice and xenophobic violence was still part of America in the 1950s. Migration and increasing visibility in suburbia was especially rife with tensions. As African Americans migrated into northern cities amid the war and postwar industrial booms, they were met with antagonism and harassment from working-class whites who resented black encroachment into their labor and housing markets. Racial conflicts and riots subsequently erupted in cities like Detroit, Philadelphia, and Chicago throughout the 1940s and 1950s (Wood 263–4).

Images of "peaceful black protestors facing angry white mobs, fending off police dogs" (Wood 265) would resonate in the viewers watching how the Mole Men were hunted down by white people (there are no African Americans among the townspeople depicted through the film) with dogs and rifles. In one key scene, Luke Benson (Jeff Corey), the man leading the mob and the xenophobic prejudices with stories of dangerous attackers who came from within the Earth, says he wants to find the creature to "hang it." The reference to "hang" from a tree a creature who wears his body covered in black clothes evokes the haunting of lynching and hangings motivated by racial hate. In a later scene, Superman takes a wounded Mole Man to the town's hospital. A young doctor makes his best efforts to help the creature. The old director of the hospital, however, wants "that monster" out of his building immediately. According his words, the hospital is not there to attend this kind of "thing," less-than-human, non-white-skin creature.

The masses move pushed by fear and racial hatred, Superman being the only reasonable man amidst this uprising of prejudice. It is only at this moment that the film presents the first appearance of Superman. The superhero shows up not to stop the Mole Men, but to antagonize the mob hunting the little underground creatures. In other words, Superman, the American Boy Scout par excellence, is needed not to stop monsters but Americans. His main foe is Luke Benson; he tries to push Superman aside, but the Man of Steel bends his rifle with his bare hands. Later, taking Benson by his shirt, Superman angrily says that are men like Benson who make it hard for people to understand each other. These words, which are almost the first ones Superman pronounces in the film, confirms the American values he is upholding: equality. Against the seeds of fear and paranoia dominating the era—seeds sown, in part, through the medium of popular culture—Superman advocates for integration against the evils of xenophobia.

The townspeople as Superman's main foes is emphasized by the film's poster. Superman is depicted at the center; Lois Lane is localized at the inferior left corner, sharing space with an image of Superman beating one of Silsby's citizens. Some of the film's promotional material sustained this reading. Periodicals such as *The Southeast Missourian*, dated December 13, 1951, make a brief reference to the film. The photo illustrating the article is one of Superman facing Luke Benson. The epigraph reads: "George Reeves, as the bullet-proof champion of justice, dares the pistol of Jeff Corey in a tense scene" (21). There is no Mole-Man seen.

The American values held by this version of Superman identifies the problem within America and attacks it (literally): conformity may lead to a degree of mistruth which, in turn, may lead to shut down other people's voices. The problem does not lie in the underground creatures, but in the complete lack of understanding and empathy by part of the townspeople. Mass hysteria and paranoia is explicitly mentioned when Lois wants to communicate the news about Mole Men running amok. It takes convincing from Superman before she agrees not to send in the story to Metropolis, as the Man of Steel fears spreading further panic nation-wide. Superman knows that (real) America is co-opted by paranoia, and he is ready to put an end to this particular evil.

The cruelty of the mob led by Luke Benson emphasizes the xenophobia as an ill. Benson shoots Superman with his gun twice, even if he (presumably) knows who the superhero is and what he represents. Later, Benson and his men have one creature cornered in a little hut in the middle of the desert. The men put the wood hut on fire with the mole-man inside, who is able to escape (without the hunting mob noticing it) through a tunnel excavated with his bare hands. Killing difference is the only goal in their collective, hive-like mind.

When the mob arrives to the hospital to hang the wounded creature, Superman stops them. One citizen insinuates that maybe Superman should be hanged, too; a statement rife with racial intolerance. In the film's climax, Superman makes a bold statement before the mob: it was the white men who invaded the creatures' world with a driller (as a way to obtain resources, it should be added). It is not white men's prerogative to invade other's people habitats, as everyone must share the planet with equality regardless of external appearance or thinking. In the film's last scene, the Mole Men shut downs the oil pit with an explosion, foreclosing further attempts of invasion. As she stands alongside Superman and watches the oil well burn, Lois delivers the last line of the film: "It's almost as if they were saying, 'You live your lives, and we'll live ours,'" thus echoing, for the first time, Superman's sentiments.

As stated by the loyalty program installed by Truman, one American value dominating the 1950s was a patriotic sentiment that should lead citizens to denounce any sign of suspicious difference. The people of Silsby embrace this ethical principle, while Superman stands at the side of "evil": the creatures whose difference may make them dangerous to national security. Further, Superman wants to keep the American government oblivious of the existence of the creatures, a clear example of the Man of Steel acting against the status quo and the law.

It is undeniable that Superman acted heroically and to support American values, but not those sustained by the Truman administration. In fact, he acted explicitly *against them*, allowing creatures marked by difference to run away and advocating for the right of every person to live without feeling oppressed. This was a bold statement to make in the 1950s, but Superman was the hero who can make it.

Peace and Global Interventionism: Facing Reaganomics in the Reagan Era

Superman IV: The Quest for Peace is the last installment of the Christopher Reeve Superman franchise of the 1980s. Produced with a smaller budget that its predecessors, the film was considered "dreadful" (Hanley 151). Tim Hanley explains the ordeal the film suffered: "as a result of *Superman III*'s poor performance, the Salkinds sold the rights to Superman to Cannon Films, a production company best known for making B-movies. The cast agreed to return for a fourth Superman film; Reeve was swayed when the producers allowed him to have input on the story." However, "shooting went badly on every level. Cannon continually slashed the film's budget, and the end result looked shoddy, with subpar special effects and reused stock footage throughout" (150). Reeve's input and belief that there was no better heroism that having the Man of Steel assisting global disarmament helped the creation of a storyline that involves Superman being conflicted over what to do about the world's nuclear weapons after a small child asks him to get rid of them all.

In the 1980s, the world was still enduring the effects of the Cold War, with nuclear weapons being by far the most dangerous aspect of the conflict. Ronald Reagan, elected president in 1981 and re-elected in 1984, "talked about the need to negotiate with the Soviet Union in order to reduce the high levels of arms, particularly nuclear weapons, and to do so with strict verification" (Matlock 60). However, Reagan kept criticizing and demonizing of all things communist, so most efforts for a global disarmament were quickly short-circuited. In his first press conference as president, Reagan "announced that he favored 'an actual reduction in the numbers of nuclear weapons'" (60), thus addressing the arms race as a hot problem. The general impression, however, was that Reagan was adamant in retarding or directly invalidating any real, concrete attempt at disarmament. In brief, "Reagan was eager to reach an agreement that would reliably reduce nuclear arsenals" but "he was in no particular hurry to start the negotiations" (60). Contradictorily, he believed that U.S should be strong in arms and nuclear power before starting to even think about the possibility of global disarmament.

In this scenario, the Man of Steel of *Superman IV* seems less radical: he is only complying with Reagan's agenda. The world is emptied of nuclear weaponry but America has the most extreme of arms of mass destruction—Superman—at its side. The film opens with Russian "comrade" astronauts working on a space station. One of them is singing (in Russian) a Frank Sinatra's song, a subtle way to hint at the superiority of America presence through the world. An accident occurs and one of the astronauts is stranded into deep space. Superman arrives to rescue him and take him again into his ship. Superman salutes, the Russians salute back, and the opening sequence ends. The opening may read as simple, but it reveals much about the Reaganomic mind. Superman has no qualms in saving Russian astronauts who, arguably, could be replaced by American ones, as they have no further weight in the plot: the incident is not mentioned again. The communist astronauts, in the other hand, show no reserve in being rescued by Superman, a striking feat if we keep in mind that Russians in the era were mostly depicted as villains who clashed with American superheroes. Here, the relationship is depicted in nuanced tones, as Superman retires before the communist astronauts can say something to him (either good or bad). The relationships between U.S and the Soviet Union are warmer but kept in suspension.

After the opening scene, Clark is seen in Smallville, where he denies selling his childhood farm to a multinational conglomerate. There is no further elaboration on this point,[2] but it is enough to code Superman—the alien—as American. The mention of a transnational corporation indicates a desire to keep the America soul free from foreign influence and thus healthily attached to its small-town roots. To further emphasis his Americanness, Clark ends the scene in his natal Smallville playing baseball.

If Ronald Reagan enthroned a capitalist-fueled frame to the decade (an ethos of individualism, free market, and accumulation of capital), the film and its main character, Superman, opposes the Reaganomic mindset. *The Daily Planet* has been sold to new owners whose main ethical principle is "making money" rather than telling the truth. All the workers at *The Daily Planet* are shocked, including Lois Lane (Margot Kidder), but it is Clark who actually says something against this policy of indiscriminate accumulation of capital. When news about the failure of global disarmament comes to *The Daily Planet*, the new owner, David Warfield (Sam Wanamaker), is clearly happy: global crisis increases the sales of newspapers by millions, making him richer. The surname "War-field" also emphasizes this linkage between war and capitalism.

The President of the U.S in the fiction (Robert Beatty) parallels Reagan's attitudes regarding nuclear arms disarmament. In a message to all America, the president states that "because the summit has failed, we have no choice but to strive to be second to none in the nuclear arms race." In other words, the Soviet coalition is unyielding in keeping the nuclear arms race going forward, situation that "obliges" America to, at least, "try" to be second to none. It is all the communists' fault. A group of children seeing the news on TV are asked by their teacher for suggestions on what to do at the face of such a crisis. The teacher (Jayne Brook) suggests writing letters to the congressmen on Washington. Jeremy (Damian McLawhorn), however, suggests writing a letter to someone *who really cares* about nuclear disarmament (Superman), implying that politicians were only "performing" their interest on global peace, a sentiment probably shared by many in the audience at the time. The assignment written on the blackboard behind the teacher asks the children to write 200 words on the Statue of Liberty, thus uniting together two American values: freedom and the search for peace. The lack of commitment towards global disarmament, however, insinuates that this particular value is not held as high as declared. Even Lois dismisses the nuclear crisis in two scenes, calling Clark a "pessimist." Only Superman and Jeremy, the kid who writes a letter to the Man of Steel, seem genuinely worry about the weight that this particular American value—peace—holds in contemporary America.

After consulting with the ghosts of his ancestors from Krypton (whom advise him to remain neutral in the global nuclear arms race), Superman makes the decision to start an interventionist, pro-active approach to disarmament. Interventionism and Superman were linked together already from the conception of the character by two Jewish creators (writer Jerome "Jerry" Siegel and artist Joseph "Joe" Shuster) in a context of Nazi anti–Semitism. Superman was "obliged" to intervene in the conflicts between democracy in one hand and fascism in the other. Not surprisingly, Superman was widely discussed as a Golem-like figure of justice. As retold by Martin Lund, a two-page story "How Superman Would End the War," published in *Look* magazine on February 27, 1940, revolved around the Man of Steel grabbing both Adolf Hitler and Joseph Stalin to stand trial in front of the League of Nations. This interventionism, however, "was not framed as a call for the USA to do the same" but mere wish fulfillment by Siegel and Shuster (Lund 27, 107). With Reagan promising nuclear disarmament and later pedaling back at his own promises, however, the Superman of Furie's film seems to be "softly" pushing the American president to the ultimate decision: end the arms race once and for all.

After meeting Jeremy, Superman talks to a global audience at the UN headquarters. As a man who represents no nation in particular, Superman needs the endorsement of at least one member of the ONU; everyone in the saloon agrees with letting him speak. The naiveté of depicting all members of the ONU granting Superman the power of speech (although Superman clearly stands for America) illustrates a society willing to give voice to someone outside common politics. There, Superman states his decision of taking away the nuclear weapons from every country which has them. Even more naïve, everyone in the saloon cheers Superman's interventionist declaration, thus obscuring in part the political implications brought by a man who represents America overruling the sovereignty of foreign nations. To avoid favoritism, Superman is depicted in the next scene snatching away nuclear missiles from both America and Russia and later throwing them to the sun to be consumed. Next, Lex Luthor (Gene Hackman) proposes to defeat Superman with a villain of his own creation, Nuclear Man (Mark Pillow). His intention is continuing the production of nuclear missiles to sell in the black market. Interestingly, the proposition is made to characters who represent gangsters rather than leaders from foreign nations. This way, the nuclear arms are desired by "evil" people rather than countries such as Russia or U.S. In the world of *Superman IV*, every nation of the world agrees with Superman's interventionism, further obliterating any contradiction through the lens of Manichean evilness. In the (rushed) ending, Superman defeats Nuclear Man through a battle on the Moon, returns Luthor to jail and gives a speech to the press about global peace and the responsibility of citizens worldwide in demand it from their governments.

Arguably, global peace is a transnational moral value rather than just American, even if Reagan emphasized this particular principle as part of his electoral campaign (White 16). Still, it is the American hero who takes care of this extreme step, acting, apparently, in behalf of America. Through Superman's interventionist adventures, the president is nowhere to be seen, his absence very telling by virtue of ambiguity. Is he agreeing with Superman's actions? If so, why he does not say so or have acted before? In this scenario, Superman follows Reagan's desires for peace but, unlike the president, the Man of Steel steps out from the shadows of bureaucracy and diplomatic relationships to ensure world peace, even if that means "doing the right thing" without waiting for the president's explicit endorsement. As Reagan established peace as one of his goals, Superman's decisions seem to stem from his president's agenda. Unlike Reagan, the Man of Steel really did what he has promised Jeremy and the entire world he will do, sidestepping through the process the president's prudency.

Conclusions

Umberto Eco famously argued that with Superman "we have a perfect example of civic consciousness, completely split from political consciousness" as the Man of Steel is "busy by preference, not against blackmarketing drugs, nor, obviously, against corrupting administrators or politicians, but against banks and mail truck robbers" (22). To Eco, these crimes are the most visible forms of evil. In other words, Superman will attack global hunger by defeating criminals who want to steal the food rather than fight social inequalities represented by capitalism or particular democracies. For Eco, this is a problem stemming from the nature of the plots, as they do little to upset hierarchies; doing otherwise may label the plotlines as "subversives." Thus, "the plot must be static and evade any development because Superman must make virtue consist of many little activities on a small scale, never achieving a total awareness" (22).

But Superman does so in both Sholem's *Superman and the Mole Men* and Furie's *Superman IV: The Quest for Peace*. Coincidentally, both film productions have been overlooked in critical analysis. The former is mostly forgotten except for die-hard fans, while the latter is considered as the proverbial nail in the coffin of the franchise. In the films, Superman continues being the incarnation of American values: equality and peace. However, his support for these values—supposedly better represented by Truman and Reagan, as they were elected to lead the country to its best form—clash with other American values: patriotism and the right of defense. Thus, rather than sustaining the status quo, Superman subverts them. The "official" voice, that of the presidents, remains silent. In fact, in *Mole Men*, Superman asks Lois to keep secrecy on what had happened in Silsby. It seems that even the president cannot be trusted.

Like Eco stated, Superman represents a civic conscience. But that does not mean the uncritical support for the status quo, not that the plots are so much simplistic as Eco mentions. Superman is the embodiment of American values, but the ambiguous nature of these principles makes hard to pin down a concrete definition. Rather than a deficit, this lack of clarity makes Superman's stories and myth richer to readers and viewers.

Notes

1. Their skin tone is, in fact, gray, as the film was made in black and white. The posters, however, suggest the mole men's skin is greenish. This would answer why Lois Lane screams in horror after seeing them.

2. Many scenes and subplots were left at the cutting room, as the film was heavily excised to run under the hour and a half mark.

Works Cited

Carlisle, Rodney. *Postwar America, 1950 to 1969*. FactsonFile, 2009.
Eco, Umberto. "The Myth of Superman: The Amazing Adventures of Superman." *Diacritics*, Vol. 2, No. 1 (Spring, 1972), pp. 14–22.
Gordon, Ian. *Superman: The Persistence of an American Icon*. Rutgers University Press, 2017.
Hanley, Tim. *Investigating Lois Lane: The Turbulent History of the Daily Planet's Ace Reporter*. Chicago Review Press, 2016.
Jackson, John, Jr. *Racial Paranoia: The Unintended Consequences of Political Correctness. The New Reality of Race in America*. Basic Civitas, 2009.
Jellinek, Glenn. "The Task of the Adaptation Critic." *Adaptation in Visual Culture: Images, Texts, and Their Multiple Worlds*, edited by Julie Grossman and R. Barton Palmer, Palgrave Macmillan, 2017, pp. 37–52.
Kohl, Paul. "Superman's Difficult Transition into the Age of Relevance." *The Ages of Superman: Essays on the Man of Steel in Changing Times*, edited by Joseph Darowski, McFarland, 2012, pp. 103–114.
Lund, Martin. *Re-Constructing the Man of Steel: Superman 1938–1941, Jewish American History, and the Invention of the Jewish–Comics Connection*. Palgrave Macmillan, 2016.
Matlock, Jack., Jr. "Ronald Reagan and the End of the Cold War." *Ronald Reagan and the 1980s: Perceptions, Policies, Legacies*, edited by Cheryl Hudson and Gareth Davies, Palgrave Macmillan, 2008, pp. 57–80.
Nayar, Pramod. *Reading Culture: Theory, Praxis, Politics*. SAGE, 2006.
Romagnoli, Alex, and Gian Pagnucci. *Enter the Superheroes: American Values, Culture, and the Canon of Superhero*. Scarecrow Press, 2013.
Sanabria, Kim, and Carlos Sanabria. *Academic Listening Encounters: American Studies. Teacher's Manual*. Cambridge University Press, 2008.
Theoharis, Athan. *Seeds of Repression: Harry S. Truman and the Origins of McCarthyism*. Quadrangle Books, 1971.
Toth, Justine. "People Have Had Enough Tragedy: The Spectacle of Global Heroism in *Superman Returns*." *The War on Terror and American Popular Culture: September 11 and Beyond*, edited by Andrew Schopp, Matthew B. Hill, Matthew Hill, Fairleigh Dickinson University Press, 2009, pp. 167–186.
Trapp, Larry. *American Values, 1960–2000: What Went Wrong?* Xlibris, 2002.
"A Week at the Cape Theatres." *The Southeast Missourian*. 13 Dec. 1951, pp. 21.
White, John Kenneth. *The Values Divide: American Politics and Culture in Transition*. Seven Bridges Press, 2003.
Wood, Amy Louise. *Lynching and Spectacle: Witnessing Racial Violence in America, 1890–1940*. The University of North Carolina Press, 2009.

A European Superman

Lars Konzack

In 1990, the Danish comic book company Interpresse (partly owned by the Swedish publishing house Semic), under license from DC Comics, published the one and, to this date, only Superman comic originally produced outside the United States (Rhode and Bottorff, Jr. 267). It was a world divided between two super powers, the United States of America and NATO vs. the Soviet Union and the Warsaw Pact. Each was willing to destroy the world with nuclear weapons if necessary to prove their economic and political system was the correct one. In the end, the Soviet Union and the Warsaw Pact collapsed (December 1991). In 1988 when work on the graphic novel began, however, little did the world know that the collapse of the Soviet Union was imminent. People imagined that this conflict would last until the world ended in a devastating nuclear war of total annihilation. When the graphic novel *Superman og Fredsbomben* was published in 1990, it was just after the fall of the Berlin Wall and, I am sorry to say, the plot was suddenly outdated.

In celebration of the 50th anniversary of Superman in 1988, DC Comics encouraged overseas publishers to produce an original story with Superman. Only Henning Kure and Ove Høyer, the Interpresse editors from Denmark, took the challenge (the graphic novel is dedicated to Henning Kure and Ove Høyer for that very reason) because the company could see an opportunity for a profit. The result was a 48-page graphic novel *Superman og Fredsbomben* (directly translated: *Superman and the Peace Bomb* aka *Superman: A Tale of Five Cities*, inspired by Charles Dickens' *A Tale of Two Cities*). Writer Niels Søndergaard and visual artist Teddy Kristiansen were inspired by the Cold War plot and the artwork from the 1986 graphic novel *Batman: The Dark Knight Returns* by Frank Miller—including illustrations of television screen panels—but the tone and story were more influenced by Keith Giffen and J.M. deMatteis, as we shall see later. The only requirement from the company Semic that owned Interpresse, according to Niels Søndergaard, was that the story should take place in the five countries in which Semic published comics.

Superman: A Tale of Five Cities had a different take on the Man of Steel than the typical American comic. In this graphic novel, Superman visits five European capitals (Amsterdam, Copenhagen, Oslo, Stockholm, and Helsinki) and meets local superheroes like The Little Mermaid in Copenhagen and the Icemaiden and Iceflower of Norway. Superman is used to exemplify European self-image during the last decade of the Cold War. There is a double bind in this communication (Bateson 271–278). The reader gains awareness of a distinct Northern European culture but in the context of an American cultural imperialism. In a sense, the European culture becomes more visible as seen through the eyes of this former European colony. Still, it is created by Danes looking at Europe as if they were Americans (or an alien from another planet raised in United States) coming to visit Europe. This creates closeness and distance at the same time when producing and reproducing the myth of Superman in a European context.

The plot is as follows: *The Daily Planet* reporter Lois Lane is on a European tour following peace activist Theodore P. Wyatt. LexCorp has invented a device, the "Peace Monger," that can render nuclear weapons harmless by turning the radioactive material into lead. Wyatt, a peace activist funded by LexCorp., travels from Amsterdam to Copenhagen, Oslo, and Stockholm, and ends up in Helsinki in order to tell the world about the "Peace Monger." Wyatt is not only followed by Lois Lane but, to her dissatisfaction, Clark Kent, who she thinks is only there to steal her story. CIA and KGB keep a close eye on their journey ... and so does Superman. Superman protects Wyatt against KGB and CIA and any others who wants him dead, putting the security of the planet Earth above governments and corporations. Spoiler alert: Lex Luthor wants to sell the peace bomb to the Soviet Union because, if nuclear bombs become less threatening, there is more money in conventional weapons. However, Superman gets in the way and Lex Luthor demands he be killed. Superman believes the target is Wyatt but it is in fact Superman himself. Here comes the plot twist: It turns out that Wyatt is in fact a killer robot armed with kryptonite created by LexCorp for the purpose of killing Superman. By pretending to be a peace activist, Lex Luthor wants to lure Superman into the taking his guard down. The plan works but at the same time, Lex Luthor shows the effect of the peace bomb to the Russians and suddenly the kryptonite, being a radioactive material, becomes lead. Superman survives and Lex Luthor destroys the peace bomb and all knowledge about it because Lex Luthor would rather live in an unsafe world with nuclear weapons than remove the ultimate weakness of Superman.

Superman og Fredsbomben was originally written in Danish and then translated into six other languages: Swedish, Norwegian, Finnish, Dutch, Spanish, and Italian; an English translation has never occurred. The Dutch title emphasized Superman coming to Europe, while the Swedish, Norwegian, and Finnish title focused on selling Superman as coming to local cities and countries. The Dutch cover is titled "Superman in Europa" and shows Superman flying under a bridge in Amsterdam. The Swedish cover is "Stålmannen i Stockholm" ("Man of Steel in Stockholm") and shows Superman flying above Stockholm. The Norwegian cover is "Superman i Norge" ("Superman in Norway"), showing Superman fighting in Frognerparken of Oslo. The Finnish version is "Teräsmies Supersankari Helsingissä!" ("Superman: Superhero in Helsinki"), covering Superman flying above Helsinki and the Sibelius Monument. All of them place Superman in a national context of each country. Superman visiting the local European capitals was a selling point in marketing and chosen for that very reason by the publishing house Semic, which owned comic book publishing companies in Holland, Denmark, Norway, Sweden, and Finland.

Understanding the Scandinavian market tells us why the five cities were chosen but the Danish comic creators also found inspiration in the contemporary superhero comics, drawing upon the latest comic book styles. European graphic novels and American translations of Disney comics dominated European comics culture in the 1980s; Batman and Superman were well-known characters as well. There had already been a long European tradition with popular comics like *The Adventures of Tintin*, *Lucky Luke*, *The Smurfs*, and *Asterix & Obelix*. In the 1970s and 1980s, the comics in Europe matured. A new generation of comic creators wanted to tell stories that were more than just amusing and entertaining popular culture for children. Not that they had anything against popular culture or being entertaining, they just wanted more depth. In 1974, the French comic magazine *Métal Hurlant* (licensed in the United States as *Heavy Metal*) began exploring the boundaries of comics as a visual medium, emphasizing filmic graphics, complicated imagery, and unreal plots (Couch 209). *Métal Hurlant* inspired many visual artists and European graphic novels such as *Valérian* and *Laureline* by Pierre Christin and Jean-Claude Mézières, *Corto Maltese* by Hugo Pratt, *The Incal* by Alejandro Jodorowsky and Jean "Moebius" Giraud, and *Cities of the Fantastic* by François Schuite and Benoît Peeters. The European experimental comic book scene was a backdrop for the creation of *Superman og Fredsbomben*. But, of course, they also looked towards American comics.

The Dark Age is the name of this era in the history of superhero comics (Voger 6). The Golden Age of Superheroes began in 1938 with Superman. It was followed by the Silver Age in 1956, with more elaborate characters and advanced plots inspired by science fiction. This again was followed by the social realism of the Bronze Age in the 1970s. The Dark Age (sometimes referred to as the Iron Age or Modern Age) starting with two superhero comics in 1986, namely Frank Miller's *Batman: The Dark Knight Returns* and Alan Moore's *Watchmen* (Jenkins 16; Holston 10; Fagan and Fagan 41; Johnson 140–149). As has already been established, *Superman: A Tale of Five Cities* is directly inspired by Frank Miller's *Batman: The Dark Knight Returns* and consequently it is a part of the Dark Age of superhero comics.

Dark Age superhero comics has been described as grim and gritty psychodrama (Voger 9), baroque self-consciousness (Jenkins), and the rebirth of hardboiled anti-heroes (Holston 11). It was to some extent a reaction, maybe even an over-reaction, to the Comics Code Authority of the Silver Age that began in the Bronze Age and continued into in the Dark Age (Holston 10–11). It is worth noting the revisions to the Comics Code in 1971, allowing for the social commentary of the Bronze Age, and in 1989, allowing for the grim-and-gritty aesthetic. However, the Comics Code, of course, did not bind European publishers. That said, according to Niels Søndergaard, the manuscript had to be approved by DC. The necessary changes DC required was that Superman should rebuild any destroyed buildings and monuments and The Little Mermaid should not have her head sawed off; in the original manuscript, she would have been brutally slaughtered.

The superhero was growing up in the 1980s and it became obvious to visionaries that the superhero genre was able express more than juvenile power fantasies. Comic book writer Kurt Busiek famously argues:

> If a superhero can be such a powerful and effective metaphor for male adolescence then what else can you do with them? Could you build a superhero story around a metaphor for female adolescence? Around mid-life crisis? Around the changes adults go through when they become parents? Sure why not? And if a superhero can exemplify America's self-image at the dawn of World War II, could a superhero exemplify America's self-image during the less confident 1970s? How about the emerging national identity of a newly independent African nation? Or a non-national culture like the drug culture or "greed-is-good" business culture of the go-go Eighties? Of course. If it can do one, it can do the others (8).

Busiek suggests that it is possible to address mature themes in superhero comics. *Superman og Fredsbomben* has indeed a mature theme. It is a gaze into Cold War dilemmas and how America, personified by Superman, is at the same time perceived as a protector of Western democracies and as an exponent of American cultural imperialism (Bertrand

51). The protection of NATO countries by the American nuclear arsenal symbolized in Superman is at the same time built on mutual assured destruction.

It is important to note that while Holland, Denmark, and Norway were part of NATO, Sweden and Finland were not. Only four years earlier in 1986, the Prime Minister of Sweden, Olof Palme, had been shot. Olof Palme had represented a Western criticism of the Vietnam War and the Cold War (Olesen 157). The Nordic countries and Holland were geographically close to the intersection of the Cold War. If it had ever turned warm, then these countries risked being nuked, if not from the Soviet Union then maybe from their allies in an attempt to stop the enemy from advancing further. In any case, a nuclear war between NATO and the Warsaw Pact could turn Holland and the Nordic countries into a nuclear wasteland. This knowledge of an upcoming apocalypse lead to pacifist movements (Evan 290). Moreover, in Scandinavia and especially in Sweden there was widespread disapproval of American cultural imperialism or Americanization (O'Dell 43). The graphic novel refers directly at cultural imperialism when Superman encounters Swedish protesters accusing him of being an exponent of American cultural imperialism. Superman answers, "I am not an exponent of anything. I am…. I am just me." Lois Lane cynically concludes, "I know that. You know that. They know that. It's is just a tradition" (p. 28). The American/European relationship was not always friendly during the Cold War. They shared the same enemy but there was still competition between the countries and they did not always have the same political priorities (van Heuven 5). This explains the hostility Superman is met with in Norway and Sweden but also that he is accepted as part of the free world.

In the comic, Superman is the United States of America personified. He is as potentially destructive as the American nuclear bombs. As long as he is your friend, it is splendid; but what if this alien being someday turned on humanity? Then it could be the end of human civilization like a nuclear Ragnarök. During the Cold War, the NATO allies were dependent on American willingness to support and protect the European democracies from the Communist authoritarian regimes of the Eastern Bloc (van Heuven 3). Seen from a Western European perspective, Superman is the personified American nuclear bomb that the NATO countries are dependent on for world peace. Nevertheless, Superman may also be the very reason for ending world peace in a nuclear all-encompassing catastrophe.

Superman himself comes from the planet Krypton that suffered a similar cataclysmic event, annihilating the entire planet. Superman's America is at the same time both where he grew up and an alien world. In a sense, it is just like many Americans born from European ancestry, living in the new world as both aliens and natives at the same time. When *Daily Planet* photographer Jimmy Olsen visits Norway, he is returning to his place of origin. Superman is not. He is a symbol of America, a superhero representing a global superpower; still, he is an alien not only to America but Europe as well.

There is no reference to Superman's fictional hometowns of Metropolis and Smallville. Instead, the graphic novel presents real European cities. According to Theodore P. Wyatt, LexCorp chose these Northern European countries because they would provide the utmost attention due to their well-known humanitarian position (11). The reason for this self-image stems from political decisions. Holland and the Nordic countries had during the Cold War been developing social-liberal welfare states in an attempt to take the best from free market economy and combine with the best from socialism, supporting universal health care and free education (Farnsworth). They were rejecting *laissez-faire* capitalism as well as totalitarian communism, introducing a third type of political economy based on democracy and freedom of the individual. In the 1980s, the Nordic countries and Holland also had a high rate of foreign aid to third world countries (Lundsgaarde 4). Furthermore, they felt obliged to receive refugees from countries all over the world, defending the human rights. However, this positive attitude towards immigrants from Africa and the Middle East has since changed in the twenty-first century towards a more hostile position (Widfeldt). This, of course, tells a lot about the self-image of Holland and the Nordic countries feeling morally superior to other nations.

Additionally, there is an exhibition of famous tourist attractions throughout the graphic novel. Superman flies into the Canals of Amsterdam (pp. 6–8). There is a view of the Little Mermaid statue (14), damage to the Copenhagen City Hall tower, and a visit to Tivoli (p. 17). Iceflower (Isblomst) attacks Superman at Frognerparken in Oslo, leading to the destruction of Gustav Vigeland's monolith (pp. 22–24). There is a glimpse of The Royal Palace in Stockholm (p. 29) and Superman flys by Stockholm City Hall tower (p. 30). In addition, the killer robot Wyatt demolishes the Sibelius Monument in Helsinki by throwing the Superman into the sculpture during their final fight (39–40). Normally, the readers of Superman would only witness American monuments and buildings and, of course, the fictional city of Metropolis. It strengthens patriotic self-esteem to see national monuments and buildings portrayed in a superhero comic with a strong brand even though they are shattered and rebuilt. Some people might even find it amusing, like when children feel the thrill of building and destroying sandcastles.

The reader is expected to already know Superman/Clark Kent and Lois Lane because their introduction is superficial. In Denmark, strips of Superman were translated in 1940 for the weekly magazine *Illustreret FamilieJournal* and later, in 1950, the first Superman comic was translated into Danish. Episodic narratives like Superman and many other superhero storylines make use of this approach. It is a break from Aristotelian poetics, insisting on the unity of the story (Aristotle). Though bear in mind, Aristotle created his theory for drama—not episodic narratives, e.g., Homer's *The Odyssey*. The producers of the graphic novel also expect the reader to know Lex Luthor as a villain and there is even a chance meeting with Jimmy Olsen wearing a Norwegian folk costume. Lois Lane encounters Jimmy Olsen at the hotel asking, "What are you doing here, and what kind of ridiculous outfit is that?" Jimmy answers, "Eh ... it is a family tradition. I am going to visit my aunt and uncle in Hardanger." Lois continues, "Do you have family here?" to which Jimmy replies, "Do you know any Olsen from Botswana?" (p. 21).

As an episodic narrative, it is important for the Superman character to stay the same (Eco and Chilton 16). If the character and plot develop too much, it will influence later episodes. This does not mean, however, the Superman character has been static. In fact, many writers have developed the character little by little and sometimes with significant changes. The arch-nemesis Lex Luthor received his first appearance in *Action Comics* #23 (Apr. 1940)—two years after Superman's initial release and the very same year that Superman got his ability to fly, which did not come from the comics but in the second episode of the radio serial *The Adventures of Superman*.

Additionally, this radio serial introduced kryptonite in 1943 (Tye 91, 109; Hayde). In *Action Comics* #300 (May 1963), readers learn that yellow sunlight activates all of his powers including strength and his powers deactivates by red sunlight akin to the sun of Krypton. Not all developments of the Superman universe work well and are therefore either forgotten or reversed. *Superman* #61 (Nov./Dec. 1949) introduced kryptonite to the comics' mythos, but kryptonite was initially red until two years later in *Action Comics* #161 (Oct. 1951) when it got its legendary green glow. Lots of different colored kryptonite appeared with distinctive effects on Superman but only the green kryptonite that makes Superman vulnerable has been consistent. This is only to show that Superman and his universe have not been static since its conception in 1938. Rather it is an innovative process over time based on the contributions of the various content providers.

In *Superman: A Tale of Five Cities*, two new female superhero characters are introduced. One is The Little Mermaid (Den Lille Havfrue) from Denmark, based in name only on the fairy-tale by Hans Christian Andersen; the other is Iceflower (Isblomst) from Norway. The Little Mermaid has telepathic powers. Because of her talent, she recognizes Theodore P. Wyatt as a robot; that is why the robot attacks her with a chainsaw. Fortunately, Superman saves her. Almost dead, she tries to warn Superman about Wyatt but cannot tell much else before passing out. Iceflower, the sister to the DC comics character Icemaiden (Isjomfruen), camouflages herself as a statue before attacking and defeating Superman because she believes he killed The Little Mermaid. Luckily, Icemaiden interferes before Iceflower can finish him off. Iceflower then reveals her powers to turn water molecules into ice in different colors as well as telekinetic powers that makes her able to lift heavy objects and have a forceful punch. Afterwards, she tries to hit on Superman but he disappears before she knows it. The reader also picks up that Iceflower's real name is Kari Nansen and that she is not very bright. That is why her more famous sister keeps her out of the Justice League.

Not to go into issues regarding intellectual property, the two characters, The Little Mermaid and Iceflower, are technically an official part of the DC universe but forgotten in time because the graphic novel did not get an English translation. Icemaiden, on the contrary, is an existing character in the DC universe. She first appeared in *Super Friends* #9 (Dec. 1977) as a blue, Norwegian superheroine with cryokinesis. Later, she reappeared in *Infinity Inc.* #32 (Nov. 1986). Her real name is Sigrid Nansen, and it makes sense that her sister Iceflower bears the name Kari Nansen. It gets a bit complicated because another character named Ice with magical ice powers takes over from Icemaiden. Her name is Tora Olafsdotter and she had her first appearance in *Justice League International* #12 (Apr. 1988). Just to complicate things even more, Ice for a while went by the name of Ice Maiden, taking over from the original Icemaiden. The sharp-witted reader would notice that Icemaiden has the appearance of Ice and the family name of the original Icemaiden. Therefore, the character Icemaiden (Isjomfruen) in *Superman: A Tale of Five Cities* is an amalgam of Icemaiden (Sigrid Nansen) and Ice (Tora Olafsdotter). Possibly, Niels Søndergaard and Teddy Kristiansen mixed up the two characters Icemaiden and Ice.

What is more important, though, is the fact that a character from *Justice League International* is present in *Superman: A Tale of Five Cities*. This is because while the visual arts and the plot is certainly inspired by Frank Miller's *Batman: The Dark Knight Returns*, the dialogue and the tone of the story is not. It is much more lighthearted, humorous, and witty. I have already shown some of this witty dialogue in Lois Lane's comment on protesters and Jimmy Olsen's on having Norwegian family. Another example is in the beginning of the graphic novel in Holland when Superman flies around, a man yells, "It's a bird!" a woman replies, "It's a plane!" and a child shouts, "It's a Flying Dutchman!" (p. 6). This joke of course paraphrases "Look! Up in the sky!" "It's a bird!" "It's a plane!" "It's

Superman!" from *The Adventures of Superman* radio show in the 1940s and the television series in the 1950s. Later, in Copenhagen, Tivoli, a man shouts, "Look! It is a bird!" and a woman replying, "No, it is a plane!" and a child yelling, "No, a space alien from another planet!" (p. 17).

Keith Giffen together with John Marc (J.M.) DeMatteis famously created the unorthodox humorous, lighthearted tone in *Legion of Substitute Heroes* from 1985 and continued the witty dialogue in *Justice League International* from 1987. *Legion of Substitute Heroes* was a group of rejected applicants to the *Legion of Super-Heroes*, trying to prove their special powers are not as useless as the Legionnaires claim. It is safe to assume that Niels Søndergaard and Teddy Kristiansen read *Justice League International*, because the title would be the natural choice to look for inspiration regarding Non-American superheroes such as Icemaiden. Consequently, Niels Søndergaard's witty dialogue in all probability found inspiration in Keith Giffen's *Justice League International*.

The main character in *Superman: A Tale of Five Cities* is of course Superman himself. Nevertheless, he surrounds himself with strong female characters. I will not say the graphic novel is a feminist manifesto. The theme of the story is nuclear war and if that ever happens then feminist concerns become less relevant. That said, there are some feminist issues present in the narrative. Lois Lane is the first female character the reader sets eyes on—even before Superman. She is a career woman, working as a reporter for *The Daily Planet*. She is madly in love with Superman and has no respect for Clark Kent. When Clark Kent shows up in Europe, she automatically assumes he wants to steal her scoop, reporting about the peace activist Theodore P. Wyatt and the peace bomb, especially because Clark Kent follows her through all five cities. When confronted with this in Copenhagen, Clark Kent answers, "I am here to visit a famous Danish … eh … astronaut." Of course, Denmark did not have a famous astronaut before 2015 when Andreas Mogensen journeyed to the International Space Station. Anyway, rather than being an active feminist, Lois Lane represents a professional woman with control of her life situation within the limits of middle-class lifestyle and norms (Roeder 37).

Readers do not really get to know The Little Mermaid. She is a mere plot device and damsel in distress. She does not really work as an example of liberated Scandinavian feminism. Nordic countries are considered the leaders on gender equality (Holli et al. 148). The difference between American feminism and Scandinavian feminism is that feminism is considered a part of the welfare model (Borchorst 30) and sexual openness with comprehensive sex education in public schools (Svendsen 139). In 1969, Denmark was the first country in the world to legalize visual pornography. Readers get to know Iceflower and Icemaiden better, and they represent super powers in the same league as Superman. Iceflower was truly subjugating Superman. The sisters are talented and empowered but has nothing to do with the actual plot and the reader is left wondering why they are depicted other than as bravura and Norwegian local color. From a Scandinavian feminist perspective, Iceflower is very open about her sexuality, telling Superman she is no longer a virgin when she unsuccessfully tries to seduce him.

The graphic novel passes the Bechdel test from the comic strip "Dykes to Watch Out For" by Alison Bechdel (Murphy). The Bechdel test states that a movie has to have: (1) at least two women in it, (2) who talk to each other, (3) about something besides a man. Lois Lane and Icemaiden have a short conversation without talking about a man but rather about Icemaiden's sister (p. 26). It is imperative to emphasize the test is not academic but originally meant as a joke and does not necessarily offer any insights into the overall content of the work in question. Nevertheless, it gives an impression of how bigoted a work is.

In 1988, in celebration of the 50th Anniversary of Superman, two Danes, Teddy Kristiansen and Niels Søndergaard, took the challenge to create a licensed official Superman graphic novel. It turned out to be a Dark Age comic with gritty visual arts inspired by Frank Miller and witty dialogue inspired Keith Giffen. The theme of the graphic novel was nuclear war and the Cold War and with unlucky timing, the graphic novel was published just after the fall of the Berlin Wall. The graphic novel presents the self-image of Holland and the Nordic countries during the late Cold War as humanitarian nations in a world on the brink of destruction, dependent on American military. This is symbolized through Superman in a double bind of at the same time being the protector of Western European democratic values and a dangerous alien being. That said, *Superman: A Tale of Five Cities* is a rare glimpse into the thoughts and feelings of late Cold War sentiment in a Northern Europe that could at any moment be at the brink of destruction.

Works Cited

Aristotle. *Poetics*. Irvine, CA: Xist Publishing, 2015 (c. 335 BC).
Bateson, Gregory. "Double Bind, 1969." *Steps to an Ecology of Mind*, edited by Gregory Bateson, University of Chicago Press, 2000, pp. 271–278.
Bertrand, Claude-Jean. "American Cultural Imperialism—A Myth?" *American Studies International*, Vol. 25, No. 1 Apr. 1987, pp. 46–60.
Borchorst, Anette. "Woman-friendly Policy Paradoxes? Childcare Policies and Gender Equality in Scandinavia." Melby, Ravn and Wetterberg. *Gender Equality and Welfare Politics in Scandinavia: The Limits of Political Ambition?* Bristol, UK: Policy Press, 2009.
Busiek, Kurt. "Introduction." *Kurt Busiek's Astro City: Life in the Big City*. Busiek (w), Brent Anderson (i), and Alex Ross (covers), Homage Comics, 1996, pp. 7–10.
Couch, N. C. "International Singularity in Sequential Art: The Graphic Novel in the United States, Europe and Japan." *Manga: An Anthology of Global and Cultural Perspectives*, edited by Toni Johnson-Woods, Continuum, 2010, pp. 204–220.
Eco, Umberto, and Natalie Chilton. "The Myth of Superman." *Diacritics*, Vol. 2, No. 1 Spring 1972, pp. 14–22.
Evan, William M. *The Arms Race and Nuclear War*. Prentice-Hall, 1987.
Fagan, Bryan D., and Jody Condit Fagan. *Comic Book Collections for Libraries*. Libraries Unlimited, 2011.
Farnsworth, Kevin. *Social versus Corporate Welfare: Competing Needs and Interests Within the Welfare State*. Palgrave MacMillan, 2012.
Hayde, Michael J. *Flights of Fantasy: The Unauthorized but True Story of Radio & TV's Adventures of Superman*. BearManor Media, 2016.
Holli, Anne Maria, et al. "Critical Studies of Nordic Discourses on Gender and Gender Equality." *NORA – Nordic Journal of Feminist and Gender Research*, Volume 13, 2005, pp. 148–153.
Holston, Alicia. "A Librarian's Guide to the History of Graphic Novels." *Graphic Novels and Comics in Libraries and Archives: Essays on Readers, Research, History and Cataloging*, edited by Robert G. Weiner, McFarland, 2010, pp. 9–16.
Jenkins, Henry. "'Just Men in Tights': Rewriting Silver Age Comics in an Era of Multiplicity." *The Contemporary Comic Book Superhero*, edited by Angela Ndalianis, Routledge, 2009, pp. 16–43.
Johnson, Jeffrey K. *Super-History: Comic Book Superheroes and American Society, 1938 to the Present*. McFarland, 2014.
Lundsgaarde, E. *The Domestic Politics of Foreign Aid*. New York: Routledge, 2013.
Murphy, Katherine J. "Analyzing Female Gender Roles in Marvel Comics from the Silver Age (1960) to the Present." *Discussions*, Vol. 12, No. 2, 2016.
O'Dell, Tom. *Culture Unbound: Americanization and Everyday Life in Sweden*. Lund: Nordic Academic Press, 1997.
Olesen, Thorsten B. *The Cold War and the Nordic Countries: Historiography at a Crossroads*. Odense: University Press of Southern Denmark, 2004.
Rhode, Michael, and Ray Bottorff, Jr. "The Grand Comics Database (GCD): An Evolving Research Tool." *International Journal of Comic Art*, 3:1 Spring 2001, pp. 263–74.
Roeder, Joshua. "Lois Lane: In Step with Second-wave Feminism." *Fairmount Folio: Journal of History #16*, 2015, pp. 36–48.

Svendsen, Stine H. Bang. "The Cultural Politics of Sex Education in the Nordics." *The Palgrave Handbook of Sexuality Education*, edited by Louisa Allen and Mary Lou Rasmussen, Palgrave-Macmillan, 2018, pp. 137–56.
Tye, Larry. *Superman: The High-Flying History of America's Most Enduring Hero*. Random House, 2012.
van Heuven, Marten. *The U.S. Role in Post-Cold War Europe*. RAND, 1994.
Voger, Mark. *The Dark Age: Grim, Great & Gimmicky Post-Modern Comics*. TwoMorrows Publ., 2006.
Widfeldt, Anders. *Extreme Right Parties in Scandinavia*. Routledge, 2015.

Superman vs. The Soap Opera

The Success of Lois & Clark:
The New Adventures of Superman

NICOLE FREIM

Introduction

In June 1938, Jerry Siegel and Joe Shuster's creation Superman entered the public consciousness for the first time in *Action Comics* #1. Brandishing a car overhead as he rescued Lois Lane from a gangster and fighting characters like an abusive husband and a corrupt senator, Superman jumped (not quite flying yet) into our lives. A man who is more than a man, Clark Kent joined the *Daily Planet* and set about living his double life in four-color glory. As this volume shows, the character of Superman is one of the most heavily adapted comic book characters to date. This may be because he was the first and so has a head start. Or it may be rooted in wish fulfillment fantasies; Superman is incredibly powerful, something many of us would like to be. The numerous appearances of the character may also lie in the core of who he is—a genuinely decent person who cares and continually strives to do what is right. While many of us wish we had more power in life, we can also respect a character who is a *good* person.

During Superman's history, another constant that anchors the character is his relationship with Lois Lane. Also introduced in *Action Comics* #1, Lois has been with Clark all along, evolving and changing with the times just as he did. The romantic triangle of Lois, Clark, and Superman was based for decades on Lois's yearning for Superman and Clark's yearning for Lois. Though this has varied over the years as each character had different storylines and love interests, these three characters are the heart of the story; their relationships are a large part of the characters' appeal.

Starting with the short cartoon films in 1941, Superman, Lois, and Clark have been on screen (large or small) in every decade. Changes, ranging from subtle to blinding, creep in to every production, just as the tone of the comics can shift with each new writer and storyline. While the films with Christopher Reeve were popular in the late '70s and early '80s and a television series centering on Superboy debuted in 1988, major changes were taking place in the character's comic. Superboy was eliminated in *Crisis on Infinite Earths* (Apr. 1985–Mar. 1986), and John Byrne rewrote Superman in his *Man of Steel* series (July–Sept. 1986). After the success of *Watchmen* (Sept. 1986–Oct. 1987) and *The Dark Knight Returns* (Feb.–June 1986), the overall tone of the comics industry was shifting into a darker and grittier world. While this bled into film, as seen with Tim Burton's *Batman* (1989), the character of Superman had always been seen as a bit of a goody-two-shoes. A slightly dark turn for the character did occur in *Superman III* (1983), with the junkyard fight between Clark and an "evil" Superman being the highlight of the film, but that film did fail miserably. So how to create a fresh take on the character for audiences?

In the early 90s, Warner Bros. started to develop a new television series for Superman, heavily influenced by Byrne's version of the character. Comic book historian Les Daniels notes in his book *Superman: The Complete History* (1998) that then-DC president Jeanette Kahn "had been working for years to sell the concept for a new kind of Superman program"—with the working title *Lois Lane's Daily Planet* (166). This series, ultimately called *Lois & Clark: The New Adventures of Superman* (1993–1997; hereafter *L&C*), was helmed by Deborah Joy LeVine, a woman who had not read any Superman comics. In the documentary "From Rivals to Romance: The Making of *Lois and Clark*," LeVine talks about how she did not want to write a show about Superman but said she "wouldn't mind writing a romantic comedy called Lois and Clark." This approach may be what helped the series be initially successful and be seen as reinvigorating for the characters. Teri Hatcher, who played Lois Lane on *L&C*, says in the same documentary that LeVine wrote a pilot about two characters, and it was almost "secondary that they were Lois and Superman." LeVine's approach was just the vision needed for the decades old characters.

While an emphasis on romance was not new—Lois has always been smitten with Superman and Clark has always been smitten with Lois—reorienting the romance to Lois and Clark allowed the show to present a new take on the old story. Lois became a leading figure in her own right: strong, skilled, and unapologetically feminist. Clark (Dean Cain) became the other main character, a charming, handsome, kind, and eminently dateable leading man. Superman became the means to an end for Clark to help where he can. The lighter tone of a romantic comedy and a strong supporting cast let the writers and producers revel in a soap opera atmosphere for the show. Indeed, comic book characters are perfect for the outlandish events often associated with soap operas; the emphasis on romance fits into that genre as well, paving the way for additional romantic rivals and dramatic turns of events. These key shifts in telling a (by now) familiar story—the soap-opera nature and plots, the emphasis on strong female characters and feminist stories, and prioritizing the character of Clark over Superman—were the secret to producing a vision of the characters that was and remains quite popular.

Superheroes as Soap Operas

In the mid-twentieth century, the introduction of the television helped to give rise to the genre of the soap opera. These serial stories, which played during the day and focused largely on family and relationships to target female viewers, came to be called soap operas due to the commercials for cleaning products often played during the shows, something started back when these types of programs were radio dramas. This could also be viewed as the natural progression from works like those of Charles Dickens, which were published in serial form, often with dramatic endings to chapters in order to keep audiences eager for the next installment. (Plus, the longer he could stretch the story out, the more money Charles could make from the publication.)

Comic books are similar in that regard; the monthly titles center on a few main characters but often have large supporting casts and weave multiple narratives through a single issue and develop those narratives over the course of months. Indeed, one website devoted to television tropes argues that soap operas are the "distaff counterpart to comic books"—meaning the "feminine" version of comic books (the sexism in that idea is the topic for another paper)—and points out that Marvel Comics and *Guiding Light* had a "crossover comic book made in 2006" ("Soap Opera"). One of the main characters, Harley Davidson Cooper (Beth Ehlers), has an accident which gives her light and electrical superpowers. After putting on a costume and taking the codename Guiding Light, a short eight-page comic book commemorated this event. George Gustines wrote in *The New York Times* about the unique crossover and mentions that it "certainly helped that David Kreizman, the head writer of *Guiding Light*, is a longtime comics fan." While more of a pet project than an attempt to get new viewers for the show, the blend of the two genres does help underscore how similar they are.

Following LeVine's inclination to write *L&C* as a romantic comedy, the show leaned into some of the more common soap opera tropes, most of which had little to do with Superman's powers. Kidnapping happens repeatedly; Lois, Clark, Martha Kent (K. Callan), Jonathan Kent (Eddie Jones), Perry White (Lane Smith), Jimmy Olsen (Michael Landes/Justin Whalin), and Lex Luthor (John Shea) all experience this trauma at some point, though Lois more often than the others. Lois also survives frequent assassination attempts, and people who seem dead return from the grave—including Lex, Lois, and Clark at varying times. After Lois and Clark have gotten engaged in the third season, the episode "Chip Off the Old Clark" tests their relationship with the appearance of Superman's supposed "lovechild"—causing Lois to doubt Clark's honor and integrity; the child is later shown to have received Superman's powers through an accidental transfer and they fade. Two of Lex's illegitimate children, Jaxon Xavier (Andy Berman) in season 3 ("Virtually Destroyed") and Lex Luthor, Jr. (Keith Brunsman) in season 4 ("Faster than a Speeding Vixen," "Shadow of a Doubt," and "Voice from the Past"), show up hoping to avenge their father, though neither succeed. The end of season three sees the appearance of Clark's long-lost wife Zara (Justine Bateman), the woman from Krypton who was "promised" to him at birth. The band of Kryptonians looking to establish New Krypton want Clark as their leader, and this causes a delay in his wedding to Lois and a temporary split for the couple ("Big Girls Don't Fly"). A former boyfriend, Patrick Sullivan (Julian Stone), arrives in town and pursues Lois, later trying to sacrifice her in a Druidic ritual ("When Irish Eyes Are Killing"). Both Superman and Lois are sent to jail; Superman for contempt of court in season one's "The Man of Steel Bars" and Lois in season four for murder in "The People vs Lois Lane." After Lois is sentenced to death, Clark helps her escape to prove her innocence ("Dead Lois Walking"). Kidnappings, previously unknown children and spouses, jealous exes, sudden resurrections, and death sentences are fairly par for the course in soap operas.

One often-used soap opera plot point—amnesia—afflicted both Lois and Clark. In season one's "All Shook Up," Superman is knocked back to Earth after trying to destroy a huge meteor on course to devastate the planet. The impact gives Clark amnesia and he spends the episode trying to remember who he is and what exactly his relationship with Lois is while everyone else wonders what happened to Superman. Lois gets amnesia in season three, though she has it as part of a five-episode arc. She hits her head in "Double

Jeopardy" and winds up thinking she is a character in the novel she is writing; Lex plays along and attempts to convince her that he is the man she loves ("Seconds"). Superman rescues her from that but then has to check Lois into a hospital, where she winds up falling for Dr. Maxwell Deter (Larry Poindexter), who is treating her and who uses a bit of hypnosis on her to convince her that she loves him ("Forget Me Not"). Finally, in "Oedipus Wrecks," a villain's mind control machine is able to jog loose her memories, and Lois and Clark's love is restored.

Another common standby for maximum drama is the evil twin trope. While L&C didn't use this in the strict sense of a birth twin, the show did make use of it several times. Lex manages to clone Superman and raises the clone as his "son" with the philosophy "might makes right" and the "old Superman has outlived his usefulness" and must be killed. Superman manages to befriend the clone, who dies (clones sadly have short life spans) without telling Lex about Clark's true identity ("Vatman"). Lois had to deal with imposters twice. The first time, Lex's ex-wife Arianna Carlin (Emma Samms) is looking for revenge on Lois for letting Lex fall to his supposed death. Arianna has a double of Lois made with the help of plastic surgery in order to discredit Lois and make her appear crazy when she denies doing things her double has been seen doing ("Madame Ex"). The more complicated version happens when Lois gets amnesia in season three. Before the accident which causes the amnesia, she had been kidnapped by Lex and replaced with a clone, who then married Clark in Lois's place. After being found out, the clone attempts to convince Clark that because she learns fast, she can be just as good as the "real" Lois if he gives her the chance to learn ("Seconds"). He declines since there can only be one Lois. All these identity struggles heighten tension and give the viewer the chance to see and understand what makes up the essence of the character as they rediscover themselves.

In classic soap opera fashion, L&C also has a handsome, charismatic villain masquerading as a hero. The show goes one step further than Byrne's Man of Steel, which changed Lex Luthor from a mad scientist into a powerful and wealthy businessman. Although that version of Lex was also interested in Lois romantically, she knew that he was a person of questionable morals and so rejected him. In order to ratchet up the tension, L&C depicts Lex as a romantic lead—with a full head of hair. Executive producer Robert Singer described John Shea, the actor who played Lex, as "handsome, romantic, and erudite." Teri Hatcher talked about this Lex being sexy and evil at the same time. Shea pointed out, "of course Lex is rich enough to cure baldness"—though he did sport a polished dome in his seasons two and three appearances after his hair fell out from the process of being revived from death ("From Rivals…"). Viewers learn in the first episode that Lex is not what he seems. The pilot revolves around a proposed space shuttle launch that may be sabotaged, and the viewers—and Superman—know that Lex is behind the plot, as well as the murder of the scientist working for him. Lois, however, remains in the dark. Even Lex admits in a later episode that his persona is a facade; when his assistant pretends to be Lex for a meeting and says afterwards, "it's not easy playing you," Lex responds, "Nonsense. I do it every day" ("Barbarians at the Planet"). Presenting Lex in this way lets the audience root more for Clark, wanting the average nice-guy persona to triumph over the villainous one-percenter. Mike Carlin, an editor at DC Comics, describes the contrast in characters as being about what you do with what you have: "if you try to do good, you're Superman. If you do bad, you're Lex Luthor" ("From Rivals…"). Letting the audience in on the real situation makes Lex's eventual demise more satisfying.

The biggest perk, however, of portraying Lex as handsome and charismatic is that it paves the way for the soapiest aspect of the show—the romantic triangles. Audiences familiar with the story are prepared for the love triangle of Clark adoring Lois who shuns him and adores Superman, who cannot be with her lest she discover his secret. Comics scholar Gerard Beritela takes the view that it is "this convoluted triangle of romance, deception, and irony that fuels the human interest of the early stories, and it is this same triangle that significantly changes over the decades as a reflection" of issues in society (52). Indeed, *L&C* took that triangle, spun it around, and exploded it into a bunch of other triangles. That dynamic between Clark-Lois-Superman is there to an extent, but the portrayal of both Clark and Lex as charming, eligible bachelors and expanding the cast to include plenty of young, attractive romantic possibilities for men and women lets the show dial up the interpersonal tension. In the pilot episode, when Lois and Clark are talking to a female scientist, Dr. Antionette "Toni" Baines (Kim Johnston Ulrich), the woman clearly softens in her willingness to answer their questions thanks to Clark's attractiveness—so much so that Lois rolls her eyes over it. In "Pheromone, My Lovely," Morgan Fairchild plays the chemist Miranda, who is in love with Lex and tries to remove Lois as her competition. Cat Grant (Tracy Scoggins) spends multiple episodes trying to land a date with Clark; when she first sees him, she whistles, asking Lois, "Who's the new tight end?" Lois replies with "Why don't you throw your usual forward pass and find out?" ("Pilot"). Cat does get him back to her apartment once, but nothing happens.

The main love triangle for the first season is more of a square: Clark is pining for Lois while Lois is pining for Superman—and dating Lex Luthor. Rather than trying to choose between a "god in tights" and a nebbish colleague, this Lois is pursued by a handsome billionaire philanthropist, as Lex appears, and a handsome, intelligent, genuinely decent, talented reporter. Dramatic irony lets the audience know that Lex is really a villain and not the man Lois should be with, helping us root for Clark while acknowledging the appeal of Lex's persona. Lois pursues Lex in the beginning, although from a professional standpoint. Starting with the pilot, Lois is determined to land the first one-on-one interview with the reclusive, wealthy Lex Luthor "if it kills" her. Meeting at a charity ball that Lex is giving, Lois, hair upswept elegantly, dressed in a dark blue ball gown with a deep neckline, confronts him:

> LOIS: "Lex Luthor. (beat) Why haven't you returned my call? Lois Lane, Daily Planet."
> LEX (KISSING HER HAND): "Well, I can assure you I'll never make that mistake again" ["Pilot"]

While they dance, Lex says he "finds boldness attractive" but that he's hesitant to give interviews since he's had "bad experiences" with the media. Lois looks him directly in the eye and says, "but not with me" and Lex asks her to dinner. Sadly, Clark then cuts in, earning a dirty look from Lois as she was getting so close to her dream. But the viewers can understand Clark's impulse as Lex's first appearance did come off a bit smarmy. However, as Lois fails to fall immediately under his spell, Lex becomes more enamored of her as the season wears on. Lex spends season one wooing Lois and finally—after covertly ruining the *Daily Planet* and breaking her away from her friends—convincing her to marry him; she does, however, say no at the altar. When he returns in seasons two and three, he is still obsessed with Lois; "winning" her back and killing Superman are his two purposes in life.

Clark is also smitten with Lois from the first as she barges in to Perry's office during Clark's interview; after Clark finally gets the job, Perry pairs them for a story. Lois had asked for a task force and instead gets "a hack from Smallville—I couldn't make that name up." As Lois and Clark are leaving the newsroom, she lays down the rules:

> LOIS: "I did not work my buns off to become an investigative reporter for the *Daily Planet* just to babysit some hack from nowheresville. And one other thing, you are not working with me—you are working for me. I call the shots, I ask the questions. You are low man—I am top banana—and that's the way I like it. Comprende?"
> CLARK: "You like to be on top. Got it."
> LOIS [GLARING]: "Don't push me, Kent. You are way out of your league." ["Pilot"].

As they get on the elevator, Clark is smiling. The tension increases from there. During a late night in the newsroom over Chinese food [that is startlingly hot and tastes amazingly authentic, almost like it was flown in from China], Lois says she thinks she has Clark figured out. But as they exchange a steamy look, she follows with, "Don't fall for me, farm boy. I don't have time for it" ("Pilot"). She may not want to have time for it, but the sparks are flying all the same.

During the course of the season, we see more moments between the two of them. In one episode, both of them wind up undercover at a night club owned by the mob. The Taylor mob family is having a power struggle between brother Johnny (Michael Milhoan) and sister Toni (Jessica Tuck) as to who should take over. Clark blows Lois's cover in order to keep his own intact and later asks if she was jealous about Toni. When Lois gets home, she is ranting to herself, "Jealous? Ha! That'll be the day! Like I really care." As she sits digging into a carton of ice cream, she says out loud that she is jealous (though this seems to surprise her). Lex, who saw Lois sing at the club, turns up at her door and tells her that she was magnificent: "It was the real you—passionate, sultry, seductive," before giving her a kiss on the cheek and a longing stare. At the end of the episode, Clark asks Lois to tell him "honestly" if she wasn't "the slightest bit jealous of me and Toni?" Lois replies, "You'd like that, wouldn't you? Me, home alone in a schlumpy robe crying into a tub of rocky road" over him and tells him it would only happen in his dreams ("I've Got a Crush on You"). Between Lois's realization of her jealousy over Clark and the intense looks between Lois and Lex, this episode was fraught with tension.

The love triangle of Lois, Lex, and Superman comes to a head when Lex proposes to Lois towards the end of season one. She asks for time to think it over, but in this process, she wants to talk to Superman. She confesses to him that she is totally in love with him (something she is sure he has guessed) and asks if there is any chance for them. Superman hangs his head and sighs. Although Lois assures him that she would still love him "even if you were just a regular person," Superman/Clark clearly doubts that. His rejection sends her to accept Lex's proposal; after watching from outside while she puts on the engagement ring, Superman flies off to the Arctic to scream in anguish ("Barbarians at the Planet"). As Clark and the gang are gathering evidence that Lex was responsible for the *Daily Planet* going under, Clark also confesses to Lois that he is in love with her. She rejects him at the time, but later, as she is standing in her wedding gown and crying, she tries out names like "Mrs. Lex Luthor" and "Lois Lane Luthor" before landing on "Lois Lane.... Kent." When she arrives at the altar, she tries to answer "I do" but winds up saying she can't—right before the wedding is interrupted by police arriving to arrest Lex (an interrupted wedding being yet another soap opera trope). Later, Lois does try to admit her feelings to Clark, but he says he would have said anything to stop her wedding, while crossing his fingers behind his back to make up for this lie, and they agree to be friends ("The House of Luthor").

In the second season, Lois and Clark start dating, which had its own set of problems, not least of which were Clark's frequent departures to deal with Superman-related crises. But the show also introduced competing love interests for each character. As competition for Lois, Mayson Drake (Farrah Forke) arrives. She is a city attorney who has a wild crush on Clark—and little regard for Superman. When speaking with Superman, Mayson points out that he is not a member of the police force, he does not read criminals their Miranda rights, and he's a vigilante who operates outside the law. She asks Clark out repeatedly, including for a weekend getaway to a cabin in the woods. Clark misses that meeting since he, as Superman, is dealing with temporary blindness—which is also quite a soap opera thing to happen ("The Eyes Have It"). As the season goes on, eventually Clark has to confess that while he cares for Mayson, he cares for Lois as well. Mayson says she knows he is hiding something from her, and at the end of the episode, as she is dying from a bomb exploding in her car, she sees the Superman suit under his shirt and realizes that is what he's been hiding ("Lucky Leon"). While investigating Mayson's death, Lois and Clark encounter Dan Scardino (Jim Pirri), a government agent who chases Lois for multiple episodes. The character was young and handsome, and while he was known as a loose cannon, even Clark has to admit that Dan is also a highly decorated agent. Unlike Clark, Dan is not constantly darting away from dates with Lois. Lois began dating him after getting fed up with Clark's disappearances ("Target: Jimmy Olsen!"). However, by the end of the season, she says goodbye to Dan and even tells Superman that she is giving up on her dream of him—so that she can focus on her relationship with Clark.

Overall, the problems of the show feel closer to those of a soap opera than of a drama. Relationship problems only last for a few episodes. Difficulties like evil twins or kidnappings or a murderous ex are generally resolved fairly quickly. While the show does contain serious moments and some serious messages, it lacks the tone and intensity of contemporaneous dramas like *Law and Order* (1990–2010) or *ER* (1994–2009). Not everything is played for laughs, but the viewers know that, as in comic books, the hero will triumph. And in this case, Lois and Clark are the heroes. We know that their relationship will come through and they will be okay, no matter what life throws at them.

The Feminist Mystique

Lois Lane has always been something of a feminist. Making her debut in *Action Comics #1* alongside Clark and Superman, she responds to Clark's date invitation in that issue with a rousing "I suppose I'll give you a break ... for a change" (Siegel and Shuster 6). When gangster Butch tries to cut in on their dance, Clark wants her to simply dance with the man; he's trying to adhere to his "role of a weakling." Lois replies, "You can stay and dance with him but I'm leaving now!" Butch responds that she'll dance with him and like it, which prompts Lois to slap him in the face (7). Sadly, this does get her kidnapped by three thugs and in need of rescue by Superman, but that's beside the point. Lois has always been a character willing to stand up for herself. And considering that she's been a career woman from the start, this intrepid journalist is something of a standout among non-powered supporting characters in comic books.

The second wave of feminism was strong through the 1960s and 1970s, which is when Margot Kidder's Lois Lane appeared (Reger xvi). In 1978's *Superman*, Lois speaks with Perry as an equal, talks circles around Clark, refuses to give in to a mugger, and figures out that Clark is Superman. As the backlash to the second wave hit in the 1980s, the new version of Lois might have been toned down a bit to more of the damsel-in-distress trope. But the 1990s were kicking off the third wave of the feminist movement (Reger xvi). *L&C* builds on the feminist slant of previous incarnations to seed bits of woman power throughout the entire show. While Lois is clearly a feminist and there are a few strongly feminist themed episodes, some of the flavor comes in subtle forms—including in the villains and female actors playing parts ranging from single episode appearances to supporting characters—which adds to the way the series embraces feminism.

In comics, often the villains match the hero. If the main character is female, she may have more female villains than a male hero would. The majority of Superman's villains in the comics are male. But this show has a higher percentage of female villains; in 88 episodes, approximately 22 episodes feature women as the primary villain or as part of a husband-and-wife team. Some of these women are out for revenge (like a woman scorned), and others are after power. Lois does fight and/or outthink several of these—just as she does with some of the male villains. Most of the female villains are shown to be clever and skilled. We see scientists who use their creations for such ends as stealing Superman's powers ("Ultra Woman"), turning regular people into assassins ("Target: Jimmy Olsen!"), and shrinking people and keeping them in a cage ("It's a Small World After All"). Intergang, the mob-like organization which is trying to take over Metropolis and the world, is originally run by a father and son, Bill Church, Sr. (Peter Boyle) and Bill Church, Jr. (Bruce Campbell). The father remarries to the young, attractive, blonde Mindy (Jessica Collins), who wears skin tight dresses and high heels and speaks in a childlike way. The tables soon turn, though, and we find out that it is all an act as Mindy frames both father and son so that she can take over Intergang ("We Have a Lot to Talk About"). This is not to say that the male villains are not also clever and skilled, but it is nice to see the women able to formulate their own plans and weapons rather than simply borrowing them from men.

A number of background characters—people who appear in one or two episodes—are women in positions of power and authority. In the first episode, the scientist in charge of the space shuttle launch, Dr. Baines, is a woman who considers herself on par with Lex; it does get her killed, but that's no different than many male villains ("Pilot"). When a heat wave in November is argued to be linked to Superman's use of powers, Dr. Katherine Goodman (Elaine Kagan) helps Lois figure out that the real culprit is Lex's power plant ("Man of Steel Bars"). Before the culprit is revealed, Metropolis sought an injunction against Superman to stop using his powers, and in the courtroom, Judge Angela Diggs (Rosalind Cash) is played by an African American woman and the prosecutor (Haunani Minn) by a Hawaiian woman ("The Man of Steel Bars"). In "Wall of Sound," the current mayor of Metropolis, Mayor Sharpe (Pamela Roberts), is a woman, and in "Chi of Steel," the Robin Hood figure who is a martial arts master is initially believed to be a man but is an Asian woman, Lin Chow (Leila Lee Olsen). Mayson Drake, a prosecutor for the city, takes the initiative several times to ask Clark out, trying to be more assertive in going after what she wants. Cat Grant's character is unabashedly forward about reveling in her femininity and her enjoyment of physical pleasures.

In "The Ides of Metropolis," the officer hunting down an escaped murderer (albeit wrongly convicted) is a woman, Detective Betty Reed (Melanie Mayron). Reed and Lois do have a scene where they fight briefly, throwing a few kicks at each other, and another where they have been captured and are talking to pass the time. During this,

Reed mentions how the police force is "a boys' club" and Lois says, "tell me about it." The women then share admiration—Reed says she wishes she could get her hair to do that curl and flip thing that Lois's does. Lois volunteers that she wishes she could get her nails to look as good as Reed's—and is astonished when Reed admits they are press-on nails available at LexMart. While this conversation about hair and nails might seem less than empowering, the fact that the women can be proud of their looks is a plus. Not to mention that they break out of their confinement and apprehend the villains without Superman's help.

Martha Kent is also quite a strong character, capable of many things, including fixing Clark's kitchen sink ("The Source"). She takes a variety of adult education classes and explores different types of hobbies. While her husband rolls his eyes and complains about a lack of home cooked meals since "your mother has become an ar-teest," Martha proudly displays her metal sculpture: "I call it 'Too Much Too Soon Tortured Heart Waning Moon.' What do you think—too cerebral?" and Clark responds that it is very creative ("Pilot"). Martha dabbles in painting—and allows the instructor to paint a nude portrait of her, which later causes Jonathan to worry that she's having an affair ("Ides of Metropolis"). Another class works with lasers to create art, a skill which allows her to create a hologram of Superman and help him to be "present" at the same time as Clark—saving him when someone has found out Superman's secret identity ("Top Copy"). She also has modern sensibilities; when she is helping Clark with his costume, she says, "one thing's for sure—no one's going to be looking at your face." When Clark protests, she points out, "Well, they don't call them tights for nothing" and she hugs him ("Pilot"). When Jonathan and Martha are kidnapped, Martha is the one searching the room for ways out ("And the Answer Is..."). Martha is in many ways an older role model for Lois—a woman who is married and happy and yet still has her own goals and life.

With her top billing on the show, Lois is naturally the heart of the feminist statements being made on *L&C*. The lovely Teri Hatcher—known before this for small roles in television and film, including a spot on *Seinfeld* for an episode which revolved around the question of whether her very attractive breasts were the result of implants ("The Implant")—first appears on screen in disguise as a man. The camera goes from top to bottom revealing her knit cap, mustache and beard, flannel shirt, pea coat, jeans, and work boots. The first thing she does is drop her bag at her desk and reach under her shirt with scissors to cut off a bandage which has been concealing her breasts. Her first line to Jimmy as she hands over some film is "I nailed them cold" and she proceeds to shake out her hair and grin widely. The next camera shot pans up from the floor, showing Lois has changed into heels with ankle straps, hose, a skirt slit to above the knee, blouse and suit jacket, and perfectly done makeup and sleek hair. She is walking into the newsroom, into a celebration of her story exposing a million-dollar car theft ring. When Jimmy says, "I still can't believe they thought you were a boy," Lois replies, "the mustache helped—and thanks for showing me how to boost a car." Jimmy proposes a toast "to Lois Lane—going where no reporter has gone before" ("Pilot").

This introduction sets up Lois's character fairly well. She will stop at nothing to get a story; going undercover as a man fazes her not at all. During what may be the most feminist episode of the series, Lois goes undercover as a man in order to get into Perry White's men's club. The doorman would not let her in, and she would not let Clark go in without her, claiming "If you go in there without me, it's as if you're saying there's nothing wrong with this kind of discrimination" ("Chi of Steel"). Perry is distraught that Lois, in a suit with a fake mustache again, managed to get into his club, traipse all about, and even use the restroom. In this same episode, Lois is visiting a martial arts studio and comments that she has studied karate and tai chi and would love to take a class—only to be told that women are not allowed in the master classes. The episode also features Lois having a dream about the men at the *Planet* sending her for coffee, the granddaughter of the martial arts master as the Robin Hood figure helping people, and Martha and Jonathan switching chores to demonstrate how much Martha does. Placed halfway through the second season, the episode pulled into sharp focus some of the issues that women face.

Despite her willingness to cross-dress, Lois is still coiffed, attractive, and quite feminine. Most of her outfits evoke a classic look which Hatcher described as "20's and 40's–*His Girl Friday*" sort of style ("From Rivals…"). Her skirts do get shorter in the second season, and Lois is not afraid to work her feminine assets to get a story. When she goes undercover at a nightclub, she gets the part of a chorus girl easily. Mob boss Johnny is auditioning dancers/singers and calls out for the girl in the back, "yeah you—with the legs," to come forward. Lois, clad in a white button-down shirt opened low, black hot pants, and heels, strolls forward in a seductive manner—which is all it takes for Johnny to hire her ("I've Got a Crush on You"). She also dons a red suit which is cut to show the lace of her camisole and features a short skirt with black hose and high heels when she goes to interview a scientist who is a notorious womanizer.

> CAT: "That explains the vain attempt to look sexy."
> CLARK: "Are you planning to exploit your femininity to get the interview—"
> LOIS: "Of one of the strangest and most reclusive scientists of our time? You bet" (leaves with an exaggerated hip swivel) ["Witness"].

Lois also dresses in black leather to get close to a rock star after she figures out that he's into "trashy brunettes" ("Wall of Sound"). While she may not use her attractiveness as a weapon often, she knows it's there, she's secure in it, and she will use it if she needs to. And she enjoys her femininity. When the Prankster (Bronson Pinchot) freezes everyone in the newsroom, Lois's dress is removed and put on Jimmy, and she is left in her lingerie, posed with a cigarette ("Return of the Prankster"). Lingerie under the work clothes is a subtle comment on her underlying sensuality.

The damsel-in-distress epithet has often been applied to Lois Lane. While this Lois is frequently put in danger, she does not always wait for Superman to save her. She is a fighter, routinely engaging in light combat: kicking her assailants, tripping them, and wrestling away weapons. She does not merely sit tied to a chair and wait to be rescued; she engages the enemy when she can. When she has been kidnapped by the Prankster and his associate (who is wildly in love with her), she manages to disable the men. She is holding a gun on the criminals when Superman shows up and says, "I guess you don't need me." Lois replies, "Not this time, but don't go far, big fella" ("The Prankster"). She also becomes a superhero when an incident with red kryptonite transfers Superman's powers to her. Martha helps her with a costume (pink and aqua—and including a domino mask), and Superman awkwardly introduces her as "Ultra-gir … uh, woman. Ultra Woman." After spending a few days in Superman's boots, Lois comes to appreciate the tough choices he has to make. That episode also features a story from Jonathan and Martha about the time he was laid up from back surgery; Martha went out, got a job as a secretary and ended up running the whole office with two secretaries of her own ("Ultra Woman"). Lois takes the initiative to help Superman when he needs it; often Lois is the one figuring out what exactly is going on and giving Clark the information he needs to be able to stop the villain.

Aside from her appearance and her fighting skills, Lois's personality is both feminist and feminine. The first episode shows us Lois at home, in bed, watching a sappy romance called "The Ivory Tower" and crying over the show. A few episodes later, a woman comes to Lois for help, saying, "You spoke at my women's group last October—'The Weaker Sex: Fact or Fiction.' It was a terrific speech" ("I'm Looking Through You"). Lois is both emotional and strong. Once Lois and Clark get engaged, she contemplates changing her name; Perry even gives her a name plate for her desk which reads "Lois Kent." Lois pairs it with the name plate she already has, viewing the two and trying the combination of Lois Lane Kent. In the end, she keeps her name, telling Clark that she's worked hard for her reputation and is fond of Lois Lane. Clark agrees with her decision, saying that he's fond of Lois Lane, too ("It's a Small World After All"). Her reputation is at the forefront of much of the series; she wins various writing prizes, gets a promotion to editor in chief, and is the only reporter to land an interview with the President when he visits Metropolis ("Return of the Prankster"). She is a bit consumed with her own greatness, though, and can barely manage to be gracious when Clark is nominated for an award that she assumed she would be nominated for. Since they had made plans to go to the awards dinner together (back when Clark thought he would be her plus one), Lois reluctantly agrees to be his date. Afterwards, she asks for a report.

> LOIS: "So how did I rate as a date?"
> CLARK: "Oh, A+."
> LOIS: "I hung on your arm decoratively."
> CLARK: "You did."
> LOIS: "Fawned appropriately."
> CLARK: "Absolutely."
> LOIS: "And just faded into the background during your big moment."
> CLARK: "You were beautiful yet invisible."
> LOIS: "Mm—make me go through another night like that, and I'll rip out your spleen" ["Wall of Sound"].

Lois's drive to be the best shows her as her own fully realized character, with or without a man. Her strength comes out the most, however, in her love life. In the beginning of the series, she is a bit of a stereotype. LeVine wanted her to have a lousy social life as a sort of commentary: "she's worked herself up to the top and now what does she have? She's alone in her apartment, dreaming of a man in a cape" ("From Rivals..."). Hatcher also thinks of Lois as someone who has a secret identity in that "she's not presenting her true self either. She's this 'I've got it all handled—I can do everything—I'm in control' persona where inside, she's a lonely, needy, 'I need to be loved' person" ("From Rivals..."). While this perspective of Lois may be true in the beginning, as the show goes on, she develops a mastery of her emotions. Season one Lois says yes to marrying Lex because she gets swept up in his power and charm. Season Two Lois takes the scary step of being the one to admit how she really feels; she tells Dan Scardino and Superman that she is letting go of both of them because Clark is the one she really wants to be with ("Whine, Whine, Whine"). Season Two ends with Clark asking her to marry him, and Season Three starts off with Lois saying "who's asking—Clark or Superman?" ("We Have a Lot to Talk About"). She tells him that she cannot marry him because she just figured out that he is Superman and wants time to think. At the end of the episode, their relationship is back on—but not at marriage level yet. Two episodes later, Clark breaks up with her for her own safety, worried that she will be targeted by Superman's enemies ("Contact"). A single episode after that, which features one of Lois's ex-boyfriends, Clark realizes that he doesn't want to be without her (not to mention that she can find plenty of dangerous situations on her own), and he tries to get back together with her. Despite her feelings for him, Lois stands firm and says no. She points out that it might be temporary, and if he thought it was "for the best," he would break up with her again. She is wise enough to know that she could not survive having him break her heart again ("When Irish Eyes Are Killing"). This takes a strength of character and level of self-awareness that season one Lois didn't have. Choosing to make the best decision for herself, even if it is painful, shows how far Lois has come.

Lois represents strong women in every sense of the word. From her success at work to her ability to stand up for herself to doing what's best for her regardless of how much it hurts in the moment, Lois embodies a new feminist role model. The show supports this with characters like Martha Kent and Cat Grant and dozens of other small parts that could have been cast as men but were instead given to women. This is actually embracing more realism since women are half the population.

Clark and His Imaginary Friend, Superman

For years, the standard view was that Superman was the important character while Clark Kent was a necessary evil which Superman endured in order to achieve his goals. In *The Myth of the American Superhero* (2002), John Shelton Lawrence and Robert Jewett describe Superman as "the redemptive god with superhuman strength" and Clark as the "plebeian alter ego" within the "bounds of democratic ordinariness" (42). While the character has undergone many changes over the years (let's not even get into the ridiculousness of all the different kryptonites), that particular perspective probably depends a lot on who is writing the comic. After the ending of *Crisis on Infinite Earths* wiped out many characters developed by DC Comics over nearly fifty years, the editors began looking for a writer who could helm the flagship character of Superman. In 1986, writer/artist John Byrne began his mini-series *The Man of Steel*. Daniels writes about this new direction for the character as more of a return to some old ideas that had been lost or altered over the decades. Byrne wanted to "return to Siegel and Shuster's original idea that Clark Kent didn't put on the costume until he was grown" (159). This revamp also eliminated such things as Superboy, Supergirl, the Super Pets, and the death of the Kents. While not all of Byrne's proposed alterations made it into the comic, the series was a wild success. Lex Luthor was no longer a mad scientist but a crafty, corrupt businessman, partly based on Donald Trump (Cronin). Lois Lane became a weight-lifting, fashionable ace reporter. Along with these changes, Byrne wanted to make Clark cooler and more important than Superman. The writer's view was "Clark Kent was who he really was, who he'd been most of his life. Superman was just a red and blue suit he wore" (Daniels 161). This view of the character would be conscripted for the show *L&C*, and was the last key to making the show a success.

As evidenced by receiving billing above Superman, the character of Clark Kent was central to the soap opera romance designed to catch a new crop of viewers. Unlike the future series *Smallville* (2001–2011), which refused to put Clark into the red-and-blue outfit, *L&C* embraced the idea right away. Martha Kent sews the suit for Clark in the pilot episode, but as in that episode and the majority of others, Superman is a secondary character. Dean Cain, who played Clark, switched the style of Christopher Reeve's Superman, styling Superman's hair with the severe, slicked back look and keeping the tousled, sexy look for Clark. This Clark was not mild-mannered or awkward; he was more than a match for the spunky Lois Lane. And viewers saw right away that Clark was definitely super without the red suit. When Lois arrives at Clark's dingy rented room to pick him up, he's clad only in a towel. Her shock is apparent, and after getting a good look at his bare, muscled chest, says, "I said nine. I thought you'd be naked—um, ready." Clark explains that he was on the phone and excuses himself to get dressed ("Pilot"). This is not the only time we get shots to satisfy the female gaze; when Mayson Drake comes to Clark's apartment to go over his testimony, she is similarly awe-struck at his bare chest. Clark says he'll put something on and Mayson quickly demurs, insisting that she does not want him to be uncomfortable and agrees that it's hot, taking off her jacket to reveal a shapely tank top ("Church of Metropolis"). Even though Clark spends most of his time in suits, his easy smile and "smoldering eyes" (as described by Mayson in her journal) are more attractive than the Superman outfit. (Let's be honest—it's underwear on the outside—there's only so attractive that can be.)

Various instances throughout the series serve to remind us that, in many ways, Clark's life is perfectly ordinary. The Fortress of Solitude, where Clark hides a Kryptonian device from his spaceship, is in fact an old treehouse marked with a sign written by a young Clark. He flies home once a week for dinner with his parents, and they visit him regularly in Metropolis. When he is upset or needs advice, home is the first place he calls, often speaking to both parents at once on two phone extensions. His mother nags him about eating and asks him about girls. When Superman falls under the influence of a magician who has hypnotized him, Clark tells his parents how he is worried about the damage he could do while in these trances. They point out to him that he was raised as a human, so of course something like hypnosis could have an effect on him, but they encourage him to fight it, saying he must have superior ability to resist ("Illusions of Grandeur"). When Lois demands that he tell her a big secret so that she has leverage over him before she tells him her secret, he says that his mother might be having an affair ("Ides of Metropolis"). Aside from his identity as Superman, this is actually the most major thing happening in his life.

The line drawn between Clark and Superman is a clear one, if one that is sometimes hard to maintain. Some versions of the story have featured Lois trying relentlessly to uncover just who Superman is. *L&C* borrows again from Byrne, who got rid of the idea that "Superman had led people to believe he had another identity," asking why the Man of Steel would dangle such a thing in the face of brilliant reporter Lois (Daniels 160). Superman's persona is, at first, portrayed as a recently arrived alien. Even Lex Luthor is surprised to find out that Superman was sent here as an infant; after discovering this, he tells his personal assistant Nigel St. John (Tony Jay) "he walks among us. When I discover his Earthly identity, as I will, he and everyone that shares his secret will be at my mercy" ("Foundling"). This accidental stumbling on the secret is used multiple times in the series and they have to find some creative ways out of it. These include plot points like a hologram Superman talking to Clark, Clark using ketchup to fake an injury, Clark's conveniently timed loss of powers from kryptonite, and the appearance of a Clark/Superman from an alternate dimension. In most episodes, we see Clark more than we see Superman. He might use his powers, but they are simply a tool for Clark. In the pilot, he stops a runaway bus. In other episodes, his superpowers are employed for such things as reheating cold coffee ("I've Got a Crush on You"), blowing out matches to keep a man from lighting a cigarette inside the *Daily Planet* ("Barbarians at the Planet"), and playing baseball against himself ("Requiem for a Superhero"). As Clark says to Lois when he is trying to explain his deception, "Superman is what I can do. Clark is who I am." She does not react well, and Clark mumbles to himself "glasses, secret identity ... it seemed like a good idea at the time" ("Tempus Fugitive"). Overall, the power that Clark has is less important than who he is.

And this is at the core of the show. By highlighting Clark, the series tells us over and over that he is a decent person. Viewers care much more about Clark than they do about Superman because Clark is the worthy party; Superman is just some fancy tricks. When other people get superpowers, they cannot handle it as well because being a hero is not about the powers. It's about the person. In "A Bolt from the Blue," a lightning strike transfers some of Superman's powers into a random man at a cemetery. William Wallace Webster Waldecker (Leslie Jordan) declares himself "Resplendent Man" and sets about rescuing people—for a fee. Superman tries to talk sense into him, convince him that he should be using his powers for good rather than for profit, and to his credit, William eventually comes to agree that he should not have superpowers. When Lois becomes Ultra Woman, she struggles greatly with her inability to save everyone. She cannot stand being a minute too late to stop a mudslide: "...what makes me a good reporter is that I DON'T accept things. And I'm always questioning, and I'm never satisfied ... and I'm never gonna be satisfied with getting there five seconds too late" ("Ultra Woman"). While she might have made peace with it in time, she knows that Clark was born to do this. His innate goodness and strength of character is what make him super, not the ability to light things on fire with his eyes.

In the first episode, when Clark is interviewing for a position at the *Planet*, Perry asks Lois, "What happened to that mood piece I gave you about the razing of that old theater?" Lois says she was not in the mood, but after Clark has been turned down for the job, he goes to the old theater. He disables the wrecking ball and sits quietly, listening to an older actress recite lines from *The Cherry Orchard*. Later in the same episode, when a cop is joking about an apparent suicide, Clark jumps in to say, "The man's name was Samuel Platt. He was brilliant—a scientist and someone who cared about others. Under the circumstances, I don't believe that kind of humor is appropriate." The cop is abashed and Lois is impressed. And this is what the show gives us over and over—Clark as a good man. He consistently displays concern for others and a strong sense of responsibility for his extraordinary powers. Even his jealousies and insecurities make him more human. This is the real appeal of the character of Superman. Not being all powerful and able to do anything he wants, but being strong enough to protect weak and good enough to be deserving of the powers.

Conclusion

Lois & Clark was relatively successful for several seasons. The heightened soap opera approach to the familiar trio of Lois, Clark, and Superman was a hit with viewers. In the first three seasons, the show averaged around 18 million viewers, according to Nielsen ratings ("List..."). Hatcher was a sexy and savvy reporter; in 1995, as the show's popularity was cresting, a picture of Lois draped in Superman's cape was reportedly the most downloaded picture on the internet (and since it was still dial up at the time, that says something about the fans' dedication). Cain was a gorgeous and endearing Clark, and arguably more attractive as Clark than as Superman.

So what happened? Some would say that the show fell victim to the "Moonlighting curse" and fell apart once Lois and Clark finally tied the knot, the loss of the romantic tension in the "will they get together" question. Others might say that watching Lois and Clark negotiate how to handle life as a married couple was just less interesting. Wondering if Clark can ever let his Superman persona go long enough to be present for a whole date with Lois apparently went over better than watching Lois and Clark make friends with another married couple—even if that couple was revealed to be a superpowered assassin and his scientist wife ("Bob and Carol and Lois and Clark"). Ratings for the fourth season fell to half of what the viewership had been: from 18.3 million viewers for the pilot episode down to 4.9 million viewers of the last episode of season four ("List..."). The show did end on a cliffhanger, with a child being left for Lois and Clark—who had recently found out that they might not be able to have children ("The Family Hour"). With the falling ratings, however, ABC decided not to have the fifth season.

Despite its flaws, *L&C* was a compelling entry into the mythos of Superman. Placing Lois front and center and embracing the romance between her and Clark allowed the show to reach a new audience. People who might not have been interested in something based on a superhero comic might give a romantic comedy a try. The feminist Lois was a complement to other characters of the '90s like *Xena: Warrior Princess*, *Buffy the Vampire Slayer*, and Agent Scully from *The X-Files*. Focusing on the humanity of Clark, letting him be a real person rather than an all-powerful alien, let audiences connect with him on a level beyond wish fulfillment. Seeing him struggle with dating, dealing with his parents, juggling his life responsibilities—all of it made him into a more appealing character, one that the audience could admire **and** empathize with. *L&C* in some ways paved the way for *Smallville*, which focused on Clark rather than his heroics, keeping him human and not "Superboy." While not universally admired, as a version of Superman, *Lois & Clark* had just the right touch for the time and managed to fly.

Works Cited

"All Shook Up" (2 Jan. 1994). *Lois & Clark: The New Adventures of Superman: The Complete First Season*, story by Jackson Gillis, teleplay by Bryce Zabel, directed by Félix Enriquez Alcalá, Warner Bros., 2005.
"And the Answer Is..." (21 May 1995). *Lois & Clark: The New Adventures of Superman: The Complete Second Season*, written by Tony Blake and Paul Jackson, directed by Alan J. Levi, Warner Bros., 2006.
"Barbarians at the Planet" (1 May 1994). *Lois & Clark: The New Adventures of Superman: The Complete First Season*, written by Dan Levine and Deborah Joy LeVine, directed by James R. Bagdonas, Warner Bros., 2005.
Beritela, Gerard F. "Super-Girls and Mild-Mannered Men: Gender Trouble in Metropolis." *The Amazing Transforming Superhero!*, edited by Terrence Wandtke, McFarland, 2007, pp. 52–69.
"Big Girls Don't Fly" (12 May 1996). *Lois and Clark: The New Adventures of Superman: The Complete Third Season*, written by Brad Buckner and Eugene Ross-Leming, directed by Philip Sgriccia, Warner Bros., 2006.
"Bob and Carol and Lois and Clark" (17 Nov. 1994). *Lois and Clark: The New Adventures of Superman: The Complete Fourth Season*, written by Brian Nelson, directed by Oz Scott, Warner Bros., 2006.
"A Bolt from the Blue" (21 Nov. 1994). *Lois & Clark: The New Adventures of Superman: The Complete Second Season*, written by Kathy McCormick, directed by Philip J. Sgriccia, Warner Bros., 2006.
"Chi of Steel" (8 Jan. 1995). *Lois & Clark: The New Adventures of Superman: The Complete Second Season*, written by Hilary Bader, directed by James Hayman, Warner Bros., 2006.
"Chip Off the Old Clark" (19 Nov. 1995). *Lois & Clark: The New Adventures of Superman: The Complete Third Season*, written by Michael Jamin and Sivert Glarum, directed by Michael Watkins, Warner Bros., 2006.

"Church of Metropolis" (23 Oct. 1994). *Lois & Clark: The New Adventures of Superman: The Complete Second Season*, written by John McNamara, directed by Robert Singer, Warner Bros., 2006.
"Contact" (1 Oct. 1995). *Lois and Clark: The New Adventures of Superman: The Complete Third Season*, written by Chris Ruppenthal, directed by Daniel Attias, Warner Bros., 2006.
Cronin, Brian. "Comic Legends: Was Lex Luthor in Man of Steel Based on Donald Trump?" *Comic Book Resources*, 5 Feb. 2018, https://www.cbr.com/superman-lex-luthor-donald-trump/. Accessed 20 May 2020.
Daniels, Les. *Superman: The Complete History*. Chronicle Books, 1998.
"Dead Lois Walking." (10 Nov. 1996). *Lois and Clark: The New Adventures of Superman: The Complete Fourth Season*, written by Brad Bickner and Eugene Ross-Leming, directed by Chris Long, Warner Bros., 2006.
"Double Jeopardy" (18 Feb. 1996). *Lois & Clark: The New Adventures of Superman: The Complete Third Season*, written by Brad Buckner and Eugenie Ross-Leming, directed by Chris Long, Warner Bros., 2006.
"The Eyes Have It" (22 Jan. 1995). *Lois & Clark: The New Adventures of Superman: The Complete Second Season*, written by Kathy McCormick and Grant Rosenberg, directed by Bill D'Elia, Warner Bros., 2006.
"The Family Hour" (14 June 1997). *Lois and Clark: The New Adventures of Superman: The Complete Fourth Season*, written by Brad Bickner and Eugenie Ross-Leming, directed by Robert Ginty, Warner Bros., 2006.
"Faster Than a Speeding Vixen" (12 Apr. 1997). *Lois and Clark: The New Adventures of Superman: The Complete Fourth Season*, written by Brad Kern, directed by Neal Ahern, Warner Bros., 2006.
"Forget Me Not" (10 Mar. 1996). *Lois & Clark: The New Adventures of Superman: The Complete Third Season*, written by Grant Rosenberg, directed by James Bagdonas, Warner Bros., 2006.
"Foundling" (20 Feb. 1994). *Lois & Clark: The New Adventures of Superman: The Complete First Season*, written by Dan Levine, directed by Bill D'Elia, Warner Bros., 2005.
"From Rivals to Romance: The Making of *Lois and Clark*." *Lois & Clark: The New Adventures of Superman: The Complete First Season*, Warner Bros., 2005.
Gustines, George Gene. "Pulpy TV and Soapy Comics Find a Lot to Agree On." *The New York Times*, 31 Oct. 2006, https://www.nytimes.com/2006/10/31/arts/pulpy-tv-and-soapy-comics-find-a-lot-to-agree-on.html. Accessed 27 Feb. 2020.
"Home Is Where the Hurt Is" (17 Dec. 1995). *Lois & Clark: The New Adventures of Superman: The Complete Third Season*, written by William M. Akers, directed by Geoffrey Nottage, Warner Bros., 2006.
"The House of Luthor" (8 May 1994). *Lois & Clark: The New Adventures of Superman: The Complete First Season*, written by Deborah Joy LeVine and Dan Levine, directed by Alan J. Levi, Warner Bros., 2005.
"The Ides of Metropolis" (6 Feb. 1994). *Lois & Clark: The New Adventures of Superman: The Complete First Season*, written by Deborah Joy LeVine, directed by Philip J. Sgriccia, Warner Bros., 2005.
"Illusions of Grandeur" (23 Jan. 1994). *Lois & Clark: The New Adventures of Superman: The Complete First Season*, written by Thania St. John, directed by Michael Watkins, Warner Bros., 2005.
"I'm Looking Through You" (10 Oct. 1993). *Lois & Clark: The New Adventures of Superman: The Complete First Season*, written by Deborah Joy LeVine, directed by Mark Sobel, Warner Bros., 2005.
"It's a Small World After All" (28 Apr. 1996). *Lois and Clark: The New Adventures of Superman: The Complete Third Season*, written by Pat Hazell and Teri Hatcher, directed by Philip Sgriccia, Warner Bros., 2006.
"I've Got a Crush on You" (24 Oct. 1993). *Lois & Clark: The New Adventures of Superman: The Complete First Season*, written by Thania St. John, directed by Gene Reynolds, Warner Bros., 2005.
Lawrence, John Shelton, and Robert Jewett. *The Myth of the American Superhero*. William B. Eerdmans Publishing Company, 2002.
"List of *Lois & Clark: The New Adventures of Superman* Episodes." *Wikipedia*, https://en.wikipedia.org/wiki/List_of_Lois_%26_Clark:_The_New_Adventures_of_Superman_episodes. Accessed 28 May 2020.
"Lucky Leon" (12 Mar. 1995). *Lois & Clark: The New Adventures of Superman: The Complete Second Season*, written by Chris Ruppenthal, directed by Jim Pohl, Warner Bros., 2006.
"Madame Ex" (18 Sept. 1994). *Lois & Clark: The New Adventures of Superman: The Complete Second Season*, written by Tony Blake and Paul Jackson, directed by Randall Zisk, Warner Bros., 2006.
"The Man of Steel Bars" (21 Nov. 1993). *Lois & Clark: The New Adventures of Superman: The Complete First Season*, written by Paris Qualles, directed by Robert Butler, Warner Bros., 2005.
"Oedipus Wrecks" (24 Mar. 1996). *Lois and Clark: The New Adventures of Superman: The Complete Third Season*, written by David Simkins, directed by Kenn Michael Fuller, Warner Bros., 2006.
"The People vs. Lois Lane" (27 Oct. 1997). *Lois and Clark: The New Adventures of Superman: The Complete Fourth Season*, written by Grant Rosenberg, directed by Robert Ginty, Warner Bros., 2006.
"Pheromone, My Lovely" (28 Nov. 1993). *Lois & Clark: The New Adventures of Superman: The Complete First Season*, written by Deborah Joy LeVine, directed by Bill D'Elia, Warner Bros., 2005.
"Pilot" (12 Sept. 1993). *Lois & Clark: The New Adventures of Superman: The Complete First Season*, written by Deborah Joy LeVine, directed by Robert Butler, Warner Bros., 2005.
"The Prankster" (9 Oct. 1994). *Lois & Clark: The New Adventures of Superman: The Complete Second Season*, written by Grant Rosenberg, directed by James Hayman, Warner Bros., 2006.
Reger, Jo. "Introduction." *Different Wavelengths: Studies of the Contemporary Women's Movement*, Edited by Jo Reger, Routledge, 2005, pp. xv–xxx.

"Requiem for a Superhero" (17 Oct. 1993). *Lois and Clark: The New Adventures of Superman: The Complete First Season*, written by Robert Killebrew, directed by Randall Zisk, Warner Bros., 2005.

"Return of the Prankster" (26 Feb. 1995). *Lois & Clark: The New Adventures of Superman: The Complete Second Season*, written by Grant Rosenberg, directed by Philip J. Sgriccia, Warner Bros., 2006.

"Seconds" (25 Feb. 1996). *Lois & Clark: The New Adventures of Superman: The Complete Third Season*, written by Philip W. Chung and Corey Miller, directed by Alan J. Levi, Warner Bros., 2006.

"Shadow of a Doubt" (19 Apr. 1997). *Lois and Clark: The New Adventures of Superman: The Complete Fourth Season*, written by Grant Rosenberg, directed by Philip J. Sgriccia, Warner Bros., 2006.

Siegel, Jerry (w), and Joe Shuster (w). "Superman," *Action Comics* #1 (June 1938). DC Comics, 1938.

"Soap Opera." *TV Tropes*, https://tvtropes.org/pmwiki/pmwiki.php/Main/SoapOpera. Accessed 27 Feb. 2020.

"The Source" (2 Oct. 1994). *Lois & Clark: The New Adventures of Superman: The Complete Second Season*, written by Tony Blake and Paul Jackson, directed by John T. Kretchmer, Warner Bros., 2006.

Superman. Directed by Richard Donner, performances by Gene Hackman, Margot Kidder, and Christopher Reeve, Warner Bros., 1978.

"Target: Jimmy Olsen!" (2 Apr. 1995). *Lois & Clark: The New Adventures of Superman: The Complete Second Season*, written by Tony Blake and Paul Jackson, directed by David S. Jackson, Warner Bros., 2006.

"Tempus Fugitive" (26 Mar. 1995). *Lois & Clark: The New Adventures of Superman: The Complete Second Season*, written by Jack Weinstein and Lee Hutson, directed by James Bagdonas, Warner Bros., 2006.

"Top Copy" (19 Feb. 1995). *Lois & Clark: The New Adventures of Superman: The Complete Second Season*, written by John McNamara, directed by Randall Zisk, Warner Bros., 2006.

"Ultra Woman" (12 Nov. 1995). *Lois & Clark: The New Adventures of Superman: The Complete Third Season*, written by Gene O'Neill and Noreen Tobin, directed by Mike Vejar, Warner Bros., 2006.

"Vatman" (13 Mar. 1994). *Lois & Clark: The New Adventures of Superman: The Complete First Season*, story by H.B. Cobb, teleplay by H.B. Cobb and Deborah Joy LeVine, directed by Randall Zisk, Warner Bros., 2005.

"Voice from the Past" (26 Apr. 1997). *Lois and Clark: The New Adventures of Superman: The Complete Fourth Season*, written by John McNamara, directed by David Grossman, Warner Bros., 2006.

"Wall of Sound" (25 Sept. 1994). *Lois & Clark: The New Adventures of Superman: The Complete Second Season*, written by John McNamara, directed by Alan J. Levi, Warner Bros., 2006.

"We Have a Lot to Talk About" (17 Sept. 1995). *Lois & Clark: The New Adventures of Superman: The Complete Third Season*, written by John McNamara, directed by Philip J. Sgriccia, Warner Bros., 2006.

"When Irish Eyes Are Killing" (15 Oct. 1995). *Lois & Clark: The New Adventures of Superman: The Complete Third Season*, written by Grant Rosenberg, directed by Winrich Kolbe, Warner Bros., 2006.

"Whine, Whine, Whine" (14 May 1995). *Lois & Clark: The New Adventures of Superman: The Complete Second Season*, written by Kathy McCormick and John McNamara, directed by Michael Watkins, Warner Bros., 2006.

"Witness" (9 Jan. 1994). *Lois & Clark: The New Adventures of Superman: The Complete First Season*, written by Bradley Moore, directed by Mel Damski, Warner Bros., 2005.

Adaptation, Fandom and Gender

What Counts, Who Counts and Why

ANNA F. PEPPARD

Introduction

The television show *Lois & Clark: The New Adventures of Superman*, a superhero romantic comedy that aired for four seasons on ABC from 1993 to 1997, has affected my life in ways I am still accounting for. As the first television show starring mature professionals my 12-year-old self regularly watched, *Lois & Clark* helped shape my view of adult relationships and gender roles. It was also my first fannish interaction with a genre that has helped shape my career. At 28, I began research for a PhD dissertation on superhero comics. Subsequently, I have, like my one-time idol, Lois Lane, spent a significant amount of my professional life writing, talking, and thinking about Superman.

This connection to Lois went strangely unobserved until a nostalgic re-watch of *Lois & Clark* in and around my 30th birthday. I then spent weeks agonizing over the possibility I was studying superheroes for reasons that were more heteronormative than feminist; perhaps my entire dissertation was simply an excuse to spend time with the (imaginary) man I loved. Eventually, I came to realize that *Lois & Clark*, for all its inadequacies as a model of female empowerment (which I will discuss in due course), has, in fact, been essential to my feminism. A big part of why I loved *Lois & Clark* was because my best girlfriend loved it, too. I relished our post-show phone conversations almost as much as the episodes themselves. In between the squees and breathless "oh my gods" were nascent feminist critiques. Though we both crushed heavily on Dean Cain's Clark/Superman, we also agreed he was "kind of the worst," an underachiever compared to Teri Hatcher's Lois, who seemed to work twice as hard at everything (including acting), and had to, because she did not have the luxury of superpowers (which went hand-in-hand with what I would later learn to call male privilege). *Lois & Clark* also introduced me to female communities that further encouraged me to interrogate the politics of mainstream media; my combined fascination and dissatisfaction with the show prompted me to read my first fanfiction, which in turn inspired me to write my own. Years later, these experiences of fandom would inform my academic feminism. When I was researching my dissertation, book after book, essay after essay, treated the superhero genre as an exclusively male preserve; my experience as a woman whose superhero fandom began with a television show and blossomed within female friendships and fan communities was virtually invisible, even impossible. Now, I know that both my dissertation about depictions of the body in superhero comics and my continued work on issues of representation in the superhero genre are efforts to address this neglect; much of my writing and research on superhero stories strives to make visible the subversive possibilities that first drew me to the genre and get to the bottom of why those possibilities have been so grievously underexplored by creators as well as scholars.

Thankfully, both superhero stories and the scholarship done on them has diversified in recent years. Though female characters still only headline approximately 20 percent of mainstream superhero comics (Hanley), several comic book series, films, and television shows starring female superheroes and incorporating feminist messaging—many of them written, drawn, or directed by women—have found enough commercial and critical success to inspire hope for continued change. In addition, there are now many books and articles about representations of gender, race, and sexuality within superhero stories, often written by the diverse academic/fans or "aca/fans" (Jenkins, "Good News") whose voices were largely absent in that first wave of research. Yet many superhero stories remain neglected, including *Lois & Clark*. The show is rarely discussed in scholarship about Superman or adaptations of comic books, and those scholars who do discuss it often diminish or misrepresent it. For instance, the five pages Ian Gordon devotes to the show in his recent book *Superman: The Persistence of an American Icon* describes *Lois & Clark* as a nostalgia-driven property that largely "[fails] to represent current experience," except, perhaps, for "a segment" of its audience that continues to generate considerable online content, such as fanfiction (78). Gordon does not speculate on the gender of this "segment" of fans who became especially attached to the show. Indeed, Gordon's framing of the show as nostalgia-driven emphasizes its cultivation of "diverse audience appeal" (74). This might include women, but it might not; Gordon's analysis suggests there is either no way to know or no reason to care. This silence is conspicuous, given the well-documented fact that "[f]an fiction writing communities have historically been made up overwhelmingly of women" (Busse and Lothian 60). Moreover, characterizing *Lois & Clark* as primarily nostalgic ignores its relevance to then-contemporary feminist debates (see Freedman), as well as its uniqueness as the only officially sanctioned Superman adaptation developed by women—executive producer Deborah Joy LeVine from an idea by DC president Jenette Khan—to privilege romance, a connotatively feminine mode of expression.

Most of the scholarship that has been done on *Lois & Clark* exists separately from scholarship on comics or superheroes, appearing in books dedicated to female protagonists (see Wilcox) or Lois specifically (see Farghaly). While much of this scholarship is excellent, there is additional value to be gained in discussing *Lois & Clark* not only as a story about Lois, but also as a story about the Superman story. Similar to Linda Hutcheon, I am interested in adaptation as a means of interrogating "the *politics* of intertextuality" (xii, emphasis in original). In other words, I am interested in exploring which elements of a source text (or texts) an adaptation chooses to interact with, how, and especially why. The latter relates to whose desires an adaptation serves—what is it trying to achieve, and on whose behalf? As an adaptation of a traditionally male-centric storyworld created by women and consciously pitched to a female (and/or "feminine-attuned") audience, *Lois & Clark* is an especially useful text for performing such interrogations.

In the first part of this chapter, I examine *Lois & Clark*'s attempts to make the Superman storyworld more inclusive by promoting an ethic of gender equality that extends from the shared gender deviance of its title characters. I also examine the limits of this equality, which manifest in the show's ultimate faithfulness to a status quo in which Lois remains subservient to the needs and desires of Clark/Superman. In the second part of this chapter, I further interrogate the politics of adaptation by examining an adaptation of *Lois & Clark* in the form of the "Season 5 and 6" fanfiction series that was written by a female-led collective of fans in the wake of the show's cancellation in 1997. Fanfiction is one of the few forms of creative production Hutcheon discounts as a type of adaptation. "There is a difference," says Hutcheon, "between never wanting a story to end … and wanting to retell the same story over and over in different ways" (9). This sounds reasonable on its surface, yet the particularly tangled transmediality of a character such as Superman complicates matters. Most Superman adaptations are not based on any particular story but rather on a mythos that is at once ubiquitous and diffuse, formed out of many interactions between multiple media forms over the course of more than eighty years. Superman stories have long since become "'heteroglossic' in that they [contain] all the elements or utterances of previous versions or variants of *Superman*" (Berger 89). One consequence of this heteroglossia is that Superman adaptations are always, in part, reiterations and extensions; in other words, continuations of an ongoing and possibly never-ending storyworld—much like fanfiction. Because fanfiction offers "a means for marginalized groups and especially female fans to construct a discursive space within hegemonic culture to express themselves in meaningful and personally fulfilling ways" (Bonnstetter and Ott 352), treating the "Season 5 and 6" fanfiction series as an adaptation is essential to developing a more complete understanding of Superman, both as a character and as a transmedia property with diverse meanings for diverse fans. Focusing on a three-part story by fanfiction author Sheila Harper in which Clark and a postpartum Lois switch bodies for several days, I examine how the "Season 5 and 6" fanfiction series addresses the feminist failures of both *Lois & Clark* and the academic discourse that has neglected it, which are united in their unwillingness to truly de-center male perspectives.

"I'm not *a normal man"* : Re-Writing Gender in Lois & Clark

Lois & Clark consistently emphasizes the shared gender deviance of its title characters as part of an effort to make space for Lois within the historically male-centric Superman storyworld and present Clark/Superman as an ideal partner for the postfeminist woman who "demands … a balanced recognition of intelligence and sexuality" (Durden 172). This strategy is established in the LeVine-penned pilot, which opens with Lois stalking through the *Daily Planet* newsroom in baggy clothes and a fake beard, having adopted male drag to expose a "million-dollar theft ring." Clark's transformation into Superman is thematically linked to this performance of drag, in part through a musical montage later in the episode in which he tries on multiple potential superhero costumes for the first time. This montage, which incorporates numerous campy style references such as hot pink tights and leopard print briefs, is set to the tune of Bonnie Tyler's 1984 hit "Holding Out for a Hero"; by the early 1990s, this song was a well-established favorite within drag culture (Morgan). The pilot also features a comedic scene involving Clark disappearing into a supply closet intending to fly out the window, only to be interrupted by *Planet* editor Perry White, who asks him, with considerable hesitancy and discomfort, "When are you coming—out of the closet?" In addition, elsewhere in the episode,

Clark responds to Lois's attempt to equate him with the deceptive and inconstant men she has known by assuring her, "I am *not* a normal man." Though the audience knows Clark is referring to the secret of his alien-ness and superpowers, this exchange nonetheless foregrounds the non-normative nature of Clark's body and identity, and links that non-normative-ness to gender. Similarly, while Clark's transformation into Superman does not involve literal drag, and while Clark does not openly express, in the pilot or elsewhere, any same-sex desire, *Lois & Clark* nonetheless foregrounds its title characters as compelled to adopt actually or potentially deviant gender performances in order to be the best versions of themselves. The intent to thematically link Lois's actual performance of drag with Clark's metaphorical performance of drag is further suggested by these performances' placement within the pilot; Lois's performance is the opening scene, while Clark makes his first appearance as Superman at the end of the episode.

Personality-wise, too, each character is introduced as possessing gender deviant traits. This has always been at least potentially true of Superman, whose foundational duality and aforementioned alien-ness make him "a monster" (Carroll 8) with an "indeterminate identity" (Pitkethy 218) that fluctuates "between self-effacement (Clark Kent) and flamboyance (Superman) … leading easily to the queering of this mostly male-addressed genre" (Hatfield 110). *Lois & Clark* consciously exploits this potential for deviance by changing Clark from a "a timid, socially inept, physically weak, clumsy, sexually ineffectual quasi intellectual" (Brod 7) into a stylish and sensitive epitome of the "New Man" ideal. John Benyon could be talking about *Lois & Clark's* version Clark when he describes the New Man as "a refugee from the hardline masculinity epitomized by the paranoid, macho men with stifled emotions" of earlier eras, who evinces "a willingness to take on a supportive role in a woman's career" (100). Clark earns his job at the *Daily Planet* by writing what Lois derides as a "mood piece" about the planned demolition of an historic theatre, which involves him sympathetically commiserating with an older actress as she gives an emotional performance of Chekov's *The Cherry Orchard* on an empty stage; the normally gruff Perry White is nearly brought to tears by Clark's rendition of the story, and hires him on the spot. Lois, meanwhile, begins the series with an exaggeratedly aggressive demeanor. She repeatedly informs Clark, in some shape or form, that she is "top banana," and is lectured by her sister, Lucy, that she "needs to stop being so *smart* all the time, so intense" if she wants to hold on to a man; according to Lucy, Lois "scared off" a previous boyfriend by "dragging" him to a "women in journalism seminar" titled "Weak Men and the Wise Women Who Love Them." Privately, though, Lois is shown crying over romantic movies, hoping to be swept off her feet by a sexually confident Prince Charming. Lois and Clark's romance involves them learning to appreciate each other's deviance and uncover each other's dualities; Clark must uncover the sensitivity hidden beneath Lois's prickly façade, while Lois must uncover the bold hero hidden beneath Clark's writerly veneer. Uncovering commonalities within differences is a convention of the romance genre in its late twentieth-century form. Henry Jenkins, for instance, argues that for female fans of the television show *Beauty and the Beast* (1987–1990), "Romantic consummation … did not entail simply the fulfillment of the viewers' erotic fantasies, but rather posed an ideological solution, a reconciliation of differences, the possibility of trust and intimacy between two people who are so different and yet so alike" (*Textual Poachers* 142). Importantly, though, in *Lois & Clark*, the characters' realer selves are their more gender deviant ones. Whereas the original Superman stories presented Clark Kent as a disguise for Superman, *Lois & Clark* follows in the footsteps of John Byrne's

1986 comic book miniseries *The Man of Steel*, which rebooted canon to show how Superman "became the disguise for Clark Kent" (Robinson 88). Similarly, it is precisely Lois's aggressiveness that makes Clark fall in love with her. In the pilot, Clark describes Lois to his adoptive parents as "complicated. Domineering, uncompromising, pig-headed ... brilliant." His dreamy intonation of "brilliant" prompts a wide-eyed expression from his match-making mother.

The show's commitment to exploring the relationship between gender deviance and equality becomes especially apparent in its third season. In this season, Lois's knowledge of Clark's dual identity inspires a self-conscious, season-long debate about whether a truly equal partnership between these characters is possible, and if so, what such a partnership might look like. A looming marriage provides the context for this debate. At the conclusion of the season two finale, "And the Answer Is....," Clark asks Lois to marry him, and Lois responds by revealing she has learned his dual identity; the season ends with a cliffhanger in which Lois removes Clark's glasses and says, "Who's asking—Clark, or Superman?" The season three premiere, "We Have a Lot to Talk About," proceeds from this revelation, which informs Lois's decision to (temporarily) reject Clark's proposal. The general context, then, for season three is an intensified courtship/engagement period that functions metatextually as a justification of the show's premise. Showing that Lois can trust Clark attempts to prove *both* that Lois does not have to sacrifice her journalistic career to succeed in love *and* that women in the audience do not have to choose between personal empowerment and dreaming about being swept off their feet by the (super)man of their dreams. This negotiation reflects postfeminist ideals regarding the "'New Woman' of the 1990s," who was "distinguished from all other versions of the New Woman by a cultural climate in which women can now be traditionally 'feminine' and sexual in a manner utterly different in meaning from either pre-feminist or non-feminist versions demanded by phallocentrically defined female heterosexuality" (Sonnet 170). In the postfeminist 90s, the ideal of "having it all" reigned supreme; the supposed achievement of gender equality meant that women were able (and obligated) to be both empowered and traditionally feminine, both strong and sexy. Similarly, showing that loving Lois makes Clark stronger rather than weaker attempts to prove *both* that Clark does not need to sacrifice his superheroic career to succeed in love *and* that the Superman story does not have to choose between romance and action in order to succeed with audiences. This negotiation reflects ideals discussed above regarding the New Man of the 1980s and '90s, who was newly attuned to both femininity and feminism. If ratings are anything to go by, many viewers enjoyed these negotiations. This was the show's most popular season; individual episodes attracted as many as 22 million viewers a week ("Nielsen Ratings"), and contemporary entertainment reporting described the show as "dominating" the Sunday evening timeslot it shared with *The Simpsons*, *Cybill*, and *Mad About You* (Tucker 53). Significantly, the episode "Ultra Woman," in which Lois briefly becomes a superhero after Clark's powers are accidentally transferred to her, was the most popular entry of the show's most popular season ("Nielsen Ratings") and features its most direct embrace of gender deviance as a component of Lois and Clark's bond. It also powerfully illustrates the limits of the show's equality; this important episode concludes with a justification of Clark/Superman's primacy within the narrative.

When Lois first acquires Clark's powers via a red kryptonite laser built by a pair of scheming sisters trying to disable Superman, she is not enthusiastic. While discussing costume ideas with Clark's adoptive parents, Martha and Jonathan, Lois declares herself unfit to be a superhero, and worries about the effect her empowerment might have on Clark. Says Lois, "I don't think I can do this…. It's just, it's not me—it's Clark. You know he's putting on this brave face, but inside I know this is eating him alive. If he sees me in a cape and tights, how do you think that's going to make him feel?" Jonathan reassures her, "Lois, Clark is strong. And I'm not just talking about how much he can bench press. He's strong where it counts, when it counts." Jonathan proves correct. Clark is consistently depicted as supportive rather than jealous or hurt; he helps Lois learn to use her new powers, and repeatedly talks her through the emotional burden of superheroism. Yet in the immediate wake of her first outing as Ultra Woman, Lois does not feel burdened; instead, she is emboldened, and expresses this in overtly gender deviant ways.

After saving the Daily Planet from a potential explosion, Lois returns to work in a skirt suit that combines connotatively masculine and feminine references. The suit is dark brown with white pinstripes, and features an oversize jacket worn with a white shirt with large French cuffs, accessorized with a menswear tie. The bottom half of the suit is a long column skirt that requires Lois to sashay as she walks. Upon entering the office, she is greeted with dozens of enormous flower bouquets addressed to Ultra Woman, many of them from celebrity male admirers such as Fabio, Brad Pitt, Deion Sanders, and Antonio Banderas. Lois spends a few moments relishing this attention before perching confidently on the edge of Clark's desk and popping open the bottle of orange juice he had been struggling to open. In response, Clark jokes, "Please don't tell me that I loosened it for you." When Lois discusses the strangeness of wearing her superhero costume under her clothes, Clark admits that he misses it, which provokes more gender play. Lois asks, "You don't like just wearing your boxers?" "Boxers?" Clark asks. "I wear briefs." Lois cocks a knowing smile as she quips, "I know." A scandalized Clark lets his jaw drop open as he hisses, "Lois, did you *x-ray* my—" "I was just kidding," Lois interrupts, with a smile and a laugh. She sashays away, but as soon as Clark stands to reach across his desk, she does perform a generous x-ray of his rear end. Shortly thereafter, Lois's super-hearing picks up a distress call. Clark urges her to answer it, to which Lois replies, "There's something I gotta finish first." She then seizes Clark's tie, kisses him hard on the mouth, drops him with a "thud" back into his office chair, and turns to leave, smirking as she loosens her tie. Clark is left blinking after her, exhaling a not-displeased "Whoa." Subsequent scenes feature Clark playing the classic damsel in distress role; he is beaten up by muggers, kidnapped by the scheming sisters, tied to an elaborate bomb, and told to call Ultra Woman for help. Though Clark manages to disentangle himself from the bomb, he does end up collapsing on a park bench and calling Lois. She arrives promptly and effortless tears open the wire binding his wrists.

This role reversal would seem to provide a context for building a new kind of understanding between the characters. But in the end, it is Lois, rather than Clark, who seems to do the most learning. Shortly after rescuing Clark, Lois breaks into tears about her inability to respond to every call for help. Clark attempts to reassure her, saying, "No matter how strong you are, and no matter how fast, sometimes, it just isn't enough. You have to accept that." Lois protests, "But what makes me a good reporter is that I *don't* accept things. I'm always questioning, and I'm never satisfied. And I'm never going to be satisfied with getting there five seconds too late. And no matter what you say, I know it doesn't make you feel good to watch me do what you were *born* to do." Finally, she pleads, "Can we just bag these lunatics and get things back to normal?" This exchange celebrates Lois's passion and perfectionism while simultaneously retreating from gender deviance as a vehicle of empowerment or equality. Lois is, ultimately, too emotional (i.e., too feminine) to be a good superhero, and her emphasis on Clark's superheroism as something that is "normal" and that he was "born to do" situates male possession of superpowers as natural while female possession of superpowers is unnatural and, as such, rightfully temporary.

In keeping with the New Man and postfeminist-inspired negotiations of gender discussed above, "Ultra Woman" frames its final embrace of traditional gender roles as an empowering choice rather than a draconian imposition. After the eventual restoration of Clark's powers, the episode concludes with Lois and Clark returning to the park where Clark first proposed at the end of season two. As they stroll, the couple has the following exchange:

> LOIS: "You know, if someone had asked me three days ago who the one person in the world I admired most was, I'd have said—you. But without really knowing what that meant. And without really understanding that the hardest part about being you, is all the things you can't do. All the cries for help that you can't answer, and how that quietly tears you apart. It never stops you. And after living a little of that myself, I realized something—something that I never thought was possible."
> CLARK: "What?"
> LOIS: "I love you more. More than I ever have, and more than I ever thought I could love anyone. And so, I want to ask—" [Lois gets down on one knee, and presents the ring Clark had presented to her.] "—will you marry me?"
> CLARK [JOKINGLY]: "Who's asking—Lois, or Ultra Woman?"
> LOIS [SMILES BACK]: "Who's answering—Clark, or Superman?"
> CLARK: [NOW SERIOUS] "I'm answering."
> LOIS: "I'm waiting."
> CLARK: "Yes."
> Clark slides the ring onto her finger, and they kiss. Fade to black.

Those inclined to be generous might see this scene as emphasizing the importance of compromise; in this reading, the revelation of Clark's constant compromises inspires the defiantly independent Lois to embrace the inevitable compromises that come with marriage. Alternatively, experiencing the boundlessness of Clark's love—which extends beyond Lois or Metropolis to include the entire world—inspires Lois to be more open to a deeper form of love. Both readings can be supported by the continued use of gender deviance to emphasize equality, with Lois proposing to Clark and the reversal and repetition of the "Who's asking?" line from the season two finale. This scene also, however, highlights what Rhonda Wilcox argues is one of *Lois & Clark*'s most significant feminist failures. According to Wilcox, the show is "occupied with showing Lois's education to worthiness" while Clark, in contrast, "changes very little" (111). In this episode, Lois learns that Clark is even more super than she once thought, specifically because he is capable of managing his emotions more effectively than she is; Clark may be a New Man, but he is still definitely a man. Clark, meanwhile, does not seem to learn anything; he does not offer a reciprocal reflection on his experience of losing his powers. Clark, it seems, was already perfect, and Lois can only become less imperfect by accepting this perfection.

Clark's perfection reflects Superman's value as a brand, which in turn reflects the male privilege that informs his desirability both as someone to be and someone to *be with*. In this scene, and as a general rule, *Lois & Clark* attempts to include feminist/female desires while maintaining Superman's centrality by showing that Clark/Superman is worthy of the self-sacrificing devotion of a postfeminist woman such as Lois. It is seeing first-hand how truly *good* Clark is—specifically in terms of how hard he works to protect others—that finally convinces Lois she does not need to be afraid of surrendering her power (or powers) to Clark. *Lois & Clark* acknowledges that there are bad patriarchs, like the power-hungry Lex Luthor. But it also encourages successful but lonely career women to look for salvation in the arms of good patriarchs who may be hiding in plain sight. To be fair, Clark is substantially more emotionally attuned and progressively minded than the "supreme example of unchallenged, autonomous masculinity" that Janice A. Radway argues dominated the mass market romance novels of the 1980s; where such romance novels almost invariably "avoid[ed] having the hero openly declare his dependence on a woman" (Radway 148), Clark often tells Lois that he would "lose everything" if he lost her love ("Just Say Noah"). And yet, *Lois & Clark* nonetheless communicates a similar overarching message, inasmuch as "a potential argument for change is transformed into a representation and recommendation of the status quo" (Radway 148).

This is, admittedly, a lot of rhetorical weight to place on a single episode. But the descent into heteronormativity that follows Lois and Clark's marriage near the beginning of season four bolsters Wilcox's argument that Lois changes a great deal while Clark remains the same. The season one version of Lois, who would rather become her own man than ask a man for help, is deeply uncomfortable around children ("Smart Kids"), and considers domesticity incompatible with her professional goals, is nearly unrecognizable in the season four version of Lois, whose major life events involve getting married in a church in a traditional white dress ("Swear to God, This Time We're Not Kidding"), moving out of her downtown apartment into a suburban house with a white picket fence ("The People vs. Lois Lane"), learning to cook for her husband with the help of a domestically gifted ghost ("Ghosts"), giving up a promotion because it negatively affects her relationship with her husband ("Stop the Presses"), and, finally, having a baby (more precisely, having a baby wrapped in a Superman blanket dropped off at her suburban doorstep in the series finale, "The Family Hour"). Lois would have to be a superhero to take on so many additional responsibilities without sacrificing her relationship or career, yet she never again acquires actual superpowers. Because it is Clark, rather than Lois, who begins the series with ambitions to have a family, and Clark who first proposes to Lois and most vocally extols the virtues of marriage, Lois's domestication is, at best, a symbol of the transformative power of love. At worst, it is a surrender to Clark's desires at the expense of her own. Significantly, season four was the series' least popular; its steadily declining ratings led to *Lois & Clark*'s cancellation.

"[Lois, I'm sorry,] he thought. [I didn't understand.]" : Re-gendering Writing in "Lois & Clark Season 5 and 6"

The "Season 5 and 6" fanfiction series features 34 chapters or "episodes" of approximately 15,000 words each written by a collective of about 25 largely—thought not exclusively—female-identified fans who met through a *Lois & Clark* discussion listserv and fanfiction mailing list. Different solo authors or small groups of authors are responsible for different episodes that fit within a larger story arc, the organization of which is credited to Leanne Shawler. Though different authors inevitably have their own strengths and things they enjoy focusing on (some stories contain more descriptive passages than others, for instance), the style of the series is largely consistent, and maintains the show's "PG" rating. The series introduces some new characters, but is primarily committed to moving the story forward rather than fundamentally restructuring or deconstructing it; all creative choices are carefully justified within established canon, and each chapter has a theoretical "air date" to generate a sense of authenticity. In addition, many of the changes the series does make are couched in the wider Superman mythos. For instance, the newly created wife of Clark's grandson in the future, who appears in several stories, is named Lori—presumably a reference to Lori Lemaris, a recurring love interest of Superman during the Silver Age of comics. The intended faithfulness of this series is informed by the nature of the group that produced it. The *Lois & Clark* discussion listserv interacted directly with the creators of the show; according to Fanlore, "on the Monday after first-run episodes aired, digests [of the Sunday discussions on the listserv] were printed out and distributed to the cast and crew." The list also spawned several fan gatherings in Los Angeles, at least one of which featured a tour of the *Lois & Clark* set in which listserv members met the actors and production staff ("LOISCLA"). In other words, this was a group that actively sought out, and was granted, a significant measure of "official" approval.

Nonetheless, this series does re-write *Lois & Clark* in notable ways, with significant implications for its representations of gender. Aspects of this rewriting can be read as extending from the "Season 5 and 6" fanfiction series' incorporation of many additional female voices. Though the central tenants of *Lois & Clark* were established by LeVine—who wrote the pilot as well as six additional season one episodes—after LeVine left the show at the end of season one, it had exclusively male producers and was, like virtually every other network show of its era, heavily dominated by male writers and directors. The introductory author's notes for the first story in the "Season 5 and 6" series, "Back to the Future" by Barbara, interestingly ignores (or perhaps, chooses to displace) this male dominance in favor of spotlighting LeVine as a guiding creative force: "This story continues the legacy created by Deborah Joy Levine [sic] and all of the wonderful writers of Lois and Clark, The New Adventures of Superman [sic]." The female-oriented nature of the "Season 5 and 6" fanfiction series is reflected in its expanded focus on female subjectivity. In the show, Clark has privileged access to discussing his feelings because he has a set of confidants Lois does not, in the form of his ever-understanding parents. Lois has no confidants of her own; the burden of Clark's secret, combined with a lack of female friends (her sister Lucy disappears after the pilot), means she can only voice her doubts and frustrations to Clark and his family. The switch from a visual medium to a textual one allows the "Season 5 and 6" series to make Lois's perspective considerably more visible. Many stories in the "Season 5 and 6" series extensively detail Lois's emotional responses to the day-to-day struggle of dealing with Clark's recurring and unpredictable absences from both the newsroom and the home. These passages can be read metatextually as female fans negotiating their own place within the traditionally male-centric Superman storyworld, and expressing frustration with the necessity of those negotiations.

This expanded focus on female subjectivity is readily evident in the "Season 5 and 6" series' most substantial deviation from the source. This series explains the baby that is left on Lois and Clark's doorstep as a great-great-grandson from the future who was sent back in time to protect him from a supervillain. This in turn reveals that, contrary to the show's claim that Lois and Clark are "biologically incompatible" ("The Family Hour"), the couple can, in fact, have biological children. While this does not change the domestic thrust of the show's fourth season, returning the baby to the future and slowing down Lois and Clark's journey through fertility struggles to pregnancy and post-pregnancy does enable the "Season 5 and 6" series to more fully explain and justify Lois's change of heart regarding marriage, children, and domesticity. The writers of this series ensure that motherhood is no longer the end of Lois's journey, but rather a context informing many more journeys, including many more discussions about the meaning of equality with marriage. These discussions are especially evident in Sheila Harper's "Season 6" trilogy "Turn Around," "Walk in My Shoes," and "Mirror, Mirror," in which a super-scientific device called a "cognitive facilitator" causes Lois and Clark to switch bodies for several days, uncertain throughout about whether they will be able to switch back. Harper's trilogy both maintains fidelity to the source text and forces Clark to change more dramatically than the show was ever able or willing to do.

Harper's trilogy is part of the popular "genderswap" subgenre of fanfiction. There are many reasons for the popularity of this subgenre, most of them related to the fact that fanfiction has historically been dominated by female fans re-writing connotatively masculine genres, such as science fiction and action-adventure. Indeed, gender transformation stories would seem to quite obviously align with what media fan "Obsession_inc." calls "transformational" fandom. In contrast to "affirmational" fandom, which closely follows rules developed by a source text's creators, "transformational" fandom practices are "all about laying hands upon the source and twisting it to the fans' own purposes'" (quoted in Tosenberger 7). As Catherine Tosenberger observes, "Since the vast majority of English-language Western literature and entertainment assumes a default straight, white, cisgender male audience, it's not surprising that transformational fandom is often populated by those considered marginal audiences, who are more likely to feel a need to rework a beloved story to suit their own desires" (8). Genderswap fanfiction often addresses desires related to social and cultural inequities and exclusions. Anne Kustriz, for instance, argues that in both genderswap fanfiction and the fairy tales and myths about gender transformation that preceded and influence it, "Characters who undergo sexual transformations … allow authors and artists to reflect upon the relationship between biology, performance, and subjectivity. They also enable reflection on the cultural conditions that structure the lives of those socially recognized as women and men" (323). Kristina Busse and Alex Lothian concur that genderswap fanfictions often "highlight multidimensional intersections of sex, gender, desire, and embodiment" (57). That Harper's trilogy shares these goals is made especially apparent through its main intertextual reference—the *Lois & Clark* episode "Ultra Woman." Harper's trilogy makes many direct references to "Ultra Woman" and features a concluding scene that actively revisits the themes of that episode's own conclusion.

At the point of the "Season 5 and 6" series where Harper's trilogy takes place, Lois and Clark's biological daughter, Laura, is nine months old and attends employee daycare at the Daily Planet while Lois and Clark are at work. Though Clark is committed to participating equally in parenting responsibilities, his duties as Superman routinely prevent him from making good on these intentions. Throughout Harper's trilogy, Lois struggles with this state of affairs. In a scene from the first story of the trilogy, "Turn Around," which takes place prior to the characters' body-swap, Lois has the following thoughts during a press conference for the Metropolis Public School System (a symbolically significance choice of organization):

> She suddenly heard that thought in isolation: I almost wish the building would catch on fire or something. What was she thinking? Oh God, maybe she really was an adrenaline junkie…. Was that the real reason she felt disgruntled when Clark took off on a rescue and left her to handle the childcare and housework? Because he was doing "exciting stuff" and she was stuck in a boring routine of changing diapers and washing laundry and cooking meals?

Though Lois voices similar thoughts and fears within *Lois & Clark*, during season four, she effectively transforms from a woman dedicated to questioning heteronormativity to one terrified of being excluded from it. By resurrecting Lois's doubts, Harper's trilogy—and the "Season 5 and 6" series as a whole—re-engages with, and adds additional complexity to, the gender inequities *Lois & Clark* attempted to present as resolved.

In Harper's trilogy, however, the consequences of gender inequity are experienced most forcefully by Clark in Lois's body. This choice risks sidelining Lois, but, as in other genderswap fanfictions, it also reflects a desire "to explore women's situation by transferring it onto a male character" (Busse and Lothian 60). Harper's trilogy shares with *Lois & Clark* a compulsion to make Clark a perfect partner for the postfeminist woman. Yet the nature of this perfection is importantly different. In Harper's trilogy, Clark's perfection lies in his ability to cope with change, and use it to become an even better partner. Clark becomes, over the course of Harper's trilogy, the one man who truly "gets it"; "it" being the challenge of successfully performing female-ness in a postfeminist world that enables, but also requires, women to be at once sexy, feminine, and professional, juggling ideal relationships, families, and careers.

Interestingly, Clark's greatest struggles while existing in Lois's body do not involve highly visible, generic manifestations of gender inequity; he does not get kidnapped or deal with street harassment. Instead, he struggles with the types of excessively mundane events that are common in the lives of working mothers but were rarely depicted on network television during the era in question. For instance, in "Turn Around," Clark is confronted with the seemingly impossible task of carrying his "baby, diaper bag, insulated milk bag, and purse" from the daycare to his car. A substantial paragraph documents his process of thinking through the mechanics of the task, concluding with Clark "wondering how Lois ever managed to carry baby and bags and still maintain her balance in high heels. And people thought his flying and super strength were miraculous!" After a long day of pounding the pavement as a (female and non-superpowered) star reporter for a major metropolitan newspaper, Clark finds bathing his baby daughter a similarly Herculean undertaking:

> Bathing Laura was harder than it had been the night before. Kneeling in front of the tub made Clark's knees sore; leaning over the side of the tub dug into his ribs; and lifting Laura from this position made his arms and shoulders ache. She slipped in his hands when he picked up her water-slick body, and catching her nearly wrenched his upper back. He laid her on a towel on the bathroom floor to dry her and put a lightweight sleeper on her, but standing up and lifting her hurt his lower back. Groaning as he carried her down into the kitchen to fix her bottle, he wondered if this was why Lois still used the baby bath on the dressing table ["Walk in My Shoes"].

In three substantial scenes, Clark also struggles with breastfeeding. The trilogy's breastfeeding scenes represent Clark's most meaningful engagement with corporeal difference; they also represent the only instances in which occupying Lois's body brings Clark genuine pleasure. At first, Clark has difficulty relaxing enough to be able to breastfeed, which results in Laura painfully biting him. But like the hero he is, he perseveres:

> Clark turned to [Laura], cradling her in his other arm. Woebegone brown eyes drowned in tears looked up at him, and he stroked her hand as she tried nursing again. When her small fingers curled around his thumb, he smiled down at her—and suddenly felt an odd tingling in his chest. Laura's tentative gumming grew strong and assured, her frown easing into contentment, and they both sighed.
> As she relaxed in his arms, he rocked her, stroking her soft hair with one hand and smoothing the other forefinger over the back of the silky-skinned hand clasping his thumb. He talked to her softly and

smiled into her drowsy brown eyes while he enjoyed the sweetly pleasurable sensation of her nursing and felt peace soak into his heart. "I love you, baby girl," he murmured, and his throat tightened when she pulled away long enough to give him a wide, milky smile before she returned to the serious business of eating.

When she finally drifted to sleep, he held her for a long moment, studying her face tenderly. He had loved her before she was even born, but somehow … this created a bond that he had never expected. No wonder Lois had fought so hard for the childcare center at the Planet. The only wonder was that she had been able to tear herself away from Laura to go to work at all [Harper, "Walk in My Shoes"].

This passage features some potentially problematic glorifications of breastfeeding as an essential aspect of motherhood, and female experience in general. On the other hand, Clark's struggle to breastfeed and his consistent mix of emotions while doing so (he never truly stops being "embarrassed" by the act) can also resonate with real-life experiences of either/both female-presenting and identifying mothers, transgender parents, or even male-presenting and identifying fathers who may have psychological or physical difficulty with breastfeeding. Thus, in addition to strengthening Clark's bond with both Lois and his daughter, this trilogy's breastfeeding scenes can be viewed as using the science fiction convention Darko Suvin calls "cognitive estrangement" (18) to discuss an issue in the lives of many parents in a different and potentially more accessible way than more directly "realistic" portrayals.

Lois, too, finds that occupying Clark's body has positive and negative aspects. In some instances, she enjoys the sense of freedom she had been missing. In "Walk in My Shoes," when Clark insists—much as Lois would customarily do—on accompanying her on "a quick fly-by" of a house owned by a man they are investigating ("'I thought we were partners,'" he complains), Lois replies, "'I just thought it might be better if we didn't both leave [Laura] unless we had to—and I can check it faster.'" In other words, it is easier—and, indeed, more natural—for the male-presenting person who happens to have superpowers to work outside the home, and for the female-presenting, non-superpowered person to stay home with the child. Lois also, however, finds herself struggling to control Clark's awkwardly large and frighteningly strong body. In "Walk in my Shoes," she tells Clark, "'I didn't like that kind of responsibility when I was Ultra Woman, and it's worse when it isn't even my own body. I have to think every minute *how* to do things because my reach is wrong or it's too far to the ground.'" She likens the experience to "'walking downstairs when you're reading something and you fall down that last step because you put your weight down on the same level as the last step, but there's nothing under you.'"

This mix of positive and negative experiences is reminiscent of what Jenkins, referencing Patricia Frazer Lamb and Diana L. Veith's research, describes as the "play with androgyny" within slash fanfiction. In slash stories, male characters often "mix and match traditionally masculine and feminine traits, sliding between genders as they struggle for intimacy" (Jenkins, *Textual Poachers* 193). In Harper's trilogy, however, this sliding between genders is limited by the fact that the characters never lose sight of their preferred gender identities. A particularly clear example of this occurs at the beginning of the final story of the trilogy, "Mirror, Mirror." Following an emotionally trying scene in which Clark and Lois confront the seeming death of the scientist who transformed them, suggesting they may be permanently stuck in each other's bodies, Clark's has the following thoughts:

His gaze slid downward, past smoothly swelling breasts, down long, slender legs to small, neatly shod feet. He clenched one slim hand into a fist. He couldn't do this. In every way he defined himself, even during those frightening years when his powers were first appearing and he didn't know if he was even

human or not, he had clung to one thing: he was a man. Dimly he remembered an echo of one of his earliest conversations with Lois:
> You ... seem to have all the ... parts of a man.
> Well, I am a man, Lois. Just like you're a woman.

And now that had been torn from him. Vulnerable to all the ills and injuries humans were prone to, stripped of his enormous speed and strength, banished—he cast a quick, aching glance upward—from the sky that had been his retreat and his joy: those were problems he had faced before and could deal with again. But not this. Dammit, he *wasn't* a woman!

This passage notably compares the experience of having a female-presenting body to becoming literally disempowered; this highlights Clark's superpowers as an extension of his maleness. It also, however, misogynistically situates having a female-presenting body as *worse* than losing access to one's superpowers. Yet Clark quickly acknowledges the unfairness of his response, and learns from it, using his heightened emotional awareness to better understand his male-presenting wife: "He should have realized it earlier, but since he thought of his own body as being the 'right one,' it hadn't occurred to him that being trapped in his body was as distressing to Lois as being trapped in hers was to him." Clark's "anger and despair" are described as "fading into the background" in place of "concern for how Lois was handling [the experience]." In addition, by having Lois and Clark remain certain of their true gender identities and declining to eroticize their transformations, Harper's trilogy can be read as more understanding than many genderswap fanfictions are of what is, for many people, the deeply felt reality of gender identity. Genderswap fanfiction's tendency to exploit the erotic potential of sexual transformation can be both subversive and problematic, sometimes simultaneously. In a blog post for *Fanfic Magazine*, Malory Beazley notes that even as "testing the waters of sex and gender is enjoyable and certainly the main appeal of [genderswap] fics, the often one-dimensional focus on sexual gratification usually comes at the expense of transgender readers: traditional genderswap fics often gloss over tangible sex and gender issues that pertain to transgender individuals." What Busse and Lothian describe as genderswap fanfiction's frequent privileging of "female desires and fantasies at the expense of transrealism" (74) is implicit in the term "genderswap." As Beazely notes, this subgenre "should really be called 'sexswap' because in the vast majority of these fics," including Harper's trilogy, "it is the biological sex that is switched." Harper's trilogy does not solve these issues; the magical and temporary nature of Lois and Clark's transformations hardly constitutes a realistic depiction of transgender experience. Nonetheless, this story's investigations of gender are complex and thoughtful, with the potential to be useful for many different readers navigating a diversity of experiences.

Having Lois and Clark remain certain of their gender identities is also, of course, a conservative choice. This conservatism extends, in part, from the "Season 5 and 6" fanfiction series' aforementioned fidelity to its source; because this series is rated "PG" it can only be so titillating, and because its primary goal is to extend the source, it can only make so many changes to it. Conservative impulses are common within fanfiction, but remain underexplored. The privileging of slash fiction within existing scholarship on fanfiction has resulted in some scholars not paying sufficient attention to the fact that "Fidelity to the canon is, for many fans, the prime directive of fan fiction" (Bonnstetter and Ott 350). This commitment to fidelity means "activities often thought to be emancipatory," such as re-writing television shows, "can, in fact, reproduce hegemony" (Scodari 111). This is certainly a concern with Harper's trilogy, which, like "Ultra Woman" before it, eventually restores a status quo in which men save the world while women preserve the home. In some instances, however, asserting faithfulness can be its own kind of rebellion. The conclusion of Harper's trilogy, which finds Lois and Clark back in their own bodies and lounging in each others' arms on the beach of a secluded island, functions as a case in point.

Initially, Harper's conclusion asserts faithfulness to *Lois & Clark* by effectively re-stating the "Ultra Woman" conclusion. In the conclusion of Harper's trilogy as in the conclusion of "Ultra Woman," Lois says that becoming Superman has helped her better appreciate Clark's goodness. Says Lois, "'[T]hese past few days I realized *again* ... that being Superman also tears you away from things you want to do. Being with Laura and me. Doing the ordinary things that—that connect you to everyone else on this planet. All those things you wanted when you created Superman.'" In other words, Lois realizes (again) that she is wrong to be frustrated with Clark's absences because they are actually an extension of his goodness, and may, in fact, be harder on him than on her. Yet Harper's conclusion also differs from that of "Ultra Woman" by having Clark offer a reciprocal reflection, accompanied by a promise of continued change. When Lois tries to apologize for complaining, Clark says, "'No, honey, I'm glad you did. I needed to hear it,'" then proceeds to discuss what he learned: "'When I take care of Laura by myself, I use super speed to do a lot of chores or heat vision to warm her bottle.... I hardly ever get tired, either, so I didn't realize how hard it is for you to juggle so many things when I'm off being Superman ... or how tiring it is.'" "'I've gotten pretty good at it,'" says Lois, "'but it's nice having you recognize the effort.'" In response, Clark says he wants to "'do more than just acknowledge it,'" and proposes a host of changes to lighten her load, such as hiring a professional cleaner and taking responsibility for pre-preparing meals. This in-depth discussion of the distribution of domestic chores functions as a form of foreplay; the scene ends with the couple kissing, preparing to do more. Part of this scene's faithfulness to its source is located in its re-justification of a return to the main features of the status quo. But another part of its faithfulness involves taking inspiration from *Lois & Clark*'s purported representation of gender equality to articulate meaningful compromise—and make it sexy.

Unfortunately, neither Harper's trilogy nor most of the other stories in the "Season 5 and 6" fanfiction series substantially redress what Wilcox and Durden identify as perhaps the central feminist failure of *Lois & Clark*, which is its lack of representations of female community. Wilcox notes that Lois is virtually the only working woman *Lois & Clark* does not eventually reveal as a villain (104), while Durden observes, "Although Lois is established as a feminist character, the lack of female friendships ... demonstrates that *Lois & Clark* might not be quite so progressive after all" (185). In Harper's trilogy, Lois once again finds herself completely dependent on Clark and his parents as outlets for her emotional struggles. And yet, she does have the writers and readers of this and many other fanfictions who speak with her by talking through her, sharing her frustrations and making small, albeit significant, steps to alleviate them. For some fans, this may not be enough to make the "Season 5 and 6" fanfiction series a sufficiently feminist text. I share this doubt; if presented with the opportunity to travel back in time and choose between giving my 12-year-old self the "Season 5 and 6" fanfiction series, *Lois & Clark*, or the CW's *Supergirl* (2015–present), I would likely opt for the latter. But even if *Lois & Clark*'s depictions of gender equality were seldom truly convincing, the show did provide a useful context for discussing the meaning of equality. The "Season 5 and 6" fanfiction series, meanwhile, provides a useful space for deepening those discussions. Even if these discussions are (inevitably) imperfect, they are valuable, and worthy of being continued.

Conclusion

Before writing this chapter, I had not read Harper's trilogy in over twenty years. Despite this, I remembered it clearly enough that when I heard about this collection, it immediately occurred to me to write about it. I worried it would be difficult to track down, but found it as the first result of my initial Google search; it seems that both *Lois & Clark* and the "Season 6 and 6" series remain popular, despite many newer Superman adaptations. Or perhaps, they remain popular *because of* newer adaptations creating interest in the past. When considering adaptations of transmedia characters, it is especially important to consider the ways in which "[m]ultiple versions [of a text] exist laterally, not vertically" (Hutcheon xiii), and the implications therein. As Liam Burke argues, "Adaptation studies today favors a poststructuralist approach that positions each adaptation at the center of a spider's web of intertextual relations, which includes—but is not limited to—the source text" (129). If this is true, there is no good reason to exclude fanfiction as a form of adaption, and many good reasons to include it. Some fanfiction writers would undoubtedly reject the adaptation label, which could be seen as limiting their ability to re-write the source to suit themselves. But denying the *possibility* that fanfiction might be a form of adaptation can be understood as linked to the historical—and ongoing—policing of which texts, readers, and ways of reading "count" and which do not. As Busse observes, fans fail to be "good fans, and thus embarrass other fans, by liking the wrong things and liming them in the wrong ways" (74). Such distinctions between "good" and "bad" fans are routinely gendered. "Underlying all these analyses," writes Busse, "is a gender binary that identifies certain behaviors as *masculine* or *feminine*, with the former usually connoting active, intellectual, aggressive, and objective, and the latter, passive, emotional, sensitive, and subjective" (74, emphasis in original). The fact that the 2006 film *Superman Returns*, which extends the Superman filmic universe of the 1970s and 80s, is generally accepted as a legitimate adaptation, while the "Season 5 and 6" fanfiction series is not, reflects this gendered divide. *Superman Returns* is an action film (i.e., "aggressive") and officially sanctioned by DC Comics (i.e., "objective"), while the "Season 5 and 6" fanfiction series is romantically oriented (i.e. "sensitive," "emotional") and not officially sanctioned (i.e., "subjective"). If we discount fanfiction as a form of adaptation, we risk perpetuating the same gendered hierarchies and exclusions that have historically informed both the superhero genre and its academic scholarship.

Excluding fanfiction as a form of adaption also risks neglecting the full complexity of intertextual storytelling in the digital era. Though I watched *Lois & Clark* before I read Harper's fanfiction trilogy, I saw the show differently after reading it, and know that both *Lois & Clark* and Harper's stories continue to shape my view of Superman—and superheroes in general—despite the dozens of superhero movies and television shows I have seen and the thousands (yes, thousands) of superhero comics I have read since I was a tween. My fandom of both *Lois & Clark* and its fanfiction will also certainly inform my reading of the forthcoming CW television show *Superman & Lois*, which, according to its initial synopsis, promises to follow the personal, professional, and fantastic adventures of "the world's most famous superhero and comic books' most famous journalist as they deal with all the stress, pressures and complexities that come with being working parents in today's society" (Beedle). The producers of this show are far more likely to have watched *Superman Returns* than to have read the *Lois & Clark* "Season 5 and 6" fanfiction series. But for those of us who have read and loved the "Season 5 and 6" series—which, like *Superman & Lois*, involves Lois and Clark not simply having a child (as in *Lois & Clark*), but also raising that child, and doing so together, rather than apart (as in *Superman Returns*)—this new CW show sounds a lot like an adaptation of fanfiction. And we will likely adjudicate its goodness based, in part, on expectations established by the "emotional, sensitive, and subjective" stories we perceive as a logical source.

In the end, regardless of whether we see ourselves as formalists or poststructuralists, we all, inevitably, make value judgements about which adaptations matter. This chapter has argued that decisions about which adaptations matter are also decisions about what counts as an adaptation, as well as who is allowed to make such decisions. Interrogating these realities is likely more feasible than overcoming them. In the future, then, we might work harder to acknowledge that every time we situate one origin story as more legitimate than another, our own origin stories matter a great deal. This is why this chapter incorporates mine. To some, a lactating Superman sighing with the rhythm of his daughter's mouth on his nipple might seem like a radical, irreconcilable deviation from the source. But from where I am sitting, it is entirely sensible, and even correct. For any of us, the "real" Superman is inseparable from our favorite one. Seeing and accepting the validity of more fan favorites might give us all a different, and considerably more diverse, understanding of Superman and his world—which is also our world, whoever we are.

Works Cited

Barbara. "Back to the Future." *Lois & Clark* Fanfic Archive. http://www.lcfanfic.com/stories/1998/html/s5-01.html.
Beazley, Malory. "The Trouble with Genderswap." *Fanfic Magazine*, 31 Jan. 2016. https://fanslashfic.com/2016/01/31/the-trouble-with-genderswap/.
Beedle, Tim. "Breaking News: The CW's *Superman & Lois* Gets a Series Order." DC Comics website, 14 Jan. 2020. https://www.dccomics.com/blog/2020/01/14/breaking-news-the-cws-superman-lois-gets-a-series-order.
Benyon, John. *Masculinities and Culture*. Open University, 2002.
Berger, Richard. "'Are There Any More at Home Like You?': Rewiring *Superman*." *Journal of Adaptation in Film & Performance*, vol. 1, no. 2, 2008, pp. 87–101.
Bonnstetter, Beth E. and Brian L. Ott. "(Re)Writing Mary Sue: *Écriture Féminine* and the Performance of Subjectivity." *Text and Performance Quarterly*, vol. 31, no. 4, 2011, pp. 342–367.
Brod, Harry. *Superman is Jewish?: How Comic Book Superheroes Came to Serve Truth, Justice, and the Jewish-American Way*. Free Press, 2016.
Burke, Liam. *The Comic Book Film Adaptation: Exploring Modern Hollywood's Leading Genre*. University Press of Mississippi, 2015.
Busse, Kristina. "Geek Hierarchies, Boundary Policing, and the Gendering of the Good Fan." *Participations: Journal of Audience and Reception Studies*, vol. 10, no. 1, 2013, pp. 73–91.
_____, and Alex Lothian. "Bending Gender: Feminist and (Trans)Gender Discourses in the Changing Bodies of Slash Fan Fiction." *Framing Fan Fiction: Literary and Social Practices in Fan Fiction Communities*, by Kristina Busse. University of Iowa Press, 2017, pp. 57–77.
Carroll, Noël. *The Philosophy of Horror, or, Paradoxes of the Heart*. Routledge, 1990.
Durden, Mary E. "It's a Bird! It's a Plane! It's Lois Lane!: The Construction of a Super(ior) Woman in *Lois & Clark*." *Examining Lois Lane: The Scoop on Superman's Sweetheart*, edited by Nadine Farghaly, The Scarecrow Press, 2013, pp. 171–188.
Farghaly, Nadine, editor. *Examining Lois Lane: The Scoop on Superman's Sweetheart*. The Scarecrow Press, 2013.
Freeman, Matthew. "Woman on Top: Postfeminism and the Transformation Narrative in *Lois & Clark: The New Adventures of Superman*." *Examining Lois Lane: The Scoop on Superman's Sweetheart*, edited by Nadine Farghaly, The Scarecrow Press, 2013, pp. 189–210.

Gordon, Ian. *Superman: The Persistence of an American Icon*. Rutgers University Press, 2016.
Hanley, Tim. "Gendercrunching January 2017—Counting Lead Female Characters at Marvel And DC." *Bleeding Cool*, 14 Mar. 2017. https://www.bleedingcool.com/2017/03/14/gendercrunching-january-2017-counting-lead-female-characters-at-marvel-and-dc/.
Harper, Shiela. "Mirror, Mirror." *Lois & Clark* Fanfic Archive. http://www.lcfanfic.com/stories/1999/html/s6-10.html.
_____, "Turn Around." *Lois & Clark* Fanfic Archive. http://www.lcfanfic.com/stories/1999/html/s6-08.html.
_____, "Walk in My Shoes." *Lois & Clark* Fanfic Archive. http://www.lcfanfic.com/stories/1999/html/s6-09.html.
Hatfield, Charles. *Hand of Fire: The Comics Art of Jack Kirby*. University Press of Mississippi, 2011.
Hutcheon, Linda. *A Theory of Adaptation*. Routledge, 2006.
Jenkins, Henry. "Good News for Aca/Fan." Confessions of an Aca/Fan Blog, 20 Aug. 2006. http://henryjenkins.org/blog/2006/08/good_news_for_acafen.html.
_____. *Textual Poachers: Television Fans and Participatory Culture*. Updated Twentieth Anniversary Edition. Routledge, 2013.
Kustritz, Anne. "Meet Stephanie Rogers, Captain America: Genderbending the Body Politic in Fan Art, Fiction, and Cosplay." *Supersex: Fantasy, Sexuality, and the Superhero*, edited by Anna F. Peppard, University of Texas Press, 2020, pp. 317–339.
"LOISCLA." Fanlore. https://fanlore.org/wiki/LOISCLA.
Morgan, Joe. "Know Your Herstory: Relive the Most Epic Lip Sync to Holding Out for A Hero Ever." *Gay Star News*, 20 Apr. 2017. https://www.gaystarnews.com/article/know-herstory-relive-epic-lip-sync-holding-hero-ever/#gs.5XG29pgB.
"Nielsen Ratings." *USA Today*. Fall 1995. p. D3.
Peppard, Anna F. "'No One's Going to be Looking at Your Face': The Female Gaze and the New (Super)Man in *Lois and Clark: The New Adventures of Superman*." *Supersex: Sexuality, Fantasy, and the Superhero*, edited by Anna F. Peppard, University of Texas Press, 2020, pp. 221–243.
_____, "'This Female Fights Back!': A Feminist History of Marvel Comics." *Make Ours Marvel: Media Convergence and a Comics Universe*, edited by Matt Yockey, University of Texas Press, 2017, pp. 105–137.
Pitkethy. Clare. "Straddling a Boundary: The Superhero and the Incorporation of Difference." *What Is a Superhero?* edited by Robin S. Rosenberg and Peter Coogan, Oxford University Press, 2013, pp. 25–30.
Radway, Janice A. *Reading the Romance: Women, Patriarchy, and Popular Literature*. The University of North Carolina Press, 1991.
Robinson, Michael G. "*Lois & Clark*: What's New About *The New Adventures of Superman*?" *Studies in Popular Culture*, vol. 21, no. 1, 1998, pp. 83–98.
Rossen, Jake. *Superman vs. Hollywood: How Fiendish Producers, Devious Directors, and Warring Writers Grounded an American Icon*. Chicago Review Press, 2008.
Scodari, Christine. "Resistance Re-Examined: Gender, Fan Practices, and Science Fiction Television. *Popular Communication*, vol. 1, no. 2, 2003, pp. 111–130.
Sonnet, Esther. "'Erotic Fiction by Women for Women': The Pleasures of Post-Feminist Heterosexuality." *Sexualities*, vol. 2, no. 2, 1999, pp. 167–187.
Suvin, Darko. *Metamorphoses of Science Fiction: On the Poetics and History of a Literary Genre*. Yale University Press, 1979.
Tosenberger, Catherine. "Mature Poets Steal: Children's Literature and the Unpublishability of Fanfiction." *Children's Literature Association Quarterly*, vol. 39, no. 1, 2014, pp. 4–27.
Tucker, Ken. "Hearts and Powers." *Entertainment Weekly*, no. 304, Dec. 1995, p. 53.
Wilcox, Rhonda V. "Lois's Locks: Trust and Representation in *Lois and Clark: The New Adventures of Superman*." *Fantasy Girls: Gender in the New Universe of Science Fiction and Fantasy Television*, edited by Elyce Rae Helford, Rowman & Littlefield, 2000, pp. 91–114.

The Man of Steel

A Modern Hero in Crisis

SIMON HAROLD WALKER

In the 2019–2020 "Crisis on Infinite Earths" Arrowverse crossover, Brandon Routh's emotionally-scarred *Kingdom Come* Superman quips after battling with his multiverse doppelganger, Tyler Hoechlin's virtuous Superman from *Supergirl*, "this is actually the second time I've gone crazy and fought myself" (*Batwoman*). Routh's return as Superman, together with his call-back to the events of *Superman III* (1983) and the use of John William's Superman theme, draws a canonical connection between the classic Christopher Reeve *Superman* films and the *Kingdom Come*–devastated version depicted by Routh, building on his adoption of the mantel (ahem, cape) in the widely-critiqued 2006 film, *Superman Returns* (Topel). This confirmation comes after nearly two decades of increasingly bleak depictions and reimaging's of the "Blue Boy Scout" (Sharpe 38).

This chapter considers the characterization of Superman as he is redefined under the gaze of twenty-first-century reality. In *Smallville* (2001–2011), Tom Welling desperately fights his inner darkness to become a beacon of hope. In *Supergirl* (2015–2021), Tyler Hoechlin has portrayed the brightest and most likable Superman since Dean Cain in the 1990s *Lois and Clark* (1993–1997). Yet even in the alternative reality in which *Supergirl* is set, his character seems oddly out of place. The Arrowverse, built initially upon the gritty reality established by *Arrow* (2012–2020), has spun a range of successful TV series centering on a range of DC superheroes, including *The Flash* (2012–present), *Supergirl*, *The Legends of Tomorrow* (2016–present), and most recently *Batwoman* (2019–present). While many episodes within the various series have had consistent comedic tones, more often each show has increasingly dealt with dark plot lines, including the deaths and murder of family members, torture of the main protagonists, loss of key characters without return, and various degrees of public mistrust for the heroes. *The Flash* and *Legends of Tomorrow* have historically retained aspects of their characteristic levity; yet as events moved towards the end of *Arrow* as part of the unprecedented "Crisis on Infinite Earths" crossover event, darker themes have overshadowed the traditional lighter tone. Still, the Arrowverse remains a light-hearted romp in comparison to the current DC Extended Universe, including *Man of Steel* (2013), *Batman v Superman: Dawn of Justice* (2016), and *Justice League* (2017), within which Superman is a murderer, has already died and been buried, remained more alien than human in nature, and mostly divided his time between being dead, moping, and grimacing. These newest depictions stand in shocking contrast to the bright blue-and-red paragon of heroics that has been the standard of the character for so long. However, these are not as surprising to the long-term readers of the various comic versions of Superman, as over the last century the character has been reinvented and reinterpreted in ways significantly darker than has so far been imaginable on screen. This has included a fascist Superman (*Multiversity Guidebook* #1 [Mar. 2015]), a murderous, revenge-driven Superman (*Injustice: Gods Among Us* #1 [Mar. 2013]), and in *Kingdom Come* (May–Aug. 1996), a disenfranchised, morally-questionable Superman, similar in kind to his alter ego in Mark Millar's *Superman: Red Son* (June–Aug. 2003), who turns away from his good-natured persona following a murderous gas attack at the *Daily Planet* and the subsequent public celebration of the murder of the Joker by another hero in retribution.

However, as the trend continues to humanize, deconstruct, and present a fractured version of the eponymous hero, such versions may soon enter the public perception. It is this darkening of the character that is the focus of this chapter. Within current popular fiction, there remains an expectation for heroes to be as flawed as the viewer and blur the line between moral and just. Richard Donner's bright blue, square-jawed wonder-man seems no longer believable. The original belief that "a man can fly" may remain but in a world where corrupt businessmen can become world leaders, where nations are torn apart by lies told for the profit of the elite, and where physical agency is increasingly removed, our "belief" in bright, glittering heroes is on the wane.

To consider how the post-modern Superman can be recognized through the blackened mirror of twenty-first-century culture, this chapter will consider three core aspects of the character on paper and particularly on screen. Firstly, the suit which has defined the Man of Steel for nearly a century will be analyzed. From the birth of the character to the heights of brightest blue to darkest maroon, the role of the super-suit will draw a link between behavior, audience expectation, and reflection of the cultural mood. Next, the behavior of the titular hero will be examined. Superman is traditionally considered a paragon of truth and justice. His moral compass has historically been unwavering, yet over the last century his character increasing shifted, first on the page before finally on screen. With this transformation came the loss of assurance in the virtuousness of the character and his acts; this change enables audiences to question the very validity of the character they are engaging with. Finally, the role of music and themes will be explored. While muted on the page, on screen sound is as important to the narrative and characterization as an action. Music instructs the audience how to feel about the characters and story unfolding around them. Increasingly, the orchestral accompaniment has darkened along with the interpretations of the character. This chapter will therefore illustrate how this has affected the views understanding and acceptance of the Man of Steel as he strives to relevance within the context of the twenty-first century.

Costume and Colors: Clothes Maketh the Man

In 2013, Henry Cavill's version of Superman took to the skies, breaking both the ground he leapt from and cinematic tradition as the typical brightness of his suit's red, blue, and yellow were significantly reduced to darker hues. This shift followed a decade of suit alterations across the various incarnations of Superman. In the CW's *Smallville*, Clark Kent (Tom Welling)'s teenage progression into the titular superhero was marked by numerous costume changes, beginning with casual parings of red and blue and ending with Clark adopting the classic costume, although the audience is treated to only a fleeting glimpse after ten seasons of waiting. Significantly, midway through Clark's transformation, he adopted a solid black suit to reflect his increasing internal battle between morality and justice. Over several seasons this association with black continued as many of Clark's actions take place under the cover of darkness, particularly as his actions become morally questionable. This association between morality and darkness stretches beyond modern fiction and is a recognizable parable in fiction and religious testimony for thousands of years.

The link between black and negative actions, however, is relatively new within the canonized Superman mythology. The most famous of the black suits was introduced after the "Death of Superman" (1992–1993) where, following the rise of several "pseudo-supermen," the original was resurrected and adopted a dark black suit with a silver shield. This suit was introduced as a "regeneration suit" designed to restore Superman before he could once again adopt his classic visage. This costume returned briefly in 1996 during *Final Night* as Superman lost his powers, as did a variation of the suit in *Batman Beyond* television series (1999–2001), *Flashpoint* comic book event mini-series (2011), and *Man and Superman* comic book one-shot (2019). In almost all cases, the black suit is reflective of a loss of status, power, or association with the original version of Superman. Within various stories, the black suit has often served as a visual dissociation and distinction from the traditional characterization. This allows Superman to act in different ways, immediately visually distinguishable to the reader, freeing him from the norms and behaviors that canonically restrict his character.

This correlation between clothing and behavior is not limited to superhero fiction. Long before the black super shield, Spider-Man's symbiote costume (*Amazing Spider-Man* #252 [May 1984]), the speedster grim reaper Black Flash (*The Flash* Vol. 2 #138 [June 1998]), or Captain America's Nomad (*Captain America* #180 [Dec. 1974]), real humans have been able to psychologically excuse their change in normative behavior through a radical change of clothes. During the First World War, the first of the new technologically and geographically all-encompassing wars in the twentieth century, millions of civilians around the world exchanged their typical clothes for a military uniform. Historian Jayne Tynan argues the adoption of a military uniform was central to establishing the masculine identity of the soldier, allowing for a disassociation from the normative behavior that was typically expected of them (19). British First World War soldier Private Johnson best summed this transition up poetically in his diary as he wrote at the end of the war: "I had served 4 years and 8 months in His Majesty's Forces. In May month, I took up once more the threads of civilian life so hastily thrown down in the dark days of 1914" (IWM 12383.). In his book *War Bodies,* Simon Walker clarifies how behaviors drastically changed according to dress, as the uniform worn by British enlistees in the First World War psychologically and socially enabled them to act and speak in ways previously not permitted by acceptable standards, including killing, sexual acts, and drinking (22).

As a character, Superman has a long history of distorted reflections. From Bizzaro to Clark Kent's identity struggle made solid when the Clark and Superman personalities split and fight as a result of kryptonite poisoning in *Superman III* (1983), negative versions of the character have typically been depicted wearing subdued versions of the recognizable suit. In 2003, writer Mark Millar broke new ground by asking the question of what could have happened if Superman had landed somewhere other than Kansas, USA. *Superman: Red Son* presents the character as growing up within the communist

Soviet Union, rejecting the American Dream that he had symbolized in all other depictions and instead utilizing his powers to "save and protect" through totalitarianism. *Red Son* mirrors many tragic-hero narratives as the moral ground on which Superman resides increasingly slips beneath him. His quest to protect and save the Earth increasingly reflects the development of a totalitarian approach where his actions, including war, physical abuse, and experimentation, and the abuse of idolism, inspire acts of self-destruction in others. Spurning the American flag's colors in favor of grey, red, and black, the Soviet Superman's uniform grows increasingly more militaristic as the story progresses.

This reinterpretation of the costume also occurs in the multiverse versions of the character where Superman is bought up as part of Nazi regime in Germany. This version of the character lands in the Nazi-owned territory in 1938 and become instrumental in the Third Reich's victory and domination of Earth. Two versions of the character exist: The first, a black-and-red uniformed, blond Kryptonian who wore a swastika on his shield and led the JL-Axis established by Fuehrer Adolf Hitler (*52* #52 [July 2007]); the other is Overman, AKA Karl Kant/Kal-L, who retains the same dark hair and complexion of the original Superman but wears a fully black and grey uniform with a red lightening shield (*Multiversity Guidebook* #1). Both versions are totalitarian killers whose ideologies are reflected by their clothing. These are recognizably evil versions of the character, just as was presented in *Superman III* as the jaded alter ego attempts to kill Clark or in *Smallville* where the dark-suited teenage Kent battles his own morality and pains. Darker versions of the costume reflect for the viewer and reader signs of moral conflict within the soul of the wearer. This is particularly the case for the *Kingdom Come* version of the character, whose classic suit is again reduced in brightness and, more importantly, has the S-shield changed to red against black, in keeping with the suffering and anger of the battle-worn Superman dragged out of retirement. In the Arrowverse, the *Kingdom Come* version of character is reinterpreted with a similar backstory and the same costume that stands in significant contrast to that worn by Tyler Hoechlin's Superman.

It is difficult to consider the Soviet and Nazi versions of Superman next to the standard paragon version in bright blue. Yet, these versions are not as unalike as perhaps first thought. Post–Second World War, American psychologist Stanley Milgram attempted to test the validity of claims that Nazi collaborators lacked agency for the horrendous actions during the tyrannical rule of Adolf Hitler. His experiment demonstrated the role of uniforms in establishing authority and acceptable behavior. Later, in 1971, Philip Zimbardo, another American psychological researcher, conducted his infamous Stanford Prison Experiment during which the random assignment of clothes designating between pseudo-guard or pseudo-prisoner almost immediately prompted radical changes in behavior in both parties. For the character of Superman, his adopted upbringing is as formative within his socialized identity as his powers or his Kryptonian heritage. He may have originated from an alien planet, but it is the formative grounding of his rural American adoptive parents who instill within Kal-El his sense of moral purpose and internalized ethics. Often it is the blue-and-red suit that accompanies the actualization of these moral internalizations, combining with acceptance of Kal-El's powers, to give him purpose.

This is particularly evident in Richard Donner's *Superman* series, where frequently the emergence of the suit accompanies actualization or restoration of the recognizable character. In *Superman: The Movie* (1978), young Clark Kent, played by Jeff East, transforms into Christopher Reeve's costumed Superman after he wanders the globe seeking to understand his purpose. In the finale of *Smallville*, Clark Kent is told by the remnants of his birth father's consciousness within the Fortress of Solitude that he had finally earned the right to wear the red-and-blue suit that had been locked away from him for so long. Jor-El (Terence Stamp) tells his son "Your abilities may be of my blood, but it is your time in Smallville with Jonathan and Martha Kent, and all the people there, that made you a hero, Kal-El" ("Finale—Part 2"). The pursuit of the final suit was one of the primary aspects of this version of Clark's character arc, an event that dragged audiences on for ten seasons as they waited to see Clark self-actualize only to be disappointed as Tom Welling is never fully visible in the suit. In *Lois and Clark*, the adoption of the super suit is a comedic montage which cements Dean Cain's Superman personality and persona. Set to the theme "I Need a Hero" by Gloria Gaynor, Cain's Superman tries on a series of bright suits designed to draw attention and avoid recognition. Having made each of his trial suits, his adopted mother Martha (K. Callan) hugs her son, now dressed in the trademark bright blue and red, and laughs "One thing's for sure. Nobody's going to be looking at your face!" ("The Pilot"). This is similarly repeated in 2010's *Superman: Earth One* Vol. 1 by J. Michael Straczynski and Shane Davies, where Clark is depicted as a younger and more rash new hero attempting to adjust to his life in the city of Metropolis. This version of Clark combines elements from *Smallville* and *Lois and Clark*, as his suit is yet again made by his mother but Clark worries about his actions, safety, and purpose. Almost paraphrasing the words spoken on screen two decades previous, Martha tells her son in response to his lack of mask, "When people see how powerful you are, all the things you can do, they're going to be terrified ... unless they can see your face, and see there that you mean them no harm. The mask [indicating his face] is what you are going to have wear the rest of your life" (76).

This subtle shift in the purpose of the suit, from inspiring hope to reassurance of intent, encapsulates the modern interpretations of the suit and Superman's numerous incarnations in the twenty-first century. Cavill's Superman tells Lois Lane (Amy Adams) in 2013's *Man of Steel* that the red *S* on his subdued uniform meant hope; however, the costume and the subsequent actions of the most recent movie version of the character convey a different message both to the audience and the fictional world within which he resides.

Morally Questionable—You Will Believe That a Man Can Fly, Lie and Die

In *Man of Steel*, Henry Cavill's Superman appears to cross a line that would divide the fandom. Faced with an impossible choice during the finale, Superman snaps General Zod (Michael Shannon)'s neck as he is held immobile in a headlock. As Zod traces his heat vision towards a cowering family, Superman is forced to kill one of the last survivors of his home planet to save his adopted people. In a 2016 podcast for *Nerdist*, script writer David S. Goyer claimed that his and Christopher Nolan's decision to have Superman murder Zod at the conclusion of the film was a deliberate divergence from tradition orchestrated by the needs of the narrative.

> You have to do what's right for the story. In that instance, this was a Superman who had only been Superman for like, a week. He wasn't Superman as we think of him in the DC Comics or even in a world

that conceived of Superman existing…. If you take Superman out of it, what's the right way to tell that story? … [T]he moral, horrible situation to be in is to actually be forced to kill, not wanting to, the only other person from your race. Take Superman aside, I think that's the right way to tell that story [qtd. in Lockett].

Elsewhere, director Zac Snyder also took credit for the decision, claiming that he wanted to establish a no-win scenario for the hero that would force a character-defining moment for future films.

> David [S. Goyer], Chris[topher Nolan] and I had long talks about it, and I said that I really feel like we should kill Zod, and that Superman should kill him. The "Why?" of it for me was that if was truly an origin story, his aversion to killing is unexplained…. I wanted to create a scenario where Superman, either he's going to see [Metropolis' citizens] chopped in half, or he's gotta [sic] do what he's gotta do [Outlaw].

This superhero version of the Kobayashi Maru (the famous no-win scenario in *Star Trek* that maverick starship captain James T. Kirk cheated to win at Starfleet Academy) proved particularly controversial as it appeared in contrast to the expected behavior of epitome of moral action in bright blue-and-red that Superman had been regarded being for so many decades.

This shift in the characterization of Superman on the silver screen was accompanied by an increasing shift in the attitudes and behaviors of various heroes within popular culture. Beloved characters such as Iron Man, Captain America, and Green Arrow were reinvented for new audiences baring visible physical and psychological scars. Playboy Tony Stark (Robert Downey, Jr.) was portrayed in *Iron Man* (2008) as a morally bankrupt, possibly alcoholic hedonist whose redemption arc constantly offset his genius against his narcissism. Captain America, aka Steve Rogers (Chris Evans), evolves in the Marvel Cinematic Universe in a story arc that is vaguely reminiscent to the changes to Superman on the silver screen. First established as the bright-blue moral compass of the Avengers (*The Avengers* [2012]), even providing comedic relief by criticizing the use of bad language (*The Avengers: Age of Ultron* [2015]), his later darker-suit version opposed the system he swore allegiance to before leading a team of renegades hunted by friends and enemies (*Captain America: Civil War* [2016]). At the end of *Avengers: Infinity War* (2018), Steve's unshakable moral code lays shattered as he has continued to compromise and react to the tragic world that arose following Thanos's extermination of half of the universe. In *Avengers: Endgame* (2019), Captain America's inflexibility and self-righteous determination in condemning Stark's attempt to implement the Ultron defense system to protect the planet is laid bare as Stark confronts him, arguing that for all of Steve's expressive moral diatribes, they still "lost together." Steve also takes the morally ambiguous action of displacing himself in time to return to life in the past with Peggy Carter. While the end of *Endgame* does not make this clear, the philosophical conundrum remains that if Steve lived through the same period twice, then his future knowledge makes him complicit in the deaths and destruction that occur in his personal past, including the rise of Hydra, the destruction of New York, and murder of half the sentient population of the entire universe. On television, the reinterpretation of Green Arrow marked one of the most drastic departures from previous depictions of the character as the DC's Arrowverse began in 2012. Like Superman, his costume colors were toned down to reflect the change in character as much of the humor of the most recent version portrayed on screen by Justin Hartley in *Smallville* was replaced by trauma and grief.

These different and grittier versions of famous characters on screen were again less of a surprise to comic book fans. Within the vast history of comic book interpretations of the characters, morally questionable actions are common within darker-toned storylines. For DC, Green Arrow has been both one of the most cartoonish and the grittiest heroes across their line-up. In 1970, in attempt to revive the ailing health of the Green Lantern series, Green Arrow and Green Lantern were paired and dispatched to deal with "real American issues," which soon included the first Speedy (Roy Harper)'s heroin addiction (*Green Lantern* Vol. 2 #85 [Sept. 1971]). Later, Green Arrow continued to challenge social issues, commonly depicted as a socialist akin to Robin Hood, the Arrow comics included storylines about his own personal flaws, including infidelity, which lead to his break-up with Black Canary (Dinah Lance) (*Green Arrow* Vol. 2 #90 [Sept. 1994]) as well as his next Speedy sidekick (Mia Dearden) having contracted HIV after years of child abuse (*Green Arrow* Vol. 3 #43 [Dec. 2004]). It was during this period that the utility belt-style quiver that held cartoonish weapons, such as the infamous boxing glove arrow (*Adventure Comics* #118 [July 1947]), the chimney sweep arrow (*Adventure Comics* #263 [Aug. 1959]), and the baby rattle arrow (*Adventure Comics* #265 [Oct. 1959]), was phased out. The more realistic and dangerous standard arrow replaced it, albeit with numerous upgrades over the years, which maimed and later killed the Green Arrow's enemies. One of the most poignant of these was the conclusion of O'Neil and Adam's socially aware *Green Arrow/Green Lantern* series (*The Flash* #217–219 [Sept. 1972–Jan. 1973]), where Oliver accidently kills a criminal and attempts to give up his Green Arrow persona through guilt. These examples of darker and, crucially, more realistic storylines, at least in terms of thematic reaction if not reality, were increasingly rife within the comic books across the board.

These darker storylines were often praised for their engagement with modern societal issues. Whilst often receiving acclaim within the comic book world, their impact was limited upon zeitgeist in general, as the film and television versions of the characters lagged behind in terms of innovation and reality. This is very much the case within depictions of the character of Superman on screen in relation to the pages of comic books. In literature, Superman has killed on several occasions. In his earliest incarnations, less powerful than he would later be depicted and preceding the moral code set by editor Whitney Ellsworth in 1940, Superman took a significantly more aggressive stance against criminals and villains. In his first few issues in 1938, Superman was presented as closer to the stance later taken by the Green Arrow as an anti-establishment social crusader fighting for common people against the abuse of the rich and powerful. Blue-suited and able to leap ran than fly, Superman faced wife beaters, lynch mobs, and political and business corruption. In *Action Comics* #2 (July 1938), he carelessly throws an enemy soldier high over a forest, insinuating the man's death, and destroys a plane with the pilot trapped inside. In *Superman* #2 (Fall 1939), he gleefully watches a criminal die, chocking on the poison gas the man has thrown down to kill them both. As the man gasps for air, Superman tells him with a smile "The gas doesn't affect my physical structure." In the introduction to *Superman in the Fifties* (2002), comic book writer and Superman expert Mark Waid makes the distinction between the earliest incarnation of the character from his future idealistic version by describing him as a "diamond in the rough: a quick-tempered social activist whose dedication to the ideals of truth and justice apparently put him above the rules and regulations of society" (5). In "The True *Übermensch*: Batman as Humanistic Myth," C.K. Robertson argues that this version of Superman represented the original Nietzschean *Übermensch* version of the character (52), set as the pinnacle of human ability and somewhat above morality. This characterization would later transfer to Batman as Superman developed into the peak of morality over humanity. Robertson concluded within the that later attempts to return Superman to "a darker and harsher [version] would feel forced and inappropriate" (58).

Yet, sixty years on from the original introduction of the character, that is exactly what happened. Versions of the character, as well as many other superheroes, in the comics grew darker, inspired by the 1986 devastating duo of Alan Moore and Dave Gibbons' anarchic and brooding *Watchmen* and Frank Miller's dystopic and genre-changing *The Dark Knight Returns*. Over the subsequent decades Superman would die and be resurrected, commit murder, and reject his role as savior. In the computer game *Injustice: Gods Amongst Us* (2013) and the accompanying prequel comic book, Batman looks upon horrified as Superman punches through the Joker's chest to exact revenge for murdering his friends, blowing up Metropolis, and tricking Superman into murdering his own wife and unborn child (*Injustice: Gods Among Us* #1). In *Kingdom Come*, Superman's rejection of society ends with his creation of a more authoritarian response to crime which brings him to blows with other heroes over the loss of his values and subsequent actions. The comic book stories "Whatever Happened to the Man of Tomorrow?" (*Superman* #423/*Action Comics* #583 [Sept. 1986]), *Infinite Crisis* (Dec. 2005–June 2006), *Superman Unchained* (Aug. 2013–Jan. 2015), and "What's So Funny About Truth, Justice, & the American Way?" (*Action Comics* #775 [Mar. 2001]), as well as the animated films *Superman: Doomsday* (2007) and *Superman: Unbound* (2013), to name just a few of the darkest stories in Superman's recent history, all depict the character acting in violent, morally questionable, or unlawful ways; many of which owe much to the original work and vision of Moore and Millar.

On screen, this transformation has been more gradual. As noted, the end of the twentieth century witnessed a live-action shift from jovial bright stories of *Lois and Clark* and the wholesome heroics of Reeve's Superman to the darker teen depiction of Tom Welling's Clark Kent/Kal-El in *Smallville*. Routh's only screen outing as Superman may be as colorful as the original films, but it presented an out-of-place Superman who abandoned his son and repented for his past mistakes. Henry Cavill's three screen outings as the character have seemed to produce more time moping and screaming than anything else. Even his return from the dead in *Justice League* is tempered by his irresponsibility, as he ups and abandons the fight to save humanity to answer the calls for help captured by his super hearing. While there is a moral argument to made for both sides, his decision seems illogical to save a few at the potential cost of the many. Only Tyler Hoechlin's version of the character in *Supergirl* seems reminiscent of the beloved character, yet even his version has quickly succumbed to portrayals of darker aspect of the character, including a dark-suited antagonist version within the 2018 Arrowverse "Elseworlds" crossover event ("Elseworlds, Part 3" [2018]). Lynette Porter argues in *Tarnished Heroes, Charming Villains, and Modern Monsters* (2010) "…in the 2000's, situational ethics seem [more] common, and few legal of moral behavioral proscriptions are perceived as absolute" (66). As future versions of the character continues during the era of prestige television, the argument remains that audiences seem capable of suspending their disbelief if their heroes are presented as vulnerable and damaged. Screen depictions of heroes have begun to catch up with the reality overladen portrayals within many graphic novels, leading to, paraphrasing Harvey Dent (Aaron Eckhart) in *The Dark Knight* (2008), a need "to die a hero or live long enough to become the villain" to retain audience interests.

Sounds About Right—Setting the Tone

The results of an experiment on the relationship between music and emotion by Nidhya Logeswaran and Joydeep Bhattacharya, published in 2009 in *Neuroscience Letters*, found substantial evidence of "cross-modal influences by musical emotion," demonstrating that visual subjective interpretation could directly coerced through the pairing of types of music (133). Simply, when paired with music, action on the screen can be extremely subjectively interpreted. In the brutally brilliant YouTube Series *Epic Rap Battles*, a faceoff between Stephen Spielberg and Alfred Hitchcock includes the dismissal of Spielberg's ability with the line "Half your billions should go to John Williams." Satire aside, the power of film music and themes accompanying the action on screen to set the tone of the imagery cannot be overstated. John Williams remains one of the most famous composers of film themes in cinematic history, responsible for the iconic soundtracks to *Star Wars* (1977–2019), *Superman: The Movie* (1978), *E.T.* (1982), *Home Alone* (1990–1992), *Jurassic Park* (1993–1997), and *Harry Potter* (2001–2004). Williams has created scores that immediately create mental images of the film in seconds within the memory of the listener. His scores have also added the emphasis to a scene that was lacking prior to musical accompaniment. In the documentary series *The Movies that Made Us* (2019), *Home Alone* editor Raja Gosnell explains that the first music arranged for the film did little to transform the cartoon type violence from terrifying to funny. In a desperate bid, the director Chris Columbus turned to the famous composer John Williams, and according to Gosnell, the film immediately changed tone: "suddenly it all comes to life ... you put this music on top of it, which changes the whole movie." This effect is not limited to John William's work, but he remains one of the greatest of all time having written the scores for so many well-known classic films.

This subjectivity becomes apparent in the two separate cinematic encounters between General Zod and Superman. In *Man of Steel*, during the final showdown as Superman kills Zod, the music over the action is somber, uncomplicated, and reduced to a piano solo rendition of "If You Love These People" composition by Hans Zimmer, who composed the score for the entire film. The scene is maximized to draw a darker emotional reaction. Superman screams agonizingly over the corpse of his fallen foe before sobbing into the lap of Lois Lane. This action confirms the tone for Cavill's ongoing portrayal of the character as another typically Zimmer theme, majestic but darkly atmospheric, accompanies him high into the air as Superman and bespectacled and clumsy as Clark Kent. Zimmer is famous for his brooding, grandiose themes that often homage to the previous musical arrangements that preceded and inspired them. Dan Golding argues in his chapter "The Sound of the Cinematic Superhero" in *The Superhero Symbol: Media, Culture, and Politics* (2020) that Zimmer's theme for *Man of Steel* shares many similarities to the iconic Williams theme as both use a perfect fifth as the basis of their introduction. He refers to this as a "mutation" of previous musical identities to create the auditory "superhero identity" on the screen (171). Typically, Zimmer writes in D-minor, adding a melancholy aspect to the score. He also regularly employs the Phrygian mode, which is the use of a scale similar to a natural minor scale with inclusion of a minor second interval ("What Are Musical Modes"). This is generally accepted as a method of adding further melancholy to the already fairly somber standard minor chords. It also adds a touch of grandeur, therefore it is commonly found both in heavy metal guitar solo and file soundtracks. Zimmer's theme "What Are You Going to Do When You Are Not Saving the World" begins somberly and grows slowly to a majestic crescendo, adding in loud horns for the chorus accompanied by almost militaristic drumming. This is a powerful auditory image implying supremacy and majesty of Cavill's Superman. The theme is both regal and aloof, theoretically encapsulating the characterization envisaged by Snyder and Christopher Nolan perfectly. Yet, it is more likely that the theme and the character are symbiotic; Zimmer's theme reiterates to the audience how different this version of the character is from the previous film incarnations they are accustomed to. The new Superman for the twenty-first century bears little resemblance to smiling, bright-blue boy scout played by Christopher Reeve, even audibly.

In contrast, John William's iconic Superman theme is immediately recognizable, beginning first with the triumphant horn fanfare before building with a militaristic drumming to a dramatic crescendo. The theme is jovial and powerful. In an interview with *Gramophone* in 2017, John Williams confirmed his rationale behind the composition:

> [the theme is] an attempt to make a connection with an audience, and (in the case of Superman) about what a hero is—what we think in the year 1980, or whatever it was, a hero should be represented by. Probably, in very conventional terms, a trumpet to begin with, or some drums if you like. And the music should be tonal and heraldic and heroic and so on [Mangan].

John Williams's theme has provided the sustaining music associated with Superman since 1978. The distinctive themes share similarities to Sammy Timberg's brass fanfare "Superman March" from the Fleischer Superman cartoons (1941–1942) and the opening theme for the 1950s *Adventures of Superman* (1951–1958), credited to Leon Klatzkin, which first established the use of the musical triad which matched the three syllables in the character's name. While William's incorporated these into his own composition, his theme was much more than a homage as it became the iconic theme associated with the character that has provided the underlying basis for all following both on television and in cinema as all versions have included rhythmic, militarist, march-like drumming and a crescendo of horns. This also includes Superman-related series such as the 1980s much-maligned television show *Superboy* (1988–1992); *Smallville*, which frequently used horns and drums for dramatic effect; and the Arrowverse *Supergirl*, which includes a slightly different, lower version for Tyler Hoechlin's Superman when he was first revealed in the season two opener ("The Adventures of Supergirl"). This association with majestic horns and drums is also present in the numerous animated films focused on Superman, ranging from the acclaimed '90s television series *Superman: The Animated Series* (1996–2000) through to the most modern interpretations of comic books stories such as the animated films *Superman: Unbound* (2013), *The Death of Superman* (2018), *Reign of the Supermen* (2019), and *Superman: Red Son* (2020), amongst many others, all carry the pairing of heroic horns and pounding drums to establish the recognizability of the protagonist.

In *Lois and Clark*, the overlaid music is often essential to the story in a way that make the series unique to the other portrayals. In an interview in 2017, Jay Gruska, the composer for *Lois and Clark*, explained that his approach had been instructed to capture the duality of the action and romance that made up each episode. He explained: "Two things were stressed in the meeting about musical approach, the heroic/muscular side of Superman music, alongside both the romantic and tongue in cheek relationship between Lois and Clark" (Baxter). Often in the series, bluesy, wry piano riffs were used to accentuate the comedic actions of a character, more often than not following an interaction between Lois and Clark, complete with a final nonplussed look in the vague direction of the camera. Lois and Clark also opened with a homage to the William's theme, with a dramatic horn, string, and drum theme accompanied with a flying bright red cape, once again unifying the light-hearted tone of the series to the jovial heroic Reeve version that preceded it rather than presenting a darker perspective as the contextual graphic novels published around the same time were glorifying in.

The power of the music accompanying the character's behavior on screen can be extraordinary. This theory is particularly open to validation within the final scenes of *Superman II* (1980), where Reeve's Superman tricks Zod (Terence Stamp) and his allies into becoming depowered and turns the tables on them. Believing that he has the upper hand, Zod demands that Superman kneels before him and swear eternal loyalty to Zod while holding his hand. The reveal comes as Superman begins to crush Zod's hand and the bone popping sounds are accompanied by the John Williams' fanfare. The theme continues as Superman lifts Zod into the air, smirks at him, shakes his head sarcastically, and, still smiling, throws Zod across the room where he smashes against the wall and then falls, apparently to his death, into the cavernous depths below. Zod's compatriots follow him, with Ursa (Sarah Douglas) being punched by Lois Lane (Margot Kidder) and falling in as a result. Lois and Superman then happily hug accompanied by the romantic theme synonymous to the couple in the Reeve films. In both movie versions of Superman's final showdown with Zod it appears that the character goes against his set moral code and kills him. Yet, whilst the killing in *Man of Steel* is accompanied by anguish and devastation, the *Superman II* is accompanied by smiles and laughter. However, far from regarding Lois and Superman to be psychopathic at the blatant killing of three people, the jovial theme allows the audience to celebrate with them and enjoy the finale as a positive end. *Man of Steel* makes no such allowance and forces the audience to share the anguish and internalize the moral quandary that Superman faced. In essence, *Man of Steel* and the subsequent DC follow up films *make* the moment more realistic, drawing the audience in to consider the ramifications of the heroes' actions, almost humanizing Superman through his demonstration of fallibility.

In modern television, it is the fallibility of the hero that is increasingly important. To maintain interest and relatability from the modern audience fallible characters must follow the mantra of realism and responsibility, in way that any previous incarnations in various guises on screen, page, or story did not. Like Superman, in the twenty-first century our heroes' music, like their clothing and indeed their behavior, is required to be darker in order to be realistic and believable.

Conclusion

While the comic book version of Superman has been experimenting with his angst phase for a long time, it is only in the last couple of decades that live action screen versions of Superman have caught up. Certainly, the angsty television version of Superboy of the 1980s had some darker and more hot-headed tendencies, but compared to the trials and tribulations that teenage Clark would face in *Smallville*, which opened with him being crucified in a cornfield with a painted S on his chest, *Superboy* was practically a pre-school cartoon. The most recent versions of the Superman series have included an already once-deceased, darker-suited, particularly alien version who oscillates between grief and aloofness (*Man of Steel*), a confused and incredibly dangerous genetic experiment (Superboy in *Titans* [2018–present]), and an updated version of the original Superman, resplendent in blue and red, played by Tyler Hoechlin in *Supergirl*. In the new Superman & Lois television series (2021), this preference for darker themes has continued. In the new *Superman & Lois* television series (2021), this preference for darker themes has continued. In the first episode ("Pilot"), Clark loses both his job at *The Daily Planet* and his adoptive mother Martha Kent on the same day, resulting in moving his wife and twin sons, Jonathan and Jordan, to Smallville. While still retaining a family positive persona similar to other Arrowverse shows like *The Flash*, this uprooting and disruption of family life also echoes the dysfunction and catastrophe witnessed in darker comic book-based shows such as *Locke and Key* (2020–present) and *The Umbrella Academy* (2019–present).

Within the modern medium for screen entertainment, darker storylines imbued with fallible reality seems to be the most popular. In 2019, *Game of Thrones* (2011–2019), *Stranger Things* (2016–present), *The Umbrella Academy,* and *The Boys* (2019–present) were amongst the most popular watched shows according to Google (Venable). Each of the shows mentioned feature antagonistic main characters that swear, act in ways unbecoming to a traditional hero, and involve storylines that include abuse, rape, kidnap, death, and loss. Given the competition, it is unreasonable to expect future screen depictions of Superman not to incorporate emotive and hard-hitting realistic themes into the narrative. As the character evolves, he will continue to shift to reflect the attitudes and viewing tastes of the audience or he faces the potential to become obsolete. Prior to be cast as Superman, Christopher Reeve attempted to visualize how he would bring the character of Superman to the silver screen as he flew to the audition for the part in London. Reeve later reflected in an interview that he spent much of the time considering the world in which his *Superman* was going to inhabit and how that would affect his portrayal: "By the late 1970s, the masculine image had changed.... Now it was acceptable for a man to show gentleness and vulnerability. I felt that the new Superman ought to reflect that contemporary male image" (Hughes 195). Reeve's interpretation contextually provided one of the most beloved versions of the character; the question remains of how the Man of Steel must continue to change to reflect the audience expectations of the future.

Since the beginning of the twentieth-first century, much of the world has been affected by war and terrorism. America suffered the greatest loss in its recent history on the 11th of September 2001, the European Union was fractured in 2020, and leaders once considered unlikely to take power occupied positions of authority around the globe. Poverty, suicide rates, and reliance on charity to survive has increased over the course of two decades. Given the state of the world politically, socially, and economically as it stands, it is highly likely that Reeve was right in saying that Superman should reflect the contemporary culture within which he is developed. To that end, it is hardly surprising that the Man of Tomorrow is somewhat more desolate today.

Works Cited

"The Adventures of Supergirl." *Supergirl*, season 2, episode 1, The CW, 10 Oct. 2016.
The Avengers. Directed by Joss Whedon, Marvel Studios, 2012.
Avengers: Age of Ultron. Directed by Joss Whedon, Marvel Studios, 2015.
Avengers: Endgame. Directed by Joss Whedon, Marvel Studios, 2019.
Avengers: Infinity War. Directed by Joe Russo and Anthony Russo, Marvel Studio, 2018.

Batman v Superman: Dawn of Justice. Directed by Zack Snyder, Warner Bros. 2016.

Baxter, Daryl. "Interview: Jay Gruska." *Daryl Baxter*, 12 Sept. 2017, https://darylbaxter.com/2017/09/12/interview-jay-gruska/. Accessed 12 Dec. 2019.

"Bruce Wayne." *Titans*, season 2, episode 7, DC Universe, 18 Oct. 2019.

Burton, Bonnie. "New Superman and Lois Lane TV series flying over to The CW." *CNET*, 28 Oct. 2019, https://www.cnet.com/news/new-superman-lois-tv-series-flying-over-to-the-cw/. Accessed 12 Jan. 2019.

Captain America: Civil War. Directed by Joe Russo and Anthony Russo, Marvel Studio, 2016.

"Crisis on Infinite Earths: Part 2." *Batwoman*, season 1, episode 9, CW, 9 Dec. 2019.

"Dinosaurs on a Spaceship." *Doctor Who*, series 7, episode 2, BBC, 8 Sept. 2012

Dooley, Kevin (w), and Eduardo Barreto (p/i). "Cross Roads, Part Ten: He Who Hesitates…," *Green Arrow* Vol. 2 #90 (Sept. 1994). DC Comics, Inc., 1994.

"Elseworlds, Part 3." *Supergirl*, season 4, episode 9, The CW, 11 Dec. 2018.

Englehart, Steve (w), Mike Friedrich (w), Sal Buscema (p), and Vince Colletta (i), "J'Accuse," *Captain America* Vol. 1 #170 (Feb. 1974). Marvel Comics, 1974.

"Finale—Part 2." *Smallville*, season 10, episode 21, The CW, 13 May 2011.

Golding, Dan, "The Sound of the Cinematic Superhero." *The Superhero Symbol: Media, Culture, and Politics*, edited by Liam Burke, Ian Gordon, Angela Ndalianis, Rutgers University Press, 2019, pp.164–173.

Gruenwald, Mark (w), Ron Lim (p), and Danny Bulanadi (i). "With Friends Like These…," *Captain America* Vol. 1 #380 (Dec. 1990). Marvel Comics, 1990.

"Home Alone." *The Movies That Made Us*, written by Benjamin J. Frost, directed by Brian Volk-Weiss, Netflix, 29 Nov. 2019.

Hughes, Libby. *Christopher Reeve*. iUniverse, 2004.

Iron Man. Directed by Jon Favreau, Marvel Studios, 2008.

IWM, 12383. Private Papers of J. A. Johnson.

Johns, Geoff (w), Grant Morrison (w), Greg Rucka (w), Mark Waid (w), Keith Giffen (p), et al. "A Year in the Life," *52* #52 (July 2007). DC Comics, Inc., 2007.

Jurgens, Dan (w/a), Karl Kesel (w), Jerry Ordway (w), Louise Simonson (w), Roger Stern (w), et al. *Superman: Reign of the Supermen*. DC Comics, Inc., 2016.

Justice League. Directed by Zack Snyder, Warner Bros. 2017.

Lockett, Dee. "David S. Goyer Has a Good Reason Why Superman Killed Zod (and Half of Metropolis) in Man of Steel." *Vulture*, 29 Oct. 2015, https://www.vulture.com/2015/10/why-superman-killed-general-zod-in-man-of-steel.html. Accessed 12 Dec. 2019.

Logeswaran, Nidhya, and Joydeep Bhattachara. "Cross Modal Transfer of Emotion by Music." *Nueroscience Letters*, vol. 455, issue 2, 2009, pp. 129–133.

Man of Steel. Directed by Zack Snyder, Warner Bros., 2013.

Mangan, Timothy. "John Williams Interview: 'It's not hard work that makes success; it's sustained hard work that makes success." *Gramophone*, 20 Feb. 2017, https://www.gramophone.co.uk/features/article/john-williams-interview-it-s-not-hard-work-that-makes-success-it-s-sustained-hard-work-that-makes-success. Accessed 11 Mar, 2019.

"Maps and Legends." *Star Trek: Picard*, season 1, episode 2, CBS All Access, 30 Jan. 2020.

Millar, Mark (w), and Dave Johnson (a). *Superman: Red Son*. DC Comics, Inc., 2004.

_____, and Steve McNiven (p). *Civil War—Collected Edition*. Panini Publishing, 2018.

Milgram, Stanley. *Obedience to Authority: An Experimental View*. 1974. Harper and Row, 2017.

Morrison, Grant (w), et al. *Multiversity*. DC Comics, Inc., 2015.

O'Neil, Dennis (w), and Neal Adams (p/i). "Snowbirds Don't Fly," *Green Arrow* Vol. 2 #85 (Aug. 1971). DC Comics, Inc., 1971.

Outlaw. Kofi. "*Man of Steel* Ending Controversy and The *Superman II* Hypocrisy." *Screenrant*, 18 June 2013, https://screenrant.com/man-steel-ending-superman-kills-zod-death-discussion/. Accessed 24 Dec. 2019.

"The Pilot." *Lois and Clark: The New Adventures of Superman*, season 1, episode 1, ABC, 12 Sept. 1993.

"Pilot." *Superman & Lois*, season 1, episode 1, The CW, 23 Feb. 2021.

Porter, Linda. *Tarnished Heroes, Charming Villains and Modern Monsters: Science Fiction in Shades of Grey on 21st Century Television*. McFarland, 2010.

Quesada, Joe (w), Sean Chen (p), Alitha Martinez (p), and Rob Hunter (i). *Iron Man: The Mask in the Iron Man*. Marvel Comics, 2001.

"Revelations." *Battlestar Galactica*, season 4, episode 10, Syfy, 12 June 2008.

Robertson, C.K. "The True *Übermensch*: Batman as Humanistic Myth." *The Gospel According to Superheroes: Religion and Pop Culture*, edited by B.J. Oropeza, Peter Lang, 2005, pp. 49–66.

Sharpe, Robert. "Could Superman Have Joined the Third Reich? The Importance and Shortcomings of Moral Upbringing." *Superman and Philosophy: What Would the Man of Steel Do?*, edited by Mark D. White, Wiley Black, 2013, pp. 37–46.

Siegel, Jerry (w), and Joe Shuster (p). "War in San Monte," *Action Comics* #2 (July 1938). DC Comics, 1938.

_____. "Superman Champions World Peace!" *Superman* #2 (Fall 1939). DC Comics, 1939.

Spencer, Nick (w), and Jesus Saiz (p/i). *Captain America: Steve Rogers* #1 (July 2016). Marvel Comics, 2016.

"Steven Spielberg vs. Alfred Hitchcock." *YouTube*, uploaded by Epic Rap Battles of History, 15 Dec. 2014, https://www.youtube.com/watch?v=_wYtG7aQTHA. Accessed 11 Jan. 2019.
Straczynski, Michael J. (w), and Shane Davies (a). *Superman: Earth One*. DC Comics, Inc., 2010.
"Superman on Earth." *Adventures of Superman*, season 1, episode 1, syndication, 19 Sept. 1952.
"Superman." Directed by Dave Fleischer, Paramount, 1941.
Superman: The Movie. Directed by Richard Donner, Warner Bros. 1978.
Superman III. Directed by Richard Lester, Warner Bros., 1983.
Superman Returns. Directed by Bryan Singer, Warner Bros., 2006.
Taylor, Tom (w), et al. *Injustice: Gods Among Us* #1 (Mar. 2013). DC Comics, 2013.
Topel, Fred. "Jim Lee Fought for Brandon Routh to Play Superman Again in Crisis on Infinite Earths Crossover [Exclusive]." *Slashfilm*, 5 Aug. 2019, https://www.slashfilm.com/crisis-on-infinite-earths-crossover/. Accessed 1 Feb. 2020.
Tynan, Jane. *British Army Uniforms and the First World War: Men in Khaki*. Palgrave Macmillan, 2013.
Venable, Nick. "The 10 Most Popular TV Shows of 2019, According to Google." *Cinema Blend*, 12 Dec. 2019, https://www.cinemablend.com/television/2486624/the-10-most-popular-tv-shows-of-2019-according-to-google. Accessed 1 Jan 2020.
Waid, Mark. Introduction. *Superman in the Fifties*. DC Comics, Inc., 2002, pp. 5–8.
_____ (w), and Alex Ross (a). *Kingdom Come*. DC Comics, Inc., 1997.
Walker, Simon. *Physical Control, Transformation, and Damage in the First World War: War Bodies*. Bloomsbury, 2020.
"What Are Musical Modes." *Masterclass*, 2019. Accessed 1 Jan. 2019.
Winnick, Judd (w), Phil Hester (p), and Ande Parks (i). "New Blood, Part IV: In Custody," *Green Arrow* Vol. 3 #24 (Dec. 2004). DC Comics, Inc., 2004.
Zimbardo, Philip. *The Lucifer Effect: Understanding How Good People Turn Evil*. Random House, 2008.

No Tights, No Flights
How Smallville *Put the "Human" in "Superhuman"*

CHRISTOPHER MAVERICK

Superheroes are relics of a bygone era; at least, superheroes as we have always known them are. They are a twentieth-century invention that have the same cultural relevance as the vinyl record, rotary phone, or butterfly collar: at best, curious collectors' items adored by hipsters for their retro kitsch; at worst, laughably obsolete and mostly forgotten fossils with the slightest passing resemblance to their much superior descendants. Perhaps the most outdated is Superman, an overpowered paragon of virtue, traversing a ridiculous array of fantasy scenarios with an ever-expanding collection of godlike powers and an ideological sensibility that seems as anachronistic as the telephone booths in which he changes clothes. Yet, somehow in the twenty-first century, superheroes seem more popular than ever, dominating both the cinema box office and the television airwaves. That said, the current crop of "superhero" narratives is a fundamentally different invention than their predecessors, serving a different purpose. Where the classic superhero served as an ethical template and hopeful inspiration to find the courage and power to confront injustices that plague the reader, the contemporary version illuminates the limits of power to solve human problems and inadequacies. The demarcation between the twentieth and twenty-first-century incarnations can be seen in the 2001 television series *Smallville*.

Ostensibly a reboot of the Superman origin story, *Smallville* (2001–2011) is in many ways the origin of the current explosion of superhero media. While live-action superhero adaptations had long been a part of the American media landscape, their presence was relatively sparse in 2001 compared to what they would become only a decade later. Before *Smallville*, there was typically at most a single live-action superhero adaptation on American television at a time, and often gaps of years between the cancellation of one program and the beginning of the next. The television series *Adventures of Superman* ran from 1952 through 1958. *Batman* was on the air from 1966 until 1968. The 1970s saw *Wonder Woman* airing from 1975 through 1979, briefly overlapping *The Incredible Hulk* production of 1978 through 1982. *Superboy* ran in syndication from 1988 through 1992, followed by *Lois & Clark: The New Adventures of Superman* airing from 1993 through 1997. During this same period, superheroes made sporadic appearances in wide-release films. Christopher Reeves starred in four commercially successful *Superman* films between 1978 and 1987, with a poorly received *Supergirl* spinoff (starring Helen Slater) that was released in 1984. Between 1989 and 1997, Tim Burton and Joel

Schumacher directed a series of four *Batman* films. The first *Blade* movie was released in 1998 and *X-men* premiered in 2000, just a year before *Smallville*. However, the premiere of *Smallville* marked a turning point in superhero media in the United States. The films and television programs before it tended to focus on the miraculous feats that a superhero could perform. In contrast, *Smallville* focused on the human story behind the superhero. It asked what humanity looked like in a superhuman world. *Smallville* can therefore be seen as a sort of bridge that connects that older age of sporadic superhero media to the constant stream of franchised cinematic universes of the twenty-first century. It restructured the way in which we think about the superhero and revitalized its popularity for twenty-first-century media. At least one adaptation of an existing comic book superhero franchise has been on American television or in first run theatrical release ever since.

Right or wrong, we often think of Superman as the definitive superhero of the genre. Indeed, it is hard to even think about the very concept of "superheroes" without The Man of Steel. He's arguably not the first superhero; Lee Falk's Phantom had been gracing the pages of newspapers for more than two years before Superman's first appearance in *Action Comics* #1 (June 1938). He wasn't the first superhero to venture off of the comics page either; Walter B. Gibson's The Shadow began starring in his own radio adventures in 1937, predating the 1940 premiere of *The Adventures of Superman* radio program. Batman, Captain America, and Captain Marvel, as well as the Shadow and the Phantom, all had their own live-action film appearances before the 1948 *Superman* serials began. Regardless, since *Action Comics* #1, Superman has become ubiquitous in American pop culture and around the world.

In 1962, literary critic Umberto Eco argued that the key to the character's success was "Superman cannot 'consume' himself, since a myth is 'inconsumable'" (150). That is to say that the continuous narrative of Superman over several generations of readers has led to a character that transcends the concept of time (153). Eco believed that a myth must be viewed in its contemporary context, seeming current within the immediate text but also predate the text and exist after the text is complete. That is, Superman of 1940, 1980, and 2020 must speak to different contemporary audiences but at the same time remain the same character across time. As a result, he exists not as a distinct character, but a kind of mythic gestalt. A fan's platonic ideal of what Superman represents—and transitively their understanding of what superheroes in general should be—is largely defined by the era and media in which the fan first encountered the character. However, each fan's mythic gestalt is also informed by countless iterations they have encountered in various media over time, and no two fans can have the exact same exposure. For his first six decades of existence, Superman's adventures were designed to create a mythic gestalt that represented an aspirational vision of what ethical behavior should be for the reader.

The original Superman was more hardboiled pulp hero than big blue boy scout. Debuting in 1938, he was a hard-hitting crusader confronting the threats that creators Jerry Siegel and Joe Shuster—two young Jewish men who came of age during the Great Depression in Cleveland, Ohio—saw in their everyday lives. Superman inspired hope in the reader. He fought poverty, government corruption and organized crime long before he ever confronted any "supervillains." His early stories gave little diegetic justification for why he felt the need to help people. He was simply devoted to virtue. Inspired by Nietzsche's concept of the *Übermensch* from *Also Sprach Zarathustra*, Siegel and Shuster's

Superman argued that power, rather than corrupting, was an opportunity to put objective justice before subjective legality. Superman did not so much believe might made right as he believed there was morality that existed beyond the law and it was his duty to serve it. He sometimes used questionable tactics and often found himself in opposition to legal authorities, but always in the service of the downtrodden. In "Superman in the Slums," from *Action Comics* Vol. 1 #8 (Jan. 1939), Superman deduces that much juvenile crime is caused by impoverished inner-city youth being forced to steal to provide for their families. As such, he decides to destroy the city's decrepit tenements in order to force government aid to rebuild more acceptable housing. When the military is called in to stop him, Superman fights them off and continues his demolition. This Superman was a call to action for the reader to stand with the disempowered by any means necessary. In effect, the 1930s Superman espouses a sort of ethical utilitarianism. If injustice existed in the world, it was his moral imperative to address it any way he could; the ends always justifying the means.

As time went on, Superman grew away from his grass roots antihero origins towards a more patriotic persona. By the mid–1940s, Superman increasingly turned his attention to the growing threat of World War II. While his adventures seldom pitted Superman in direct opposition to the Axis powers—instead preferring to protect the American home front while the military dealt with overseas threats—comic covers of the day depicted him as a staunchly American hero, often facing off against German or Japanese soldiers. He became a protector of not only Metropolis or America but the planet and faced off against extraterrestrial threats and would-be world conquerors. As his sphere of influence grew, Superman drifted away from his ethical utilitarian roots into a kind of Socratic virtue ethics. By the time the Comics Code Authority (CCA) was introduced in 1954, which essentially mandated that comic book heroes maintain an impeccable moral code, Superman rarely operated outside of the law and instead attempted to serve the public good while maintaining strict respect for legal authority and social norms. At the same time, successive writers boosted Superman's power set with greater strength and additional abilities. Where his early comics claimed he could "leap tall buildings in a single bound" and "nothing short of a bursting shell could pierce his skin" (Siegel and Shuster, "Superman, Champion of the Oppressed" 1), by mid-century Superman was capable of unassisted interstellar flight and could shrug off heavy artillery and missile strikes. He developed additional abilities like X-ray vision and freeze breath as he began to confront more powerful and fantastic supervillains.

While analyzing Superman as ethical allegory, Audrey L. Anton notes that the Man of Steel is subject to Immanuel Kant's edict that *ought implies can*. That is, Anton states, "if we say Superman *ought* to prevent a powerless helicopter from falling onto a crowd of people, then we have to assume that Superman *can* do so. If he weren't able to do so— as I can't, and I assume you can't either—it would be unfair to hold him (or us) responsible for catching the falling helicopter" (158). Anton's purpose here is to absolve Superman of moral responsibility for events that are beyond his control. However, she in effect discovers a philosophical justification for the ever-increasing powerset that twentieth-century writers gifted him. If Superman is to be definitionally the greatest of all superheroes, then he necessarily must be capable of handling any threat. This sets up a sort of circular reasoning—*ought implies must*. If Superman feels that he *ought* to confront any evil that he can reasonably defeat, and if he possesses such immense power that he *can*, his virtue ethics dictate he *must* use it in public service. As such, by the end of the century,

Superman became a nigh perfect being with incorruptible character, and the narrative began to imply that his power and morality were interchangeable. However, with that abundance of power and morality came a sense of stagnancy. His perfection of virtue—mired in the idealistic, 1950s sensibilities of the CCA—and unmatched power were not conducive to storytelling that addressed contemporary fears.

In the mid–1980s, two prestige superhero DC Comics series, Alan Moore and Dave Gibbons' *Watchmen* (1986–1987) and Frank Miller's *Batman: The Dark Knight Returns* (1986), revitalized the industry by exploring contemporary Cold War and Reagan-era politics and deconstructing the superhero genre. Moore and Gibbons used a collection of new characters, loosely based on classic Charlton Comics heroes, to question what would happen if a single superhuman being were inserted into a realistic world. Thus, while *Watchmen* lacks the classic Superman, there is an analogue in the form of Doctor Manhattan, referred to as "the superman"—like Siegel and Shuster's creation, a reference to Nietzsche's *Übermensch*—in the narrative. As the sole superhuman on the planet, Doctor Manhattan drastically alters the geopolitical stage. His service as an omnipotent agent of the United States government disrupts the balance of power with other countries. America's status as a *political superpower* is unquestioned and feared because of their association with the planet's sole actual superpower. However, while his reality warping abilities make him even more powerful, unlike Superman, Manhattan lacks a dedication to virtue ethics. In fact, throughout the series, he becomes increasingly detached from human concerns. He begins to exhibit extreme philosophical pragmatism, perhaps extending into Nietzschean meta-ethical moral relativism and eventually fatalism, as he perceives time non-linearly. In contrast to the classic Superman who is defined by ultimate power in service of humanity, Dr. Manhattan's superiority to humanity argues that a superman is beyond human concerns.

In contrast, Miller's *The Dark Knight Returns* reimagines Superman as an extreme Kantian deontologist, albeit one still in devoted service to the United States government, in direct opposition against a Batman who now embodies the teleological utilitarian ideal. Where Dr. Manhattan's powers evolved him beyond his humanity, Miller argued that tying Superman's undeniable power to unflinching ideology would eventually lead to fascism. In contrast, Miller's Batman displays a heightened version of the ideology of the 1930s Superman. He has no strict code of conduct as his methods are always adaptable to what he sees as seeking justice. The two superheroes eventually come into physical combat with Superman serving as an agent of the State in opposition to Batman as an avatar of individual liberty. Unlike the world of *Watchmen*, where there is only a single superhuman being that the rest of the world must react to, the comic book Superman frequently interacts with other superpowered individuals. He cannot be above humanity, as others exist on his *Übermensch* level. Therefore, within the world of *The Dark Knight Returns*, Superman's moral philosophy did not necessarily seem superior to Batman's. Instead, Miller presented a narrative where the deontological mandate to do the right thing was at odds with the teleological desire to do them for the right reason. While the personal relationships between Batman, Superman, and the other characters played into this conflict, their personal lives barely come into play; Bruce Wayne's status as a billionaire and Clark Kent's occupation of reporter are largely irrelevant. Instead, Miller's work postulates that the nature of the superhero was, and always had been, to explore ideology rather than humanity.

Though both *Watchmen* and *Dark Knight* offer relatively bleak outlooks on the removal of humanity from the superhero genre, ironically their popularity caused their implicit critiques to be ignored as the comics industry increasingly copied the surface level violence that Moore and Miller's stories offered. Thus, throughout the 1990s, superhero comics began turning towards darker, gritty storylines that rejected the optimistic heroism of the past. For a time, this led to experiments with massive status quo changing events such as the "Death of Superman" story arc in 1992, which temporarily replaced the character with four lesser-powered, and less morally didactic, counterparts. Similarly, 1998's "Superman Red/Superman Blue" storyline saw the character having his normal power set replaced with lesser energy wielding abilities and splitting into two distinct beings, neither of which possessed the totality of his normal moral fortitude and impeccable character. While these changes did boost sales for the comics, the effects were always temporary, and the returns were diminishing with each attempt. In the mid-1990s, Superman comic titles averaged sales of roughly 100,000 copies each (J. Miller) and were already considered a market disappointment in comparison to more successful, morally ambiguous, lesser-powered, street-level characters. By the end of the millennium, with a general decline in popularity for comics as a whole, sales on Superman comics were typically well under 40,000 copies per issue. Though the character maintained his worldwide brand recognition, the actual traditional narratives of Superman stories, and superhero stories in general, had grown stale to the readership. No matter what era Superman had appeared in he had always represented a sense of hope and virtue that was becoming increasingly incompatible with the post-modern cynicism that the most popular superheroes of the era espoused.

At the same time, the American television landscape was in midst of a vast cultural shift. Television critic Alan Sepinwall argues that the start of the twenty-first century began a second "golden age of television." Where once television was seen as an artistically inferior and intellectually unsophisticated substitute to the theatrical experience, Sepinwall contends that a shift in focus towards big-budget, spectacle-based blockbusters in Hollywood cinema eliminated much of the perceived prestige bias in story quality. This was concurrent with the rise of DVD, DVR, and on-demand streaming-based media decoupling television programming from specific viewing time appointments. Thus, television became a prime medium for long form serialized visual storytelling. In his analysis, Sepinwall focuses on innovative dramas that highlighted the human experience in unique situations or careers, noting for instance that *The Sopranos* (1999–2007) challenged its audience, rather than coddling it. Tony Soprano (James Gandolfini) was not only a bad guy, but an increasingly unapologetic one as the series aged and "where previous dramas had humanized edgy characters over time, The Sopranos did the opposite" (50). While Sepinwall never refers to *Smallville* specifically, I would argue that by humanizing Superman rather than idolizing him, *Smallville* recontextualized superheroes in the same way that *The Sopranos* reconstructed the gangster genre.

Premiering on October 16, 2001, *Smallville* attempted to redefine the concept of Superman for a new millennium. Producers Alfred Gough and Miles Millar maintained many aspects of the base Superman mythology that are common to other versions. The one-hour pilot episode ("Pilot") opens in 1989, as a freak meteor shower decimates the quaint town of Smallville, Kansas. A local couple, Martha (Annette O'Toole) and Jonathan Kent (John Schneider), wreck their truck but are saved by a miraculously strong toddler who lifts them from the wreckage. The Kents then find a crashed spaceship nearby and, reasoning that the toddler is an alien, adopt him and name him Clark. Twelve years later, Clark (Tom Welling) is a high school freshman learning to cope with his emerging alien powers. While the base origin presented in the opening episode matches that which had been attached to the character ever since *Action Comics* #1, the story quickly deviates from more familiar incarnations of the Superman mythos. Welling's Clark is aware of his heightened strength and his superhuman speed but does not yet possess many of Superman's other abilities and is unaware of his alien origins; up until the pilot, the Kents have kept Clark's otherworldly heritage a secret from even him.

A benefit of the inconsumable mythic gestalt is that fans approaching any new incarnation of Superman have a base model to compare him to. It is not necessary to inform the viewers who the character of Clark Kent is; instead, the creators may foster interest by exploring the changes they make to the assumed default narrative. In *Action Comics* #1, Superman's origin of being rocketed to Earth as a baby from a doomed planet is dispensed within a single page so that readers can join a story in medias res of Superman racing against the clock to free an innocent woman wrongly sentenced to death. He then foils a succession of other crimes and by his second issue has already established a reputation that makes him feared by the criminals he faces. The 1952 television series *Adventures of Superman* gives more details, building on fourteen years of established lore from the comics, radio series and a 1942 novel, to use the bulk of its pilot episode ("Superman on Earth") detailing Superman's Kryptonian origin and early life on Earth. However, by the second episode, Superman (George Reeves) is again already a famous and easily recognizable hero. The 1978 *Superman* film similarly moves through Superman (Christopher Reeve)'s younger years as quickly as possible to segue into Superman revealing himself to the world by saving Lois Lane (Margot Kidder) from a helicopter accident. Likewise, the pilot episode of 1993's *Lois & Clark* ("Pilot") sees Superman (Dean Cain) debut by saving Lois Lane (Terri Hatcher) and several others from an explosion on a space shuttle. In both of the latter cases, Lois gives him the name Superman when she writes a story about her experience and his public identity quickly becomes a worldwide celebrity. Even the 1988 *Superboy* series dispenses with the origin story altogether and presents a college-aged Clark (John Haymes Newton) who has apparently been active as Superboy for quite some time before the first episode ("The Jewel of Techacal") begins and is well known to authorities and the press. That Superboy differed from Superman only because he was physically younger; the series assumes the viewer is already aware of the mythic gestalt of the character from other sources.

In each of these cases, the storyline assumes that Superman is experienced and competent with his powers. He has already mastered his abilities and displays a confidence that marks him as a dashing hero in contrast to his "mild-mannered reporter" secret persona. Furthermore, he is decidedly dedicated to using his abilities to serve humanity. His ethical code is set; his dedication to his philosophical ideology is unquestioned. Virtue is an inherent part of his character. For most versions of the Superman narrative, the duality of Clark Kent and Superman is arguably one of the most important elements of the character. It was key to his aspirational nature. Being a hero is Superman's true occupation; Clark Kent's job as a reporter is merely a means to an end. It is a cover that allows him greater access to information so that he may effectively serve the ideological good. However, since Clark is the very definition of an every-man, the message behind most Superman incarnations is that any reader or viewer can be a hero if they have a strong enough ethical code. *Lois & Clark* reversed the typical narrative to focus on Clark and his romantic relationship with Lois Lane to observe how being a superhero interfered with his domestic life. In either case, one of the identities, either Superman or Clark, is a masquerade that the other performs.

Conversely, *Smallville*'s Clark lacks a dual identity altogether. Rather than being introduced as a competent superhero with full mastery of his powers, *Smallville*'s Clark spends much of the first several seasons exploring his emerging powers and discovering his alien heritage. Furthermore, where the breakthrough 1978 theatrical film based its entire marketing campaign around the slogan "you will believe a man can fly," *Smallville* featured a more grounded Clark Kent, both literally and figuratively as the producers abided by what they called the "no tights, no flights" motto. That is to say, Gough and Millar's very premise explicitly removed arguably the three most recognizable signifiers of the character. Thus, while the entire *Smallville* series serves as an extended origin for Superman, it is a Superman that is uncannily both familiar and foreign to the viewer. There was no iconic red and blue figure streaking overhead while onlookers exclaimed "Look, up in the sky! It's a bird! It's a plane! It's Superman!"—a chant that had been synonymous with the character since the 1940s radio show. Instead, the series focused on Clark Kent as he first navigates high school, and later college and adult life, while trying to protect the secret of the alien powers that he was still struggling to control. With this struggle came complications to his moral code.

The "no tights, no flights" edict was met with reservations by fans and critics before the series even began. Comic book historian Bradford Wright expressed concern over the lack of the uniform, saying "nothing really compares to that costume. Not Santa Claus' red suit or the Elvis jumpsuit—nothing is as recognizable" (qtd. in Boucher). Similarly, legendary comic writer Stan Lee echoed, "superhero stories are the fairy tales of today and they require a lot of color and sense of fantasy, and that's what the costumes have done" (qtd. in Boucher). Screenwriter Kevin Smith has frequently alleged that producer Jon Peters' insistence that Superman neither fly nor wear his iconic costume was among the many reasons that the proposed 1998 film *Superman Lives* never made it past pre-production (*An Evening with Kevin Smith*). Nevertheless, the "no tights, no flights" approach was an immediate success, with *Smallville*'s debut setting a ratings record for the WB network. Ultimately, the series would run for ten seasons, making series lead Tom Welling the longest-tenured live-action actor to star in the role to date and *Smallville* becoming the longest-running live-action superhero program on American television.

The reservations against the loss of costume, powers, and name were understandable. Wright is correct in speaking to the iconic nature of the Superman uniform. The removal of the costume and other elements specifically served to divorce *Smallville* from the superhero genre in the minds of some viewers. In *Superhero: The Secret Origin of a Genre* (2006), comic scholar Peter Coogan argues that the superheroic protagonist requires three key elements: a prosocial *mission*, extraordinary *powers*, and a heroic *identity* (39), or MPI. While *Smallville*'s Clark Kent does display some level of the first two elements of Coogan's genre definition, the "no tights" edict and lack of Superman name immediately sever him from the final element of Coogan's framework. Especially in the case of Superman, Coogan contends that the costume is essential to identity, saying "although Superman was not the first costumed hero, his costume marks a clear and striking departure from those of pulp heroes[…]. The slouch hat, black cloak, and red scarf of the Shadow or the mask and fangs of the Spider disguise their faces but do not proclaim their identities. Superman's costume does, particularly through his 'S-chevron'"

(33). Clark's lack of costume or alter ego seems to hamper any real consideration of him having a heroic identity.

Comic book author Kurt Busiek offers a similar prescriptive definition of superheroness that *Smallville* seems to resist. To Busiek, "the primary hallmarks of the superhero are superpowers, costume, code name, secret identity, heroic ongoing mission, and superhero milieu. If the character has three of those six, he or she is probably a superhero" (133). Here, *Smallville*'s Clark fares a little better as he again has the mission and the powers, and the argument of superhero milieu is at least questionable. For Busiek, "superhero milieu" is something of a catch-all term that allows for the inclusion in the superhero genre if there are enough nebulous superhero tropes in the story. That is to say, that Lois Lane may not be a superhero by any reasonable metric; however, the presence of Superman and other clearly recognizable superheroes in her stories makes them acceptable as superhero comics. While *Smallville* did build a superhero milieu over time with the inclusion of clearly costumed heroes like Green Arrow (Justin Hartley) and Hawkman (Michael Shanks), this only came as Clark also adopted more traditionally superhero elements into his own persona as "the Blur" in the later seasons. Eventually, as the Blur, Clark would wear a proto-Superman uniform that included a leather jacket with the S-chevron. However, when the series premiered, no such costume existed.

In their semiotic analysis of superhero costumes, Barbara Brownie and Danny Graydon point to comic book Clark as their definitive example of clothes making the man—or Superman, as it were. They argue "Superman's otherness is firmly established in a costume that is identical from day to day. Wearing only one costume, Superman reduces his core values to a single, consistent message which is not compromised by daily adjustments to his wardrobe" (12). Superman's costume establishes his *brand*. The iconography of Superman is so powerful that the visual signifiers attached to him have become more indicative of his history, ideology, and power than any other aspect of his character. The S-chevron and red and blue costume are so iconic, that explaining the back story and origin of the Superman character is not necessary for a successful adaptation. In a sense, it signifies the mythic gestalt. Given the appearance of a character dressed like Superman, viewers will simply fill in the blanks with what they know from other incarnations. This is why the 1988 Superboy series was able to dispense with an origin pilot episode. Presenting the character with the visual identifiers of Superman establishes a connection with the mythic gestalt for the viewers. To dress as Superman is to be Superman; background and morality are simply assumed. However, at least until he officially adopts the Blur identity, *Smallville*'s Clark actively avoids any obvious visual performance of superheroism.

That is not to say, however, that *Smallville*'s Clark is completely divorced from his Superman origins. Indeed, his specific visual presentation is indicative of the new phase of superheroism that *Smallville* represents, an implied superheroism that draws from the classic MPI framework but does not rely on it. Typically, in the Superman mythos, Clark Kent is as much of a performance through costume as Superman. Brownie and Graydon suggest "when Superman steps out of red, yellow, and blue, and into black or gray, or when Spider-Man exchanges spandex for cotton and denim, he is not removing his disguise, he is substituting one costume for another" (70). Where Superman is Kal-El's performance of masculine heroism, Clark Kent is his performance human mundanity. As the titular character in Quentin Tarantino's *Kill Bill Vol. 2* (2004) says, "Clark Kent is Superman's critique on the whole human race." The blue suit, sensible haircut, and thick spectacles are meant to create the impression of ordinariness, something that Kal-El is naturally anything but. Just as he originally had no superhero costume, Welling's character wore no Clark Kent disguise either. Instead, *Smallville*'s Clark typically opted for a comfortable array of T-shirts, denim and flannel. His shaggy mop of hair was conventionally stylish for teen boys of the day. No eye glasses were to be found. In short, *Smallville*'s Clark dressed as an average American youth. However, the color scheme of his clothing featured prominent blues and reds, visually recalling the classic Superman iconography. In the latter seasons, Clark adopts an official superhero uniform of sorts. This costume, consisting of blue jeans, a blue t-shirt, and a stylized red leather jacket, continues to evoke the same basic fashion sense of his earliest non-superhero appearances while still allowing him greater access to the idea of the standard superhero aesthetic theorized by Coogan, Busiek, and Brownie and Gradyon.

Similarly, Clark lacks a codename for the bulk of the *Smallville* narrative. This again serves to separate him from the classic tropes of the superhero genre. Clark hides his powers and alien origins from the public. While he often uses his abilities to help others, he usually attempts to do so without directly revealing his involvement. Thus, he lacks the need of a dual identity. Even in the later seasons, once the general public becomes aware of a superhuman protector looking over them, his makeshift codename of "The Blur" is predominantly an identifier used only by the press to refer to their unseen protector. Clark's colleagues in the Justice League, a team of superheroes he works with in the latter seasons, rarely refer to him by the codename, despite using alter egos themselves. As with his lack of costume, Clark's lack of dual identity not only distances him from superhero genre conventions, it privileges his personal character development above his heroic mission. The effect of the downplayed costuming and superheroic identity was to create a hybrid between the traditionally dual identities of Clark and Superman. *Smallville*'s Clark was not actively performing either role. He was neither paragon of heroic virtue nor critique of mundane humanity. Instead, what *Smallville* presented was a unified character that represented his true self. Rather than serving as a symbol for a philosophical stance, this Clark was merely a young man coming of age, albeit in extraordinary circumstances. For the first time in the history of the character, *Smallville* allowed creators to truly and fully explore Clark's humanity.

Superman, at his essence, has always been a wish-fulfillment myth meant to empower the reader. Siegel and Shuster's classic version asked the readers to consider what they would do with the gift of ultimate power. The simplistic MPI tropes from which Superman was constructed were key to his success. He postulated that any mild-mannered, socially-awkward young man might secretly be hiding an all-powerful, hypermasculine hero. Throughout most versions of the Superman narrative, Clark's personal life is of relatively little importance next to his career as Superman. In story, Clark typically served only as an inciting incident, either allowing Superman to gain information or providing a personal relationship to supporting cast members, like Lois Lane and Jimmy Olsen, who Superman may need to rescue. Extra-diegetically, the Clark Kent identity exists to create an avatar of wish fulfillment for the reader to connect to. However, since Clark is the protagonist of *Smallville* rather than a storyline convention, it is Clark's mission rather than Superman's that must speak to the viewer.

This refocus in Clark's heroic mission further separates him from the classic construction of superherodom and reconstructs a contemporary one. *Smallville*'s Clark does engage in altruistic superheroic activity for the benefit of the community, but the true focus of the story is usually on the ways in which Clark's heroic responsibilities interfere with his day-to-day life. Where the classic Superman myth appeals to a reader with aspirations that their actions could make a difference and save the world, *Smallville*'s version presented a hero with grand responsibilities who yearned for a simpler life. Clark existed in a post–9/11 world; a world with school shootings, hate crimes, and mental illness; a world where there were constant difficulties that were beyond the control of a teenage boy, but not beyond his concern. And despite all of those twenty-first-century external concerns, he still had to contend with typical adolescent problems of school, peer pressure, high school cliques, and dating. This was not a Superman who wanted to save the world. It was a Clark Kent who wished he didn't have to.

There was certainly no lack of superhuman action on *Smallville*. Any given episode saw Clark attempting to save a friend or family member from an assortment of "meteor freaks"—humans granted superpowers by exposure to the radioactive kryptonite scattered throughout the town during the same meteor shower that brought Clark to Earth. Clark sees protecting the town from meteor freaks as his duty as he inexplicably blames himself for the meteor shower, an event that was beyond his control. In particular, he feels a sense of guilt towards his love interest, Lana Lang (Kristen Kreuk). The pilot episode reveals that a young Lana was orphaned when, as a toddler, she witnessed her parents' car being struck by a meteor, killing them instantly—a traumatic event that colors the rest of her life. Clark feels as though he must atone for this tragedy and countless others that affected the town, not simply because he has the power to do so but because he feels responsible for their occurrence in the first place. This sense of guilt only grows over the course of the series as Clark learns that Krypton's destruction was in part due to civil war and mismanagement of natural resources from his ancestors. In this way, Welling's Clark was not a paragon of virtue as other Supermans before him. He does not act out of a moral or ideological need to do good but instead is driven to accomplish the tasks assigned to him, reluctant though he may be, as a matter of obligation. Like so many millennials living suddenly in a post–9/11, twenty-first-century world, Clark feels a responsibility to correct the sins of past generations even though he would prefer to simply live out his adolescence in peace and deal with the problems that are typically incurred by a boy of his age. Most notably, he would prefer to focus on one thing, his relationship with Lana. Instead of ethical virtue, *Smallville* Clark's biggest motivation is a girl.

Smallville was not the first Superman adaptation to attempt to investigate his humanity through romance, though it did do it to a greater extreme. *Lois & Clark* similarly focused on the eponymous characters' relationship. However, *Lois & Clark* featured a fully formed Superman, confident in his abilities and dedicated to his pro-social mission. That series explored how a romantic relationship might fit into the busy life of a superhero and the powers and the responsibilities that came with it. There, Clark would often use his powers to his advantage in his personal life. For instance, in the pilot episode of *Lois & Clark*, he flies to China to procure authentic Chinese food to impress Lois for a late-night dinner. In contrast, *Smallville* Clark's powers and alien nature were often a hindrance rather than an advantage. During the pilot episode, Clark reveals his desire to try out for the high school football team—a typical adolescent boy's wish. However, his parents forbid him from doing so out of fear that he might accidentally harm another player. This is further complicated by Clark's romantic feelings towards Lana, who has a boyfriend on the team, Whitney (Eric Johnson). Lana frequently wears a necklace containing a fragment of the kryptonite meteor that killed her parents, a poignant if somewhat morbid reminder of her loss. The kryptonite charm weakens Clark whenever he is near Lana, resulting in him often stumbling and falling—acts of clumsiness that others read as adolescent awkwardness caused by his attraction to her. Aware of Clark's crush on his girlfriend, Whitney chooses Clark as the target for an annual freshman hazing ritual. Because Whitney happens to be wearing Lana's necklace, he and his teammates are able to easily overpower Clark, stripping him to his boxer shorts, and hanging him on a scarecrow post in a mock crucifixion. Not only can his powers not save him from bullying, his Kryptonian origins are indirectly the cause. Clark is thus othered on multiple levels. He is an immigrant—a literal alien from another world—and at the same time a typical high school student dealing with the pressures of social exclusion common to all teenagers. In effect, the trials of adolescence are a bigger threat to Clark than any supervillain.

That is not to say that the series was without supervillains. As a trope of the series, Clark fights a "villain of the week" in nearly every episode. Often, especially in the first four seasons which focused on his high school life, these villains are allegorical signifiers of coming-of-age issues. Clark found himself engaged against foes representing alcohol, drug use, mental illness, homosexuality, and sexual assault. Furthermore, he encountered additional social issues that were not symbolically represented by supervillains. Over the course of the series, Clark was forced to confront political corruption, terrorism, war, and the death of a parent. Unlike other incarnations of Superman who found some way to use his powers to fight through any situation, this Clark learned that there were some problems that could not be solved by any of his gifts.

This does not mean that he did not try. Unlike prior versions of Superman, *Smallville*'s Clark is often tempted to use his powers for personal gain or even revenge. In the pilot, after escaping from his scarecrow crucifixion and finding Lana dancing with Whitney at the Homecoming dance, Clark alleviates his jealousy by using his super-strength to stack several of the football players cars on top of each other. His self-serving use of his powers was not limited to revenge and jealousy; it was, however, often fueled by typical teenaged desires. In season one episode three ("Hothead"), Clark decides to join the football team against his parents' wishes and uses his powers to excel above his teammates, much to his father's disapproval. Similarly, when Clark accidentally discovers his power of X-ray vision during gym class in the fourth episode ("X-Ray"), he is unable to resist spying on Lana showering in the girls' locker room. On occasion he is tempted to use his powers secretly in order to impress Lana or other girls that he is interested in, particularly when under the influence of red kryptonite, which acts as a drug that lowers his inhibitions. However, using his powers for personal gain seldom works out the way Clark wishes. His retaliation against Whitney with the car stacking makes him feel momentary joy that is quickly quashed when he finds Whitney and Lana dancing together at the Homecoming dance and himself still being a social outsider. Joining the football team does not give Clark the peer acceptance that he desires, and he soon quits in order to find his own individualism. He always regrets his careless and dangerous actions while under the influence of red kryptonite, often because he has inadvertently brought physical harm to others. Though he clearly enjoys peaking at a nude Lana in the moment, he immediately feels guilt over the invasion of privacy.

Lana and Clark's romantic relationship provided the driving narrative core of the show. As Clark's primary love interest, Lana serves not only as a damsel in distress to be rescued—as was typical of both her and Lois Lane in previous incarnations—but also, through her relationship problems with Clark, an opportunity to highlight his lack of perfection, both physical and emotional. Despite the presence of superpowered threats, the show owed as much if not more, of its structure to contemporary teen soap opera dramas like *Beverly Hills, 90210* (1990–2000) and *Dawson's Creek* (1998–2003). Lana provided an opportunity to see Clark as not only human, but deeply flawed in typical adolescent ways. During season two, episode two ("Heat"), Clark discovers the power of heat vision, only to learn that he cannot control it whenever he is sexually excited. Soon after, Lana simply implying to him that she was interested in pursuing their mutual romantic attraction causes him to scorch a nearby wall in an allegorical premature ejaculation. While this example highlights his sexual and physical immaturity, Lana more frequently serves to call attention to Clark's emotional immaturity.

Clark often stands Lana up when they make plans together because he has been sidetracked by a superpowered threat. Even after she and Whitney break-up, Clark's secrets prevent them from being together. While the show never gives a compelling reason why Clark cannot share his secret with Lana—other friends do learn about Clark's nature and Lana knows other superpowered individuals and protects their secrets—the fact that she is aware he is keeping a secret from her prevents them from becoming closer. Furthermore, whenever Lana comes close to discovering his secrets or asks him to trust her, Clark often changes the subject and chastises her for her own trust issues. This continues even after Clark loses his powers in the fifth season premiere ("Arrival"). Believing himself to be permanently human, Clark decides that his obligation to protect the world at his own expense has ended and he can lead a normal life. In Kantian terms, if *ought* implies *can*, then *can't* implies *does not have to*. Clark and Lana finally become a couple and in the following episode lose their virginity to each other, continuing the coming-of-age theme of the series. However, he still neglects to tell her of his alien origins. This implies that there is more to his secrecy that is not tied his powers or the danger that they might bring to loved ones. He is simply unable to open up emotionally to a person he is dating. Furthermore, even without his abilities, Clark is still drawn into dangerous circumstances and his morality causes him to do his best to intervene, thus implying that his personal obligations exist regardless of whether he has power to perform them easily. His assumption about an inverse of the Kantian ought was incorrect. His responsibilities were never what kept him from a life with Lana. It was always his emotional unavailability.

When Clark's powers are returned in the season five episode three ("Hidden"), he begins distancing himself from Lana again, fearing that with his enhanced strength he will injure her during lovemaking. Here he alludes to Larry Niven's satirical 1971 essay "Man of Steel, Woman of Kleenex" but also an enhanced version of sexual performance anxiety common in newly sexually active teens. When their mutual friend Chloe (Allison Mack), who unlike Lana is aware of Clark's secrets, encourages him to be truthful with Lana and work through their issues as a couple, Clark resists. By the tenth episode ("Fanatic"), Lana has grown frustrated with Clark's distant behavior and their sudden lack of sexual intimacy. When she questions him, Clark once again attempts to shift the blame to her trust issues. However, Lana refuses to be sidetracked and calls Clark on his attempt at gaslighting her. Their disagreement shows that not even Superman is above mundane relationship problems. Many of the problems that Clark faces, both with Lana and in the rest of his life, are born of his own psychological issues and anxiety. Unlike previous versions of Superman, he is not infallible and, in fact, his lapses in judgement cause as many problems as he solves. His powers do not put him above human errors and, if anything, only serve to exacerbate them.

While Clark's powers may be an accelerant to his problems, they are not the cause. His vast array of abilities allows him to dispatch most supervillains by the end of a single episode. However, his struggles with interpersonal relationships persist for seasons. The ongoing narrative threads that pervade each season typically deal with Clark's more personal relationships with Lana, his parents, Chloe, Lex Luthor (Michael Rosenbaum), and eventually Lois Lane (Erica Durance). Despite Clark's fallibility, his sense of responsibility constantly drives him to put his heroic missions before his personal life. His neglect often makes his personal problems worse. This creates the impression that unlike previous Supermans, Clark's greatest conflicts are not existential threats to humanity but personal conflict. This was a Superman who was not a perfect being. He was deeply flawed, yet he persisted in spite of his imperfections.

In this way, *Smallville* was not the origin story for Superman but instead the template for the twenty-first-century incarnation of the superhero. By the time *Smallville* aired its final episode ("Finale") in May 2011, two-thirds of Christopher Nolan's *Batman: The Dark Knight* film trilogy was complete. The Marvel Cinematic Universe (MCU), which premiered in 2008, was preparing to release its fifth film. In 2012, a year after its cancellation, *Smallville*'s network, the CW, premiered *Arrow*, chronicling the adventures of another DC Comics superhero. A cavalcade of comic superhero adapted television shows and movies would follow in the next several years. Though none of these adaptations would be as stringent about the "no tights, no flights" rule as *Smallville*, the spirit of the rule became the backbone of the modern superhero narrative. Where superhero films and TV shows before *Smallville* followed the perils a costumed adventurer faced, those afterwards focused on the hero's civilian identities. Bruce Wayne (Christian Bale) does not appear in costume until more than an hour into the 140-minute runtime of Nolan's *Batman Begins* (2005) and his total time in costume is less than 73 minutes throughout the entire seven-and-a-half-hour trilogy (Travesty). Similarly, Tony Stark (Robert Downey, Jr.) and his fellow Avengers appear out of costume far more often than not in the MCU movies and only seldomly address each other by their codenames. In fact, Stark rejects the very notion of having a dual identity entirely by the end of the first *Iron Man* film (2008) and most of his fellow heroes follow suit in their films. The CW *Arrowverse* shows follow this same pattern; while their characters have secret costumed identities, the shows primarily focus on the interpersonal relationships between the teams of heroes assembled on each. Like *Smallville*, this allows them to explore internal conflict that infallible heroes could not address. Nolan's Batman is plagued by issues of inadequacy. The MCU's Tony Stark struggles with PTSD. *Arrow*'s Oliver Queen (Stephen Amell) is obsessed with atoning for his past failures. Like Clark, all three allow their personal demons to interfere with their love lives. Rather than an inspiration, the superhero story has become a critique of twenty-first-century mental anguish.

Over the course of ten seasons, *Smallville* bent the "no tights, no flights" rule to its limit. Clark encountered several other Kryptonians with the ability to fly and was temporarily able to accomplish it himself when possessed by his alternate evil personality, Kal-El, but is unable to do so without the influence of mind-altering and performance-enhancing red kryptonite. At the end of the ninth season, Clark receives the iconic Superman costume but declines to actually wear it and adopt the Superman name until the series finale a year later. Even then, viewers only see the briefest glimpse of Tom Welling as a full-fledged Superman. The series ends with Clark ripping open his shirt to reveal the Superman sigil on his costume and fly off to face some great threat. He is in control of his powers; he has his dual identity; he is dedicated to his heroic mission. His bildungsroman complete; he will now be a perfect being and paragon of virtue. Effectively, Clark had at long last transformed into a superhero of the classic mold, embarking on new adventures. These are adventures that we as viewers will never see on screen but can imagine because they are represented by the decades of Superman stories that came before. Clark had now truly become the classic Superman, and Superman—and other classic superheroes—are of no interest in our modern world. The superhero story of the twenty-first century is a different creation from its twentieth-century counterpart. It is meant to assure rather than inspire. It is the story that tells us that we are not defined by our responsibilities but by our interpersonal relationships. *Smallville* and the movies and television programs it inspired are as much about superheroes as *ER* (1994–2009) is about doctors or *Law & Order* (1990–2010) is about cops and lawyers. Where once the superhero narrative was philosophical allegory, now it has become an analysis of the human condition. Superheroing is simply a job, one held by imperfect characters who struggle despite their extraordinary careers. In the twenty-first century, the superhero fan no longer requires the inspirational wish-fulfillment myth that tells us we can be exceptional. Instead, we look to a grounded narrative that assures us we do not have to be.

Works Cited

"Arrival" (29 Sept. 2005). *Smallville: The Complete Fifth Season*, written by Todd Slavkin and Darren Swimmer, directed by James Marshall, Warner Bros., 2006.

Boucher, Geoff. "Cape Fear: Superman Sheds Get-Up." *Orlando Sentinel*, 1 Sept. 2001, www.orlandosentinel.com/news/os-xpm-2001-09-01-0108310457-story.html. Accessed 5 Mar. 2020.

Brownie, Barbara, and Danny Graydon. *The Superhero Costume: Identity and Disguise in Fact and Fiction*. Bloomsbury Academic, 2016.

Busiek, Kurt. "The Importance of Context: Robin Hood Is Out and Buffy Is In." *What Is a Superhero?*, edited by Robin S. Rosenberg and Peter M. Coogan, Oxford University Press, 2013, pp. 133–138.

Coogan, Peter M. *Superhero: The Secret Origin of a Genre*. MonkeyBrain Books, 2006.

Eco, Umberto. "The Myth of Superman." Translated by Natalie Chilton. *Arguing Comics: Literary Masters on a Popular Medium*, edited by Jeet Heer and Kent Worcester, Univ. Press of Mississippi, 2005, pp. 146–164.

"Episode List: Smallville." *TV Tango*, TVTango.com, www.tvtango.com/series/smallville/episodes. Accessed 27 Mar. 2020.

"Fanatic" (12 Jan. 2006). *Smallville: The Complete Fifth Season*, written by Wendy Mericle, directed by Michael Rohl, Warner Bros., 2007.

"Finale" (13 May 2011). *Smallville: The Final Season*, written by Turi Meyer, Brian Peterson, Alfredo Septién, and Kelly Souder, directed by Greg Beeman and Kevin Fair, Warner Bros. 2011.

"Heat" (1 Oct. 2002). *Smallville: The Complete Second Season*, written by Mark Verheiden, directed by James Marshall, Warner Bros., 2004.

"Hidden" (13 Oct. 2005). *Smallville: The Complete Fifth Season*, written by Brian Peterson and Kelly Souders, directed by Whitney Ransick, Warner Bros., 2007.

"Hothead" (30 Oct. 2000). *Smallville: The Complete First Season,* written by Greg Walker, directed by Greg Beeman, Warner Bros., 2003.

"The Jewel of Techacal." *Superboy*, Season 1 Episode 1, syndication, 8 Oct. 1988. *DC Universe*, https://www.dcuniverse.com/videos/watch/the-jewel-of-the-techacal/dce18587-8d80-4ca9-9eac-1f26996061d0/. Accessed 27 Mar. 2020.

Jurgens, Dan (w), et al. *Superman Transformed!* DC Comics, 1998.

Kill Bill Vol. 2. Written and directed by Quentin Tarantino, Miramax Films, 2004.

Miller, Frank (w/p) and Klaus Janson (i). *The Dark Knight Returns*. DC Comics, 1986. *DC Universe*, https://www.dcuniverse.com/comics/book/batman-the-dark-knight-returns-1986-1/1ef201a2-81a2-4339-b5ee-669de432618f/dk-returns-books. Accessed 27 Mar. 2020.

Miller, John Jackson. "Comic Book Sales by Month." *Comichron*, www.comichron.com/monthlycomicssales.html. Accessed 5 Mar. 2020.

Moore, Alan, (w) and Dave Gibbons (a). *Watchmen*. DC Comics Inc., 1987.
Niven, Larry. "Man of Steel, Woman of Kleenex." *All the Myriad Ways*, Ballantine Books, 1983.
Nyberg, Amy Kiste. *Seal of Approval: The History of the Comics Code*. University Press of Mississippi, 1998.
"Pilot." *Lois and Clark: The New Adventures of Superman*, Season 1, Episode 1, ABC, 12 Sept. 1993. *DC Universe*, https://www.dcuniverse.com/videos/watch/pilot/660b2b18-df8e-44cd-be53-54cd14615aa4/. Accessed 27 Mar. 2020.
"Pilot" (16 Oct. 2001). *Smallville: The Complete First Season*, written by Alfred Gough and Miles Miller, directed by David Nutter, Warner Bros., 2003.
Sepinwall, Alan. *The Revolution Was Televised: How the Sopranos, Mad Men, Breaking Bad, Lost, and Other Groundbreaking Dramas Changed TV Forever*. Simon & Schuster, 2013.
Siegel, Jerry (w), and Joe Shuster (a). "Superman, Champion of the Oppressed." *Action Comics* Vol. 1 #1 (June 1938). DC Comics, pp. 1–13. *DC Universe*, https://www.dcuniverse.com/comics/book/action-comics-1938-1/f5f6ab2b-0746-4a95-bf79-039a529bbb50. Accessed 5 Mar. 2020.
_____. "Superman in the Slums," *Action Comics* Vol. 1 #8 (Jan. 1939). DC Comics, pp. 1–13. *DC Universe*, https://www.dcuniverse.com/comics/book/action-comics-1938-8/4fbf5099-3820-4a40-ae62-c060b90a2fd1. Accessed 5 Mar. 2020.
Smith, Kevin. *An Evening with Kevin Smith*. Sony, 2002.
Superman. Directed by Richard Donner, performance by Christopher Reeve, Warner Bros., 1978.
"Superman on Earth." *Adventures of Superman*, season 1, episode 1, syndication, 19 Sept. 1952. *DC Universe*, https://www.dcuniverse.com/videos/watch/superman-on-earth/1f7ebc81-3eef-4e3e-85d8-163e2a7f2765/. Accessed 1 Mar. 2020.
Travesty. "Which Movie Has the Most Bat Screen Time?" *The SuperHeroHype Forums*, Evolve Media, 12 Mar. 2010, forums.superherohype.com/threads/which-movie-has-the-most-bat-screen-time.335105/. Accessed 5 Mar. 2020.
Wright, Bradford W. *Comic Book Nation: The Transformation of Youth Culture in America*. Johns Hopkins University Press, 2003.
"X-Ray" (6 Nov. 2001). *Smallville: The Complete First Season*, written by Mark Verheiden, directed by James Frawley, Warner Bros., 2003.

Through the Lens of Dr. Frankenstein
Luthor as Prometheus
Daniel Peretti

When Victor Frankenstein gave life to a concatenation of corpses in Mary Shelley's 1818 novel, he recoiled in horror at the abomination he had made. His rejection of the monster sets the tragedy in motion, shaping every element of both characters' lives from that moment onward. *Frankenstein* is subtitled *The Modern Prometheus*. In rejecting the monster, Frankenstein simultaneously ensured that he would identify with that allusion, and that he would irreversibly distance himself from it; he would endure Promethean suffering while failing to fulfill Promethean benevolence toward his creation. As one of the most popular stories of the modern world, Doctor Frankenstein can count among his literary descendants the villain Lex Luthor.

Luthor's many incarnations across media throughout the last century inflect the Frankenstein story in interesting ways. These incarnations—which adapt extant material, combine plot points, and invent whole cloth—can illuminate contemporary conceptions of heroism and villainy. This chapter will examine two such incarnations of Luthor from *Superman Returns* (2006) and *Batman v Superman: Dawn of Justice* (2016). In each, Luthor's use of the Prometheus myth in the form of dramatized oral narration draws attention to Promethean and Frankensteinian themes. These films, released only ten years apart, nonetheless have different writers, directors, producers, and actors. The embedded narratives told by Luthor reveal him to be a unique character in each film, with different goals and methods—differences that are philosophical and result from adapting the character from separate eras of comics. Though neither of these films could be called adaptations of specific comic book stories, they have nonetheless been influenced by the trends in superhero comic books, so some brief analysis of these trends is necessary. Following that is an analysis of how two other related Superman films, *Superman: The Movie* (1978) and *Man of Steel* (2013), adapt a conversation between young Clark Kent and his adoptive parents; focusing on these conversations furthers the discussion of the same story being told in different eras by different filmmakers. After a brief analysis of the 2011 comic book *Superman: The Black Ring* (Cornell), in which Luthor is the protagonist, I conclude that Luthor's use of Prometheus is dramatically ironic, since Superman himself is the more clearly Promethean of the two.

A Different Type of Adaptation

Cinema allows for a variety of types of embedded narrative (Nelles 134; Slethaug 1–11; Leitch 93–126; Griffith), which can take any of several forms that are worth describing in brief. First, the tale can be presented extra-narratively, such as the short story about a dybbuk that precedes *A Serious Man* (2009); this is prologue. Such an embedded narrative could include voice-over narration or may be narrated by one of the characters in the film. It can also occur as a flashback. Second, a story can be quoted; in this case, a different film can be shown in brief clips. This occurs in *Gods and Monsters* (1998) when the characters watch the film *Bride of Frankenstein* (1935). Third, there are instances in which something like an entire short film is shown within feature-length films, such as the presentation of *The Little Prince* in the 2016 film of that title. Finally, there is the type of embedded storytelling that dramatizes an oral performance of a tale: an onscreen character narrates a story, which may be edited to include reaction shots of other characters or sequences that show the events told in the story. The Prometheus story adapted for the two Superman films takes the form of oral performance, without any dramatization of the events it describes.

Thomas Leitch, in *Film Adaptation and its Discontents*, wants to develop a "detailed grammar" of the types of adaptation; in doing so, he also hopes to show the sliding scale between adaptation and allusion. He sees a gap between these types of intertextuality, and notes that adaptation studies have not quite fully characterized how they relate. Leitch defines allusion as "microtexts embedded in a film's larger structure" (121), and that definition—a microtext—fits how Luthor tells the story of Prometheus in these films. Both versions of the myth are short; neither is more than 125 words.

Adaptation studies has, in the last several decades, broken free of the need to analyze an adaptation in terms of its fidelity to a source (Griffith 38–70), which is fortunate for this study because the story of Prometheus varies greatly in antiquity; we can only speak of an earliest known source (in this case, the poems of Hesiod), not of an "original" source. It is entirely possible that earlier writers put the story onto paper, but it is even more likely that Prometheus circulated in oral traditions for centuries prior to the earliest written version. Removing fidelity to a source as an analytical necessity also affords scholars greater flexibility when analyzing superhero adaptations, which rarely adapt a single story; instead, they commonly take elements from disparate comic book stories and combine them into something new. The tale told by a character such as Lex Luthor compounds these adaptational intricacies: Luthor himself is not a single character; as the DC Comics' superhero universe has splintered into different forms (Friedenthal), so has Luthor. Furthermore, Luthor in feature films has been different characters.

Luthor: Pre–Crisis, Post–Crisis

Audience members cannot help but know that Luthor is at the least untroubled by ethics, at the most a murderer and megalomaniac. Yet other aspects of his personality and biography have changed greatly over time. Following the 1986 comic series *Crisis on Infinite Earths* (Wolfman; see O'Rourke and O'Rourke), the Superman titles received a fresh start, with a new telling of Superman's origin and his initial encounter with Luthor in the series *Man of Steel* (Byrne). The new version of Luthor presented a public persona of respectable wealth and enterprise. Part of this change can be explained by an evolution of the character to fit with comic book stories developing greater depth in their narrative structures and themes. Simple megalomania was no longer sufficient to hold an audience's attention, so Luthor shifts from overt opposition to society to a prominent, albeit corrupt, proponent of the status quo. Superman films display the same shift in Luthor's villainy. *Superman: The Movie* makes Gene Hackman's Luthor a classic villain: his motive is purely venal, he has an underground lair, and the public and law enforcement are aware of his crimes. This film was released during the pre–*Crisis* era, and its Luthor reflects the comic book character of the time; importantly, it serves as the template for the Luthor of *Superman Returns*. Though it was released twenty years after the post–*Crisis* Superman made his debut, *Superman Returns* is a sequel to the first two Superman films of the 1970s and 1980s (Toh 172). Luthor in the Zack Snyder films *Man of Steel* and *Batman v Superman* fits with the post–*Crisis* conceptualization of Luthor as someone who conceals his criminal activity through the substantial means at his disposal. Some characters regard him with suspicion, but his image is one of a respectable, philanthropic entrepreneur.

While it might not seem strange that both of these versions of Luthor tell the Prometheus story, it is surprising that they both seem to identify with Prometheus. Before discussing the traits at the heart of the identification, it is necessary to survey the versions of Prometheus that have come down to us from antiquity.

Prometheus: Hesiodic vs. Aeschylean

Like Luthor, Prometheus has changed significantly, though the changes were evident in Classical Greece. The events of the story remain constant: Prometheus steals fire from Mount Olympus and gives it to men against the wishes of Zeus. Because of this transgression, Zeus chains Prometheus to a rock, where an eagle daily tears open his belly to eat his liver. Zeus then punishes men by introducing woman, in the form of Pandora, who unleashes misery and misfortune. Carol Dougherty describes the story of Prometheus as "richly ambiguous," a myth that accounts for both "the human condition as a triumph of the human intellect, imagination, and technology over all that nature can throw our way" and "why it is that back breaking toil, oppressive political conditions, and endless suffering define our daily life" (20). According to Dougherty, the myth of Prometheus "helps us reflect upon and even reimagine our own human experience" (2).

The two most prominent ancient texts recounting the Prometheus story, Hesiod's *Theogony* (c. 700 BCE) and Aeschylus's *Prometheus Bound* (c. 430 BCE), display opposite attitudes toward this myth. In Hesiod's version, Prometheus got what he deserved for his deceit and disobedience. Hesiod writes of Prometheus in uniformly negative terms—"shifty" (*Works and Days* 66) and "devious" (*Theogony* 548)—despite the boons he provides for humanity. For Aeschylus, however, Prometheus possesses a "nobility of character wholly lacking in Hesiod" (Ziolkowski 36). This is Prometheus the culture hero, who teaches arts and sciences to humanity, and this version of the character is the most commonly referenced version in the modern, Western world (Peretti).

Text 1: Superman Returns

In *Superman Returns*, Luthor plans to use Kryptonian crystal technology to dominate the real estate market by creating a new continent. To obtain this technology, he travels to Superman's Arctic fortress. Along the way, he explains his plan to his companion, Kitty:

> LUTHOR: "Do you know the story of Prometheus? No, of course you don't. Prometheus was a god who stole the power of fire from the other gods and gave control of it to mortals. In essence, he gave us technology. He gave us power."
> KITTY: "So we're stealing fire? In the arctic?"
> LUTHOR: "Actually, sort of. You see, whoever controls technology controls the world. The Roman Empire ruled the world because they built roads. The British Empire ruled the world because they built ships. America, the atom bomb, and so on and so forth. I just want what Prometheus wanted."
> KITTY: "Sounds great, Lex, but you're not a god."
> LUTHOR: "Gods are selfish beings who fly around in little red capes and don't share their power with mankind. No. I don't want to be a god. I just want to bring fire to the people. And I want my cut."

Kitty looks over at the wall, and the camera pans to follow her eyeline to show a relief of an angelic being carrying a star downward from clouds toward the Earth. The version in *Superman Returns: The Complete Shooting Script* lacks the relief on the wall, but there is no major difference between the two. However, when writing the novelization, Marv Wolfman takes advantage of the ability of prose to render a character's thoughts and give readers a brief glimpse into Luthor's attitude. Arriving at the fortress, Luthor gains access to all of Superman's Kryptonian information: "Luthor thought for a moment. He had the secrets of the universe in front of him. He could ask for the knowledge to cure all diseases. How famous would he be then? *My god, how the masses would worship me. But then, I've always hated their kind*" (92, italics in original).

Prometheus' motive for stealing fire is not clear in Hesiod's versions of the myths. Aeschylus, however, presents a Prometheus who sees himself as "the last free mind in the universe, the sole remaining consciousness that can distinguish between absolutes of good and evil" (Harris and Platzner 122). He opposes Zeus because of a commitment to morality, but he does so by giving fire to men because of his "excessive love for Man" (Aeschylus Line 123). In *Superman Returns*, Luthor wants revenge on Superman but, as Justine Toh points out, he also envies Superman's media coverage and public adoration (173). Luthor may claim a democratic desire "to bring fire to the people," but his thoughts reveal his motive to be anti–Promethean; he is contemptuous rather than benevolent, egomaniacal rather than self-sacrificing. As an embedded narrative, the telling of the myth in *Superman Returns* allows us to see Luthor's hypocrisy—it is what narratologist Patrick Hogan calls a psychological embedded narrative, which completely limits the primary narrator to the knowledge and emotional orientation of the embedded narrator (247–248). Luthor apparently cannot see his own motives for what they are. With that in mind, let's turn to the next text.

Text 2: Batman v Superman: Dawn of Justice

Ten years after *Superman Returns*, *Batman v Superman* includes a scene in which Luthor holds a fundraiser for the Library of Metropolis at his home. Introduced as "philanthropist, bibliophile, true friend" of the library, Luthor comes to a small stage and gives a speech:

> Me? Ah. Okay. Thank you. Umm, you're embarrassing me. Speech, speech! Ah, blah, blah, blah, open bar, then end. Uh, heh heh. The word philanthropist comes from the Greek, meaning a lover of

humanity. Uh, it was coined about twenty-five hundred years ago. […]between gods and men. Prometheus went with us, and he ruined Zeus's plan to destroy mankind, and for that he was given a thunderbolt. Choo! Hm, that seems unfair. On a serious note, the Library of Metropolis[…]. But at one time, dad could not buy them. No, my father could not afford books growing up. He had to root through the garbage for yesterday's newspaper. […] Books are knowledge, and knowledge is power. And I'm…. No … no, what am I? … I … what was I saying? No. The bittersweet pain among men is having knowledge with no power, because that is paradoxical, and…. Thank you for coming.

This telling of the Prometheus story barely comes through as a narrative because of interruptions, so the reference to Prometheus is little more than an allusion. Yet it is specific in its allusive intent: we are told that Prometheus was a philanthropist and that he suffered for humanity. The resonance becomes clear when considered alongside a speech from later in the film. Confronting Superman near the film's climax, Luthor says:

Boy do we have problems up here. The problem of evil in the world. The problem of absolute virtue. […] The problem of you on top of everything else. You above all. Cause that's what god is. Horus, Apollo, Jehovah, Kal-el. Clark Joseph Kent. See, what we call god depends upon our tribe, Clark Joe. Cause god is tribal. God takes sides. No man in the sky intervened when I was a boy to deliver me from daddy's fist and abominations. I figured out way back, if god is all powerful, he cannot be all good. If he is all good, then he cannot be all powerful. And neither can you be. They need to see the fraud you are, with their eyes, the blood on your hands. […] And tonight they will.[1]

In this latter speech, Luthor places himself in the role of Prometheus in two ways. First, he is performing a philanthropic duty, to side with humanity against a god. Second, he suffers. His suffering, however, does not have to do with his philanthropy; instead, it is the suffering of childhood abuse. He is motivated to Promethean philanthropy because he was denied it himself. The god in his scattered story is a father figure. Yet Luthor also has another agenda, which, like the Luthor of the post–Crisis comics, is existentialist (Donovan and Richardson). When he reveals that he has kidnapped Superman's mother and will only set her free if Superman kills Batman (thus showing the world that Superman is morally compromised), Luthor declares, "And now god bends to my will."

Luthor's retelling of Prometheus is embedded in a larger narrative of Luthor's attempt not merely to defeat Superman but to discredit him. His is ideologically motivated in his opposition to Superman in a way that the Luthor of *Superman Returns* is not. In the latter film, Luthor argues repeatedly that humanity cannot trust Superman, and only toward the end of the film do we begin to understand his motivations. Yet Luthor brings up the poverty of his father's youth, revealing perhaps too much about himself in the process of apparently losing his train of thought. He claims that knowledge is power and yet that human beings can have knowledge with no power. In his speech to Superman as his plan comes to fruition, Luthor attempts to correct the paradox apparent in his possession of knowledge (i.e., of Superman's secret identity and vulnerability to Kryptonite). It's easy enough to root his perception of this paradox in his childhood: his intelligence did not give him power over his father's physical abuse.

Binary Oppositions

An embedded text, such as Luthor's Prometheus story, can serve to explain the primary text (Bal 58). The Prometheus story is a useful one; the roles of Prometheus and Zeus provide a short-hand relationship that can be used to characterize power and rebellion. We notice several differences in these portrayals of Luthor that contribute to their versions of the Prometheus story, differences that are also evident in their attitude toward Superman. In *Superman Returns*, Luthor's true goal is acquiring wealth through, ultimately, a real-estate scheme, and his enmity stems from Superman's ability to stop him; he declares a democratic motive based on the sharing of power. The Luthor of *Batman v Superman*, on the other hand, hates Superman's existence independent of any specific plan or goal of his own. Superman has not opposed Luthor in any way when Luthor alludes to Prometheus at the fundraiser, so there is no enmity or revenge involved. This is the existentialist Luthor: he hates what Superman represents.

Despite these differences, both versions of Luthor feel affinity for the heroic, Aeschylean Prometheus. Culture heroes give culture to humanity in the form of art, navigation, science, and a variety of cultural desiderata that make human life possible in its current form. The Luthor in *Batman v Superman* brings up Prometheus in the context of donating money to build libraries, a center of culture. Later, in trying to rid humanity of Superman, Luthor acts less like a culture hero; though many culture heroes do slay monsters, that is not what defines them in the role, and Luthor's position as a corrupt, self-serving antagonist makes any reading of him as a culture hero too much of a stretch. His speeches reveal his real motives. His speech at the library fundraiser sounds like it's building to an admission that he feels powerless in the face of Superman's presence. His later speech, when he thinks he is about to defeat Superman, equates his relationship with his father to his relationship with Superman. Luthor begins by listing problems: evil, absolute virtue, and Superman. "You above all," he says, "Cause that's what god is."

Yet Luthor waffles between calling Superman a god and calling him a demon or devil. In an earlier scene, Luthor points to a painting that depicts devils rising up out of the ground and says, "That should be upside down. We know better now, don't we? Devils don't come from Hell beneath us, no. No, they come from the sky." When Luthor sees that his plan has failed, he says, "So, if man won't kill god, the devil will do it." Specifically, he's referring to a monster that he has created using Kryptonian technology to resurrect to the body of Zod (whom Superman killed in *Man of Steel*), mixed with his own DNA, in the form of a monster. Luthor's conflation of god and devil demonstrates his incoherent philosophy, which sees him ostensibly want to kill Superman for humanity's benefit—as a deterrence against possible future conflict—while simultaneously releasing a monster he cannot control: the monster's first response is to lash out at Luthor. His creation of a nonverbal monster that wreaks havoc on the community descends from the cinematic rather than the literary Frankenstein tradition, but the reference is not made explicit in the scene. Yet it also echoes the similar impulse of the Luthor seen in *Superman Returns*, who uses Kryptonian technology to create a monstrous landmass that Superman must excise from the planet. Both Luthors' creations echo the taboo science of Mary Shelley's novel. The Luthor of *Superman Returns* conceptualizes sharing of power in a single way: distribution of technology. He says that Superman doesn't share "his power" with the rest of humanity, but this isn't, strictly speaking, accurate; we could say that Superman shares his power in the form of service—a form of sharing that Luthor cannot conceptualize. Where the Aeschylean Prometheus is selfless to the point of sacrifice, Luthor is more like the Hesiodic Prometheus.

Beyond the difference in the Luthors' motives, the films present different attitudes toward Superman and the concept of the superhero. Both films were met with extensive criticism for their portrayal of Superman (Barber; Buchanan). Some audience members appreciate the Superman of these films; others say this Superman is not true to the character's history of optimism, inspiration, and hope. Superman's popularity and the availability of the films mean that they are revisited by critics from time to time, and for *Superman Returns*, the criticisms have remained constant since its release. One writer notes the fact that its Superman doesn't meet audience expectations: "The issue is that Superman is having such a tough time emotionally that his morality strays.... Superman has oft been criticized for being too clean cut and boring, but no one expected (or wanted) him to act like this" (Delaney). Similarly, an article in *Forbes* argues that *Man of Steel* and the films that followed it "didn't feel true to Superman's personality," evident in the dark colors of the costume and how "seriously" Snyder's film took Superman in general (Di Placido). The Luthors of these two cinematic portrayals reflect the tones of the films themselves, and I believe that the differences in Luthor's motives demonstrate the differences in contexts of when they were released. The following section will explore this difference in relation to a more straightforward instance of adapting material from comics.

The Burden of Being Superman

In both *Superman: The Movie* and *Man of Steel*, Clark Kent's adoptive father instructs him on the moral question arising from his powers. *Superman Returns*, because it follows Richard Donner's *Superman: The Movie*, does not include such as scene. The films of the 1970s and 1980s are nostalgic in their vision and reflect the unabashed delight and goodness presented in previous Superman animated shorts, serials, and television portrayals (Yockey). Governmental and law enforcement agencies in the Donner films and in *Superman Returns* do not question Superman's role. Authorities discuss neither Superman's problematic status as a vigilante, nor the need to prepare in case he betrays them. His reception is, with the exception of criminal opinion, a happy one. In the Snyder films, however, authorities greet Superman with suspicion and outright hostility. This is a product of the postmodern turn in the superhero genre that became popular in the wake of comics such as *Watchmen* (Moore [1986–87]) and *Dark Knight Returns* (Miller [1986]) and has become a prominent storytelling crutch (O'Rourke and O'Rourke 118). Specifically, the conventions of the genre have veered away from the notions of delight and fantasy common in the 1960s toward a "realism" that grounds the superhero in a world more like what readers might expect to live in if superheroes actually existed. The difference is best illustrated by an examination of those similar scenes in which Superman receives instructions from his parents.

The precedent for this type of scene goes all the way back to *Superman* #1 (June 1939). In that earliest version, both Superman's adoptive parents are present. His father says, "Now listen to me, Clark! This great strength of yours—you've got to hide it from people or they'll be scared of you!" His mother is the one to suggest benevolence: "But when the proper time comes, you must use it to assist humanity" (Siegel 195). *Superman: The Movie* includes a similar conversation between Clark and his adoptive father (Glenn Ford). When Pa Kent notices Clark showing off his powers, even though no one saw him do it, he says:

> When you first came to us, we thought that people would come and take you away because when they found out the things you could do. It worried us a lot. But then a man gets older and he thinks very differently and things get very clear. And there's one thing I do know, son, and that is you are here for a reason. I don't know whose reason, whatever the reason is, maybe it's because ... um, I don't know, son. But I do know one thing, it's not to score touchdowns.

They laugh at the end of this speech. The meaning is clear: Clark should eschew self-aggrandizement for virtue.

Man of Steel includes a similar scene between Clark and his father Jonathan (Kevin Costner). When Clark saves a bus full of children from drowning, some of them notice his powers. One of the mothers expresses concern, prompting Jonathan to tell him the following:

> There's more at stake here than just our lives, Clark, or the lives of those around us. When the world … when the world finds out what you can do, it's going to change everything. Our … our beliefs, our notions of what it means to be human. Everything. You saw how Pete's mom reacted, right? She was scared, Clark[…]. People are afraid of what they don't understand. […] When we found you, we were sure the government was going to show up at our doorstep, but no one ever came[…]. You're the answer, son. You're the answer to are we alone in the universe[…]. It'd be a huge burden for anyone to bear, but you're not just anyone, Clark. And I have to believe that you were, that you were sent here for a reason. All these changes that you're going through, one day, one day you're going to think of them as a blessing. And when that day comes, you're going to have to make a choice. A choice of whether to stand proud in front of the human race or not…. But somewhere out there you, you have another father, too, who gave you another name. And he sent you here for a reason, Clark. And even if it takes you the rest of your life, you owe it to yourself to find out what that reason is.

Notice the difference in tone. This isn't a father reprimanding a son for showing off; Jonathan counsels caution because of the ramifications Clark's existence. He frames Clark's presence on Earth as something that must be hidden. Ford's Pa Kent brushes that worry aside as the fear of a new father who lacks the proper perspective; his concern is for Clark's sense of ethics. Costner's Jonathan Kent frames Clark's powers as potentially damaging to the world. He doesn't tell Clark that humanity can learn from him or that it might be a good thing to question what it means to be human—he lacks confidence in the moral choices Clark will make as an adult. He is so focused on secrecy that he dies to preserve his son's privacy.

Snyder splits his adaptation of the conversation from the comic across two films. The *Man of Steel* lacks any comment from Martha Kent (Diane Lane). In *Batman v Superman*, Superman (and it's relevant that he *is* Superman at this point in the story) flies back to Smallville to discuss his purpose in the world with his mother. She tells him, "People hate what they don't understand. But they see what you do and they know who you are. You're not a killer, a threat. I never wanted this world to have you. Be their hero. Be their monument. Be their angel. Be anything they need you to be. Or be none of it. You don't owe this world a thing. You never did." Thematically, Martha's words align with Jonathan's from the previous film, but they run contrary to both *Superman: The Movie* and the comics. Jonathan questioned whose purpose Superman would fulfill. According to Martha, Superman's purpose is his own.

It's easy to see *Man of Steel* as a more "realistic" depiction of Superman: it shows both the fears of Superman's parents and how a confrontation between Superman and the US governmental military and law enforcement might play out. Its Superman is plagued by doubt because everyone doubts him, including his own father. Doubt saturates the entirety of *Man of Steel*, and it stretches into *Batman v Superman* as well: a montage of news clips uses real public figures to voice this doubt. These soundbites create a tone of moral ambiguity against which Superman must react. Luthor's ideological, philosophical, and ultimately religious rejection of Superman is voiced throughout the film by legislators, law enforcement, and military leaders, all of whom, it seems, would feel better if Superman weren't around. Much of the criticism of these films focused on their tone, and Snyder has said that the response to the first two films led him to "make an adjustment" to the tone of his subsequent work with the characters in *Justice League* (qtd. in Buchanan).

Expanded Origins

James Griffith, in *Adaptations as Imitations*, lays out a method for evaluating adapted novels that can apply to adaptations of sequential art as well. Griffith suggests an inductive approach that begins with the original authors' "shaping cause" and evaluates the adaptation on whether the adapting artist has chosen to pursue the same shaping cause in the new medium: "Films, as artificial objects, embody an intention (or unifying principle, or shaping cause); that embodiment or structure, imposed to bring about the intention for the audience, is the work's form" (69). The 1978 Donner film maintains Siegel and Shuster's original shaping cause: Superman receives essentially the same lesson from his adoptive parents, and he spends the rest of the film enacting a heroism that does not interrogate it. His education in and commitment to ethics is complete at the end of Jonathan Kent's speech. Donner isn't interested in a long period of introspection as Superman tries to figure out what his role on Earth will be. Snyder's films, on the other hand, diverge from Siegel and Shuster's shaping cause for the Superman story. There is some evidence that Snyder's films were intended to show Superman eventually embracing the type of heroism embodied by the character in the Donner films. Snyder indicates as much in an interview: "What's really great is that where we were going is kind of what the audience was wanting, which is a good thing. We just had to take the characters from somewhere [dark] to bring them up to where they are now" (qtd. in Buchanan). This is relevant not to the films themselves—they must stand or fail on their own, not on how they might potentially be informed by films as yet unmade—but to the nature of the Superman films and how they have evolved.

Looking at how the Superman origin stories have changed over the decades, the most obvious difference is perhaps the lengthened period prior to Clark Kent donning the costume and becoming a public figure. In *Action Comics* #1 (June 1938), for example, the entirety of his origin consists of a single page. Superman's commitment to virtue was "absolute and *a priori*" (Saunders 32). As creators are given more and more room (in terms of page lengths and screen time) to tell their stories, the origin expands. *Superman: The Movie* devoted fifty minutes of screen time building up to the first time Superman puts on his costume. In the twenty-first century, the television show *Smallville* spent ten years—217 hour-long episodes—before Clark Kent becomes Superman. Snyder's choice to spread this story over several films keeps with the trend not only to prolong the period but to dramatize it, showing the audience how Superman makes and comes to question his decisions. The major difference is that Snyder's Clark Kent wears the Superman suit while continuing his ethical edification.

Promethean Resonance

When analyzing embedded narratives, William Hansen suggests we find points of contact between the larger text and the tale told within it; these resonant qualities can lead us to understand the larger text in new ways (15–16). Commonly, the resonance is thematic. Hogan describes theme as "any norm—particularly an ethical or political norm—that carries over from the narrative to the real world" (18). Embedded narratives add a dimension to that relationship between narrative and real world because the embedded narrative has its first points of contact with the framing narrative. So the Prometheus narratives told by Luthor in the films show us that he sees himself as an Aeschylean Prometheus, but the audience's knowledge of Luthor as a villain adds irony to that, making the inclusion of the myth a comment on the dangers of hubris.

Between these two films, *Superman: The Black Ring* by Paul Cornell and Pete Woods told a story of Luthor and an android that looks like Lois Lane (made with Kryptonian technology) seeking cosmic power. Luthor's consciousness is attacked by an alien caterpillar called Mister Mind, whose goal is to prompt Luthor to think specific thoughts to lead him on his quest for power. In the process, Mister Mind allows Luthor to fantasize several different scenarios. In the first of these, Luthor imagines himself as an analogue to Prometheus: we first see him standing with a group of fur-clad men and women staring up at a massive temple. As he sums up their situation—miserable in comparison to those who had the temple built—he holds an apple in his hand to evoke forbidden fruit. He sneaks into the temple and steals a brazier of fire. At this point, the fantasy shifts to Luthor as Dr. Frankenstein—an allusion that fits with Luthor's pre–Crisis past as a mad scientist as well as with Shelley's subtitle: *The Modern Prometheus*. Shelley's reference leads readers to understand Victor Frankenstein as both creative and suffering because of his acts, and Luthor seems to see himself as suffering in a variety of ways that will become clear below. In this fantasy, the Lois android works as his lab assistant, though her hairstyle invites us to read her as the Monster's Mate from *The Bride of Frankenstein*. Luthor and Lois debate whether or not to unveil the figure Luthor has created. He hesitates, saying, "Whatever it is, this thing isn't really human. It could snap a person like matchwood. It could kill with a **look**." When Lois taunts him, he says, "I know myself. I don't know what it is, but I am not—afraid of—!—Myself." Tearing away the sheet, Luthor sees himself lying on the slab.

Seeing that Luthor has imprecated himself as Superman, Lois claims that he "**represent**[s] the human race." The scene shifts to a Western town, which Luthor, now a sheriff, must save through a shootout with Superman. Realizing that he is being manipulated, Luthor is able to take control of the fourth fantasy, in which he attacks Mister Mind as Superman would, yelling, "This is a job for—Lex Luthor" while ripping open his shirt to reveal not the Superman chevron but his chest. The chevron's shape is still present, since opening a shirt as Superman does creates four sides of the pentangle. Instead of an alien heritage, the act exposes Luthor's humanity, which in this case consists of a bare and hairless chest. Yet the panel is not devoid of significant iconography. When Luthor says his own name, the words appear in what we might read as comic book title or, perhaps more appropriately, a business logo. The rest of the story follows Luthor's quest for omnipotence, which he does obtain; however, he can only use it if his intentions are purely benevolent. We have seen Luthor fantasize about that kind of exercise of power in his Prometheus fantasy, but when the time comes to enact his plan, he cannot move past his enmity toward Superman. He finishes his quest but is prevented from realizing his goals.

According to Theodore Ziolkowski, the story of Frankenstein has crystallized the cultural myths of Adam and Prometheus into a modern myth about "knowledge and responsibility" (50)—that is, about ethics. In all the Superman stories discussed in this chapter, Luthor steals Kryptonian technology and unleashes it without fully comprehending its consequences. In creating Doomsday for *Batman v Superman*, Luthor becomes a Frankensteinian mad scientist, an analogy also prominent in *The Black Ring*. In the comic, the result is merely unfortunate: he does not use the power he gains to make the cosmos better, but he does not make it worse. In the film, he sets loose a monster that could have destroyed much of the world if not for superheroic intervention. Peter Conrad sums up Luthor's situation nicely when writing about the evolution of Prometheus: the myth "is reinterpreted in a sequence of orthodox rebuttals and atheistic denials, twisting into a dangers self-inquisition for the writers involved. Can an artist arrogate the creative power of the God who made the world or the parent who engenders new life, or does he only mock and sterilely mimic that potency? Does his method of continuing ensure renewal, or is it an unnatural after-life, like the animation of corpses by Mary Shelley's latter-day Prometheus, Victor Frankenstein?" (6). Luthor, unable to get past his grudge against god, fails himself and the humanity he claims to champion.

Luthor sees himself as an Aeschylean Prometheus when he is in fact Hesiodic. Superman, on the other hand, demonstrates the Aeschylean qualities; he is Promethean in his benevolence and sacrifice. What separates pre- and post–Crisis Superman stories, I think, is the focus on Promethean suffering—Superman's burden; the fact that Luthor is the one identifying himself with Prometheus makes the contrast all the more apparent. Superman of the Donner films suffers, but he smiles more than he frowns. While there *is* joy in the Superman of the Snyder films, such as when he first discovers he can fly, for much of the films he wears a dour expression; the tone is set by the color palate, and it varies only rarely. The authorities are suspicious of him, and he does not clearly articulate his motives. Luthor sees himself through the lens of Dr. Frankenstein—a lens distorted by ambition, occluded by selfishness, and restricted by tunnel vision. He tells his own story and takes no one else's advice. Superman, on the other hand, sees himself through the eyes of others. He listens to the criticisms made in public discourse, he asks authority figures for advice, and he listens to Lois Lane. His morality is a work in progress, but that allows him to change. If, as Ben Saunders proposes, Superman is an ongoing challenge to imagine what "an absolute commitment to virtue might look like" (31–32), recent Superman stories have done so by exploring how that commitment becomes established in the first place.

Note

1. The bracketed ellipses indicate moments when the filmmaker cut away from Luthor's speech. The script for this film is more difficult to find than that of *Superman Returns*. The copy I have access to, dated 2014 (two years prior to the film's release), does not include reference to Prometheus at all.

Works Cited

Aeschylus. *Prometheus Bound. The Complete Greek Tragedies: Aeschylus II*. Translated by David Greene, Washington Square Press, 1973."
Bal, Mieke. *Narratology: Introduction to the Theory of Narrative*, Third Edition. University of Toronto Press, 2009.
Barber, Nicholas. "Ignore the Backlash—Batman v Superman Is a Four-Star Epic." BBC.com. 23 Mar. 2016. http://www.bbc.com/culture/story/20160323-is-batman-v-superman-a-winner. Accessed 13 Dec. 2019.
Batman v Superman: Dawn of Justice. Directed by Zack Snyder, performances Diane Lane, Henry Cavill, Ben Affleck, Jesse Eisenberg. Warner Bros., 2016.
The Bride of Frankenstein. Directed by James Whale, performances by Elsa Lanchester and Boris Karloff. Universal, 1935.
Buchanan, Kyle. "Zack Snyder Faces His Haters on the Set of Justice League." *Vulture*. 21 June 2016. https://www.vulture.com/2016/06/zack-snyder-set-justice-league.html. Accessed 13 Dec. 2019

Byrne, John (w/a). *The Man of Steel* (1986). DC Comics, Inc., 2003.
Conrad, Peter. *To Be Continued: Four Stories and Their Survival*. Clarendon Press, 1995.
Cornell, Paul (w), and Pete Woods (a). *Superman: The Black Ring*, 2 volumes. DC Comics, Inc., 2011.
Curran, Brad. "Justice League's Snyder Cut Has Won Over DCEU Critics." *Screen Rant*. 22 Oct. 2019. https://screenrant.com/justice-league-movie-snyder-cut-dceu-critics/. Accessed 16 Nov. 2019.
Delaney, Jack. "How Superman Returns Screwed up the Man of Steel." *Screen Rant*. 12 Mar. 2016. https://screenrant.com/superman-returns-screwed-up-man-of-steel/. Accessed 23 Dec. 2020.
Di Placido, Dani. "DC Films Still Doesn't Know What to Do with Superman." *Forbes*. 27 Nov. 2019. https://www.forbes.com/sites/danidiplacido/2019/11/27/dc-films-still-doesnt-know-what-to-do-with-superman/#4f6da6e86ce1. Accessed 13 Dec. 2019.
Donovan, Sarah K., and Nicholas Richardson. "Lex Luthor as Existentialist Anti-Hero." *Superman and Philosophy*, edited by Mark D. White. Wiley Blackwell, 2013, pp. 121–130.
Dougherty, Carol. *Prometheus*. Routledge, 2006.
Friedenthal, Andrew J. *The World of DC Comics*. Routledge, 2019.
Gods and Monsters. Directed by Bill Condon, performances by Ian McKellan and Brendan Fraser. Lionsgate, 1998.
Grene, David, and Richmond Lattimore. *Aeschylus II: The Suppliant Maidens, The Persians, Seven Against Thebes, Prometheus Bound*. Washington Square Press, 1973.
Griffith, James. *Adaptations as Imitations: Films from Novels*. University of Delaware Press, 1997.
Hansen, William. "Reading Embedded Narration." *Myth and Symbol II: Symbolic Phenomena in Ancient Greek Culture*, edited by Sunnøve Des Bouvrie. Papers from the Norwegian Institute at Athens 7, 2004.
Harris, Stephen, L., and Gloria Platzner. *Classical Mythology: Images and Insights*. McGraw-Hill, 2012.
Hesiod. *Works and Days* and *Theogony*. Translated by Stanley Lombardo. Hackett Publishing, 1993.
Hogan, Patrick Colm. *Narrative Discourse: Authors and Narrators in Literature, Film, and Art*. The Ohio State University Press, 2013.
Justice League. Directed by Zack Snyder, performances by Henry Cavill, Ben Affleck, and Gal Gadot. Warner Bros., 2017.
Leitch, Thomas. *Film Adaptation and Its Discontents: From* Gone with the Wind *to* The Passion of the Christ. The Johns Hopkins University Press, 2007.
The Little Prince. Directed by Mark Osborne, performances by Jeff Bridges and Mackenzie Foy. Onyx Films, 2015.
Lincoln, Bruce. *Theorizing Myth*. University of Chicago Press, 1999.
The Lord of the Rings: The Fellowship of the Ring. Directed by Peter Jackson, performances by Elijah Wood and Ian McKellan. New Line, 2001.
Man of Steel. Directed by Zack Snyder, performances by Henry Cavill and Michael Shannon. Warner Bros., 2013.
Miller, Frank (w/p), and Klaus Janson (i). *Batman: The Dark Knight Returns*. DC Comics, Inc., 1986.
Moore, Alan (w), and Dave Gibbons (a). *Watchmen*. DC Comics, Inc., 1986.
Nelles, William. "Embedding." *Routledge Encyclopedia of Narrative Theory*. Routledge, 2010.
O'Rourke, Daniel J., and Morgan B. O'Rourke. "'It's Morning Again in America': John Byrne's Re-Imagining of the Man of Steel." *The Ages of Superman: Essays on the Man of Steel in Changing Times*, edited by Joseph J. Darowski. McFarland, 2012, pp. 115–124.
Peretti, Daniel. *The Modern Prometheus: The Persistence of an Ancient Myth in Contemporary American Culture, 1950–2007*. Ph.D. Thesis, Indiana University, 2009.
Saunders, Ben. *Do the Gods Wear Capes?: Spirituality, Fantasy, and Superheroes*. Continuum International Publishing Group, 2011.
A Serious Man. Directed by Ethan Coen and Joel Coen, performances by Michael Stuhlbarg and Richard Kind. Focus Features, 2009.
Slethaug, Gordon E. *Adaptation Theory and Criticism: Postmodern Literature and Cinema in the USA*. Bloomsbury, 2014.
Siegel, Jerry (w), and Joseph Shuster (a). "Origin of Superman," *Superman #1* (July 1939). *Superman Chronicles* Vol. 1. DC Comics, Inc., 2006.
Superman: The Movie. Directed by Richard Donner, performances by Christopher Reeve and Gene Hackman. Warner Bros., 1978.
Superman Returns. Directed by Bryan Singer, performances by Brandon Routh, and Kevin Spacey. Warner Bros., 2006.
Toh, Justine. "'People Have Had Enough Tragedy': The Spectacle of Global Heroism in *Superman Returns*." *The War on Terror and American Popular Culture: September 11 and Beyond*, edited by Andrew Schopp and Matthew B. Hill. Farleigh Dickenson University Press, 2009, pp. 167–186.
Wolfman, Marv (w), and George Perez (p). *Crisis on Infinite Earths*. DC Comics, Inc., 1986.
Wolfman, Marv. *Superman Returns: The Novelization*. Warner Books, 2006.
Yockey, Matt. "Somewhere in Time: Utopia and the Return of Superman." *The Velvet Light Trap*. Vol. 61 no. 1 2008, pp. 26–37.
Ziolkowski, Theodore. *The Sin of Knowledge: Ancient Themes and Modern Variations*. Princeton University Press, 2000.

Lois Lane in Three Acts

Zack Snyder's Key to a Modern Portrait of The Daily Planet's *Reporter*

SANDRA ECKARD

Director Zack Snyder's foray into the DC Extended Universe (DCEU)[1] has had mixed results. While many agree his casting choices, such as Gal Gadot as Wonder Woman, are spot on, his three films—*Man of Steel* (2013), *Batman v Superman* (2016), and *Justice League* (2017)—were met with such a mixed bag of critical and fan reactions. Though many loathe his direction and story construction, there was also a die-hard following of fans who persisted in arguing for the "Snyder Cut" of his final film in the trilogy, which had re-shoots and was edited by Joss Whedon.[2] This chapter will not focus on the merits—or not—in the films' content, but rather will examine the arc of *The Daily Planet* reporter and Superman's love interest, Lois Lane. Zack Snyder's vision of Lois Lane begins with a clear construction of a modern woman, and not only does he place her at the forefront of the first film, *Man of Steel*, he also deliberately constructs her as "the key" to Superman's journey in the second film *Batman v Superman*. Although we don't get to see where Snyder's now-cancelled five-movie arc might have gone, we do have three films to analyze this version of the famous reporter.

Snyder's version of Lois Lane, a character first constructed by Siegel and Shuster in *Action Comics* #1 (June 1938), is just the latest in a character who evolves and changes with each generation. In the 1940s, she was a career-minded reporter; in the 1950s, she was more of a love interest; and in the 1970s, she was a social justice advocate who was often pushing boundaries. Her latter experiences often mirrored issues and offered social commentary, such as with the "I am Curious (Black)!" (*Superman's Girl Friend Lois Lane* #106 [Nov. 1970]), where Lois undergoes a transformation to change her skin color to experience the world as a black person.

The most recognizable versions of Lois outside of comics might be Margot Kidder from the Christopher Reeve *Superman* cycle (1978–1987), whose strong-willed and personable version became a beloved incarnation that balanced being the love interest with a likeable representation of a modern woman of the time. However, casting Lois isn't just a matter of finding a pretty face; Kate Bosworth's 2006 take was a complete misfire. Starting fresh with a new version after Kidder needs to honor the parts of Kidder that audiences related to (dogged truth-seeker, worthy love interest) while still updating her character for today's audiences. Snyder's vision, then, for an independent, strong-willed female character has both hits and misses, but overall, helps to move Lois successfully into a modern heroine.

Man of Steel

The audience first meets Lois Lane (Amy Adams) as she exits a helicopter in 2013's *Man of Steel*, and right away, we see a Lois Lane in action: she is in the middle of investigating a story about a mysterious ship that has been discovered in the Artic. This scene allows us to learn about her not only from her actions, but also through other characters' eyes. Jed Eubanks (Tahmoh Penikett), the soldier in charge of Artic Cargo for the military, greets her warmly, stating, "I got to confess Miss Lane, I'm not a fan of *The Daily Planet*. But those pieces you wrote when you were embedded with the First Division were, well, they were pretty impressive." She takes the praise lightly, responding with, "Well, what can I say? I get writer's block if I'm not wearing a flak jacket!" Right away, audiences get a sense that she enjoys her job and courts adventure—thriving, even, on the adrenaline.

Not all of the military is enamored of her, for when she meets Colonel Hardy (Christopher Meloni), he criticizes her for being early. She's ready with one of the most memorable scenes from the film: "Look, let's get one thing straight, guys, okay? The only reason I'm here is because we're on Canadian soil and the appellate court overruled your injunction to keep me away. So, if we're done measuring dicks, can you have your people show me what you found?" This response shows that this version of Lois is a straight shooter, confident in what she does—traveling to the Artic—and in what she says. In an interview for *Parade* in 2016, Amy Adams reinforces her take on Superman's favorite reporter, asserting that "Lois is a superwoman in her own way." She continues by explaining her take on the character: "I love how willing Lois is to put her fears aside…. It's not about being fearless; it's about overcoming your fears and trying anyway" (Spenser).

While her capabilities might not be the same as Superman's, Lois can be more than a damsel in distress. In *Superman Returns,* for example, Bosworth's Lois needed to be "saved" multiple times, and in one of the key scenes, faints at the sight of a long-missing Superman. While the character seems to be written as a Pulitzer Prize–winning journalist, scenes such as this fainting one illustrate that a supposedly modern heroine was, in fact, not. However, Snyder's Lois is built to contrast this version. When General Zod (Michael Shannon) requests Lois to join Superman (Henry Cavill) on his space ship, she immediately consents to go. While there, she learns from the AI version of Jor-El (Russell Crowe) how to stop Zod. Once safely on the ground, she immediately finds Clark: "I know how to stop them!" Instead of falling apart or worrying about her own safety, Lois is focusing on helping save the world. She, unlike Bosworth's Lois Lane, doesn't faint—she instead uses the information that the hologram Jor-El gives her to help craft a plan to stop the villain.

Throughout the film, Lois is placed in at least two moments where she is in need of rescue. And both times, Superman must save her—providing the obligatory flying scenes with the iconic "Superman carries Lois Lane" moments that are ubiquitous throughout every comic, television, or film version over the last eighty years. However, what modernizes these scenes in *Man of Steel* is that in both of these "damsel" moments, Lois isn't just a passive abductee or victim. She is actively working to solve problems with her own skill set. From the beginning, what connects the plot together is her desire to publish a story about the stranger with mysterious powers who saved her life in the Artic. She traces his path and helps to uncover how he has been helping people for years. It is Lois in the end who uncovers Clark Kent's secret through her dogged, determined investigation. When he then tells her his reasons why he wants to keep his identity a secret, Lois listens. While she is intrigued by him, she doesn't focus on his words like a love-struck damsel. Instead, she hears him as he tells her the story of how his father died—and he could have prevented it. And, in the end, she saves Superman, too, in a very important way: she keeps his secret.

Unlike most versions of the story, Lois doesn't just have a memory loss or have some spell cast on her that evaporates. In the *Adventures of Superman* television series (1952–1958), a pattern develops that viewers have become familiar with: an evil scientist is determined to figure out Superman's identity. During her investigation, Lois (Phyllis Coates) is questioning the scientist and drinks a cup of coffee that is laced with a truth serum. Viewers get what we want—because of the serum's effects, she mumbles, "You are Clark Kent!" However, once the serum's effects wear off, the story is reset and Lois doesn't remember ("The Secret of Superman"). This plot device is used many times in various Superman stories, where Lois is incapacitated or unable to see that Clark Kent and Superman are the same person. In most versions, even if Lois learns the truth, something happens and the potion fades or Superman realizes that he has to protect her and "take back" the truth—such as in *Superman II* (1980). Clark realizes that he can't choose Lois over having the power to save the world, and he then kisses her, using his ability to wipe her memory of his secret identity.

In Snyder's vision, Lois is strong enough to not only learn the truth—but also keep the secret. Tim Hanley argues in *Investigating Lois Lane* (2016) that not only does Clark land a job at *The Daily Planet* because of Lois pulling strings to get him on staff, "the franchise seems poised to skip the secret identity shenanigans that have traditionally undermined her intellect and instead portray Lois as a smart, capable partner to both Clark and Superman" (156). Adams argues that what attracts her to the role "is that she [Lois]'s been very consistently strong, successful, independent" (Davidson).

In *Man of Steel*, Lois Lane is powerful enough, then, and smart enough to not only follow the trail to figure out Clark's true background and identity—she is strong enough to keep the secret and become a strong, modern partner, not just a love interest, for both Clark and Superman.

Batman v. Superman: Dawn of Justice

Much like *Man of Steel*, the audience first sees Lois Lane as a journalist in her first scene in 2016's sequel. Snyder makes a deliberate parallel here, helping to craft her persona with action—she is once again on assignment—this time in the fictional nation of Nairomi, Africa. She is there to interview the elusive leader Amajagh (Sammi Rotibi), who many view as a terrorist. Amajagh takes one look at Lois and states, "They did not tell me the interview was with a lady." Ready, unflappable, Lois replies, "I'm not a lady. I'm a journalist." Amy Adams seems to have grown even more confident in her portrayal the second time around, describing her character as even more "fearless" ("*Batman v. Superman*: Amy Adams on Playing Lois Lane"). This scene—which rapidly escalates—is the set up for a conflict that pits The Dark Knight of Gotham against his perceived next threat: Superman.

The Africa incident gains international attention, forcing everyone, including Lois, to reflect on Superman's role in the world.

> LOIS LANE: They held hearings about what happened. They're saying that…
> CLARK KENT: I don't care. I don't care what they're saying. The woman I love could have been blown up or shot. Think of what could have happened.
> LOIS LANE: Well, think about what did happen.
> CLARK KENT: I didn't kill those men if that's what they think. If that's what you're saying.
> LOIS LANE: No, I'm saying I want to understand what happened. I'm saying, thank you for saving my life. I'm saying there's a cost…. I just don't know if it's possible.
> CLARK KENT: Don't know what's possible?
> LOIS LANE: For you to love me and be you.

In previous incarnations, both in comic and on screen, Lois spent much of her time focusing on her relationship with Superman. Many of the comics within *Superman's Girl Friend Lois Lane* (Apr. 1958–Oct. 1974) focus on her love of Superman or her attempts to get him to love her in return. In issue #5's "The Fattest Girl in Metropolis" (Dec. 1958), Lois is accidentally zapped with a growth ray while interviewing a famous scientist about his newest design. When she wakes up the next day, she is twice the size and cannot fit in any of her clothes. Rather than her health or side effects, her biggest worry is that Superman won't love her: "What if Superman, the man I love, saw me now? I must avoid him at all costs!" The entire story is focused on her attempts to avoid him, and it sets up a common theme for the 1950s and early 1960s that her primary focus was not her career, but rather her love (or adoration) of Superman.

In contrast, Zack Snyder's vision in this second act builds on the vision of the *Daily Planet* reporter, focusing on her independence and her desire—since she knows who Superman is—to balance what she wants and what the world needs. However, she does still have damsel-in-distress moments. Elaina Dockterman asserts in "Wonder Woman's Epic Introduction is Undercut by a Helpless Lois Lane" (2016) that, in addition to a flashback to *Man of Steel*, there are three additional times that Lois needs Superman to save her: when she is taken hostage, when she is thrown by Lex Luthor (Jesse Eisenberg) off a roof, and when she is trapped under water. In each of these instances, she is doing her job by interviewing or investigating. However, as Dockterman argues: "Heck, even when Lois tries to help, she gets into trouble." Her criticism is fair—but I believe Lois's strength is that she is a different kind of female character. Lois Lane is not designed to compete with a goddess such as Diana Prince/Wonder Woman; instead, she is there as a relatable avatar for the female viewers in the audience. Lois, then, is human—complete with weaknesses and limitations that any woman has. Despite her human flaws and her rescue moments in the film, Snyder also paints Lois—especially in the Ultimate Edition with additional scenes cut from the theatrical release—as a *human* who uses her intelligence and persistence to figure out Lex Luthor's grand plan to frame Superman.

Snyder's version of Lois, then, doesn't just wallow in being saved by Superman— or loved by him—as she immediately goes back to investigating after the big incident in Africa. While interviewing the suspected terrorist, shots rang out and people died. During the follow-up investigation by the U.S. government, witnesses—erroneously— blamed Superman. Later unpacking her suitcase, Lois finds a mysterious bullet in her journal, prompting her to travel to D.C. in hot pursuit of the truth behind the bullet's origin. After he dodges her calls, Lois even follows General Swanwick (Harry Lennix) into the men's bathroom. Annoyed, he retorts, "You know, with balls like yours, you belong in here." But it's her persistence that uncovers the truth, as she works with a crime lab expert to discover proof that Superman wasn't working with Lex Luthor—it's only through her investigation that it is revealed that Lex had gifted the primary witness in the hearings a new wheelchair; this wheelchair was lined with lead so that Superman's x-ray vision couldn't spot the danger before the bomb went off, blowing up the U.S. Capitol Building. Lois, then, ties together the pieces to clear Superman's name and solve the mystery.

However, Lois doesn't just function as a reporter. She also serves as a sounding board for Superman. Their connection is actually the primary relationship in the film other than Clark's with his mother, so her role as his sounding board is important; since they are the only ones in on the secret of his identity, from Snyder's vision, it feels as though they are not just lovers but confidants as well. As Clark struggles to see himself as part of Earth or as an alien, she attempts to reassure him that the truth will come out, that the work that he does helping others does matter:

> Lois Lane: Clark, there are people behind this.
> Superman: I'm afraid I didn't see it because I wasn't looking. All this time. I've been living my life the way my father saw it. Righting wrongs for a ghost. Thinking I'm here to do good. Superman was never real. Just the dream of a farmer from Kansas.
> Lois Lane: That farmer's dream is all some people have. It's all that gives them hope. [presses the insignia on Superman's chest] This means something.

The most important impact that Lois has on the plot, though, is to unite Batman (Ben Affleck) and Superman. In the heat of their battle, Superman is losing to Batman and his Kryptonite weapons. It is Lois who—with no superpowers—gets a helicopter to go to Gotham to help. Here, she intervenes and reveals to Batman that Martha is Clark's mother's name, giving him pause and allowing Superman time to explain Luthor's manipulative plot. In addition, she also hunts down the Kryptonite spear that, earlier, had been used against Superman—but in the end, might just be the only tool that could be used to defeat Doomsday. This spear, with a Kryptonite tip, affects both Superman and the creature because they both originate from Krypton. Despite the fact that it weakens him— and Lois has to juxtapose retrieving it for him and keeping it far enough away from him so he can regather his strength—Superman realizes that Lois, and the people of Earth, are worth any sacrifice. His love for her, and her's for him, gives him the strength to wield the spear and kill Doomsday; because of his weakened state, he dies as well. However, the internal conflict in the film—on whether or not he belonged on Earth, on whether or not he is "human enough" to lead a full life—has been resolved specifically because of Lois, who he declares is "his world."

Although there are the, once again, the traditional scenes where Superman rescues Lois Lane, the number of times that she helps—either by rescuing him or investigating on her own—provide a positive balance that solidifies Snyder's vision of Lois as a strong, modern heroine. *Batman v. Superman* gives Lois Lane a solid second act, allowing her character to fully develop as a woman, as a journalist, and as a love interest. Though the close of the film does focus on her as Clark Kent's love interest, her overall role is well developed in the film. While *Batman v Superman* centered on introducing Diana Prince's Wonder Woman, the fierce Amazonian warrior, it's hard to imagine that a human female character could hold the screen in contrast, but Zack Snyder does his best to provide

Amy Adams different paths to use her own superpowers as a journalist and as a woman to flesh out this modern take on Lois Lane.

Justice League

In 2017's *Justice League*, the audience first meets Lois as she deals with the aftermath of Superman's—and Clark Kent's—death. We see her in a montage of dreary images of how everyone in the world is either acting out by committing crimes or mourning the death of their hero. This film opens this worldwide despair that even Bruce Wayne cannot move past, as he decides to use the Kryptonian ship's otherworldly tools to resurrect Superman to help them fight a new foe, Steppenwolf (Ciarán Hinds). As the film that centers on building the League of superheroes—individuals with special powers—it doesn't leave much room for an ordinary reporter who only has ordinary skills.

Lois Lane's first real scene involves a teary coffee chat with Martha Kent (Diane Lane) as they talk about their lives and reminisce about Clark. We see a very different Lois here—she's not spunky or eager to chase a story. She's sad and still mourning. When Martha suggests that she should follow a lead that another reporter mentions, she dismisses it, declaring "I'm not ready yet. I'm perfectly happy doing fluff pieces…. It was hard coming back here at all." The Lois we meet here is not the Lois that we met in the previous two installments.

Through a brief connecting scene, we do get a bit of Lois's decision making and mindset for why she can't get back to work effectively: "Stories just made sense. It was more than just a puzzle; it was about the truth. It was about seeing the engine of the world … when it still ran." She has no interest in tackling larger stories because she believes the world is broken, and she can't yet make sense of her purpose without Clark—or the world's purpose without Superman.

What is confusing about this scene is that it is in stark contrast with both Adams's—and Snyder's—focus on Lois as a powerful woman. While we can give some leeway in cultural expectations (there is always one scene where Lois needs saved in almost every version of the comic, television, or cinematic variation of the character over time), and while we can also allow some wiggle room with Lois as a different kind of female character, it is sad that in this third act for the character we see her have not one of her first scenes pass the Bechdel Test. The test is named after illustrator Alison Bechdel who, in 1985, outlined three questions to measure the representation of women in fiction:

1. Does the movie contain two or more (named) females?
2. Do these characters talk to each other?
3. If so, do they discuss something other than a man? [Racic]

Sadly, the whole conversation between Lois and Martha involves Clark and the loss of the man they both loved. Interestingly, Martha Kent seems more willing to grow and move on than Lois. She has sold the Kent farm and now works in a café in Metropolis, allowing her to be self-sufficient (even if still in mourning). While Amy Adams crafts Lois to be likeable, this scene feels tonally awkward and out of character. Perhaps part of this lack of consistency is due to the Zack Snyder and Joss Whedon mash up that became the theatrical release of *Justice League*. For anyone who doesn't know—or who didn't cringe at the CGI mustache debacle of Henry Cavill reshoots for *Justice League*—Zack Snyder didn't finish the editing and final production elements of the movie because of the death of his daughter. Warner Bros. turned over the final filming and editing to Joss Whedon, who received a writing credit but not a directing credit; however, much of the film was re-shot, and the directors' styles and humor noticeably clashed. This scene is rumored to be one of Whedon's, not Snyder's (Johnston).

The next time Lois arrives—much later in the film—is as the main ingredient in Bruce's "contingency plan" for bringing back Superman; "if the plan goes south" he states, he will "bring in the big guns." Bruce's plan to resurrect Superman means playing with death, and as Diana warns him, "You lose something when you die." So, when Superman returns to life but is missing his soul, Bruce has Lois on back-up so that she could spark his memories and bring him fully back.

This, though, makes Lois a plot device; her primary role, then, in the story is to be the "key" to Superman's humanity, to bring him back to himself, his morals as Clark Kent, and his role as the world's savior.

> LOIS LANE: What was it like…?
> SUPERMAN: Coming back? Itchy. I mean, honestly … weird. In so many ways. But, mostly, just…
> LOIS LANE, SEARCHING FOR THE WORDS: I wasn't strong. I didn't … umm … you would've been very disappointed in me. I wasn't … Lois Lane, dedicated reporter. I… I just…
> SUPERMAN: It's okay. I'm the idiot who left. But I'm back now … and I'm going to make things right.

With the return of the love of her life, it seems that the spark within her to find hope has returned. And it is Lois who then moves the plot forward, reminding Clark why he was resurrected in the first place: "I was hoping it would take you longer to recover … because now I have to send you away."

At the end, Lois's famous power suit returns—as does her spirit and her writer's view of the world as her voice, her article, provides the closing of the film. She has grown, then, from a fiancée stuck in the past and consumed by loss to a new view of herself and the world, filled with hope:

> LOIS LANE, voiceover: Darkness. The truest darkness … is not about the absence of light. It is the conviction that the light will never return. But the light always returns … to show us things familiar. Home. Family. And things entirely new. Or long overlooked. It shows us new possibilities…. And challenges us to pursue them.
> This time, the light shone on the heroes coming out of the shadows to tell us we won't be alone again. Our darkness was deep and seemed to swallow all hope. But these heroes were here the whole time to remind us that hope is real. That you can see it. All you have to do is look … up in the sky.

While the second half of *Justice League* feels more promising for an overall vision of Lois Lane—perhaps because it feels more in line with Snyder's overall vision—it's important to note that Zack Snyder originally wanted a five-film arc for Superman and the DCEU. However, it's clear with the lack of success for *Justice League* and rumors of behind-the-scenes drama at Warner Bros. that Snyder will not direct any more connected films in the universe. Many films will now be stand-alone; in February 2019, Warner Bros. CEO Kevin Tsujihara "confirmed the future of the studio's superhero movies rests in individualized stories and not an interconnected movie universe" (Sharf) under the official label Worlds of DC.

In *Batman v Superman*, we hear the Flash (Ezra Miller) from the future say that "Lois is the key," but Snyder didn't reveal exactly what that meant until years later in 2019. Chris Terrio's original *Justice League* script was to focus on connecting back to this moment, showing why Superman becomes evil: the villain Darkseid kills Lois (Saavedra).

This trope is known as fridging, from Gail Simone's analysis of Women in Refrigerators, wherein a love interest or character is killed in a comic world to motivate the hero to kill or seek revenge (Hatch). Zack Snyder believes in strong women, especially Lois Lane, and argues that she "doesn't need Superman or Clark; the fact that Clark likes her makes him smarter, cooler, better! The more badass Lois is, the better Clark gets" (Harrington). Snyder starts off well, but between studio demands, script changes, rewrites, and multiple directors, Lois's independence and vision become muddled.

So, perhaps, it's better that Lois Lane's story here is told in only three acts. She starts off as a modern interpretation of a classic character, returning her to the original Siegel and Shuster's 1938 version who was more focused on her work than her love life. These three acts are a few steps forward, a few steps back. While we can enjoy some scenes and see some sparkles in Snyder's vision, in the end, we are left with an incomplete, unsatisfying character arc. Perhaps with the next incarnation, we will be able to move past tropes and into new ground for one of the oldest, and most deserving, female characters.

In a recent twelve-issue, limited-run comic book series titled *Lois Lane* (2019–2020), Lois is married to Clark, and her love life is not the center of the story; rather, a conspiracy involving the death of a fellow reporter. Lois "has a laptop, a bunch of pencils, and a raft of notepads.... That's more than enough to get her into deep trouble, and used effectively, more than enough to get her out of it" (Gustines). This new series is simply titled *Lois Lane*; there is no need to add the details of *Superman's Girl Friend*, as with the long-running series from an earlier time. This new Lois can stand on her own, without Superman in the title. Maybe soon, she can be her own superhero after all.

Notes

1. The DC Extended Universe is the unofficial designation for the shared universe of Warner Bros. films based on the characters from DC Comics.
2. The four-hour cut of *Zack Snyder's Justice League* was released in Mar. 2021

Works Cited

"*Batman v. Superman:* Amy Adams on Playing Lois Lane, Shirtless Scenes with Henry Cavill." *ABC News.* 25 Mar. 2016. https://abcnews.go.com/Entertainment/batman-superman-amy-adams-playing-lois-lane-shirtless/story?id=37924576. 2 Dec. 2019.
Batman v. Superman: Dawn of Justice Ultimate Edition. Directed by Zack Snyder, Warner Bros., 2016.
Binder, Otto (w), and Kurt Schaffengerger (p/i). "The Fattest Girl in Metropolis," *Superman's Girl Friend Lois Lane* #5 (Dec. 1958). *Lois Lane: A Celebration of 75 Years,* DC Comics, Inc., 2013, pp. 86–94.
Davidson, Danica. "Lois Lane Is 'A Powerful Woman' Says Amy Adams." *MTV.com.* 31 Mar. 2011. http://www.mtv.com/news/2598546/amy-adams-lois-lane-superman/. Accessed 3 Jan. 2020.
Dockterman, Eliana. "Wonder Woman's Epic Introduction Is Undercut by a Perpetually Helpless Lois Lane." *Time.* 27 Mar. 2016. https://time.com/4269943/batman-v-superman-wonder-woman-lois-lane/. Accessed 4 Jan. 2020.
Gustines, George Gene. "Lois Lane Fights for Justice in New Comic Book Series." *The New York Times.* 2 Jul. 2019. https://www.nytimes.com/2019/07/02/arts/design/lois-lanes-comic-book.html. Accessed 4 Feb. 2020.
Hanley, Tim. *Investigating Lois Lane: The Turbulent History of The Daily Planet's Ace Reporter.* Chicago Review Press, 2016.
Harrington, Donnia. "Exclusive: An Interview with Zack Snyder." *Comic Book Debate.* 20 May 2019. https://comicbookdebate.com/2019/05/20/exclusive-an-interview-with-zack-snyder/. Accessed 5 Feb. 2020.
Hatch, Aaron. "Women in Refrigerators: Killing Females in Comics." *The Artifice.* 11 Oct. 2015. https://the-artifice.com/women-in-refrigerators-killing-females-in-comics/. Accessed 5 Feb. 2020.
Johnston, Rich. "Thirsty…The 'Mewling Quim' and 'Prima Nocta' Moment of *The Justice League.*" *The Bleeding Cool.* 16 Nov. 2017. https://www.bleedingcool.com/2017/11/16/thirsty-mewling-moment-justice-league/. Accessed 27 Jan. 2020.

Justice League. Directed by Zack Snyder, Warner Bros., 2017.
Kanigher, Robert (w), Werner Roth (p), and Vince Colletta (p). "I am Curious (Black)!" *Superman's Girl Friend Lois Lane* #106 (Nov. 1970). *75 Years of Lois Lane*, DC Comics, Inc., 2013, pp. 115–129.
Man of Steel. Directed by Zack Snyder, Warner Bros., 2013.
Racic, Monica. "Do This Year's Best Picture Nominees Pass the Bechdel Test?" *The New Yorker Online*. 3 Mar. 2018. https://www.newyorker.com/culture/culture-desk/do-this-years-best-picture-oscar-nominees-pass-the-bechdel-test. Accessed 3 Jan. 2020.
Saavedra, John. "*Justice League:* Darkseid Killed Lois Lane in Original Script." *Den of Geek*. 26 Mar. 2019. https://www.denofgeek.com/movies/justice-league-lois-lane-dead/. Accessed 3 Feb. 2020.
"The Secret of Superman." 1952. *Adventures of Superman*, season 1, episode 10, syndication, 17 Nov. 1952."
Sharf, Zack. "Warner Bros. Pulls Back on DCEU: Shared Universe No Longer Top Priority." *IndieWire*. 28 Feb. 2019. https://www.indiewire.com/2019/02/warner-bros-pulls-back-dceu-no-shared-universe-1202047994/. Accessed 25 Jan. 2020.
Spenser, Amy. "Amy Adams: Lois Lane Is a Superwoman." *Parade Magazine*. 18 Mar. 2016. https://parade.com/464337/parade/amy-adams-lois-lane-is-a-superwoman/. Accessed 2 Jan. 2020.

Branded a Tyrant

Rescuing Superman Video Games with the Injustice *Series*

CARL WILSON

With the release of video game *Injustice 2* in 2017, published by Warner Bros. Interactive Entertainment, Guinness World Records recognized Superman as the "Longest-running videogame character," noting that he has been "officially enduring longer than gaming megastars such as PAC-Man and Mario" (Daultrey). While *Action Comics #1* saw the first appearance of Superman over 80 years ago in 1938, the first super hero video game *Superman* (1979) was developed and published over 40 years ago by Atari to coincide with the Warner Bros. movie release of *Superman* (1978). Yet, despite his historically significant position within the medium, Superman is absent from academic collections such as *100 Greatest Video Game Characters*, edited by Robert Mejia, et al., or Taschen's more expansive art-book *1000 Game Heroes*. In *The League of Super Hero Games*, one of the few books on the subject, taking flight as Superman in the mobile video game *Man of Steel* (2013) ranks at a lowly 28 out of 30 "Most Heroic Moments Ever," behind playing as Alfred the Butler in 2014's *Lego Batman 3: Beyond Gotham* (Albigès 13). According to video game database MobyGames, Superman has appeared in at least 21 games where he has been granted a starring role, although this pales in comparison to Batman's hundred-plus roles (Kartanym). In terms of quality, Superman has also been largely neglected. Video game websites such as *Kotaku* have run articles with exploratory titles such as "Let's See If Superman 64 Really Is The Worst Game Of All Time" (Totilo), while British daily newspaper *The Guardian* featured the same game, *Superman: The New Superman Adventures* (1999), in their overview "So bad they're good: five terrible video games that people loved anyway" (Marsh). The *Injustice* series spans the video games *Injustice: Gods Among Us* (2013), which sold 424,000 units on launch, making it the best-selling game of April and May 2013 (Makuch), and *Injustice 2*, which was the "highest-grossing console game in the second quarter of 2017" (Strickland). The series also includes their mobile and arcade iterations, where the first mobile game surpassed $1 million "just nine days after its launch," despite being free-to-play (Nouch). The *Injustice* franchise also includes 60 and 36 issue comic book runs serving as prequel narrative frameworks for *Injustice: Gods Among Us* and *Injustice 2*, respectively, with further spin-off tie-in short series including the *Masters of the Universe* franchise or a recounting of events from the perspective of Harley Quinn. Yet, while Superman's name is never on the cover, the diegesis and the actions of those within the critically and commercially well-regarded reality of *Injustice* are firmly only possible because of Superman and his critical, pivotal presence adapted to fit the franchise.

For Superman to endure, especially with his resurgence in the successful *Injustice* series, he has been transformed through a number of intersecting points: the technology and genre preferences available at the point of inception; contemporary video game tropes, including cultural discourses of violence and representation; and the imperatives of the commercial entertainment companies and their prior intertextual media products. Considering the industrial development of Superman video games from a 1979 origin story through to the brand's incorporation of popular game-styles and gritty direction, largely dictated by the shifting positions of the license holders and game developers within the evolving strategies of subsidiary studios, the focus of this chapter will be on how these shared histories and determining factors are inextricable, and in being so, they are directly responsible for creating and shaping the emergent Superman villain found within *Injustice*. To entirely shift the context of the headline provided by *The Guardian*, Superman is now so bad, he is finally good.

Injustice: Assemblages

Set in a new parallel universe to the pre-existing versions of Superman published by DC Comics, the transtextual narrative of *Injustice* (2013) opens with a series of actions that shift away from any established DC Universe. Confusing Superman with green kryptonite gas to think he is fighting Doomsday in a rematch from *The Death and Return of Superman* (1992–93), Joker encourages the Man of Steel to kill a pregnant Lois Lane. Lane's heart has also been attached to a trip switch for a nuclear device, which detonates and wipes out Metropolis when her heart stops beating. Superman's collective history of killing is not extensive but is informative in understanding his motivations, and the variations contained within, when pushed to his limits. In the films *Superman II* (1980) and *Man of Steel* (2013), for example, Superman is resigned to killing General Zod when it is painfully apparent that his relentless counterpart will never stop trying to subjugate humanity. In comic tale "Whatever Happened to the Man of Tomorrow?" (1986), after killing Mr. Mxyzptlk, Superman willingly depowers himself to have a life and child with Lois, explaining "I just couldn't risk letting anything that powerful and malignant survive [....] I broke my oath. I killed him" (Moore 56). The *Kingdom Come* (1996) version of Superman is dissuaded by Lois Lane in her dying breath from seeking revenge on Joker and retires, only to re-emerge and engage in what Batman calls "down and dirty, quick and fast totalitarian 'solutions' [within a] new regime" (Waid 72), with Superman realizing in the end that "Every choice I've made so far has brought us here—has been wrong!" (181). Bouncing off these influential narrative trajectories in different ways, the Superman of *Injustice* is a distorted and divergent version of these past incarnations. In a fit of rage, Superman punches straight through Joker, killing him without the off-frame or shadow-filled ambiguity of Batman's attempts in *The Dark Knight Returns* (1986) and *The Killing Joke* (1988). He then installs and maintains a new world order where crime is absent, along with personal freedom. Superman is a fascist, Zod-like leader in an unravelling plot where any remaining heroes are imprisoned or outright murdered for non-compliance; there are no return-of-the-hero epiphanies for this Superman, although his actions do allow others to grow. Echoing *Flashpoint* (2011),

Wonder Woman's Amazonians and Aquaman's Atlanteans are brought into the conflict, as are gods, magic users, and a variety of competing Lantern Corps colors. With comparisons to *Knightfall* (1993), Superman breaks Batman's back. Eventually, heroes from a parallel universe are pulled in to assist the Batman-led resistance (analogous to Frank Miller's *The Dark Knight* series and the multiverse plot of *JLA: Earth 2* [2000]) and Superman is contained at the end of *Injustice: Gods Among Us*. The narrative of *Injustice 2* introduces Brainiac and Supergirl, retelling their entwined post–*Crisis on Infinite Earths* (1985–1986) narrative from the *Superman: Brainiac* arc of *Action Comics* #866–#870 (2008); the B-plot charts the rise of an alternate version of the Secret Society of Super Villains, in contrast to the disbanded Justice League, calling themselves "The Society." Superman is released to contain these new threats to Earth, where he again seeks authoritative control.

In providing a synopsis of the narrative, it is easy to fall back on comparing key plot-beats to past occurrences from Superman's collective histories. As Linda Hutcheon notes: "Pastiche will often be an imitation not of a single text [...] but of the indefinite possibilities of texts" (Hutcheon 38); the *Injustice* series is both an overlapped pastiche of genre style from within the same mode and, based on the frequency of allusions, a self-reflexively conscious retelling of defining moments transposed from classic DC Comics stories and film events. Critically, while the superhero genre remains the same, the recontextualized borrowings at work in *Injustice* are also filtered through the lens of a video game medium (so conflict with Superman, the end-of-game boss, and his cohorts must be inevitable and competitive and frequent). Further complicating this dynamic, in some aspects the *Injustice* games adopt from the output of other subsidiaries such as Warner Bros. Animation. Harley Quinn, for example, is brought in via both her villainous presentation in the *Batman: Arkham* video games and her more sympathetic developments within recent DC Comic book titles, but in opposing Superman becomes something entirely new in *Injustice*: a member of the Justice League. The *Injustice* series also takes inspiration from the cinema, developing parallel to the aesthetics and darker themes of *Man of Steel*, also released in 2013, which itself has been influenced by the Dark Knight works of director Christopher Nolan and comic book writer and artist Frank Miller, among others. With the *Injustice* prequel comics by writers Tom Taylor and Brian Buccellato and various artists, these influences on character development, design, and execution are also adapted back again into the original source medium making circular references several-times removed from where they were invented, with the difference between pastiche and specific intertextual deployment becoming further entangled.

Regarding comic book movies heavily leaning on the "mythic" aspects of the source material, Liam Burke offers that "the choice to borrow only the characters and setup, and not a particular story, allows for a more all-encompassing adaptation" (Burke 13). Past Superman video game adaptations forced the protagonist to fit within the confines of the genre/culture and format/industry at hand to create severely contained types of Superman; in KEMCO's *Superman* (1987), for example, the hero travels between levels by subway instead of flying, reflecting both the Japanese influences of the developer and that it would have also been easier to code. Tom De Haven affirms that "Superman is forever a work in progress, changing, sometimes subtly, other times radically [....] certain parts of his makeup—his essence, the crux of him—have never altered. Or when they have, corrections soon have been made, his integrity reconfirmed" (De Haven 4). With the *Injustice* franchise, this type of adaptation still takes place as a necessity of genre and format (Superman still cannot fly wherever he wants), but there is also an explicitly aware engagement with what Henry Jenkins, through considering the work of Roberta Pearson and William Uricchio, called "a moment of transition from continuity to multiplicity" (Jenkins). As universes collide, the *Injustice* series literally features multiple versions of the same characters (Superman vs. Superman is the climax of *Injustice: Gods Among Us*) and the DLC builds out from this acceptance of a shared and tethered diversity of representation. In "Red Son" for *Injustice: Gods Among Us*, there is an adapted Superman costume and 20 exclusive missions based around the comic book storyline (2003); with "The Man of Steel Pack," there is a new outfit for Superman where he looks like Henry Cavill's iteration from the movie *Man of Steel*; based on the 2011–2016 comic revamp at DC Comics, there is also "New 52," which can be bought as a part of the Collector's Edition, Battle Edition, New 52 Pack; the 2009–2010 comic book crossover storyline "Blackest Night" costume also features as a part of the "Blackest Night Costume Pack 1"; and "Cyborg Superman" from *The Death and Return of Superman* is free with the Zatanna Compatibility Pack. Despite the variety of these different "skins," the multiple ways in which they may be obtained, and the diverse intertextual references from which they draw upon, they are based on the same Superman character model underneath and the same skill-set of moves; they are still fundamentally tied to the Superman presented within the narrative of *Injustice*. The Superman of the *Injustice* games is voiced by George Newbern, who also provides Superman's voice in the *Justice League* (2001–2004), *Justice League Unlimited* (2004–2006), and *The Batman* (2007–2008) animated series, as well as the animated films *Superman vs. the Elite* (2012), *Justice League: War* (2014), *Justice League: Throne of Atlantis* (2015), and *Justice League vs. the Fatal Five* (2019). To reconcile the industrial and cultural sensibility behind a clearly strategized divergence and convergence around the figure of Superman, Jim Collins refers to such groupings as *"aggregate narratives"* because "they appeal to disparate but often overlapping audiences, by presenting different incarnations of the superhero simultaneously, so that the text always come trailing its intertexts and rearticulations." There is, therefore, "an assemblage of intertextual representations rather than a set definition" (Collins 180). In not only identifying the deeply varying notions of Superman's superhero canonicity as it has been delineated and evolved over time, but in playing with these shifting characters and set-ups as though they were from parallel DC Universes to be borrowed from in the formation of a new diegesis—which in its self-contained and self-reflexive variances across a plurality of texts can barely be considered canonical unto itself, let alone a fixed concept of who Superman is—this pliable, aggregate assemblage is the foundation of the *Injustice* franchise.

In seeking to move beyond fidelity to traditional DC Comics narratives, Will Brooker offers that "those limits end when DC Comics ends and Warner Brothers, the overarching conglomeration, begins. There can be no continuity enforced between DC's comics and Warner's films" (*Batman Unmasked* 279). With the *Injustice* series, narrative continuity from the already varied output of DC Comics' pre-existent comic releases, such as *Action Comics*, is broken. This is further complicated by the *Injustice* comics, which are officially tied-in with the video game, feature artwork and writing by DC staff and are published by DC Comics. The *Injustice* comics were originally released in digital format, but in addition to subsequent single-issue releases, printed compilation volumes of the *Injustice* series have also featured in *The New York Times*' Best Sellers list (Taylor). As such, the popularity of the *Injustice* comics challenge and compete with DC Comics' own core releases, which regularly refresh and rewrite their own universes, often with multiple divergent titles based on the same character running simultaneously. The two series of *Injustice* comics serve as prequels to the actions within the two video games, which echoes the recent release strategies of Warner Interactive video games based on DC Comics franchises, such as the comics *Batman: Arkham City* (five issues, 2011) and *Batman: Arkham Unhinged* (58 issues, 2011–2013) acting as a prequel to the events of the video game *Batman: Arkham City* (2011) and *DC Universe Online: Legends* (26 issues, 2011–2012) being set before the actions within *DC Universe Online* (2011). Further studies might compare the role of Superman in the *Injustice* comics with his *Injustice* video game iteration, as he fulfils separate criteria dictated by the functions of the media he inhabits. As Anthony N. Smith notes: "these comic-book titles serve not only DC Comics' objective of appealing to videogame enthusiasts but also its parent company Warner Bros.' goal of generating synergies between the content that its various divisions produce" (Smith 155). Justin Mack uses the label "paratexts" to "distinguish the *Arkham* games from those pieces of licensed Batman content which exist primarily to promote another text" (Mack 152). The *Injustice* games do not purely function as paratexts despite behaving like one at times, such as with DLC to promote other active franchises. Equally, the *Injustice* comic books encourage readers to buy the video game to get the complete story and, through the use of advertising in the single-issues, they direct the consumer to a variety of other games, comics, and action-figures all aligned with the brand. The cover of *Superman: The Game!* (1985) gestures towards other texts: "You have *seen* the film … and *read* the comic … now *play* the game." But significantly, unlike with these earlier Superman tie-in games, the term paratext cannot be consistently affixed to the *Injustice* comics and games because the franchise they form is a discrete multi-textual entity, or "pillar" to borrow from Mack, produced by a more sophisticated alignment of corporate and artistic goals.

Moving on from a consideration of textual assemblages and the contradictions they embrace, the focus from here will be on the industrial conditions, synergies and maneuverings that have created such a space for the *Injustice* series to not only exist, but thrive where other games that feature Superman and attempt meaningful brand activations have failed to make an impact. As Roberta Pearson and Anthony N. Smith suggest, "convergence and globalization do not render the consideration of specificities invalid; indeed, a full understanding of these forces requires not only challenging boundaries but also acknowledging continuities" (Pearson 9). Through all the potential variants, assemblages, and Supermen-in-progress, the *Injustice* series and the production of a tyrant Superman originated not from any creative or corporate decision to merchandise a novel Superman, but through a highly specific set of industrial and cultural circumstances emerging within the era of media convergence, which in turn forms an integral part of the enduring legacy of Superman himself.

The Dearth and Return of Superman

In a period facilitating the first act of corporate synergy to include films, superhero comics, and video games, in 1979 parent company Warner Communications, Inc. owned Superman creators DC Comics, Hollywood film studio Warner Bros. Pictures, Inc., and video game company Atari, Inc., who they had recently bought in 1976 in their first period of Atari ownership (Hanson 82). During the expansive success of the Atari 2600 home video game platform where "Around 30 million of the consoles were sold"

(Titcomb), "the market for comic books was shrinking, and, for the first time, licensing of characters became more profitable" (O'Rourke 117). Additionally, for DC Comics, the sub-million-dollar sales from "the comic book paled in comparison, then, with the $140 million in film rentals alone Warner-DC took in for the 1978 *Superman* film" (Gordon 165). Yet, while *Superman*, the 1979 game, could have signaled the start of a long and successful story of in-house video game adaptations being integrated alongside comic book and cinema releases produced by other subsidiary companies within a controlled corporate structure, this dynamic was abruptly challenged by internal and external forces.

Following a business culture clash between the parent company and its subsidiary, several key developers left Atari, Inc. in 1978 and 1979, which is when "the new managers at Atari realigned company focus to favor marketing and advertising" (Williams 95). In Tristan Donovan's *Replay: The History of Video Games*, the 1979 Superman game is briefly mentioned as a side-note in Atari management's partially failed attempt to entirely repurpose Warren Robinett's ground-breaking *Adventure* mid-development, the first action-adventure game and one that "sold more than a million copies worldwide" (Donovan 92). According to Jessica Aldred, the "middling success [of *Superman*] was at least in part responsible for the relative dearth of movie-licensed titles until 1981" (Wolf 93). In producing a quick and compromised tie-in at the behest of marketing imperatives, Nick Monfort and Ian Bogost also note that the game "expunged the movie's social and emotional relationships—and those of the comic books—choosing action sequences instead. Games licensed from movies have continued to follow this early VCS game in this regard" (Montfort 63). Continuing in this vein of financial abstraction, after the video game market collapsed in 1983, Warner Communications divided and sold Atari in 1984 and 1985, leaving them without control over a video game subsidiary (Sanger). Once the market began to quickly recover, for the following two decades of involvement with the video games industry Warner focused exclusively on licensing out their DC Comics properties to third party game developers and publishers. The former Chief Creative Officer of DC Entertainment and co-writer of online video game *DC Universe Online* Geoff Johns believes that to make a good Superman title, "all games come down to gameplay and the right studio, I'm sure the right studio could crack it" (Narcisse). But, as Justin McElroy notes in his article "A brief history of crappy Superman games," the quality of all of these games without exception is poor, with the adapted characters being a "pretty thoughtless way of bringing Superman into gaming."

Warner's commercial strategies shifted again with the founding of Warner Bros. Interactive Entertainment in 2004: a video game subsidiary "Signaling an increased commitment to the fast-growing interactive gaming world" with a "focus on the creation, development, production and distribution of games that will be marketed to consumers under the Warner Bros. Games brand," according to their press release (Warner Bros.). With a new in-house approach to video games that demonstrated a cohesive industrial logic behind their licensing deals, Warner Bros. Interactive Entertainment quickly came under the aegis of the broader parent-company, Warner Bros. Home Entertainment, Inc., when it was formed in 2005. Speaking in 2007, Samantha Ryan, senior vice president of Warner Bros. Interactive Entertainment, specified that they had a "5 year slate plan" for expansion, so "are bullish about acquiring more internal development" with a "focus on diversity" beyond the first-person shooters that their only subsidiary acquisition, Monolith Productions, were making at this point (Alexander). TT Games Limited was also bought in 2007 and, within a year, their subdivision Traveller's Tales had released family-friendly action game, *Lego Batman: The Videogame* (2008), the first in a series of DC Comics based LEGO games (released 2012, 2014, and 2018), within a pre-existing series of licensed adaptations that later included games based on the rival properties of DC Comics competitors, Marvel. While Warner Bros. Interactive Entertainment began to expand in scope, in September 2009, DC Comics became a subsidiary of the newly formed DC Entertainment, Inc. with a mission statement to "strategically integrate the DC Comics business, brand and characters deeply into Warner Bros. Entertainment and all its content and distribution businesses" (Outlaw). Building on this corporate structure, which is a direct reaction to the successes of Marvel Studios, LLC, (the Walt Disney Company went on to purchase Marvel Entertainment in December 2009), 2010 became a significant year for Warner Bros. Interactive Entertainment as they "purchased a majority stake in Rocksteady Studios" (Plunkett), who by that point had already developed two critically acclaimed action-adventure games in the Arkham series: *Batman: Arkham Asylum* (2009) and *Batman: Arkham City* (2011). Under Warner Bros. Interactive Entertainment, Rocksteady Studios developed *Batman: Arkham Knight* (2015) then *Batman: Arkham VR* (2016). In 2010, Warner Bros. Interactive Entertainment also bought Turbine, Inc., who later released the PC online game *Infinite Crisis* (2015) and the mobile online game *Batman: Arkham Underworld* (2016). In the same year, Warner Bros. Interactive Entertainment founded studio WB Games Montréal, who made *Batman: Arkham Origins* (2013) to fill a gap in the *Arkham* release schedule while Rocksteady worked on *Batman: Arkham Knight*. Monolith also released a Batman game, *Gotham City Impostors* (2012), which was a first-person shooter. Continuing to explore their licensing options, Telltale, Inc. used the Batman universe to create two series of episodic narrative adventures, *Batman: The Telltale Series* (2016) and *Batman: The Enemy Within* (2017), based on their Telltale Tool engine, which was highly popular with brand licensors. Gameloft S.A. published a mobile adaptation of *The Dark Knight Rises* (2012) with a game engine very similar to their earlier release of Marvel's *The Amazing Spider-Man* that same year. Phosphor Games, LLC, adapted the *Man of Steel* movie for mobile platforms in 2013, which, notably, is the only entirely Superman focused game in the Warner Bros. Interactive Entertainment era. In 2015, Phosphor Games, LLC. then co-created the mobile game *WWE Immortals* with NetherRealm Studios, using the *Injustice* mobile engine to create a game where wrestler superstars had special powers. Armature Studio, LLC developed *Batman: Arkham Origins Blackgate* (2013) with DC Comics writer Adam Beechen for handheld consoles, after being asked by Warner Bros. Interactive Entertainment to make a "game that was in the Metroidvania flavor" based on the production history of the studio's employees (Miller).

To understand the significance of Superman's brand resurrection and central positioning within the *Injustice* series, it is important to see that apart from the tie-in mobile games, none of the video games made around the time of *Injustice* were created in isolation but to cross-promote a comic book narrative, cartoon, or movie. Furthermore, these games were largely constructed based on past game engines, the genre experiences of diverse development teams, the cultural demands of video game playing audiences, and were influenced by the grittier world of *Arkham* Batman (or were a direct reaction to it, as with the LEGO games), itself informed by, but not beholden to, Nolan's *Dark Knight* trilogy of films (2005–2008). After their outsourced attempt to adapt *Superman Returns* in 2006 was critically unsuccessful, without these same, sequential breakthroughs for

Superman, there was little reason for Warner Bros. Interactive Entertainment to make in-house video games with him as the central character (Paprocki).

Writing about Batman, Brooker offers that "It is this sense of Batman as myth that comprises all his contradictory variants, but is loose and flexible enough for the contradictions not to matter," while the brand is "a smaller, more contained and more controlled network of texts, defined by their current status as Warner Bros. Batman products: expressions of the contemporary corporate template, rather than a broader, folk identity" (*Hunting the Dark Knight* 152). The games released by Warner Bros. Interactive Entertainment during this period not only tap more directly into Brooker's delineation of the terms "myth" and "brand" as they can be understood in critical terms, but they indicate an industrial strategy that is formulated on an understanding of this very difference. The earlier quoted press releases for the creation of Warner Bros. Interactive Entertainment and DC Entertainment both invoke the term "brand" as quality markers to demonstrate an awareness of their corporate legacies and custodial responsibilities in shepherding all types of content without being drawn into any specifics. Breaking this down further, Warner Bros. Interactive Entertainment's subsidiaries function as individual brand developers, with little overlap between their apportioned territories except for when they are called on to bolster the most popular brands in divergent ways. This shift in strategy and synergy has directly led to a period where profitable premises and platforms within the video game medium are explored, with brands (in this context: certain versions of superheroes) being deployed from the wider DC mythos (all the versions of superheroes) where appropriate. Comics and animated films are now based on the video game universes made by Warner Bros. Interactive Entertainment, but even these are as transmedia extensions of the separate digital universes with their plurality of coherent narrative streams contributing to an accumulated DC mythos. For Superman to prosper, he does not need to significantly alter his myth; as evidenced by Batman and the litany of post–2005 games released with his starring presence, Superman needs one of his brands to be relevant to the types of games that are being made.

Krypton Kombat

In February 2009, between the release of two of their most critically and financially fertile franchises (*LEGO Batman* in September 2008 and *Batman: Arkham Asylum* in August 2009), Warner Bros. Interactive Entertainment were presented with the opportunity to possess a top-tier fighting game franchise. During the early '90s, Time Warner Interactive attempted to capitalize on the arcade fighting game phenomenon that had exploded with Capcom's *Street Fighter II: The World Warrior* (1991), making approximately $1.5 billion revenue in home console adaptations and merchandising by 1993 and $2.3 billion dollars in arcades by 1995 (Rignall). As competition in the US, Midway Games under WMS Industries Inc., released *Mortal Kombat* (1992), with the sequel, *Mortal Kombat II* (1993), also generating more than $1 billion in arcade revenue alone (Ali 115–116). Despite limited success in the market, but with debts of $19.5 billion in 1995, parent company Time Warner sold "assets that were not part of its core businesses," such as Atari Games to WMS Industries Inc., in 1996 (Bloomberg). However, since having been spun off from WMS Industries Inc. in 1998, Midway Games Inc. consistently failed to make a profit and filed for bankruptcy with their assets for sale, including their Atari

Games rights and the *Mortal Kombat* series of games (Ali 188). By July 2009, Midway Games belonged in the Warner Bros. Interactive Entertainment stable (McWhertor); by April 2010 they were renamed, via WB Games Chicago, NetherRealm Studios.

While the Atari license rights may have played a role in their purchase, based on their experiences and track-record, NetherRealm had three primary objectives as a subsidiary company. One task was to make fighting games for mobile platforms, adapted from Rocksteady's *Arkham* series (*Batman: Arkham City Lockdown* was released in 2011, *Batman: Arkham Origins* [mobile] was released in 2013). Their two flagship responsibilities were to reboot and continue to make the profitable *Mortal Kombat* fighting games (starting with *Mortal Kombat*, the ninth game in the series, released in 2011), and through adapting the same heavily modified Unreal Engine 3, develop a DC Comics fighting game with an alternate release pattern of every two years, the first game being *Injustice: Gods Among Us* in 2013.

When their licenses were first distributed, games featuring Superman or the rest of the Justice League were action-platformers and side-scrolling action games, moving on to action-adventure games and action-RPGs once the medium had developed the capacity for exploratory 3D worlds. Viewed from this perspective, *Injustice* is an anomaly of adaptation. There are DC Comics fighting game precedents, but in a far smaller number, such as *Justice League: Task Force* (1995) and a cancelled game that was going to be a tie-in to George Miller's cancelled Justice League film which instead became *Green Lantern: Rise of the Manhunters*, a tie-in for the 2011 *Green Lantern* film (Farrell). And then there is *Mortal Kombat vs. DC Universe* (2008): the last public release from Midway Games Inc. before being bought by Warner Bros. Interactive Entertainment. Among their bankruptcy filings, Midway stated that "During 2005, we signed publishing agreements with Warner Bros. Interactive Entertainment, licensing several properties to develop video games based on both television programs and films in the children's market" (Booty). *Mortal Kombat vs. DC Universe* can be seen as an extension of the older licensing style engaged in by Warner to occupy a market space with their own branded product, in this context against the *Marvel vs. Capcom* series that had almost entirely dominated the comic crossover fighting genre unchallenged until this point, spanning 16 titles since 1996 and with sales of 9.3 million units as of September 2019 (Capcom). In adapting the home territory of the *Mortal Kombat* universe to accommodate the DC Comics universe, "fatalities" (violent finishing moves) were toned down and the game was rated T "Teen" by the ESRB, instead of the M "Mature" rating of the *Mortal Kombat* series. To deploy his branding identity in the novel narrative environment of the crossover genre, Superman is still identifiable as the traditional good guy. If *Mortal Kombat vs. DC Universe* can be seen as an exercise in demonstrating that Midway games and Warner Bros. Interactive Entertainment were two companies capable of working in a configuration that would only be possible due to their industrial positioning at that moment, to play on the strengths of their shared histories and licenses against their joint competition, Marvel and Capcom, then *Injustice* is the evolution of a process having shakily started when Atari released *Superman* for Warner Communications, Inc. in 1979. Without the sales and buy-outs of subsidiaries, often happening multiple times with the same company, the movement from in-house to third party licensing and back again, the development of DC Comics properties and the varying successes of their integration across the variously named Warner subsidiary networks, and the shifting demands of audience tastes and genre expectations, there would not have been the industrial or cultural opportunities for *Injustice* to be created and for Superman to be required.

Despite the box art introducing the video game as "From the Creators of *Mortal Kombat*" and not "From DC Comics," to make Superman and his new alternate-universe meaningfully resonate in such a stark departure from his past identities, *Injustice: Gods Among Us* had to be created with the permissions and specialized assistance that were largely absent during earlier Superman adaptations. Working on *Injustice: Gods Among Us*, DC Comics writers Justin Gray and Jimmy Palmiotti served as story consultants (Sarkar). According to Lead Designer John Edwards, "DC Comics was fairly easy to work with [on *Injustice 2*]. Everything had to pass through an approval process, but rarely did any of the team's ideas get rejected. In the end, coming up with the many, many different costume variations was easy […] because of the depth and breadth of DC lore" (Hall). Conversely, *Injustice* comics writer for DC Comics, Tom Taylor, explains, "the challenge is not 'how do I make this interesting?' but how do I complement what these guys [NetherRealm] have done? How do I too find that perfect balance between emotional, epic storytelling and sudden, irreparable spine removal?" (Esposito). Within the transmedia collaborative environment, there is less emphasis on retaining an exclusionary idea of what a medium must contain, than there is in exploring the possibilities afforded by the elements that are being newly introduced.

According to the in-game tips and the official game guide, *Injustice* Superman is classed as a "power character" who uses brute force and strength, but he also possesses the fastest attack in the game, has an Air Dash maneuver that can cover great distances, can use heat vision despite its risks, and has super breath for pushing an advantage against attack blocked opponents (Bishop 207). In addition to dozens more options, including the more clearly signaled Superman Punch and special moves such "Kryptonian Crush" and "Fury of Krypton," thematically, these sophisticated fighting moves come from within the DC Universe without them needing to be dampened or reshaped to fit the fighting game genre. In this regard, the Superman brand in *Injustice* is brought into alignment with aspects of the wider Superman mythos in ways that his narrative does not. Here, Superman does not travel by subway; he punches through the planet.

Where Superman was held back in *Mortal Kombat vs. DC Universe*, throughout *Injustice*, this deployment of the Superman brand is irreparably altered the more he is engaged with as a narrative device: he is still motivated by the traditional concerns he always has at his core, but in the same way that Midway Games/NetherRealm are experts in creating tainted hero mythologies and epoch shifting narratives, this new configuration of tyrant Superman follows a trajectory that is a necessary output of the games made by their studio. Moving beyond the mechanics of fatalities and the spectacle of bloody violence, in comparison to *Injustice*, the Earthrealm in *Mortal Kombat* is also consistently under threat from invading armies seeking world dominance and servitude, and in *Mortal Kombat X* (2015), Liu Kang, the hero of the franchise is also turned into a dark supreme leader while other heroes die around him. Magnified by a central core of unwavering righteousness, Superman is arguably the only DC Comics character capable and powerful enough to bring out the best and worst in everyone he comes into contact with, necessary for a fighting game where sides are taken and violence is compulsory. However, despite the apparent limitations of the genre, predicated on the spectacle of two figures fighting, the social and emotional relationships that were expunged in past games have emphatically returned and are now the centerpiece of the franchise. With *Injustice*, NetherRealm took a similar approach to the innovative story mode they introduced in *Mortal Kombat vs. DC Universe* then fully explored with *Mortal Kombat* and its cinematic, cutscene-filled, multi-hour narrative campaign. The *Injustice* story mode is the equivalent core narrative pillar, but the game also borrows from the challenge towers of *Mortal Kombat*, offering character-based trials with divergent narrative endings that function as retcons, reversions, or perversions of the core story. In the central story, there are also two endings: the canon ending where Superman is defeated again at the end of *Injustice 2* and the non-canon ending where Superman continues his reign. In the same way that the trials expand upon the world within the game, but in potentially conflicting and impossible ways, the spin-off six-issue comic series *Injustice vs. Masters of the Universe* (2018) is entirely based on the non-canon ending. In this addendum, Superman kills Skeletor in the exact same way that he kills Joker. Within the DLC there are also cross-over characters from games such as *Mortal Kombat* and other non–DC Comics properties, such as the *Teenage Mutant Ninja Turtles* (owned by IDW Publishing), fulfilling not only the remit of comic "event" narratives to include as diverse a cast of characters as possible, but also the fighting game genre's modern appeal in drip-feeding character reveals for a social-media savvy video game audience (see: Cabrera).

Within the *Injustice* series then, with all the intertextual repetition, narrative echoes, and character rewriting, understanding Brooker's delineation of myth and brand is useful in not only unpacking how the series operates within the broader configuration of DC Comics/Warner Bros. Interactive Entertainment/NetherRealm transmedia operations around their tent-pole products, but also offers a useful framework in determining the multi-varied appeal within modern branded clusters themselves. Unlike the *Superman* of 1978, *Injustice* does not need to rely on an existence as a paratextual franchise tie-in to carry on, as it is recognized by its various owners as an aggregate franchise, a nexus of narrative possibilities that do not always conjoin at their start or end points, but offer something both subjectively malleable and objectively epic, always escalating and always *in media res*. The strategy of reincorporating subsidiary game studios within Warner's business structure is integral to the success of the DC Comics licensed games post-2005. These games are not created individually, rather they are mythos-imbued node points demonstrative of a wider, coordinated strategy of market appeal. Building on intertextual cultural history as much as evolving industrial practices, the new heroes resonate with interpretations of their past constructions and constrictions as much as the forces that shape their contemporary presentations and motivations. However, without Superman, the first digital superhero, turning heel to play his part as a supervillain there would be no exploratory space labelled *Injustice* or a need for a Superman to endure in modern video games.

Works Cited

Albigès, Luke, et al. *The League of Super Hero Games*, Scholastic Inc., 2017.
Aldred, Jessica. "A Question of Character: Transmediation, Abstraction, and Identification in Early Games Licensed from Movies." *Before the Crash: Early Video Game History*, edited by Mark J. P. Wolf, Wayne State University Press, 2012, pp. 90–104.
Alexander, Leigh. "Q&A: Warner Bros' Ryan Talks Expansion, Acquisition, Superheroes." GamaSutra, 19 Oct. 2007, https://www.gamasutra.com/php-bin/news_index.php?story=15928. Accessed 5 May 2020.
Ali, Reyan. *NBA Jam*, Boss Fight Books, 2019.
Bishop, Sam, et al. *Prima Official Game Guide: Injustice: Gods Among Us*, Random House, Inc., 2013.
Bloomberg News staff. "Time Warner to Sell Part or All of Its Stake in Atari." *The New York Times*, 25 Mar. 1995, https://www.nytimes.com/1995/03/25/business/time-warner-to-sell-part-or-all-of-its-stake-in-atari.html. Accessed 5 May 2020.

Booty, Matthew V. "Form 10-K: MIDWAY GAMES INC." United States Securities and Exchange Commission, 6 Apr. 2009, https://www.sec.gov/Archives/edgar/data/1022080/000095015209003529/c50336e10vk.htm. Accessed 5 May 2020.
Brooker, Will. *Batman Unmasked: Analyzing a Cultural Icon*, Continuum, 2000.
_____. *Hunting the Dark Knight: Twenty-First Century Batman*, I.B. Tauris, 2012.
Burke, Liam. *The Comic Book Film Adaptation*, University Press of Mississippi, 2015.
Cabrera, David. "Fighting Games Don't Need to Be Saved from Goofy Characters." *Polygon*, 29 Nov. 2017, https://www.polygon.com/2017/11/29/16710588/injustice-teenage-mutant-ninja-turtles-final-fantasy-tekken. Accessed 5 May 2020.
Capcom IR (Investor Relations). "Game Series Sales." Capcom, 30 Sept. 2019, http://www.capcom.co.jp/ir/english/finance/salesdata.html. Accessed 5 May 2020.
Collins, Jim. "Batman: The Movie, Narrative: The Hyperconscious." *The Many Lives of the Batman: Critical Approaches to a Superhero and his Media*, edited by Roberta E. Pearson and William Uricchio, BFI Publishing, 1991.
Daultrey, Stephen. "Release of *Injustice 2* Sees Superman Take Longest-running Character in Videogames Record." Guinness World Records, 17 May 2017, https://www.guinnessworldrecords.com/news/2017/5/release-of-injustice-2-sees-superman-take-longest-running-character-in-videogames-472260. Accessed 5 May 2020.
De Haven, Tom. *Our Hero: Superman on Earth*, Yale University Press, 2010.
Donovan, Tristan. *Replay: The History of Video Games*, Yellow Ant, 2010.
Esposito, Joey. "Injustice: Gods Among Us Gets a Comic Book Prequel." IGN, 14 Jan. 2013, https://uk.ign.com/articles/2013/01/14/injustice-gods-among-us-gets-a-comic-book-prequel. Accessed 5 May 2020.
Farrell, Blair. "Footage of The Cancelled Double Helix Justice League Game Surfaces." Comic Gamers Assemble, 24 Jan. 2015, https://comicgamersassemble.com/2015/01/24/footage-of-the-cancelled-double-helix-justice-league-game-surfaces/. Accessed 5 May 2020.
Gordon, Ian. *Superman: The Persistence of an American Icon*, Rutgers University Press, 2017.
Hall, Charlie. "*Injustice 2* Gear System Revealed, and Introducing Dr. Fate." *Polygon*, 2 Mar. 2017, https://www.polygon.com/2017/3/2/14786160/injustice-2-gear-system-dr-fate-reveal. Accessed 5 May 2020.
Hanson, Christopher. "Bushnell, Nolan (1943-)." *Encyclopedia of Video Games: A-L*, edited by Mark J. P. Wolf, ABC-CLIO, 2012, pp. 80–83.
Hutcheon, Linda. *A Theory of Parody: The Teachings of Twentieth-Century Art Forms*, University of Illinois Press, 2000.
Injustice: Gods Among Us. Directed by Ed Boon, Warner Bros. Interactive Entertainment, 2013.
Injustice 2. Directed by Ed Boon, Warner Bros. Interactive Entertainment, 2017.
Jenkins, Henry. "Just Men in Capes? (Part One)." Confessions of an Aca-Fan, 14 Mar. 2007, http://henryjenkins.org/blog/2007/03/just_men_in_capes.html. Accessed 5 May 2020.
Kartanym, et al. "Superman Licensees." Moby Games, https://www.mobygames.com/game-group/superman-licensees. Accessed 5 May 2020.
Mack, Justin. *Superhero Synergies: Comic Book Characters Go Digital*, Rowman & Littlefield, 2014.
Makuch, Eddie. "Analyst: Injustice: Gods Among Us Sales hit 424,000 in US." *GameSpot*, 13 May 2013, https://www.gamespot.com/articles/analyst-injustice-gods-among-us-sales-hit-424000-in-us/1100-6408267. Accessed 5 May 2020.
Marsh, Calum. "So Bad They're Good: Five Terrible Video Games That People Loved Anyway." *The Guardian*, 27 Aug. 2018, https://www.theguardian.com/games/2018/aug/27/so-bad-theyre-good-five-terrible-video-games-that-people-loved-anyway. Accessed 5 May 2020.
McElroy, Justin. "A Brief History of Crappy Superman Games." *Polygon*, 9 July 2015, https://www.polygon.com/2015/7/9/8924443/superman-game-rocksteady. Accessed 5 May 2020.
McWhertor, Michael. "Warner Bros. Now Owns Midway, Mortal Kombat." *Kotaku*, 10 July 2019, https://kotaku.com/warner-bros-now-owns-midway-mortal-kombat-5312018. Accessed 5 May 2020.
Miller, Matt. "Batman Meets Metroid in Arkham Origins Blackgate." *Game Informer*, 19 Apr. 2013, https://www.gameinformer.com/b/features/archive/2013/04/19/batman-meets-metroid-in-arkham-origins-sister-game.aspx?PostPageIndex=1. Accessed 5 May 2020.
Montfort, Nick, and Ian Bogost. *Racing the Beam: The Atari Video Computer System*, The MIT Press, 2009.
Moore, Alan (w), and Kurt Swan (p). "Whatever Happened to the Man of Tomorrow?" (Sept. 1986). *Whatever Happened to the Man of Tomorrow? The Deluxe Edition*, DC Comics, 2009, pp. 10–61.
Morrison, Grant. *Supergods: What Masked Vigilantes, Miraculous Mutants, and a Sun God from Smallville Can Teach Us About Being Human*, Spiegel & Grau, 2011.
Mortal Kombat. Directed by Ed Boon, Warner Bros. Interactive Entertainment, 2011.
Mortal Kombat vs. DC Universe. Directed by Ed Boon, Midway Games Inc., 2008.
Narcisse, Evan. "Geoff Johns Says a Great Superman Video Game Needs the 'Right Studio.'" *Kotaku*, 14 Feb. 2012, https://kotaku.com/geoff-johns-says-a-great-superman-video-game-needs-the-5885093. Accessed 5 May 2020.
Nouch, James. "The Charticle: How *Injustice: Gods Among Us* hit $1 million in US App Store revenue." Pocket

Gamer.biz, 15 Apr. 2013, https://www.pocketgamer.biz/the-charticle/50113/the-charticle-how-injustice-gods-among-us-hit-1-million-in-us-app-store-revenue. Accessed 5 May 2020.

O'Rourke, Daniel J., and O'Rourke, Morgan B. "It's Morning Again in America: John Byrne's Re-Imaging of the Man of Steel." *The Ages of Superman: Essays on the Man of Steel in Changing Times*, edited by Joseph J. Darowski, McFarland, 2012, pp. 115–124.

Outlaw, Kofi. "Warner Bros. Creates DC Entertainment Inc." *Screen Rant*, 10 Sept. 2009, https://screenrant.com/warner-bros-creates-dc-entertainment-inc-diane-nelson/. Accessed 5 May 2020.

Paprocki, Matt. "Superman Returns: What Went Wrong." *Polygon*, 7 Feb. 2017, https://www.polygon.com/features/2017/2/7/14537590/superman-returns-what-went-wrong. Accessed 5 May 2020.

Pearson, Roberta and Anthony Smith. "Introduction: The Contexts of Contemporary Screen Narratives: Medium, National, Institutional and Technological Specificities." *Storytelling in the Media Convergence Age: Exploring Screen Narratives*, edited by Roberta Pearson and Anthony N. Smith, Palgrave Macmillan, 2015, pp. 1–17.

Plunkett, Luke. "Warner Buys Batman: Arkham Asylum Devs." *Kotaku*, 23 Feb. 2010, https://kotaku.com/warner-buys-batman-arkham-asylum-devs-5477933. Accessed 5 May 2020.

Rignall, Jaz. "Top 10 Highest-Grossing Arcade Games of All Time." *USgamer*, 1 Jan. 2016, https://www.usgamer.net/articles/top-10-biggest-grossing-arcade-games-of-all-time. Accessed 5 May 2020.

Sanger, David E. "Warner Sells Atari to Tramiel." *The New York Times*, 3 July 1984, https://www.nytimes.com/1984/07/03/business/warner-sells-atari-to-tramiel.html. Accessed 5 May 2020.

Sarkar, Samit. "*Injustice: Gods Among Us* Developers Expanding Upon All Aspects of Mortal Kombat." *Polygon*, 15 Oct. 2012, https://www.polygon.com/2012/10/15/3509028/injustice-gods-among-us-netherrealm-expanding-upon-mortal-kombat. Accessed 5 May 2020.

Smith, Anthony N. *Storytelling Industries: Narrative Production in the 21st Century*, Palgrave Macmillan, 2018.

Strickland, Derek. "*Injustice 2* Was Highest-grossing Game of Q2 2017." *TweakTown*, 2 Aug. 2017, https://www.tweaktown.com/news/58633/injustice-2-highest-grossing-game-q2-2017/index.html. Accessed 5 May 2020.

Taylor, Tom. "Injustice: Gods Among Us Year One: The Deluxe Edition." *Tom Taylor Made*, http://www.tomtaylormade.com/comics/injustice-gods-among-us-year-one-the-deluxe-edition/. Accessed 5 May 2020.

Titcomb, James. "Atari to Make First Console in Over 20 Years." *The Telegraph*, 19 June 2017, https://www.telegraph.co.uk/technology/2017/06/19/atari-make-first-video-games-console-20-years/. Accessed 5 May 2020.

Totilo, Stephen. "Let's See if Superman 64 Really Is the Worst Game of All Time." Kotaku, 18 Jan. 2011, https://kotaku.com/lets-see-if-superman-64-really-is-the-worst-game-of-all-5736742. Accessed 5 May 2020.

Waid, Mark (w), and Alex Ross (a). *Kingdom Come* (May-Aug. 1996). DC Comics, 2008.

Warner Bros. Entertainment. "Newly Created Warner Bros. Interactive Entertainment Inc. Dedicated to Interactive Gaming Business to Be Headed by Technology Executive Jason Hall." Warner Bros. Entertainment Inc., 14 Jan. 2004, https://www.warnerbros.com/news/press-releases/newly-created-warner-bros-interactive-entertainment-inc-dedicated-to-interactive-gaming/. Accessed 5 May 2020.

Williams, Andrew. *History of Digital Games: Developments in Art, Design and Interaction*, CRC Press, 2017.

Superman, a Super Freak

Returning the Man of Steel to the Circus in DC Bombshells

CHRISTINA M. KNOPF

Clad in tight red trunks and red boots, the muscle-bound figure stops a cannon ball in its flight, using only his nerves of steel, lightning-fast reflexes, his hands, and his broad chest. No, this show of strength is not by Superman, but by strongman John Holtum in 1870. Throughout the late nineteenth and early twentieth centuries similarly impressive feats, such as breaking chains by expanding one's rib cage or biting through them, bending iron bars, lifting horses, elephants, and cars, and driving railroad spikes with bare fists, were accomplished by muscular men in tights and briefs throughout circuses, sideshows, and follies around the world (Blogball). The likes of Siegmund Breitbart (1883–1925), known as the "Strongest Man in the World," Eugen Sandow (1867–1925), considered the "Father of Bodybuilding," and Joseph Greenstein (1893–1977), the so-called "Mighty Atom," were inspirational to Superman's creators Jerry Siegel and Joe Shuster when they designed the Man of Steel's image and costume in the 1930s (Brownie & Graydon 12–13; Ricca 122); indeed, Superman accomplished Holtum's cannonball-catching stunt himself in 1940 in *Superman* #4. Thus, when Superman was adapted by DC Collectibles in 2016 and by writer Marguerite Bennett in 2017 as a circus performer for the *DC Comics Bombshells*, his new role was not without precedent. The Bombshell characterizations of Superman exemplifies how adaptation can work in consort with an original text while also subverting or reframing the text to resonate with contemporary culture and concerns.

In 2011, DC Collectibles decided to reimagine its classic DC Comics superheroines as vintage pin-up girls. They began by studying World War II, period fashion, and military nose art. To keep a modern feel, they also looked to rockabilly culture (DC). In 2013, the first nine-inch statue of the DC Comics Bombshells, created from the artwork of Ant Lucia and sculpted by Tim Miller, was released. Wonder Woman led the line; reflecting the "can-do attitude" of the 1940s, the Amazonian warrior was reimagined as Rosie the Riveter. In statues and variant covers, action figures and artwork, other characters followed suit: Supergirl was given a USO showgirl style; Harley Quinn became a nose art victory girl; Aquawoman was glamorized as a beach-bunny; Batwoman was cast as ballplayer; Poison Ivy appeared as a lingerie model; Catwoman looked the part of a femme fatale; Ravager was made-up as a pirate; Lois Lane was turned into a papergirl; Big Barda became a roller derby diva; Bumblebee a cheerleader; Flash a carhop; Starfire was a firefighter; Green Lantern a policewoman; Batgirl a vampire; Hawkgirl a dieselpunk rocketeer; and Power Girl and Superman were re-imagined as an acrobatic team.

The retro character images inspired, and were in turn inspired by, two series of comic books written by Marguerite Bennett: *DC Comics Bombshells* and the follow-up *DC Comics Bombshells: United*. The sculpted and print media interacted visually and thus narratively to adapt the iconic Superman character. Transmedia and adaptation studies share a common interest in transtextuality, repositioning original and adapted texts as nodes, or redistribution points, in a larger transmedial network that encompasses proliferations, peripherals, and paratexts. As Zoë Shacklock suggests, an adaptation is "content flow within a continuing narrative" (263). Thus, the many popular (and academic) discussions that focus on fidelity or authenticity of assorted superhero adaptations miss the mark; transmedia adaptations provide flexibility in producing and consuming narratives that allow for nuanced contextual understandings.

The queer, feminist, female-centric series used the changing role of women during World War II as their premise. Bennett established an alternate-history storyline and a cast of characters in a retro, parallel universe in which well-known heroines like Supergirl, Batwoman, and Aquawoman existed in a world where they were not derivatives of male superheroes but instead were characters and heroes in their own right. Indeed, in the comic, Batwoman's heroism saves the lives of Thomas and Martha Wayne and thus prevents the tragedy that would have spurred Bruce Wayne to become Batman. Supergirl is the only known Kryptonian on Earth and both Power Girl and Superman are cloned from her blood.

Of her approach in these retellings, Bennett explained, "In this story, in this universe, I wanted the women to be the ones to define what heroism is going to be for this coming century" (quoted in Rogers para. 7). Characters were thus shaped by their wartime roles: Batwoman played for the All-American Girls Professional Baseball League until she enlisted; Supergirl and Stargirl were part of the Russian bomber pilot regiment known as the Night Witches; Wonder Woman joined the Army; Aquawoman worked reconnaissance with the Navy; Zatanna was a cabaret singer; Huntress was a member of the German youth underground; Catwoman and Poison Ivy were black market smugglers; and Power Girl and Superman were circus performers. To add authenticity to the alternate-history storyline Bennett looked to vintage art styles and media formats (Ratcliffe). In the original, digital–first run, each individual story worked as a separate ten-page chapter focusing on a different heroine, and each heroine was given her own narrative genre. As Bennett described, Wonder Woman was part of a war story; Batwoman's story was developed as a pulp adventure radio serial; Catwoman was a *noir* character; Zatanna's story was a Hammer film; Aquawoman was in a romance; Harley Quinn was a Looney Tunes farce; and Supergirl and Stargirl were in a propaganda reel (Rogers; Ratcliffe; Barksdale). In turn, readers might further understand Cheetah as part of pulp jungle adventure, Lois Lane as a Horatio Alger figure, Batgirl as a Val Lewton character, and Superman as a star of the Ringling Bros. and Barnum & Bailey Circus.

The multi-media/mixed-medium adaptation of the original Superman image to a circus-styled statue, and the re-adaptation of the statue into a circus performing comic book character, is both restorative and transformational. Styled as a twentieth-century circus performer, the image speaks to the strongman-inspiration behind the Man of Steel's original costuming in 1938, and thus carries with it all the nationalistic and racialized weight of social Darwinism and biological superiority that was bound to ideals of physical development at the turn of the century. This new old-fashioned look also embraces the costuming of the circus aerialist, whose ability to transcend Earthly confines was once perceived as godly, connecting the Bombshell to the philosophical concept that bears his name—the *Übermensch*. But the strongman and the aerial contortionist were also part of the human oddities in circuses often referred to as "freaks." This marks the Bombshell Superman as transformational, allowing him to be a symbol not only of male power fantasies, human ideals, or the American way, but also of transgendered identities, human fears, and complex international civics.

Strength, Power, and the American Way

During the late nineteenth century, strongmen, acrobats, and aerialists around the world were creatively flexing their muscles and showcasing their skills in circuses and sideshows, deploying nationalistic symbolism within global concerns about racial ideologies and Darwinian evolution (Tait loc. 388; Gerstle 1281). In America, people such as Theodore Roosevelt were explicitly promoting athleticism as integral to Americanism, believing physical development and moral development to be intertwined (Kasson; Dorsey). Thus, the defeat of white boxers Tommy Burns in 1908 and Jim Jeffries in 1910 to the black Jack Johnson signaled to many a decline of white masculinity and superiority (Kent). Two decades later, the superhero helped to re-establish and reinforce the fantasy of white, masculine, physical superiority. "The genre of the superhero is very much a white-male-dominated power fantasy that is itself very much based in ideas around physical performance and power in relation to the negotiation of identity" (Gateward & Jennings loc. 170). The superhero, "informed by white supremacist visuality" (Scott 295), is depicted as a singular, usually white and masculine, embodiment of the country. "Nationalist superhero comics have been, and continue to be, embedded within racialized understandings of the nation-state" (Dittmer 49).

The creation of Superman grounded the superhero as the embodiment of male power fantasies, offering an enactment of the physical perfection displayed by strongman Bernarr MacFadden and promised by bodybuilder Charles Atlas (Landon 201). As Grant Morrison wrote:

> The real insight into Superman's distinctive look arrived [...] when I discovered some photographs of circus strongmen in the 1930s. There among the [...] painted caravans [was the] overpants-belt combo, here worn by men with handlebar mustaches, pumping dumbbells in their meaty fists and staring bullishly at the camera. [...] Underpants on tights were signifiers of extra-masculine strength and endurance in 1938. [...] Shuster had dressed the first superhero as his culture's most prominent exemplar of the strongman ideal [...] [14].

But "The cape, showman-like boots, belt, and skintight spandex" being "derived from circus outfits" also "helped to emphasize the performative, even *freak-show-esque*, aspect of Superman's adventures" (Morrison, 14; emphasis added). And this deviant side of Superman is brought to bear in Marguerite Bennett's *Bombshells* adaptation of the character.

Freaks, Wonders and Physical Oddities

"Being a freak," Robert Bogdan suggests "is not a personal matter, a physical condition that some people have." Instead, "'freak' is a frame of mind, a set of practices, a way of thinking about and presenting people. It is the enactment of a tradition, the performance of a stylized presentation" (5). While the rise in popularity of American freak shows in the nineteenth century can be linked to nationalist ideologies of the American cultural self, offering a point of reference against which to construct the normalcy and physicality of the ideal citizen (Garland-Thomson 10), such freakery was a performance that made the distinction between Oddity and Conformity not only visible but obvious (Adams 6). Many freaks of the circus sideshow were not exhibits but actors who invited audiences not to observe them but to interact, even converse, with them, thus actively defining their differences within society (Durbach 9). Superman, with the "carnival flair implied by skintight spandex" (Morrison 14), similarly takes ownership of his otherness; asserting "pride in his difference" through costume (Brownie & Graydon 18–19).

In Bennett's *DC Comics Bombshells,* Superman is a result of genetic experiments during World War II in the quest for the ultimate soldier. He is cloned from the DNA of Kara Starikov, an alien raised by a Russian family who joins the Soviet Air Force and becomes a figure of Soviet propaganda as Supergirl. As an experiment, he is considered a failure by creator Dr. Hugo Strange because he is too kind and gentle to serve as a warrior. Eventually rescued, along with his cloned "sister" Power Girl, by Supergirl and fellow Bombshells including Lois Lane, the quiet flyer joins Harley Quinn's "monster carnival"—a European traveling circus the Bombshells rescued from Nazi occultists—as an aerialist. (In keeping with the female-centered storyline, Superman remains but a mere supporting player in the series, essentially as a sidekick to Power Girl, never even having a line of dialogue.)

According to classifications used in showbusiness, and beyond, the Bombshells Superman is both a "born freak" who came by his physical anomalies, such as his super strength and the power of flight, naturally, and a "novelty act" who boasts an unusual performance of acrobatics and feats of strength (see Bogdan 8). Aerial skills, or trapeze artistry, is grouped with other "dynamic circus skills steeped in acrobatic action" with performances that present "artistic and physical displays of skillful action by highly rehearsed bodies that also perform cultural ideas: of identity, spectacle, danger, transgression" (Tait loc. 202 & loc. 200). Like other forms of freakery, it is a performance that suggests a particular identity realized through costume, action, and staging; through the stylized repetition of actions, identities of gender, national origin, ethnicity, and sexual identification were both reinforced and destabilized (Adams 6, 31; Davies loc. 96; Tait 661).

Aerialists in the late nineteenth into the early twentieth centuries "were attributed physical qualities that mixed up their gender identity" (Tait loc. 255). Male aerialists were praised not only for masculine daring but also for feminine gracefulness; female aerialists were notable not only for their feminine elegance but also for masculine courage. Both were admired for their muscular development, for in overcoming limits to gravity and physical action, they exemplified ideals of Darwinian evolution. But the same musculature also challenged prevailing assumptions about the gendered body; muscled women and lithe men were visually similar and were gendered primarily through costume and name. In fact, many male aerialists performed as women to give their feats an added sense of wonder and increased danger, and some women performed as men to get better opportunities (Tait loc. 661, 1374, 1410, 1432). By the turn of the twenty-first century, performances like Cirque du Soleil, Circus Oz, and Arachaos established an aesthetic in which queer identity was integral and "internationally controversial for its reinterpretations of sideshow freakery, anti-establishment politics and sexually explicit performance" (Tait loc. 159). And it is during this era that recognized, celebrated, and exploited the transgressions of circus through popular culture that Superman was adapted as, or more accurately returned to, a sideshow performer in *DC Comics Bombshells*.

The Greatest "Show of Force"

The *Bombshells* and subsequent *Bombshells: United* story is a response to, and enabled by, heightened attention to contested public spaces with active debates about who is/not allowed to participate in civic life. The alternative version of World War II offers a reminder that the contributions of women and minorities in the past, and present, is often undervalued or dismissed. Commander Amanda Waller describes her Bombshells unit saying, "While the good gentlemen are relying on traditional warfare—we have engaged an independent organization that makes use of '*unexpected and unsuspected resources*'"—women (Bennett, Andolfo, & Braga, vol. 3; emphasis added). It is accordingly significant that Superman is narratively derived from Supergirl, a departure from the historical creation of Supergirl as a spinoff of Superman, and that he is rescued by Lois Lane, rather than his canonical role of rescuing her. Moreover, Lois falls in love not with Superman but with Supergirl, undermining the character's creation as the embodiment of ideal masculinity as attractive to women (see Avery-Natale 72).

The focus on Supergirl over Superman in the Bombshells adaptation is reflective of DC Comics' response to second wave feminism in the 1970s. At this time, as Thomas C. Donaldson noted, "DC moved Supergirl from being a secondary feature in *Action Comics* to the lead (cover) feature in *Adventure Comics*" (63). Additionally, female superheroes were (re)created as "avatars of liberal feminism" (64) who were not only the active protagonists in their own stories but who were also "physically more powerful" than their predecessors demonstrating that they were "dependent on no man" (65). But unlike the Supergirl of the 1970s whose civilian career as a journalist was made possible only through the influence of Superman, the Bombshells Supergirl is neither derivative of nor dependent on the Bombshells Superman.

In the assorted Bombshells lines of collectibles, Superman appears both as an acrobat, teamed up with Power Girl, and as a solo strongman. While the latter role is more in line with Superman's creative origins, the former role marks Superman's introduction into Bennett's *Bombshells* universe. As a strongman, or as a superhero in a strongman-inspired costume, Superman provides both a creation and performance of masculinity and hypermasculinity—an exhibition of physical superiority through extraordinary size and muscle tone (Brownie & Graydon 14). As an aerialist, he advances the gender-bending of Bennett's story. Perched atop the broad shoulders of Power Girl, the duo reverses the usual gender roles of acrobatic teams in which the male lifts and catches his female partner. Seated on her shoulders, Superman's size is visually smaller than that of his female partner, thereby undermining the character's normal demonstration of hypermasculinity.

Beyond serving as a backdrop for Superman's aerialist costume, the circus plays an important role in advancing Bennett's particular adaptation of the Man of Steel. Circus literature of the mid-twentieth century represented circus as an "other"—a carnivalesque form against which the bourgeois defined themselves (Carmeli, "Invention of

Circus" 214). According to Mikhail Bakhtin, the Carnival creates a transitional space in which regular conventions are suspended or overturned and hierarchies are inverted; the Carnivalesque is a mockery of the serious, often featuring bodily grotesquery, characterized by laughter and the temporary dismissal of a serious reality (5–7, 19–21). The death-defying feats of trapeze artists often invoked a mixture of admiration and repulsion; "leaping and diving actions no doubt induced psychic fears of maimed if not fatally injured bodies" (Tait loc. 589)—a marked contrast to the outward cheerfulness of the circus atmosphere—and contortion performances "could make the body seem bizarre with positions that induced fascination and fear" (Tait loc. 596). Circus performances banked on the delivery of fantasy pantomimes that delivered both the macabre, as with human-fly acts, and the romantic, as in performances of flight (Tait loc. 649). The circus was thus perceived as existing outside the usual social order, indeed outside of history and social time, with its own code, traditions, and family structures (Carmeli, "Invention of Circus" 217–218).

So, too, Superman and the *DC Comics Bombshells*. The Carnivalesque atmosphere of mockery and subversion in Harley Quinn's circus is captured in the words of Power Girl who observes, "Nothing like taking a show of force and making it a show of fun, right?" (Bennett, Aneke, Andolfo & Braga, vol. 6). Bennett's alternative history was created without the real-world power and hierarchical constraints faced by women of the past (or present). Though prejudices were found in the *Bombshells* universe, they did not limit the activities of the women, allowing historically oppressed persons (women, people of color, and queers) to be heroic without first having to prove themselves (Rogers para. 11). This disruption to the social hierarchy also established a timeless, yet nostalgic, quality, found in circus literature (Carmeli, "Invention of Circus" 218). The backdrop of World War II, with its apparent clarity of purpose, is a popular media frame for subsequent conflicts (Crampton & Power 245) and in *Bombshells* it offers a useful parable for exploring the social changes of the present day, allowing the characters to straddle multiple eras; shifting gender roles of the 1940s works as a metaphor for the shifting gender identities of the 2010s. In 1941, the workforce became gender integrated; in 2016, bathrooms did. In 1943, women were allowed to serve in all branches of the military; in 2010, gays were allowed to openly serve, and in 2016, combat jobs were opened to women. From 1942 to 1946, internment camps held over 100,000 Japanese Americans; in 2018 immigration detention centers in the United States held about 40,000 people per day (Sands).

In *American Carnival*, Phillip McGowan proposed a United States–based idea of the carnivalesque that, rather than disrupting the normal social structures through laughter, sought to reinforce hegemonic identities of race, sexuality, and social position by reassuring audiences, through the act of looking at the exotic "Other," of their own normality. But through these rituals of exclusion, of Othering, the dispossessed, create "a space to present, and re-present, their own identities outside of the normalizing framework beyond the walls of this public sphere" (Stephan 6; also: Bacon 211; Peinado-Abarrio 1). Superman's adaptation as an aerialist, rather than a strongman, is again significant in this regard. As Yoram Carmeli ("Circus Play") notes of the circus as a site of transformation:

> The circus play of human life both invoked and crystallized the spectators' anxieties in the disenchanted fragmented order. If the freak is human, the boundaries of the "human" are shattered; and *when a human body is played and perceptually objectivated*, **through the acrobatic display**, *the ontological bases of human identity are experientially problematized* [158: emphasis added].

This is the essence of the DC Comics Bombshells adaptation of Superman—problematizing what it means to be a hero, to be gendered, to be sexual, in society and in comics.

Tell Your Own Story

A recurring theme throughout Bennett's writing is the idea of individuals being true to themselves. The words of Aquawoman early in the series establishes this message, "I am the teller of my own story. I belong to myself alone" (Bennett, Braga & Andolfo, vol 2). It is, therefore, fitting that the Bombshells adaptation of Superman, and other DC Comics icons, developed from pin-up and nose art glamour girls with rockabilly influence, to faux war-era advertising and propaganda, to alternate herstory inspired by period genre is reflective of participatory practices in fandom.

Material practices in fan communities, from fan-fic to role play, often emphasize reproduction. Fan-creators customize and extrapolate, crafting new material to fill in gaps in canon and beyond. These practices reproduce ideas and items in order to create transformative narratives, which call attention to characters and stories and their co-construction between source and receiver, producer and consumer, artist and audience (Godwin 1.4, 1.6; Lamerichs 0.1). Cosplay is one such activity. As a fan practice, cosplay creates an intimate and complex relationship between the fan and a character (Reysen et al 1). Nicole Lamerichs argues that "cosplay emphasizes the personal enactment of a narrative" (1); in other words, it is a way for fans to be tellers of their own story. It can be understood as a form of, or at least akin to, Judith Butler's notion of performativity that suggests identity (particularly gender identity) is the temporary result of imitation—that it is consciously constructed and subverted (45).

Within this construction or subversion of identity in cosplay is crossplay and gender-bending cosplay (GBC). By either cross-dressing or shifting the identified gender or biological sex of a character to match that of the player, crossplay and GBC articulates gender and sexuality in a way that defies and erodes conventional discourses (Leng 89–90, 107). But more than that, GBC and crossplay represent artistic expression of performative fan identity. Similarly, cosplay mashups permit fans to defy genre categories, expressing their love for and identification with multiple fandoms and aesthetics in a single costume. Variants that deviate from the source material may exhibit fans' cultural aesthetics or emphasize different key personality traits essential to characters' narrative arcs and development (King 367–368).

Participatory fandoms collaborate to interpret and reinterpret performativity, materiality, and society (for example, Brough & Shresthova 2.3). The DC Comics Bombshells designs encapsulate the spirit of such material fan practices. They gender-bend the DC Universe. They defy both genre and era, bringing together comedy of the 1930s, action of the 1940s, style of the 1950s, and horror of the 1960s. They mashup aesthetics, bringing superheroics into contact with glamour and gothic, professional and piratical, athletic and artistic, diesel and derby, function and fashion. As such, the Bombshells Superman can be read in accordance with André Bazin's definition of adaptation which perceives "the refraction of one work in another creator's consciousness" (20) as "content flow within a continuing narrative" (Shacklock 263), with the circus/carnival/sideshow serving as the hypertext (Genette) that unites the aerialist Bombshell Superman to the original Superman in his strongman-inspired costume.

Conclusion

Because new stories featuring Superman have been told continually since his creation in 1938, his evolution, re-creations, and adaptations reflect not only changes in entertainment media but also, as Joseph Darowski has noted, "changes in American society" (2). The Bombshells adaptation of Superman, challenging gender norms and performance in the twenty-first century, is an exemplar. Grant Morrison argued:

> We can never change him too much, or we lose what he is. There is a persistent set of characteristics that define Superman through decades of creative voices and it's that essential, unshakeable quality of Superman-ness the character possesses in every incarnation, which is divinity by any other name [14].

Morrison further suggests that as generations of writers and artists offer their interpretations, "something persists, something that is always Superman" (13). In the Bombshells, that something is Superman's Otherness that is also his Humanness, captured by his origins in the sideshows and circuses that, like the Man of Steel, raised questions about truth, justice, and the American Way.

WORKS CITED

Adams, Rachel. *Sideshow U.S.A: Freaks and the American Cultural Imagination*. The University of Chicago Press, 2001.

Avery-Natale, Edward. "An Analysis of Embodiment Among Six Superheroes in DC Comics." *Social Thought and Research*, vol. 32, 2013, pp. 71–106.

Bacon, Helen. "*They're Just People, That's All*: American Carnival, the Freakish Body and the Ecological Self in Daniel Knauf's *Carnivàle*." *Otherness: Essays and Studies*, vol. 6, no. 1, 2018, pp. 193–220.

Bakhtin, Mikhail. *Rabelais and His World*. 1968. Translated by Hélène Iswolsky. Indiana University Press, 1984.

Barksdale, Aaron. "DC Comics' 'Bombshells' Is a Blast from the Past but with Queer Characters." *Huffington Post*, 20 Aug. 2015, www.huffingtonpost.com/entry/dc-bombshells-queer-superhero_us_55d35c10e4b055a6dab18890. Accessed 27 Aug. 2015.

Bazin, André. "Cinema as Digest." *Film Adaptation*, edited by James Naremore, Rutgers University Press, 2000, pp. 19–27.

Bennett, Marguerite (w), Laura Braga (ill.), and Mirka Andolfo (ill.). *DC Comics Bombshells, Volume 2: Allies*. DC Comics, 2016.

_____. *DC Comics Bombshells, Volume 3: Uprising*. DC Comics, 2017.

_____, and Aneke (ill.). *DC Comics Bombshells, Volume 6: War Stories*. DC Comics, 2018.

Blogball. "10 Amazing Strongman Feats of the Past." *Listverse*, 14 Jun. 2014, https://listverse.com/2008/11/04/10-amazing-strongman-feats-of-the-past/. Accessed 19 Oct. 2019.

Bogdan, Robert. *Freak Show*, Kindle ed., University of Chicago Pres, 1988.

Brough, Melissa M., and Sangita Shresthova. "Fandom Meets Activism: Rethinking Civic and Political Participation." *Transformative Works and Cultures*, vol. 10, 2012, doi:10.3983/twc.2012.0303. Accessed 4 Nov. 2019.

Brownie, Barbara, and Danny Graydon. *The Superhero Costume: Identity and Disguise in Fact and Fiction*, Kindle ed., Bloomsbury Publishing, 2015.

Butler, Judith. *Gender Trouble: Feminism and the Subversion of Identity*. 1990. Routledge, 1999.

Carmeli, Yoram. "Circus Play, Circus Talk, and the Nostalgia for a Total Order." *Journal of Popular Culture*, vol. 35, no. 3, 2001, pp. 157–164.

Carmeli, Yoram S. "The Invention of Circus and Bourgeois Hegemony: A Glance at British Circus Books." *Journal of Popular Culture*, vol. 29, no. 1, 1995, pp. 213–221.

Crampton, Andrew, and Marcus Power. "Frames of Reference on the Geopolitical Stage: *Saving Private Ryan* and the Second World War/Second Gulf War Intertext." *Geopolitics*, vol. 10, no. 2, 2005, pp. 244–265.

Darowski, Joseph J. Preface. *The Ages of Superman: Essays on the Man of Steel in Changing Times*, edited by Darowski, Kindle ed., McFarland, 2012, pp. 1–4.

Davies, Helen. *Neo-Victorian Freakery: The Cultural Afterlife of the Victorian Freakshow*. Kindle ed., Palgrave Macmillan, 2015.

DC. "DC Comics Bombshells: From Concept to Collectible." *YouTube*, 22 Jan. 2015, https://www.youtube.com/watch?time_continue=7&v=fysFQEP3EsA. Accessed 18 Sept. 2019.

Dittmer, Jason. *Captain America and the Nationalist Superhero: Metaphors, Narratives, and Geopolitics*. Temple University Press, 2013.

Donaldson, Thomas C. "The Inflexible Girls of Steel: Subverting Second Wave Feminism in the Extended Superman Franchise." *The Ages of Superman: Essays on the Man of Steel in Changing Times*, edited by Joseph J. Darowski, Kindle ed, McFarland, 2012, pp. 62–77.

Dorsey, Leroy G. *We Are All Americans, Pure and Simple: Theodore Roosevelt and the Myth of Americanism*. University of Alabama Press, 2007.

Durbach, Nadja. *Spectacles of Deformity: Freak Shows and Modern British Culture*. University of California Press, 2010.

Garland-Thomson, Rosemarie. "Introduction: From Wonder to Error—A Genealogy of Freak Discourse in Modernity." *Freakery: Cultural Spectacles of the Extraordinary Body*, edited by Rosemarie Garland-Thomson, New York University Press, 1996, pp. 1–19.

Gateward, Frances, and John Jennings. "Introduction: The Sweeter the Christmas." *The Blacker the Ink: Constructions of Black Identity in Comics and Sequential Art*, edited by Frances Gateward, Kindle ed., Rutgers University Press, 2015, loc. 87–421.

Genette, Gerard. *Palimpsests: Literature in the Second Degree*. Translated by Channa Newman and Claude Doubinsky, University of Nebraska Press, 1997.

Gerstle, Gary. "Theodore Roosevelt and the Divided Character of American Nationalism." *The Journal of American History*, vol. 86, no. 3, 1999, pp. 1280–1307.

Godwin, Victoria. "Mimetic Fandom and One-Sixth-Scale Action Figures." *Transformative Works and Cultures*, vol. 20, 2015, https://doi.org/10.3983/twc.2015.0686. Accessed 18 Sept. 2019.

Kasson, John F. *Houdini, Tarzan, and the Perfect Man: The White Male Body and the Challenge of Modernity in America*. Kindle ed., Hill and Wang, 2001.

Kent, Graeme. *Great White Hopes: The Quest to Defeat Jack Johnson*. Kindle ed., The History Press, 2005.

King, Emerald L. "Tailored Translations—Translating and Transporting Cosplay Costumes." *Signata*, vol. 7, 2016, doi:10.4000/signata.1243. Accessed 18 Sept. 2019.

Lamerichs, Nicolle. "Stranger Than Fiction: Fan Identity in Cosplay." *Transformative Works and Cultures*, no. 7, 2011, doi:10.3983/twc.2011.0246. Accessed 18 Sept. 2019.

Landon, Richard. "A Half-Naked Muscleman in Trunks: Charles Atlas, Superheroes, and Comic Book Masculinity." *Journal of the Fantastic in the Arts*, vol. 18, no. 2, 2008, pp. 200–216.

Leng, Rachel. "Gender, Sexuality, and Cosplay: A Case Study of Male-to-Female Crossplay." *The Phoenix Papers*, vol. 1, 2013, pp. 89–110.

McGowan, Philip. *American Carnival*. London, Greenwood Press, 2001.

Morrison, Grant. *Supergods: What Masked Vigilantes, Miraculous Mutants, and a Sun God from Smallville Can Teach Us About Being Human*. Kindle ed., Spiegel & Grau, 2012.

Peinado-Abarrio, Rubén. "Of Monsters and Men: Masculinities in HBO's *Carnivàle*." *Oceánide*, vol. 9, no. 4, 2017, http://oceanide.netne.net/articulos/art9-4. Accessed 4 Nov. 2019.

Ratcliffe, Amy. "Marguerite Bennett Discusses WWII Female Heroes in 'DC Comics Bombshells.'" *Comic Book Resources*, 29 Jul. 2015, www.cbr.com/marguerite-bennett-discusses-wwii-female-heroes-in-dc-comics-bombshells. Accessed 26 Oct. 2015.

Reysen, Stephen, Courtney N. Plante, Sharon E. Roberts, and Kathleen C. Gerbasi. "'Who I Want to Be': Self-Perception and Cosplayers' Identification with Their Favorite Characters." *The Phoenix Papers*, vol. 3, no. 2, 2018, pp. 1–7.

Ricca, Brad. *Super Boys: The Amazing Adventures of Jerry Siegel and Joe Shuster—the Creators of Superman*. St. Martin's Press, 2013.

Rogers, Vaneta. "*DC Comics Bombshells* Creates World Where Women Were Heroes of World War II." *Newsarama*, 24 Jul. 2015, www.newsarama.com/25336-dc-bombshells-creator-creates-world-where-women-were-heroes-of-world-war-ii.html. Accessed 15 Oct. 2016.

Sands, Geneva. "This Year Saw the Most People in Immigration Detention Since 2001." *CNN*, 12 Nov. 2018, www.cnn.com/2018/11/12/politics/ice-detention/index.html. Accessed 23 Aug. 2019.

Scott, Anna Beatrice. "Superpower vs. Supernatural: Black Superheroes and the Quest for a Mutant Reality." *Journal of Visual Culture*, vol. 5, 2006, pp. 295–314.

Shacklock, Zoë. "'A Reader Lives a Thousand Lives Before He Dies': Transmedia Textuality and the Flows of Adaptation." *Mastering the Game of Thrones: Essays on George R.R. Martin's* A Song of Ice and Fire, edited by Jes Battis and Susan Johnstons, E-book, McFarland, 2015, pp. 262–279.

Stephan, Matthias. "Introduction." *Otherness: Essays and Studies*, vol. 6, no. 1, 2018, pp. 1–10.

Tait, Peta. *Circus Bodies: Cultural Identity in Aerial Performance*. Kindle ed., Routledge, 2005.

Forging Kryptonite

Lex Luthor's Xenophobia as Societal Fracturing, from Batman v Superman *to* Supergirl

Ian Boucher

"My plan? To send the nations of the Earth at each other's throats, so that when they are sufficiently weakened, I can step in and assume charge!"
—Lex Luthor, *Action Comics* #23 (Apr. 1940)

"Now we know better now, don't we? The devils don't come from Hell beneath us, no. No, they come from the sky."
—Lex Luthor, *Batman v Superman: Dawn of Justice* (2016)

"I've always been interested in our genes. Strengths, weaknesses ... alcoholism."
—Lex Luthor, *Supergirl*, "The House of L" (2019)

Lex Luthor: Humanity's Kryptonite

The 2016 United States presidential election has had significant implications for American society. It occurred during a time of expanding customized media,[1] increasing partisanship,[2] and a worldwide escalation in far-right rhetoric and policies,[3] and was centered around overtly racist, sexist, and Islamophobic rhetoric[4] from a candidate-to-president who was supportive of an effort by the Russian government to divide Americans.[5] After the election, hate crimes increased and hateful policies were enacted, such as reducing transgender rights, banning Muslims from entering the United States, and separating families of asylum seekers at the United States border.[6] This environment seeped into the lives of people in the United States to varying degrees, but nevertheless more significantly than previous elections. Scholars began researching the toll on people identifying as LGBTQ, Latinx, Muslim, and living within mixed-status families,[7] on the dominant culture's perception of quality of life as a whole,[8] and on personal relationships with family and friends.[9]

With any societal event, fiction plays a crucial role in helping culture unpack it. This has certainly been true of superheroes. As the first superhero and one with continued relevance, Superman has represented different things to different generations and continues to respond to this process of cultural dialogue. Always first in pursuing the demise of this paragon, however, has been the criminal genius Lex Luthor. As the greatest nemesis of America's greatest hero, Lex has been representative of issues that American society has struggled against.

At his core, Lex Luthor represents jealousy. As Superman is a defender of the common person, Lex Luthor is an oppressive power who is furious that Superman can't be affected by him and will stand against him. "*Who does Superman think he is?*" Luthor asks in *All-Star Superman* #5 (Sept. 2006) (Morrison et al. 16). As Superman is popularly regarded as the ultimate immigrant, Lex Luthor's jealousy has throughout his history led him to use xenophobia to demean his opponent, exploiting fear in others to shape society according to his wishes. To humanity, Lex Luthor has come to represent his favorite weapon, Kryptonite, forging poisonous fragments to fracture planet Earth more effectively than his hijacked missiles in the film *Superman* (1978).

In the years surrounding the 2016 United States presidential election, Lex Luthor served as a representation exploring the cultural effects of encroaching xenophobia in live-action Superman media, from society in the film *Batman v Superman: Dawn of Justice* (2016) to the family in the fourth season of the television series *Supergirl* (2018–2019). Both adaptations situate Luthor's xenophobia within character relationships that were socially relevant for the times they were produced. Developed in the years leading up to the election, *Batman v Superman* focuses on polarization of the characters on a societal level. *Supergirl*'s fourth season, produced a few years after the election and continuing the series' focus on relatives and friends of Superman, reflects an intensification of Luthor's xenophobia into the creation of pervasive divisions within the familial arena. Lex Luthor's increasingly invasive disruption of superhero relationships in these adaptations acts as a Kryptonite reflecting a poisonous fracturing of relationships in the real world.

Lex Luthor's Xenophobia: Jealousy Exploiting Fear

Lex Luthor has reflected societal discord since the beginning, exploiting fear for his own gain. His first appearance in *Action Comics* #23 as a power-hungry criminal and "just an ordinary man—but with th' brain of a super-genius!" (Siegel et al. 10) is the opposite of Superman. Luthor seeks to pit two countries against one another as journalist Clark Kent "seeks to warn the two warring countries of the greater menace that faces them" (7). As Luthor developed in further publications, so did his motivation of jealousy. From prison in *Superman* #164 (Oct. 1963), he muses: "I'm locked up in this cage, but *he* roves the whole world! He … Superman … the man who put me here because he's really jealous of my scientific genius, which I use for crime!" (Hamilton et al. 2). In *The Man of Steel* #4 (Nov. 1986), Luthor has become one of the most powerful business leaders in the world.[10] After Superman publicly humiliates him by placing him under arrest for putting people in danger to test the Man of Steel's abilities, Lex vows to "*remind*" Metropolis who is in charge and "show them" that Superman is "*nothing*" (Byrne et al. 22). In *Adventures of Superman* Vol. 2 #15 (Sept. 2013), Luthor explains that "you can think of me as a sort of Johnny Appleseed … spreading a healthy disdain for Superman's nonsense" (Killen et al. 20).

As the comics continue, Luthor increasingly exploits Superman's status as the ultimate immigrant with xenophobia. For the most part, Luthor isn't actually afraid, but merely finds ways to stir up controversy about Superman. In *Superman: Birthright* (2003–2004), Lex is "utterly fascinated by the possibility of alien lifeforms" (Waid et al., #6 [Mar. 2004] 12). But when Superman stands against him (#5 [Jan. 2004]; #9 [June 2004]), Lex calls him a "*freak*" (#9 19) and an "*interplanetary extremist*" (20). He frames Superman as an "*advance scout*" (#10 [July 2004] 18) for a false alien invasion from Krypton, and employs extremists (#11 [Aug. 2004] 11; #12 [Sept. 2004] 22) to save Metropolis using his "Earth-First Security Force" (#11 17). Lex knows what he is doing, for he refers to his own actions as a "scam" (#9 17) and "slander" (#10 8). While battling Superman, he asserts, "Last of your race. Which makes this *genocide*" (#12 19). In *Lex Luthor: Man of Steel* (2005), Lex refers to Superman as "Not a *man*. Not even *close*" (Azzarello et al., #1 [May 2005] 11) and "isn't *natural*" (#3 [July 2005] 12), and declares to Superman that humanity "can drive you back out to the *blackness* from which you came" (#5 [Sept. 2005] 25). Lex regards Superman's Otherness as a direct threat to his vision for humanity, which he regards as owing him (#4 [Aug. 2005] 16). He exploits fear about Superman as an alien to get Batman to fight the Man of Steel (#3), and tries to unite humans as a species against Superman by arranging for the death of civilians and police officers in order to stage Superman's murder of an ostensibly human, though in reality robotic, hero named Hope (#5). In *All-Star Superman* #5, Lex refers to Kryptonians as "opportunistic alien vermin" who "*dump*[ed]" their "*trash*" on Earth (Morrison et al. 7), and Superman as "an alien invader" he "*refuse*[s] to bend the knee to" (16). Superman's "very *presence*" reduces humanity (6). But eventually, Lex's real motivations come out: "*If it wasn't for Superman, I'd be in charge on this planet!*" (22).

Batman v Superman: *Xenophobia on a Societal Level*

Polarization in the United States didn't begin in 2016, but was building for many years leading up to the election in a vitriolic media landscape catering to people's beliefs. A sequel to *Man of Steel* (2013), *Batman v Superman: Dawn of Justice* introduces a Lex Luthor (Jesse Eisenberg) who represents the stoking of the flames of division on a societal level, taking the form of the mind behind the algorithms that exacerbate society's divisions in real life (Noble). Lex is established as a young, trendy figure, reminiscent of Silicon Valley and recalling Eisenberg's role in *The Social Network* (2010), playing basketball on a colorful court as his more streamlined outraged gatekeeping of Superman plays out behind the scenes through his experiments with Kryptonite. Lex orchestrates society's fears largely from afar by exploiting legitimate debate around two figures who are in the societal spotlight for unilaterally enacting justice: Superman (Henry Cavill) and Batman (Ben Affleck). Lex Luthor is adapted as a Johnny Appleseed who sows the seeds of hostility for Superman on society's stage by corrupting Congress, the media, and Batman himself. This chapter analyzes the extended "Ultimate Edition" of the film, which according to director Zack Snyder is the originally intended version.

The Sin of Existence

Like many of the comics, Lex Luthor's plans in the film are rooted in jealousy and manifested as xenophobia. Lex reveals his resentment to Superman on a LexCorp rooftop: "You above all. Ah, 'cause that's what God is." Since no deity rescued Lex as a child from abuse at the hands of his father, Lex intends to expose Superman as a "fraud" to the world. But as much as Lex talks about gods, Superman, however extraordinary he is, is not a god but a person in a real body. Adding to this is the paradox that Lex, by discussing his father's oppression living in East Germany elsewhere in the film and his desire to keep his father's room "just the same," exhibits a devotion to his abuser and regards Superman as an oppressive foreign power. He tells Senator June Finch (Holly Hunter) that "the oldest lie in America" is "that power can be innocent"; much like one of Lex's mercenaries in *Birthright* #11 (Waid et al. 12). Lex further indicates his perspective on Superman by prefacing his statement about his childhood with "God is tribal, God takes sides." Lex isn't just resentful of an abstract concept, but considers prosperity to be a result of competition between social groups and is directly threatened by a person from another group on a genetic level. By calling Superman a god, Lex applies a label that dehumanizes a living person. When he makes Superman "above all," it's not just as superior in the abstract, but as literally both outside and against humanity.

The scene on the rooftop ends with the true implications of Lex's arguments—the kidnapping of Superman's mother, Martha Kent (Diane Lane): "Why, the mother of a flying demon must be a witch. And the punishment for witches, what is that? That's right. Death by fire." Lex throws Superman's family contemptuously at him with photographs of Martha gagged and labeled with the word "Witch" scrawled across her forehead, a term that exudes something both more and less than human, and overshadows and oppresses any gifts that Superman may have, much as Lex's false invasion in *Birthright* nullifies the Man of Steel's "ability … to help anyone" (Waid et al., #10 16). Lex later makes Superman's existence offensive on a religious level when he calls it a "sin." The film indicates that Lex's ideology extends to Kryptonians as a species. When Lex requests the remains of General Zod (Michael Shannon) that are in the government's custody, he refers to Zod as "the dead alien." A scoffing Senator Barrows (Dennis North) asks rhetorically, "You want Zod's body?" Lex emphasizes a lack of acknowledgment of Zod's personhood by reacting not to the question, but to the terminology. He considers it, nods, and allows it with the reply, "Okay." Lex later sprinkles his own blood in Zod's face and remarks, "You flew too close to the sun. Now look at you," as he pushes him underwater to use for genetic engineering. Lex seeks to annihilate Superman based on deeply held, visceral hatred of him as a Kryptonian and capitalizes on the film's professed pettiness of "man"-kind to instill xenophobia in the societal paragons of Truth, Justice, and the American Way—Congress, media, and Batman.

Stoking Congress, Media, and Superheroes

In *Batman v Superman*, Lex manipulates government, media, and superheroes into doing his xenophobic bidding. The film opens with the destruction of Metropolis in *Man of Steel* from Bruce Wayne's perspective of rushing into the wreckage of Wayne Enterprises. This establishes a destructive foundation for Batman's misgivings toward Superman that Lex builds on to bring into the mainstream. Lex orchestrates a situation that puts Lois Lane (Amy Adams) in danger from African rebels, forces Superman to act unilaterally to rescue her, and leads to the murder of the rebels by "private security contractors" in order to implicate Superman.

In Lex's first scene, he blankets xenophobic language in a magnanimous demeanor and intellect. He meets with U.S. senators to discuss an import license for Kryptonite as a deterrent against Superman, who he maintains is just one of many metahumans:

"Now you don't have to use a silver bullet. But if you forge one … well then. We don't have to depend upon the kindness of monsters." Lex implies that Superman is a monster, and the first of many at that, but Senator Barrows is more concerned with status and gets Lex access to Kryptonian technology and a Kryptonian body that are in government custody. Senator Finch, however, confronts Lex with her decision to block the license: "You can call me whatever you like. Take a bucket of piss and call it Granny's Peach Tea. Take a weapon of assassination and call it deterrence. You won't fool a fly or me. I'm not gonna drink it." Lex responds by pointing out a painting in his father's room that contains demons storming Heaven: "[T]hat should be upside-down. Now we know better now, don't we? The devils don't come from Hell beneath us, no. No, they come from the sky." He directly connects Superman to the iconography of evil invaders. When Lex can't fully corrupt the system, he visits the U.S. Capitol to protest the committee on Superman as being "soft on security," before destroying his opposition, the civil societal discourse Finch calls for, and the U.S. government itself by blowing up everyone in the room.

News media has a constant presence in the film, and Lex's orchestrations in Africa make Superman the center of the conversation. The Senate debates the Man of Steel's actions with legitimate questions, as Senator Finch makes statements like "The world has been so caught up with what Superman can do, that … no one has asked what he should do," and "How far will he take his power? And does he act by our will, or by his own?" However, while Lois Lane investigates, characters surround themselves with screens or cameras rather than engage with their problems directly, and Lex acts as an Iago who shepherds the conversation toward xenophobic rhetoric. A sequence where Superman listens to Spanish-speaking workers and media to rescue a girl from a fire in Mexico transitions to media pundits debating Superman's actions, and the sequence ends with a question from Charlie Rose, "Must there be a Superman?" The validity of Superman's existence is called into question. Senator Finch mindfully responds, "There is," but later, at the U.S. Capitol, a mass of protestors outside carries signs like "Superman = Illegal Alien," "Aliens are Un-American," "This is Our World. Not Yours!," "Aliens Doom Nations," and "God Hates Aliens." Senator Finch calls for societal conversation—"This is how a democracy works. We talk to each other."—but is killed in Lex's explosion that escalates the conversation to its next stage, of the media implicating Superman with "anonymous and credible tips" implied to be from Lex as Superman's effigy is burned in the street. Superman is increasingly impacted over the course of the film, and Lex revels in the permeation of his poison on his rooftop by tossing a blue ball that he had earlier used to signify a delicate world. Lex's dialogue succeeds in stirring up mass distrust of an "exceptional" person, different and with power, who, in one pundit's speculation, is "trying to do the right thing."

Throughout the film, the effects particularly stoke the hatred of an already violent superheroic figure of society, Batman, through Lex's manipulation of Bruce's guilt over Metropolis. As Lex tells Superman, "Ripe fruit, his hate. Two years growing but it did not take much to push him over actually. Little red notes, big bang, you let your family die!" In addition to shaping the news cycle, Lex sends Batman and Superman their own customized media of notes, news clippings, and photographs that widen the heroes' division, and Bruce's love for humanity becomes pitted against a perceived Other. Alfred Pennyworth (Jeremy Irons) uses footage from *Man of Steel* to warn Bruce about the increasing violence of Batman's methods: "That's how it starts, sir. The fever. The rage. The feeling of … powerlessness. That turns good men … cruel." After Lex brings Clark and Bruce together as societal figures of journalist and businessperson at a benefit for the Library of Metropolis ("I love bringing people together!" he greets), Bruce pivots on Clark's critical questioning about Batman's violence and impunity to a statement about "an alien, who, if he wanted to could burn the whole place down," even deflecting his own earlier claim to Alfred that "We've always been criminals." Batman spends the early part of the film tracking Luthor's Kryptonite, but reveals to Alfred that he intends to use it to "destroy" Superman. Bruce becomes adamant that Superman is an "absolute" "enemy" because of the mere potential of the Man of Steel to be so. After watching the Capitol explosion on the news, Bruce becomes so bombarded with his own customized media that his fears are weaponized and he no longer considers the reality in front of him when Superman pleads for his help. The film's titular battle adapts the comic *The Dark Knight Returns* (Miller et al., #4 [Dec. 1986]) into a statement on polarization and xenophobia, and Batman becomes blind with his armored suit's electric eyes to all else but the destruction of Superman. He hates Superman not as an individual person or neighbor, but as a Kryptonian on an existential level with condemnations like, "You're not brave. Men are brave," and, "You were never a god. You were never even a man." Bruce allows his pain to be brandished against another within a hateful spear of Kryptonite. Rather than forming an alliance based in personhood, Bruce lets himself become a pawn. He becomes more like Lex Luthor than Batman, forging the Kryptonite and brandishing his hardships under xenophobic dialogue. As in *Adventures of Superman* #15, Lex is acting as a Johnny Appleseed, and his "ripe fruit" is on display.

But the Bell's Already Been Rung

The conflict between Batman and Superman is resolved when the peril of Superman's mother traumatically reminds Batman of the murder of his own mother, Martha Wayne (Lauren Cohan), and Bruce realizes how far he's let his hatred go before seeing Clark as a person. He tosses his spear aside, his inner heroism rekindled with the possibility for redemption. However, although Lex underestimates society's heroes, he further escalates the film into the personified societal hatred of the monster Doomsday, which gains strength from violence. Even though Superman, Batman, and Wonder Woman (Gal Gadot) come together and Superman drives Luthor's poison into the heart of Doomsday, the film doesn't shy from the consequences of Luthor's actions. Lex's hatred and societal polarization kill a paragon, extraterrestrial, human, reporter, and, as Wonder Woman reflects, "soldier." The camera pans across a *Daily Planet* headline of John F. Kennedy's assassination, harkening back to an era of less polarized media and echoing Perry White's (Laurence Fishburne) amendment of *The Dark Knight Returns*, "The American conscience died with Robert, Martin, and John" (Miller et al., #1 [June 1986] 36: "The American conscience died with the Kennedys"). America regains its clarity as the United States holds a state funeral mourning an international figure from Krypton while a son and fiancé is buried in Smallville, united by the song "Amazing Grace." People of a wide diversity of backgrounds hold candles, and Bruce, implicated personally, vows that "men" and metahumans must "stand together," "rebuild," and "do better." The film is a warning against a worldwide building of polarization and xenophobia.

Meanwhile, Lex Luthor's actions make him into the Lex Luthor of the comics. His head is shaved, he has created a fissure in the Kent family, he has communicated with Steppenwolf of Apokolips to create his own alien invasion in preparation for *Justice*

League (2017; 2021), and he is hopeless for the world as "it all caves in. Civilization on the wane, manners … out the window." Society in real life continued unheeding, and Lex plotted further accordingly. As Lex tells Batman, "the bell's already been rung."

Supergirl: *Xenophobia on a Personal Level*

As the effects of the 2016 presidential election seeped further into American society, the fourth season of the television series *Supergirl* used Lex's poison to depict a progression of societal pain fomenting further division among characters in Superman media, splintering them on a much more personal level than *Batman v Superman*. As a longform narrative focused on Superman's cousin Kara Zor-El (Melissa Benoist), and on exploring xenophobia in socially relevant ways, *Supergirl*'s approach to these themes was always going to be more personal. But as the series unfolded, its fourth season adapted its characters to navigate more intricate ground than previous seasons, which had referenced political events ("How did anyone even vote for that other guy?" Supergirl asks dismissively in her excitement to meet a female president played by Wonder Woman herself, Lynda Carter, in Season 2's "Welcome to Earth," which aired the week before the election) or had the characters fight outside forces, some of which were family (Season 2's xenophobic renegade organization Cadmus). Season 4 reflects an intensification in live-action Superman media of Lex Luthor's xenophobia from the societal arena into the formation of pervasive divisions within the family. This chapter will primarily focus on the three episodes of the season in which Lex appears.

Like the comics starring Kara Zor-El, the first four seasons of the *Supergirl* television series feature characters affiliated with Superman (and frequently played by actors from throughout the DC media multiverse) who branch off and develop their identities, from Supergirl herself to the relationships she builds with Jimmy (now James) Olsen (Mehcad Brooks), Cat Grant (Calista Flockhart), Livewire (Brit Morgan), the Legion of Super-Heroes, and beyond. Characters become significant not just based on who they are, but who they are to one another. Superman, for instance, also becomes Kara's cousin Kal/Clark. *Supergirl* builds unique connections between adapted and original characters and creates a show about relatives and friends who become Kara's family.

Central to this is Lena Luthor (Katie McGrath), Lex's sister. Lena is a quintessential representation of adaptation in *Supergirl*, as her inclusion and development emphasizes family while also going beyond her name. Her relationship with Kara quickly becomes more complex than her brother's relationship to Kal, evolving from being investigated by Kara and Clark (Tyler Hoechlin) in Season 2 to becoming Kara's best friend. Despite Lena's struggles with the legacy of her family, her trust with Supergirl, and her own ambiguity, she generally strives to do the right thing. After being referenced many times and introduced as a child in previous seasons (Aidan Fink, "Luthors"), Lex (Jon Cryer, who previously played Lex's nephew Lenny in 1987's *Superman IV: The Quest for Peace*) appears as a supervillain late in Season 4. Supergirl's relationship with Lena serves as the entry point to develop Lex's relationship with Supergirl as the effects of the 2016 election permeated the lives of families in the United States. Lex is brought in as family to splinter a show about Supergirl's family. In this adaptation, Lex isn't introduced as an observer manipulating others from afar but as Lena's brother, and works through the deep personal connections between the Luthor and El families.

Supergirl focuses heavily on xenophobia. Many of the superpowered characters are extraterrestrials, and Supergirl works with a secret government organization known as the Department of Extranormal Operations (DEO) to keep Earthlings safe from extraterrestrial threats, frequently manifesting as people who committed crimes on other planets. As the series progresses, further emphasis is placed on protecting many aliens as refugees—Kara herself is framed as a refugee in the opening credit sequences beginning with Season 3 ("Far from the Tree")—as well as the integration of aliens into society through the Alien Amnesty Act. In Season 4, however, the hatred of aliens boils over from the fringes and immerses the daily life of the American mainstream. The primary villains are two humans at political extremes: Agent Liberty (Sam Witwer [*Smallville*'s Davis Bloome/Doomsday]), a former professor who becomes radicalized against aliens and builds widespread support using "Earth First" rhetoric following the death of his father (DC veteran Xander Berkeley) in the episode "Man of Steel," and Manchester Black (David Ajala), a former football hooligan who becomes radicalized against the Children of Liberty human supremacist organization following the murder of his alien fiancé (Tiya Sircar) in the episode "Ahimsa." Supergirl becomes increasingly exasperated about what the division between humans and aliens is doing to society and her family, most significantly to her relationship with her adopted human sister, DEO director Alex Danvers (Chyler Leigh), who sacrifices her memory of Kara's superhero identity so as not to reveal it to the government and subsequently loses a crucial part of their bond. Lena, for her part, must experience a horrendous confrontation with her own brother, for the season's turmoil turns out to be manipulated by Lex Luthor. As this version of Lex takes advantage of society across the political spectrum in order to seek out the destruction of Superman, he makes the Supergirl family his final battleground, intertwining his hatred and eroding the characters' relationships. Lex Luthor's xenophobia becomes more pervasive, disturbing, and hurtful alongside real-life international discourse, and hits way too close to home.

Furthermore, Season 4 adapts the prestige comic book series *Superman: Red Son* #1–3 (Millar et al. [June–Aug. 2003]). *Red Son* is a story in which the rocket of baby Kal-L—a reference to the original spelling of the name—crashes in Soviet Ukraine instead of Kansas. This causes Superman to become a totalitarian leader and severs Kal's connections within himself, those he protects, and the entire DC Universe. The spelling of Kal-L in this version also ultimately represents Superman's relationship to Lex Luthor, as Kal turns out to be a descendent of Lex's sent from the future.[11] In *Supergirl*, Lex goes further than Doomsday in *Batman v Superman* to create a deeply personal personification of family division. He forges a warped sibling connection with a clone of Supergirl, who at the end of Season 3 landed in the fictional Eastern European nation of Kaznia. Lex creates a Supergirl severed from her identity and based on division known as Red Daughter, who represents the effects of the fissures that Lex's encroaching xenophobia has created among the characters.

Fracturing the Family

In the episode "O Brother, Where Art Thou?," Lex Luthor's xenophobia intertwines with Supergirl's family. He is introduced in a flashback as having turned the Sun red, with a stunned and appalled Lena tied to a chair. This time, as Lex protests about Superman being "a false god" and "not … a man!," he is not just a villain out to destroy a superhero but a brother whose hatred is destroying his relationship with his sister. In the present, Lex is dying of cancer and is given a "mercy furlough" from prison, during which he uses every opportunity to appeal to his relationship with Lena to find a cure. The episode explores the effects of Lex's xenophobia on his family, even as Lex poisons it further by transferring his division into Supergirl's family.

As the episode's title implies, Lex's actions as a supervillain have created a personal aftermath for the Luthors, with societal pain tied to a deep family history. Regardless of Lex's actions, and *Supergirl*'s motif about shaping one's own family, Lena is bound to Lex as more than a hostage in a chair. As Lex and Lena discuss Lex's actions, it is as siblings:

> LEX: But now I wonder if you didn't want to just pull up a front row seat to watch me wither away and die?
> LENA: I'm not the one who accidentally poisoned myself with Kryptonite in a quixotic attempt to kill an invincible man. And while I do find the irony that you now need Black Kryptonite to cure yourself just delicious … You are my brother, Lex. I do wanna save you. Besides, how can you pay your debt to society if you're already dead?
> LEX: (laughs) Mm, now there's my sister.

Lex needs a superpower serum being developed by Lena from Black Kryptonite, or the Harun-El, and he further poisons his bond with his sister to get her to finish it. He utilizes strategies great and small to rekindle his relationship with Lena, quickly endearing himself as an irritating brother through comic relief—whining "I'm pathetic"—and generating as much empathy as he can muster about his condition with an oxygen mask, bloody coughs, and abuse by a guard: "I'm used to it. I'm not very … popular in prison." He uses the term "sis," recalls the memory of an abusive childhood tutor, and argues over the effectiveness of taunts in their sibling collaborations. Lex reshapes his bond with Lena under his control. He gets her to use his term "superpowers," and puts it in Lena's mind that she has always sought his approval. For a time, Lex is able to normalize their situation, as they make progress in finalizing the serum with a simultaneous exclamation of "We've almost got it!"

The reason they are working together is not for Lex, but to heal Lena's ex-boyfriend James Olsen, who had been in the thick of the turmoil of the season as a journalist and editor-in-chief of *CatCo Magazine* and had just been shot during an assassination attempt. Unbeknownst to Lena, Lex had arranged this attempt for Lena to test the serum on James, and the severe harm of Lex's actions extends to the main cast of *Supergirl*. As the Legion of Super-Heroes' Brainiac 5 or "Brainy" (Jesse Rath) observes, the attempt on James aggravates the comprehensive personal strain of the characters: "I think this event has-has forced me to process every difficult thing I have ever experienced." Lena goes from tending Lex to visiting James in the hospital, and Lex's cancer symbolically spreads when Lena embraces Kara standing among the familiar cast of characters. When Kara decides to help the Martian Manhunter J'onn J'onzz (David Harewood) fight Manchester Black, Alex, with her lost memory, feels like Kara betrays their family by leaving. When Kara asks over the phone, "What is happening?" Alex responds, "Well you would know if you were here." Their relationship is at the center of the Supergirl family, and is being driven apart.

As in *Batman v Superman*, Lex gets Lena to do what he wants, but this time it is more personal by poisoning the very nature of family. It is Alex who inspires Lena as a friend to finish the Harun-El serum to cure James, due to Lena's self-described "sheer force of will." Most disconcertingly, Lex tells Lena a story that strengthens their bond by severing it. He recounts the story of Lena's mother, who their father had an affair with, and reveals that while Lex's origins were the "poison" of two hateful parents, Lena's were "love" from her mother: "And if the rest of this family stands steadily in darkness, you will always fall into the light." As Lena leaves the room, she puts a hand on her brother's shoulder, which evokes everything they have lost and regained, even as the regretful satisfaction on Lex's face reveals that he knows what he has harmed in service of his agenda. Lex's exploitation of Lena's love affirms that Lena is both a Luthor and not a Luthor.

And much like *Batman v Superman*, as Lex breaks down bonds, he underestimates how heroes can rebuild new ones. This episode introduces another sister affected by Lex's actions, James's sister Kelly Olsen (Azie Tesfai). When James needs a relative to make medical decisions and the Supergirl family rallying around him is able to do nothing, Kelly appears. She builds a connection with Alex as "Kara's sister," and with the rest of the characters when she tells the hospital, "And these people are family too." Kelly shines a light on both the bonds that are strained—when she asks Alex where Kara is, an unconscious James starts convulsing in his nearby hospital bed—and the families we make. She explains to Alex that "James has always been more of a chosen family kinda guy," and the Supergirl family officially becomes James's family. Moreover, Kelly is a psychologist who begins to help the characters overcome their trauma by helping Alex with Kara through a discussion of James's coping mechanisms. Kelly, who had misgivings about Lena based on James's dating and super-friend experiences, in turn learns through Alex that Lena is more than her family name. And by the end of the episode, Kelly gets James to reach out to his biological family by speaking with their mother over the phone. The *Supergirl* family begins to be reconstructed.

When Lena becomes aware of Lex's plan, she returns from saving James only to find that the abusive guard and even her longtime assistant Eve Teschmacher (Andrea Brooks) are really working for Lex, and that Lex has taken the finished serum. Lex has turned Lena's entire world upside down all around her. Not only did Lex's actions confirm and deepen the damage to their family, but such actions were not isolated or on the margins—Lena's workplace and government are also not what she thought they were, and in service of Lex's hatred. Lex breaks forth destructively from the Luthor mansion, murders the actual guards, and comes face to face with Supergirl as the Last Daughter of Krypton's new nemesis. Lex's orchestrations represent the poison of xenophobia burning through society's structures and pervasively disrupting the bonds of family. Kryptonite has made family its casualty.

Division Personified

In Lex's next episode, "The House of L," he develops a warped sibling relationship with Red Daughter, creating a severed Supergirl representative of Lex's widening of the distance between siblings in the Supergirl family. The episode begins with the damage that Lex's xenophobia has caused Supergirl's world. A Harun-El superpowered Lex slams Supergirl with the *Daily Planet* globe and the words, "[T]his time, the Planet hits back." A flashback depicts Lex's trial for turning the Sun red, where Lena testifies that Lex used to tell her "it was just me and him against the world," but "One disagreement over his obsession, and he shut me out." Lex's hatred had caused their circle to rupture, and the expressions of both siblings convey their broken family. James's testimony reveals that, like the comics, Lex "kept offering Superman a place in his organization" and "didn't take the rejection well," indicating that Lex's xenophobia grew from jealousy. Lex quotes himself from *All-Star Superman* #5 with the words, "*Superman* made me do it" (Morrison et al. 2), uses the concepts "paradigm shift" and aliens being among humans from *Batman v Superman* to justify his argument that he is "protecting mankind from an extinction event," and, much like that film, Lex kills the judge and jury, this time under Frank Sinatra's "My Way." Lex then corrupts the prison system by bribing the warden, and he infiltrates *CatCo* through Eve Teschmacher due to James's connection "to the second Kryptonian." After having effectively taken over the rest of society, he prepares to take on the family arena. The rest of the episode continues in flashback to focus on the personification of Lex's division.

The end of *Supergirl*'s third season led to a small amount of Harun-El creating a Supergirl clone who landed in Kaznia ("Battles Lost and Won"). In "The House of L," Lex agrees to help the Kaznian government in a way that critically explores the Russian government's real-life role in playing the right and the left of the United States against one another that contributed to the deepening divisions during the 2016 election (Farrington; United States). Lex impersonally stokes the emotional divisions of the season, not because he cares about the Kaznian government's politics of bringing "back the glory days of the Soviet Union," or about the politics of Agent Liberty or Manchester Black, but because he wants to profit from all of them. And he shapes Red Daughter in the process.

Supergirl is an idealist and an optimist, so when Lex meets Red Daughter, he sets out to "bend" Kara's counterpart in the opposite direction in a way that parallels the season by distancing her from her personal connections and poisoning her against them. The title of the episode emphasizes the name "L" from *Red Son* that is both El and Luthor. Lex and Red Daughter are both adopted siblings searching for connections who become a warped, Bizarro-esque family forged through fracture in which Red Daughter is a representation of the damage of Luthor's xenophobia. She is an anti–Supergirl reflecting Kara's own crisis of family and society. Red Daughter is positioned against her country, family, and herself, and is a sister who does Lex's bidding for impersonal motivations ultimately directed toward the destruction of a Kryptonian.

As a clone of Kara without her memories, Red Daughter remembers only the name "Alex" from her previous life. She holds onto it with everything she has as the defining point of her identity. Family, specifically through sisters, is also the connection point between her and Lex, where Supergirl has a positive relationship with her sister and Lex has a negative one. Lex claims that he is Alex, and that he and Red Daughter were once "besties." Red Daughter yearns for connection, and Lex fulfills that need with divisive ideology, training her to be a Kaznian soldier by poisoning her strengths in a veritable fortress of isolation.

Early in Red Daughter's training, Lex gives her a bag of Chocos cookies, which become a vehicle for digesting us-versus-them language when Lex instructs, "You need to see the world as they do." Kara is an idealist, an optimist, and a romantic who perceives the nuance and hope in life and rejoices in its beauty, so Red Daughter enjoys not only the cookies, but the "lush" language of a copy of *The Great Gatsby* given to her by Lex. Lex, however, destroys her romantic impressions of America when he scolds her that the book is "about vapid, profligate fools." Kara has a very strong connection with and need for her sister Alex, so when Red Daughter indicates interest in Lena over chess after Lex brings her up, Lex in turn indicates that Red Daughter can replace Lena. He says that Red

Daughter reminds him of her, and that he thought he was "inseparable" from his sister, but Lena was a disappointment. Kara pursues peace and equality, so Lex claims that Red Daughter will achieve them when he puts her in a box flashing images of excess, weapons, protests, fast food, pollution, and homelessness contrasted with Supergirl's "S" reflected at her backwards against her pupil. The Kryptonian symbol for hope, which represents Kara's personality as well as her cultural background, becomes contextualized by Lex as standing in Red Daughter's way. When Red Daughter asks who is Supergirl, she emphasizes her search for connection with the words "to me," and Lex replies that Supergirl is her "sister" who "usurped" her, which Red Daughter then compares to Lena. Lex gets Red Daughter to feel betrayed by Supergirl, and, rather than a sister loved by Alex, Red Daughter is aligned against Supergirl as her artificial Alex is aligned against Lena. Lex gives Red Daughter a tour of decadence in Supergirl's home, National City, to show her the worst sides of the United States. Red Daughter isn't just a Supergirl separated on a cellular level. Lex widens the chasm, poisoning her into a divisive version of Kara, personifying his effect on the Supergirl family. Family becomes weaponized.

However, when Lex takes Red Daughter to Kara's apartment, entering Supergirl's life underscores Red Daughter's separation and she begins to get back to who she is. Red Daughter sees a photograph attached to the refrigerator of Kara and Alex alongside a Game Night score card listing, "Team Name: Danvers Sisters; Players: Kara + Alex." Kara and Alex are a distant, abstract concept, rediscovered through a historical artifact. Lex, meanwhile, is consumed with a framed picture of Supergirl. When Alex enters the apartment, Red Daughter impersonates Kara, and Lex stands around the corner with his gun drawn. Alex's memory loss separating her from her sister is accentuated by an interaction with a stranger doing a perfect impression. They, along with Lex, are false relatives. But they are all searching for reconnection. Red Daughter seeks out answers about herself and analyzes her world by reconnecting with Kara's identity through holding onto Kara's things, reading her journal, putting on her glasses, and visiting Lena.

Yet although Red Daughter inherently pursues nuance and truth, her dependence on Lex to put things into context as family makes her even more powerless to overcome Lex's manipulation than Bruce Wayne in *Batman v Superman*. Lex's underestimation of Kara through Red Daughter leads him to further sever Supergirl's nature by destroying Red Daughter's only real friend, a Kaznian boy named Mikhail (Gabriel Gurevich). Mikhail represents the battle for Supergirl's soul in a scene in Mikhail's cabin where he stands between Red Daughter and Lex discussing family. Red Daughter is in sunshine, focusing on the positive of visiting Mikhail, while Lex is in shadow, focusing on the negative of his and Mikhail's mutually bad fathers. Lex muses that he "used to pray for a hero like the one [Mikhail] got," and says with veiled venom toward Red Daughter, "Here you are," continuing to affirm her with unease. Lex ultimately makes it look like Mikhail is killed by a missile from the U.S. Navy.

Lex realizes that this was again an underestimation and tries to keep Red Daughter aligned as family with the words, "Luthors bide their time." But Kara's emotions are important to her and Red Daughter becomes a warped reflection of El, Danvers, and Luthor when, in her rage, she murders American sailors. When Red Daughter questions Lex about her identity and Kara's connections with Alex and Lena, it is as an estranged sister challenging her family's narrative. She links Lex's motivations to Lena, which hits a nerve of truth through the world Lex has created and causes Lex to leave. Even Lex's new divisive family has become divided. Furthermore, as much as Lex has used his feelings of rejection to his advantage, he is nevertheless resentful, whether of society or family.

Soon afterward, Red Daughter begins to physically break down. Lex doesn't intend this family to last, but while he needs it, he finds a way for it to do so. To keep Red Daughter alive, he gives himself cancer in order to manipulate Lena for the Harun-El serum. In doing so, he becomes a cancer to the world of Supergirl. His actions are represented when he appears to Lena as a hologram, stressing the Luthors' rift as he continues to try to bring them together without love. He emphasizes their genetic connection, painful childhoods, similarity of "obsession," and that "Love is valueless, I respect you."

In the present, Lex uses his new Harun-El blood, its own synthetic sibling of Kryptonite, to revive Red Daughter through a transfusion. This stabilizes her, fuels her, and brings them together through the destabilizing substance that split Supergirl and now powers a destabilizing man. Lex's xenophobia has succeeded in creating a new, warped Supergirl family based in division. He affirms, "This is not about Lena. This is about you and me," and Red Daughter becomes her own self by turning away from emotion and embracing her clinical relationship with Lex to destroy Supergirl. Lex cements their connection by invoking an earlier anecdote about Alexander the Great realizing his father Philip of Macedon's legacy, and Lex and Red Daughter become a family united by militancy. Lex has literally cultivated division in Supergirl's family and rebuilt it as a weapon, and Lena, his actual family, is now replaced and discarded, once again tied to a chair.

State of Reunion

From the show's perspective of family, the fourth season finale "The Quest for Peace" realizes the escalation of Lex Luthor's jealousy as American policy, confronts that escalation, and considers possibilities for resolution. As Red Daughter battles Supergirl, Kaznia attacks the United States and Lex takes to the skies at his highest point. He swoops in, catches a missile, winks to the people, and makes himself the savior of the United States as he gleefully decimates the Kaznians while singing the last verse of "My Way," heralding his complete vindication. While Lex had seemed to be building Red Daughter toward the *Red Son* comic and the "L" legacy, he was, of course, pandering. After all, as Lex might say, he may not have been the real Alex, but he is the real Alexander. Even a devoted member of Lex's family like Red Daughter is not immune to Lex's poison. Lex betrays her, captures her, and makes it look like he killed Supergirl. Lex admonishes, "You had my history at your disposal. Internet accessible," as he reiterates his hatred of Kryptonians.

Lex's jealousy is imposed on society as xenophobic government rhetoric and policy. The President (Bruce Boxleitner), revealed to be appointed by Lex and under his control—Lex even straightens the leader of the free world's flag pin to suit him—uses the word "invaders" toward Kaznia and "terrorist" toward Supergirl, pardons Lex, and appoints him to a White House position as the new Secretary of Alien Affairs. Lex is credited by the media with "magnanimity" after donating energy to restore power lost during the Kaznian attack. Unknown to the public, this energy is being harnessed from aliens who are being "rounded up" and placed in internment—as Lex puts it, "supercharged disposable batteries … Vile and viable." Among the captives are Red Daughter, as well as J'onn and Dreamer (Nicole Maines), a superhero who further emphasizes the impact of hateful policies, both as a person bridging cultural divisions with human and alien parents, and as the first transgender superhero on television. Lex's first test of the harnessed energy is to charge up a gauntlet to liquefy one of the humans working for him.

Much like in *Batman v Superman*, Lex's actions have sown division in the United States for his own ends. They echo the longstanding American political strategy of using race to pit people against one another (Alexander). This was utilized in 2016 and has been exemplified by such policies as the War on Drugs, which began not based on need or public opinion but on the desire of politicians for votes from "people who believe they are white" (Boucher; Coated 42). In the words of Khalil G. Muhammad illustrating this philosophy in the documentary *13th* (2016): "*I* will be the savior and protector of the white population." Lex's actions also parallel the United States' exploitation of people in other countries to maintain American wealth. Although racially and economically exploitative policies have always been embedded in the United States, in the years surrounding the 2016 election they created alarm in the dominant culture with a more distinct face. Lex no longer hides behind a veneer of neutrality.

And Lex's actions are represented as pettiness itself, as beyond resources, money, and power, the entire season was a means to an end in service of using the energy from the aliens to, of course, destroy Superman. The energy powers a satellite to attack the off-planet Kryptonian community Argo City, where Superman, as well as Kara's biological mother Alura Zor-El (Erica Durance [*Smallville*'s Lois Lane]),[12] live depowered. When Lena warns it will be "genocide" and links xenophobia to political expediency and false information with the words, "The public will find out the truth," Lex replies:

> The truth is meaningless. The people of Earth believe I am their savior. They needed a human hero and I fulfill that need. Nothing will ever change their minds. Facts are irrelevant. All that matters is spin. People are so stupid, they don't even read. And even when they do, they certainly don't think. I am the leader of this nation now. And nothing can stop me. Prost.

Lex knows he is not dealing in truth, and in the previous episode, "Red Dawn," Lex's actions bring Supergirl to the brink of death at the hand of Red Daughter.

These developments are experienced through the vantage point of family. Kara's family acts as a unifying force. In "Red Dawn," as Supergirl battles Red Daughter in a forest at night, the stress is too much for an onlooking Alex's struggling mind. Her memories come flooding back, and in another scene reminiscent of *The Dark Knight Returns*, she fully returns to revive Kara by stuffing blades of grass into her sister's hand and imploring her to harness the sunlight in the plants around them.[13] Reconnecting with her sister goes hand in hand with reconnecting with the world. Upon her resurrection, Kara doesn't hesitate for a moment. After recuperating in "The Quest for Peace," her first reaction is to stop Lex. When discussing it with Alex and her adopted mother Eliza Danvers (Helen Slater, 1984's Supergirl), Eliza and Alex respectively point out that "Lex and the President have succeeded in convincing the people that all aliens are dangerous, that Supergirl is the enemy" and "Lex is the hero." Supergirl replies, "Well I guess it's my job to show them who Lex really is. Show them the truth. ... I will not let fear win. And with my sister by my side, anything is possible." Justice and family are intertwined.

This is true even for the Luthors, where family is a force of anxiety. Lena's familial concerns are taken to their most extreme and represented on a world stage as she attends a family gathering enveloped in a White House invitation, so that Lex won't "come after the people [she cares] about." And instead of Supergirl witnessing the big villain speech, it's a quintessential Luthor meeting with Lena, Lex, and Lex's villainous mother Lillian

(Brenda Strong) parrying one another—as Lillian stresses, "This is the first family gathering we've had in ages." When Lena retorts, "Your murderous son has duped the world into thinking he's Earth's hero. This is hardly Thanksgiving dinner," Lillian counters, "Sounds perfectly normal for our family." Lex claims that he did everything for their family "to take its rightful place in history," and quotes Hitler to justify his treatment of aliens (Lillian chides, "It'll hurt the brand," as she tries to poison him). When Lena refuses a drink from Lex, it is simultaneously as a hero confronting a villain at the end of a television season and as a relative confronting disturbing political views at a family gathering. Family concerns are fused with society in a battle for a national home governing international discourse, and Lex Luthor's supervillain xenophobia is personally appalling, relevant, and a true encroachment, represented at the highest level of society. As Kara realizes, "He's gonna wipe out my family."

Like *Batman v Superman*, Lex underestimates people. As a superhero series, the season is also about how personal relationships can serve as a reminder for overcoming the societal divisions closing in around them. When Supergirl's family reconnects, the tide turns. Lex's speech about truth is intercut with citizens both for and against him responding to an article by Kara revealing Lex's machinations. Lena and Lillian subdue Eve and two guards, and Lillian affirms, "That's my girl." Brainy, who had been completely cut off from his emotions in "Red Dawn" and become an unfeeling version of himself, painfully regains his emotions while witnessing J'onn and Dreamer standing together for others in the face of the odds, and he confesses his love for Dreamer. And as Lex insults Supergirl's cousin, Kara responds that Lex can "thank" his sister for a suit that repels Lex's Kryptonite gauntlets. The final battle features a kick-butt battle track of Mötley Crüe's "Kickstart My Heart."

At the end of the battle, a freed Red Daughter flies to Supergirl's aid and takes a hit from one of Lex's gauntlets. As she lay in Supergirl's arms, she imparts, "You were right. My Alex was nothing like your Alex. Protect your people, as I protected mine." Red Daughter sacrifices herself for her connections, and is absorbed back into Supergirl, simultaneously a casualty, a melting away of divisions, and a rebuilding of clarity. Whole again, Supergirl is able to repel Lex with her heat vision. Before damaging his supersuit, she says, "This is for Red Daughter," and when Lex's suit fails in midair, Supergirl offers to save him. Unable to grasp such a notion, he replies, "Saved? By a Kryptonian? I'd rather die," and lets go.

Of course, Lex is never as selfless or beleaguered as he lets on, so he transports himself into his lair. Waiting for him, however, is a disappointed Lena, the real collateral that doesn't go away with a triumphant superheroic punch. Shortly after Lex muses, "You can only count on blood," Lena grows cold and shoots him, breaking her own heart with the tearful words, "The world will never be a safe place with you in it." As Lex dies, he delivers his final blow—and likely what he intended anyway—by turning Lena against any human connection she could have, revealing that all of her friends and her adopted mother had been hiding from her that Kara is Supergirl. Lex leaves her "with no one … and nothing!," not a brother, family, friends, or faith in any of them, just like him. Lex's family is destroyed.

Societally, Kara rejoices in "the Fourth Estate [saving] the day." Her article about Lex inspires the government to remove the President from office, Agent Liberty goes to prison, and as Dreamer says, "[p]eople are talking again. And, you know, listening to facts." Kara reaffirms the power of not giving up to bring "the truth to light." The Alien Amnesty Act is reinstated, and like in *Batman v Superman*, the government apologizes for doubting Supergirl, only this time the hero is there to receive it. Lex exerted his will on society through the destruction of family connections, and Supergirl's family doesn't just reconnect, but rebuilds, as two new couples are created, of Alex/Kelly and Brainy/Dreamer. Agent Liberty's son, George Lockwood (Graham Verchere), torn throughout the season, ends with the following as his father reflects behind a barred television in prison:

> Turning against each other has only led to more division, more hate, and more violence. There must be a better way. ... I've seen firsthand how that kind of anger can, can tear a family apart. I've lived that heartbreak. And I wanna make sure nobody else has to. If humans and aliens can just listen to each other then we can stand up, united, against those who seek to divide us.

From Alex and Kelly's first kiss to this moment, the underlying music extols the power of a society based in love and partnership, and Supergirl looks on and smiles.

Despite this happy ending, *Supergirl*'s quest for peace, much like *Batman v Superman*, realizes that reality has been far less simple, and knows that any kind of societal reunion requires attention to the far greater damage under the surface. In this television series, where the answers to justice are ultimately held by the families within society, the transition into the fifth season is driven by supremely personal shifts emphasizing further implications. As J'onn proclaims their new family, Lena says that she is with Kara always, and there is a pang. An organization called Leviathan is spurred by Lex's failure; Kara's connection with Lena is shattered as Lena slams a glass down on a picture of her, Kara, and Alex; J'onn's estranged brother Malefic is brought to Earth (DC veteran Phil LaMarr, the voice of Static and Green Lantern John Stewart); and Lex is brought back to life, presumably to continue his personally societal divisions.

Lex Luthor in *Batman v Superman: Dawn of Justice* and the fourth season of *Supergirl* utilizes xenophobia in service of his own personal jealousy. These live-action depictions reflect a continuously relevant character who has explored and developed understandings about the American political experience in the years surrounding the 2016 United States presidential election. How audiences, researchers, lawmakers, and policy will continue to unfold, connect, or splinter remains to be determined.

Notes

1. See: Alberto Ardèvol-Abreu and Homero Gil de Zúñiga, "Effects of Editorial Media Bias Perception and Media Trust on the Use of Traditional, Citizen, and Social Media News." *Journalism & Mass Communication Quarterly*, vol. 94, no. 3, 2017, pp. 703–24; Barry A. Hollander, "Tuning Out or Tuning Elsewhere? Partisanship, Polarization, and Media Migration from 1998 to 2006," *Journalism and Mass Communication Quarterly*, vol. 85, no. 1, Spring 2008, pp. 23–40; Yonghwan Kim, "Does Disagreement Mitigate Polarization? How Selective Exposure and Disagreement Affect Political Polarization," *Journalism & Mass Communication Quarterly*, vol. 92, no. 4, 2015, pp. 915–37; Emily Vraga, "Party Differences in Political Content on Social Media," *Online Information Review*, vol. 40, no. 5, Sept. 2016, pp. 595–609; and Benjamin R. Warner, "Modeling Partisan Media Effects in the 2014 U.S. Midterm Elections," *Journalism & Mass Communication Quarterly*, vol. 95, no. 3, 2018, pp. 647–69.

2. See: Carroll Doherty and Jocelyn Kiley, "Key Facts About Partisanship and Political Animosity in America," *Pew Research Center*, 22 June 2016; "On Eve of Inauguration, Americans Expect Nation's Deep Political Divisions to Persist," *Pew Research Center*, 19 Jan. 2017; and "The Partisan Divide on Political Values Grows Even Wider," *Pew Research Center*, 5 Oct. 2017.

3. See: "Europe and Right-Wing Nationalism: A Country-by-Country Guide," *BBC News*, 13 Nov. 2019; and Prebble Q. Ramswell, "Derision, Division–Decision: Parallels between Brexit and the 2016 US Presidential Election," *European Political Science*, vol. 16, no. 2, 2017, pp. 217–32.

4. See: Christian S. Crandall, Jason M. Miller, and Mark H. White II, "Changing Norms Following the 2016 U.S. Presidential Election: The Trump Effect on Prejudice," *Social Psychological and Personality Science*, vol.

9, no. 2, 2018, pp. 186–92; and "Trump Has Long History of Offensive Comments About Women," *PBS NewsHour*, 9 Oct. 2016.

    5. See: Alana Abramson, "President Trump Just Acknowledged Russian Meddling in the 2016 Election," *Time*, 17 July 2018; Dana Farrington, "READ: The Mueller Report, With Redactions," *NPR*, 18 Apr. 2019; and Ashley Parker and David E. Sanger, "Donald Trump Calls on Russia to Find Hillary Clinton's Missing Emails," *The New York Times*, 27 July 2016.

    6. See: "Hate Crime Statistics," *Federal Bureau of Investigation Uniform Crime Reporting*; Katayoun Kishi, "Anti-Muslim Assaults Reach 9/11-era Levels, FBI Data Show," *Pew Research Center*, 21 Nov. 2016; Christian S. Crandall, Jason M. Miller, and Mark H. White II, "Changing Norms Following the 2016 U.S. Presidential Election: The Trump Effect on Prejudice," *Social Psychological and Personality Science*, vol. 9, no. 2, 2018, pp. 186–92; Kirsten A. Gonzalez, Johanna L. Ramirez, and M. Paz Galupo, "Increase in GLBTQ Minority Stress Following the 2016 US Presidential Election," *Journal of GLBT Family Studies*, vol. 14, no. 1–2, 2018, pp. 130–51; Miriam Jordan, "How and Why 'Zero Tolerance' Is Splitting Up Immigrant Families," *New York Times*, 12 May 2018; and Mark Sherman, "High Court OKs Trump's Travel Ban, Rejects Muslim Bias Claim," *AP News*, 26 June 2018.

    7. See: Wahiba Abu-Ras, Zulema E. Suárez, and Soleman Abu-Bader, "Muslim Americans' Safety and Well-Being in the Wake of Trump: A Public Health and Social Justice Crisis," *American Journal of Orthopsychiatry*, vol. 88, no. 5, 2018, pp. 503–15; Laurie A. Drabble, Cindy B. Veldhuis, Angie Wootton, Ellen D. B. Riggle, and Tonda L. Hughes, "Mapping the Landscape of Support and Safety Among Sexual Minority Women and Gender Non-conforming Individuals: Perceptions After the 2016 US Presidential Election," *Sexuality Research and Social Policy*, vol. 16, no. 4, 2019, pp. 488–500; H. Kenny Nienhusser and Toko Oshio, "Awakened Hatred and Heightened Fears: 'The Trump Effect' on the Lives of Mixed-Status Families," *Cultural Studies↔Critical Methodologies*, vol. 19, no. 3, 2019, pp. 173–83; and Laura Wray-Lake, Rachel Wells, Lauren Alvis, Sandra Delgado, Amy K. Syvertsen, and Aaron Metzger, "Being a Latinx Adolescent under a Trump Presidency: Analysis of Latinx Youth's Reactions to Immigration Politics," *Children and Youth Services Review*, vol. 87, Apr. 2018, pp. 192–204.

    8. See: Heather C. Lench, Linda J. Levine, Kenneth A. Perez, Zari Koelbel Carpenter, Steven J. Carlson, and Tom Tibbett, "Changes in Subjective Well-Being Following the U.S. Presidential Election of 2016," *Emotion*, vol. 19, no. 1, Feb. 2019, pp. 1–9.

    9. See: M. Keith Chen and Ryne Rohla, "The Effect of Partisanship and Political Advertising on Close Family Ties," *Science*, vol. 360, no. 6392, 1 June 2018, pp. 1020–24; Kirsten A. Gonzalez, Lex Pulice-Farrow, and M. Paz Galupo, "'My Aunt Unfriended Me': Narratives of GLBTQ Family Relationships Post 2016 Presidential Election," *Journal of GLBT Family Studies*, vol. 14, no. 1–2, 2018, pp. 61–84; Amy Janan Johnson, Eryn N. Bostwick, and Ioana A. Cionea, "Talking Turkey: Effects of Family Discussions About the 2016 Election Over the Thanksgiving Holiday," *Journal of Family Communication*, vol. 19, no. 1, 2019, pp. 63–76; and Kevin S. McCarthy and Joshua V. Saks, "Postelection Stress: Symptoms, Relationships, and Counseling Service Utilization in Clients Before and After the 2016 U.S. National Election," *Journal of Counseling Psychology*, vol. 66, no. 6, 2019, pp. 726–35.

    10. In the mid-1980s, DC Comics rebooted their continuity and reintroduced their characters following the *Crisis on Infinite Earths* event mini-series (Apr. 1985–Mar. 1986). Writer/artist John Byrne revamped and updated the Superman mythos in the *Man of Steel* limited series (July–Sept. 1986). This included transforming Lex Luthor from a mad scientist to the quintessential 1980s villain: the corporate businessman. Byrne stated: "I built the character as a cross between Donald Trump, Ted Turner, Howard Hughes and maybe Satan himself!" (Cronin).

    11. This was likely inspired by Siegel's early attempts to get Superman published as a comic strip before it became a comic book. Believing that he might have more success with an artist other than Joe Shuster, Siegel submitted proposals to established comic strip artists. In a script to Leo O'Mealia, artist of the *Fu Manchu* comic strip, Superman was a scientist-adventurer who used a time machine one minute before the Earth was destroyed to send himself back to 1934 (Tye 18).

    12. Durance played the role beginning in Season 3. In the first two seasons, Alura was played by Laura Benanti. Benanti also played Alura's sister, Astra.

    13. In *The Dark Knight Returns* #4, Superman uses the sunlight stored by a flower to begin rejuvenating after being caught in the explosion of a Soviet nuclear warhead that he had diverted into a desert (Miller et al., #4, Dec. 1986).

Works Cited

"Ahimsa" (4 Nov. 2018). *Supergirl: The Complete Fourth Season*, story by Eric Carrasco, teleplay by Katie Rose Rogers and Jessica Kardos, directed by Armen V. Kevorkian, Warner Bros. Television, 2019.

Alexander, Michelle. *The New Jim Crow: Mass Incarceration in the Age of Colorblindness*. Kindle ed., The New Press, 2012.

Azzarello, Brian (w), Lee Bermejo (a), Dave Stewart (c), and Rob Leigh (l). *Lex Luthor: Man of Steel* #1 (May 2005). DC Comics, 2005

_____. *Lex Luthor: Man of Steel* #3 (July 2005). DC Comics, 2005.
_____. *Lex Luthor: Man of Steel* #4 (Aug. 2005). DC Comics, 2005.
_____. *Lex Luthor: Man of Steel* #5 (Sept. 2005). DC Comics, 2005.
Batman v Superman: Dawn of Justice: Ultimate Edition. Directed by Zack Snyder, Warner Bros., 2016.
"Battles Lost and Won" (18 June 2018). *Supergirl: The Complete Third Season*, written by Robert Rovner and Jessica Queller, directed by Jesse Warn, Warner Bros. Television, 2018.
Berlanti, Greg, Ali Adler, and Andrew Kreisberg, developers. *Supergirl: The Complete Third Season*. Warner Bros., 2017–2018.
_____. *Supergirl: The Complete Fourth Season*. Warner Bros., 2018–2019.
Boucher, Ian. "Introduction." *Humans and Paragons: Essays on Super-Hero Justice*, edited by Ian Boucher, Sequart Research and Literacy Organization, 2017, pp. 1–14.
Byrne, John (w/p), Dick Giordano (i), Tom Ziuko (c), and John Costanza (l). "Enemy Mine…" *The Man of Steel* Vol. 1 #4 (Nov. 1986). DC Comics, 1986.
Coates, Ta-Nehisi. *Between the World and Me*. Spiegel & Grau, 2015.
Cronin, Brian. "Comic Legend: Was Lex Luthor in *Man of Steel* Based on Donald Trump?" *CBR.com*, 5 Feb. 2018, https://www.cbr.com/superman-lex-luthor-donald-trump/. Accessed 12 Mar. 2020.
"Far from the Tree" (23 Oct. 2017). *Supergirl: The Complete Third Season*, written by Jessica Queller and Derek Simon, directed by Dermott Downs, Warner Bros. Television, 2018.
Farrington, Dana. "READ: The Mueller Report, With Redactions." *NPR*, 18 Apr. 2019, https://www.npr.org/2019/04/18/708850903/read-the-full-mueller-report-with-redactions. Accessed 6 Jan. 2020.
Hamilton, Edmond (w), Curt Swan (p), and George Klein (i). "The Showdown Between Luthor and Superman!" *Superman* Vol. 1 #164 (Oct. 1963). DC Comics, 1963.
"The House of L" (24 Mar. 2019). *Supergirl: The Complete Fourth Season*, written by Dana Horgan and Eric Carrasco, directed by Carl Seaton, Warner Bros. Television, 2019.
Killen, Kyle (w), Pia Guerra (a), Matthew Wilson (c), and Wes Abbott (l). "The Way These Things Begin," *Adventures of Superman* Vol. 2 #15 (Aug. 2013), DC Comics. *ComiXology*, 5 Aug. 2013, https://www.comixology.com/Adventures-of-Superman-2013-2014-15/digital-comic/45511. Accessed 3 Sept. 2019.
"Luthors" (13 Feb. 2017). *Supergirl: The Complete Second Season*, written by Robert L. Rovner and Cindy Lichtman, directed by Tawnia McKiernan, Warner Bros. Television, 2017.
"Man of Steel." *Supergirl: The Complete Fourth Season*, written by Rob Wright and Derek Simon, directed by Jesse Warn, Warner Bros. Television, 28 Oct. 2018.
Millar, Mark (w), Dave Johnson (p), Andrew Robinson (i), Paul Mounts (c), and Ken Lopez (l). "Red Son Rising," *Superman: Red Son* #1 (June 2003). DC Comics, 2003.
Millar, Mark (w), Davie Johnson (p), Kilian Plunkett (p), Andrew Robinson (i), Walden Wong (i), Paul Mounts (c), and Ken Lopez (l). "Red Son Ascendant," *Superman: Red Son* #2 (July 2003). DC Comics, 2003.
Millar, Mark (w), Killian Plunkett (p), Walden Wong (i), Paul Mounts (c), and Ken Lopez (l). "Red Son Setting," *Superman: Red Son* #3 (Aug. 2003). DC Comics, 2003.
Miller, Frank (w/p), Klaus Janson (i), Lynn Varley (c), and John Costanza (l). "The Dark Knight Returns," *Batman: The Dark Knight Returns* #1 (Jun 1986). DC Comics, 1986.
_____. "The Dark Knight Falls," *Batman: The Dark Knight Returns* #4 (Dec. 1986). DC Comics, 1986.
Morrison, Grant (w), Frank Quitely (p), Jamie Grant (i/c), Phil Balsman (l). "The Gospel According to Lex Luthor," *All-Star Superman* #5 (Sept. 2006). DC Comics, 2006.
Noble, Safiya Umoja. *Algorithms of Oppression: How Search Engines Reinforce Racism*. New York University Press, 2018.
"O Brother, Where Art Thou?" (17 Mar. 2019). *Supergirl: The Complete Fourth Season*, written by Derek Simon and Nicki Holcomb, directed by Tawnia McKiernan, Warner Bros. Television, 2019.
"The Quest for Peace" (19 May 2019). *Supergirl: The Complete Fourth Season*, story by Robert Rovner and Jessica Queller, teleplay by Rob Wright and Derek Simon, directed by Jesse Warn, Warner Bros. Television, 2019.
"Red Dawn" (12 May 2019). *Supergirl: The Complete Fourth Season*, story by Lindsay Sturman, teleplay by Gabriel Llanas and Eric Carrasco, directed by Alexis Ostrander, Warner Bros. Television, 2019.
Siegel, Jerry (w), Joe Shuster (p), and Paul Cassidy (i). *Action Comics* Vol. 1 #23 (Apr. 1940). DC Comics, 1940.
Superman. Directed by Richard Donner, Warner Bros., 1978.
Superman IV: The Quest for Peace. Directed by Sidney J. Furie, Warner Bros., 1987.
13th. Directed by Ava DuVernay, Netflix, 2016.
Tye, Larry. *Superman: The High-Flying History of America's Most Enduring Hero*. Random House Trade Paperbacks, 2013.
United States, Office of the Director of National Intelligence, National Intelligence Council. *Assessing Russian Activities and Intentions in Recent US Elections*. 6 Jan. 2017. https://www.dni.gov/files/documents/ICA_2017_01.pdf. Accessed 4 Jan. 2020.
Waid, Mark (w), Leinil Francis Yu (p), Gerry Alanguilan (i), Dave McCaig (c), and Comic Craft (l). *Superman: Birthright* #5 (Jan. 2004). DC Comics, 2004.
_____. *Superman: Birthright* #6 (Mar. 2004). DC Comics, 2004.

_____. *Superman: Birthright* #9 (June 2004). DC Comics, 2004.
_____. *Superman: Birthright* #10 (July 2004). DC Comics, 2004.
_____. *Superman: Birthright* #11 (Aug. 2004). DC Comics, 2004.
_____. *Superman: Birthright* #12 (Sept. 2004). DC Comics, 2004.
"Welcome to Earth" (24 Oct. 2016). *Supergirl: The Complete Second Season*, written by Jessica Queller and Derek Simon, directed by Rachel Talalay, Warner Bros. Television, 2017.

Anxiety Burning Bright

Exploring the Genealogy of the Evil Superman in Brightburn

DEBADITYA MUKHOPADHYAY

Can an alien with limitless power gladly become a selfless protector of the people whom he could have easily ruled forever? While the entire canon of Superman's adventures keeps saying yes, David Yarovesky's *Brightburn* (2019) says the opposite and the present study will focus on explaining why it does so. Not only does this alteration by *Brightburn* give the Superman film franchise a new direction by initiating a unique storyline but it also highlights the entire canon's underlying politics of valorizing the alien attributes of this character. Aliens are conventionally shown to be "devils incarnate" functioning just like "ghosts, ghouls, and things that go bump in the night" because of their "difference and otherness" (Sardar 6). Though a few of these aliens are at times shown to co-operate and even help humans in different ways, they are never imagined to co-exist with humans without being secretive about their superior strength or intellect. Only Superman is exempted from this pattern and is shown to be heartily welcomed by humanity in general despite publicly showing his flying ability or formidable heat vision. In the case of Superman, these unearthly features are never viewed as a threat; instead they are hailed as the signs of a messiah.

The whole Superman canon marks a major departure from the typical portrayal of aliens. Unlike many other stories featuring aliens, the tales of Superman never present the idea of human-alien co-existence to be out of the norm. Rather, as per the norms of the Superman canon, "the best case scenario" is Superman "helping millions of people." This, however, becomes possible only because such a scenario "does not take into account the notion of Superman using his powers to rule the earth by force" (Buchenberger 192). The very first comic book featuring Superman, *Action Comics* #1 (June 1938), ruled out the possibility of the alien child getting corrupted by showing him taking the decision to utilize "his titanic strength" in the service of humanity like a Good Samaritan (Siegel and Shuster 2). When eventually the series started expanding the character's world by focusing on Superman's formative years, the stories forestalled the emergence of the notion further by showing how wisely the Kents guided their ward and how obediently this mighty alien followed all the advices of his foster parents even after knowing his true heritage.

Comic books focusing on Superman's growing up like *Superman* #53 (Aug. 1948), *The Man of Steel* (July–Sept. 1986), *Superman: Birthright* (Sept. 2003–Sept. 2004), etc., two films, namely Richard Donner's *Superman* (1978) and Zack Snyder's *Man of Steel* (2013), and the television series *Smallville* (2001–2011) indeed serve as the key foundation of this character's heroic image. By recurrently presenting the Kents to be ideal parents who accept their adopted child's alien nature without hesitation and the alien Kal-El gladly choosing to obey his foster parents despite noticing his physical as well as intellectual superiority over them, these aforementioned origin stories always encourage the audience to ignore the possibility of Superman turning into a conquering alien with great success. Instead of continuing this tradition of imagining Superman to be a well-meaning alien or an obedient son, Yarovesky's film marks a watershed moment of the character's history by separating Superman from both of these long-celebrated templates and shows a sinister outcome of the mighty alien child's arrival and co-existence with humans. This chapter will analyze how and why *Brightburn* made way for the anxiety about this iconic superhero's alienness to burn so brightly all over its plot whereas the other Superman stories mentioned above treat it in their respective manners, thereby showing what these varying treatments of alienness have to tell about their corresponding milieus.

As mentioned above, Superman's otherwise problematic presence gets normalized in the majority of his early stories because they showed him to be a benevolent alien voluntarily choosing to be the guardian angel of humanity. Interestingly, the very first story of Superman did not exactly do so. Instead, *Action Comics* #1 gave full prominence to these unearthly attributes of the character. It presented him to be a savior only after highlighting how intimidating his differences from human beings actually are. And yet it effortlessly cemented the character's heroic image in its contemporary readers' mind. Amongst the eleven stories featured in the opening issue of *Action Comics*, it was the thirteen-page story featuring an alien by Joe Shuster and Jerry Siegel that stole the limelight. Though the story earnestly attempts to present its eponymous alien-hero to be the epitome of messianic qualities, it never portrays him to be meek and mild when he appears as Superman. It always shows Superman at the peak of his brute strength but keeps reminding readers of his good intentions through all the authorial comments accompanying each of his acts and celebrating his emergence as the arrival of a true leader of mankind. For instance, the very first appearance of the character in costume accompanied a note that described him to be "champion of the oppressed" (Siegel and Shuster 2).

Still, Superman's actions and their impact as shown in the story recurrently betray the threatening nature of his alien attributes to a great extent. During each of the cases handled by Superman, human beings coming in contact with him get intimidated by his paramount strength. He lifts a man off the ground and breaks the governor's steel door to save the innocent Evelyn Curry from execution (Siegel and Shuster 3–5). When saving a housewife from her abusive husband, Superman looks all set to rough up the violator and stops only when the police arrive (6–7). The third incident in particular makes him look threatening when, even after saving Lois and capturing her abductors, he smashes their car just to vent his anger (10). In the last of the four cases featured in the story, Superman snoops about the residence of Senator Barrow and after identifying the man trying to manipulate the Senate, instead of handing him over to the law, the mighty hero goes on tormenting him in an insouciant manner by picking him up and running along telephone wires (13–14). In each of these cases, Superman seems to show off the unearthliness of his powers, fully knowing how they are likely to scare the good and the bad alike.

Impact of these terrorizing acts of Superman is shown in the comics through the reaction of all the human characters who cross their path with him in the four cases outlined above. The Governor and his attendant appear to be scared beyond their wits when they see Superman effortlessly tearing a steel-door apart or when a bullet fired at a point-blank range fails to penetrate his skin (Siegel and Shuster 4). Similarly, the abusive husband gets knocked senseless after his chopper blade breaks like a toy at its first contact with Superman's body (7). The reactions of Lois Lane's abductors or the person who tries to manipulate the Senator too attest the petrifying nature of the character. Even the very cover of *Action Comics* #1 might be counted as a case in point for its choice of subject. Instead of using any of the panels showing Superman protecting the helpless, the cover featured a magnified version of the most problematic moment of the whole story, when he lifts the car over his head and smashes to the ground (10). By presenting this scene out of its context, the cover created a genuinely fearsome first impression of the character. Grant Morrison points out the allusion to Edvard Munch's iconic painting *The Scream* (1893) by referring to the man placed at "the bottom left corner." According to Morrison, this man "clutching his head" resembles the central figure of Munch's painting not only due to the similarity of their postures but also for having a face that looks like "a cartoon of gibbering existential terror" and being "a man driven to the city limits of sanity by what he has just witnessed"(6).

Co-presence of Siegel's valorization of the character and these scattered acknowledgments of Superman's intimidating nature throughout their story betray its creators' latent anxiety about the very decision of imagining an alien as a superhero. A number of publishers had rejected this story because they found "the idea of a superpowered alien too crude," which even led Siegel to re-imagine Superman as a human child from the future instead of an alien (Weldon 16). Eventually, Siegel and Shuster decided to stick to their alien child version of the character simply because the editorial team of *Action Comics* insisted them to do so (Scivally 8). As per the account of Larry Tye in *Superman: The High-Flying History of America's Most Enduring Icon* (2012), even this team was quite unsure of Superman's success. In fact, they had to conduct a survey for knowing whether "it was Joe and Jerry's caped hero who had driven those sales" (Tye 50). The publishers as well as the creators of Superman basically gambled when they passed off this alien character as a superhero. Their gamble paid off so tremendously because the character clicked perfectly with its contemporary audience.

The apparently problematic content of the story garnered a phenomenal response because it immediately struck a chord with the Americans of the Depression Era who wanted to keep faith in the notions of the American Dream even amidst the bleakness of their time. Robert C. Hauhart opines that faith in American Dream persisted "even during periods when no financial security [was] to be had" (85). Superman offered sustenance to these believers of the American Dream because the very "idea of Superman making the world a better place gave people a hope about the future" (Krensky 20). Despite the unmistakable rowdiness, Superman's activities in his first adventure are indeed shown to be always beneficial for the good citizens of America. He does act recurrently like a vigilante but neither the creators nor their audience felt that to be problematic because they were experiencing "a loss of trust and belief in the country's central institutions" (Johnson 7). As a whole, the idea of a mighty alien arriving in America, becoming one with the place, and always going the extra mile for its protection helped immensely in kindling the hope for a better future in Americans because it implied

America to be the chosen land worthy of the arrival and dwellings of friendly aliens. Another interesting reason behind the positive response about the character's alien identity emerges when this alienness is read in the light of a prevalent American discourse regarding migrants. In *The Epic of America* (1931), James Truslow Adams suggested that the only way Americans can overcome the crisis of Great Depression is by "progress[ing] together" and draws attention to the importance of all migrants of America in this whole by reminding how the very idea of American Dream "evolved from the hearts and hardened souls" who came to America "from all the nations" (qtd. in Hauhart 71). Therefore, Siegel and Shuster created "Superman as the ultimate immigrant" (Weldon 59) and showed their alien-immigrant character helping Americans by working both as an honest reporter and a dauntless savior; they showed him doing precisely what the American intelligentsia envisioned the immigrants should do.

Alternatively, the co-existence of this rowdiness and absolute power in Superman, as shown by *Action Comics* #1, may be understood as a result of his creators' desperate revision of ideas gathered from Philip Wylie's *Gladiator* (1930). Prior to the comic, Siegel came up with a short story entitled "The Reign of the Super-Man," illustrated by Shuster for his self-published pulp magazine *Science Fiction: The Advance Guard of Future Civilization* #3 (1933). According to Glen Weldon, this story in turn was heavily inspired by Philip Wylie's novel *Gladiator*, which featured a boy, Hugo Danner, born with supreme strength due to his scientist father's experiments. Danner, just like Superman of the first *Action Comics* issue, wanted to "lift up" mankind but unlike his comic book counterpart, was "feared and loathed" by common men (Weldon 9). In Weldon's words, Siegel "ate [...] up" Wylie's novel and "spat it out" (9) while writing "The Reign of the Super-Man." But the plotline of *Gladiator* appears to have been utilized by Siegel for building up the plot of the comic as well. For the short story, Siegel used the idea of the serum and a scientist who creates the same. Subsequently, in case of the comic, the figures of the boy with amazing powers, his scientist father, and features like the lifting of "tremendous weights" or the armor-resistant body of the superhero were borrowed from the novel.

Apart from the plot and characters, Siegel also drew inspirations from the theme of Wylie's novel for the story and the comics, albeit in different ways. *Gladiator* showed the hubristic nature of an individual with Icarian aspirations and Siegel expanded the idea by showing these to be an inherent feature of mankind. In the novel, it is only the boy hero Hugo Danner who "dares to confront God" (Weldon 9) after getting empowered by the serum his father makes while Siegel's short story shows an incredibly talented researcher, Professor Smalley, and a vagabond, Richard Dunn, fighting each other for getting hold of an extract that can give its consumer the "rule of the universe" (Fine 12). Besides, Danner gets misdirected only after his rejection by humanity but the desire to rule the earth seems to be innate in case of Siegel's Professor Smalley and Richard Dunn. The formula for superpower does not actually corrupt them; rather, it brings out their lust for power by emerging as the best possible means for fulfilling their desire.

According to Bruce Scivally's account of the comic character's genesis in *Superman on Film, Television, Radio and Broadway* (2008), Siegel and Shuster turned the tyrannous Superman into a hero because they realized that in order to get rich by creating comic book characters they must make sure that their character was "admired by the public" (6). Larry Tye's book too interprets Siegel's decision along similar lines. When referring to Siegel's "unpublished memoir," Tye says: "Jerry decided his only hope lay in crafting a hero so super that no publisher could resist, one whose story was just unbelievable enough to be credible. He vowed to stay up as late as it took" (32). Interestingly, a possible reason behind the aforementioned revising of the ur-text, as well as the source of the ur-text, appears to contribute significantly in making America look great or, to be more exact, greater than a number of European nations driven by Fascist ideals. While the idea of creating a superhuman entity through scientific experimentation as in *Gladiator* or "The Reign of Superman" appear to resemble what Germany was doing throughout the 1930s by intensively researching on performance-enhancing drugs for military purposes (Reinold and Hoberman 873–74), the idea of America getting blessed all of a sudden by the arrival of an alien who is far more superior than any German fascist could ever be, even after getting empowered by the drugs they strived to create, certainly connotes the greatness of America.

Keeping its primary goal of analyzing how *Brightburn* subverts the major templates of the Superman's canon in mind, even at the risk of being reductionist, this study will now read the subsequent development of this canon by explaining only how the end of the Great Depression created an obligation of bringing in new templates that the Depression-Era Superman adventures hardly required and outline only a select few of these templates that will be relevant for showing what exactly gets subverted by Yarovesky's film.

The apt revisions of the character by its creators during the post–Depression Era saved it from getting questioned for its reckless nature by readers of the next generation which were no longer driven by the urge to celebrate vigilantism like the readers of previous era. Larry Tye aptly sums up this transition saying: "When the nation was mired in economic doldrums it had needed a combative hero. Now that its economy and spirit were rebounding, the new attitude was a return to normalcy. For Superman that meant toning down the violence and adhering to a stricter set of rules." (61). The first comics issue to show Superman's formative years, 1953's *Superman #53*, contributed significantly to the cementing of this gentlemanly image of the character when it expounded the first six panels of Siegel and Shuster's *Action Comics* feature by offering an eight-page story. Though it drew heavily upon the first solo issue of the self-titled *Superman* (June 1939)'s two page back-story as well as George Lowther's novel *The Adventures of Superman* (1942) that offered the first in-depth account of Clark Kent's youth and the growth of his powers, the difference in length and detailing show the additional importance given by the 1953 issue. A wide range of writers carried on the trend of re-imagining Superman's origin and coming-of-age in the following years in comics as well as the films, producing no less than seven comic books and two film versions of it, but none of them made an attempt to explore how the emergence of Superman's power could have affected his adolescence and by extension, his very nature. The only exception is the television series *Smallville*, where a hormonal Clark is shown to literally misuse his X-ray by enjoying a sneak peek at Lana's naked body during his gym class ("X-Ray") or simply lose control over his heat vision when he gets sexually aroused ("Heat"). Though these episodes of *Smallville* offered a notable problematization of Superman's genteel image, they refrained from showing him essentially as a threat.[1] Rather, they always showed him to be basically good at heart and, moreover, they always showed how the Kents' parenting and Lana's love immediately brought Clark back to normal.

Along with emphasis on the seminal influence of the Kents' parenting or the love offered by Lana and at times Lois, the post–Depression Superman stories also counterbalanced Superman's alienness by recurrently introducing super-villains. Entries in the third volume of *The Original Encyclopedia of Comic Book Heroes* (2007), devoted to Superman, inform that the character the Ultra-Humanite, first appearing in *Action Comics* #13 (June 1939), to be the first villain with meta-human strength that Superman faced. Putting together the dates mentioned against each of Superman's villains, a notable rise in the number of super-villains maybe noted in the post–Depression Era stories. While the Depression Era stories showed the character fighting only one super-villain,[2] the early World War II years saw three major super-villains arriving in quick succession: The Prankster (*Action Comics* #51 [Aug 1942]), The Toyman (*Action Comics* #64 [Sept 1943]), and Mister Mxyzptlk (*Superman* #30 [Sept 1944]). The post–World War II years showed a greater recurrence of villains. When the *Giant Superman Annual* #2 (Jan. 1961) was published, its cover presented six villains with super powers, including characters like Brainiac and Metallo. The comics also featured Bizarro, first appearing in *Superboy* #68 (Nov. 1958) and subsequently appearing in regular intervals during 1950s and '60s (Gordon 53). This character Bizarro who was "an imperfect copy of Superman"(Gordon 53) indeed helped in underlining Superman's heroic "self" by being its corresponding "other." The purpose served collectively by these super-villains in obliviating Superman's alienness may be understood by drawing upon the key findings of Jack Fennell's insightful study of super-villains. Fennell finds the superheroes to be a present day equivalent of "mediaeval royalty" with "the right to punish transgressors" (321) whose acts of meting out justice "reaffirm" the readers' sense of being "moral" (325) and adds that in order to entertain the readers like this the hero always needs "unambiguously evil or non-human villain[s]" (326). The arrival of these villains was therefore highly necessary for the post–Depression Superman stories. These stories made these villains serve a totemic purpose by encouraging readers to associate villainy or tyranny exclusively with them and ignore the potentially harmful nature of Superman without a second thought.

Brightburn marks a departure from the templates utilized by the two major eras analyzed above from the very beginning. At first it creates a proper distancing from the entire canon of Superman adventures through its choice of title, characters, setting, and timeline. Then it goes on subverting the standard origin story of Superman by foregrounding the character's alien attributes and their ramifications unlike any other comic book or film. Superman arrived on earth in a spaceship and yet most versions of the origin stories showed this arrival to take place without much of a ripple. In most cases, the very scene of its landing is downplayed. For instance, in Superman #53 when the Kents come across the Kryptonian rocket beside the road, it is shown to have landed quite peacefully for a spaceship that has run across galaxies. Among the comic book stories, only *Birthright* showed the arrival to be partly alarming by showing the life battery rapidly going downhill as the Kryptonian ship struggles to reach its destination (Waid 13–14). Likewise, the on-screen versions of the event rarely showed it to be horrific. Only the opening episode of *Smallville* portrayed this with some degree of scariness by showing a meteorite shower that leaves people of Smallville shocked and kills Lana Lang's parents ("Pilot"). Following *Smallville*, *Brightburn* becomes the first film to bring out the horrific impact of the alien child's arrival to the fullest by showing the Breyers suddenly experiencing a tremor followed by a power-cut when the spaceship arrives.

After showing how shocking the moment of the alien child's arrival could actually be, the film starts exploring the impact of this arrival on both the child and humanity in general. In all the comic books and films about Superman's origin, this foundational moment of the character's life is shown to have a positive impact on the child and humanity only when the arrival takes place in America. Otherwise, as shown in *Superman: The Dark Side* (Aug.–Oct. 1999) and *Superman:Red Son* (June–Aug. 2003), Kal-El (or Kal-L) eventually becomes a killing machine when, instead of being raised in America by the Kents, he gets raised by Darkseid in Apokolips or by Stalin in the Soviet Union, respectively. In other words, the orphaned alien is not led astray by his condition because he lands amidst the ideal citizens of an ideal nation. *Brightburn* deals with this template by retaining it with a subtle twist. The Breyers and the place Brightburn unmistakably mirror the Kents and Smallville, respectively, but as their very names suggest, they are literally something else.

Jor-El selects earth to be the destination of Kal-El's spaceship in John Byrne's *The Man of Steel* because he wanted to give his son "the fullness of life" that the "cold and heartless society" of Krypton had stopped offering (Byrne 10). When he shows a scene of rural Kansas to his wife Lara to give her a clear idea about their son's future, the place is shown to be a land of hardworking people giving their honest labor in the fields (Byrne 11). This clearly presented America as a land of opportunities for all the deserving à la the American Dream. In the words of Glen Weldon: "Siegel and Shuster had created the Man of Steel as the ultimate immigrant" (59). All these origin stories basically showed how the ultimate immigrant gladly becomes an ideal immigrant by gladly choosing to contribute to making America the greatest nation. Since the Kents play the key role in this crucial transformation of the alien Kal-El into the ideal citizen by teaching him "their American middle-class ethic" (Engle 85), these origin stories always show them to be ideal figures. *Brightburn* subverts this long-nourished template consisting of ideal figures by showing the Breyers as well as their alien foster-child to be flawed individuals.

The ideal nature of the Kents becomes apparent from their very appearance. They are mostly shown as bespectacled and white-haired, resembling the typical sagacious guardian figures. Conversely, Tori and Kyle Breyers appear to be more restless right from their first appearance.

Kyle Breyer (David Denman), in particular, is very different from Jonathan in his strained relationship with the foundling child Brandon (Jackson A. Dunn). Jonathan is shown to become worried about the future of the Kents' relationship with their adopted son only in *The Man of Steel* (1986) and *Birthright* (2003). But even in these instances, when he admits of it to the young Clark, the air is immediately cleared. Moreover, neither of these stories show Jonathan actually regretting their decision to bring home Clark. Kyle, on the other hand, clearly has a suppressed anxiety about the very decision to adopt the foundling. When he gets worried about Brandon, the hidden anxiety comes out in the form of a shocking nightmare in which he sees the alien baby transforming into a menacing, red-eyed terror. Jonathan is always shown to be an ideal teacher for Clark but Kyle is shown struggling all along with Brandon. Each of the Superman adventures show Jonathan revealing Clark's true origin but Kyle is shown faltering even when speaking of hormonal changes with Brandon. Unlike Jonathan, Kyle remains confused about the possible ways to tackle his ward and what is more important, he goes on insisting that Brandon should never find the space ship he arrived in. Jonathan is shown to have no issue with Clark's actual origin at all. When he reveals the great secret of Clark's life, he always concludes his talk reminding Clark how much he believes in him. Kyle's reluctance to tell Brandon about his origin and his ultimate decision to shoot Brandon reveal how he little he believed in his adopted son.

Just like Jonathan, Martha too is always shown to love Clark irrespective of his alienness. If Jonathan had a strictness befitting an ideal father, Martha embodied the archetypal mother by always showering her unconditional love on Clark. Additionally, in *Superman #146* (July 1961) and *The Man of Steel* (1986), she is shown to be guiding Clark in taking the decision to become a superhero just like Jonathan does in many other stories. In *Superman #53*, Jonathan Kent gives Clark the name Superman and instructs him to "become a powerful force for good" by using his powers (10). Similarly, Martha Kent is shown to knit Superman's iconic uniform in both *Superman #146* and *The Man of Steel* (1986). Tori Breyer (Elizabeth Banks)'s approach to Brandon, however, appears to be faulty for her inability to accept Brandon to be anything other than the little boy she wanted him to be. As shown in Kyle's nightmare, Tori was desperate to believe Brandon's arrival to be a gift for them. In reality, she goes on refusing to change her opinion when Kyle shows her ample proofs of their son's growing sinister nature. While its preceding Superman origin film, Snyder's *Man of Steel* (2013), showed Martha's voice soothing the adolescent Clark's rage instantly, Tori's repeated utterance: "You'll always be my baby boy" fails to calm Brandon. Instead, her final attempt to kill Brandon shows that, just like her husband, she too could never come to terms with Brandon's alienness and trusted him very little.

Brandon himself epitomizes the strangeness lying underneath the character of Kal-El or Clark Kent all along. The series *Smallville* made Clark appear to be out of place amongst children of similar age by showing him to be "somewhere between a high school freak and geek" (Jagodzinski 173) but Brandon is a bigger misfit. His classmates laugh at him for his outstanding intelligence. None of them are shown to make any attempt to befriend Brandon. Even Caitlyn (Emmie Hunter), whom Brandon feels attracted to, starts treating him with repulsion as soon as she gets a hint about Brandon's powers. Unlike Clark, Brandon is shown to find out about his true heritage all by himself. Since his parents provide him very little direction about what he should do with his powers, he starts to explore everything around, including humans, with a clinical indifference. He clearly develops a low opinion about his parents after seeing how Tori interprets the significance of his arrival. The Kents too were unable to answer Clark's queries with clarity but they never made the mistake of telling Clark that someone simply sent him down because the Kents wanted a child as Tori did. Superman never lied to his parents but Brandon lies frequently because he wanted to use them as cover. He pressures his aunt Merilee (Meredith Hagner) to not report about his lack of remorse and tries to maintain peace with the Breyers because he knows as long as he has them by his side, he would always have a very strong alibi.

Clearly, Brandon is a polar opposite of Clark who shows what the character imagined by Siegel and Shuster could actually become if he was not shaped into a hero by several great narratives that came into existence in response to their respective milieus. As long as notions like America being an ideal place for the immigrants or America as a polar opposite of fascism pervaded, they helped the idea of portraying an alien becoming a self-less protector of humanity to work. A serious anxiety regarding immigrants and an imminent rise of fascism in America took over the nation since 2017 due to the debates surrounding the rhetoric used by President Donald Trump. Researchers on the notion of rising fascism in America find it to resemble "classic fascism" despite noting that "it has significant differences" from fascism, too (Harris et al. 14). A similarity of observation is found in Banu Gökarıksel and Sara Smith's article "Making America Great Again?: The Fascist Body Politics of Donald Trump" (2016), which reads: "Trump does not reject democracy outright" but also adds that "he deploys a viscerally embodied language of sexist, racist, and xenophobic hate" (80). An oft-cited study of the effects of America's post–2017 policies about the immigrants, "U.S. Immigration Policy Under Trump: Deep Changes and Lasting Impacts" (2018) by Sarah Pierce, Jessica Bolter, and Andrew Selee, confirms the ramification of such problematic rhetoric or policy making, by informing that significant and alarming "behavioral changes" have been noticed in the immigrants. They state: "There is strong evidence that the prevalence of harsh rhetoric about immigration and policy change on the ground have had serious effects on the behavior of individuals both inside and outside the United States" (10).

Though none of the analyses referenced above accept or reject the notion of fascism's emergence in America, they make it very clear that anxieties about immigrants as well as the latent fascist elements that gave rise to such hated viewing of the immigrants are looming large in the American society. Anxiety about the nature and condition of immigrants had already made its presence felt in superhero films through James Mangold's *Logan* (2017), which showed mutants as immigrants and depicted the superhero Wolverine battling with his evil self. In *Brightburn*, these contemporary anxieties of America find a more nuanced expression. Geoff Klock opined that the "implied threat of large-scale fascistic control" always lies beneath superhero narratives (41). Superman, being no exception, bore fascistic overtones as suggested by Frederic Wertham's study *Seduction of the Innocent* (1954), for his "S" sign which, according to Wertham, is quite close to the infamous "S.S." as well as his ability to "solve all […] social problems—by force" (34). In a society where the American policies about immigrants or the very nature of its administration were not feared as xenophobic or fascistic, these problematic sub-texts of the Superman canon went mostly unnoticed. But in 2019, the prevalence of these two anxieties shaped the alien character of *Brightburn* to a significant extent by making such anxieties take over the character in an unforeseen manner.

Brightburn, however, does not simply demonize the alien-immigrant, showing it to be a threat on his own. Rather it shows how Brandon's circumstances make him convinced that an outsider like him can never actually be loved or trusted and his only option is to kill anyone who is afraid of him. Even if he wants to do something good, as he earnestly confesses towards the end to Tori, whispering "I want to do good, Mom," he only meets with betrayal. He ultimately kills both of his adoptive parents but does so only when he becomes sure about their murderous intent. Tori and Kyle, on the other hand, appear to be more problematic. They desperately try to create a norm for the alien to fit in. Kyle wants him to be exactly like he was at his adolescence and Tori keeps reminding him how "tiny and fragile he was" or how he will always be her "little baby boy." Both wanted to kill him because they realized that Brandon would never be what they wanted. Thus, Brandon Breyer's transformation into his alter ego Brightburn actually speaks of a fear that rises chiefly from the feeling that it is no longer possible to imagine America becoming a home for the alien-immigrants and, more importantly, from the realization that instead of a protector figure the contemporary milieu of America can only give rise to a fascist.

Notes

1. For more on *Smallville*, see Christopher Maverick's "No Tights, No Flights: How *Smallville* Put the 'Human' in 'Superhuman'" in this collection.

2. Though Superman's arch-enemy Lex Luthor made his first appearance in Action Comics #23 (Apr. 1940), he is not mentioned here because, unlike Ultra-Humanite or the succeeding villains, Luthor never had any meta-human powers.

Works Cited

Binder, Otto (w), and Al Plastino (p/i). "The Story of Superman's Life!" *Superman* Vol. 1 #146 (July 1961). DC Comics, 1961.
Brightburn. Directed by David Yarovesky, performances by Elizabeth Banks, David Denman, and Jackson A. Dunn, Sony Pictures, 2019.
Buchenberger, Stefan. "Supreme and the Corruption of Power." *The Ages of Superman Essays on the Man of Steel in Changing Times*, edited by Joseph J. Darowski, McFarland, 2012, pp. 166–176.
Byrne, John (w/p), and Dick Giodarno (i). *The Man of Steel*, Titan Books, 1986.
Engle, Gary. "What Makes Superman So Darned American?" *Superman at Fifty: The Presence of a Legend*, edited by Gary Engle and Denis Dooley, Cleveland, 1987, pp. 85–91.
Fennell, Jack "The Aesthetics of Supervillainy." *Law Text Culture*, special issue of Justice Framed: Law in Comics and Graphic Novels, vol. 16, 2012, pp. 305–328, https://ro.uow.edu.au/ltc/vol16/iss1/13/. Accessed 26 Apr. 2020.
Fine, Herbert S. "The Reign of the Super-Man." *Science Fiction the Advance Guard of Future Civilization*, vol. 1, no. 1, 1933, pp. 4–14. University of Florida Digital Collections, https://ufdc.ufl.edu/UF00077088/00001/4x. Accessed 26 Apr. 2020.
Finger, Bill (w), Wayne Boring (p), and Stan Kaye (i). "The Origin of Superman," *Superman* Vol. 1 #53 (Aug. 1948). DC Comics, 1948. Read Comic Online,https://readcomiconline.to/Comic/Superman-1939/Issue-53?id=16293#1. Accessed 26 Apr. 2020.
Fleisher, Michael L. *The Original Encyclopedia of Comic Book Heroes*, Volume Three: Superman. DC Comics, 2007.
Gökarıksel, Banu, and Sara Smith. Editorial. "'Making America Great Again'? The Fascist Body Politics of Donald Trump." *Political Geography*. vol. 54, 2016, pp. 79–81, https://doi.org/10.1016/j.polgeo.2016.07.004. Accessed 26 Apr. 2020.
Gordon, Ian. *Superman: The Persistence of an American Hero*. Rutgers University Press, 2017.
Harris, Jerry et al. "Trump and American Fascism." *International Critical Thought*. vol. 7, 2017, pp. 1–17, https://www.researchgate.net/publication/321808701_Trump_and_American_Fascism. Accessed 26 Apr. 2020.
Hauhart, Robert C. *Seeking the American Dream A Sociological Inquiry*. Palgrave Macmillan, 2016.
"Heat" (1 Oct. 2002). *Smallville: The Complete Second Season*, written by Mark Verheiden, directed by James Marshall, Warner Bros., 2004.
Jagodzinki, Jan. *Television and Youth Culture Televised Paranoia*. Palgrave Macmillan, 2008.
Johnson, Jeffrey K. *Super-History: Comic Book Superheroes and American Society 1938 to the Present*. McFarland, 2012.
Klock, Geoff. *How to Read Superhero Comics and Why*. Continuum International Publishing Group, 2002.
Krensky, Stephen. *Comic Book Century: The History of American Comic Books*. Twenty-First Century Books, 2008.
Man of Steel. Directed by Zack Snyder, performances by Henry Cavill, Amy Adams, and Michael Shannon, Warner Bros., 2013.
Millar, Mark (w), Dave Johnson (p), et al. *Superman: Red Son*. DC Comics, 2004.
Moore, John Francis (w), Kieron Dwyer (p), Hilary Barta (i), et al. *Superman: The Dark Side*. DC Comics, 1999.
Morrison, Grant. *Supergods: What Masked Vigilantes, Miraculous Mutants, and a Sun God from Smallville Can Teach Us about Being Human*. Spiegel and Grau, 2012.
Pierce, Sara et al. "U.S. Immigration Policy Under Trump Deep Changes and Lasting Images." *Migration Policy Institute*, 2018, pp. 1–24, https://www.migrationpolicy.org/research/us-immigration-policy-trump-deep-changes-impacts. Accessed 26 Apr. 2020.
"Pilot" (16 Oct. 2001). *Smallville: The Complete First Season*, written by Alfred Gough and Miles Miller, directed by David Nutter, Warner Bros., 2003.
Reinold, Marcel, and John Hoberman. "The Myth of the Nazi Steroid." *The International Journal of the History of Sport*, vol. 31, no. 8, 2014, pp. 871–883, https://www.tandfonline.com/doi/abs/10.1080/09523367.2014.884563. Accessed 26 Apr. 2020.
Sardar, Ziauddin. Introduction. *Aliens R Us: The Other in Science Fiction Cinema*, edited by Ziauddin Sardar and Sean Cubitt, Pluto Press, 2002, pp. 1–17.
Scivally, Bruce. *Superman on Film, Television, Radio and Broadway*. McFarland, 2008.
Siegel, Joe (w), and Joe Shuster (p/i). "Superman, Champion of the Oppressed," *Action Comics* #1 (June 1938). DC Universe, https://www.dcuniverse.com/comics/book/action-comics-1938-1/f5f6ab2b-0746-4a95-bf79-039a529bbb50/. Accessed 26 Apr. 2020.
Swan, Curt (a), Stan Kaye (i), et al. *Giant Superman Annual #2* (Jan. 1961). DC Comics, 1961.
Tye, Larry. *Superman: The High-Flying History of America's Most Enduring Hero*. Random House, 2012.
Waid, Mark (w), Leinil Francis Yu (a), et al. *Superman: Birthright*. DC Comics, 2013.
Weldon, Glen. *Superman the Unauthorized Biography*. Wiley, 2013.
Wertham, Fredric. *Seduction of the Innocent*. Main Road Books, 2004.
"X-Ray" (6 Nov. 2001). *Smallville: The Complete First Season*, written by Mark Verheiden, directed by James Frawley, Warner Bros., 2003.

Appendix I
Adaptations Starring Superman or the Superman Family

Adaptations starring Superman or characters created for the Superman family of comic books.

Comic Books

Superman-Tim. 90 issues. Tim Publications, Inc. and National Periodical Publications, Inc., 1942–1950.
 A combination Superman activity book and boys' clothing catalog published in a black-and-single-color, 5½" × 8" booklets and sold in conjunction with the Superman-Tim Club.
Superman III. 1 issue. Cary Bates (w), Curt Swan (p), and Sal Amendola (i). DC Comics, Nov. 1983.
 A comic book adaptation of the film.
Supergirl Movie Special. 1 issue. Joey Cavalieri (w) and Gray Morrow (a). DC Comics, Feb. 1985.
 A comic book adaptation of the film.
Superman IV: The Quest for Peace. 1 issue. Bob Rozakis (w), John Beatty (a), Dick Giordano (a), Don Heck (a), Frank McLaughlin (a), Curt Swan (a), and Al Vey (a). DC Comics, 1987.
 A comic book adaptation of the film.
Superboy/The Adventures of Superboy. 22 issues. John Moore (w), Jim Mooney (p), Ty Templeton (i), et al. DC Comics, Feb. 1990–Feb. 1992.
 A companion comic book series to the *Superboy/Adventures of Superboy* syndicated television series. The comic book series changed its name from *Superboy* (#1–10) to *The Adventures of Superboy* (#11–22).
The Adventures of Superboy Special #1. 1 issue. Stan Berkowitz (w), Curt Swan (p), and Mike Machlan (i). DC Comics, 1992.
 A companion comic book special to the *Superboy/The Adventures of Superboy* syndicated television series.
Superman Adventures. 66 issues, 1 annual. Paul Dini (w), Rick Burchett (p), Terry Austin (i), et al. DC Comics, Nov. 1996–Apr. 2002.
 A companion comic book series to *Superman: The Animated Series*. The series is notable for containing the first comic book writing by Mark Millar.
Batman and Superman Adventures: World's Finest. 1 issue. Paul Dini (w), Joe Staton (a), and Terry Beatty (a). DC Comics, Nov. 1997.
 An adaptation of *The Batman Superman Movie: World's Finest* animated film.
Superman Adventures Special: Superman vs Lobo—Misery in Space. 1 issue. David Michelinie (w), John Delaney (p), and Mike Manley (i). DC Comics, Feb. 1998.
Smallville. 11 issues, 1 special. Mark Verheiden (w), Clint Carpenter (w), Kilian Plunkett (p)., and Mark Morales (i). DC Comics, 2003–2005.
 A companion comic book series to the *Smallville* television show.

Smallville Season 11. 139 digital chapters/35 issues, 5 specials. Brian Q. Miller (w), Pere Perez (p/i), et al. DC Comics, May 2012–Mar. 2015.

An in-continuity continuation of the *Smallville* television series wherein the now costumed Superman met other heroes from the DC Universe that were not included in the tv series, including: Batman, Nightwing, Green Lantern, and Wonder Woman. The series was initially published as digital chapters before being collected in issues and then trade paperbacks. After the first 69 chapters/19 issues, publication switched from an ongoing series to a series of mini-series.

Superman Returns: Prequel. 4 issues. Jimmy Palmiotti (w), Justin Gray (w), Marc Andreyko (w), Ariel Olivetti (p/i), Karl Kerchel (p/i), Rick Leonardi (p), Nelson DeCastro (i), Wellington Diaz (p), and Doug Hazelwood (i). DC Comics, Aug. 2006.

A limited series prequel to the film with each issue focusing on a different character.

Superman Returns: The Movie Adaptation. 1 issue. Martin Pasko (w), Mike Haley (p), Mike Collins (p), Ron Randell (p), and Matt Haley (i). DC Comics, Sept. 2006.

A comic book adaptation of the film.

Krypto the Superdog. 6 issues. Jesse Leon McCann (w), Min S. Kiu (p), Jeff Albrecht (i). DC Comics, Sept. 2006–Feb. 2007.

A comic book companion series to the *Krypto the Superdog* animated series.

Man of Steel: The Prequel. 1 issue. Story by David S. Goyer, Geoff Johns, and Zack Snyder. Sterling Gates (w), Jerry Ordway (p/i), Bob McLeod (i), Joe Rubenstein (i), and Bob Wiacek (i). DC Comics, May 2013.

A comic book prequel to the film, featuring an appearance by Kara Zor-El (Supergirl).

Batman v Superman: Dawn of Justice Prequel. 5 digital chapters/1 issue. Christos Gage (w) and Joe Bennett (a). DC Comics, Jan. 2016.

Prequel comic book to the film. The 5 chapters were released online as part of a tie-in promotion with Dr. Pepper.

Batman v. Superman: Dawn of Justice—Upstairs/Downstairs. 1 digital issue. Christos Gage (w) and Joe Bennett (a). DC Comics, Feb. 2016.

Digital comic companion to the film. The comic was released online as part of a tie-in promotion with Doritos and Wal-Mart.

General Mills Presents Batman v Superman: Dawn of Justice. 4 mini comics. Jeff Parker (w), R.B. Silva (a), José Marzan, Jr., et al., DC Comics and General Mills, Feb. 2016.

A companion comic book mini-series to the film. The four mini comics were found in specially marked boxes of General Mills cereals as part of a promotional tie-in.

Superman Smashes the Klan. 3 issues. Gene Luen Yang (w) and Gurihiru (p/i/c). DC Comics, Oct. 2019–Feb. 2020.

A comic book adaptation of the storyline "The Clan of the Fiery Cross" from *The Adventures of Superman* radio show.

Comics Strips

Superman. Jerry Siegel (w), Joe Shuster (a), et al. McClure Syndicate. 5 Nov. 1939–May 1966.

Lois Lane, Girl Reporter ran sporadically as a topper to the *Superman* Sunday pages from 24 Oct. 1943–27 Feb. 1944.

The World's Greatest Superheroes; *The World's Greatest Superheroes Present Superman*; *Superman/Superman Sunday Special.* Martin Pasko (w), George Tuska (p), Vince Colletta (i), et al. Chicago Tribune/New York News Syndicate. 3 Apr. 1978–10 Feb. 1985.

The focus was on Superman, but the strip also featured Batman, Robin, Wonder Woman, the Flash, and Black Lightning.

Films

Superman and the Mole Men. Directed by Lee Sholem, written by Richard Fielding, performances by Phyllis Coates (Lois Lane), George Reeves (Superman/Clark Kent), et al., Lippert Pictures, 1951.

Superman in Scotland Yard. Directed by George Blair and Thomas Carr, written by Jackson

Gillis, performances by John Hamilton (Perry White), Jack Larson (Jimmy Olsen), Noel Neill (Lois Lane), George Reeves (Superman/Clark Kent), Robert Shayne (Inspector Henderson), et al., Motion Pictures for Television, 1954.

Compilation of three episodes of *The Adventures of Superman* television series shown theatrically: "A Ghost in Scotland Yard" (Episode #34), "Panic in the Sky" (Episode 38), and "Lady in Black" (Episode #49).

Superman in Exile. Directed by George Blair and Thomas Carr, written by David T. Chantler and Jackson Gillis, performances by John Hamilton (Perry White), Jack Larson (Jimmy Olsen), Noel Neill (Lois Lane), George Reeves (Superman/Clark Kent), Robert Shayne (Inspector Henderson), et al., Motion Pictures for Television, 1954.

Compilation of three episodes of *The Adventures of Superman* television series shown theatrically: "Superman in Exile" (Episode #33), "The Face and the Voice" (Episode #36), and "The Whistling Bird" (Episode #51).

Superman and the Jungle Devil. Directed by George Blair and Thomas Carr, written by David T. Chantler and Peter Dixon, performances by John Hamilton (Perry White), Jack Larson (Jimmy Olsen), Noel Neill (Lois Lane), George Reeves (Superman/Clark Kent), Robert Shayne (Inspector Henderson), et al., Motion Pictures for Television, 1954.

Compilation of three episodes of *The Adventures of Superman* television series shown theatrically: "Shot in the Dark" (Episode #31), "The Machine That Could Plot Crime" (Episode #39), and "Jungle Devil" (Episode #40).

Superman/Superman: The Movie. Directed by Richard Donner, screenplay by Robert Benton, David Newman, Leslie Newman, and Mario Puzo, performances by Ned Beatty (Luthor's henchman Otis), Marlon Brando (Jor-El), Jackie Cooper (Perry White), Glenn Ford (Pa Kent), Gene Hackman (Lex Luthor), Margot Kidder (Lois Lane), Marc McClure (Jimmy Olsen), Valerie Perrine (Eve Teschmacher), Christopher Reeve (Superman/Clark Kent), Phyllis Thaxter (Ma Kent), et al., Warner Bros. 1978.

Kirk Alyn and Noel Neill, who portrayed Superman/Clark Kent and Lois Lane in the film serials *Superman* (1948) and *Atom Man vs Superman* (1950), with Neill reprising her role in seasons 2–6 of the *Adventures of Superman* television show, had a cameo as Lois Lane's parents that was cut from the theatrical release but later restored.

Süperman Dönüyor/The Return of Superman. Directed by Kunt Tulgar, screenplay by Necdet Tok, performances by Güngör Bayrak (Alev), Seref Çokseker (Tayfun's Earth Mother), Tayfun Demir (Tayfun/Superman), Yildimir Gencer (Ekrem), Rasit Hazar, Esref Kolçak (Prof. Centinel), Nejat Özbek (Haydar), Reha Yurdakul (Tayfun's Earth Father), et al., Kunt Films, (1979).

Unauthorized film adaptation from Turkey; also known as "Turkish Superman."

Superman II. Directed by Richard Donner and Richard Lester, screenplay by David Newman, Leslie Newman, and Mario Puzo, performances by Ned Beatty (Luthor's henchman Otis), Jackie Cooper (Perry White), Sarah Douglas (Ursa), Gene Hackman (Lex Luthor), Margot Kidder (Lois Lane), Marc McClure (Jimmy Olsen), Jack O'Halloran (Non), Valerie Perrine (Eve Teschmacher), Christopher Reeve (Superman/Clark Kent), Terence Stamp (General Zod), Susannah York (Lara), et al., Warner Bros., 1980.

The Richard Donner Cut was released in 2006.

Superman III. Directed by Richard Lester, screenplay by David Newman and Leslie Newman, performances by Jackie Cooper (Perry White), Margot Kidder (Lois Lane), Marc McClure (Jimmy Olsen), Annette O'Toole (Lana Lang), Richard Pryor (Augustus "Gus" Gorman), Christopher Reeve (Superman/Clark Kent), Annie Ross (Vera Webster), Pamela Stephenson (Lorelei Ambrosia), Robert Vaughn (Ross Webster), et al., Warner Bros., 1983.

Supergirl. Directed by Jeannot Szwarc, screenplay by David Odell, performances by Hart Bochner (Ethan), Peter Cook (Nigel), Faye Dunaway (Selena), Mia Farrow (Alura In-Ze), Marc McClure (Kimmy Olsen), Peter O'Toole (Zaltar), Helen Slater (Supergirl/Linda Lee), Maureen Teefy (Lucy Lane), Brenda Vicarro (Bianca), Simon Ward (Zor-El), et al., Warner Bros., 1984.

Superman IV: The Quest for Peace. Directed by Sidney J. Furie, screenplay by Lawrence Konner and Mark Rosenthal, performances by Jackie Copper (Perry White), Jon Cryer (Lenny Luthor), Gene Hackman (Lex Luthor/voice of Nuclear Man), Mariel Hemingway (Lacy Warfield), Margot

Kidder (Lois Lane), Marc McClure (Jimmy Olsen), Marc Pillow (Nuclear Man), Christopher Reeve (Superman/Clark Kent), and Sam Wanamaker (David Warfield), Warner Bros., 1987.

Superman. Directed by B. Gupta, screenplay by Sunil Priyadarshi, performances by Dharmendra (Superman's Biological Father), Puneet Issar (Superman/Shekhar), Shakti Kapoor (Verma), Rajeeta Kaur (Superman's Biological Mother), Ashok Kumar (Superman's Foster Father), Sonia Sahni (Editor), et al., 1987.

Unauthorized Bollywood version of Superman in Hindi.

Steel. Directed by Kenneth Johnson, written by Kenneth Johnson, performances by Annabeth Gish (Susan Sparks), Judd Nelson (Nathaniel Burke), Shaquille O'Neal (John Henry Irons/Steel), et al., Warner Bros., 1997.

Superman Returns. Directed by Bryan Singer, screenplay by Michael Dougherty and Dan Harris, performances by Kate Bosworth (Lois Lane), Marlon Brando (Jor-El), Sam Huntington (Jimmy Olsen), Frank Langella (Perry White), James Marsden (Richard White), Parker Posey (Kitty Kowalski), Brandon Routh (Superman/Clark Kent), Eve Marie Saint (Martha Kent), Kevin Spacey (Lex Luthor), et al., Warner Bros., 2006.

Superman Returns acts as a sequel to *Superman: The Movie* and *Superman II*, ignoring the continuity of *Superman III*, *Supergirl*, and *Superman IV: The Quest for Peace.* Unused dialogue and footage of Marlon Brando as Jor-El from *Superman: The Movie* was utilized. Noel Neill, who played Lois Lane in the film serials *Superman* (1948) and *Atom Man vs. Superman* (1950), as well as in season 2–6 of the *Adventures of Superman* television show (1952–1958), has a cameo as Lex Luthor's elderly wife Gertrude Vanderworth. Jack Larson, who portrayed Jimmy Olsen on the *Adventures of Superman* television show, has a cameo as a bartender.

Man of Steel. Directed by Zack Snyder, screenplay by David S. Goyer, performances by Amy Adams (Lois Lane), Henry Cavill (Superman/Clark Kent), Kevin Costner (Jonathan Kent), Russell Crowe (Jor-El), Laurence Fishburne (Perry White), Diane Lane (Martha Kent), Michael Shannon (General Zod), et al., Warner Bros. 2013.

Batman v Superman: Dawn of Justice. Directed by Zack Snyder, written by David S. Goyer and Chris Terrio, performances by Amy Adams (Lois Lane), Ben Affleck (Batman/Bruce Wayne), Henry Cavill (Superman/Clark Kent), Kevin Costner (Jonathan Kent), Jesse Eisenberg (Lex Luthor), Laurence Fishburne (Perry White), Gal Gadot (Wonder Woman/Diane Prince), Holly Hunter (Senator June Finch), Jeremy Irons (Alfred), Diane Lane (Martha Kent), et al., Warner Bros., (2016).

Brightburn. Directed by David Yarovesky, written by Brian Gunn and Mark Gunn, performances by Elizabeth Banks (Tori Breyer), David Denman (Kyle Breyer), Jackson A. Dunn (Brightburn/Brandon Breyer), Meredith Hagner (Merrilee McNichol), Emmie Hunter (Caitlyn Connor) Matt Jones (Noah McNichol), Becky Wahlstrom (Erica Connor), et al, Sony Pictures, 2019.

A subversive homage to the Superman mythos that reimagines the young extraterrestrial gaining his powers a la Superboy but without empathy, turning him into a murderous villain.

Film Serials

Superman. 15 chapters. Directed by Thomas Carr and Spencer Gordon Bennet, written by Lewis Clay, Royal K. Cole, Arthur Hoerl, George H, Plympton, and Joseph F. Poland, performances by Kirk Alyn (Superman/Clark Kent), Tommy Bond (Jimmy Olsen), Virginia Caroll (Martha Kent), Edward Cassidy (Eban Kent), Carol Forman (Spider Lady), Nelson Leigh (Jor-El), Noel Neill (Lois Lane), Luana Walter (Lara), Pierre Watkin (Perry White), et al., Columbia Pictures, 1948.

Atom Man vs. Superman. 15 chapters. Directed by Spencer Gordon Bennet, written by David Mathews, George H. Plympton, and Joseph F. Poland, performances by Kirk Alyn, (Superman/Clark Kent), Tommy Bond (Jimmy Olsen), Noel Neill (Lois Lane), Lyle Talbot (Lex Luthor/Atom Man), Pierre Watkin (Perry White), et al., Columbia Pictures, 1950.

Films, Animated

The Batman Superman Movie: World's Finest. Directed by Toshihiko Masuda, screenplay by Stan

Berkowitz, Alan Burnett, Paul Dini, Rich Fogel, and Steve Gerber, voice performances by Joseph Bologna (Dan Turpin), Kevin Conroy (Batman/Bruce Wayne), Robert Costanza (Harvey Bullock), Tim Daly (Superman/Clark Kent), Dana Delaney (Lois Lane), George Dzundza (Perry White), Lisa Edelstein (Mercy Graves), Mark Hamill (The Joker), Bob Hastings (Comissioner Jim Gordon), Arleen Sorkin (Harley Quinn), Lauren Tom (Angela Chen), Efrem Zimbalist Jr. (Alfred Pennyworth), et al., Warner Bros. Animation, 1997.

Compilation of three episodes of *Superman: The Animated Series* (Season 2 episodes 16, 17, and 18) which features the cast of *Batman: The Animated Series*.

Superman: Brainiac Attacks. Directed by Curt Geda, written by Duane Capizzi and Christopher Simmons, voice performances by Powers Boothe (Lex Luthor), Tim Daly (Superman/Clark Kent), Dana Delany (Lois Lane), George Dzundza (Perry White), Shelley Fabares (Martha Kent), Mike Ferrell (Jonathan Kent), Lance Henricksen (Brainiac), David Kaufman (Jimmy Olsen), Tara Strong (Mercy Graves), et al., Warner Bros. Animation, 2006.

Superman: Doomsday. Directed by Lauren Montgomery, Bruce Timm, and Brandon Vietti, screenplay by Duane Capizzi, voice performances by Adam Baldwin (Superman/Clark Kent), John DiMaggio (Toyman), Anne Heche (Lois Lane), Tom Kenny (The Robot), Swoosie Kurtz (Martha Kent), James Marsters (Lex Luthor), Cree Summer (Mercy Graves), Ray Wise (Perry White), Adam Wylie (Jimmy Olsen), et al., Warner Bros. Animation, 2007.

An adaptation of comic book storylines *The Death of Superman* (1992–1993), and *The Reign of Supermen* (1993).

Superman/Batman: Public Enemies. Directed by Stan Liu, written Stan Berkowitz, Voice performances by Clancy Brown (Lex Luthor), Kevin Conroy (Batman/Bruce Wayne), Tim Daly (Superman/Clark Kent), Alison Mack (Power Girl), John C. McGinley (Metallo), Alan Oppenheimer (Alfred Pennyworth), C.C.H. Pounder (Amanda Waller), Calvin Tran (Toyman/Hiro Okamura), et al., Warner Bros. Animation, 2009.

An adaptation of comic book storyline "The World's Finest" from *Superman/Batman* #1–6 (2003–04).

Superman/Batman: Apocalypse. Directed by Lauren Montgomery, written by Tab Murphy, Voice performances by Ed Asner (Granny Goodness), Andre Braugher (Darkseid), Kevin Conroy (Batman/Bruce Wayne), Tim Daly (Superman/Clark Kent), Susan Eisenberg (Wonder Woman/Diana Prince), Summer Glau (Supergirl/Kara Zor-El), Julianna Grossman (Big Barda), et al., Warner Bros. Animation, 2010.

An adaptation of the comic book storyline "The Supergirl from Krypton" from *Superman/Batman* #7–13 (2004), and a sequel to the animated film *Superman/Batman: Public Enemies*.

Superman/Shazam!: The Return of Black Adam. Directed by Joaquim Dos Santos, written by Michael Jelenic, voice performances by Zack Callison (Billy Bastion), James Garner (Shazam) George Newbern (Superman/Clark Kent), Jerry O'Connell (Captain Marvel), Michael Kevin Richardson (Tawky Tawney), Arnold Vosloo (Black Adam), et al., Warner Bros. Animation, 2010.

Animated short film released as part of the *DC Original Showcase Shorts Collection*.

All-Star Superman. Directed by Sam Liu, written by Dwayne McDuffie, voice performances by Ed Asner (Perry White), Frances Conroy (Martha Kent), Alexis Denisof (Dr. Leo Quintum), Jamie Denton (Superman/Clark Kent), Matthew Gray Gubler (Jimmy Olsen), Christina Hendricks (Lois Lane), Anthony LePaglia (Lex Luthor), et al., Warner Bros. Animation, 2011.

An adaptation of the comic book mini-series *All-Star Superman* (2005–2008).

Superman vs. The Elite. Directed by Michael Chang, written by Joe Kelly, voice performances by Catero Colbert (Coldcast), Grey DeLisle (Young Manchester Black), Disney (Menagerie), Robin Atkins Downes (Manchester Black), Paul Eiding (Pa Kent), Marcella Lentz-Pope (Ver Black), David Kaufman (Jimmy Olsen), Andrew Kishino (The Hat), George Newbern (Superman/Clark Kent), Paula Perrette (Lois Lane), Fred Tatascoire (Perry White), Tara Strong (Young Vera Black), et al., Warner Bros. Animation, 2012.

An adaptation of "What's So Funny About Truth, Justice, and the American Way?" from DC Comics' *Action Comics* #775 (Mar. 2001).

Superman: Unbound. Directed by James Tucker, screenplay by James Tucker, voice performances by

Matt Bomer (Superman/Clark Kent), Frances Conroy (Martha Kent), Alexander Gould (Jimmy Olsen), Stana Katic (Lois Lane), John Noble (Brainiac), Molly Quinn (Supergirl/Kara Zor-El), Stephen Root (Zor-El), Wade Williams (Perry White), et al., Warner Bros. Animation, 2013.

An adaptation of comic book storyline "Superman: Brainiac" from *Action Comics* #866–870 (2008).

The Death of Superman. Directed by Sam Liu and James Tucker, written by Peter J. Tomasi, voice performances by Jonathan Adams (Mayor Booker), Rosario Dawson (Wonder Woman), Paul Eiding (Jonathan Kent), Patrick Fabian (Hank Henshaw), Nathan Fillion (Green Lantern), Christopher Gorham (Flash), Charles Haiford (Bibbo Bibbowksi), Jennifer Hale (Martha Kent), Matt Latner (Aquaman), Max Mittelman (Jimmy Olsen), Shermar Moore (Cyborg), Nyambi (Martian Manhunter), Jerry O'Connell (Superman/Clark Kent), Jason O'Mara (Batman/Bruce Wayne), Rick Pasqualone (Dan Turpin), Rebecca Romijn (Lois Lane), Amanda Troop (Maggie Sawyer), Cress Williams (John Henry Irons), Rainn Wilson (Lex Luthor), et al., Warner Bros. Animation, 2018.

An adaptation of comic book storyline *The Death of Superman* (1992). Part of the DC Animated Movie Universe.

Reign of the Supermen. Directed by Sam Liu, written by Jim Krieg and Tim Sheridan, voice performances by Rocky Carroll (Perry White), Rosario Dawson (Wonder Woman), Paul Eiding (Jonathan Kent), Patrick Fabian (Cyborg Superman/Hank Henshaw), Nathan Fillion (Green Lantern), Christopher Gorham (Flash), Jennifer Hale (Martha Kent), Charles Halford (Bibbo Bibbowksi), Erica Luttrell (Mercy Graves), Max Mittelman (Jimmy Olsen), Cameron Monaghan (Superboy/Conner Kent), Shemar Moore (Cyborg), Nyambi (Martian Manhunter), Jerry O'Connell (Superman/Clark Kent), Jason O'Mara (Batman/Bruce Wayne), Rebecca Romijn (Lois Lane), Tony Todd (Darkseid), Cress Williams (Steel/John Henry Irons), Rainn Wilson (Lex Luthor), et al., Warner Bros. Animation, 2019.

An adaptation of comic book *The Reign of the Supermen* (1993). Part of the DC Animated Movie Universe.

Superman: Red Son. Directed by Sam Liu, screenplay by J.M. DeMatteis, voice performances by Amy Acker (Lois Lane), Diedrich Bader (Lex Luthor), Jason Isaacs (Superman), Phil LaMarr (John Stewart), Vanessa Marshall (Wonder Woman), Jim Meskimen (John F. Kennedy), Phil Morris (Jimmy Olsen), Sasha Roiz (Hal Jordan), William Saylers (Joseph Stalin), Roger Craig Smith (Batman), Paul Williams (Brainiac), Travis Willingham (Superior Man), Winter Ave Zoli (Svetlana), at al., Warner Bros. Animation, 2020.

An adaptation of the comic book mini-series *Superman: Red Son* (2003).

Superman: Man of Tomorrow. Directed by Chris Palmer, written by Butch Lukic, voice performances by Ike Amadi (Martian Manhunter), Darren Criss (Superman/Clark Kent), Alexandra Daddario (Lois Lane), Brett Dalton (Parasite), Neil Flynn (Jonathan Kent), Ryan Hurst (Lobo), Zachary Qunito (Lex Luthor), Bellamy Young (Martha Kent), Warner Bros. Animation, 2020.

Film, Animated Short

Superman. 17 short films. Voice performances by Joan Alexander (Lois Lane), Bud Collyer (Superman/Clark Kent), et al. Paramount Pictures, 1941–1943.

The first nine cartoons were produced by Fleischer Studios and the final eight by Famous Studios.

Musical

It's a Bird…. It's a Plane…. It's Superman! Music by Charles Strouse, Lyrics by Lee Adams, Book by David Newman and Robert Benton, 1966.

Original Broadway production directed by Harold Prince, choreography by Ernest Flatt, performances by Jack Cassidy (Max Menken), Jerry Fujikawa (Father Ling), Bob Holiday

(Superman/Clark Kent), Linda Lavin (Sydney Carlton), Patricia Maynard (Lois Lane), Eric Mason (Perry White), and Michael O'Sullivan (Dr. Abner Sedgwick). Played on Broadway for four months (29 Mar.-17 July 1966) and 129 performances.

Novels

The Adventures of Superman by George Lowther, illustrations by Joe Shuster, Random House, 1942.
Superman: The Last Son of Krypton by Elliot S. Maggin, Warner Books, 1978.
Superman: Miracle Monday by Elliot S. Maggin, Warner Books, 1981.
Superman III by William Kotzwinkle, Warner Books, 1983.
    Novelization of the film.
Supergirl by Norma Fox Mazer, Warner Books, 1984.
    Novelization of the film.
Superman IV by B.B. Hiller, Scholastic, Inc., 1987.
    Young Adult Novelization of the film.
The Death and Life of Superman by Roger Stern, Spectra, 1993.
    An adaptation of *The Death of the Superman* (1992), *Funeral for a Friend* (1993), and *Reign of the Supermen* (1993) storylines.
Superman: Doomsday and Beyond by Louise Simonson, illustrations by Dan Jurgens and José Luis García-López, Bantam Books, 1993.
    Young adult novelization of *The Death and Life of Superman*.
Lois and Clark: The New Adventures of Superman—Heat Wave by Michael Jan Freidman, HarperCollins, 1996.
Lois and Clark: The New Adventures of Superman—Exile by Michael Jan Freidman, HarperCollins, 1996.
Lois and Clark: The New Adventures of Superman—Deadly Games by Michael Jan Freidman, HarperCollins, 1996.
Lois and Clark: A Superman Novel by C.J. Cherryh, Prima Publishing, 1996.
Steel by Dean Wesley Smith, Tom Doherty Association Book, 1997.
    Novelization of the film.
Smallville: Arrival by Michael Teitelbaum, Little, Brown Books for Young Readers, 2002.
    Young adult novelization of television series' pilot episode.
Smallville: Strange Visitors by Roger Stern, Warner Books, 2002.
Smallville: See No Evil by Cherie Bennett and Jeff Gottesfeld, Little, Brown Books for Young Readers, 2002.
Smallville: Dragon by Alan Grant, Warner Books, 2002.
Smallville: Flight by Cherie Bennett and Jeff Gottesfeld, Little, Brown Books for Young Readers, 2002.
Smallville: Hauntings by Nancy Holder, Warner Books, 2003.
Smallville: Animal Rage by David Cody Weiss and Bobbi J.G. Weiss, Little, Brown Books for Young Readers, 2003.
Smallville: Whodunnit by Dean Wesley Smith, Warner Books, 2003.
Smallville: Speed by Cherie Bennett and Jeff Gottesfeld, Little, Brown Books for Young Readers, 2003.
Smallville: Buried Secrets by Suzan Colon, Little, Brown Books for Young Readers, 2003.
Smallville: Shadows by Diana G. Gallagher, Warner Books, 2003.
Smallville: Runaway by Suzan Colon, Little, Brown Books for Young Reader, 2003.
Smallville: Silence by Nancy Holder, Warner Books, 2003.
Smallville: Greed by Cherie Bennet and Jeff Gottesfeld, Little, Brown Books for Young Readers, 2003.
Smallville: Curse by Alan Grant, Warner Books, 2004.
Smallville: Temptation by Suzan Colon, Little, Brown Books for Young Readers, 2004.
Smallville: City by Devin Grayson, Warner Books, 2004.

Smallville: Sparks by Cherie Bennett and Jeff Gottesfeld, Little, Brown Books for Young Readers, 2004.

Superman: The Never-Ending Battle by Roger Stern, Pocket Star Books, 2005.
    A part of the Justice League of America novel series. Full-cast audio book directed by Richard Rohan, performances by Terence Aselford (Alfred Pennyworth), Lily Beacon (Cat Grant), Tim Carlin (Perry White), Andy Clemence (The Atom), David Coyne (Aquaman), Colleen Delany (Wonder Woman), Michael Glenn (The Flash), James Konicek (Superman), Eric Messner (Green Lantern), Thomas Penny (J'Onn J'Onzz), Faith Potts (Martha Kent), Michael Replogle (Jonathan Kent), Richard Rohan (Batman), Nanette Savard (Lois Lane), et al., Graphic Audio, 2008.

It's Superman by Tom de Haven, Ballentine Books, 2005.
    Audiobook narrated by Scott Brick, Blackstone Audiobooks, 2006.
    Full-cast audiobook directed by Scott McCormack, performances by Lily Beacon (Martha Kent), Laura C. Harris (Lois Lane), David Lynch (Jonathan Kent), Richard Rohan (narrator), Joel David Santner (Superman/Clark Kent), et al., Graphic Audio, 2014.

Superman Returns by Marv Wolfman, Warner Books, 2006.
    A novelization of the film. Audiobook narrated by Scott Brick, Blackstone Audiobooks, 2006.

Superman: The Last Days of Krypton by Kevin J. Anderson, Harper Entertainment, 2007.
    Audiobook narrated by William Dufris, Tantor, 2007.

Enemies & Allies: A Novel by Kevin J. Anderson, William Morrow, 2009.
    Full-cast audiobook directed by Richard Rohan, performances by Terrence Aselford (Alfred Pennyworth), Tim Carlin (Perry White), Steven Carpenter (Jimmy Olsen), James Keegan (Lex Luthor), James Konicek (Superman), Faith Potts (Martha Kent), Richard Rohan (Batman, narrator), Nanette Savard (Lois Lane), et al. Graphic Audio, 2013.

Man of Steel by Greg Cox, Titan Books, 2013.
    A novelization of the film.

Man of Steel: The Early Years by Frank Whitman, HarperFestival, 2013.
    Junior novel prelude to the film.

Lois Lane: Fallout by Gwenda Bond, Switch Press, 2015.

Batman v Superman: Dawn of Justice—Cross Fire by Michael Kogge, Scholastic, 2016.
    Junior novel prelude to the film.

Lois Lane: Double Down by Gwenda Bond, Switch Press, 2016.

Supergirl at Super Hero High by Lisa Yee, Random House Books for Young Readers, 2016. Novelization of the *DC Super Hero Girls: Super Hero High* animated television special. Part of the *DC Super Hero Girls* middle grade book series. Audiobook narrated by Anais Fairweather, Listening Library, 2017.

Lois Lane: Triple Threat by Gwenda Bond, Switch Press, 2017.

Supergirl: Age of Atlantis by Jo Whittemore, Harry N. Abrams, 2017.
    Book One in middle grade series based on the television series.

Supergirl: Curse of the Ancients by Jo Whittemore, Harry N. Abrams, 2018.
    Book Two in middle grade series based on the television series.

Supergirl: Master of Illusion by Jo Whittemore, Harry N. Abrams, 2019.
    Book Three in middle grade series based on the television series.

Superman: Dawnbreaker by Matt de la Pena, Random House Books for Young Readers, 2019.
    Part of the DC Icons young adult book series. Audiobook narrated by Andrew Eiden, Penguin Books, 2019.

Poetry

Dietrich, Bryan D. *Krypton Nights: Poems*. Zoo Press, 2003.
    The 2001 winner of the Paris Review Prize in Poetry.

Radio

Superman. 353 episodes. Produced by Frank Chase, directed by Jack Johnstone, et al., written by

Jack Johnstone, George Lowther, George Ludlam, et al., voice performances by Joan Alexander (Lois Lane; 9 June 1940–1951), Rollie Bester (Lois Lane; 26 Feb.–8 Mar. 1940), Helen Choate (Lois Lane; 18 Mar.–26 Apr. 1940), Bud Collyer (Superman/Clark Kent), Jackie Kelk (Jimmy Olsen), George Lowther (narrator), Julian Noa (Perry White), et al., WOR, New York City, 12 Feb. 1940–Feb. 1942.

Superman was syndicated as 15-minute episodes three days a week from 12 Feb. 1940–9 May 1941. After a hiatus, it returned on a five day a week schedule from 15 Aug. 1941–20 Feb. 1942.

The Adventures of Superman. 1735 episodes. Produced by Whitney Ellsworth, Jessica Maxwell, and Robert Maxwell, directed by Allen Ducovny, Mitchell Grayson, George Lowther, et al., written by Olga Druce, Ben Peter Freeman, Edward Langley, George Lowther, et al., voice performances by Joan Alexander (Lois Lane), Jackson Beck (narrator, Beanie Martin, Alfred Pennyworth; 14 Oct. 1943–21 Jan. 1950), Bud Collyer (Superman/Clark Kent; 12 Feb. 1940–21 Jan. 1950), Matt Crowley (Inspector Henderson, Batman/Bruce Wayne), Michael Fitzmaurice (Superman/Clark Kent; 5 June 1950–1 Mar. 1951), Earl George (Inspector Henderson), Jack Grimes (Jimmy Olsen; 5 June 1950–1 Mar. 1951), Jackie Kelk (Jimmy Olsen; 1940–1949), George Lowther (narrator, 31 Aug. 1942–13 Oct. 1943), Ross Martin (narrator; 5 June 1950–1 Mar. 1951), Julian Noa (Perry White), Ned Wever (Jor-L, Inspector Henderson), et al., Mutual Broadcasting System (1942–1949), ABC (1949–1951), New York City, 31 Aug. 1942–1 Mar. 1951.

The Adventures of Superman was a 15-minute serial airing five days a week on the Mutual Broadcasting System from 31 Aug. 1942–Feb. 1949. It switched to a self-contained, half-hour show airing three days a week from 7 Feb. 1949–17 Dec. 1949. ABC produced thirteen half-hour episodes targeting an adult audience that were produced 29 Oct. 1949–21 Jan. 1950. ABC revived the series, re-using all the half-hour scripts with a new cast, as a twice-weekly show from 5 June 1950–1 Mar. 1951. Guest appearances included Stacy Harris (Batman/Bruce Wayne), Ronald Liss (Robin), Gary Merrill (Batman/Bruce Wayne), and Agnes Moorhead (Kal-L's mother Lara),

Superman. Approximately 1040 episodes. Voice performances by Alfred Bristow (Perry White), Margaret Christensen (Lois Lane), Reginald Collins (Perry White), Ron Faulkner (Jimmy Olsen), Douglas Herald (Inspector Henderson), John Meillon (Jimmy Olsen), Leonard Teale (Superman/Clark Kent), Morris Unicombe (Jimmy Olsen), et al., 2GB, Sydney, 30 May 1949–30 May 1954.

An Australian production re-using scripts from *The Adventures of Superman* radio show with a new cast. The 15-minute episodes aired four days a week. Guest appearances by Batman and Robin were voiced by Bruce Beeby (Batman) and Trader Faulkner (Robin).

Superman on Trial. 1 episode. Directed by Neil Cargill, written by Dirk Maggs, voice performances by David Graham (Jonathan Kent), Dave Gibbons (himself), Garrick Hagon (Jor-El, Perry White), William Hootkins (Lex Luthor), Jeanette Kahn (herself), Lorelei King (Martha Kent, Lana Lang), Vincent Marzello (Jimmy Olsen), Stuart Milligan (Superman), Bob Sessions (Batman), Shelley Thompson (Lois Lane, Lara), and Adam West (himself), BBC, 1988.

As part of the 50th anniversary celebration of the Man of Steel, BBC Radio 4 produced this docudrama which revisits Superman's past as part of a trial to determine his humanity.

The Adventures of Superman. 2 seasons, 12 episodes. Directed by Dirk Maggs, written by Dirk Maggs, voice performances by Barbara Barnes (Lucy Lane), Garrick Hagon (Perry White), William Hootkins (Lex Luthor), Lorelei King (Lois Lane), Burt Kwouk (Doctor Teng), Vincent Marzello (Jimmy Olsen), Stuart Milligan (Superman/Clark Kent), Shelley Thompson (Lana Lang), Simon Treves (Metallo), and Dick Vosburgh (Jor-El), BBC, 1990–1991.

Adaptation of John Byrne's 1986 *Man of Steel* mini-series. These series were originally broadcast as five-minute episodes on BBC Radio 4 and then rebroadcast as half-hour episodes on BBC Radio 4.

Superman: Doomsday and Beyond. 5 episodes. Directed by Dirk Maggs, written by Dirk Maggs, voice performances by Denica Fairman (Maggie Sawyers), Garrick Hagon (Jonathan Kent), Leon Herbert (John Henry Irons), William Hootkins (Lex Luthor), Lorelei King (Lois Lane), Burt Kwouk (Doctor Teng), Vincent Marzello (Jimmy Olsen), Eric Meyers (Guy Gardner),

254   Appendix I

Stuart Milligan (Superman/Clark Kent, The Kryptonian), Liza Ross (Supergirl), and Kerry Shale (Superboy, The Cyborg), BBC Radio, 1993.

An adaptation of the comic book storylines *The Death of Superman* (1992) and *The Reign of the Supermen* (1993). Originally aired on BBC Radio 5 and rebroadcast on BBC Radio 1. The radio series was released in the U.S. as *Superman Lives!*

Records/Cassettes

Superman's Christmas Adventure. One 78 rpm vinyl record. Directed by Jack Johnstone, written by Allen Ducovny and Jerry Mason, voice performances by Joan Alexander (Lois Lane), Bud Collyer (Superman/Clark Kent), George Lowther (Narrator), et al., Decca Records, 1941.

Superman. One 78 rpm vinyl record. Freddie "Schnickelfritz" Fisher and His Orchestra, Decca Records, 1941.

Novelty waltz with lyrics by Robert Maxwell and music by Freddie Fisher. The record states the song is "From Paramount's Cartoon 'Superman,'" though this is not the case.

Superman: The Flying Train. Two 78 rpm vinyl records. Voice performances by Joan Alexander (Lois Lane), Jackson Beck (Narrator), Bud Collyer (Superman/Clark Kent), Musette Records, 1947.

Features read-along comic booklet.

Superman: The Magic Ring. Two 78 rpm vinyl records. Voice performances by Joan Alexander (Lois Lane), Jackson Beck (Narrator), Bud Collyer (Superman/Clark Kent), Musette Records, 1947.

Features read-along comic booklet

The Official Adventures of Superman. One 33⅓ rpm vinyl record. Directed by Herb Gale, written by Ronald Liss, voice performances by Joan Alexander (Lois Lane), Jackson Beck (Narrator), Peter Fernandez, Jack Grimes (Jimmy Olsen), Bob Holliday (Superman/Clark Kent), Ronald Liss, and George Petrie, Metro Records, 1966.

The Origin of Superman. One 33⅓ rpm vinyl record. Directed by Hamilton O'Hara, voice performances by Ronald Liss, Hamilton O'Hara, Dan Ocko, Nat Polen, and Jim Stevens, Golden Records, 1966.

Features read-along comic book.www

Children's Treasury of Superman Musical Stories. One 45 rpm vinyl record. Tifton, 1966.

Superman: Alien Creatures. One 33⅓ rpm vinyl record. Power Records, 1975.

Features read-along comic book.

Superman: Weatherspoon's Catalyst. One 33⅓ rpm vinyl record. Power Records, 1975.

Superman: P.O. Box 65. One 33⅓ rpm vinyl record. Power Records, 1975.

Superman: Mystery of the Mad Minnows. One 33⅓ rpm vinyl record. Power Records, 1975.

Superman: The Best Cop in the World. One 33⅓ rpm vinyl record. Power Records, 1975.

Features read-along comic book.

Superman: The Mxyzptlk Up Menace. One 33⅓ rpm vinyl record. Power Records, 1975.

Superman: Tomorrow the World. One 33⅓ rpm vinyl record. Power Records, 1975.

Features read-along comic book.

Superman: City Under Siege. One 33⅓ rpm vinyl record. Power Records, 1975.

Features read-along comic book.

Superman: The Killer Bees. One 33⅓ rpm vinyl record. Power Records, 1975.

Superman: Star of Bangalore. One 33⅓ rpm vinyl record. Power Records, 1975.

Superman: The Man from Krypton. One 45 rpm vinyl record. Power Records, 1978.

Features read-along comic book.

Superman: Light Up the Tree, Mr. President. One 33⅓ rpm vinyl record. Power Records, 1978.

Superman from Krypton to Metropolis. One audio cassette. Fisher-Price, 1982.

Features read-along book.

The Adventure of Superman. One audio cassette. I.J.E., Inc., 1984.

Features read-along book.

Superman and the Neutron Nightmare. One audio cassette. Written by Marv Wolfman. EMI/Golden Wonder, 1984.

Superman versus the Solatron Belt. One audio cassette. Written by Cary Bates. EMI/Golden Wonder, 1984.
Superman and the Conqueror of the Past. One audio cassette. EMI/Golden Wonder, 1985.
Superman in Death from a Distant Galaxy. One audio cassette. EMI/Golden Wonder, 1985.
Superman: Double Trouble. One audio cassette. Ladybird, 1989.
  Features read-along book.
Superman: Man of Steel No. 1–6. Six audio cassettes. Written by John Byrne. MPI, 1989.
  Full-cast adaptation of John Byrne's 1986 *Man of Steel* mini-series.

Short Stories

"Superman in Radio." *Radio and Television Mirror*. 16 short stories, illustrated. Vol. 15, No. 3-Vol. 17 No. 6, Jan. 1941–Apr. 1942.
  Two to three page illustrated short story companions to *The Adventures of Superman* radio show.
The Further Adventures of Superman. Edited by Martin H. Greenberg, Spectra, 1993.
  Short story collection containing: "The Riddle of Superman's Mask" by Will Murray; "Apparitions" by Diane Duane; "Lucifer over Lancaster" by Elizabeth Hand and Paul Witcover; "Dateline: Metropolis" by Karen Haber; "Mine Enemy Grows Older" by Joe Calavieri; "Forget Me Not" by Mark Waid; "Déjà vu All Over Again" by Edward Wellen; "Excerpt from the Diary of Dr. Morris Finkelstein" by Mike Resnick; "I Now Pronounce You Superman and Wife" by Henry Slesar; and "The Warrior of the Final Dawn" by Garfield Reeves-Stevens.
"Starwinds Howl" by Elliot S! Maggin, *https://www.maggin.com/Lancer/StarwindsHowl.pdf*, 1999.
  A self-published novelette recounting the origin of Krypto by the *Superman* comic book and novel scribe.

Television Shows

Adventures of Superman. 6 seasons, 104 episodes. Developed by Robert J. Maxwell and Whitney Ellsworth, performances by Phyllis Coates (Lois Lane, Season 1), John Hamilton (Perry White), Jack Larson (Jimmy Olsen), Noel Neill (Lois Lane, Seasons 2-6), George Reeves (Superman/Clark Kent), Robert Shayne (Inspector Henderson), et al., Motion Pictures for Television, 1952–1958.
  Seasons 1 and 2 (episodes 1–52) were filmed in black and white. Seasons 3–6 (episodes 53–104) were filmed in color.
Superboy/The Adventures of Superboy. 4 seasons, 100 episodes. Developed by Alexander Salkind and Ilya Salkind, performances by Jim Calvert (Trevor Jenkins "T.J." White), Gerard Christopher (Superboy/Clark Kent, Seasons 2–4), Stacey Haiduk (Lana Lang), Sherman Howard (Lex Luthor, Seasons 2–4), Salome Jens (Martha Kent), John Haymes Newton (Superboy/Clark Kent, Season 1), Scott James Wells (Lex Luthor, Season 1), Stuart Whitman (Jonathan Kent), et al., Viacom Enterprises, 1988–1992.
  The title changed from *Superboy* to *The Adventures of Superboy* in the third season.
Lois & Clark: The New Adventures of Superman. 4 seasons, 88 episodes. Developed by Deborah Joy LeVine, performances by Dean Cain (Superman/Clark Kent), K Callin (Martha Kent), Teri Hatcher (Lois Lane), Eddie Jones (Jonathan Kent), Michael Landes (Jimmy Olsen, Season 1), Tracy Scoggins (Cathrine "Cat" Grant), John Shea (Lex Luthor), Lane Smith (Perry White), Justin Whalin (Jimmy Olsen, Season 2–4), et al., ABC, 1993–1997.
  Other proposed titles included *Lois Lane's Daily Planet* and *Metropolis*
Smallville. 10 seasons, 217 episodes. Developed by Alfred Gough and Miles Millar, performances by Aaron Ashmore (Jimmy Olsen), Erica Durance (Lois Lane), Cassidy Freeman (Tess Mercer), John Glover (Lionel Luthor), Justin Hartley (Oliver Queen/Green Arrow), Sam Jones III (Pete Ross), Kristin Kreuk (Lana Lang), Allison Mack (Chloe Sullivan), Annette O'Toole (Martha Kent), Michael Rosenbaum (Lex Luthor), John Schneider (Jonathan Kent), Lara Vandervoort (Kara), Tom Welling (Clark Kent), et al., Warner Bros. Television, 2001–2011.
Supergirl. Ongoing, 5 Seasons, 109 episodes. Developed by Ali Alder, Greg Berlanti, and Andrew

Kreisberg, performances by Melissa Benoist (Supergirl/Kara Danvers), Mehcad Brooks (James Olsen/Guardian), John Cyer (Lex Luthor), Calista Flockhart (Cat Grant), David Harewood (Martian Manhunter/J'Onn J'Onzz), Jeremy Jordan (Winslow "Win" Schott Jr.), Chyler Leigh (Alex Danvers), Katie McGrath (Lena Luthor), et al., Warner Bros. Television, 2015–present.

Superman/Clark Kent and Lois Lane have guest-starred in *Supergirl*, played by Tyler Hoechlin and Elizabeth Tulloch, respectively.

Krypton. 2 seasons, 20 episodes. Developed by David S. Goyer, performances by Georgina Campbell (Lyta-Zod), Elliot Cowan (Daron-Vex), Cameron Cuffe (Seg-El), Wallis Day (Nyssa-Vex), Rasmus Hardiker (Kem), Ian McElhinney (Val-El), Ann Ogbomo (Jayna-Zod), Aaron Pierre (Dev-Em), Blake Ritson (Brainiac), Colin Salmon (General Dru-Zod), Emmett J. Scanlan (Lobo), Shaun Sipos (Adam Strange), Hannah Waddingham (Jax-Ur), et al., Warner Bros. Television, 2018–2019.

Superman & Lois. Ongoing, 1 season. Performances by Tyler Hoechlin (Superman/Clark Kent), Elizabeth Tulloch (Lois Lane), et al., Warner Bros. Television, 2020.

Spin-off of *Supergirl* focusing on Superman and Lois Lane as parents.

Television Specials

It's a Bird.... It's a Plane.... It's Superman! Directed by Jack Regas, performances by Allen Ludden (Perry White), Kenneth Mars (Max Mencken), Al Molinaro (Father Ling), Loretta Swit (Sydney Carlton), Leslie Ann Warren (Lois Lane), David Wayne (Dr. Abner Sedgewick), David Wilson (Superman/Clark Kent), ABC, 1975.

Shortened adaptation of the Broadway musical that aired on the late-night *Wide World of Entertainment*.

Superman 50th Anniversary. Directed by Robert Boyd, performance by Dana Carvey (Chief Historian Junior Supermen of America), et al., CBS, 1988.

A prime-time special of skits and clips celebrating the 50th anniversary Man of Steel.

Television Series, Animated

The New Adventures of Superman; The Superman-Aquaman Hour of Adventure; The Batman-Superman Hour. 4 seasons, 68 six-minute segments. Directed by Hal Sutherland, voice performances by Joan Alexander (Lois Lane, 1966–1967, 1969–1970), Jackson Beck (Lex Luthor, Narrator, Perry White), Julie Bennett (Lois Lane, 1967–1969), Bud Collyer (Superman/Clark Kent), Jack Grimes (Jimmy Olsen), Gilbert Mack (Mr. Mxyzptlk), Cliff Owens (Brainiac), et al., Filmation, 1966–1970.

The Adventures of Superboy. 3 seasons, 34 six-minute segments. Directed by George Blair, voice performances by Bob Hastings (Superboy/Clark Kent), Ted Knight (Krypto, Narrator), Janet Waldo (Lana Lang), et al., Filmation, 1966–1969.

The Adventures of Superboy aired as part of *The New Adventures of Superman* series on CBS.

Superman. 1 season, 13 episodes. Directed by Cosmos Anzilotti, Bill Hutton, and Tony Love, voice performances by Michael Bell (Lex Luthor), Tress MacNeille (Martha Kent), Ginny McSwain (Lois Lane), Alan Oppenheimer (Jonathan Kent), Stanley Ralph Ross (Perry White), Lynne Marie Stewart (Jessica Morganberry, Young Clark Kent), Mark Taylor (Jimmy Olsen), Beau Weaver (Superman/Clark Kent), Bill Woodson (opening narration), et al., CBS, 1988.

Released to coincide with Superman's 50th anniversary.

Superman: The Animated Series, The New Batman/Superman Adventures. 3 seasons, 54 episodes. Voice performances by Joseph Bologna (SCU Lt. Dan "Terrible" Turpin), Victor Brandt (Dr. Emil Hamilton), Clancy Brown (Lex Luthor), Corey Burton (Brainiac), Joanna Cassidy (Inspector Maggie Sawyer), Daly (Superman/Clark Kent), Dana Delany (Lois Lane), George Dzundza (Perry White), Lisa Edelstein (Mercy Grave), Shelley Fabares (Martha Kent), Mike Ferrell (Jonathan Kent), Joely Fisher (Lana Lang), Michael Ironside (Darkseid), David Kaufman (Jimmy Olsen), Lauren Tom (Angela Chen), et al., Warner Bros. Animation, 1996–2000.

Krypto the Superdog. 2 seasons, 39 episodes. Directed by Scott Jeralds, voice performances by Michael Daingerfield (Superman), Brian Dobson (Lex Luthor), Brian Drummond (Streaky the

Supercat), Alberto Ghisi (Kevin Whitney), Scott McNeil (Ace the Bat-Hound, Ignatius), Tabitha St. Germain (Andrea Sussman), Sam Vincent (Krypto the Superdog), et al., Warner Bros. Animation, 2005–2006.

Video Games

Superman. Atari 2600, Atari, Inc., 1979.
Superman: The Game. Commodore 64, First Star Software, 1985.
Superman. NES, Kemco, 1987
Superman. Arcade game, Taito, 1988.
Superman: The Man of Steel. Commodore 64 and Atari ST, Tynesoft/First Star Software, 1989.
Superman. Sega Mega Drive and Genesis, Sunsoft, 1992.
    Released in the European market in 1993 as *Superman: The Man of Steel.*
The Death and Return of Superman. Sega Genesis and Super NES, Sunsoft, 1994.
Superman. Game Boy, Titus Software, 1997.
Superman Activity Center. MacOS and Microsoft Windows, Knowledge Adventure, 1998.
    Educational game
Superman: The New Superman Adventures. Nintendo 64, Titus Interactive, voice performances by Victor Brandt (Dr. Emil Hamilton), Clancy Brown (Lex Luthor), Corey Burton (Brainiac), Tim Daly (Superman), Dana Delany (Lois Lane), Michael Ironside (Darkseid), Brion James (Parasite), David Kaufman (Jimmy Olsen), and Malcolm McDowell (Metallo), 1999.
    Based on *Superman: The Animated Series.*
Superman: Shadow of Apokolips. Nintendo Gamecube and Playstation 2, Infogrames, 2002.
    Based on *Superman: The Animated Series.*
Superman: The Man of Steel. Xbox, Infogrames, 2002.
Superman: Countdown to Apokolips. Game Boy Advanced, Infogrames, 2003.
    Prequel to the video game *Superman: Shadow of Apokolips.* Based on *Superman: The Animated Series.*
Superman: The Greatest Superhero. V-Smile, VTech, 2005.
    Educational game.
Superman Returns. Nintendo DS, Playstation 2, and Xbox 360, Electronic Arts, 2006.
    Based on the film *Superman Returns.*
Superman Returns: Fortress of Solitude. Game Boy Advanced, Electronic Arts, 2006.
    Puzzle game based on the film *Superman Returns.*
Superman. IOS, Chillingo, 2011.
Man of Steel. Android and IOS, Phospor Games, 2013.

Other

"Stamp Day for Superman." Directed by Thomas Carr, performances by Noel Neill (Lois Lane) and George Reeves (Superman/Clark Kent), U.S. Department of the Treasury, 1954.
    A short film distributed to schools to promote the purchase of U.S. Saving Bonds.
The Multipath Adventures of Superman. 75 episodes. Directed by Ben Lee, Craig Saunders, et al., written by Janet Harvey, Paul Kupperberg, et al., voice performances by Harry Goz (Perry White), Lois Markle (Lois Lane), Fred Melamed (Lex Luthor), Barton Tinapp (Superman/Clark Kent), et al., Brilliant 3D, 1999–2001.
    Animated choose-your-own-adventure series available on the Warner Bros. website. The first story, "The Menace of Metallo," was released as a CD-ROM.
Smallville: Chloe Chronicles. 4 mini-episodes. Developed, directed, and written by Mark D. Warshaw, performance by Allison Mack (Chloe Sullivan), et al., Warner Bros. Television, 2003.
    Mini-series of short investigative reports by Chloe Sullivan released on the web as a promotional tie-in with AOL. The mini-series is included on the *Smallville* Season Two DVD box set (2003).

Smallville: Chloe Chronicles Volume Two. 7 mini-episodes. Developed and directed by Mark D. Warshaw, written by Brice Tidwell and Mark D. Warshaw, performances by Sam Jones III (Pete Ross), Allison Mack (Chloe Sullivan), et al., Warner Bros. Television, 2004.

Mini-series of short investigative reports by Chloe Sullivan and Pete Ross released on the web as a promotional tie-in with AOL. The mini-series is included on the *Smallville* Season Three DVD box set (2004).

Smallville: Vengeance Chronicles. 7 episodes. Developed, directed, and written by Mark D. Warshaw, performance by Allison Mack (Chloe Sullivan), et al., Warner Bros. Television, 2006.

Mini-series of short investigative reports by Chloe Sullivan released on the WB's website. The mini-series is included *Smallville* Season Five DVD box set (2006).

Smallville Legends: The Oliver Queen Chronicles. 6 mobisodes. Warner Bros. Television, 2007.

Five-minute CGI-animated episodes recounting the early life of Green Arrow/Oliver Queen. Released as a promotional tie-in with Sprint, the episodes were made available on Sprint cellphones before appearing on The CW website. The mini-series is included on the *Smallville* Season Six DVD box set (2007).

Smallville Legends: Justice and Doom. 5 chapters. Stephen Nilson (w) and Steve Scott (a). Warner Bros. Television, 2007.

A mini-series of on-screen comic strips which aired as interstitial during episodes of *Smallville* as a promotional tie-in with Toyota. The story expanded on adventures of the Justice League (Green Arrow, Cyborg, Aquaman, Impulse, and Watchtower). The mini-series is included on the *Smallville* Season Six DVD box sets (2007).

Smallville Legends: Kara and the Chronicles of Krypton. 6 mobisodes. Directed by David Molina and Terry Shakespeare, written by Christopher Hanada and Tanner King, Warner Bros. Television, 2008.

A mini-series of animated shorts recounting the life of Supergirl/Kara before she was sent to Earth. Released as a promotional tie-in with Sprint, the episodes were made available on Sprint cellphones before appearing on the CW website. The mini-series is included on the *Smallville* Season Seven DVD box set (2008).

Smallville: Visions. 5 chapters. Stephan Nilson (w), Andie Tong (p), and James Offredi (i), Warner Bros. Television, 2008.

Promotional webcomic with Stride Gum wherein viewers voted on two possible outcomes to resolve the cliffhanger at the end of each chapter. The webcomic mini-series is included on the *Smallville* Season Seven DVD box set (2008).

Appendix II
Adaptations Featuring Superman or the Superman Family

Adaptations featuring Superman or characters created in the Superman family of comic books.

Comic Books

Super Friends. 47 issues. E. Nelson Bridwell (w), Ric Estrada (p), Joe Orlando (i), Vince Colletta (i), et al., DC Comics, Nov. 1976–Aug. 1981.
    Companion comic book series to the animated television series.

Justice League Adventures. 34 issues. Ty Templeton (w), Min S. Ku (p), Dan Davis (i), et al., DC Comics, Nov. 2001–Aug. 2004.
    Companion comic book series to the animated television series.

Justice League Unlimited. 46 issues. Adam Beechen (w), Carlo Barberi (a), Walden Wong (i), et al., DC Comics, 2004–May 2008.
    Companion comic book series to the animated television show.

Young Justice. 26 issues. Kevin Hopps (w), Greg Wiseman (w), Mike Norton (p/i), et al. DC Comics, Jan. 2011–Feb. 2013.
    Companion comic book series to the animated television series.

Injustice: Gods Among Us Years 1–5. 153 digital chapters/60 issues, 4 annuals. Brian Buccelleto (w, Year Three #8–Year Five), Tom Taylor (w, Year One–Year Three #7), Jheremy Raapack (a), et al. DC Comics, Jan. 2013– Jan. 2017.
    Prequel comic book series to the video game.

DC Comics Bombshells. 100 digital chapters/33 issues, 1 annual. Marguerite Bennett (w), Marguerite Sauvage (a), et al. DC Comics, July 2015–June 2017.
    A comic book series inspired by the DC Collectables line of superheroine figurines.

Injustice: Ground Zero. 12 digital chapter/6 issues. Christopher Sebela (w), Brian Buccelleto (w), Pop Mhan (a), Tom Derenick (a), and Daniel Sampere (a). DC Comics, Dec. 2016–July 2017.
    A comic book mini-series recounting the events of the *Injustice: Gods Among Us* video game from the point of view of Harley Quinn.

Injustice 2. 72 digital chapters/36 issues, 2 annuals. Tom Taylor (w), Bruno Redondo (a), et al., DC Comics, Apr. 2017–Oct. 2018.
    Prequel comic book series to the video game.

Injustice vs. Master of the Universe. 6 issues. Tim Seeley (w) and Freddie E. Williams II (p/i). DC Comics, Sept. 2018–Jan. 2019
    Comic book crossover between the *Injustice* video game universe and *He-Man and the Masters of the Universe*.

Young Justice: Outsiders. 2 digital chapters/1 issue. Greg Wiseman (w) and Christopher Jones (p/i). DC Comics, Jan. 2019.
    Prequel comic book to the third season of the animated television series.

DC Super Hero Girls Giant. 2 issues. Amy Wolfram (w), Agnes Garbowska (a), et al. DC Comics, Nov. 2019- Jan. 2020.
   Comic book companion to the television animated series based on the Mattel DC Super Hero Girls toy line featuring Supergirl.

DC Super Hero Girls: Infinite Frenemy. Amanda Deibert (w), Erich Owen (a), et al. DC Comics, Apr.–May 2020.
   Companion digital series to the television animated series based on the Mattel DC Super Hero Girls toy line featuring Supergirl.

Teen Titans Go!/DC Super Hero Girls Giant. 1 issue. Amanda Deibert (w), Derek Fridolfs (w), Agnes Grabowska (a), Erich Owen (a), et al. DC Comics, May 2020.
   Comic book companion to the television animated series based on the Mattel DC Super Hero Girls toy line featuring Supergirl.

Film

Justice League. Directed by Zack Snyder, screenplay by Chris Terrio and Joss Whedon, performances by Amy Adams (Lois Lane), Ben Affleck (Batman/Bruce Wayne), Henry Cavill (Superman/Clark Kent), Ray Fisher (Cyborg/Victor Stone), Gal Gadot (Wonder Woman/Diana Prince), Amber Heard (Mera), Ciarán Hinds (Steppenwolf), Jeremy Irons (Alfred Pennyworth), Diane Lane (Martha Kent), Jason Mamoa (Aquaman/Arthur Curry), Ezra Miller (The Flash/Barry Allen), Connie Nielsen (Queen Hippolyta), J.K. Simmons (Commissioner James Gordon), et al., Warner Bros., 2017.

Films, Animated

Justice League: New Frontier. Directed by Dave Bullock, written by Stan Berkowitz and Darwyn Cooke, voice performances by David Boreanaz (Green Lantern/Hal Jordan), Miguel Ferrer (Martian Manhunter/J'Onn J'Onzz), Neil Patrick Harris (The Flash/Barry Allen), Lucy Lawless (Wonder Woman/Diana Prince), Kyle MacLachlan (Superman/Clark Kent), Kyra Sedgwick (Lois Lane), Brooke Shields (Carol Ferris), Jeremy Sisto (Batman, Bruce Wayne), et al., Warner Bros. Animation, 2008.
   Adaptation of Darwyn Cooke's mini-series *DC: The New Frontier* (2004).

Justice League: Crisis on Two Earths. Directed by Sam Liu and Lauren Montgomery, written by Dwayne McDuffie, voice performances by Jonathan Adams (Martian Manhunter/J'Onn J'Onzz), William Baldwin (Batman/Bruce Wayne), Brian Bloom (Ultraman), Bruce Davison (President Slade Wilson), Richard Green (Jimmy Olsen), Mark Harmon (Superman/Clark Kent), Josh Keaton (The Flash/Wally West), Vanessa Marshall (Wonder Woman/Diana Prince), Chris Noth (Lex Luthor), Nolan North (Green Lantern/Hal Jordan), Freddi Rogers (Rose Wilson), James Patrick Stuart (Johnny Quick), Gina Torres (Superwoman), James Woods (Owlman), Cedric Yarbrough (Firestorm), et al., Warner Bros. Animation, 2010.
   Based on the unproduced animated film *Justice League: Worlds Collide.*

Justice League: Doom. Directed by Lauren Montgomery, written by Dwayne McDuffie, voice performances by Carlso Alazraqui (Bane), Claudia Black (Cheetah/Barbara Ann Minerva), Paul Blackthorne (Metallo/John Corben), Kevin Conroy (Batman/Bruce Wayne), Olivia d'Abo (Star Sapphire/Carol Ferris), Tim Daly (Superman/Clark Kent), Grey DeLisle (Lois Lane), Susan Eisenberg (Wonder Woman/Princess Diana), Nathan Fillion (Green Lantern/Hal Jordan), David Kaufman (Jimmy Olsen), Carl Lumbly (Martian Manhunter/J'Onn J'Onzz), Bumper Robinson (Cyborg/Victor Stone), Michael Rosenbaum (The Flash/Barry Allen), et al., Warner Bros. Animation, 2012.
   An adaptation of the comic book storyline "Tower of Babel" from *JLA* #43–46 (2000). It is a sequel to the animated film *Justice League: Crisis on Two Earths* (2010).

Batman: The Dark Knight Returns Part 2. Directed by Jay Oliva, written by Bob Goodman, voice performances by Maria Canals-Barrera (Commissioner Ellen Yindel), Robin Atkin Downes (Oliver Queen), Michael Emerson (The Joker), Tress MacNeille (Selina Kyle), Jim Meskimen (President Ronald Regan), Mark Valley (Superman/Clark Kent), Peter Weller (Batman/Bruce Wayne), Ariel Winter (Robin/Carrie Kelley), et al., Warner Bros. Animation, 2013.
   An adaptation of the 1986 *Batman: The Dark Knight Returns* mini-series.

Lego Batman: The Movie—DC Superheroes Unite. Directed by Jon Burton, screenplay by David A. Goodman, voice performances by Lauren Bailey (Harley Quinn, Poison Ivy, Wonder Woman), Troy Baker (Batman/Bruce Wayne, Two-Face, Brainiac), Brian Bloom (Cyborg), Clancy Brown (Lex Luthor), Steve Blum (Bane, The Penguin), Cam Clarke (Green Lantern/Hal Jordan, Martian Manhunter/J'Onn J'Onzz), Townsend Coleman (Commissioner James Gordon), Rob Paulsen (Riddler), Charlie Schlatter (The Flash/Barry Allen, Robin), Christopher Corey Smith (Joker), Katherine Von Till (Catwoman, Batcomputer), Travis Willingham (Superman/Clark Kent), et al., Warner Bros. Animation and The Lego Group, 2013.
    Based on the video game *Lego Batman 2: DC Superheroes*.

Justice League: The Flashpoint Paradox. Directed by Jay Oliva, written by Jim Krieg, voice performances by Steve Blum (Lex Luthor), Justin Chambers (The Flash/Barry Allen), Kevin Conroy (Batman/Bruce Wayne), Sam Daly (Superman/Clark Kent), Dana Delany (Lois Lane), Cary Elwes (Aquaman/Arthur Curry), Nathan Fillion (Green Lantern/Hal Jordan), C. Thomas Howell (Professor Zoom/Eobard Thawne), Danny Huston (General Sam Lane), Michael B. Jordan (Cyborg/Victor Stone), Vanessa Marshall (Wonder Woman/Princess Diana), Kevin McKidd (Batman/Thomas Wayne), et al., Warner Bros. Animation, 2014.
    An adaptation of the 2011 comic book limited series *Flashpoint*.

JLA Adventures: Trapped in Time. Directed by Giancarlo Volpe, screenplay by Michael Ryan, voice performances by Diedrich Bader (Batman), Laura Bailey (Dawnstar), Dante Basco (Karate Kid), Corey Burton (Time Trapper, Captain Cold), Jack DeSena (Robin), Tom Gibis (Toyman, Jonathan Kent), Grey DeLisle-Griffin (Wonder Woman, Superbaby), Michael David Donovan (Bizarro), Peter Jessop (Superman), Erica Luttrell (Cheetah, Martha Kent), Liam O'Brien (Aquaman), Kevin Michael Richardson (Black Manta, Solomon Grundy), Jason Spisak (The Flash), Fred Tatasciore (Lex Luthor), Avery Waddell (Cyborg), Travis Willingham (Gorilla Grodd), et al., Warner Bros. Animation, 2014.

Justice League: War. Directed by Jay Oliva, written by Heath Corson, voice performances by Sean Astin (Shazam), Steve Blum (Darkseid), Zach Callison (Billy Baston), Christopher Gorham (The Flash/Barry Allen), Justin Kirk (Green Lantern/Hal Jordan), Michelle Monaghan (Wonder Woman/Diana Prince), Jason O'Mara (Batman/Bruce Wayne), Shemar Moore (Cyborg/Victor Stone), Alan Tudyk (Superman/Clark Kent), et al., Warner Bros. Animation, 2014.
    An adaptation of DC Comics' New 52 storyline "Origin" from *Justice League* Vol. 2 #1–6 (Nov. 2011–Apr. 2012). This marks the start of shared continuity among the DC Universe animated original movies known as the DC Animated Movie Universe (DCAMU).

Lego DC Comics Super Heroes Batman: Be-Leaguered. Directed by Rick Morales, screenplay by James Krieg, voice performances by Troy Baker (Batman), Dee Bradley Baker (Aquaman, Man-Bat), Grey Delisle (Lois Lane, Wonder Woman), John DiMaggio (Joker, Lex Luthor), Tom Kenny (Penguin), Nolan North (Superman, Alfred Pennyworth), Khary Payton (Cyborg), Paul Reubens (Bat-Mite), Kevin Michael Richardson (Black Manta, Captain Cold), James Arnold Taylor (The Flash), et al., Warner Bros. Animation and The Lego Group, 2014.

Justice League: Throne of Atlantis. Directed by Ethan Spaulding, written by Heath Corson, voice performances by Sean Astin (Shazam/Billy Baston), Stephen Blum (Lex Luthor), Patrick Cavanaugh (Jimmy Olsen), Rosario Dawson (Wonder Woman/Diana Prince), Nathan Fillion (Green Lantern/Hal Jordan), Christopher Gorham (The Flash/Barry Allen), Sirena Irwin (Queen Atlanna), Jay K. Johnson (Sam Lane), Juliet Landau (Lois Lane), Matt Lanter (Aquaman/Arthur Curry), Harry Lennix (Black Manta), Sumalee Montano (Mera), Shemar Moore (Cyborg/Victor Stone), George Newbern (Steve Trevor), Jerry O'Connell (Superman/Clark Kent), Jason O'Mara (Batman/Bruce Wayne), Khary Payton (John Henry Irons), Sam Witwer (Ocean Master/Orm), et al., Warner Bros. Animation, 2015.
    An adaptation of the "Throne of Atlantis" storyline from *Aquaman* Vol. 7 #14–17 (Jan.-Apr. 2013) and *Justice League* Vol. 2 #15–17 (Feb.-Apr. 2013). Part of the DC Animated Movie Universe.

Lego DC Comics Super Heroes: Justice League Vs. Bizarro League. Directed by Brandon Vietti, screenplay by Michael Jelenic, voice performances by Diedrich Bader (Green Lantern/Guy Gardner, Greenzarro), Troy Baker (Batman/Bruce Wayne, Batzarro), John DiMaggio (Lex Luthor, Deathstroke), Tom Kenny (Plastic Man, Penguin), Phil Morris (Green Arrow, Hawkman), Nolan

North (Superman/Clark Kent, Bizarro), Khary Payton (Cyborg, Cyzarro), Kevin Michael Richardson (Captain Cold, Gorilla Grodd), James Arnold Taylor (The Flash, Desaad), Tony Todd (Darkseid), Kari Wahlgren (Wonder Woman, Bizarra), April Winchell (Giganta), et al., Warner Bros. Animation and The Lego Group, 2015.

Justice League: Gods and Monsters. Directed by Sam Liu, Screenplay by Alan Burnett, voice performances by Benjamin Bratt (Superman/Herman Guerra), Paget Brewster (Lois Lane), Larry Cedar (Pete Ross), Trevor Devall (Emil Hamilton, Lightray), Michael C. Hall (Batman/Dr. Kirk Langstrom), Jason Isaacs (Lex Luthor), Yuri Lowenthal (Jor-El, Jimmy Olsen), Khary Payton (John Henry Irons, Granny Goodness), Tamara Taylor (Wonder Woman/Bekka), Bruce Thomas (Darkseid, General Zod), et al., Warner Bros. Animation, 2015.

Lego DC Comics Super Heroes: Justice League—Attack of the Legion of Doom. Directed by Rick Morales, screenplay Jim Krieg, voice performances by Troy Baker (Batman), Dee Bradley Baker (Martian Manhunter, Man-Bat), John DiMaggio (Joker, Lex Luthor), Grey Griffin (Wonder Woman, Lois Lane), Mark Hamill (Trickster, Sinestro), Josh Keaton (Green Lantern), Tom Kenny (Penguin), Nolan North (Superman), Khary Payton (Cyborg), Kevin Michael Richardson (Black Manta, Captain Cold, Gorilla Grodd), Cree Summer (Cheetah), James Arnold Taylor (The Flash, General Sam Lane), Tony Todd (Darkseid), et al., Warner Bros. Animation and The Lego Group, 2015.

Lego DC Comics Super Heroes: Justice League—Cosmic Clash. Directed by Rick Morales, screenplay by Jim Krieg, voice performances by Troy Baker (Batman), Jessica DiCicco (Supergirl), Grey Griffin (Wonder Woman), Josh Keaton (Green Lantern), Phil LaMarr (Green Lantern), Yuri Lowenthal (Cosmic Boy), Andy Milder (Lightning Lad), Phil Morris (Vandal Savage), Nolan North (Superman), Khary Payton (Cyborg), Jason Spisack (Captain Fear), James Arnold Taylor (The Flash), Kari Wahlgren (Saturn Girl), et al., Warner Bros. Animation and The Lego Group, 2016.

Justice League vs. Teen Titans. Directed by Sam Liu, screenplay by Alan Burnett and Bryan Q. Miller, voice performances by Stuart Allen (Robin/Damian Wayne), Jake T. Austin (Blue Beetle/Jaime Reyes), John Bernthal (Trigon), Steve Blum (Lex Luthor, Toyman), Terrence C. Casron (Ra's al Ghul), Rosario Dawson (Wonder Woman/Diana Prince). Taissa Farmiga (Raven), Christopher Gorham (The Flash/Barry Allen), Shemar Moore (Cyborg/Victor Stone), Jerry O'Connell (Superman/Clark Kent), Jason O'Mara (Batman/Bruce Wayne), Brandon Soo Hoo (Beast Boy/Garfield Logan), Kari Wahlgren (Starfire), Rick D. Wasserman (Atomic Skull, Solomon Grundy, Weather Wizard), Warner Bros. Animation, 2016.

Part of the DC Animated Movie Universe.

Lego DC Comics Super Heroes: Justice League—Gotham City Breakout. Directed by Matt Peters and Melchior Zwyer, voice performances by Troy Baker (Batman), Eric Bauza (Bane, Commissioner Gordon), Greg Cipes (Beast Boy), John DiMaggio (Deathstroke, Scarecrow), Will Friedle (Nightwing/Dick Grayson), Grey Griffin (Wonder Woman), Sarah Hyland (Bargirl), Vanessa Marshall (Poison Ivy), Scott Menville (Robin/Damian Wayne), Nolan North (Superman), Tom Kenny (Penguin), Khary Payton (Cyborg), Jason Spisack (Joker), Tara Strong (Harley Quinn), Hynden Walch (Starfire), et al., Warner Bros. Animation and The Lego Group, 2016.

DC Super Hero Girls: Hero of the Year. Directed by Cecilia Aranovich, written by Shea Fontana, voice performances by Dean Cain (Jonathan Kent), Teala Dunn (Bumblebee), Anais Fairweather (Supergirl), Grey Griffin (Wonder Woman, Giganta), Stephanie Sheh (Katana), Helen Slater (Martha Kent), Tara Strong (Harley Quinn, Poison Ivy), Mae Whitman (Batgirl), Alexis G. Zall (Lois Lane), et al., Warner Bros. Animation and Mattel, 2016.

DC Super Hero Girls: Intergalactic Games. Directed by Cecilia Aranovich, written by Shea Fontana, voice performances by Romi Dames (Lena Luthor), Teala Dunn (Bumblebee), Anais Fairweather (Supergirl), Grey Griffin (Wonder Woman, Platinum), Stephanie Sheh (Katana, Bleez), Tara Strong (Harley Quinn, Poison Ivy), Fred Tatascoire (Brainiac, Kryptomites), Mae Whitman (Batgirl/Barbara Gordon, Speed Queen), Alexis G. Zall (Lois Lane), et al., Warner Bros. Animation and Mattel, 2017.

Lego DC Super Hero Girls: Brain Drain. Directed by Todd Grimes, written by Jeremy Adams, voice performances by Romi Dames (Lena Luthor), Teala Dunn (Bumblebee), Anais Fairweather (Supergirl), Grey Griffin (Wonder Woman, Lois Lane), Ashlyn Selich (Batgirl), Stephanie Sheh (Katana), Tara Strong (Harley Quinn), et al., Warner Bros. Animation, The Lego Group, and Mattel, 2017.

Lego DC Super Hero Girls: Super-Villain High. Directed by Elsa Garagarza, written by Jeremy Adams, voice performances by Romi Dames (Lena Luthor, Divide), Teala Dunn (Bumblebee), Anais Fairweather (Supergirl), Grey Griffin (Wonder Woman, Lois Lane), Cristina Milizia (Green Lantern/Jessica Cruz), Ashlyn Selich (Batgirl), Stephanie Sheh (Katana), Tara Strong (Harley Quinn, Poison Ivy), et al., Warner Bros. Animation, The Lego Group, and Mattel, 2018.

Lego DC Comics Super Heroes: The Flash. Directed by Ethan Spaulding, written by Jeremy Adams and Jim Krieg, voice performances by Dee Bradley Baker (Aquaman, Captain Boomerang), Troy Baker (Batman), Eric Bauza (Atom, B'dg, Jimmy Olsen), Grey Griffin (Wonder Woman, Lois Lane), Troy Kenny (Plastic Man, Penguin), Phil LaMarr (Firestorm), Nolan North (Killer Croc, Superman), Khary Payton (Cyborg), Dwight Schultz (Reverse Flash), James Arnold Taylor (The Flash), et al., Warner Bros. Animation and The Lego Group, 2018.

Lego DC Comics Super Heroes: Aquaman—Rage of Atlantis. Directed by Matt Peters, written by Jeremy Adams and Jim Krieg, voice performances by Jonathan Adams (Atrocious), Dee Bradley Baker (Aquaman, Dex-Starr), Troy Baker (Batman), Eric Bauza (Jimmy Olsen), Trevor Devall (Ocean Master), Susan Eisenberg (Mera), Grey Griffin (Wonder Woman, Lois Lane), Cristina Milizia (Jessica Cruz), Scott Menville (Robin/Damian Wayne), Nolan North (Superman), Khary Payton (Cyborg), Aylson Stoner (Batgirl), Fred Tatasciore (Lobo), Warner Bros. Animation and The Lego Group, 2018.

DC Super Hero Girls: Legends of Atlantis. Directed by Cecilia Aranovich and Ian Hamilton, written by Shea Fontana, voice performances by Teala Dunn (Bumblebee), Anais Fairweather (Supergirl), Grey Griffin (Wonder Woman), Erica Lindbeck (Mera, Siren), Max Mittelman (Aquaman), Khary Payton (Cyborg), Stephanie Sheh (Katana), Tara Strong (Harley Quinn, Poison Ivy, Raven), Mae Whitman (Batgirl), et al., Warner Bros. Animation, 2018.

Justice League vs. The Fatal Five. Directed by Sam Liu, screenplay by Alan Burnett, Eric Carrasco, and Jim Krieg, voice performances by Phillip Anthony-Rodriguez (Mano), Daniela Bobadilla (Miss Martian), Kevin Conroy (Batman/Bruce Wayne), Susan Eisenberg (Wonder Woman), Diane Guerrero (Green Lantern/Jessica Cruz), Peter Jessop (Tharok), Matthew Yang King (The Persuader), Sumalee Montano (Emerald Empress), George Newbern (Superman/Clark Kent), et al., Warner Bros. Animation, 2019.

Batman: Hush. Directed by Justin Copeland, screenplay by Ernie Altbacker, voice performances by Sachie Alessio (Lady Shiva), Stuart Allan (Robin/Damian Wayne), Geoffrey Arend (Riddler), Chris Cox (Scarecrow), James Garrett (Alfred Pennyworth), Adam Gifford (Bane, Clayface), Peyton List (Poison Ivy), Peyton R. List (Batgirl/Barbara Gordon), Sean Maker (Nightwing/Dick Grayson), Jennifer Morrison (Catwoman/Selina Kyle), Jerry O'Connell (Superman/Clark Kent), Jason O'Mara (Batman/Bruce Wayne), Rebecca Romijn (Lois Lane), Jason Spisak (The Joker), Maury Sterling (Thomas Elliot), Bruce Thomas (Commissioner James Gordon), Hynden Walch (Harley Quinn), Vanessa Williams (Amanda Waller), Rainn Wilson (Lex Luthor), et al, Warner Bros. Animation, Aug. 2019.

An adaptation of the "Hush" storyline in *Batman* Vol. 1 #608–619 (Oct. 2002–Sept. 2003). Part of the DC Animated Movie Universe.

Justice League Dark: Apokolips War. Directed by Matt Peters and Christina Sotta, screenplay by Mairghread Scott, voice performances by Stuart Allan (Robin), Sachie Alessio (Lady Shiva), Sean Astin (Shazam/Billy Baston), Jon Berthal (Trigon), Ryan Chase (Jason Blood/Etrigan), Roger Cross (Green Lantern John Stewart, Swamp Thing), Rosario Dawson (Wonder Woman), John DiMaggio (King Shark), Taissa Farmiga (Raven), Nathan Fillion (Green Lantern Hal Jordan), Christopher Gorham (The Flash), Matt Lanter (Aquaman), Nyambi Nyambi (Martian Manhunter), Camilla Luddington (Zatanna), Sean Maher (Nightwing), Liam McIntyre (Captain Boomerang), Sumalee Montano (Mera), Shemar Moore (Cyborg), Jerry O'Connell (Superman), Jason O'Mara (Batman), Matt Ryan (John Costantine), Rebecca Romijn (Lois Lane), Yvonne Strahovski (Batwoman), Tony Todd (Darkseid), Nicholas Turturro (Deadman), Colleen Villard (Black Orchid), Hynden Walch (Harley Quinn), Rain Wilson (Lex Luthor), et al., Warner Bros. Animation, May 2020.

The conclusion of the DC Animated Movie Universe.

Lego DC: Shazam! Magic and Monsters. Directed by Matt Peters, script by Jeremy Adams, voice performances by Sean Astin (Shazam), Dee Bradley Baker (Dr. Sivana, Jeepers, Crocodile Man), Troy Baker (Batman), Zach Callison (Billy Baston, Jimmy Olsen), Ralph Garman (The Wizard), Grey Griffin (Wonder Woman, Lois Lane), Jennifer Hale (Mary Baston), Tom Kenny (Penguin, Perry White), Christina Milizia (Green Latern Jessica Cruz), Nolan North (Superman), Fred Tatasciore (Lobo, Oom), Jonny Rees (Mr. Mind), James Arnold Taylor (The Flash), Imari Williams (Black Adam), et al., Warner Bros. Animation and The Lego Group, June 2020.

Graphic Novels

DC Super Hero Girls Vol. 1: Finals Crisis by Shea Fontana (w) and Yancey Labat (a), DC Comics, 2016.
    A graphic novel based on the Mattel DC Super Hero Girls toy line featuring Supergirl.

DC Super Hero Girls Vol. 2: Hits and Myths by Shea Fontana (w) and Yancey Labat (a), DC Comics 2016.
    A graphic novel based on the Mattel DC Super Hero Girls toy line featuring Supergirl.

DC Super Hero Girls Vol. 3: Summer Olympus by Shea Fontana (w) and Yancey Labat (a), DC Comics, 2017.
    A graphic novel based on the Mattel DC Super Hero Girls toy line featuring Supergirl.

DC Super Hero Girls Vol. 4: Past Times at Super Hero High by Shea Fontana (w) and Agnes Garbowska (a), DC Comics, 2017.
    A graphic novel based on the Mattel DC Super Hero Girls toy line featuring Supergirl.

DC Super Hero Girls Vol. 5: Out of the Bottle by Shea Fontana (w) and Yancey Labat (a), DC Comics, 2017.
    A graphic novel based on the Mattel DC Super Hero Girls toy line featuring Supergirl.

DC Super Hero Girls Vol. 6: A Date with Disaster by Shea Fontana (w) and Yancey Labat (a), DC Comics, 2018.
    A graphic novel based on the Mattel DC Super Hero Girls toy line featuring Supergirl.

DC Super Hero Girls Vol. 7: Search for Atlantis by Shea Fontana (w) and Yancey Labat (a), DC Comics, 2018.
    A graphic novel based on the Mattel DC Super Hero Girls toy line featuring Supergirl.

DC Super Hero Girls Vol. 8: Spaced Out by Shea Fontana (w) and Agnes Garbowska (a), DC Comics, 2019.
    A graphic novel based on the Mattel DC Super Hero Girls toy line featuring Supergirl.

DC Super Hero Girls: At Metropolis High by Amy Wolfman (w) and Yancey Labat (a), DC Comics, 2019.
    A graphic novel based on the Mattel DC Super Hero Girls toy line featuring Supergirl.

DC Super Hero Girls: Powerless by Amy Wolfram (w) and Agnes Garbowska (a), DC Comics, 2020.
    A graphic novel based on the Mattel DC Super Hero Girls toy line featuring Supergirl. Originally released as a digital mini-series.

DC Super Hero Girls: Weird Science by Amy Wolfman (w) and Agnes Garbowska (a), DC Comics, 2020.
    A graphic novel based on the Mattel DC Super Hero Girls toy line featuring Supergirl. Originally released as a digital mini-series.

Novels

Kingdom Come by Elliot S! Maggin with Mark Waid and Alex Ross, Aspect, 1999.
    Novelization of the 1996 comic book prestige mini-series. Full-cast audiobook, directed by Kevin Thompson, voice performances by Mike Arkin, Kent Bronthurst, Chuck Cooper, John Cunningham, Birgitte Darby, Jeff David, MacIntyre Dixon, Mark Findely, Harry Gauss, Igor Golden, Mike Lilliard, Mike Marion, Peter Newman, Chloe Patelis, Don Peoples, Barbara Rosenplatt, Garrett Scott, Craig Zakarian, Hachette Audio, 1998.

Batman: The Stone King by Alan Grant, Pocket Star Books, 2001.
    Part of the Justice League of America novel series. Full-cast audiobook directed by

Richard Rohan, voice performances by David Coyne (The Stone King), Colleen Delany (Wonder Woman), Michael Glenn (The Flash), James Konicek (Superman), Eric Messner (Green Lantern), Thomas Penny (J'Onn J'Onzz), Richard Rohan (Batman), et al., Graphic Audio, 2008.

Wonder Woman: Mythos by Carol Lay, Pocket Star Books, 2002.
    Part of the Justice League of America novel series. Full-cast audiobook directed by Richard Rohan, voice performances by Colleen Delany (Wonder Woman), Michael Glenn (The Flash), James Konicek (Superman), Eric Messner (Green Lantern), Thomas Penny (Martian Manhunter), Richard Rohan (Batman), Nanette Savard (Lois Lane), et al., Graphic Audio, 2009.

Justice League: Secret Origins by Michael Teitelbaum, Bantam Books for Young Readers, 2002. Junior novelization of the animated series' pilot episode.

Justice League: In Darkest Night by Louise Simonson, Bantam Books for Young Readers, 2002.

Justice League: Wings of War by Michael Jan Freidman, Bantam Books for Young Readers, 2002.

Justice League: The Gauntlet by Louise Simonson, Bantam Books for Young Readers, 2002.

Justice League: Red Justice by Michael Teitelbaum, Bantam Books for Young Readers, 2003.

Justice League: Wild at Heart by Louise Simonson, Bantam Books for Young Readers, 2003.

Justice League: No Man Is an Island by Alan Grant, Bantam Books for Young Readers, 2003.

Justice League: A Golden Opportunity by Michael Teitelbaum, Bantam Books for Young Readers, 2003.

Justice League: A League of His Own by Michael Jan Freidman, Bantam Books for Young Readers, 2003.

Justice League: Speed Trap by Brian Augustyn, Bantam Books for Young Readers, 2003.

Flash: Stop Motion by Mark Schultz, Pocket Star Books, 2004.
    Part of the Justice League of America novel series. Full-cast audiobook directed by Richard Rohan, voice performances by David Coyne (Plastic Man), Colleen Delany (Wonder Woman), Michael Glenn (The Flash), James Konicek (Superman), Eric Messner (Green Lantern), Thomas Penny (J'Onn J'Onzz), Richard Rohan (Batman), et al., Graphic Audio, 2008.

JLA: Exterminators by Christopher Golden, Pocket Star Books, 2004.
    Part of the Justice League of American novel series. Full cast audiobook directed by Richard Rohan, voice performances by Andy Clemence (The Atom), David Coyne (Aquaman), Elliot Dash (Steel), Colleen Delany (Wonder Woman), Michael Glenn (The Flash), James Konicek (Superman), Dylan Lynch (Hal Jordan), Eric Messner (Green Lantern), Thomas Penny (J'Onn J'Onzz), Richard Rohan (Batman), Nanette Savard (Lois Lane), et al., Graphic Audio, 2008.

Green Lantern: Hero's Quest by Dennis O'Neil, Pocket Star Books, 2005.
    Part of the Justice League of America novel series. Full-cast audiobook directed by Richard Rohan, voice performances by Andy Clemence (The Atom), David Coyne (Plastic Man), Colleen Delany (Wonder Woman), Michael Glenn (The Flash), Dylan Lynch (Hal Jordan), James Konicek (Superman), Eric Messner (Green Lantern), Thomas Penny (J'Onn J'Onzz), Richard Rohan (Batman), et al., Graphic Audio, 2009.

Crisis on Infinite Earths by Marv Wolfman, iBooks, 2005.
    Novelization of the 1985–86 comic book mini-series. Full cast audiobook directed by Richard Rohan, voice performance by Colleen Delany (Wonder Woman), Michael Glenn (The Flash), Kames Konicek (Superman), Eric Messner (Green Lantern), Richard Rohan (Batman), Nanette Savard (Lois Lane), et al., Graphic Audio, 2009.

DC Universe: Last Sons by Alan Grant, Grand Central Publishing, 2006.
    Full-cast audiobook direct by Richard Rohon, voice performances by David Coin (Lobo), James Konicek (Superman), Thomas Penny (J'Onn J'Onzz), et al., Graphic Audio, 2010.

Infinite Crisis by Greg Cox, Ace Books, 2006.
    Novelization of the 2005–2006 limited comic book series. Full-cast audiobook directed by Richard Rohan, voice performances by Colleen Delany (Wonder Woman), James Konicek (Superman), Richard Rohan (Batman), Nanette Savard (Lois Lane), et al., Graphic Audio, 2007.

DC Universe: Trail of Time by Jeff Mariotte, Grand Central Publishing, 2007.
    Full-cast audiobook directed by Richard Rohan, voice performances by Jeff Allin (Jason Blood), Steven Carpenter (Jimmy Olsen), James Konicek (Superman), Scott McCormick (Etrigan), Bruce Allen Rauscher (Phantom Stranger), Richard Rohan (Jonah Hex). Nanette

Savard (Lois Lane), Christopher Sheeren (Vandal Savage), et al., Graphic Audio, 2010.

52: The Novel by Greg Cox, Ace Books, 2007.
   Novelization of the 2006–2007 weekly comic book series *52*. Full cast audiobook directed by Richard Rohan, voice performances by Tim Carlin (Perry White), David Konicek (Clark Kent), Richard Rohan (narrator), Nanette Savard (Lois Lane, Whisper A'Daire), et al. Graphic Audio, 2007.

Countdown by Greg Cox, Ace Books, 2009.
   Novelization of the 2007–2008 weekly comic book series *Countdown to Final Crisis*. Full cast audiobook directed by Richard Rohan, voice performances by Tim Carlin (Perry White), Steven Carpenter (Jimmy Olsen), James Konicek (Superman), et al., Graphic Audio, 2010.

Final Crisis by Greg Cox, Ace Books, 2010.
   Novelization of the 2008–2009 comic book limited series. Full cast audiobook directed by Richard Rohan, voice performances by Terrence Aselford (Dan Turpin), Jeff Baker (Lex Luthor), Tim Carlin (Perry White), Wren Casey (Supergirl), Colleen Delany (Wonder Woman), James Konicek (Superman), Richard Rohan (Batman), Nanette Savard (Loid Lane), et al., Graphic Audio, 2010.

Wonder Woman at Super Hero High by Lisa Yee, Random House Books for Young Readers, 2017.
   Part of the DC Super Hero Girls novel series. Features and appearance by Supergirl.
   Audiobook narrated by Ashley Eckstein, Listening Library, 2017.

Batgirl at Super Hero High by Lisa Yee, Random House Books for Young Readers, 2017.
   Part of the DC Super Hero Girls novel series. Features an appearance by Supergirl.
   Audiobook narrated by Mae Whitman, Listening Library, 2017.

Katana at Super Hero High by Lisa Yee, Random House Books for Young Readers, 2017.
   Part of the DC Super Hero Girls novel series. Features an appearance by Supergirl.
   Audiobook narrated by Stephanie Sheh, Listening Library, 2017.

Harley Quinn at Super Hero High by Lisa Yee, Random House Books for Young Readers, 2018.
   Part of the DC Super Hero Girls novel series. Features an appearance by Supergirl.
   Audiobook narrated by Tara Sands, Listening Library, 2018

Bumblebee at Super Hero High by Lisa Yee, Random House Books for Young Readers, 2018.
   Part of the DC Super Hero Girls novel series. Features an appearance by Supergirl.
   Audiobook narrated by Teala Dunn, Listening Library, 2018.

Records/Cassettes

Justice League of America: The Lunar Invaders. One audio cassette. Directed by Christopher Cerf, narrated by Kathy Mullen, Fisher-Price, 1982.
   Features read-along book.

Super Powers Collection: The Darkseid Saga. One 33⅓ rpm vinyl record. Kenner Products, 1984.
   Mail-in promotion with the Kenner Super Powers Collection toy line.

Super Powers: Battle at the Earth's Core. One vinyl record/audio cassette/VHS tape, Kid Vid Productions, 1985.
   Features read-along book.

Super Powers: Darkseid … of the Moon. One vinyl record/audio cassette/VHS tape, Kid Vid Productions, 1985.
   Features read-along book.

Super Powers: The Battle for Apokolips! One vinyl record/audio cassette/VHS tape, Kid Vid Productions, 1986.
   Features read-along book.

Television Series

Titans. Ongoing, 2 seasons, 24 episodes. Developed by Greg Berlanti, Akira Goldsman, and Geoff Johns, performances by Teagan Croft (Raven/Rachel Roth), Anna Diop (Starfire/Koriand'r), Minka Kelly (Dove/Dawn Granger), Conor Leslie (Wonder Girl/Donna Troy), Esai

Morales (Deathstroke/Slade Wilson), Joshua Orpin (Subject 13/Conner), Ryan Potter (Garfield "Gar" Logan), Alan Ritchson (Hank Hall/Hawk), Brenton Thwaites (Robin/Nightwing/Dick Grayson), Curran Walters (Robin/Jason Todd), and Chelsea Zhang (Rose Wilson), Warner Bros., 2018–present.

Subject 13/Conner, based on Superboy/Conner Kent, and Krypto are featured in the second season.

Television Series, Animated

Super Friends/The All-New Super Friends Hour/Challenge of the Super Friends/The World's Greatest Super Friends/Super Friends/Super Friends: The Legendary Super Powers Show/The Super Powers Team: Galactic Guardians. 9 seasons, 104 episodes. Produced by Lewis Marshall and Iwao Takamoto, voice performances by Norman Alden (Aquaman, 1973–74), Bill Callaway (Aquaman, 1977–1986), Connie Cawlfield (Wonder Woman, 1984–85), Danny Dark (Superman), Shannon Farnon (Wonder Woman, 1973–1983), Casey Kasem (Robin), Ola Soule (Batman, 1973–1983), B.J. Ward (Wonder Woman, 1985–86), Adam West (Batman, 1984–1986), et al., Hanna-Barbera, 1973–1986.

Justice League/Justice League Unlimited. 5 seasons, 91 episodes. Developed by Bruce Timm, voice performances by Maria Canals (Hawkgirl/Shayera Hol), Kevin Conroy (Batman/Bruce Wayne), Susan Eisenberg (Wonder Woman/Princess Diana), Phil LaMarr (Green Lantern/John Stewart), Carl Lumbly (Martian Manhunter/J'Onn J'Onzz), George Newbern (Superman/Clark Kent), Michael Rosenbaum (The Flash/Wally West), et al., Warner Bros. Animation, 2001–2006.

Legion of Super Heroes. 2 seasons, 26 episodes. Developed by Amy Wolfram, voice performances by Michael Cornacchia (Bouncing Boy), Shawn Harrison (Timber Wolf), Heather Hogan (Phantom Girl), Yuri Lowenthal (Superman/Superman X), Andy Milder (Lightning Lad), Alexander Polinksy (Chameleon Boy), Kari Wahlgren (Saturn Girl/Triplicate Girl), Adam Wylie (Brainiac 5), et al., Warner Bros. Animation, 2006–2008.

Young Justice. Ongoing, 3 seasons, 72 episodes. Developed by Brandon Vietti and Greg Wiseman, voice performances by Stephanie Lemelin (Artemis/Tigress), Jesse McCarthy (Robin/Nightwing/Dick Grayson), Danica McKeller (Miss Martian/M'gann M'orzz), Nolan North (Superboy/Conner Kent), Khary Peyton (Aqualad/Kaldur'ahm), Jason Sispack (Kid Flash/Wally West), et al., Warner Bros. Animation, 2010–2013, 2018–present.

Guest appearances by Superman are voiced by Nolan North.

Justice League Action. 1 season, 52 episodes. Produced by Alan Burnett, Jim Krieg, and Butch Lukic, voice performances by Kevin Conroy (Batman/Bruce Wayne), John de Lancie (Brainiac), John DiMaggio (Lobo, Mogul), Gilbert Gottfreid (Mr. Mxyzptlk), Rachel Kimsey (Wonder Woman/Diana Prince), Jason J. Lewis (Superman/Clark Kent, General Zod, Krypto, Streaky the Supercat), Piotr Michael (Perry White, Kalibak), Max Mittelman (Jimmy Olsen, Parasite), Joanne Spracklen (Supergirl), Tara Strong (Lois Lane, Harley Quinn), Travis Willingham (Bizarro), James Woods (Lex Luthor), et al., Warner Bros. Animation, 2016–2018.

DC Super Hero Girls. 2 seasons, 52 episodes. Directed by Natalie Wetzig, developed by Lauren Faust, voice performances by Kimberly Brooks (Bumblebee/Karen Beecher), Grey Griffin (Wonder Woman/Diana Prince), Tara Strong (Batgirl/Barbara "Babs" Gordon), Nicole Sullivan (Supergirl/Kara Danvers), Myrna Velasco (Green Lantern/Jessica Cruz), Kari Wahlgren (Zatanna "Zee" Zatara), et al., Warner Bros. Animation, 2019–present.

Reboot of the web series as a television series.

Television Special, Animated

DC Super Hero Girls: Super Hero High. Directed by Jennifer Coyle, written by Shea Fontana, voice performances by Teala Dunn (Bumblebee), Anais Fairweather (Supergirl), Grey Griffin (Wonder Woman), Stephanie Sheh (Katana), Helen Slater (Martha Kent), Tara Strong (Poison Ivy/Harley Quinn), Mae Whitman (Batgirl), et al., Warner Bros. Animation, 2016.

Video Games

Justice League Task Force. SNES and Mega Drive/Genesis, Sunsoft, 1995.
Justice League: Injustice For All. Game Boy Advanced, Saffire Corporation, 2002.
Justice League: Chronicles. Game Boy Advanced, Full Fat, 2003.
Justice League Heroes. PlayStation 2 and Xbox, Snowblind Studios, 2006.
Justice League Heroes. Nintendo DS, Sensory Sweep Studio, 2006.
Justice League Heroes: The Flash. Game Boy Advanced, WayForward Technologies, 2006.
Mortal Kombat vs. DC Universe. PlayStation 3 and Xbox 360, Midway Games, 2008.
Justice League Heroes United. Arcade game, Global VR, 2009.
DC Universe Online. Microsoft Windows, Nintendo Switch, PlayStation 3, Playstation 4, and Xbox 360, Dimensional Ink Games, 2011–present.
Lego Batman 2: DC Super Heroes. Android, IOS, Mac OS XMicrosoft Windows, Nintendo 3DS, Nintendo DS, PlayStation 3, PlayStation Vita, Wii, Wii U, Xbox 360, voice performances by Clancy Brown (Lex Luthor), Bridget Hoffman (Lois Lane, Supergirl), Travis Willingham (Superman, Bizarro, Gorilla Grodd, Captain Marvel), et al., Traveller's Tales, 2012.
Justice League: Earth's Final Defense. Android and IOS, Netmarble, 2012.
Injustice: Gods Among Us. Android, IOS, Microsoft Windows, PlayStation 3, PlayStation 4, PlayStation Vita, Wii U, and Xbox 360, voice performances by George Newbern (Superman), Nolan North (General Zod), Mark Rolston (Lex Luthor), et al., NetherRealm Studios, 2013.
Young Justice: Legacy. Microsoft Windows, Nintendo 3DS, PlayStation 3, and Xbox 360, voice performances by Stephanie Lemelin (Artemis), Jesse McCartney (Nightwing), Danica McKellar (Miss Martian, Batgirl), Nolan North (Superboy, Superman), Khary Peyton (Aqualad, Black Manta), Mark Rolston (Lex Luthor, Blockbuster), Jason Spisak (Beast Boy, Kid Flash, Riddler), et al., Freedom Factory Studios, 2013.
Scribblenauts Unmasked: A DC Comics Adventure. Microsoft Windows, Nintendo 3DS, Nintendo Switch, PlayStation 4, Wii U, and Xbox One, 5th Cell, 2013 and 2018.
Lego Batman 3: Beyond Gotham. Android, IOS, Mac OS X, Microsoft Windows, Nintendo 3DS, PlayStation 3, PlayStation 4, PlayStation Vita, Wii U, Xbox 360, and Xbox One, voice performances by Dee Bradley Baker (Brainiac, Krypto, et al.), Clancy Brown (Lex Luthor), Gilbert Gottfried (Mr. Mxyzptlk), Scott Porter (Superboy, Aquaman), Kari Wahlgren (Supergirl, et al.), Travis Willingham (Superman, Composite Superman, Cyborg Superman, Doomsday, Metallo, Parasite, Ultra-Humanite, et al.), et al., Traveller's Tales, 2014.
Infinite Crisis. Microsoft Windows, performances by Troy Baker (Superman), Camilla Luddington (Supergirl), Fred Tatasciore (Doomsday), Travis Willingham (Mecha Superman), et al., Turbine, 2015.
DC Legends. Android, IOS, Microsoft Windows, and Mac OS X, WB Games, 2016.
Injustice 2. Android, IOS, Microsoft Windows, PlayStation 4, and Xbox One, voice performances by Laura Bailey (Supergirl), Jeffrey Combs (Brainiac), George Newbern (Superman), Patrick Seitz (Bizarro), et al., NetherRealm Studios, 2017.
Justice League VR: The Complete Experience. Oculus Rift, PlayStation VR, Warner Bros. Interactive, 2017.
Lego DC Super-Villains. Mac OS, Microsoft Windows, Nintendo Switch, PlayStation 4, Xbox One, voice performances by Eric Bauza (Parastie, et al.), Clancy Brown (Lex Luthor), Corey Burton (Brainiac, et al.), Gilbert Gottfried (Mr. Mxyzptlk), Cissy Jones (Lois Lane), Yuri Lowenthal (Superboy), Max Mittelman (Jimmy Olsen), Nolan North (Ultraman/Kent Clarkson, Bizarro), Frank Tatasciore (Doomsday, Mogul, Perry White, et al.), Gina Torres (Superwoman), Travis Willingham (Superman, Eradicator, General Zod, Metallo, Ultra-Humanite, et al.), et al., Traveller's Tales, 2018.
DC Unchained. Android and IOS, FourThirtyThree, Inc., 2018.

Other

DC Super Hero Girls. 5 seasons, 112 episodes. Created by Shea Fontana, Aria Moffly, and Lisa Yee, voice performances by Romi Dames (Lena Luthor), Teale Dunn (Bumblebee), Grey Griffin

(Wonder Woman), Anais Fairweather (Supergirl), Erica Lindbeck (Batgirl/Barbara Gordon, second voice), Stephanie Sheh (Katana), Helen Slater (Martha Kent), Tara Strong (Harley Quinn/Poison Ivy), Fred Tatascoire (Brainiac/Kryptomite), Mae Whitman (Batgirl/Barbara Gordon, first voice), Alexis G. Zall (Lois Lane), et al., Warner Bros. Animation, 2015–2018.

Web series tie-in to the toy line.

DC Super Hero Girls: Super Shorts. 52 episodes. Directed by Steve Stefanelli, developed by Lauren Faust, voice performances by Kimberly Brooks (Bumblebee/Karen Beecher), Grey Griffin (Wonder Woman/Diana Prince), Tara Strong (Batgirl/Barbara "Babs" Gordon), Nicole Sullivan (Supergirl/Kara Danvers), Myrna Velasco (Green Lantern/Jessica Cruz), Kari Wahlgren (Zatanna "Zee" Zatara), et al., 2019–present

Series of web cartoon shorts released in conjunction with the *DC Super Hero Girls* animated television series (2019–present).

Guest Appearances/Cameos

I Love Lucy (television series, "Lucy and Superman," Season 6 episode 13, performance by George Reeve [Superman], 1957); *Batman and Robin the Boy Wonder* (comic strip, 1966-1973); *Aquaman* (animated television series, voice performance by Bud Collyer [Superman], 1967) *Let's All Dance with Super Friends* (disco album, 1978); *Adventures in the DC Universe* (comic book series in the style of *Superman: The Animated Series*, #1 [Apr. 1997], #7 [Oct. 1997], #12 [Mar. 1998], #14 [Mar. 1998], #18 [Sept. 1998], Annual #1 [Nov. 1997]); *Batman Beyond* (animated television series, voice performance by Christopher McDonald [Superman/Clark Kent], 1999–2001); *Static Shock* (animated television series, voice performance by George Newbern [Superman/Clark Kent], 2004); *The Batman* (animated television series, voice performance by George Newbern [Superman/Clark Kent], 2007–2008); *Batman: The Brave and the Bold* (animated television series, voice performances by Dee Bradley Baker [Krypto the Super-Dog], Sirena Irwin [Lois Lane], Richard McGonagle [Brainiac, Perry White], Alexander Polinsky [Jimmy Olsen], Kevin Michael Richardson [Lex Luthor, Mr. Mxyzptlk], Roger Rose [Superman/Clark Kent], 2008–2011); *DC Nation Shorts* (animated televisions shorts: "DC Super Pets," voice performances by David Kaye [Krypto the Superdog] and Debra Wilson [Streaky the Supercat]; "DC's World's Funnest"; "Farm League," voice performance by David Kaye [Supermanatee]; "Super Best Friends Forever," voice performance by Nicole Sullivan [Supergirl]; "Tokyo/Baby Superman," voice performances by Jeff Bennett [baby Kenta] and Blair Underwood [Superman of Tokyo]; "Tales of Metropolis," voice performances by Maria Bamford [Lois Lane], Brian Doyle-Murray [Brainiac], David Kaye [Bizarro], Elisha Yaffe [Jimmy Olsen]; 2011–2014); *Arrow* (television show, performances by Melissa Benoist [Supergirl, Overgirl], Tyler Hoechlin [Superman], Elizabeth Tulloch [Lois Lane], 2012–2020); *Teen Titans Go!* (animated television series, 2013–present); *The Lego Movie* (animated film, voice performance by Channing Tatum [Superman], 2014); *The Lego Movie Videogame* (2014); *Teen Titans Go!* (digital comic book, #5 [Apr. 2014], #9 [July 2014]), *Scooby-Doo Team Up* (comic book, #6 [Nov. 2014]); *The Flash* (television show, performances by Melissa Benoist [Supergirl], Tyler Hoechlin [Superman], and Elizabeth Tulloch [Lois Lane], 2014–present); *Lego Dimensions* (video game, Superman, Supergirl, Superboy, and Lois Lane, 2015); *Legends of Tomorrow* (television show, performances by Melissa Benoist [Supergirl], Tyler Hoechlin [Superman], Brandon Routh [The Atom, Superman/Clark Kent], Elizabeth Tulloch [Lois Lane], 2016–present); *Justice League Dark* (animated film, voice performance by Jerry O'Connell [Superman], 2017); *The Lego Batman Movie* (animated film, voice performance by Channing Tatum [Superman], 2017); *Teen Titans Go! To the Movies* (animated film, voice performance by Nicholas Cage [Superman], 2018); *Shazam!* (film, 2019); *The Lego Movie 2: The Second Part* (animated movie, voice performance by Channing Tatum [Superman], 2019); *Batwoman* (television series, performances by Melissa Benoist [Supergirl], John Cryer [Lex Luthor]. Erica Durance [Lois Lane], Tyler Hoechlin [Superman/Clark Kent], Brandon Routh [The Atom, Superman/Clark Kent], Elizabeth Tulloch [Lois Lane], Tom Welling [Clark Kent], 2019–present), *Harley Quinn* (animated series, voice performances by Natalie Morales [Lois Lane] and James Wolk [Superman/Clark Kent], 2020).

Appendix III
Unproduced Adaptations Starring of Featuring Superman or the Superman Family

Adaptations starring/featuring Superman or members of the Superman family of comic books which were proposed, announced, or entered some stage of pre-production but were not/have not been produced.

Films

Superman and the Ghost of Mystery Mountain/Superman and the Secret Planet. Performances by John Hamilton (Perry White), Jack Larson (Jimmy Olsen), Noel Neill (Lois Lane), George Reeves (Superman/Clark Kent), and Robert Shayne (Inspector Henderson), Motion Pictures for Television, 1954.
  Following the success of repackaging television episodes of *Adventures of Superman* for movie theaters, two scripts were commissioned for original films for the cast but never produced.
Superman V. Performance by Christopher Reeve (Superman/Clark Kent), Cannon Films 1988.
  Announced sequel to *Superman IV: The Quest for Peace*. It would have utilized unused footage from *Superman IV* but was never produced.
Superman: The New Movie/Young Superman. To be produced by Alexander Salkind and Ilya Salkind, script by Cary Bates and Mark Jones, Warner Bros., 1992.
Superman Reborn. Scripts by Jonathan Lemkin and Gregory Poirier, Warner Bros., 1995.
  Loosely inspired by *The Death of Superman* storyline.
Superman Lives! To be directed by Tim Burton, scripts by Kevin Smith, Wesley Strick, and Dan Gilroy, performance by Nicholas Cage (Superman/Clark Kent), Warner Bros., 1998.
  Production was cancelled in 1998 just weeks before filming would have begun. The development of the film has been recounted in the documentary film *The Death of "Superman Lives": What Happened?* (2015).
Superman: The Man of Steel. Script by Alex Ford, Warner Bros., 1998.
  First in a planned series of films, with the second film titled *Superman: The Man of Tomorrow*.
  Untitled Superman/Lobo Film. Script by Keith Griffen, Warner Bros., 1999.
Superman Lives. Script by William Wisher, performance by Nicholas Cage (Superman/Clark Kent), Warner Bros. 2000.
Superman Destruction. To be directed by McG, script by Paul Attanasio, Warner Bros., 2001.
Batman vs. Superman: Asylum/World's Finest. To be directed by Wolfgang Petersen, script by Andrew Kevin Walker and Akiva Goldsman, performances by Colin Farrell (Batman/Wayne) and Jude Law (Superman/Clark Kent), Warner Bros., 2002.
Superman: Flyby. To be directed by McG, Brett Ratner, script by J.J. Abrams, Warner Bros., 2003.
Justice League: Mortal. To be directed by George Miller, script by Kieron Mulroney and Michele Mulroney, performances by Jay Baruchel (Maxwell Lord), Adam Brody (The Flash/Barry Allen), Common (Green Lantern/John Stewart), D.J. Cotrona (Superman), Megan Gale (Wonder Woman), Arnie Hammer (Batman), and Teresa Palmer (Talia al Ghul), Warner Bros. 2008.

Untitled Superman trilogy. To be directed by Matthew Vaughn, developed with Mark Millar, Warner Bros., 2008.

In this telling, the story would have taken place mostly on Krypton, where Superman would have grown up before having to choose between the doomed planet and Earth.

Man of Steel. To be directed by Bryan Singer, script by Michael Dougherty and Dan Harris, performances by Kate Bosworth (Lois Lane) and Brandon Routh (Superman/Clark Kent), Warner Bros., 2009.

Announced sequel to *Superman Returns*.

Man of Steel 2. Performances by Amy Adams (Lois Lane) and Henry Cavill (Superman/Clark Kent), Warner Bros.

Proposed sequel to 2013's *Man of Steel*. Possible directors have included Matthew Vaughn, who would have lifted ideas from his 2008 pitch, and Christopher McQuarrie, who also pitched an interconnected Green Lantern film.

Supergirl. Written by Oren Uziel, Warner Bros., in development.

A new Supergirl film was announced in 2018 with no concrete details.

Films, Animated

Justice League: World's Collide. Performances by Maria Canals (Hawkgirl/Shayera Hol), Kevin Conroy (Batman/Bruce Wayne), Susan Eisenberg (Wonder Woman/Princess Diana), Phil LaMarr (Green Lantern/John Stewart), Carl Lumbly (Martian Manhunter/J'Onn J'Onzz), George Newbern (Superman/Clark Kent), Michael Rosenbaum (The Flash/Wally West), Warner Bros. Animation, 2004.

An unproduced direct-to-video film that would have bridged the gap between the animated series *Justice League* and *Justice League Unlimited*. Adapted as the animated film *Justice League: Crisis on Two Earths* (2010).

Film Serial

Superman. Republic Pictures, 1940/1941.

Two early attempts to create movie serials but were never produced. One set of scripts were revised and released as *Mysterious Doctor Satan* (1940).

Television Movie

The Adventures of Superboy. Performances by Jim Calvert (Trevor Jenkins "T.J." White), Gerard Christopher (Superboy/Clark Kent), Stacey Haiduk (Lana Lang), Sherman Howard (Lex Luthor), Salome Jens (Martha Kent), and Stuart Whitman (Jonathan Kent), Viacom Enterprises, 1993.

Viacom announced a series of television movies after the television series was cancelled but none were produced.

Television Series

The Adventures of Superpup. Unaired pilot. Developed by Whitney Ellsworth, directed by Cal Howard, performances by Billy Curtis (Superpup/Bark Bent), Frank Delfino (Sergeant Beagle), Ruth Delfino (Pamela Poodle), Sadie Delfino (Professor Sheepdip's dupe), Harry Monti (Professor Sheepdip), Angelo Rossitto (Terry Bite), 1958.

Set in a universe wherein the characters are dogs instead of people. Filmed on the set of *Adventures of Superman* using actors in dog suits.

Jimmy Olsen. Developed by Whitney Ellsworth, 1959.

Proposed spin-off of *Adventures of Superman* following the tragic death of George Reeves. The series would intersperse stock footage of Reeve's Superman with new material focusing on Jimmy Olsen as played by Jack Larson.

The Adventures of Superboy. Unaired pilot, 12 additional scripts. Developed by Whitney Ellsworth, performances by Bunny Henning (Lana Lang), Monty Margetts (Martha Kent), and Johnny Rockwell (Superboy/Clark Kent), 1961.

Metropolis. Produced by John Stephens and Danny Cannon, 2018.
With a similar premise to the television show *Gotham* (2014–2019), *Metropolis* would follow Lois Lane and Lex Luthor investigating fringe science before the appearance of Superman.

Television Series, Animated

Superman Family. Developed by Vinton Hueck, Warner Bros. Animation, 2019.
With a tone inspired by Silver Age comics, the family-friendly animated series would have featured Superman/Clark Kent, Lois Lane, Superboy/Jonathan Kent, Steel/John Henry Irons, Steel/Natasha Irons, Supergirl/Kara, Kenan Kong/Superman of China, and Robin/Damian Wayne.

Video Games

Superman III. Atari 5200, Atari, Inc., 1983.
Superman. NES, Sunsoft, 1992.
Superman. Playstation, Titus Software, 2000.
Superman: Battle for Metropolis. Game Boy Color, Infogrames, 2001.
Blue Steel. PlayStation 3, Xbox 360, and Wii, Factor 5, 2008.
Untitled Superman Game. WB Games, 2013–2019.
Possibly two open-world Superman games inspired by the Batman Arkham games have been cancelled, at least one by Rocksteady Studios.

About the Contributors

Ian **Boucher** is a librarian who researches the role of superhero media in developing cultural understandings of justice. He earned his BA in film studies and communication at the University of Pittsburgh, and his MLIS at Kent State University. He edited Sequart's *Humans and Paragons* and his scholarly work includes "Applying Suspense to Archetypal Superheroes: Hitchcockian Ambiguity in *Batman v Superman: Dawn of Justice*," and "Casting a Wider Lasso: An Analysis of the Cultural Dismissal of Wonder Woman Through Her 1975–1979 Television Series."

John **Darowski** is a doctoral candidate in comparative humanities at the University of Louisville. He is a member of the editorial review board for *The Journal of Popular Culture* and has previous essays published in the Ages of Superheroes series edited by Joseph J. Darowski. He was awarded the 2018 John A. Lent Best Student Paper Award from the Comics and Comic Art Area of the National Popular Culture Association/American Culture Association.

Joseph J. **Darowski** teaches English at Brigham Young University. He is a member of the editorial review board of *The Journal of Popular Culture* and has previously edited essay collections on the ages of Superman, Wonder Woman, the X-Men, the Avengers, Iron Man, the Incredible Hulk, the Flash, the Justice League, and Black Panther. Additionally, he has co-authored with Kate Darowski volumes on the television series *Cheers* and *Frasier*.

Alexandre **Desbiens-Brassard** has a Ph.D. in comparative literature from the University of Western Ontario. His doctoral thesis explored the use of monsters to criticize or comment on the intersection of scientific research and capitalism. He frequently works on novels, films and comic books. Since the completion of his Ph.D., he has worked as a professional translator while continuing to publish as an independent scholar.

Sandra **Eckard** is a professor of English at East Stroudsburg University where she teaches writing, education and literature courses. She is also the director of the Writing Studio, a tutoring space for student writers. Her research focuses are writing center theory, writing pedagogy, comic book pedagogy, reading theory and teaching with popular culture. In addition to presentations and scholarly articles, she has also published books, including *Yin and Yang in the English Classroom: Teaching with Popular Culture Texts* and the *Comic Connections* series.

Nicole **Freim** has been a part of the Comics and Comic Art area of the National Popular Culture Association for more than twenty years, serving as area chair for fifteen years. She has published articles on Wonder Woman, the Justice League, and *Supernatural*, and she is on the editorial board of *The International Journal of Comic Arts*. She is an associate professor of writing at Southwestern Oregon Community College.

Christina M. **Knopf** earned her Ph.D. in cultural sociology and political communication at the University at Albany in 2005. She is an assistant professor in communication and media studies at SUNY Cortland. She is the author of numerous articles about comics and pop culture, in addition to her book *The Comic Art of War*. Some of her most recent work can be found in the edited volumes *Monstrous Women in Comics*, *The Mignolaverse* and *Politics in Gotham*. She is a Distinguished Research Fellow of the Eastern Communication Association.

About the Contributors

Lars **Konzack** is an associate professor in information studies at the Department of Communication at the University of Copenhagen. He has an MA in information science and a Ph.D. in multimedia from Aarhus University. His field of interests are geek culture, game studies, cultural studies, aca-fandom, digital culture, imaginary worlds and transmedia storytelling. His publications include "The Origins of Geek Culture," "The Cultural History of LEGO," "Mark Rein•Hagen's Foundational Influence on 21st Century Vampiric Media."

William J. **Lorenzo** holds bachelor's degrees in both cinema studies and pure mathematics and a master's degree in film and television history. His thesis examines *Forbidden Planet* (1956) as a veiled criticism of McCarthyism in America. He has also presented papers on topics such as 1950s sci-fi film, *Star Trek*, and Italian-American film and television at national conferences. He has taught multiple film and television history courses at various New York City colleges and has also worked as an archivist in the Film Department at the Museum of Modern Art.

Christopher **Maverick** is a Ph.D. candidate in English at Duquesne University. His field is 20th-century American literature and his primary research interests include issues of race, class, gender and sexuality in American popular culture, especially television, movies, professional wrestling and comic books. He is the 2018 recipient of the Lent Award for Excellence in Graduate Studies in Comics. He is the host of *Vox Populorum*, a podcast focused on mixing an academic lens with popular criticism of contemporary media.

Debaditya **Mukhopadhyay** is an assistant professor of English at Manikchak College, affiliated to University of Gourbanga, India. He is pursuing his Ph.D. on spy fiction from Rabindra Bharati University. His areas of interest include popular literature and films, myths, adaptations, and theater. His work on Bill Condon's *Beauty and the Beast* and *Indiana Jones and the Temple of Doom* have been published in the collections *Parenting Through Pop Culture*, edited by JL Schatz, and *Excavating Indiana Jones*, edited by Randy Laist, respectively.

Fernando Gabriel **Pagnoni Berns** is a professor at the Universidad de Buenos Aires. He received his Ph.D. in audiovisual arts and teaches courses on international horror film. He is director of the research group on horror cinema "Grite" and has published chapters in the books *To See the Saw Movies*, edited by John Wallis, and *Critical Insights: Alfred Hitchcock*, edited by Douglas Cunningham, among others. He has authored a book about the Spanish horror TV series *Historias para no Dormir* and has edited a book on the Frankenstein bicentennial.

Anna F. **Peppard** is a Social Sciences and Humanities Research Council of Canada postdoctoral fellow in the department of communication, popular culture, and film at Brock University. Her writing on representations of race, gender, and sexuality in popular media appears in *Canadian Review of American Studies* and *International Journal of Comic Art*, among others, and the anthologies *Make Ours Marvel* and *#WWE: Professional Wrestling in the Digital Age*. She is the editor of *Supersex: Sexuality, Fantasy and the Superhero*.

Daniel **Peretti** teaches folklore and popular culture at Memorial University of Newfoundland. He has published scholarship on comic books, film, mythology, and holidays. In 2017 he published *Superman in Myth and Folklore*. His research projects include Santa Claus, folklore in comic books, and trickster mythology.

J. Richard **Stevens** is an associate professor of media studies at the University of Colorado Boulder and is the author of *Captain America, Masculinity, and Violence*. His research focuses on the intersection of ideological formation and media message dissemination, how cultural messages are formed and passed through popular culture, how technology infrastructure affects the delivery of media messages, communication technology policy, and related studies in how media and technology platforms are changing American public discourse.

Simon Harold **Walker** is a military historian and historical suicidologist with expertise in society, culture and behavior. He publishes on Marvel Comics, *Doctor Who*, and *Firefly*. He is an associate researcher at the University of Strathclyde, Glasgow, and has published articles on the history of disease control in the military, written pieces on suicide and military culture for *Time* and *The*

Independent. His first monograph: *Physical Control, Transformation, and Damage in the First World War* was published in 2020.

Liam **Webb** is a FT pharmaceutical proofreader and writes academic articles and fiction. He is a former itinerant tutor, adjunct English professor, and editor. He holds an MA in English, a BA in psychology, a BA in English, and various certificates. He has written several academic chapters and a dozen published stories. He has read comics for decades and has a 100-piece original comic art collection.

Carl **Wilson** is a contributing guest writer for the Eisner-nominated comic book publishers Fanbase Press and a former film editor for PopMatters.com. He has published work in over a dozen edited collections and has written chapters on video game adaptations including: the Indiana Jones franchise, the depowering of DC superheroes, the representation of women in Batman games, and digital Nosferatu.

Index

adolescence 15, 103, 167–169, 239, 242–243
ABC (American Broadcasting Company) 12, 64, 67, 78, 124, 127, 253, 255–256
Action Comics 1, 7, 9–12, 17–18, 23, 25, 29, 31–34, 41, 43, 46–49, 53, 55, 58, 60–62, 67, 70–71, 76, 78, 84, 105–106, 110, 116, 150–151, 159–160, 163, 181, 185, 194, 196, 198, 211, 216, 218, 235–240, 243, 249–250
Adams, Amy 4, 148, 186–187, 190, 220, 248, 260, 271
Adventure Comics 10, 71–72, 150, 211
The Adventures of Superman (comic book) 217, 221
The Adventures of Superman (novel) 3, 8, 14–15, 41, 50–53, 58, 60, 70, 163, 239, 251
The Adventures of Superman (radio show) 3, 8, 12–14, 17–18, 24, 32, 41, 47–48, 57–73, 76–83, 87, 105, 159, 163, 246, 252–253
Adventures of Superman (television show) 8, 17, 21–24, 59, 61, 67, 70, 153, 158, 163, 187, 247–248, 255
aggregate narrative 197, 204
Alexander, Joan 16, 63–64, 67, 71–72, 250, 253–254, 256
Alien 5, 45, 61, 64, 84–86, 93, 97, 102, 104, 107–108, 122, 124, 130, 144, 148, 154, 162–164, 166–169, 182, 189, 210, 217–221, 223, 226, 229–231, 235–243
Alyn, Kirk 19–20, 67, 247–248
American values 3, 58, 90–100
American way 2, 7, 22, 33, 37, 57, 64, 66, 79, 81, 93, 151, 209, 214, 219, 249
Atom Man 20, 65–67, 72, 83–84, 86, 248
Atom Man vs. Superman 8, 20, 67, 247–248
Arrowverse 144, 147, 149, 151, 153, 155, 170, 269
Australia 3, 58, 67–68, 72, 253

Batman 61, 66, 68 73, 86, 91, 101–103, 108, 111, 146, 150–151, 158–159, 161, 170, 177, 189–190, 194–198, 200–202, 208, 218–222, 229, 245–246, 248–250, 252–253, 256, 260–272
Batman v Superman: Dawn of Justice 4–5, 144, 173, 175–178, 180, 183, 185, 187–190, 216–231, 246, 248, 251
BBC 58, 68–70, 72–73, 253–254
Bechdel Test 107, 190
Beck, Jackson 64, 67, 71–72, 253–254, 256
Belgium 1–2, 5, 31, 36–38
Benoist, Melissa 222, 256, 269
Brightburn 5, 235–236, 239–241, 243, 248
Byrne, John 56, 69, 110–111, 113, 121–122, 130, 174, 217, 232, 241, 253, 255

Cain, Dean 111, 122, 124, 127, 144, 148, 163, 255, 262
Canada 1, 5–6, 28, 58
Carr, Thomas 20–21, 24, 248, 257
Cavill, Henry 145, 148, 151–153, 186, 190, 197, 218, 248, 260, 271

"Clan of the Fiery Cross" 3, 66, 72, 76, 78–79, 81–82, 84, 87, 246
Cold War 3, 7, 90, 92, 97, 101, 103–104, 108, 161
Collyer, Clayton "Bud" 8, 12–14, 16, 18, 20, 24, 26, 53, 61–62, 64, 67, 71, 78, 81, 250, 253–254, 256, 269
Comics Code Authority 32, 34, 103, 160
convergence 42–43, 45, 47–48, 52–53, 58, 197–198

Daily Planet 4, 8, 13, 15, 17, 21–22, 52–53, 61, 72, 78, 82, 86–87, 97–98, 102, 104, 107, 110–111, 111–115, 123, 129–130, 132, 136, 145, 185–188, 221, 225, 255,
Danvers, Kara 222–223, 224–227, 229–231, 246, 249–250, 255–256, 258, 267–269, 272
DC Bombshells (comic book) 5, 207–214, 259
DC Bombshells (statue) 4–5, 207, 211, 213
DC Comics 1, 3, 10, 12–13, 16, 18–21, 24–25, 41–46, 48, 53–55, 58–60, 68–73, 76–80, 101, 103, 106, 111, 113, 121, 128, 141, 148, 150, 161, 170, 174, 195–200, 202–204, 207–208, 210–211–213, 232, 245–246, 249, 259–261, 264
DC Extended Universe 144, 185, 192
Denmark 101, 104–107
Detective Comics, Inc. *see* DC Comics
Donenfield, Harry 10–12, 19, 21, 43, 62, 77
Donner, Richard 17, 145, 147, 179, 181, 183, 236, 247
Doomsday 69, 73, 151, 183, 189, 195, 221, 223, 249, 251, 254, 268

Eco, Umberto 34–35, 99–100, 105, 159
Ellsworth, Whitney 12–13, 16, 18–23, 25, 48, 150, 253, 255, 271–272

fandom 4, 127, 136, 141, 148, 213
fanfiction 127–129, 134–142
feminism 3, 5, 107, 111, 116–118, 120–121, 124, 127–129, 131, 133, 137, 140, 208, 211
Fleischer (animated shorts) 1, 3, 8, 16–19, 21–25, 31, 33, 37, 41, 43, 48–55, 58, 60–61, 64, 70–71, 79, 83–84, 153, 250
Fortress of Solitude 9, 122, 148, 176, 257
France 1, 5, 31
Frankenstein 4, 173–174, 178, 182–183

gender 3–5, 107, 127–141, 209–214
genderswap 136–137, 139
Germany 5, 34, 36–37, 65, 147, 160, 208, 219, 239
Gladiator (novel) 44, 47, 54, 238–239
Great Britain 3, 5, 18, 28, 35, 68, 72, 146, 176, 194
Great Depression 7, 11–12, 14, 57–58, 64, 159, 237–240

Hatcher, Teri 111, 113, 118–120, 123, 127, 163, 255
Henderson, Inspector Bill 14, 21, 48, 61, 71, 84–85, 247, 253, 255, 270

277

Hergé (George Rémi) 27, 29–31, 35–36, 38
Hoechlin, Tyler 144, 147, 151, 153, 155, 222, 256, 269
"How Superman Would End the War" 34, 64

icon 2, 4, 27–31, 34–39, 59–60, 76–77, 86, 128, 152–153, 164–166, 170, 182, 186, 208, 213, 220, 236–237, 242
iconization 3, 30–33, 35, 37
immigrant 5, 76, 84, 86, 93, 105, 168, 212, 217, 232, 238, 241–243
Injustice (comic book) 145, 151, 196–198, 203–204, 259
Injustice: Gods Among Us (video game) 5, 151, 194–198, 200, 202–204, 268
Injustice II (video game) 194–195, 203–204, 268
interventionsim 91–92, 98–99

Japan 33, 35, 37, 39, 65–66, 160, 196, 212
Jenkins, Henry 43, 58, 60, 77, 103, 128, 130, 138, 197
Joker 145, 151, 195, 204, 249, 260–263
Jor-El 11, 13–15, 24, 27, 45–46, 51, 60, 77, 148, 188, 241, 247–249, 253, 262
Justice League (film) 144, 151, 181, 185, 190–191, 202, 260, 270

Kahn, Jeanette 69, 111, 253
Kal-El 11, 13–14, 24, 47, 49, 61, 77, 147–148, 151, 165–166, 170, 177, 222–223, 236, 241–242, 253
Kara Zor-El *see* Danvers, Kara
Kelk, Jackie 63, 72, 253
Kellogg's 12, 21, 64, 66, 77, 81–82
Kennedy, Stetson 72, 76, 80, 82–83, 87
Kent, Clark 3–4, 10–13, 15–20, 22–25, 29–30, 33–34, 41, 43–55, 57, 60–62, 65, 67–71, 78–82, 84, 86, 90, 93–94, 97–98, 102, 105, 107, 110–124, 127, 129–140, 142, 145–155, 161–171, 173, 177, 179–181, 186–192, 217, 220–222, 239, 241–242, 246–257, 260–263, 266–267, 269–272
Kent, Eben 15, 48, 51, 60–61, 70, 248
Kent, Jonathan 11, 15, 51, 71, 86, 112, 118–119, 131–132, 148, 162–163, 179–181, 235–236, 239–242, 247–250, 252–253, 255–256, 262, 271
Kent, Martha 15, 51, 70–71, 86, 112, 118–119, 121, 131, 148, 155, 162–163, 180, 189–190, 219, 221, 235–236, 239–242, 247–250, 252–253, 255–256, 260–262, 267, 269, 271–272
Kent, Sarah 15, 51, 60–61, 70
Kidder, Margot 97, 116, 154, 163, 185, 247–248
Krypton 11–15, 27, 46–48, 50–51, 54, 57, 60–61, 71, 77–78, 84, 90, 93, 98, 104–105, 112, 122, 147, 163, 167–168, 170, 175–176, 178, 182–183, 189–190, 203, 208, 218–221, 224–230, 240–241, 249, 251–252, 254, 256, 258, 271
Kryptonite 14, 22, 48, 55, 61, 65–66, 71–72, 78, 83–86, 102, 105–106, 119, 121–122, 131, 146, 167–168, 170, 177, 189, 195, 216–219, 221, 224–225, 228, 230
Ku Klux Klan 3, 66, 72, 76, 80, 82, 86–87

Lane, Lois 3–4, 16, 18, 20–23, 30, 33, 45–46, 48–49, 52–55, 60, 63–65, 67–69, 71–72, 83–84, 90, 93–98, 100, 102, 104–107, 110–124, 127–142, 148, 152–155, 163, 165–168, 170, 182–183, 185–192, 195, 207–208, 210–211, 219, 229, 236–237, 239, 246–257, 260–261–272
Lang, Lana 25, 69, 167–170, 239–240, 247, 253, 255–256, 271–272
Lara 13, 16, 25, 51, 60, 77, 241, 247–2, 248, 253
Larson, Jack 21, 247–248, 270–271
LeVine, Deborah Joy 111, 113–120, 128–129, 135, 255
Liebowitz, Jack 10, 53
Lois & Clark: The New Adventures of Superman (*L&C*) 3, 110–124, 127–142, 144, 148, 153–154, 158, 163, 251, 255

Look 34, 64
Lowther, George 3, 8, 14–15, 18–20, 22, 24–25, 41, 43, 47–48, 50–54, 58, 60–61, 64, 70–71, 239, 251, 253–254
Luthor, Lena 222–231, 256, 262–263, 268
Luthor, Lex 4–5, 20, 44, 67–69, 72, 99, 102, 105, 112–115, 117, 120–123, 134, 170, 173–180, 182–183, 188–189, 216–232, 243, 247–250, 252–253, 255–257, 260–263, 266–269, 271–272

Maggs, Dirk 60, 69, 72–73, 253
Man of Steel (comic book) 69, 73, 110, 113, 121, 131, 174, 217, 235, 241–242, 253, 255
Man of Steel (film) 29, 144, 148, 152, 154, 173, 175, 178–180, 185–188, 194–197, 200, 218–220, 236, 242, 248
masculinity 130, 132, 134, 136, 138, 141, 146, 155, 165–166, 209–211
Maxwell, Robert 12, 20–22, 33, 43, 47, 59, 62, 66, 70, 78, 253–255
McCarthyism 92–93
McClure Newspaper Syndicate 10–11, 58, 246
Metropolis 14–15, 20, 30, 48, 51, 61, 66, 70, 72, 83–85, 96, 104–105, 117–118, 120, 122, 133, 136, 148–149, 151, 160, 176–177, 188, 190, 195, 217–221, 254–256, 264, 269, 272
Middleton, Ray 39, 58
Mutual Broadcasting System 12–13, 61, 64, 71, 78, 253

Neill, Noel 20–22, 247–248, 255, 257, 270
New York World's Fair 55, 58, 70–71
Noa, Julian 63, 78, 253
nuclear 3, 90–91, 97–99, 101–102, 104, 107–108, 195, 233
Nuclear Man 99, 247

Olsen, Jimmy 14, 21, 24, 48, 53, 61, 63–65, 67–69, 71–72, 78, 80–83, 104–106, 112, 116–117, 166, 222, 224, 247–250, 252–257, 260–271

Paramount Pictures 16, 19, 21, 250, 254
Philippines 1, 6, 58
postfeminism 129, 131, 133, 137
Prometheus myth 4, 173–178, 182
propaganda 30, 34–35, 64–65, 208, 210, 213

Quinn, Harley 194, 196, 207–208, 210, 212, 249, 259, 261–263, 266–267, 269
radio 1–3, 6–8, 12–22, 24–25, 33, 36, 41, 43, 47–54, 57–73, 76–81, 83–87, 93, 105, 107, 111, 159, 163–164, 208, 246, 252–254
Radio and Television Mirror 14, 25, 58, 255
Red Daughter 223, 225–230
Reeve, Christopher 1–2, 90, 96, 110, 122, 144, 148, 151, 153–155, 158, 163, 185, 247–248, 270
Reeves, George 8, 20–21, 23–24, 90, 95, 163, 246–247, 255, 257, 270–271
"Reign of the Super-Man" 7, 8, 39, 44, 239
Republic Pictures 16, 19, 271
Routh, Brandon 144, 151, 248, 270, 271

Seduction of the Innnocent 34, 243
Shayne, Robert 14, 21, 61, 247, 255, 270
Sholem, Lee 21, 90, 99, 246
Shuster, Joe 1, 3, 7–11, 14, 17, 23, 29–30, 32–36, 39, 41, 43–47, 49–50, 52, 54, 58–59, 64, 70, 86, 98, 110, 116, 121, 159–161, 166, 181, 185, 192, 207, 210, 232, 235–239, 242, 246
Siegel, Jerry 1, 3, 7–11, 23, 29–30, 32–36, 38–39, 41–50, 52–54, 58–59, 64, 70–71, 76, 86, 98, 110, 116, 121, 159–161, 179, 181, 185, 192, 207, 217, 232, 236–239, 241–242, 246

Slater, Helen 158, 230, 247, 262, 267, 269
Smallville 15, 44, 86, 94, 97, 104, 115, 148, 155, 162, 180, 221, 240–241
Smallville (television show) 4, 121, 124, 144, 145, 147–149, 151, 153–154, 158–159, 162, 164–168, 170–171, 181, 223, 229, 236, 239–240, 242–243, 245–246, 251–252, 255, 257–258
Snyder, Zack 4, 29, 149, 153, 175, 179–181, 183, 185–192, 218, 236, 242, 246, 248, 260
Superboy (character) 44, 53, 55, 70, 110, 121, 124, 155, 248, 250, 254, 256, 267–269, 272
Superboy (television show) 110, 153–154, 158, 163, 165, 245, 257, 271–272
Supergirl (character) 5, 121, 196, 207–208, 210–211, 222–231, 246–247, 249–250, 252, 254, 258, 260, 262–264, 266–269, 271–272
Supergirl (film) 158, 230, 245, 247–248, 251, 271
Supergirl (television show) 5, 140, 144, 151, 153, 155, 216–217, 222–231, 252, 255–256
Superman (animated film shorts) 3, 8, 16–19, 33, 41, 48–50, 54, 60, 65, 70, 83–84, 153
Superman (comic book) 11–12, 14–15, 17–18, 30, 32–34, 38, 41, 46–55, 61–62, 70, 78, 86, 150, 179, 207, 217, 235, 239–240, 242
Superman (comic strip) 5, 8, 10–12, 41, 46–47, 49–54, 60, 62, 71–72, 77, 246
Superman (film serial) 8, 19–20, 24, 67, 70, 159, 247–248, 250, 271
Superman II 154, 187, 247–248
Superman III 96, 111, 144, 146–147, 245, 247–248, 251
Superman IV: The Quest for Peace 3, 90–92, 96–99, 222, 245, 247–248, 254
Superman: A Tale of Five Cities 3, 101–103, 106–108
Superman & Lois 141–142, 155, 256
Superman and the Mole Men 3, 8, 20–21, 24, 90–96, 99–100, 246
Superman Day 39, 55, 58
"Superman in Radio" 14, 58, 255
Superman, Incorporated 1, 11–12, 43, 77
Superman March 17, 153
Superman og Fredsbomben 3, 101–103
Superman on Trial 68, 253
Superman Returns 4, 141–142, 144, 173, 175–179, 186, 200, 246, 248, 252, 257
Superman Smashes the Clan 3, 76, 83–87, 246
Superman: The Movie 17, 116, 148, 152, 163, 173, 175, 179–181, 194, 199, 236, 247–248

Talbot, Paul 68, 72
Tintin 3, 27–31, 35–39, 102
transgender 138–139, 209, 216, 229
transmedia 57–58, 60, 67, 70, 76–77, 83, 87, 129, 141, 201, 203–204, 208

Übermensch 5, 150, 159, 161, 209

video games 194–204, 257, 268, 272

Warner Bros. 111, 191–192, 194, 196–199, 202, 204, 247–250, 255–258, 260–264, 267, 269–272
Warner Bros. Interactive 198–202, 204, 268
Wayne, Bruce *see* Batman
Welling, Tom 144–145, 148, 151, 163–164, 166–167, 171, 255, 269
Wertham, Fredric 34, 243
Whedon, Joss 185, 190–191, 260
White, Perry 13–15, 21, 46, 48, 51–52, 61, 63, 68, 71–72, 78, 82, 85, 112, 118, 129–130, 221, 247–253, 255–257, 264, 266–270
Wonder Woman 72, 91, 158, 185, 188–189, 196, 207–208, 221–222, 246, 248–250, 252, 260–267, 269–271
WOR (radio) 12, 63, 253
World War II (WWII) 2–3, 5, 7, 11, 29, 31–32, 34, 36, 54, 57, 63–67, 69, 82, 103, 147, 160, 207–208, 210–212, 240
Wylie, Philip 44, 54, 238

Xenophobia 5, 92, 95–96, 217–219, 221–226, 228–231

Yang, Gene Luen 3, 76, 83–87, 246

Zod 148–149, 152, 154, 178, 186, 195, 219, 247–248, 262, 267–268

www.ingramcontent.com/pod-product-compliance
Ingram Content Group UK Ltd.
Pitfield, Milton Keynes, MK11 3LW, UK
UKHW050539150426
5217IPUK00026B/2002

Almost immediately after his first appearance in comic books in June 1938, Superman began to be adapted to other media.

The essays in this collection touch on subjects such as the different international receptions to the characters, the evolution of both Clark Kent's character and Superman's powers, the importance of the radio, how the adaptations interact with issues such as racism and Cold War paranoia, and the role of fan fiction in the franchise. By applying a wide range of critical approaches to adaption and Superman, this collection offers new insights into our popular entertainment and our cultural history.

JOHN DAROWSKI is a PhD candidate in comparative humanities at the University of Louisville. He is the author of several essays on the history of comic book superheroes.

Front cover image: Poster art for *Superman IV: The Quest for Peace* (1987) (Warner Bros./Photofest)